Bloom's Modern Critical Interpretations

Alice's Adventures in
Wonderland
The Adventures of
Huckleberry Finn
All Quiet on the
Western Front
As You Like It
The Ballad of the Sad
Café
Beloved
Beowulf
Billy Budd, Benito
Cereno, Bartleby the
Scrivener, and Other
Tales
Black Boy
The Bluest Eye
Cat on a Hot Tin
Roof
The Catcher in the
Rye
Catch-22
Cat's Cradle
The Color Purple
Crime and
Punishment
The Crucible
Darkness at Noon
Death of a Salesman
The Death of Artemio
Cruz
The Divine Comedy
Don Quixote
Dubliners
Emerson's Essays
Emma
Fahrenheit 451

Frankenstein
The Grapes of Wrath
Great Expectations
The Great Gatsby
Hamlet
The Handmaid's Tale
Heart of Darkness
I Know Why the
Caged Bird Sings
The Iliad
Jane Eyre
The Joy Luck Club
The Jungle
Long Day's Journey
Into Night
Lord of the Flies
The Lord of the Rings
Love in the Time of
Cholera
Macbeth
The Man Without
Qualities
The Metamorphosis
Miss Lonelyhearts
Moby-Dick
Night
1984
The Odyssey
Oedipus Rex
The Old Man and the
Sea
On the Road
One Flew Over the
Cuckoo's Nest
One Hundred Years of
Solitude
The Pardoner's Tale

Persuasion
Portnoy's Complaint
A Portrait of the Artist
as a Young Man
Pride and Prejudice
Ragtime
The Red Badge of
Courage
The Rime of the
Ancient Mariner
The Rubáiyát of Omar
Khayyám
The Scarlet Letter
A Separate Peace
Silas Marner
Song of Myself
Song of Solomon
The Stranger
A Streetcar Named
Desire
Sula
The Sun Also Rises
The Tale of Genji
A Tale of Two Cities
The Tales of Poe
The Tempest
Their Eyes Were
Watching God
Things Fall Apart
To Kill a Mockingbird
Ulysses
Waiting for Godot
The Waste Land
White Noise
Wuthering Heights
Young Goodman
Brown

Charles Dickens's
A Tale of Two Cities
Updated Edition

Edited and with an introduction by
Harold Bloom
Sterling Professor of the Humanities
Yale University

BLOOM'S
LITERARY CRITICISM
An imprint of Infobase Publishing

Bloom's Modern Critical Interpretations: A Tale of Two Cities, Updated Edition

Copyright ©2007 Infobase Publishing

Introduction © 2007 by Harold Bloom

Bloom's Literary Criticism
An imprint of Infobase Publishing
132 West 31st Street
New York NY 10001

Library of Congress Cataloging-in-Publication Data
Charles Dickens's A tale of two cities / Harold Bloom, editor. — Updated ed.
    p. cm. — (Bloom's modern critical interpretations)
  Includes bibliographical references and index.
  ISBN-13: 978-0-7910-9427-3 (hardcover)
  ISBN-10: 0-7910-9427-8 (hardcover)
  1. Dickens, Charles, 1812–1870. Tale of two cities. 2. France—History—Revolution, 1789–1799—Literature and the revolution. I. Bloom, Harold. II. Title. III. Series.

  PR4571.C48 2007
  823'.8—dc22   2006101027

Bloom's Literary Criticism books are available at special discounts when purchased in bulk quantities for businesses, associations, institutions, or sales promotions. Please call our Special Sales Department in New York at (212) 967-8800 or (800) 322-8755.

You can find Bloom's Literary Criticism on the World Wide Web at
http://www.chelseahouse.com

Contributing Editor: Pamela Loos
Cover designed by Keith Trego
Cover photo Getty Images
Printed in the United States of America
Bang EJB 10 9 8 7 6 5 4 3 2 1
This book is printed on acid-free paper.

Contents

Editor's Note   vii

Introduction   1
     Harold Bloom

Dickens and the Catastrophic Continuum
of History in *A Tale of Two Cities*   13
     J.M. Rignall

The "Angels" in Dickens's House:
Representation of Women in *A Tale of Two Cities*   27
     Lisa Robson

Language, Love and Identity: *A Tale of Two Cities*   49
     Tom Lloyd

A Tale of Two Cities   69
     John R. Reed

Domesticating History:
Revolution and Moral Management in *A Tale of Two Cities*   83
     John B. Lamb

A Tale of Two Cities   101
     Catherine Waters

A Sisterhood of Rage and Beauty:
Dickens' Rosa Dartle, Miss Wade, and Madame Defarge   129
     Barbara Black

Europe Is Not the Other: *A Tale of Two Cities*   147
    Bjørn Tysdahl

Hard Times and *A Tale of Two Cities*:
The Social Inheritance of Adultery   159
    Hilary M. Schor

Psychoanalyzing Dickens   191
    Carolyn Dever

Chronology   211

Contributors   215

Bibliography   217

Acknowledgments   221

Index   223

Editor's Note

My introduction invokes Madame Defarge's indubitable sado-masochistic appeal, and implies that she is the imaginative Muse of Dickens's quasi-historical romance, *A Tale of Two Cities*.

J. M. Rignall emphasizes the grim continuity of origin and end in the book, after which Lisa Robson fashionably presents Dickens as a patriarchal exploiter of his romance's female characters.

Linguistic codes and identity politics are Tom Lloyd's concerns, while John R. Reed explores Dickens's morality of forgiveness.

John B. Lamb sees something of Dickens's dread of revolutionary pathology, after which Catherine Waters investigates familial aspects of the novel's feminization of the French Revolution.

Virulent women, particularly Madame Defarge, fascinated the susceptible Dickens, as Barbara Black shows, while Bjørn Tysdahl finds in the book's imagery the evidence that Paris and London fuse in the novelist's vision.

Adultery and its social consequences are contrasted in *Hard Times* and *A Tale of Two Cities* by Hilary M. Schor, after which Carolyn Dever concludes this volume by courageously "psychoanalyzing" Charles Dickens, and interpreting the wrestling-into-death of Madame Defarge and Miss Pross rather differently than I do, in my introduction.

HAROLD BLOOM

Introduction

I

Courage would be the critical virtue most required if anyone were to attempt an essay that might be called "The Limitations of Shakespeare." Tolstoy, in his most outrageous critical performance, more or less tried just that, with dismal results, and even Ben Jonson might not have done much better, had he sought to extend his ambivalent *obiter dicta* on his great friend and rival. Nearly as much courage, or foolhardiness, is involved in discoursing on the limitations of Dickens, but the young Henry James had a critical gusto that could carry him through every literary challenge. Reviewing *Our Mutual Friend* in 1865, James exuberantly proclaimed that "*Bleak House* was forced; *Little Dorrit* was labored; the present work is dug out as with a spade and pickax." At about this time, reviewing *Drum-Taps*, James memorably dismissed Whitman as an essentially prosaic mind seeking to lift itself, by muscular exertion, into poetry. To reject some of the major works of the strongest English novelist and the greatest American poet, at about the same moment, is to set standards for critical audacity that no one since has been able to match, even as no novelist since has equalled Dickens, nor any poet, Walt Whitman.

James was at his rare worst in summing up Dickens's supposedly principal inadequacy:

Such scenes as this are useful in fixing the limits of Mr. Dickens's insight. Insight is, perhaps, too strong a word; for we are convinced that it is one of the chief conditions of his genius not to see beneath the surface of things. If we might hazard a definition of his literary character, we should, accordingly, call him the greatest of superficial novelists. We are aware that this definition confines him to an inferior rank in the department of letters which he adorns; but we accept this consequence of our proposition. It were, in our opinion, an offence against humanity to place Mr. Dickens among the greatest novelists. For, to repeat what we have already intimated, he has created nothing but figure. He has added nothing to our understanding of human character. He is master of but two alternatives: he reconciles us to what is commonplace, and he reconciles us to what is odd. The value of the former service is questionable; and the manner in which Mr. Dickens performs it sometimes conveys a certain impression of charlatanism. The value of the latter service is incontestable, and here Mr. Dickens is an honest, an admirable artist.

This can be taken literally, and then transvalued: to see truly the surface of things, to reconcile us at once to the commonplace and the odd—these are not minor gifts. In 1860, John Ruskin, the great seer of the surface of things, the charismatic illuminator of the commonplace and the odd together, had reached a rather different conclusion from that of the young Henry James, five years before James's brash rejection:

The essential value and truth of Dickens's writings have been unwisely lost sight of by many thoughtful persons merely because he presents his truth with some colour of caricature. Unwisely, because Dickens's caricature, though often gross, is never mistaken. Allowing for his manner of telling them, the things he tells us are always true. I wish that he could think it right to limit his brilliant exaggeration to works written only for public amusement; and when he takes up a subject of high national importance, such as that which he handled in *Hard Times*, that he would use severer and more accurate analysis. The usefulness of that work (to my mind, in several respects, the greatest he has written) is with many persons seriously diminished because Mr. Bounderby is a dramatic monster, instead of a characteristic example of a worldly master; and Stephen Blackpool a dramatic perfection, instead of a characteristic example of an honest workman. But let us not lose the use of Dickens's wit and insight, because he chooses to speak in a circle of stage fire. He is entirely right in his main drift and purpose in every book he has written; and all of them, but especially *Hard Times*, should be studied with close and earnest care by persons interested in social questions. They will find much that is partial, and, because partial, apparently unjust; but if they examine all the evidence on the other side, which Dickens seems to overlook, it will appear, after all their trouble, that his view was the finally right one, grossly and sharply told.

To say of Dickens that he chose "to speak in a circle of stage fire" is exactly right, since Dickens is the greatest actor among novelists, the finest master of dramatic projection. A superb stage performer, he never stops performing in his novels, which is not the least of his many Shakespearean characteristics. Martin Price usefully defines some of these as "his effortless invention, his brilliant play of language, the scope and density of his imagined world." I like also Price's general comparison of Dickens to the strongest satirist in the language, Swift, a comparison that Price shrewdly turns into a confrontation:

But the confrontation helps us to define differences as well: Dickens is more explicit, more overtly compassionate, insisting always upon the perversions of feeling as well as of thought. His outrage is of the same consistency as his generous celebration, the satirical wit of the same copious extravagance as the comic elaborations. Dickens' world is alive with things that snatch, lurch, teeter, thrust, leer; it is the animate world of Netherlandish genre painting or of Hogarth's prints, where all space is a field of force, where objects vie or intrigue with each other, where every human event spills over into the things that surround it. This may become the typically crowded scene of satire, where persons are reduced to things and things to matter in motion; or it may pulsate with fierce energy and noisy feeling. It is different from Swift; it is the distinctive Dickensian plenitude, which we find again in his verbal play, in his great array of vivid characters, in his massed scenes of feasts or public declamations. It creates rituals as compelling as the resuscitation of Rogue Riderhood, where strangers participate solemnly in the recovery of a spark of life, oblivious for the moment of the unlovely human form it will soon inhabit.

That animate, Hogarthian world, "where all space is a field of force," indeed is a plenitude and it strikes me that Price's vivid description suggests Rabelais rather than Swift as a true analogue. Dickens, like Shakespeare in one of many aspects and like Rabelais, is as much carnival as stage fire, a kind of endless festival. The reader of Dickens stands in the midst of a festival, which is too varied, too multiform, to be taken in even by innumerable readings. Something always escapes our ken; Ben Jonson's sense of being "rammed with life" is exemplified more even by Dickens than by Rabelais, in that near-Shakespearean plenitude that is Dickens's peculiar glory.

Is it possible to define that plenitude narrowly enough so as to conceptualize it for critical use, though by "conceptualize" one meant only a critical metaphor? Shakespearean representation is no touchstone for Dickens or for anyone else, since above all modes of representation it turns upon an inward changing brought about by characters listening to themselves speak. Dickens cannot do that. His villains are gorgeous, but there are no Iagos or Edmunds among them. The severer, more relevant test, which Dickens must fail, though hardly to his detriment, is Falstaff, who generates not only his own meaning, but meaning in so many others besides, both on and off the page. Probably the severest test is Shylock, most Dickensian of Shakespeare's characters, since we cannot say of Dickens's Shylock, Fagin, that there is much Shakespearean about him at all. Fagin is a wonderful grotesque, but the winds of will are not stirred in him, while they burn on hellishly forever in Shylock.

Carlyle's injunction, to work in the will, seems to have little enough place in the cosmos of the Dickens characters. I do not say this to indicate a limitation, or even a limit, nor do I believe that the will to live or the will to power is ever relaxed in or by Dickens. But nothing is got for nothing, except perhaps in or by Shakespeare, and Dickens purchases his kind of plenitude at the expense of one aspect of the will. T. S. Eliot remarked that "Dickens's characters are real because there is no one like them." I would modify that to "They are real because they are not like one another, though sometimes they are a touch more like some of us than like each other." Perhaps the will, in whatever aspect, can differ only in degree rather than in kind among us. The aesthetic secret of Dickens appears to be that his villains, heroes, heroines, victims, eccentrics, ornamental beings, do differ from one another *in the kinds of will that they possess*. Since that is hardly possible for us, as humans, it does bring about an absence in reality in and for Dickens.

That is a high price to pay, but it is a good deal less than everything and Dickens got more than he paid for. We also receive a great deal more than we ever are asked to surrender when we read Dickens. That may indeed be his most Shakespearean quality, and may provide the critical trope I quest for in him. James and Proust hurt you more than Dickens does, and the hurt is the meaning, or much of it. What hurts in Dickens never has much to do with meaning, because there cannot be a poetics of pain where the will has ceased to be common or sadly uniform. Dickens really does offer a poetics of pleasure, which is surely worth our secondary uneasiness at his refusal to offer us any accurately mimetic representations of the human will. He writes always the book of the drives, which is why supposedly Freudian readings of him always fail so tediously. The conceptual metaphor he suggests in his representations of character and personality is neither Shakespearean mirror nor Romantic lamp, neither Rabelaisian carnival nor Fieldingesque open country. "Stage fire" seems to me perfect, for "stage" removes something of the reality of the will, yet only as modifier. The substantive remains "fire." Dickens is the poet of the fire of the drives, the true celebrant of Freud's myth of frontier concepts, of that domain lying on the border between psyche and body, falling into matter, yet partaking of the reality of both.

II

Except perhaps for *Pickwick Papers*, *A Tale of Two Cities* always has been the most popular of Dickens's books, if we set aside also the annual phenomenon of *A Christmas Carol* and the other Christmas books. No critic however would rank it with such other later novels as *Great Expectations* and *Our Mutual Friend* or the unfinished *Edwin Drood*, or with the many earlier and middle period masterpieces. The harshest single judgment remains that of the now forgotten but formidably pungent reviewer Sir James Fitzjames Stephen, who left Dickens nothing:

> The moral tone of the *Tale of Two Cities* is not more wholesome than that of its predecessors, nor does it display any nearer approach to a solid knowledge of the subject-matter to which it refers. Mr. Dickens observes in his preface—"It has been one of my hopes to add something to the popular and picturesque means of understanding that terrible time, though no one can hope to add anything to the philosophy of Mr. Carlyle's wonderful book." The allusion to Mr. Carlyle confirms the presumption which the book itself raises, that Mr. Dickens happened to have

read the *History of the French Revolution*, and, being on the lookout for a subject, determined off-hand to write a novel about it.
Whether he has any other knowledge of the subject than a single
reading of Mr. Carlyle's work would supply does not appear,
but certainly what he has written shows no more. It is exactly
the sort of story which a man would write who had taken down
Mr. Carlyle's theory without any sort of inquiry or examination,
but with a comfortable conviction that "nothing could be added
to its philosophy." The people, says Mr. Dickens, in effect, had
been degraded by long and gross misgovernment, and acted like
wild beasts in consequence. There is, no doubt, a great deal of
truth in this view of the matter, but it is such very elementary
truth that, unless a man had something new to say about it, it is
hardly worth mentioning; and Mr. Dickens supports it by specific
assertions which, if not absolutely false, are at any rate so selected
as to convey an entirely false impression. It is a shameful thing for
a popular writer to exaggerate the faults of the French aristocracy
in a book which will naturally find its way to readers who know
very little of the subject except what he chooses to tell them; but
it is impossible not to feel that the melodramatic story which
Mr. Dickens tells about the wicked Marquis who violates one of
his serfs and murders another, is a grossly unfair representation
of the state of society in France in the middle of the eighteenth
century. That the French *noblesse* had much to answer for in a
thousand ways, is a lamentable truth; but it is by no means true
that they could rob, murder, and ravish with impunity. When
Count Horn thought proper to try the experiment under the
Regency, he was broken on the wheel, notwithstanding his
nobility; and the sort of atrocities which Mr. Dickens depicts as
characteristic of the eighteenth century were neither safe nor
common in the fourteenth.

The most palpable hit here is certainly Dickens's extraordinary reliance
upon Carlyle's bizarre but effective *French Revolution*, which is not the
history it purports to be but rather has the design, rhetoric, and vision of
an apocalyptic fantasy. No one now would read either Carlyle or Dickens
in order to learn anything about the French Revolution, and sadly enough
no one now reads Carlyle anyway. Yet Stephen's dismay remains legitimate;
countless thousands continue to receive the only impressions they ever will
have of the French Revolution through the reading of *A Tale of Two Cities*.

The book remains a great tale, a vivid instance of Dickens's preternatural gifts as a pure storyteller, though except for its depiction of the superbly ghastly Madame Defarge and her Jacobin associates it lacks the memorable grotesques and driven enthusiasts that we expect from Dickens.

The most palpable flaw in the novel is the weakness as representations of Lucie and Darnay, and the relative failure of the more crucial Carton, who simply lacks the aesthetic dignity that Dickens so desperately needed to give him. If Carton and Darnay, between them, really were meant to depict the spiritual form of Charles Dickens, then their mutual lack of gusto renders them even more inadequate. When Madame Defarge dies, slain by her own bullet, we are very moved, particularly by relief that such an unrelenting version of the death drive will cease to menace us. When Carton, looking "sublime and prophetic," goes to execution, Dickens attempts to move us: we receive the famous and unacceptable, "It is a far, far better thing that I do, than I have ever done; it is a far, far better rest that I go to than I have ever known." Dickens owes us a far, far better rhetoric than that, and generally he delivers it.

The life of *A Tale of Two Cities* is elsewhere, centered upon the negative sublimity of Madame Defarge and her knitting, which is one of Dickens's finest inventions, and is clearly a metaphor for the storytelling of the novel itself. Dickens hardly would have said: "I am Madame Defarge," but she, like the author, remorselessly controls the narrative, until she loses her struggle with the epitome of a loving Englishwoman, Miss Pross. The book's penultimate chapter, in which we are rid of Madame Defarge, is shrewdly called "The Knitting Done."

Even Dickens rarely surpasses the nightmare intensity of Madame Defarge, her absolute command of stage fire, and his finest accomplishment in the book is to increase her already stark aura as the narrative knits onwards. Here is a superb early epiphany of the lady, putting heart into her formidable husband, who seems weak only in comparison to his wife, less a force of nature than of history:

> The night was hot, and the shop, close shut and surrounded by so foul a neighbourhood, was ill-smelling. Monsieur Defarge's olfactory sense was by no means delicate, but the stock of wine smelt much stronger than it ever tasted, and so did the stock of rum and brandy and aniseed. He whiffed the compound of scents away, as he put down his smoked-out pipe.
>
> "You are fatigued," said madame, raising her glance as she knotted the money. "There are only the usual odours."

"I am a little tired," her husband acknowledged.

"You are a little depressed, too," said madame, whose quick eyes had never been so intent on the accounts, but they had had a ray or two for him. "Oh, the men, the men!"

"But my dear!" began Defarge.

"But my dear!" repeated madame, nodding firmly; "but my dear! You are faint of heart to-night, my dear!"

"Well, then," said Defarge, as if a thought were wrung out of his breast, "it *is* a long time."

"It is a long time," repeated his wife; "and when is it not a long time? Vengeance and retribution require a long time; it is the rule."

"It does not take a long time to strike a man with Lightning," said Defarge.

"How long," demanded madame, composely, "does it take to make and store the lightning? Tell me."

Defarge raised his head thoughtfully, as if there were something in that too.

"It does not take a long time," said madame, "for an earthquake to swallow a town. Eh well! Tell me how long it takes to prepare the earthquake?"

"A long time, I suppose," said Defarge.

"But when it is ready, it takes place, and grinds to pieces everything before it. In the meantime, it is always preparing, though it is not seen or heard. That is your consolation. Keep it."

She tied a knot with flashing eyes, as if it throttled a foe.

"I tell thee," said madame, extending her right hand, for emphasis, "that although it is a long time on the road, it is on the road and coming. I tell thee it never retreats, and never stops. I tell thee it is always advancing. Look around and consider the lives of all the world that we know, consider the faces of all the world that we know, consider the rage and discontent to which the Jacquerie addresses itself with more and more of certainty every hour. Can such things last? Bah! I mock you."

"My brave wife," returned Defarge, standing before her with his head a little bent, and his hands clasped at his back, like a docile and attentive pupil before his catechist, "I do not question all this. But it has lasted a long time, and it is possible—you know well, my wife, it is possible—that it may not come, during our lives."

"Eh well! How then?" demanded madame, tying another knot, as if there were another enemy strangled.

"Well!" said Defarge, with a half-complaining and half-apologetic shrug. "We shall not see the triumph."

"We shall have helped it," returned madame, with her extended hand in strong action. "Nothing that we do, is done in vain. I believe, with all my soul, that we shall see the triumph. But even if not, even if I knew certainly not, show me the neck of an aristocrat and tyrant, and still I would—"

Then madame, with her teeth set, tied a very terrible knot indeed.

"Hold!" cried Defarge, reddening a little as if he felt charged with cowardice; "I too, my dear, will stop at nothing."

"Yes! But it is your weakness that you sometimes need to see your victim and your opportunity, to sustain you. Sustain yourself without that. When the time comes, let loose a tiger and a devil; but wait for the time with the tiger and the devil chained—not shown—yet always ready."

To be always preparing, unseen and unheard, is Madame Defarge's one consolation. Dickens has made her childless, somewhat in the mysterious mode of Lady Macbeth, since somehow we believe that Madame Defarge too must have nursed an infant. Her dialogue with Defarge has overtones of Lady Macbeth heartening Macbeth, keying up his resolution to treason and a kind of parricide. What Dickens has learned from Shakespeare is the art of counterpointing degrees of terror, of excess, so as to suggest a dread that otherwise would reside beyond representation. Macbeth, early doubting, seems weak in contrast to his wife's force, but we will see him at his bloody work, until he becomes an astonishing manifestation of tyranny. Similarly, Defarge seems little in juxtaposition to his implacable wife, but we will see him as a demon of courage, skill, and apocalyptic drive, leading the triumphant assault upon the Bastille.

In his final vision of Madame Defarge, Dickens brilliantly reveals his masochistic passion for her:

Madame Defarge slightly waved her hand, to imply that she heard, and might be relied upon to arrive in good time, and so went through the mud, and round the corner of the prison wall.

The Vengeance and the Juryman, looking after her as she walked away, were highly appreciative of her fine figure, and her superb moral endowments.

There were many women at that time, upon whom the time laid a dreadfully disfiguring hand; but, there was not one among them more to be dreaded than this ruthless woman, now taking her way along the streets. Of a strong and fearless character, of shrewd sense and readiness, of great determination, of that kind of beauty which not only seems to impart to its possessor firmness and animosity, but to strike into others an instinctive recognition of those qualities; the troubled time would have heaved her up, under any circumstances. But, imbued from her childhood with a brooding sense of wrong, and an inveterate hatred of a class, opportunity had developed her into a tigress. She was absolutely without pity. If she had ever had the virtue in her, it had quite gone out of her.

It was nothing to her, that an innocent man was to die for the sins of his forefathers; she saw, not him, but them. It was nothing to her, that his wife was to be made a widow and his daughter an orphan; that was insufficient punishment, because they were her natural enemies and her prey, and as such had no right to live. To appeal to her, was made hopeless by her having no sense of pity, even for herself. If she had been laid low in the streets, in any of the many encounters in which she had been engaged, she would not have pitied herself; nor, if she had been ordered to the axe to-morrow, would she have gone to it with any softer feeling than a fierce desire to change places with the man who sent her there.

Such a heart Madame Defarge carried under her rough robe. Carelessly worn, it was a becoming robe enough, in a certain weird way, and her dark hair looked rich under her coarse red cap. Lying hidden in her bosom, was a loaded pistol. Lying hidden at her waist, was a sharpened dagger. Thus accoutred, and walking with the confident tread of such a character, and with the supple freedom of a woman who had habitually walked in her girlhood, bare-foot and bare-legged, on the brown sea-sand, Madame Defarge took her way along the streets.

We can discount Dickens's failed ironies here ("her superb moral endowments") and his obvious and rather tiresome moral judgments upon his own creation. What comes through overwhelmingly is Dickens's desire for this sadistic woman, which is the secret of our desire for her also, and so for her nightmare power over us. "Her fine figure," "that kind of beauty ... firmness and animosity," "a tigress ... absolutely without pity," "a becoming robe enough, in a certain weird way," "her dark hair looked rich," "confident tread ... supple freedom ... bare-foot and bare-legged"—these are the stigmata of a dominatrix. Loaded pistol in her bosom, sharpened dagger at her waist, Madame Defarge is the ultimate phallic woman, a monument to fetishism, to what Freud would have called the splitting of Dickens's ego in the defensive process.

That splitting attains a triumph in the grand wrestling match, where Miss Pross, a Jacob wrestling with the Angel of Death, holds off Madame Defarge in what is supposed to be an instance of Love stronger than Death, but which is all the more effective for its sexual overtones:

> Madame Defarge made at the door. Miss Pross, on the instinct of the moment, seized her round the waist in both her arms, and held her tight. It was in vain for Madame Defarge to struggle and to strike; Miss Pross, with the vigorous tenacity of love, always so much stronger than hate, clasped her tight, and even lifted her from the floor in the struggle that they had. The two hands of Madame Defarge buffeted and tore her face; but, Miss Pross, with her head down, held her round the waist, and clung to her with more than the hold of a drowning woman.
>
> Soon, Madame Defarge's hands ceased to strike, and felt at her encircled waist. "It is under my arm," said Miss Pross, in smothered tones, "you shall not draw it. I am stronger than you, I bless Heaven for it. I'll hold you till one or other of us faints or dies!"
>
> Madame Defarge's hands were at her bosom. Miss Pross looked up, saw what it was, struck at it, struck out a flash and a crash, and stood alone—blinded with smoke.

The embrace of Miss Pross clearly has a repressed lesbian passion for Madame Defarge in it, so that more than a transcendent love for Lucie here endows the force of the good with its immovable tenacity. But for the pistol blast, Madame Defarge would have been held until one or the other lady fainted or died. Miss Pross had never struck a blow in her life, but then her father Jacob had been no warrior either. Dickens, master of stage fire, destroyed Madame Defarge in the grand manner, the only fate worthy of so vivid and so passionately desired a creation.

J.M. RIGNALL

Dickens and the Catastrophic Continuum of History in A Tale of Two Cities

It is not surprising that the most remembered scene in *A Tale of Two Cities* is the last, for this novel is dominated, even haunted, by its ending. From the opening chapter in which the "creatures of this chronicle" are set in motion "along the roads that lay before them," while the Woodman Fate and the Farmer Death go silently about their ominous work, those roads lead with sinister inevitability to the revolutionary scaffold.[1] To an unusual extent, especially given the expansive and centrifugal nature of Dickens's imagination, this is an end-determined narrative whose individual elements are ordered by an ending which is both their goal and, in a sense, their source. In a historical novel like this there is a transparent relationship between narrative form and historical vision, and the formal features of *A Tale*—its emphatic linearity, continuity, and negative teleology—define a distinctive vision of history. As Robert Alter has argued in his fine critical account of the novel,[2] it is not the particular historical event that ultimately concerns Dickens here, but rather a wider view of history and the historical process. That process is a peculiarly grim one. As oppression is shown to breed oppression, violence to beget violence, evil to provoke evil, a pattern emerges that is too deterministic to owe much to Carlyle and profoundly at odds with the conventional complacencies of Whig history. Instead of progress there is something more like the catastrophic continuum that is Walter Benjamin's description of the

From *ELH* 51, no. 3 (Autumn 1984): pp. 575–587. © 1984 by the Johns Hopkins University Press.

13

historical process: the single catastrophe, piling wreckage upon wreckage.[3] And when, in the sentimental postscript of Carton's prophecy, Dickens finally attempts to envisage a liberation from this catastrophic process, he can only do so, like Benjamin, in eschatological terms. For Benjamin it was the messianic intervention of a proletarian revolution that would bring time to a standstill and blast open the continuum of history; for Dickens it is the Christ-like intervention of a self-sacrificing individual that is the vehicle for a vision of a better world which seems to lie beyond time and history. The parallel with Benjamin cannot be pressed beyond the common perception of a pernicious historical continuum and the common desire to break it, but the coexistence of these two elements in *A Tale* is, I wish to argue, important for an understanding of the novel, lending it a peculiarly haunted and contradictory quality as Dickens gives expression to a vision of history which both compels and repels him at the same time.

In Carton's final vision of a world seemingly beyond time, the paradigm of the apocalypse mediates between what is known of history and what may be hoped for it.[4] That hope is not to be dismissed as mere sentimentality, whatever the manner of its expression. However inadequately realized Carton's prophecy may be in imaginative terms, it is significant as a moment of resistance to the grimly terminal linearity and historical determinism of the preceding narrative. That resistance is not confined to the last page of the novel, for, as I shall show, it manifests itself in other places and in other ways, creating a faint but discernible counter-current to the main thrust of the narrative. This is not to say that Dickens presents a thorough-going deconstruction of his own narrative procedures and version of history in *A Tale*, for the process at work here is more ambiguous and tentative than that. There is a struggle with sombre fears that gives rise to contradictions which cannot be reduced to the internal self-contradictions of language. What the novel presents is, rather, the spectacle of an imagination both seized by a compelling vision of history as a chain of violence, a catastrophic continuum, and impelled to resist that vision in the very act of articulation, so that the narrative seems at the same time to seek and to shun the violent finality of its ending in the Terror. The nightmare vision is too grim to accept without protest, and too powerful to be dispelled by simple hopefulness, and the work bears the signs of this unresolved and unresolvable contradiction.

In his preface Dickens maintains that the idea of the novel had "complete possession" of him, and the state of imaginative obsession in which *A Tale of Two Cities* was written can be sensed in two rather different aspects of the work: in the way that it presses on relentlessly toward its violent ending, and in the way that particular scenes take on a visionary intensity, seemingly charged with obscure and powerful emotions that are neither fully controlled nor comprehended. The scenes of frenzied collective violence are the most striking examples of this kind of writing, but there are other moments, less obviously related to the main track of the story, when images and ideas erupt into the text with a spontaneous energy that arrests rather than furthers the momentum of the narrative. The first-person meditation on the death-like mystery of individuality which opens chapter 3 ("The Night Shadows") is just such an intervention:

> A wonderful fact to reflect upon, that every human creature is constituted to be that profound secret and mystery to every other. A solemn consideration, when I enter a great city by night, that every one of those darkly clustered houses encloses its own secret; that every room in every one of them encloses its own secret; that every beating heart in the hundreds of thousands of breasts there, is, in some of its imaginings, a secret to the heart nearest it! Something of the awfulness, even of Death itself, is referable to this. No more can I turn the leaves of this dear book that I loved, and vainly hope in time to read it all. No more can I look into the depths of this unfathomable water, wherein, as momentary lights glanced into it, I have had glimpses of buried treasure and other things submerged. It was appointed that the book should shut with a spring, for ever and for ever, when I had read but a page. It was appointed that the water should be locked in an eternal frost, when the light was playing on its surface, and I stood in ignorance on the shore. My friend is dead, my neighbour is dead, my love, the darling of my soul, is dead; it is the inexorable consolidation and perpetuation of the secret that was always in that individuality, and which I shall carry in mine to my life's end. In any of the burial-places of this city through which I pass, is there a sleeper more inscrutable than its busy inhabitants are, in their innermost personality, to me, or than I am to them? (44)

Both the form and the substance of this meditation set it clearly apart from the surrounding narrative. The brooding first-person voice is never heard again in the novel, even though the same sombre note is struck by the impersonal narrator. The directness and urgency of the first-person utterance invite us to look for a significant relationship between these reflections and the main themes of the novel, but it is not easy to find one. The passage is only awkwardly related to the scene on the Dover road which it punctuates, since its insistence on the essential, metaphysical mystery of individuality is out of proportion to the condition of the passengers in the coach. Their mutual suspicion and ignorance are occasioned simply by the hazards of the journey. Nor can it be said to illumine the general condition of life as it appears in this novel. Although there is some connection between the separateness of individuals and the characters and fates of Dr. Manette and Carton, Dickens's handling of character is basically at odds with such an absolute assertion of impenetrable otherness. His imperious command of his characters is never subject to epistemological uncertainty, and even the most estranged figures, like Dr. Manette and Carton, are in the end not mysterious but knowable and known. Except in its tone the excursus is altogether out of place: Dickens here steps out of his own fiction to generalize about character and individuality in life rather than in books, while paradoxically using the metaphor of the book to do so.

This reflection on character and the metaphor that it employs cast a significant light on Dickens's own practice in the novel. By implication, both his presentation of character and his use of an ending are identified as simply matters of literary convention. To see death in terms of the premature closing of a book is to raise the possibility of different relationships among death, narrative, and endings from those presented by *A Tale* itself. Discontinuity is a fact of life and, implicitly, a narrative possibility, and to imply as much is to challenge both the conventional structure of this particular narrative and the vision of historical determinism that it projects. The challenge is only momentary and implied, but the moment is not entirely isolated. Although Dickens primarily uses the death of Carton and the ending of the novel to complete a pattern of meaning rather than to effect a premature closure, there are occasions in the novel when the desire for such a closure surfaces in the text as if in reaction to the chain of violent events that leads relentlessly to the guillotine. The first-person plural dramatization of the Darnays' flight from Paris (386–7) provides, for instance, a kind of alternative premature ending for those privileged characters who are allowed to escape the logic of the historical process. The scene is both related and opposed to the "Night Shadows" meditation and Mr. Lorry's journey to Dover: this time the characters in the coach are not suspicious, but united by love and shared apprehension; they are not mysterious and unfathomable, but familiar and transparent. Nevertheless, the "awfulness of death" threatens them from without, and, as the narrative assumes the urgency and immediacy of the first-person plural and the present tense, the scene comes to suggest a flight of the imagination from the foredoomed finality of the guillotine and the novel's preordained ending. It is a flight which necessarily carries the characters beyond the boundaries of the novel, which is headed to only one conclusion, and they never again appear directly in it. Pursued not by the Revolution but, as it turns out, only by a reflection of their own fears, they may be said to be escaping from history: "the wind is rushing after us, and the clouds are flying after us, and the moon is plunging after us, and the whole wild night is in pursuit of us; but, so far we are pursued by nothing else" (387). In fleeing the ending of the novel they have fled beyond the process of history.

There is a less direct and more complex suggestion of flight from the grim logic of the historical process in the scene of the mob around the grindstone, observed by Mr. Lorry and Dr. Manette. What they witness is an appalling spectacle of bestial violence and moral degradation as Dickens lets his wildest and deepest fears rise to the surface. The chain reaction of violent oppression and violent rebellion has passed beyond human control, and in this mass frenzy all distinctions of individuality and even sex are submerged:

> The eye could not detect one creature in the group free from the smear of blood. Shouldering one another to get next at the sharpening-stone, were men stripped to the waist, with the stain all over their limbs and bodies; men in all sorts of rags, with the stain upon those rags; men devilishly set off with spoils of women's lace and silk and ribbon, with the stain dyeing those trifles through and through.

Then, as if appalled by the terrors he has let loose, Dickens, in John Gross's words, "reaches for his gun":[5]

> And as the frantic wielders of these weapons snatched them from the stream of sparks and tore away into the streets, the same red hue was red in their frenzied eyes;—eyes which any unbrutalised beholder would have given twenty years of life, to petrify with a well-directed gun.
>
> All this was seen in a moment, as the vision of a drowning man, or of any human creature at any very great pass, could see a world if it were there. They drew back from the window, and the Doctor looked for explanation in his friend's ashy face. (291–2)

Clearly signalled as the vision of a drowning man, the scene is the product of an imagination *in extremis*. It is a bourgeois nightmare of anarchy unleashed by the rebellion of the oppressed.[6] Even if it is the logical culmination of the violent oppression that has preceded it, the violence is, when it eventuates, too great to bear. The "well-directed gun," with its sudden change of focus from dramatic scene to violent, judgmental reaction, looks like an authorial intervention aimed at terminating the nightmare. The curious insistence on the eyes of the frenzied crowd emphasizes that vision is the vital element, and the urge to "petrify" those eyes can be read as the expression of a desire to put an end to that vision. The action is transposed from subject to object: it is not their eyes that Dickens the narrator wishes to close, but his own. For a moment he seeks to retreat from his own vision of the historical process.

There is, then, a form of resistance here to the catastrophic continuum of history, but at the same time Dickens reveals something about the emotional dynamics of that historical process in a way that is more penetrating than the melodramatic simplifications of Madame Defarge and her desire for vengeance. The violent reaction of the "well-directed gun," an answering of violence with violence, implicates the writer himself in the very process he is presenting. This is characteristic of the open and unguarded nature of his procedure in *A Tale*: violent fears and violent reactions are given direct, unmediated expression, so that unwitting parallels emerge between the reflexes of the author/narrator and those of the fictional characters. In this case there is an obvious affinity between the "well-directed gun," with what has been aptly termed its "true ring of outraged rate-paying respectability,"[7] and the response of the blustering bourgeois Stryver to news of the Revolution:

> Among the talkers, was Stryver, of the King's Bench Bar, far on his way to state promotion, and, therefore, loud on the theme: broaching to Monseigneur, his devices for blowing the people up and exterminating them from the face of the earth, and doing without them; and for accomplishing many similar objects akin in their nature to the abolition of eagles by sprinkling salt on the tails of the race. (267)

The reaction of the character is held firmly in focus and identified by means of irony as excessive and senseless, while the author/narrator in the grindstone passage repeats that reaction without the containing frame of any critical awareness. And both reactions have the function—the one deliberate, the other involuntary—of revealing the emotional resources that drive the catastrophic continuum of history. Dickens thus does more than simply project a deterministic vision of history; he shows how that determinism is rooted in commonplace and familiar emotions, how the potential for violence is not confined to a savage past and an alien setting, but lies very close to home. The effect is to detach history from the safety of the past and to suggest that its violent continuum may not have expired with the Revolution.

The persistence of that violence is amply demonstrated by Dickens's own susceptibility to the kinds of powerful emotions that are at work in the novel. As a caricature of the conquering bourgeois, the figure of Stryver belongs as much in the nineteenth century as the eighteenth, and Dickens himself could display distinctly Stryverish leanings in his response to contemporary events. In the same letter to Forster in which he outlines his intentions in *A Tale of Two Cities* and which he must have written about the same time as the grindstone passage,[8] there is a revealing outburst of verbal violence. The letter begins with a discussion of the case of the surgeon Thomas Smethurst, found guilty of poisoning his bigamous "wife." The trial judge, Sir Jonathan Frederick Pollock, strongly supported the verdict in the face of public unease and of moves to persuade the Home Secretary to quash or commute the sentence.[9] Dickens gives his fervent support to Pollock, and in doing so presents another example of an outraged, violent reaction to an act of violence:

> I followed the case with so much interest, and have followed the miserable knaves and asses who have perverted it since, with so much indignation, that I have often had more than half a mind to write and thank the upright judge who tried him. I declare to God that I believe such a service one of the greatest that a man of intellect and courage can render to society. Of course I saw the beast of a prisoner (with my mind's eye) delivering his cut-and-dried speech, and read in every word of it that no one but the murderer could have delivered or conceived it. Of course I have been driving the girls out of their wits here, by incessantly proclaiming that there needed no medical evidence either way, and that the case was plain without it. Lastly, of course (though a merciful man—because a merciful man I mean), I would hang any Home Secretary (Whig, Tory, Radical, or otherwise) who should step in between that black scoundrel and the gallows.[10]

The protestations of his mercifulness are convincing only as a respectable garment for his Stryverish pugnacity, and the emotional pattern of the passage recapitulates that of the grindstone scene so closely as to provide striking evidence for taking the "well-directed gun" as an authorial intervention. What is more interesting, however, is that the violence spills over into his account of his intentions in writing *A Tale*:

> But I set myself the little task of making a *picturesque* story, rising in
> every chapter with characters true to nature, but whom the story
> itself should express, more than they should express themselves,
> by dialogue. I mean, in other words, that I have fancied a story
> of incident might be written, in place of the bestiality that *is*
> written under that pretence, pounding the characters out in its
> own mortar, and beating their own interests out of them. If you
> could have read the story all at once, I hope you wouldn't have
> stopped half way.[11]

As violent an exception is taken to conventional forms of storytelling as is
taken to an alleged murderer, and when Dickens writes of "pounding" and
"beating" his characters it seems that violence is not only central to his vision
of history in this novel but is also inherent in his means of expressing that
vision. This formal violence, which could be interpreted in one sense as the
forcible subordination of character to the story of incident, is as revealingly
related to the creation of a narrative and historical continuum as is the earlier
emotional violence. The expressed intention is to prevent the reader from
stopping halfway, to maintain a compelling momentum in the narrative, and
this momentum also serves the vision of historical determinism by subjecting
individuals to a sequence of violent events that is beyond their power to
control.

What exactly Dickens means by beating his characters' own interest
out of them is open to question. It might be taken to refer to the way in
which they are forcibly harnessed to allegorical meanings, like Darnay
with the "Everyman" implications of his original family name, or the
sentimental equation of Lucie Manette with a "golden thread." But the
only character who has any real interest to be beaten out of him, Carton,
is not the object of any direct allegorizing. Indeed, in his case meaning
is deliberately withheld rather than allegorically asserted, and no cogent
reasons are offered for his alienation. This mystification has the effect of
directing the search for significance away from the personal life towards
the general condition of existence. Lukács's contention that Carton's fate
is the one that least of all "grows organically out of the age and its social
events"[12] is justified only if the wider historical process is ignored, for it is
as a victim of general social values and forces—and hence, by implication,
of the historical continuum—that interest and significance are beaten out
of him. As Lukács sees, he is a marginal figure, but he can be said to be
significant precisely for that reason: he has been marginalized, so to speak,
by the energy and values embodied in Stryver who, more properly than
Darnay, is his *alter ego*. In his gloomy estrangement Carton suggests the

neurotic price that may be exacted by the aggressive pursuit of individual success, by the bourgeois ethos of individual endeavor in its most crassly careerist form. The accusation that he levels at Stryver evinces a social as much as a personal truth: "'You were always driving and riving and shouldering and pressing, to that restless degree that I had no chance for my life but in rust and repose'" (120–1). A world dominated by the energy and purpose of such as Stryver claims its moral and psychological victims within the dominant class. The triumph of the bourgeois will creates its opposite in the aimless, drifting existence of a character whose self-image—"'I should ask ... that I might be regarded as an useless ... piece of furniture'" (237)—betrays the marks of a reified consciousness. And to the extent that Stryver partakes of the violent spirit which is at work in the larger historical events, Carton comes to stand, too, as the victim of the catastrophic continuum of history, a role which he then, at the end, consciously assumes.

To define Carton in these terms is to spell out bluntly what is only intimated indirectly, for it is Dickens's refusal to define and explain precisely that gives Carton a greater degree of density and interest than the other characters. With Carton, indeed, Dickens comes closest to creating something like the mystery and opacity of individuality that he refers to in the "Night Shadows" meditation, but only up to a point, since in the final scenes of the character's transformation there is a movement back toward conventional coherence and transparency. If, as Benjamin argues, the meaning of the life of a character in a novel is revealed in his death,[13] then Carton could be said to constitute himself as a character by choosing to die by the guillotine. He gives himself a goal and a purpose, and in so doing gives shape and meaning to his life. What has been aimless and indefinite becomes purposive and defined, and continuity is established between beginning and end, between promising youth and exemplary death. He achieves character in both a formal and a moral sense, and in the process realigns himself with the other representatives of English bourgeois life, exhibiting reflexes reminiscent of Stryver's in sensing a desire to strike the life out of the wood-sawyer (341) and reflecting on the desirability of raising Madame Defarge's arm and striking under it sharp and deep (371).

Carton's transformation is clearly intended to be read as the redemption of a wasted life, but such a reading has to ignore the qualifying ambiguities that are involved in it. As he decides on his course of action, resolution is strangely mixed with fatalism:

> "There is nothing more to do," said he, glancing upward at the moon, "until tomorrow. I can't sleep."

> It was not a reckless manner, the manner in which he said
> these words aloud under the fast-sailing clouds, nor was it more
> expressive of negligence than defiance. It was the settled manner
> of a tired man, who had wandered and struggled and got lost, but
> who at length struck into his road and saw its end. (342)

The term "end" carries a double meaning: in one sense it has to be read as "goal," stressing Carton's new-found sense of purpose and smuggling into the novel on the level of the individual life the positive teleology that is so markedly absent on the level of history. But the stronger meaning here is that of "conclusion," and a conclusion that is approached with a sense of release rather than a sense of achievement. The "tired man" is simply seeking repose, and in his desire for an end he makes explicit that resistance to the narrative and historical continuum which has been intimated elsewhere in the novel and now surfaces as the deepest yearning of a particular character.

He wishes to escape but, significantly, the mode of escape he chooses merely confirms his status as a victim of socio-historical circumstances. The act of self-sacrifice—an idea which haunts Dickens's imagination in this novel as powerfully and melodramatically as images of revolutionary violence—cannot be seen as simply the ultimate expression of altruism, since it is obscurely rooted in the same values that have significantly contributed to Carton's estrangement in the first place. The puritan ethic of disciplined personal endeavor demands renunciation such as Carton has been neurotically making all along, and its final act is the renunciation of life itself.[14] Thus the very step which makes sense of his life is as perverse as it is noble, as much a capitulation to the uncontrollable forces that have governed his life as a transcendence of them. To seek to escape sacrifice by sacrificing oneself is the expression of a truly desperate desire for an ending.

These more questionable implications of Carton's self-chosen end are largely disguised by Dickens's narrative and rhetorical strategies in the closing chapters. The polarization and pathos of melodrama are engaged to elicit acceptance of him as an exemplary altruist, while the Christian rhetoric of death and resurrection serves to present his self-sacrifice as a positive act of redemption rather than an expression of world-weary resignation. The character is, as it were, borne along by an affective and rhetorical current which obscures contradictions, and this same current is clearly intended to carry the reader, unquestioning, from Carton's death under the Terror to the resurrection of civilized order in his prophetic vision of the future. This attempt to make the historical regeneration of France and the domestic happiness of the Darnays seem continuous with what has preceded them is, however, hardly convincing, as the only element of continuity is the continuing strain of imaginative resistance to the destructive historical continuum. That the historical process of escalating violence should issue in a benign future is scarcely conceivable in this context, and Dickens passes perfunctorily over how it could come about with a casual reference to "evil ... gradually making expiation for itself and wearing out" (404). The suggestion of entropy in that last phrase is significant. It is not so much a vision of redeeming historical development that is bestowed on Carton as a vision of the end of time. "'There is no Time there'" (403), he says to the seamstress of the "better" land to which both are going; and his own vision of a better land, with its "beautiful city" and "brilliant people" (404) rising from the abyss, appears similarly otherworldly, having a greater affinity with the New Jerusalem of the Apocalypse than with nineteenth-century Paris. Indeed, the apocalyptic note in this conclusion stresses finality rather than resurrection, and death haunts even the conventional pieties of the domestic happy ending: Lorry is seen "passing tranquilly to his reward" and the Darnays, "their course done, lying side by side in their last earthly bed" (404). Lives are shown passing to a peaceful end, and all this individual and historical "wearing out" is envisaged by a man who is himself gratefully embracing death as a welcome release. Even in his famous mawkish last words it is not the heroic deed but the long-sought repose, the "far, far better rest" (404), that receives the final emphasis.

Weariness, both of character and of creative imagination, is the keynote of this ending, and it betrays the intellectual and imaginative impasse in which Dickens finds himself. Since he sees revolution as just another link in the chain of violence and oppression, and presents the efforts of individuals, like Darnay's journey to Paris, as powerless to influence the course of historical events, he can conceive no possibility, to use Benjamin's phrase, of blasting open the continuum of history by social and political action.[15] Unlike Benjamin, Dickens can advance no alternative vision of time and history. The claim once made for *Middlemarch* that it replaces "the concepts of origin, end and continuity" by "the categories of repetition, of difference, of discontinuity, of openness"[16] can certainly not be applied to *A Tale of Two Cities*. Origin and end, feudal oppression and revolutionary retribution, are linked by a causal chain which affirms the predominance of continuity. Repetition, on the other hand, as Dr. Manette's recurrent trauma illustrates, is here simply the mark of a mind imprisoned in the past, not a new, liberating category of temporal experience. Even the moments of discontinuity discussed earlier only challenge the narrative and historical continuum by revealing a desire to evade it. Carton's prophecy is simply a final evasive move, and one that gives itself away by its weary insistence on death and its eschatological suggestion of the end of time. Only by turning away from the course of human history can Dickens find a refuge for hope, and to express hope in such terms is tantamount to a confession of despair. In this novel of imprisonments and burials alive the writer himself remains imprisoned in a rigorously linear, end-determined narrative and the grimly determinist vision of history which it articulates. The resistance he offers is that of a mind vainly struggling to escape and thereby confirming the power of that which holds it captive. This vision of history as a catastrophic continuum is only made more powerful by the clear indications in the text that Dickens is expressing what is deeply repugnant to, yet stronger than, all that he can hope and wish for.

NOTES

1. *A Tale of Two Cities*, ed. George Woodcock (Harmondsworth: Penguin, 1970), 37. Further references to this edition are given after quotations in the text.

2. Robert Alter, "The Demons of History in Dickens' *Tale*," *Novel* 2 (1968–9): 135–142.

3. Walter Benjamin, "Theses on the Philosophy of History," *Illuminations*, trans. Harry Zohn, ed. Hannah Arendt (London: Fontana, 1973), 255–266 (257). See also *Gesammelte Schriften*, ed. Rolf Tiedemann and Hermann Schweppenhauser (Frankfurt, 1974), 1(3): 1244: "Die Katastrophe als das Kontinuum der Geschichte."

4. Alter, 138, gives an illuminating account of apocalyptic allusions in the novel.

5. John Gross, "*A Tale of Two Cities*," in *Dickens and the Twentieth Century*, ed. John Gross and Gabriel Pearson (London, 1962), 192.

6. Benjamin, in his opposition to the notion of historical continuity, stresses the importance of isolated moments of vision like this: "To articulate the past historically does not mean to recognize it 'the way it really was' (Ranke). It means to seize hold of a memory as it flashes up at a moment of danger. Historical materialism wishes to retain that image of the past which unexpectedly appears to a man singled out by history at a moment of danger" (*Illuminations*, 257). Whereas Benjamin was thinking of the revolutionary proletariat as the subject of such a vision, recapturing the experience of its oppressed forebears, Dickens could be said to be presenting the bourgeois counterpart of such an experience, where the man singled out by history at a moment of danger relives the perennial fears of the property-owning class.

7. Gross, 192.

8. The weekly part containing the "Grindstone" chapter was published on September 24, 1859. In this letter of August 25, Dickens tells Forster that he has asked the publisher of *All The Year Round* to send him "four weeks' proofs beyond the current number, that are in type." The current number would be that of August 20: the four weeks in proof would cover the numbers up to 17 September, leaving the "Grindstone" part as not yet in type, and most probably either just completed or still being worked on. For the letter of August 25 see *The Letters of Charles Dickens*, ed. Walter Dexter (London: Nonesuch Press, 1938), 3:117–119.

9. See Philip Collins, *Dickens and Crime*, 2nd ed. (London, 1964), 246.

10. *Letters*, 3:118.

11. Although this quotation comes from the same letter as the preceding one, I have here cited the text as given by Charles Dickens the Younger in his introduction to *A Tale of Two Cities* (London: Macmillan, 1902), xx. He points out that Forster, in quoting the letter in his *Life*, alters "bestiality" to "odious stuff." Dexter, *Letters*, 3: 118, follows Forster's diluted version.

12. Georg Lukács, *The Historical Novel*, trans. Hannah and Stanley Mitchell (Harmondsworth: Penguin, 1969), 292.

13. *Illuminations*, 100–101.

14. The irrational act of self-sacrifice could thus be said to point to a general irrationalism in history and society at large, as is suggested in a different context by Max Horkheimer and Theodor W. Adorno, *Dialectic of Enlightenment*, trans. John Cumming (London, 1973), 55: "The irrationalism of totalitarian capitalism ... has its prototype in the hero who escapes from sacrifice by sacrificing himself. The history of civilisation is the history of the introversion of sacrifice. In other words: the history of renunciation."

15. *Illuminations*, 264.

16. J. Hillis Miller, "Narrative and History," in *ELH Essays for Earl R. Wasserman*, ed. Ronald Paulson and Arnold Stein (Baltimore and London, 1975), 165–183 (177).

LISA ROBSON

The "Angels" in Dickens's House:
Representation of Women in A Tale of Two Cities

I

A Tale of Two Cities is not a woman's text; indeed, there is little chance of
its being mistaken for one. In his interpretation of the causes and effects of
the French Revolution, Charles Dickens focusses on a patriarchal world of
politics and historical development in which men dominate the scene, both
privately and publicly. Yet several women characters factor rather importantly
in the novel's development, and, as such, merit close scrutiny. The current
body of criticism concerning *A Tale of Two Cities* concentrates mainly on the
political and historical elements of the text, while conspicuously absent is a
detailed examination of the female role in Dickens's representation of the
Revolution. On the other hand, although various studies of the women in
Dickens's fiction have been offered (for example, Michael Slater's *Dickens
and Women* and Sylvia Jarmuth's *Dickens' Use of Women in his Novels*), most
are general in nature and provide little more than a cursory examination of, if
they explore at all, the women in *A Tale of Two Cities*. In this paper, therefore,
I intend to present a detailed analysis of the women in this historical novel,
particularly the two main female characters, Lucie Manette and Madame
Defarge, as well as the most prominent secondary female character, Miss
Pross.

From *Dalhousie Review* 72, no. 3 (Fall 1992): pp. 311–333. © 1993 by *Dalhousie Review*.

Specifically, I am concerned with Dickens's manipulation of the angel in the house image as a Victorian representation which idealizes women for their femininity. In terms of this ideal, these three women form a complex triangle; each woman corresponds to the other two either as some form of double or antitype. Lucie Manette and Madame Defarge, for example, represent England and France, middle-class lady and peasant, the perfect angel and her complete opposite. Miss Pross, on the other hand, is Lucie's lower-class comic counterpart, enough like her mistress to act as substitute and do what Lucie, as a middle-class woman, cannot. Finally, Madame Defarge and Miss Pross, two women of similar social standing on opposite sides of the novel's personal conflict, appear to have little in common, yet are deceivingly similar. However alike or unlike these characters may seem to be, the one quality which links them all is an apparent lack of conventionality. As participants in the turbulent French conflict of 1789, these three representatives of Dickens's female characters are often seen in unconventional situations and positions, exposing social problems and exploring new spaces for women to inhabit. Yet, although Dickens appears to allow these women to adopt nontraditional female roles, he consistently reverts to granting them representation only as passive, silent, marginal figures. In fact, *A Tale of Two Cities* seems to allow women to break free from traditional sexual boundaries only to recontain them more forcefully in their traditional positions.

When discussing representations of women in Victorian literature, the angel in the house figure, of course, is far from unconventional; she is a most traditional female representation, her image largely reflecting the highly repressive conditions governing women's activity (or the lack thereof) during the period. Like so many of his contemporaries, Dickens often turns to this stereotypical figure in his fiction. Alexander Welsh explains how, while idealizing the home and hearth as alternatives to his vision of the dark and destructive nineteenth-century city, Dickens frequently reduces women to angel figures whose role is to fill the home with comfort and a sense of security (141–63). However, in *A Tale of Two Cities* Dickens moves beyond the specifically traditional metaphor to highlight the angel's supposedly innate redemptive and regenerative abilities, her capacity to function as a type of savior figure, and the consequent elevation she receives as a spiritual creature to be worshipped. In this manner, Dickens's portrayal of women as angels in *Tale* points to a progressive potential in this Victorian ideal. While the angel figure as reflected in the women in the novel adheres to convention in its insistence on the female as the gentler, purer sex, it also emphasizes women's vital role as men's redeemers. Such a focus on women's determining capacity highlights an apparent transgression of conventional assumptions concerning the relations of gender, sexuality and activity by creating a possibility of women's intervention into history as agents of redemption and regeneration, agents who may reach beyond the novel's moral to its social sphere. To this end, Dickens presents a series of "resurrections," beginning with Dr. Manette's return to England after eighteen years of incarceration in a French prison, aided by his daughter, Lucie, who is the novel's most pronounced angel in the house.

Following the initial excitement of the Doctor's escape, Lucie reclaims her father from his mental abstraction, bringing him back to life from his living death in prison. It is Lucie's feminine attributes, her trust, her kindness, her unselfish concern, her willing self-sacrifice, which gradually coax the old man to rejoin the living world. In a description of Lucie's importance to her father, Dickens defines his feminine angel. He writes:

> Only his daughter had the power of charming this black brooding from his mind. She was the golden thread that united him to a Past beyond his misery, and to a Present beyond his misery: and the sound of her voice, the light of her face, the touch of her hand, had a strong beneficial influence with him almost always. Not absolutely always, for she could recal[l] some occasions on which her power had failed; but they were few and slight, and she believed them over. (110)

Dickens endows Lucie with "a power of charming," suggesting a sense of magic and mystery surrounding her unique restorative powers. His description renders her almost otherworldly in her capacity to transcend time, to erase the barriers of past and present for those who feel trapped within them. Although Dickens later admits that her powers of recall have limits (she is unable to reclaim her father from his relapse at the conclusion of the novel), he asserts that she "believes them [her failures] over," suggesting a religious framework of faith wherein the feminine approaches the semi-divine; in fact, by the end of the novel, Carton, her would-be lover, refers to Lucie as "Her." A woman whose very name suggests "light," Lucie's ability to redeem others depends upon her capacity to love them and sacrifice herself for them.

To reinforce her spiritual elevation and yet grant her some measure of corporeal authenticity, Dickens includes domestic and physical references in the above description. He refers to Lucie as the "golden thread" that unites, an image which gestures toward a mythic connection with the Greek Fates as the weavers of destiny. This mention of the traditionally female activities of spinning and sewing suggests the novel's metaphor of redemption, or the feminine saint image, by highlighting the domesticity of feminine figures in their roles as preservers and reconcilers of the family. Calling upon an iconographical tradition which links a woman's physical appearance with her personal and moral worth, Dickens's reference to Lucie's voice, face and hand further confirms her femininity by exposing her beauty and the healing power of her touch as outward manifestations of her inner, angelic qualities. (He also repeatedly refers to her lovely forehead as indicative of her sincerity.) Throughout the novel, Lucie appears as a dutiful daughter and wife, unwilling to marry her greatest love, should her father disapprove, standing by her husband with level-headed practicality and emotional fortitude when he faces the French Tribunal, and always maintaining a beautiful home, whether in Soho or Paris. As an idealized feminine figure, Lucie is everything to everyone; she is innocent child to her father, loving (yet pure and nonsexual) wife to her husband, and compassionate friend and moral inspiration to those who love her. Through this firm affirmation of Lucie and her redemptive capacity, Dickens offers such feminine virtue, charitable love and self-sacrifice as alternatives to the violence and inhumanity which dominate his representation of the French Revolution.

Accompanying such overt praise of Lucie, Dickens further endorses this idealized representation of women through mockery of a comical, lower-class nonconformist. Miss Pross, Lucie's faithful servant, is an ugly, wild spinster who, in the absence of a husband, has become so strong in order to survive in a patriarchal society that Mr. Lorry, the Darnays' friend and epitome of English common sense, initially takes her for a man. Lorry first encounters the bizarre woman when Lucie faints in his presence at the news of her father's survival and release. Miss Pross flies into the room like a fury, the redness of her hair and dress representative of the wildness within, and physically throws Lorry across the room. Lorry responds to Miss Pross in a typically patriarchal fashion, fascinated by her oddity but repulsed, at least initially, by her apparent masculinity. Without marriage or motherhood, supported by her strength, independence and passion, Miss Pross refuses to surrender to traditional standards of femininity, and Dickens presents her as a distortion of the feminine ideal in the novel by ridiculing the oddness of her physical appearance and her behavioral eccentricities.

Such derision, however, never becomes complete rejection because Miss Pross is masculine only in a superficial sense; in terms of her spiritual nature and moral sensitivity, she is another feminine angel. As Lorry grows to know Miss Pross, Dickens writes:

> Mr. Lorry knew Miss Pross to be very jealous, but he also knew her by this time to be, beneath the surface of her eccentricity, one

of those unselfish creatures—found only among women—who will, for pure love and admiration, bind themselves willing slaves, to youth when they have lost it, to beauty that they never had, to accomplishments that they were never fortunate enough to gain, to bright hopes that never shone upon their own sombre lives. He knew enough of the world to know that there is nothing in it better than the faithful service of the heart; so rendered and so free from any mercenary taint, he had such an exalted respect for it, that in the retributive arrangements made by his own mind—we all make such arrangements, more or less—he stationed Miss Pross much nearer to the lower Angels than many ladies immeasurably better got up both by Nature and Art, who had balances at Tellson's. (126)

Dickens affirms Miss Pross's femininity by highlighting the unselfish disposition "found only among women" which she shares, her selfless, if somewhat pathetic, devotion to that which she desires but does not have: youth, beauty, accomplishment, hope. She is a woman of "pure heart," free of "mercenary taint" or self-concern, and her maternal dedication to Lucie and her untiring, sisterly support of her undeserving brother, Solomon, confirm her spiritual goodness. However distorted and masculinized she may appear to the naked eye, such feminine self-abnegation, incessant fidelity and unqualified compassion nullify the negative effect of her masculine idiosyncrasies and gain her respect and exaltation in the mind of Lorry who, with his strong sense of practicality and dedicated business mind, is an apt representative of the English patriarchy.

As something of a feminine aberration, Miss Pross receives further vindication in terms of the novel's construction of class relations. References to her social position in the above quotation confirm her social acceptability. As a member of the English lower classes, Miss Pross knows her place and thus "binds" herself as a "willing slave" to Lucie, her social superior. She constrains herself to servitude without question, happily forfeiting her possible pleasures and goals, and in the end her hearing too, to fulfil her duty and save Lucie and her family. Although Miss Pross may love the younger woman like a daughter, Lucie remains, nonetheless, her employer, and in protecting the Darnays successfully while in France Miss Pross secures her own employment and financial security. In her "faithful service," even as an angel Miss Pross assumes her "station" among their "lower" ranks, confirming her moral superiority to those wealthy women who may have external beauty but lack this working woman's inner worth. It is in part because Miss Pross participates in Dickens's angelic ideal and happily accepts her status among the English servant classes that ridicule of her eccentricities stops short of repudiation.

In terms of both class and gender, then, Miss Pross valorizes the "thematics of suppression" (Kucich 130) in the novel and suggests the impossible position in which patriarchal society, with its hierarchical structure and masculine bias, places women. Despite their supposed elevation as agents with a redemptive, moral mission, women's subjugation to a patriarchal agenda frustrates their ability to act as feminine savior figures. In her examination of the woman-as-savior image, Nancy Klenck Hill explains: "the spiritual dimension of life which they [women] control is necessarily subservient to the material realm commanded by men, even though men recognize women's spiritual function as being higher than their own material one." (98–99). As second-class citizens, women are denied agency by a patriarchal order which demands passivity; however, hailed as idealistic, feminine redeemers, they are expected to effect salvation. Required to modify without governing, women in a patriarchal society cannot adequately meet such extravagant expectations. This impasse, in part, explains the dull and lifeless representation of Lucie in the text, because in order to survive under such circumstances Lucie must remain an "unconscious and happy" (227) heroine with little personality. By thus restricting his female characters within a patriarchal structure, Dickens places the women in his novel in an ambiguous, illogical position.

Although the effects of such ambiguity are largely masked by Lucie's initially secure, domestic happiness and by the predominantly comic treatment of Miss Pross, other similar figures in the lower classes who are represented in darker ways, grotesque rather than humorous, reveal some of the consequences of this unreasonable situation. As they attempt to fulfil their "duties" despite patriarchal constraints, women such as Mrs. Cruncher grow increasingly susceptible to male brutality. In his examination of Dickens's work in general, H. M. Daleski suggests that Dickens's characters are often related in complex patterns of analogy. Indeed, as already illustrated, Miss Pross, in many ways, can be viewed as Lucie's double, and a similar parallel can be drawn between the heroine and Mrs. Cruncher. Isolated from the main action except through the participation of her husband, Jerry, who works for Mr. Lorry in England and France, Mrs. Cruncher displays common feminine virtues such as domesticity, submissiveness and religiosity. In the end she helps successfully to redeem her husband through her example, so that he repents his un-Christian disbelief and ill-treatment of her, but throughout the novel he abuses her emotionally, psychologically and physically for her "flopping," or prayer (184). Mrs. Cruncher, then, at least in some sense, acts as a feminine savior figure like Lucie; unlike Lucie, however, Mrs. Cruncher is brutalized by her husband for her efforts. The poor woman's experience exposes the universality of female insecurity in a patriarchal culture by demonstrating that a woman's safety and well-being largely depend upon the personality of her husband. Dickens may indirectly blame Lucie for Charles's quick return to England and partial renunciation of his title in France (he returns to be with her), but never is Lucie at risk because Charles loves her and is gentle of temperament. In contrast, Mrs. Cruncher's subordinate gentleness and subjugation to her husband's violence exposes the possibilities of victimization implicit in all feminine self-sacrifice.

Dickens forces such patriarchal oppression to an extreme in Dr. Manette's letter describing the events leading to his imprisonment: the rape and subsequent death of Madame Defarge's sister. In this letter, Dr. Manette quotes the girl's brother as he explains that, despite their father's despair for their future, his sister remained optimistic. He says:

> 'Nevertheless, Doctor, my sister married. He was ailing at that time, poor fellow, and she married her lover, that she might tend and comfort him in our cottage—our dog-hut, as that man would call it. She had not been married many weeks, when that man's brother [the Marquis] saw her and admired her, and asked that man [Charles's father] to lend her to him—for what are husbands among us! He was willing enough, but my sister was good and virtuous, and hated his brother with a hatred as strong as mine.' (354–55)

Exhibiting a family loyalty shared by the girl, the brother, the speaker in this passage, does not reveal the girl's name, and this partial anonymity underscores her position as a typical representative of her gender and class. As a "good," "virtuous" and, as the Doctor soon discovers, pregnant young woman, she is another idealized angel who marries the man she loves despite his illness, in order to "tend" or nurse him, to save and comfort him. The reference to the cottage as a "dog-hut" points to the poverty among the lower classes, and the disrespect shown towards the husbands by the Marquis and his brother highlights a sense of callous, aristocratic indifference which helps to create the class hatred identified by the Defarge brother. Unaffected by the girl's virtue, Charles's uncle cruelly rapes her, an abusive act which symbolizes the aristocratic exploitation of and barbarity toward the lower classes. Although this rape generates the action which comprises the novel, rather than affirming women's agency, this event denies their ability to act. Regarded as an object or piece of property to be "admired" and "lent" by the aristocracy, the girl lies immobile on her deathbed, unable to speak save in mad ravings, acted upon by the Marquis and the Doctor, and spoken for by her brother. Madame Defarge's sister represents the epitome of feminine innocence thrust into a hostile, masculine world, exploited by abusive men and initiating action only through her violation and her death.

Such a depiction of severe male violence against women pointedly questions the novel's advocacy of feminine self-sacrifice as a means of redemption and the proposed importance of women's endless love, forgiveness and submission. Certain critics (such as Albert D. Hutter, who examines the relations between father and sons in "Nation and Generation in *A Tale of Two Cities*"), suggest that Dickens indicts the patriarchal system in *Tale*, and it is true that Dickens levels much criticism against the hierarchical social and political world of his novel. However, any criticism of the patriarchy concerns women only in a narrow sense. Although Dickens's representation of women's exploitation indicates his recognition of some of the difficulties women face and his interest in their plight, his investigation goes no further. In fact, Dickens may expose some of the ambiguities in his feminine ideal and acknowledge some of the dangers of women's subordination within a patriarchal system, but his text offers no relinquishment of its sentimentalized perception of women; rather, the novel continues to affirm and cherish a feminine ideal according to which women continue to be victims. Dickens may emphasize the angel's redemptive powers, thereby allowing for the possibility of her effective agency, but because she cannot meet the contradictory demands placed on her within a patriarchal system, she is rendered passive and silent.

II

As Dickens rather abruptly shifts the novel's focus from England to France, from the private, relatively ordered world of the Manettes and Darnays in London to the public disorder of Paris, the accompanying contrast in nationality and class presents an opportunity for a somewhat different representation of women. Although Miss Pross and several other, more minor English characters are of a lower class, Dickens mainly focusses his attention on the middle classes in England, while he concentrates on the lower classes in France and their oppression by the aristocracy. Through depiction of these French working-class women in the Revolution, Dickens's text apparently overcomes some of the limits of the woman-as-savior ideal already described by granting women an active role in public life.

From an historical perspective, the vastly different views expressed by critics regarding the positions of working women during the period serve as some indication of the complexity of women's roles in the French Revolution. Jane Abray, for instance, in "Feminism in the French Revolution," insists on the existence of a feminist movement during France's political upheaval, claiming that, "While it [revolutionary feminism] lasted it was a very real phenomenon with a comprehensive program for social change, perhaps the most far-reaching such program of the Revolution" (62). She asserts that, although revolutionary feminism began with a burst of enthusiasm, it failed as a result of tactical and strategical errors (such as the easy distraction of its members from their main concerns), political and managerial inexperience (or leaders acting in isolation from one another), and because women's general acceptance of the status quo and eighteenth-century definitions of femininity rendered feminism a minority movement (61–62). In an apparently contradictory but equally extreme view, Olwen Hufton, in "Women in Revolution 1789–1796," sees working women as responding to the Revolution solely in terms of their traditional roles as mothers and wives bereft of a feminist or political agenda, seeking involvement only when famine threatens their families with destitution (90–108).

In a sense, Hufton's conservative and chauvinistic analysis gains support from a comparative examination of women before and after the Revolution, since the minimal and often illusory gains in their social and political status seem to deny any possibility of positive feminist assessment. Mary Durham Johnson explains, for instance, that despite the rapidly changing governments and administrations from 1789–1796, women remained subject to persistently traditional, patriarchal values (132). Her description of women in pre-revolutionary France as economically dependent, legal minors, exploited in the workplace, control of their person and property transferred from father to husband upon marriage, existing to perform conjugal duties and bear healthy children (107–110), recalls conventional roles assigned women in any patriarchal system. Although the Revolution may have raised hopes for change in the status of women, governmental retaliation for female protests reasserted a paternalistic demand for obedience and dependence in order to reinforce traditional sex roles. When Napoleon came to power, his reversal of any legal and civic progress made during the Revolution regarding women's social position (in education and divorce laws, for example), and the implementation of even more sophisticated mechanisms for controlling women's behavior than had existed in the *ancien régime*, confirmed the continuation of patriarchal standards (Johnson 130–31). Such uninterrupted repression seems to illustrate a continuing failure of women's political influence.

Yet, despite their social subordination and lack of overt socio-political advancement, working women did have an impact during the Revolution, taking roles which were not strictly traditional. Harriet Branson Applewhite and Darline Gay Levy, for example, approach the period from women's perspectives in order to demonstrate that, while institutions may not have changed during the period, women's political awareness did. Finding a middle ground between Abray and Hufton as a basis for interpretation, Levy and Applewhite suggest that French revolutionary women "were not feminists, and their goals were often the age-old concerns of wives and mothers for the survival of their families, but they learned to use revolutionary institutions and democratic tactics to secure political influence" ("Women of the Popular Classes" 9). In the October insurrections of 1789, for instance, when they marched to Versailles in order to demand a stable supply of bread at affordable prices, women played an instrumental role in helping to topple the monarchy by bringing the king back to Paris with them (66). As the Revolution wore on, women made use of petitions, clubs and assemblies to gain a forum for their political views, they resorted to *taxation populaire*, or confiscation of merchants' goods to be sold at reasonable prices, and they even obtained a short-lived institutional base for their political influence in the form of the Society of Revolutionary Republican Women. Employing untraditional methods to voice traditional grievances, revolutionary women seemed to evolve from submissive subjects to participating citizens who had an impact on their government as they gained a new outlook toward themselves and their roles in society (Applewhite, Johnson and Levy 312). Even if such women were unaware of the political implications of their actions, their ability merely to act and influence public events within a patriarchal system confirms their untraditional social position.

Of course, such historical reconstructions of women's roles in the Revolution are quite recent. As for *A Tale of Two Cities* and the material to which Dickens might have been exposed when writing his novel, most scholarship confirms that Dickens's historical perspective was greatly informed by Thomas Carlyle's *The French Revolution*. The two main studies which explore Dickens's influences, Michael Goldberg's *Carlyle and Dickens* and William Oddie's *Dickens and Carlyle: The Question of Influence*, demonstrate that Dickens relied on Carlyle's text, as well as the resource material Carlyle used in writing it, as research for his historical novel (Goldberg 101; Oddie 61–63). (Oddie also leaves room for other sources, although he does not define these possibilities clearly.) L. M. Findlay explains, furthermore, that in his historical book, Carlyle portrays the women of the Revolution in a highly conservative and repressive manner, a representation which helps define the limits of his political radicalism (130–34). Nevertheless, Dickens's representation of revolutionary women in his version of the French insurrection appears strikingly modern; in fact, in many ways, it seems to echo Applewhite and Levy's discussion.

As the main representative of the French women in this rebellion, Dickens presents Thérèse Defarge, valued and trusted confidante of her husband, Ernest, and his circle of lower-class conspirators. Dickens removes Madame Defarge from a typical, domestic feminine realm to place her in the midst of the turbulent Revolution. Thus, because of her combative posture, she seems to renegotiate or redefine Dickens's feminine contradiction; as a dynamic revolutionary, she is neither submissive victim nor saintly savior. Madame Defarge demonstrates her capacity as a politically active woman responding to class suppression, for example, in the storming of the Bastille episode, when she stands out as a leader of women, forcefully declaring female equality in her sadistic cry, "We can kill as well as the men when the place is taken!" (245). Such determination, near-perfect self-control and consistency of purpose render her hateful yet admirable. Although Dickens makes no attempt to indicate Madame Defarge's political awareness, instead rendering women's involvement in the Revolution a result of hunger or a sense of personal wrong, his acknowledgement, through Madame Defarge, of women's participation and what appears to be their often powerful influence, seems to recognize the progressive nature of their role. As a politically determined and apparently determining being, Madame Defarge appears to avoid some of the restrictions placed on other women in the novel.

This inclination toward decisive action, however, finally leads Madame Defarge to seek the execution of Lucie and her family, and as she travels the Paris streets on her way to realize her desire, Dickens writes:

> There were many women at that time, upon whom the time laid a dreadfully disfiguring hand; but, there was not one among them more to be dreaded than this ruthless woman, now taking her way along the streets. Of a strong and fearless character, of shrewd sense and readiness, of great determination, of that kind of beauty which not only seems to impart to its possessor firmness and animosity, but to strike into others an instinctive recognition of those qualities; the troubled time would have heaved her up, under any circumstances. But, imbued from her childhood with a brooding sense of wrong, and an inveterate hatred of a class, opportunity had developed her into a tigress. She was absolutely without pity. If she had ever had the virtue in her, it had quite gone out of her.

It was nothing to her, that an innocent man was to die for the sins of his forefathers; she saw, not him, but them. It was nothing to her, that his wife was to be made a widow and his daughter an orphan; that was insufficient punishment, because they were her natural enemies and her prey, and as such had no right to live. To appeal to her, was made hopeless by her having no sense of pity, even for herself. (390–91)

In this passage, Dickens singles out Madame Defarge as a magnified representation of the unnatural horror of revolutionary violence; he also pointedly connects her with Lucie Manette. He begins by suggesting that Madame Defarge, like the other women of the Revolution, is disfigured by the "time." This statement implies that Madame Defarge is negatively distorted by her environment, that, had she been exposed to different circumstances, she might have turned out quite differently, perhaps even like Lucie herself. But the years leading to the Revolution turn her into a ruthless, strong, fearless, shrewd woman. Her readiness and determination render her wholly unfeminine, and the reference to her "beauty" secures her position as the fair, angelic Lucie's dark-haired antithesis. She substitutes her knitting needles of revenge, which she uses to denounce traitors, for Lucie's golden thread of harmony, and in lieu of the compassionate emotions to which Lucie often succumbs, Madame Defarge is utterly devoid of the "virtue" of pity. Certainly, she derives motivation from fidelity to her natural sister, but she distorts that devotion in order to seek vengeance and death rather than forgiveness and life. While Lucie gives birth to angelic creatures like herself and tends them with love and concern, Madame Defarge has no children, an absence which ironically connects her with the aristocratic women whom Dickens also criticizes for lacking maternal affection. (He suggests that, although upper class ladies give birth, peasant women raise the children and are, thus, more deserving of the exalted title of "Mother," 137). In short, Dickens depicts Madame Defarge as a woman of distorted potential, a woman of powerful feelings who, as the result of a lifetime of pain and oppression, turns to destruction. Because he connects her so obviously with Lucie, Madame Defarge represents a perversion of Dickens's feminine-savior figure.

The above reference to Madame Defarge's physical appearance, furthermore, while contrasting with Lucie's comeliness, also asserts that the older woman's beauty is of a different "kind," one that imbues her with, or which she transforms into, power and violence. Because only instinct can recognize the firmness and animosity behind her beauty, and because her "brooding sense of wrong" derives from her childhood, a time of innocence and lack of worldly understanding, Dickens underscores the primal nature of her desires and her basic animality. Although Dickens grants her small personal and political justification for her "inveterate hatred" in the forms of her sister's rape and her own subjection to class suppression, Madame Defarge is a "tigress" who hunts her "natural enemies" and her "prey." The way in which she toys with Foulon, for example, letting the captured aristocrat go then pulling him back several times before he is finally executed, confirms her catlike nature. (Again, Madame Defarge is connected to the aristocracy; Dickens underscores the equally brutal and basic ferocity of the upper classes by referring to the Marquis as a "refined tiger," 156). The gender-specificity of Dickens's reference to Madame Defarge as one of the "women" rather than one of the people disfigured by the times highlights female brutality as being even more disturbing than the barbarity of male revolutionaries, since such savagery contrasts so greatly with the novel's idealized perception of women's potential as realized in Lucie.

In fact, this description of Madame Defarge recalls Nina Auerbach's monster in its horrified representation of women's latent powers let loose upon the world. In her comprehensive examination of Victorian female stereotypes, Auerbach suggests that, while Victorian men traditionally valued women for their sense of morality and purity, these men also feared the metamorphic power implicit in female spirituality (1–24). Auerbach goes on to claim that literary evidence for this fear of women directly reveals itself in the dark side of the angelic metaphor, taking, for example, the form of monsters, witches, sorceresses and demons (4). In terms of Auerbach's argument, then, Madame Defarge represents one such threatening monster. Although, as the above citation indicates, she is fully cognizant of and blindly driven by patrilineal ties, seeking restitution for "the sins of his [Darnay's] forefathers," Madame Defarge heedlessly attempts to subvert the familial bonds which help support a patriarchal system in her desire to kill Charles, an act which would render Lucie and her child defenceless widow and orphan. She dares to defy time and death through her unconcern, confirming her demon-like, irrational evil in her absolute lack of pity "even for herself." As a woman she achieves status among the revolutionaries, but she does so only at the expense of human compassion and remorse. Depicting her persistent and insatiable brutality, Dickens portrays Madame Defarge as a force of nature as well as an animal, identifying her as an elemental, and hence unconquerable presence; she says to her husband, "tell Wind and Fire where to stop ... but don't tell me" (370). Such appeals to nature dehistoricize Madame Defarge, removing her from her culture and from the Revolution in order to render her effectively non-feminine and non-human, a mythic Fury.

As exaggerated as this description of Madame Defarge may appear to be, her representation echoes legends surrounding actual women of the Revolution. In *Carlyle and Dickens*, Michael Goldberg connects the activities of Madame Defarge with those of Théroigne de Méricourt (118), and Linda Kelly, in *Women of the French Revolution*, discusses various myths which grew around Théroigne as a revolutionary figure (11–23, 48–59). According to Kelly, Théroigne, who intoxicated the Revolution with her beauty, became famous for flashing through crowds in a blood-red riding habit with a sabre and pistol in hand, leading a mob to the Bastille. She subsequently came to personify the fury of the Revolution as well as women's desires to show solidarity and help in the Revolution's defense (90). However, although Théroigne apparently supported radical ideas such as a women's armed battalion, Kelly asserts that she did not help storm the Bastille, and that, in fact, much of her story is myth (11), since her eccentricity and exhibitionism denied her much revolutionary impact (35). Nevertheless, Théroigne's celebrity snowballed until she was imprisoned in connection with an attempted assassination of the Queen (47), only to be released for lack of evidence. Soon thereafter, she reportedly went mad (59). Other women such as Charlotte Corday (whose single act, the assassination of a radical journalist, Marat, supposedly performed with the intent of saving thousands of lives from the brutal measures he advocated, earned her legendary status, 100–102), Marie Antoinette (114) and Olympe de Gouges (who wrote *The Rights of Woman and the Citizen* in response to the omission of women's rights from the Revolutionary document, *The Rights of Man and the Citizen*, 122–6) were commonly depicted as monsters similar to Théroigne (102). According to such historical descriptions, therefore, the exaggeration with which Dickens depicts the brutality and inhumanity of Madame Defarge seems to owe a debt to legends concerning such revolutionary women.

More importantly, Dickens's treatment of Madame Defarge recalls the actual recontainment experienced by women in the Revolution. In the years following 1789, many men seemed to fear politically active women as subversive of male authority, suggesting that they were susceptible to manipulation by counter-revolutionary factions (Graham 247). In fact, government reaction to women's only organized seat of political power, the Society of Revolutionary Republican Women, acted upon such an apprehension. In response to public disturbances with which the Society was associated, Jacobin Deputy Amar of the Committee of General Security reportedly informed the Revolutionary Convention that women do not have the physical or moral strength to discuss political considerations and recommend resolutions; consequently, the government passed a law to restrict women from holding public meetings, from exercising political rights and from taking active roles in governmental affairs (Blum 213). As a first step in a series of repressive measures which multiplied through the reign of Napoleon, the government attempted to justify its actions through idealization of family cohesion and women's "natural" functions within the home. The political establishment promoted Rousseau's ideal of pregnant and nursing women as personifications of the regeneration of France, appealing to marriage and motherhood, to women's roles as educators within the home and family, in order to deny women political rights while exalting them as goddesses of reason (Graham 250). In partial demonstration of the limits of France's initial test of democracy (Applewhite and Levy, "Women, Democracy and Revolution" 64), the patriarchal government silenced women by legalizing female subservience in 1793.

By dismissing the unfeminine Madame Defarge as other than human and portraying women revolutionaries as beasts, Dickens apparently endorses this type of denial of women's moral and intellectual suitability for public affairs. Dickens impedes women's access to power in his representation of the Revolution by focussing on a disfigured monster whose influence is more primal than political. He thereby contains female subversion and denies women access to effective political agency by characterizing their social activities as aberrant rather than "natural" behavior. Furthermore, by endorsing only those women, such as Lucie, who do not disturb the patriarchal agenda or threaten men's supremacy, Dickens reconfirms women's subordinate status. As a half-French woman, Lucie serves as an example for her French "sisters" because she embodies Rousseau's ideal, constantly remaining a politically submissive complement to the patriarchy represented in her husband and father. Through this acceptance of Lucie and rejection of Madame Defarge, Dickens affirms the exclusion of women from political life and reveals a patriarchal fear of women becoming equal partners in the Revolution.

Beyond this bestial, demon-like version of women, at the height of the Revolution Dickens digresses even further from his ideal to blur sexual differentiation altogether. In "The Grindstone" chapter (287), for example, Dickens presents "men devilishly set off with spoils of women's lace and silk and ribbon" (291). As both sexes gather to sharpen their weapons, the general cover of blood and physical disguises prevents the accurate and easy determination of gender and identity. More pointedly, in his description of the Carmagnole, a musical celebration performed by the revolutionaries, Dickens writes:

Men and women danced together, women danced together, men danced together, as hazard had brought them together....

No fight could have been half so terrible as this dance. It was so emphatically a fallen sport—a something, once innocent, delivered over to all devilry—a healthy pastime changed into a means of angering the blood, bewildering the senses, and steeling the heart. Such grace as was visible in it, made it the uglier, showing how warped and perverted all things good by nature were become. The maidenly bosom bared to this, the pretty almost-child's head thus distracted, the delicate foot mincing in this slough of blood and dirt, were types of the disjointed time. (307–308)

The participants in this revelry recall the French peasants who rejoice in the streets at the beginning of the novel when a wine cask is spilled; however, in the Carmagnole, these people celebrate the destructive spirit of the Revolution rather than the life-giving nourishment provided by the wine. Dickens underscores the horror of this spectacle as a perversion of a religious, Christmas dance by referring to the lack of discrimination and the irrelevance of sexual distinction in the selection of dance partners. In the fever of revolutionary passion, extremes collide to enforce a disruption of the presence, or at least of the usual importance, of sexual identity.

Nevertheless, despite this temporary disintegration into androgyny, the language of this passage identifies the Carmagnole as a decidedly feminine sport. Although men participate, a woman, La Vengeance, who is Madame Defarge's second-in-command and a personification of the revolutionary spirit in the novel, leads the "terrible" dance. Dickens represents the Carmagnole as a "fallen" sport, in a reference which suggests a traditional description of prostitutes or supposedly unchaste women as having "fallen" from grace and respectability (Hutter 457). His insistence on the transformation that occurs during the dance, a conversion of what was innocent, full of grace and "good by nature," into something warped, perverted and ugly, lends further support to this conventional image of an impure woman who has distorted and abused her feminine attributes. Moreover, Dickens's reference to the celebration as affecting the blood, senses and heart suggests that this dance appeals to human emotions rather than the mind, and such feeling is conventionally recognized as the feminine equivalent of masculine intelligence. He then reduces the dancers to types, all of whom are described in feminine terms: maidens, pretty children and dancers with "delicate" feet. Sexual difference may carry little import in the Carmagnole, but Dickens's description of the event appeals to an underlying sense of gender specificity.

In fact, Dickens seems to break down sexual barriers only to re-create a negative image of the Revolution itself as feminine. L. M. Findlay suggests that Carlyle defines femininity in *The French Revolution* in part by means of Maenadic reference, a depiction which helps to perpetuate patriarchal domination (135–40).[1] Here is a point where Dickens's and Carlyle's women begin to meet, since Dickens emulates this type of representation in his historical novel. Greek mythology characterizes Maenads, or the women worshippers of the god, Dionysus, largely by their shared capacity for irrationality, for their uncontrollable, emotional, senseless, and therefore feminine, dancing and singing, and Dickens's portrait of the feminine figures in the Carmagnole echoes this description. Additionally, unreasonable and passionate French women such as Madame Defarge and La Vengeance tend to characterize most revolutionary scenes (Hutter 457), exceeding men in their savagery and strength, and dominating Dickens's representation of insurrection. It is important to note, however, that, despite their energy and fervor, and like the Maenads who depend upon their relationship to Dionysus to define their identity (Findlay 138), Dickens's women rely on men, or the circle of Jacques, to direct their activities. Therefore, while women are marginalized through denial of their independence, excessive revolutionary activity and its agents are negatively represented by reference to the feminine.

The two prevailing images which symbolize not only the effects, but also the causes of the Revolution in Dickens's analysis are, accordingly, female. Dickens presents Medusa, or "The Gorgon's Head" (149), as a symbol of the corrupt aristocracy whose misrule helps to create conditions which demand retaliation on the part of the oppressed. As a mythological female figure who turns those who look at her to stone, Medusa represents the stone-like, upper class indifference to the poor, the legacy of social and personal repression which the Marquis attempts to pass on to Charles through the "Gorgon's spell" (Frank 137).[2] Of course, Dickens includes male embodiments of the mythological figure, in particular, the Marquis, who represents the evil in the French patriarchal system, but the image itself remains female. On the other hand, Dickens personifies the consequent peasant response to this exploitation in the form of an ironic feminine savior or goddess. He says that, "Above all, one hideous figure grew as familiar as if it had been before the general gaze from the foundations of the world—the figure of the sharp female called La Guillotine" (302). Dickens raises La Guillotine to near mythic status by suggesting her timelessness and universal familiarity, and clearly identifies as female this symbol of the bloodthirstiness of revolutionary vengeance. Just as his extreme portrayal and rejection of Madame Defarge and his exaggerated depiction of Lucie as a desired feminine form demonstrates patriarchal anxiety about powerful women, so Dickens's use of feminine and female symbols to represent the French Revolution, its causes and effects, underscores a need for containment of such convulsion and a fear of revolution itself.

A careful examination of the women in Dickens's novel, therefore, clearly reveals the underlying patriarchal bias of his text. Thus, it seems rather ironic that, as the novel draws to a close, women instead of men take part in the final, decisive, climactic battle. In a revolution in which men govern activity even when women are participants in it, patriarchal traditions anticipate male orchestration and enactment of decisive action; yet Dickens allows Miss Pross and Madame Defarge to decide whether the Darnays' final flight to England will succeed. As their contest begins, Dickens writes:

> Miss Pross had nothing beautiful about her; years had not tamed the wildness, or softened the grimness, of her appearance; but, she too was a determined woman in her different way, and she measured Madame Defarge with her eyes, every inch.
>
> 'You might, from your appearance, be the wife of Lucifer,' said Miss Pross, in her breathing. 'Nevertheless, you shall not get the better of me. I am an Englishwoman.'
>
> Madame Defarge looked at her scornfully, but still with something of Miss Pross's own perception that they two were at bay. (395)

The potential irony involved in representing a physical battle between women rather than men is subdued by a recognition that these combatants are the two most masculine women in the novel, and Dickens reinforces this perception by restating Miss Pross's lack of beauty, her wildness and grimness which even time can neither tame nor soften. Once again, Dickens connects women with animals, indicating the primal nature of these two opponents in their powers of "perception," or their intuitive abilities to understand one another while "at bay" and despite their language barrier. In fact, Miss Pross's reference to Madame Defarge as the "wife of Lucifer," contrasting as it does with her own appeal to Heaven several paragraphs later, suggests that these two figures represent elemental forces more than individual women, symbolizing a revolutionary battle between evil and good, inhuman barbarity and selfless devotion. Certainly Lucie is the more obvious female embodiment of goodness, but as a woman of higher class and angelic purity, her participation in such barbaric activity would be inappropriate, so Miss Pross serves as an adequate stand-in. By suggesting that Miss Pross is determined "in her different way," a distinction which affirms her basic femininity in spite of her masculine eccentricities, Dickens carefully differentiates her from her opponent; thus, when the English woman kills Madame Defarge "with the vigorous tenacity of love, always so much stronger than hate" (397), through masculine agency Miss Pross is able to confirm the efficacy of feminine values in her certain victory over the non-feminine. (As an "Englishwoman," she also affirms England's superiority and dissociation from France's revolutionary violence.) Consequently, their individual fates pay homage to paternalistic demands for the pacification of women, as Madame Defarge, a woman who affronts femininity, experiences ultimate silencing in her death, while Miss Pross, whose feminine goodness cannot wholly atone for the murder she commits, must withdraw into the mute world of her own deafness. (Lucie, too, travels in a carriage to England in silence and passivity.) Dickens thereby allows two women to perform the climactic battle in the text without compromising patriarchal expectations.

Through manipulation of the angel in all of her various manifestations, then, Dickens is able to present women as representative of both solution and problem in the events surrounding the French insurrection of 1789 and the devastation which follows, as a source of redemption (Lucie and, to a certain extent, Miss Pross) and a symbol of revolutionary insanity (Madame Defarge). Through his paternalistic and chauvinistic polemics, he simultaneously exalts and denigrates women, exposing their ideal femininity, or lack thereof, as a measure of possible social amelioration. By twisting and distorting seemingly unconventional feminine images, Dickens recontains the women in his novel, restricting their movements and influence by forcing them to assume illogical and untenable positions in a patriarchal society. This circumscription of a potentially progressive depiction of women by a chauvinistic need for their repression and confinement underscores Dickens's gender bias.

NOTES

1. In Book Seven, chapters four through eleven of *The French Revolution* (251–89), Carlyle describes women as Maenads in reference to the October days insurrections. He refers to them as "angry she-bees" or "desperate flying wasps" (254) who need guidance and find it in the form of a man, Maillard, around whom they cluster. Carlyle paints the scene as a wild spectacle enlivened by uncontrollable women whose "inarticulate fury" Maillard miraculously manages to translate into coherent speech in order to communicate with the government and the king. In this description of the event, Carlyle displays a consistently patronizing attitude toward women and their activities, thereby somewhat restricting their revolutionary impact.

2. In "The Laugh of the Medusa," Hélène Cixous refers to the Medusa figure as a metaphor for women's uniqueness which Cixous insists needs to be expressed and released through oral and written language (245–64). As she calls for a revaluation of women's

difference, she suggests that Medusa need not seem ugly or destructive; on the contrary, in her attempt to incite women to "laugh" or speak their differences, Cixous asserts that women need to explore Medusa, look at her and recognize her beauty. Cixous suggests that Medusa is traditionally rejected as a horrible creature only because men, who fear women's uniqueness and powers as a threat to their supremacy, describe and represent her as a monster (255). To apply Cixous's argument to *A Tale of Two Cities*, then, because Dickens employs the image of Medusa in its conventionally negative connotation, the "Gorgon's head" reinforces his participation in a patriarchal fear and rejection of women.

I also find it worth noting that Medusa is destroyed by a man, Perseus, who with the aid of the gods cuts off her head with a magic sickle. This proposed resolution to the myth confirms the appropriateness of Dickens's use of the Medusa image in terms of the guillotine and his affirmation of male dominance and control over threatening women.

WORKS CITED

Abray, Jane. "Feminism in the French Revolution." *The American Historical Review* 80.1 (Feb. 1975): 43–62.

Applewhite, Harriet Branson and Darline Gay Levy. "Women, Democracy, and Revolution in Paris, 1789–1794." *French Women and the Age of Enlightenment*. Ed. Samia I. Spencer. Bloomington: Indiana UP, 1984. 64–79.

———. "Women of the Popular Classes in Revolutionary Paris, 1789–1795." *Women, War and Revolution*. Eds. Carol R. Berkin and Clara M. Lovett. NY: Holmes and Meier, 1980. 9–35.

Applewhite, Harriet Branson, Darline Gay Levy and Mary Durham Johnson, eds. and trans. *Women in Revolutionary Paris 1789–1795*. Chicago: U of Illinois P, 1979.

Auerbach, Nina. *Woman and the Demon: The Life of a Victorian Myth*. Cambridge, Mass.: Harvard UP, 1982.

Blum, Carol. "The Sex Made to Obey." *Rousseau and the Republic of Virtue: The Language of Politics in the French Revolution*. Ithaca: Cornell UP, 1986. 204–215.

Carlyle, Thomas. *The French Revolution: A History*. 1839. London: Chapman and Hill, 1900. 3 vols.

Cixous, Hélène. "The Laugh of the Medusa." Trans. Keith Cohen and Paula Cohen. *Signs: A Journal of Women in Culture and Society* 1.4 (1976): 875–93.

Daleski, Herman M. *Dickens and the Art of Analogy*. NY: Schocken, 1970.

Dickens, Charles. *A Tale of Two Cities*. 1858. Ed. and intro. George Woodcock. London: Penguin, 1988.

Findlay, L. M. "'Maternity must forth': The Poetics and Politics of Gender in Carlyle's *French Revolution*." *Dalhousie Review* 66.1/2 (1986): 130–54.

Frank, Lawrence. "The Poetics of Impasse." *Charles Dickens and the Romantic Self*. Lincoln: U of Nebraska P, 1984. 124–50.

Goldberg, Michael. *Carlyle and Dickens*. Athens: U of Georgia P, 1972.

Graham, Ruth. "Loaves of Liberty: Women in the French Revolution." *Becoming Visible: Women in European History*. Eds. Renate Bridenthal and Claudia Koonz. Boston: Houghton, 1977. 236–54.

Hill, Nancy Klenck. "Woman as Savior." *Denver Quarterly* 18.4 (1984): 94–107.

Hufton, Olwen. "Women in Revolution, 1789–1796." *Past and Present* (1971): 90–108.

Hutter, Albert D. "Nation and Generation in *A Tale of Two Cities*." *PMLA* 93.3 (1978): 448–62.

Jarmuth, Sylvia L. *Dickens' Use of Women in His Novels*. NY: Excelsior, 1967.

Johnson, Mary Durham. "Old Wine in New Bottles: The Institutional Changes for Women of the People During the French Revolution." *Women, War, and Revolution.* Eds. Carol R. Berkin and Clara M. Lovett. NY: Holmes and Meier, 1980. 107–143.

Kelly, Linda. *Women of the French Revolution.* London: Hamish Hamilton Paperback, 1987.

Kucich, John. "The Purity of Violence: *A Tale of Two Cities.*" *Dickens Studies Annual* 8 (1980): 119–37.

Oddie, William. *Dickens and Carlyle: The Question of Influence.* London: Centenary P, 1972.

Slater, Michael. *Dickens and Women.* Stanford: Stanford UP, 1983.

Welsh, Alexander. *The City of Dickens.* London: Oxford UP, 1971. 141–63.

TOM LLOYD

Language, Love and Identity:
A Tale of Two Cities

T hirty years ago G. Robert Stange criticized the 'excessive artificiality' of Charles Dickens's *A Tale of Two Cities*, writing that 'its construction constantly calls attention to itself' (74). Much has changed in the critical realm since 1957, for now this is exactly what commends the novel to the attention of those nurtured on post-structuralist ideas. A number of writers in recent years have analysed Dickens's fascination with language, including 'redoubling of the theme of writing' (Baumgarten 163), closure, hidden desires (Vanden Bossche 211), and in general the strong influence of Thomas Carlyle's Romantic Irony on Dickens's work.[1] *A Tale of Two Cities* does question the value of language divorced from feeling and experience, but in the end affirms the value of the word. By stressing the act of writing throughout the novel, Dickens creates a discomfort in the reader owing to the fact that the fiction is thereby robbed of its capacity to enchant the reader into a willing suspension of disbelief. But this is not to deny meaning; instead, it calls into question the reader's command of the word. This is especially true with Carton's ambiguous 'prophecy.'[2] Near the end of the novel we learn that the French aristocrats were unable to read the signs of the times and see how the 'powerful enchanter, Time' might turn fancy carriages into tumbrils headed for the guillotine (399). Dickens's text forces the reader to strip away the veil and explore the mysteries that lie at its heart, just as Lorry

From *The Dickensian* 88, no. 428, part 3 (Autumn 1992): pp. 154–170. © 1992 by *The Dickensian*.

and Carton must explore their inner beings and resurrect life and language. But the difficulty which interpretation entails does not presuppose the 'blankness' Dr Manette fears.

The problem with language that pervades *A Tale of Two Cities* is very similar to the one evoked by Carlyle in *The French Revolution*.[3] Like Friedrich Schlegel, Carlyle identifies a logically irreconcilable tension between words and things, interpretations and essences. He argues that in revolutionary France the Constitutionalists led by Sieyès tried to construct a 'paper' constitution too far removed from social realities, while the extremists wanted to 'govern a France free of formulas. Free of formulas! And yet man lives not except with formulas' (4:68).[4] It is necessary that we read history, or any other text, from a never-ending ironical perspective, which does not deny transcendental meaning but instead shocks us in the direction of the ineffable. Failure to do so leads to imprisonment in formulas or chaos. Thus in Dickens's novel the aristocrats are blinded by false words, while the most extreme sans-culottes try to obliterate language in their vengeance against the old order. In between are those characters who, like Lorry, Carton, and Manette, must establish identities, workable 'formulas' for themselves, amidst those varieties of fragmentation of self. Indeed, even M Defarge clings to language and meaning in the presence of his wife and the storming of the Bastille; she alone of the major characters seeks to obliterate everything and everyone, her incessant knitting of shrouds a parodic, non-verbal language which prefigures dissolution rather than the reconstruction of meaning.[5]

Throughout *A Tale of Two Cities* Dickens illustrates the precarious nature of identity in a world torn between decrepit language and destruction, where with varying degrees of success characters try to comprehend and name the 'mystery' that lies at the centre of the self. Stripped of his reason, for instance, the dignified Dr Manette becomes an 'it'; throughout the novel he alternates without control between identities as a dehumanized shoemaker partially resurrected from the Bastille, and the melancholy Doctor who seeks stability through love for his daughter Lucie.[6] The fear that he will be forgotten and his place made a 'blank' in the memories of others causes him to seek in Lucie a stable past that will formulate his identity.[7] The prison comes close to reducing Darnay to an 'it' as well when, alone in a cell, his thoughts descend into a confused stream of consciousness, scraps of his tenuously retained selfhood 'tossing and rolling upward from the depths of his mind': 'Let us ride on again, for God's sake, through the illuminated villages with the people all awake! ****He made shoes, he made shoes, he made shoes. ****Five paces by four and a half' (287).[8]

Identities need formulas, yet words can falsify if they fail to reflect the organic nature of character. After all, the sign in itself is arbitrary; personalities change, while texts can become brittle. Thus Manette's letter of vengeance against the Evrémondes comes back to haunt him at Darnay's second Paris trial. Under Lucie's influence he has rediscovered love and sympathy, and can accept as his son-in-law the heir of the family that tormented him. But the letter, buried all those years in the Bastille until discovered by Defarge, was aimed at fixing the future, which throughout the novel is presented as mysterious and ambiguous: 'I, Alexandre Manette, unhappy prisoner, do this last night of the year 1767, in my unbearable agony, denounce to the times when all these things shall be answered for. I denounce them to Heaven and to earth' (361). This is as destructive to identity, which is always in a process of change and formulation, as the superficially different sans-culottic endeavour to destroy words and naming altogether.

There is an even more frightening alternative: the autobiographical word may disappear altogether, and identity may not be preserved in the memories of others. This is the significance of the second buried letter in *A Tale of Two Cities*. Darnay tells Lucie and her father about the discovery of the almost undecipherable sign 'D.I.G.' in a Tower of London prison. Under it, many years before, a now anonymous prisoner hid some writing, which now is reduced to ashes: 'There was no record or legend of any prisoner with those initials, and many fruitless guesses were made what the name could have been' (131). Isolated from the outer world, where living memories can be generated through relations with other people, the individual must fall back on the language and memories he already has. These may be inadequate. Naturally Manette is shaken when he hears Darnay's story, not only because he recalls his own still buried writing in Paris, but because this calls to mind his old fear that, in the end, one's place may be just a 'blank' (219).[9]

The partial, parodic, and transcendent resurrections that occur in *A Tale of Two Cities* have received considerable analysis in the past.[10] Less well known is the relationship between resurrected selves and the word revivified through love, represented above all in Lucie Manette. Lorry, for instance, progresses from regarding himself as a machine bereft of feeling (54), to a more insightful man who rediscovers the meaning of the heart and his childhood. This is accomplished through Lucie's agency, for she becomes the centre of a domestic realm which draws Lorry away from his imprisoned public self.[11] In his last conversation with Sydney Carton, he acknowledges a redemption through love and memory that echoes Wordsworth's poetry of loss and redemption through the 'philosophic mind':

'I travel in the circle, nearer and nearer to the beginning. It seems to be one of the kind smoothings and preparings of the way. My

heart is touched now, by many remembrances that had long fallen
asleep ... by many associations of the days when what we call the
World was not so real with me.' (340)

Lorry's identity is not as threatened as Manette's by burial and blankness
because the business institution into which he projects himself remains
intact, even in Paris.[12] Furthermore, in his function as protector of Lucie,
which he first assumed when he carried her as a baby across the Channel,
Lorry has a perception of language denied to others. All along he can read
character and comprehend the dubieties of language. Consider how he
parries Stryver's assumption that he is 'eligible' to marry Lucie Manette. The
meretricious 'striver' avoids the truth about his suitability by formulating his
'verdict' to himself in legal jargon. Blinded by his own words, he is analagous
to those French aristocrats who place their trust in plausible formulas that
are at variance with nature:

> As to the strength of his case, he had not a doubt about it, but
> clearly saw his way to the verdict. Argued with the jury on
> substantial worldly grounds ... it was a plain case, and had not a
> weak spot in it. (171)

The detachment of Stryver's language from reality is recognized by Lorry,
who sardonically replies to his question whether he is 'eligible' to marry
Lucie: 'Oh dear yes! Yes. Oh yes, you're eligible! ... If you say eligible,
you are eligible' (174). Like the dragon in Carroll's 'The Hunting of the
Snark', he affirms the truth of Stryver's 'eligibility' by repeating it three
times. The irony is lost on the portly suitor, who then asks, 'Am I not
prosperous?'[13]

Dickens analyses the imprisonment of Stryver, the British legal system,
and above all the French aristocracy in words that deny human paradox and
mystery, or quantify them in rational forms. Like the self-satisfied empiricists
Carlyle lampoons in *Sartor Resartus* for thinking they have 'scientifically
decomposed' man's 'spiritual Faculties', the court philosophers and scientists
at the grand hotel of Monseigneur in Paris think they can control things
by controlling language.[14] But they are as wide of the mark as Johnson's
mad astronomer in *Rasselas*, who thinks he can control the movement of the
planets by thinking:

> Unbelieving Philosophers who were remodelling the world
> with words, and making card-towers of Babel to scale the skies
> with, talked with Unbelieving Chemists who had an eye on the

transmutation of metals, at this wonderful gathering accumulated by Monseigneur. (136)

But 'belief' in words and people is the key to every genuine transmutation in *A Tale of Two Cities*, above all Carton's change from wastrel to hero.[15]

Yet these rationalists believe that they believe their words, like Carlyle's philosophers with their 'dream-theorem[s]' and their 'Words well bedded ... in good Logic-mortar' (54). Dickens's analysis of the 'leprosy of unreality' (137) among the French intellectuals mirrors Carlyle's quite closely. Phoney words about the 'Centre of Truth' and the like are employed to justify a system that rests in fact on brute force, a situation dramatized by Carlyle in *The French Revolution*.[16] For example, immediately after the scene at the grand hotel, the Marquis runs down Gaspard's son without remorse or even the loss of his composure. His life centres around correct dress and composure; his face, like a 'fine mask' (140), reflects the language that has conditioned him. The narrator refers to Madame Defarge, the arch-sans-culotte, as a 'tigress' (391), and to Darnay's uncle as a 'refined tiger' who wears a mask of civility, dismissing the poor as 'dogs' but maintaining an 'unchanged front, except as to the spots on his nose' (142). Like Madame Defarge, he is obsessed with exterminating his enemies from the earth (142, 369). In fact, they are both essentially nihilists, one basing his meaning on meaningless formulas and 'repression', the other rejecting formulas altogether.

The Marquis tells Charles Darnay that his only philosophy is 'repression'. He enslaves those less powerful than he, and in turn lives in fear of Monseigneur and others above him. But his repression has another dimension as well. He has no 'within', no healthy centre of self or heart, but instead, like Friedrich Schiller's 'barbarian' in the *Aesthetic Education of Man*, has allowed culture to destroy his feelings, making him merely the inverse of the mob's 'ungovernable fury' (25).[17] He and the 'dogs' are equally given over to their material impulses. His refined sensibility denies nature its proper place in human emotions, but lets it run free in his egoistic philosophy of repression and his demonic 'assumption of indifference'. His denial of nature is evident in the fact that even his blush is not the product of an honest emotion: 'a blush on the countenance of Monsieur the Marquis was no impeachment of his high breeding; it was not from within; it was occasioned by an external circumstance beyond his control—the setting sun' (144).[18] Schiller argues that the repressed rationalist and the revolutionary mob are equally the products of a loss of psychological harmony in individuals, whether brought on by false principles or an oppressive social order. But the 'cultivated classes' are morally responsible for society's relapse into 'the kingdom of the elements' (27). Once the poor 'erupt', to cite Madame

Defarge's volcano metaphor, they are 'changed into wild beasts, by terrible enchantment long persisted in' (63). The Marquis represses his emotions and maintains his composure. The court rationalists also deny feeling, treating words as components of self-contained systems that adumbrate nature, rather than rise from it organically. His underlying brutality links Darnay's uncle with the sans-culottes, who seem to follow Carlyle's injunction to 'gather whole hampers' of 'sham Metaphors' and 'burn them' like 'pallid, hunger-bitten and dead-looking' rags (*Sartor Resartus* 73–4).

Madame Defarge embodies in its most absolute form the inevitable release of what Schiller terms the 'crude, lawless instincts' of those repressed politically and psychologically (*Aesthetic Education* 25).[19] Based on Mlle Théroigne in Carlyle's *The French Revolution*, she is like a force of nature whose instinctual patience is indicated by the 'register' she stores in her memory of who is to be saved and who executed once the energies of Saint Antoine are unleashed to sweep away the enervated aristocracy.[20] Madame Defarge seems conscious of the natural energy she represents, consistently comparing the Revolution to a natural force and denying that it can be quantified or defined.[21] For example, she tells her more conventional husband that 'it does not take a long time ... for an earthquake to swallow a town,' but stresses the inadequacy of formulas in adding the question, 'Tell me how long it takes to prepare the earthquake?' (207–8). She refuses to try to hurry the time of vengeance, saying that 'When the time comes, let loose a tiger and a devil; but wait for the time with the tiger and the devil chained' (208).

M. Defarge retains a need for clear definitions and manifestations of things, which his wife recognizes, telling him, 'you sometimes need to see your victim and your opportunity, to sustain you' (208). She regards as a weakness his desire to know when the violence will begin and end, insisting that such quantification is impossible, like trying 'to make and store the lightning' (207). Psychologically in a realm beyond formulas, she cannot set limits to her philosophy of 'extermination', and therefore opposes her husband's assertion that the Terror 'must stop somewhere' (369). But M Defarge seeks meanings even when he participates in the storming of the Bastille. Though no one is presently in the North Tower where Manette was imprisoned for eighteen years, he demands that one of the guards take him there so that he can understand the meaning of One Hundred and Five: 'Does it mean a captive, or a place of captivity? Or do you mean that I shall strike you dead?' (246). In an environment where identities are scrambled or extinguished and people are reduced to 'ghosts' of their former selves, Defarge wants a clear definition of the mystery called Manette. The 'indifference' of the Marquis and the 'absolute' extermination of Madame

Defarge are antitypes of the endeavour to connect words with things.[22] Defarge's violent destruction of the furniture in Manette's old cell to find a written or other key to his mystery reflects a paradoxical desire to obliterate and know; we later discover that he found the manuscript in the chimney, a place of ashes as well as energy.[23] His search is normally fruitless, for he finds only a dead text which no longer reflects the spiritual essence of its author.

In *A Tale of Two Cities* there is a non-verbal communication based on vengeance, and another based on love. Madame Defarge repudiates formulas in favour of absolute violence and mysterious signs based on knitting, roses in handkerchiefs, and noncommittal allusions to natural forces. But at a time when the word is falsified and dead, such signs are more efficacious than M Defarge's futile search for definitions amidst the carnage at the Bastille. Those able to read history—Dickens places his reader in this advantaged position—can read the non-verbal message contained in the Cross of Blood drawn in the air by Madame Defarge's brother (356), or the verbal sign BLOOD Gaspard scrawls on a wall with wine (61). But there are also transcendent non-verbal signs based on love and sympathy, for instance in the eyes of Darnay's mother, which give meaning to her assertion that he must 'have mercy and redress' the wrongs perpetrated by his family on the poor (154). Above all, Lucie Manette has this ability. By standing outside Darnay's Paris prison she can revitalize him, reversing his initial, precipitous slide into insanity. Madame Defarge's inability to comprehend this alternative form of communication is revealed by her plot to denounce Lucie for 'making signs and signals to prisoners' (373).

Yet she is forced to effect a non-verbal communication with Miss Pross in the climactic scene where the sans-culotte comes hunting for Lucie, who is in the process of escaping from Paris. Here her energies are thwarted, and she is spent like any natural storm or earthquake. The cessation of her power through Pross's pistol shot foreshadows the retreat of the violently daemonic and the reconstitution of the word, symbolized by the power of the signed papers to get Darnay (disguised as Carton), Manette, and Lucie out of the country. Like Thomas Mann's demonic Cipolla, Defarge is suddenly rendered lifeless, as though a violent disrobing of civilized control and language have played themselves out, leaving Pross deaf but free. In this grotesque encounter the two cannot understand each other's words: 'Each spoke in her own language; neither understood the other's words; both were very watchful, and intent to deduce from look and manner, what the unintelligible words meant' (395). Miss Pross dismisses her opponent's language as 'nonsensical' (396). Yet they communicate non-verbally, one motivated by the 'vigorous tenacity of love' (397), the other by sheer hatred. As with Darnay and his mother, and Carton and the young girl at the end of the novel, the eyes are the key to this non-rational language:

> 'It will do her no good to keep herself concealed from me at this moment,' said Madame Defarge. 'Good patriots will know what that means. Let me see her. Go tell her that I wish to see her. Do you hear?'
> 'If those eyes of yours were bed-winches,' returned Miss Pross, 'and I was an English four-poster, they shouldn't loose a splinter of me. No, you wicked foreign woman; I am your match.' (395)

Madame Defarge's attack is a parodic version of Sydney Carton's self-sacrifice in the next chapter: 'if she had been ordered to the axe to-morrow,' her only response would have been 'a fierce desire to change places with the man who sent her there' (391); rendered 'lifeless' by a pistol shot, she symbolically re-enters the unseen world when Pross locks her body in and throws the key into the same river Carton has already mentally followed to death (344).[24]

The guillotine itself symbolizes the revolutionary rage against language, for it 'hushed the eloquent, struck down the powerful, abolished the beautiful and good' (302). Foulon's execution and the glee with which the sans-culottes stuff his mouth with grass likewise illustrate the affinity between revolutionary vengeance and the obliteration of words.[25] This descent into chaos is inevitable, for the rulers' failure to read what Carlyle terms 'importunate' words necessitates both physical and perceptual destruction before meaning can be reconstituted.

In Dante's *Inferno*, Dante-pilgrim's descent through Hell involves a series of encounters with deceptive and chaotic speech forms that mirror the collapse of identity among the damned. For instance, thieves have become endlessly metamorphosing creatures that 'split words', while Satan himself inarticulately slobbers and beats his wings. Darnay has a similar experience at La Force prison, when he meets the general prison population on the way to his solitary cell. They are 'ghosts', just like their brethren who 'haunt' Tellson's in London, where their money used to be. Throughout France the very 'names' of the aristocrats are being blotted out, and yet these prisoners, most of them bound for the guillotine, desperately try to keep up civilized appearances:

> The ghost of beauty, the ghost of stateliness, the ghost of elegance, the ghost of price, the ghost of frivolity, the ghost of wit, the ghost of youth, the ghost of age, all waiting their dismissal from

the desolate shore, all turning on him eyes that were changed by the death they had died in coming there. (285)

Obsessed with naming no less than Madame Defarge is with extermination, they first ask Darnay about his 'name and condition' (285), politely echoing Farinata's fixation on learning Dante's lineage. They persist in the belief that naming, not essence, is the substance of their humanity.

Sydney Carton is also a ghost until he redeems himself; he 'haunts' Lucie Manette's neighbourhood until brought to life through an 'intention' to reveal his feelings to her (179). In the novel he moves from the 'rust and repose' for which he rebukes himself to purposeful activity, as if to illustrate Teufelsdroeckh's Aristotelian assertion that a thought is worthless until it is translated into an action.[26] Lorry's statement that Cruncher should repent 'in action—not in words' for his nocturnal activities as a 'fisherman' likewise illustrates the idea that '*The end of Man is an Action, and not a Thought*' (*Sartor Resartus* 155). But there is an intermediary step between thought and action: belief. Just as Teufelsdroeckh must translate speculation into conviction, and into conduct (195–6), Sydney Carton must discover belief before he can proceed from self-analysis to meaningful activity. Lucie Manette provides the means:

> Will you let me believe, when I recall this day, that the last confidence of my life was reposed in your pure and innocent breast, and that it lies there alone, and will be shared by one? (182)

Like Lorry, who circles back to his childhood, he seeks to revive 'old shadows' and 'old voices' (181) that have nearly expired. Lucie's belief that he might be 'much, much worthier' of himself inspires his statement that 'I would embrace any sacrifice for you and for those dear to you' (183), and is echoed in his last words (404).

His moral crisis is like that of Tennyson's Ulysses, who knows that to stop striving for new experiences is to lose the constantly replenished pasts that are vital to identity; just as Sydney Carton would like to translate his 'rust and repose' into activity, Ulysses would rather 'shine in use' than 'rust unburnished' (1. 23). Without mind-expanding experiences there can be no selfhood. Ulysses's statement that 'I am become a name' (1. 11) is conditioned by his realization that names must be constantly redefined: without memory and experience, the name becomes a hollow shell. If he decides to remain on Ithaca and never again seek 'a newer world', he will be like the 'savage race' he rules, who 'hoard, and sleep, and feed, and know not me' (11. 4,5).

The idea that one must constantly strive to redefine and affirm identity and avoid psychological burial is also important in *Faust*. Trapped in the 'prison' of his study, and conditioned by books rather than by passionate experiences, Goethe's learned Doctor is alternatively suicidal and restless for escape into the wider world. The central tenet of his blood pact with Mephistopheles is that he will be damned if he ever ceases striving to experience more of life and love: 'If I ever say to the moment, linger, you are quite beautiful, then you can put me in chains.'[27] To relax would confirm Mephistopheles' cynical statement to the Lord that for all his ideals, man is 'more beastly than any beast.'[28] But this devil is imprisoned by words, arguing that Faust needs only a poet to create the semblance of a name, and (incorrectly) that he will remain forever what he is.[29] But the moment he sees Gretchen and falls in love he is transformed into a new Faust, having commenced the activity that will both imperil his soul and open the way to redemption.[30]

Like Gretchen, Lucie Manette embodies a principle of love that inspires belief and action, in her father as well as Sydney Carton.[31] To the Doctor she is a repository of memories, the 'golden thread' that unites him 'to a Past beyond his misery, and to a Present beyond his misery' (110). Possessing the stable identity he seeks, she inspires him to try to save his imprisoned son-in-law, thereby ensuring the continuity of past, present, and future: 'As my beloved child was helpful in restoring me to myself, I will be helpful now in restoring the dearest part of herself to her,' he tells Lorry (300). In the Bastille Manette imagined two daughters, one ignorant of his existence and the other sympathetic, yet unable permanently to free him. The second one would

> show me that the home of her married life was full of her loving
> remembrance of her lost father. My picture was in her room, and
> I was in her prayers. Her life was active, cheerful, useful; but my
> poor history pervaded it all. (219–20)

This second 'and more real' daughter embodies the principles of love, remembrance, and story-telling that are essential to the affirmation of another's identity; activity is pointless if it does not have a human object and inspiration, and thereby the means of perpetuating a living fame. Thus at the novel's close, Carton projects his need for love and remembrance into the future, seeing his golden-haired namesake, the grandson of Lucie, being brought to his Paris gravesite to hear his story (404).

Lucie Manette is another of Dickens's childlike women, less a rounded character than a repository for certain ideas about memory and sympathy.

Her imaginative antecedents are to be found in Wordsworth's celebration of the child as 'best Philosopher' in the Poem 'Ode: Intimations of Immortality' and the like and, beyond that, in Schiller's concept of childhood innocence:

> They are ... not only the representation of our lost childhood, which eternally remains most dear to us, but fill us with a certain melancholy. But they are also representations of our highest fulfilment in the ideal.[32] (*Naive And Sentimental Poetry* 85)

This idealization of the idea of the child is evident in the 'childlike ingenuousness' of Sissy Jupe in *Hard Times*, who puts the cynically manipulative James Harthouse to shame and introduces an element of fellow-feeling and imagination into the utilitarian Gradgrind household.[33] Similarly, Lucie Manette is whole and, in Schiller's terms, naive, in contrast to the artificiality and the divisions that characterize London and Paris. She inspires ghosts to become people through purposeful activity, but essentially this is a passive function.[34] The struggling males perceive in her what 'sentimental' people see in nature and the idea represented by the child: 'We love in them the tacitly creative life, the serene spontaneity of their activity, existence in accordance with their own laws, the inner necessity, the eternal unity with themselves' (Schiller, *Naive And Sentimental Poetry* 85).

Soon after his conversation with Lorry about memory and childhood, Sydney Carton experiences an epiphany in the Paris streets which centres around the revivification of language. The words of Jesus reverberate through his mind as he proceeds to carry out his self-sacrifice, inspired by the belief instilled in him by Lucie: 'I am the resurrection and the life, saith the Lord: he that believeth in me, though he were dead, yet shall he live: and whosoever liveth and believeth in me, shall never die' (343). Significantly, these words come to him immediately after he carries a girl across a muddy street and asks her for a kiss.[35] By rediscovering his heart through Lucie Manette and the idea of the child she and this girl represent, he is able in his mind to transform the Biblical Word from an echo into a living symbol of his own experience, much as Lucie is able to change ghosts into people through her sympathetic influence: 'the words were in the echoes of his feet, and were in the air. Perfectly calm and steady, he sometimes repeated them to himself as he walked; but, he heard them always' (343).

Again it is helpful to turn to Carlyle for a fuller understanding of what Dickens means by a revivified word arising from belief. They both locate the transcendental experience and its symbolic language in the sympathetic marriage of minds; thus Teufelsdroeckh repeats Novalis's idea that 'my Belief gains quite *infinitely* the moment I can convince another mind thereof' (*Sartor Resartus* 214). Carlyle likewise stated that words must be read symbolically. Thus he chided his friend, the eccentric minister Edward Irving, for basing his faith in God 'on a little text of *writing* in an ancient Book.'[36] Furthermore, in *Sartor Resartus*, Teufelsdroeckh calls Jesus 'our divinest Symbol', who bodies a 'Godlike' that transcends any particular set of theological terms, including the Christian (224). That is, neither Jesus nor the Bible is final. His life is 'a Symbol of quite perennial, infinite character; whose significance will ever demand to be anew inquired into, and anew made manifest' (224). Carlyle reflects the popular German idea that Jesus was the Highest Humanity, whose example must be replicated to affirm the ideal and bring to new life the language of renunciation and belief. Each age, indeed each person, must emulate what Goethe termed the 'Worship of Sorrow' according to its own instruments and language. Jesus has to be 'anew made manifest'.

Carton's own Christ-like renunciation is confirmed by his declaration to Lorry that 'I am not old, but my young way was never the way to age. Enough of me' (340). After this, he feels no doubts about his mission to die to save his mirror-image, Charles Darnay. Hutter writes that he follows the pattern of the 'criminal-hero' of the Newgate Calendar who 'marches steadily towards his own destruction', at which point his fate and his prophecy become transcendent (20–1). Beyond this, his self-sacrifice is based on Carlyle's ecstatic dramatization of Madame Roland's death in *The French Revolution*. Carton and Roland both discover a transcendental language that contrasts with the disintegration of language around them, but to do so they must exercise a renunciation that takes them out of the world; as I have argued elsewhere, Carlyle imbues Madame Roland with Schillerian tragical traits that make hers an essentially passive and feminine ideal of conduct: he at once idealizes and dismisses his subject.[37] Sydney Carton's death bears the imprint of Schiller as well as Carlyle; since harmonious self-development and 'production' cannot be said to begin on the scaffold (*Sartor Resartus* 197), we may conclude that his renunciation is not the Goethean kind enshrined in Teufelsdroeckh's declaration that 'it is only with Renunciation (*Entsagen*) that Life, properly speaking, can be said to begin' (191).

Both of their deaths are described as 'sublime': Carton looks 'sublime and prophetic' (403), while Madame Roland is 'sublime in her uncomplaining sorrow' (*Works* 4: 209). Their sublimity removes them from their chaotic environment and makes them exemplars of noble conduct in the face of inexorable historical forces. Thus Carlyle depicts his heroine as a Grecian art work, remote from her tumultuous age, nourished 'to clear perennial Womanhood, though but on Logics, *Encyclopédies*, and the Gospel according to Jean-Jacques!' (4: 211). Similarly, Dickens suggests the transcendental apartness of Carton by distancing his narrative perspective, switching like Carlyle to the present tense, and making his prophecy an ambiguous rumour of sublimity ('They said of him ...'). To understand further the meaning of the sublime in these parallel death scenes, let us consider Schiller's theory of tragedy, which impressed Carlyle. In 'On The Sublime' the German writes that the 'morally cultivated man' is able mentally to defeat the physical forces arrayed against him 'because he has by his own free act separated himself from everything that she can reach' (*Naive And Sentimental Poetry* 195). At the moment of greatest crisis a feeling of sublimity 'suddenly and with a shock ... tears the independent spirit out of the net in which a refined sensuousness has entoiled it ... often a single sublime emotion suffices to rip this web of deceit asunder' (201–202). For instance, Schiller's Maria Stuart transcends her material and emotional 'nets' to experience a 'worthy pride' and a 'noble soul'.[38] For the first time, upon accepting the inevitability of death, she looks beyond herself to care for others, for instance Melvil (1. 3506). As with Sydney Carton, the renunciation of self leads to the rediscovery of the heart. As a sacrificial offering, Maria Stuart sets a noble 'example' for others, thus functioning the way Madame Roland and Carton do. Thus Darnay becomes 'like a young child' in Carton's hands: 'with a strength both of will and action, that appeared quite supernatural' (380), he forces the prisoner to change clothes with him. Carton's action is curiously like the role reversal in *Maria Stuart* that leaves Leicester passively doubting himself, while his former lover Maria Stuart exercises a moral will that leaves her 'transformed' on the scaffold.

In one sense Carton is closer to Maria Stuart than to Carlyle's Madame Roland: while the first two are 'sentimental' in their efforts to reconcile their mental divisions and seek the ideal, Madame Roland is a 'naive' 'noble white Vision' who naturally stands apart from the artificiality around her: she is 'serenely complete' from her youth to her death (*Works* 4: 211). Her death is a model of renunciation and composure, but she does not have to struggle to achieve either. Unlike the deeply flawed Sydney Carton and Maria Stuart, she is consistently pure and inviolate, removed from the mire of the world in which she exerts her subtle influences on the Girondins' political affairs. She is 'genuine, the creature of Sincerity and Nature, in an age of Artificiality, Pollution, and Cant' (2: 46). She is static, while Sydney Carton must pursue an ideal 'mirage of honourable ambition' through Lucie's inspiration before he can overcome the enervation of his will. In taking Darnay's place on the scaffold, he also steps into the shoes of Madame Roland and the childlike feminine transcendence she represents to Carlyle. He achieves something like the reconciled naive and sentimental visions Schiller postulates in an as yet unrealized 'Idyllic' art form, 'a free uniting of inclination with the law ... none other than the ideal of beauty applied to actual life' (*Naive And Sentimental Poetry* 153).

In their death scenes, Dickens and Carlyle are interested in the relation between writing and the ineffable. Carlyle focuses on how Madame Roland asked in vain to be allowed 'to write the strange thoughts that were rising in her ... so in her too there was an Unnameable; she too was a Daughter of the Infinite; there were mysteries which Philosophism had not dreamt of!' (*Works* 4: 211)[39] Dickens's narrator marvels that every human being is a mystery 'to every other' (44); Carton is a mystery to others, and even to himself, unable to explain to Lucie Manette the 'mystery of my own wretched heart' (180). Dickens alludes to Madame Roland's request 'to be allowed to write down the thoughts that were inspiring her' (404), just before the prophecy in which Carton enters a realm beyond reality but just short of ineffability. The narrator underscores the tentativeness, the mystery if you will, of his last words by stressing the 'if': 'if he had given utterance to his [thoughts], and they were prophetic, they would have been these' (404). Dickens leaves his reader to ponder his incapacity fully to probe the mysteries of language and personality. That the text is moving beyond language to probe transcendental mysteries is evident in a seemingly minor change Dickens makes in Carlyle's account. Madame Roland comforts the printer and Assignat-director Lamarche, emulating Maria Stuart in showing a weaker male how easy it is to die. But Sydney Carton comforts a young girl, for the second time since his final interview with Lorry. Significantly, she feels guilty because she 'cannot write', and therefore must leave her orphaned cousin ignorant about her execution (403). Their conversation while awaiting execution centres on the inefficacy of words as they prepare to enter a state where there is 'no Time' (403). Carton tells her it is better she can not write; he accepts the impermanence of words compared to love and sympathy, the positive emotions that can render language transcendental, so that (to cite Schiller's description of the aesthetic state) we have the 'dignity of free spirits' and mentally are freed from 'the degrading relationship with matter' (*Aesthetic Education* 139). Thus Dickens stresses their eye contact and the comfort it gives: 'Keep your eyes upon me, dear child, and mind no other object' (402).

There is a temptation to regard Carton's prophecy as a denial of meaning rather than an evocation of mystery, as if the reader must go away with the idea that the book's doubt is a poor thing, but its nihilism a very intense experience. Certainly it is ambiguous, but whether Carton projects his wished-for union with Lucie into the future and kills off Darnay in the process is another question. Vanden Bossche writes that 'the image of self-sacrifice created by his speech puts the authenticity of that very self-sacrifice into question by envisioning a future that nearly effaces Darnay' (211). This is perhaps true. But another explanation is that Carton envisions a unity almost beyond naming, where even his desire for perpetuation through others' memories is subordinated to a vision of a future where divisions cease. He does not refer to himself, Darnay, or Lucie Manette by name. His most forceful assertion of identity is the 'boy of my name' brought to his Paris gravesite to hear his story:

> I see that I hold a sanctuary in their hearts, and in the hearts of their descendants, generations hence. I see her, an old woman, weeping for me on the anniversary of this day.... I see that child who lay upon her bosom and who bore my name, a man winning his way up in that path of life which once was mine. I see him winning it so well, that my name is made illustrious there by the light of his. I see the blots I threw upon it, faded away. I see him, foremost of just judges and honoured men, bringing a boy of my name, with a forehead that I know and golden hair, to this place ... and I hear him tell the child my story, with a tender and a faltering voice. (404)

As is the case when Carton comforts the young girl, sympathetic eyesight now takes precedence over writing and naming. In his prophecy, only those people who have failed to transcend naming through sympathetic acts retain their names: Barsad, Cly, Defarge, and the Vengeance (404).

In *A Tale of Two Cities* Dickens suggests that people are too mysterious to be reduced to mere names and formulas. M. Defarge's search for a key to Manette at the Bastille is fruitless because the essence of selfhood is only communicable through sympathy and memory. But the mystery at the core of the self always remains; as Manette tells Darnay concerning his daughter, 'mysteries arise out of close love, as well as out of wide division' (165). But this does not presuppose an absence of ultimate meaning; to doubt is not to deny. The prophecy, like so much else in the novel, reveals an insecurity on Dickens's part about our capacity to 'name' and thus control the future, an even more precarious act than defining our identities against the onrush of contemporary events. Like the lives of George Eliot's characters in *Middlemarch*, life does not achieve finality even at death, 'but merely ceases' at the point determined by the writer. To close the text or project it into a knowable future is meretricious, for the mutability of existence precludes its ever being authoritatively 'read'. At the end of *A Tale of Two Cities* Carton, like Madame Roland, enters the transcendental realm. Beyond the mystery there may be final knowledge and identity, or only blankness. But to insist on one or the other is to become no less trapped in words than Carlyle's dream theoreticians and Dickens's Paris Projectors are. To assert the absence of stable meaning is to articulate a code which denies authoritative codes.

NOTES

1. There has been a flurry of scholarly activity in recent years on *A Tale of Two Cities*; what follows is a representative sampling. Gross analyses the partial resurrections in the novel and states that Carton 'might just as well be committing suicide as laying down his life for Darnay' (23); but for MacKay his death represents a 'transcendental achieving' and 'inviolate action' (201). See also Hutter for a study of Carton's Christ-like resurrection (20) and its parodic counterpart in Cruncher's trade, the history of which he explores. Resurrection implies unburial and exposure, according to Gallagher, whose analysis of violations of the private are in the post-structuralist vein. She writes that the Terror 'explicated the Revolution's insistence on transparency and its corollary of hidden plots' (134). Like Hutter, she compares Cruncher not only with Carton, but with the narrator, 'in that both dig up the past and uncover buried mysteries' (137).

2. Needless to say, there are differing interpretations of Carton's ambiguous prophecy. My approach emphasizes the idea of presence rather than that of absence, owing to the dynamics of the scene leading up to the prophecy and to the idealistic tradition on which Dickens draws, primarily through Carlyle. MacKay writes that his words 'are at once unspoken and yet transcendently true' (203). Baumgarten also affirms the truth of the prophecy within the terms set by the text: 'his final vision is an unwritten piece of autobiographical writing, voiced beyond any imprisoning code and opening into the prophetic realm where writing is absolute and true' (163). Rignall states that this is a 'vision of a better world which seems to lie beyond time and history' (575); see also Kuchich 168–77. But Vanden Bossche is less certain than the others about the authority of Carton's prophecy, noting that he effaces Darnay: his 'vision of a peaceful Paris is problematic in the light of the reader's knowledge of its tumultuous history and other revolutions' (211).

3. In his Preface Dickens states his debt to the 'philosophy' of Carlyle's history.

4. See Lloyd 43. Schlegel wrote that 'it's equally deadly for the mind to have a system and not to have one. Therefore it will just have to decide to combine the two'.

5. This contrasts with the non-verbal communication based on sympathy which reaches its highest expression at the end of the novel, when Carton comforts a young girl on the way to execution. See below.

6. Even Lucie is 'afraid of it' when she first sees him cobbling in his locked room in Paris (69).

7. Compare John Keats's assertion that identity is created by the interaction of intelligence, the human heart, and the external world.

8. Surrounded by aristocratic 'ghosts' and removed from any immediate human contact in his cell, Darnay is thrown upon his intelligence, which begins to disintegrate, and his heart, which momentarily is distracted from Lucie Manette's influence. Her presence outside his window eventually recreates a precarious psychological harmony.

9. When the letter is read at Darnay's trial, we learn that Manette most missed 'tidings of my dearest wife' during the eighteen years he was imprisoned (361). This would have filled his 'blankness', just as Lucie fills Darnay's by standing below his cell window.

10. Gross writes that in the novel 'the grave gives up its dead reluctantly, and the prisoner who has been released is still far from being a free man' (20).

11. 'Crush humanity out of shape once more, under similar hammers, and it will twist itself into the same tortured forms' (*Tale* 399). In a milder form, what applies to the sans-culottes applies to Lorry. Tellson's is a more benign mirror of the Bastille, including its iron bars and its air of death and suppression of personality: 'putting to death was a recipe much in vogue with all trades and professions, and not least of all with Tellson's' (84). Lorry is twisted out of shape like all the others buried here: 'When they took a young man into Tellson's London house, they hid him somewhere till he was old' (85).

12. He is not even shaken by the Paris Tellson's with its whitewashed Cupid and the bloody 'whirlings of the grindstone' in the courtyard (291).

13. Compare Gradgrind's mental imprisonment in economic jargon in *Hard Times*, illustrated by his successful mediation of Bounderby's 'proposal' to Louisa.

14. Instead of becoming trapped in our 'Philosophical Systems', Carlyle writes, we must learn to read the 'Volume of Nature': 'It is a Volume written in celestial hieroglyphs, in the true Sacred-writing; of which even Prophets are happy that they can read here a line and there a line' (*Sartor Resartus* 54, 258).

15. Lucie comforts Carton by believing in his capacity for good, and he in turn comforts the young girl at the scaffold (182, 403). Belief is contagious: see below.

16. Dickens's depiction of the Marquis and his family history owes much to Carlyle, who analyses how the ruling classes concealed their savagery beneath an apparent refinement. 'Philosophism sits joyful in her glittering saloons ... and preaches, lifted up over all Bastilles, a coming millennium' (*Works* 2: 30).

17. Schiller writes that 'man portrays himself in his actions. And what a figure he cuts in the drama of the present time! On the one hand, a return to the savage state; on the other, to complete lethargy' (*Aesthetic Education* 25).

18. The Marquis has no 'within', but Darnay's mother does. He recalls how he read both her words and her eyes, which implored him to 'have mercy and redress' his family's crimes (154).

19. Carlyle draws on Schiller's analysis in *The French Revolution*, but is more sympathetic about the motivations of the poor for rebelling. For a study of the mob psychology in Carlyle's history, see LaValley.

20. Compare also Carlyle's description of the Sphinx riddle of Nature in *Past And Present*: 'the face and bosom of a goddess, but ending in claws and the body of a lioness' (*Works* 10: 7).

21. Carlyle also uses natural imagery to describe the French Revolution, which he defines as the rebellion and victory 'of disimprisoned Anarchy against corrupt worn-out Authority' (*Works* 2: 211).

22. Like Dickens, Carlyle and Schiller point to the difficulty of connecting words with things while affirming the need to try. Thus Carlyle writes that 'words ought not to harden into things for us' (*Works* 5: 106), while Schiller points to the difficulty of finding language that can analyse, yet preserve the 'living spirit' of nature (*Aesthetic Education* 5).

23. Thus in *Hard Times*, the fire into which Louisa often stares is a reflection of the abyss as well as of her own thwarted energies. In *A Tale of Two Cities* a tipsy Lorry 'digs' in the 'live red coals' of the fireplace at his Dover hotel, as if unconsciously searching for his buried self. This follows his repeated dream of burial in the coach, where the essential relation between him and Manette becomes apparent (51, 47).

24. Once again she protects Lucie's sanctuary. See Gallagher 138.

25. Foulon told the starving poor they should eat grass; Carlyle also dwells on his execution in *The French Revolution* as a clash between false words and the rage against words. Foulon and the sans-culottes have all turned away from true language. Compare MacKay's assertion that Madame Defarge's decapitation of the governor of the Bastille 'paradoxically unifies him with the group, now an "ocean of faces" in Dickens' rhetoric of transcendence' (199).

26. Rust is an important motif in *A Tale of Two Cities.* Cruncher licks it from his fingers, for example, suggesting the symbolic failure of his 'resurrections' compared to those of Lorry and Carton. Rust and writing are connected in Manette's buried letter, which he wrote with a 'rusty iron point ... in scrapings of soot and charcoal from the chimney, mixed with blood' (348).

27. 'Werd ich zum Augenblicke sagen: / Verweile doch! du bist so schoen! / Dann magst du mich in Fesseln schlagen' (11. 1699–1701).

28.   Ein wenig besser wuerd er leben,
Haettst du ihm nicht den Schein des Himmelslichts gegeben;
Er nennt's Vernunft und braucht's allein,
Nur tierischer als jedes Tier zu sein. (11. 283–86)

29. 'Du bleibst doch immer, was du bist' (1. 1809).

30. 'Armsel'ger Faust! ich kenne dich nicht mehr' (1. 2720).

31. Lucie's power is not absolute: 'she could recall some occasions on which her power had failed; but they were few and slight, and she believed them over' (110). This is reflected in Manette's statement to her that the second, sympathetic daughter he imagined while in the Bastille 'could never deliver' him completely (220).

32. Schiller writes that it is not the physical child or nature that inspires us: 'it is not these objects, it is an idea represented by them which we love in them. We love in them the tacitly creative life, the serene spontaneity of their activity, existence in accordance with their own laws, the inner necessity, the eternal unity with themselves' (*Naive And Sentimental Poetry* 84–5).

33. But unlike Lorry, Louisa Gradgrind has no childhood to which she can return in thought: 'The dreams of childhood—its airy fables; its graceful, beautiful, humane, impossible adornments of the world beyond; so good to be believed in once, so good to be remembered when outgrown ... what had she to do with these?' (150–51).

34. Still, she seems conscious of her function and doubts her capacity to perform it. Thus she exclaims, upon being told that she will see her father, 'I am going to see his Ghost! It will be his Ghost—not him!' (57)

35. Mud is an important image in Dickens's novel: recall the mail-coach ride in the beginning, the environment of Tellson's (47), and the scramble in the mud for spilled wine outside Defarge's wine shop (43–44). Mud symbolizes a morally corrupt environment and burial, as it did for Carlyle, who recounted that he had to defeat the 'foul and vile and soul-murdering Mud-gods of my Epoch' (*Reminiscences* 281).

36. Irving became obsessed with Corinthians 13 and speaking in tongues.

37. For more information about Schiller's influence on *The French Revolution*, see my article in *Prose Studies*.

38. 'Die Krone fuehl ich wieder auf dem Haupt, / Den wuerd'gen Stolz in meiner edeln Seele!' (11, 3493–4)

39. Similarly, 'strange' thoughts appear in the mind of Tennyson's speaker in Lyric 95 of *In Memoriam*; he can not fully communicate their essence in 'matter-moulded forms of speech' (11. 25–32, 46).

WORKS CITED

Baumgarten, Murray. 'Writing the Revolution'. *Dickens Studies Annual* 12 (1983): 161–76.

Carlyle, Thomas. *The Centenary Edition of the Works of Thomas Carlyle*. Ed. H. D. Traill. 30 vols. London, 1896–99.

———. *Reminiscences*. Ed. C. E. Norton. London: J. M. Dent & Sons, 1972.

———. *Sartor Resartus*. Ed. Charles Frederick Harrold. New York: The Odyssey Press, 1937.

Dickens, Charles. *Hard Times*. New York: W. W. Norton & Company, 1966.

———. *A Tale of Two Cities*. Harmondsworth: Penguin, 1970.

Gallagher, Catherine. 'The Duplicity of Doubling in *A Tale of Two Cities*'. *Dickens Studies Annual* 12 (1983): 125–45.

Goethe, Johann Wolfgang von. *Werke*. Hamburger Ausgabe in 14 Baenden. Hamburg: Christian Wegner Verlag, 1972. Vol. 3.

Gross, John. '*A Tale of Two Cities*'. *Twentieth Century Interpretations of A Tale of Two Cities*. Ed. Charles E. Beckwith. Englewood Cliffs, New Jersey: Prentice-Hall, 1972. 19–28.

Hutter, Albert D. 'The Novelist as Resurrectionist: Dickens and the Dilemma of Death'. *Dickens Studies Annual* 12 (1983): 1–39.

Kuchich, John. *Excess and Restraint in the Novels of Charles Dickens*. Athens: University of Georgia Press, 1981.

LaValley, Albert J. *Carlyle And The Idea of the Modern*. New Haven: Yale U. P., 1968.

Lloyd, Tom. 'Madame Roland and Schiller's Aesthetics: Carlyle's *The French Revolution*'. *Prose Studies* 9 (1986): 39–53.

MacKay, Carol Hanbery. 'The Rhetoric of Soliloquy in *The French Revolution* and *A Tale of Two Cities*'. *Dickens Studies Annual* 12 (1983): 197–207.

Rignall, J. M. 'Dickens and the Catastrophic Continuum of History in *A Tale of Two Cities*'. *ELH* 51 (1984): 575–88.

Schiller, Friedrich von. *On The Aesthetic Education of Man*. Trans. Elizabeth M. Wilkinson and L. A. Willoughby. Oxford: Clarendon Press, 1967.

———. *Naive And Sentimental Poetry and On The Sublime*. Trans. Julias A. Elias. New York: Ungar, 1980.

———. *Saemtliche Werke*. 5 vols. Muenchen: Winkler Verlag, 1968. Vol. 2.

Stange, G. Robert. 'Dickens and the Fiery Past: *A Tale of Two Cities* Reconsidered'. *Twentieth Century Interpretations of A Tale of Two Cities*. Ed. Charles E. Beckwith. Englewood Cliffs, N. J.: Prentice-Hall, 1972. 64–75.

Vanden Bossche, Chris R. 'Prophetic Closure and Disclosing Narrative: *The French Revolution* and *A Tale of Two Cities*'. *Dickens Studies Annual* 12 (1983): 209–21.

JOHN R. REED

A Tale of Two Cities

Something is very wrong with justice in *A Tale of Two Cities* (1859). Both English and French legal systems seem more capable of persecuting the innocent than prosecuting the guilty. An outlaw like Jerry Cruncher may voice disgust at the inhuman legal punishment of quartering, but only from self-interest.[1] And when the mob overthrows corrupt authority in France, it imposes a mirror injustice, replacing one bloodthirstiness with another. The narrator specifically describes the self-appointed Tribunal as "unjust" (300). Many crimes in this book are punished, but not through official channels. As we have seen, this is true in much of Dickens' fiction, where public institutions rarely succeed in being just. Dickens wants a regime that combines a sense of justice with a sense of mercy, but under these requirements it is difficult to assign authority to punish. Christ recommended forgiving of offenders and advised turning the other cheek. Thus individual Christians must not exact justice. But if the unfeeling, mechanical, even corrupt state is unqualified to dispense justice, who has the moral right and the power and means to do so?

Like Carlyle and Ruskin, Dickens assumed that true justice is administered finally by providence. That does not mean that most offenses are not punished through human agency, but that the guiding power for such justice is divine. Human beings generate their deserts through their conduct

From *Dickens and Thackeray: Punishment and Forgiveness*, pp. 257–269. © 1995 by John R. Reed.

and, in that sense, all punishments are self-begotten. Most of Dickens' novels focus on punishing offenses or patterns of offense in specific institutions or individuals. But *A Tale of Two Cities* emphasizes the fates of nations rather than of individuals. Because history does not forgive, there is very little discussion of forgiveness, or even pardon or mercy, in this novel, which is overwhelmingly occupied with illustrating the consequences of unwise, unjust, and inhuman behavior.[2]

Perhaps to convey a greater sense of the tragic dimensions of the French Revolution, the novel says little about providence, but a good deal about fate and destiny. At the outset of *A Tale of Two Cities* the narrator remarks that many years before the Revolution Fate had already marked the trees that would be used to construct the guillotine (2). Madame Defarge, knitting the names of those who are to be consigned to death when the Revolution begins, works "with the steadfastness of Fate" (106), suggesting an analogy with the Greek fates who spun, measured, and cut the threads of human life. Learning that Darnay/St. Evrémonde has married Lucie Manette in England, Defarge hopes that for Lucie's sake "Destiny will keep her husband out of France" (176).

This concern for the determining power of fate is reflected in the narrator's manner, for he regularly offers confident forecasts of what is to come. Partly this is because he is telling a story whose end—the French Revolution—is in the past and thus already known to his audience. There can be no suspense about the outcome of public events. But the narrator's many proleptic passages also confirm the rigidity of the events being related. Repetition of the motif clusters of wine/blood/stain and of hastening footsteps gathering into a crowd, along with direct forecasts by the narrator ("The time was to come, when that wine [blood] too would be spilled on the street stones, and when the stain of it would be red upon many there" [28]), enhance the foreknown events in an operatic manner, like the destiny motif running through Verdi's *La Forza del Destino*, or any of the value-laden motifs that accompany and foreshadow events in Wagner's operas.

But if these and other direct forecasts of what is to come suggest a known, predictable world, a second powerful tendency of the narrative is to insist upon the mystery that is within us. Despite the many indications that life is plotted by fate, in fact not all of these signs are accurate or trustworthy. Madame Defarge does not control the destinies of others, but is herself only part of a larger force. Madame Defarge points her finger "as if it were the finger of Fate" at Lucie's child, but the implied doom never comes to pass (253). The resurrection theme in the novel is intimately related to its "psychological" kernel, but it is also linked by its overt Christian association with the idea of forgiveness and redemption. Human sympathy is the amulet by which the charmed doors of the mind and heart can be reopened. When Lucie first succeeds in penetrating the muddle of her father's mind to touch his heart, he sobs tempestuously then yields "to the calm that must follow all storms—emblem to humanity, of the rest and silence into which the storm called Life must hush at last" (45). Dr. Manette is himself emblematic of the mystery that all humans are to one another. In his confused state following his release after more than seventeen years of imprisonment, "No human intelligence could read the mysteries of his mind in the scared blank wonder of his face" (46).

The narrator candidly announces this theme of the mysterious self at the opening of chapter 3.

> A wonderful fact to reflect upon, that every human creature is constituted to be that profound secret and mystery to every other. A solemn consideration, when I enter a great city by night, that every one of those darkly clustered houses encloses its own secret; that every room in every one of them encloses its own secret; that every beating heart in the hundreds of thousands of breasts there, is, in some of its imaginings, a secret to the heart nearest it![3]

This is the inescapable condition of humanity; all efforts to fathom those nearest us are frustrated and ended by death. "In any of the burial-places of this city through which I pass, is there a sleeper more inscrutable than its busy inhabitants are, in their innermost personality to me, or that I am to them?" (10). Mystery and secrecy, as we have seen, are constant elements in Dickens' novels, but whereas in the earlier novels secrets generally have to do with concealed plots, unknown lineages, and so on, in the later novels secrets are just as often connected with internal states. The shift in this direction probably begins with *Dombey*, a pivotal novel in so many ways. In *A Tale of Two Cities*, personal and public secrets are intertwined and mysteries of the human heart are played out in public venues. In this novel as in others, secrecy is associated with suffering, death, and burial. But just as Dr. Manette, in being recalled to life from his "burial" in prison, becomes the embodied expression of a long-kept secret, so a major theme of the novel is that one way to counteract the power of death is through bringing to light the secrets within us, rooted as they are in suffering. This theme is related to Dickens' broader view that we must treasure memory—both good and bad—because out of memories come our resources for encountering the difficult experiences of life. In *A Tale of Two Cities*, secret memories are both private and communal. The communal "secrets" are already known to the reader because they are part of historical record, but the private secrets remain a mystery until the narrative exposes them to light. Thus, while the public narrative moves unswervingly toward its foreknown denouement, an accompanying narrative line presents a sequence of secrets gradually exposed to reveal the dark and bright elements harbored within human nature.

Mr. Lorry's suggestion to Dr. Manette that he might be able to defend himself against relapses in his mental health by sharing his secret with someone else is a straightforward version of Dickens' belief that the secrets of the heart may become useful when faced and shared. That which is repressed, that from which we unconsciously avert our gaze, only increases its power by being ignored. This is true in the history of nations as well as of individuals. The narrative, by temporally dislocating the order of its revelations, subtly indicates how complicated and insidious the perpetuation of evil can be, through the failure to face the secrets of the past. When Charles Darnay is arrested and "buried," "in secret," he both duplicates and anticipates Dr. Manette's history. Although Charles' confinement comes much later chronologically in the *fabula* of the novel, it is presented first in the *sjuzet*. Only after Charles' incarceration do we learn the details of Dr. Manette's unjust confinement by the St. Evrémonde brothers. Charles' imprisonment is a foreshadowing of the secret we will soon learn, and hence readable as a prolepsis or even a prophecy, but because it foreshadows a past event, it is also readable as an analepsis or recurrence, teaching us that history will rerun its scenarios until they are comprehended and consciously engaged. The two imprisonments are intimately linked. Dr. Manette recovers his full capacities in working to free his son-in-law. "For the first time the Doctor felt, now, that his suffering was strength and power" (257). His suffering having been made public, he is endowed with a productive strength that repression could never produce. Ironically, Dr. Manette is actually operating against his own scripting of history, but that revelation has yet to be made. At this point, what is important is the suggestion that torment can be transformed into triumph and that pain may be the agent of beneficial transformation.

The disclosure of our secrets is not always safe or constructive. The secret that the Doctor has himself deeply repressed comes to light and recondemns Charles to death. In the depths of his agony, Dr. Manette put in writing his curse on the whole St. Evrémonde family and now that curse has its effect. Like a prescribed fate, Dr. Manette's version of history now becomes the official text that the revolutionaries are determined to play out. Nested in this lesson on repression and revelation, suffering and salvation, is an even more basic moral ground. Hatred, rage, and vindictiveness are not the emotions that will improve human conditions. When hatred answers hatred, only more evil will be propagated in the world. Dr. Manette's cry for universal revenge against the entire family of his oppressors is as unjust as their behavior, and predictably begets additional suffering upon the victim who has become transgressor in his turn. In this way it reflects at the personal level what occurs at the public level with the violence of the revolutionaries. There are good and bad secrets in our hearts and we must learn to understand them ourselves and face them. Lucie's heart is "a mystery" to Dr. Manette, but it is clear to everyone that it is a benign mystery (128). So certain is Carton of the benignity of that heart that he wants "the last confidence of [his] life" to repose in Lucie's "pure and innocent breast" to be shared by no one else (145). This is the holy secret of another being's unselfish love.[4] Moreover, it is this love for Lucie that prompts Carton to look into "the mystery of [his] own wretched heart," and by facing its darknesses wrest from them a final shining victory (143).

Madame Defarge is the focus of error in *A Tale of Two Cities*, embodying the worst of human impulses and turning even apparent virtues into crimes. She is contrasted particularly with the Manettes, but with Darnay as well. If Madame Defarge's threads represent a terrible future, worked to its design out of the past and present, Lucie is herself "the golden thread" that unites her father's past and present over the gulf of his suppressed misery (74). And just as Lucie is the constructive force whose secret is a loving heart, so the secret in Madame Defarge's heart is an unforgiving hatred and a claim for revenge against all of the St. Evrémonde family. Dr. Manette has excluded Charles from his enmity—a form of forgiveness—but Madame Defarge has brooded on her injury until it has become a need for personal retribution. Her secret, saved until the last moment, is that the peasant family devastated by the St. Evrémonde brothers' cruelty was her family. As long as Madame Defarge labors for the oppressed she is triumphant and safe, but the moment she takes justice into her own hands she puts herself at risk, and in trying to injure Lucie and her daughter she destroys herself with her own weapon. Madame Defarge begins with a private family purpose and extends it to a public and "historical" dimension. By contrast, Lucie recovers her father, a figure publicly symbolizing historical oppression, and returns him to a rehabilitating domestic sanctuary. Lucie's love is opposed to Madame Defarge's hatred, and signifies the power of individual human effort to change events. Her golden thread is the bright line running through Madame Defarge's woven fate, and it can unravel at least a portion of that suggested destiny.

Describing the ambiguous behavior of the prisoners condemned by the revolutionary tribunal, the narrator offers a comment on human psychology that is closely related to this theme of secrecy and strength.

Similarly, though with a subtle difference, a species of fervour or intoxication, known, without doubt, to have led some persons to brave the guillotine unnecessarily, and to die by it, was not mere boastfulness, but a wild infection of the wildly shaken public mind. In seasons of pestilence, some of us will have a secret attraction to the disease—a terrible passing inclination to die of it. And all of us have like wonders hidden in our breasts, only needing circumstances to evoke them. (267–68)

We all have mysterious, even dangerous and self-destructive impulses within us, but these must be brought to light and understood. The longer they remain repressed the more dangerous they become. Dr. Manette gradually comes to realize this and transforms suffering into active, positive power; Madame Defarge does not and enjoys letting her dark urges fester in her heart until, when freed, the tigerish impulses destroy her. But perhaps Carton is the most complex example of this process. He has resigned himself to a life of slow self-destruction, an undignified and fatal dissipation, until he meets Lucie. Her own goodness and the thoughts she inspires lead Carton to explore the mystery of his heart. Recognizing its treacherous features, Carton is nonetheless able to retrieve from all of its error one shining truth of love that matures into a stunning act of generous self-sacrifice. Carton's self-recovery is also an act of self-forgiveness; he has permitted himself to be the good man he previously could not believe in.

A Tale of Two Cities is, then, a history of individual secrets and their disclosures in the context of the permanent mystery of the human heart, but it is also a history of two nations in a specific period of chronological time. In this history, as I have already noted, there are no secrets because the major events are foreknown. Yet this larger movement of the story is intimately related to the movement of individual careers.

The greatest historical guilt rests with the French aristocracy. The most obvious thing about them in this novel is that they are self-indulgent, arrogant, exploitive, and unjust. They cringe before their superiors and lord it over their inferiors. At the Monseigneur's reception in Paris there is an elegant turnout of court hangers-on. The narrator observes "that all the company at the grand hotel of Monseigneur were perfectly dressed. If the Day of Judgment had only been ascertained to be a dress day, everybody there would have been eternally correct" (101). But the whole point about Judgment Day is that all external ornament, all disguise, will be put aside and each individual will answer for his or her behavior. For most individuals some mercy will be required, since we are all fallible and likely to have some maculations to be forgiven and expunged. But the French aristocracy of *A*

Tale of Two Cities has, as a class, institutionalized injustice and will have a heavy debt of guilt to pay. The narrator provides a sample of this behavior in the Marquis St. Evrémonde as he leaves the Monseigneur's party in a foul mood. The marquis urges his coachman to make speed, and, as a consequence, the coach runs down a child in the street. The marquis reprimands the poor people in the street for not being able to tend their children and is more worried about his horses than about the child. He throws the child's distraught parent a coin as a compensation for his loss. This callous behavior is emblematic because it manifests two central abominations in Dickens' moral economy—violation of family feeling, especially when focused upon a child, and the transformation of human values into monetary terms. When he arrives back at his estate the marquis is equally callous and arrogant toward his own tenants. He refuses to provide a simple marker for the grave of a woman's dead husband.

The marquis' actions offer representative and concrete examples of abuses by the French aristocracy. They are narrated in a manner calculated to excite common human sympathies, the narrator's method of weighting his plot toward retribution. But the accumulating burden of guilt is historical, not merely national. France may be a hell of injustice and cruelty, but England is not much better. "In England," the narrator remarks, "there was scarcely an amount of order and protection to justify much national boasting" (2). Even minor crimes were punished in a vicious and bloody manner and the kings of the time "carried their divine rights with a high hand" (3). Brutal and often fatal punishment took the place of any attempt to alleviate the conditions of the poor. The Old Bailey provided no better justice than the French system. The ogreish audience at Charles Darnay's trial finds him an object of interest because, if convicted, he will be drawn and quartered. The narrator comments that "putting to death was a recipe much in vogue with all trades and professions.... Not that it did the least good in the way of prevention—it might almost have been worth remarking that the fact was exactly the reverse—but, it cleared off (as to this world) the trouble of each particular case, and left nothing else connected with it to be looked after" (50).

And yet putting to death does not clear away the midden of accumulating social guilt. Putting to death is a public way of trying to forget. With the offender dead and buried, one may forget the occasion of the crime. One need not remember that a man stole a loaf of bread because he was hungry or pinched clothing from a line to sell for food because he had no means of employment. However, it is just as unhealthy for nations to suppress their memories, to turn their eyes away from suffering, as it is for individuals. Thus in the St. Antoine neighborhood in Paris where the

Defarges have their wine shop, hunger is everywhere evident, indirectly attributable to neglect by the nation's ruling class. But this treatment has its consequences. "In the hunted air of the people there was yet some wild-beast thought of the possibility of turning at bay. Depressed and slinking though they were, eyes of fire were not wanting among them; nor compressed lips, white with what they suppressed; nor foreheads knitted into the likeness of the gallows-rope they mused about enduring, or inflicting" (29). A social evil may be repressed and forgotten, but as with the psychological operation of individuals, it will eventually find release and express itself all the more forcefully for having been so long held back.[5] The murder of the marquis is an individual event, but again symptomatic of what awaits his class when the hidden rage of the populace breaks into the open. Madame Defarge understands when she declares, "'Vengeance and retribution require a long time; it is the rule'" (170). A. O. J. Cockshut remarks that, perhaps influenced by Carlyle, Dickens treated the mobs in *A Tale of Two Cities* differently from those in *Barnaby Rudge*. The latter were "endowed with no serious meaning." By contrast the "Paris crowd is, from the start, an irresistible social force produced by inexorable causes."[6]

Madame Defarge alludes to the moral rule that evil brings its own consequences, a rule that was for Dickens a natural process as well. Thus the narrator uses images of such natural forces as storms and rising seas to describe the approach of the Revolution. As one sows so must one reap, the narrator suggests, elaborating the maxim when he explains that French aristocracy and British orthodoxy alike talk of "this terrible Revolution as if it were the one only harvest ever known under the skies that had not been sown—as if nothing had ever been done, or omitted to be done, that had led to it—as if observers of the wretched millions in France, and of the misused and perverted resources that should have made them prosperous had not seen it inevitably coming, years before, and had not in plain words recorded what they saw" (226).

And so the Revolution occurs. Secret hatred breaks into sight, becoming a kind of madness. The woman known as Vengeance typifies the unthinking violence of those who have broken from their repression with no constructive plan. They can only glory in the destruction of a power that once kept them "underground." Violent response to injustice, however, is not the answer, as Trotty Veck acknowledges in *The Chimes*. If it is not possible to pardon the outrages of the past, an individual or a people must not commit the equal error of perpetuating similar outrages in the present. The links or threads of act and consequence will in this case only fashion a continuing web of violence and retribution. Set against such a determinant sequence is the golden thread of love, forgiveness, and mercy embodied in Lucie Manette.

The connection between national and individual repression is focused in the St. Evrémondes' case. They rape a peasant girl and murder her brother. The St. Evrémonde brothers are humiliated not by the dastardly nature of these intimate crimes, but because the peasant boy dared to struggle against his oppressors on equal terms. It is to keep this embarrassing information secret that the aristocrats have Manette abducted and "buried alive." As witness to the truth, he becomes the memory they want suppressed, the secret they want hidden. But in Dickens' just universe the truth cannot be so easily concealed. The St. Evrémonde story comes to light in Charles Darnay's second trial and threatens to carry retribution to an extreme by destroying an innocent member of the family, just as the Revolution has gone to excess in slaughtering many innocent persons. Having renounced his aristocratic heritage, Darnay has immigrated to England where he lives by his own labor and is powerless to fulfill his mother's wishes, who, before her death, importuned him "to have mercy and to redress" the sins of his relatives (117). But Darnay does not know the secret crime that he is charged to redress. He inherits this secret responsibility as he inherits the name St. Evrémonde, but if he can divest himself of his name and his worldly inheritance, he cannot separate himself from his family history. When he later returns to France, he unknowingly plays two roles, though he is unaware of the private one. He hopes that he can do "something to stay bloodshed, and assert the claims of mercy and humanity," and imagines that he might have "some influence to guide this raging Revolution that was running so fearfully wild" (231–32). But his true name is a stigma dooming him to generic retribution no matter how much he has tried to renounce the abuses it represents. It appears that Darnay will unconsciously comply with his mother's appeal, redressing family derelictions with his life. National and personal patterns of trespass and retribution are made explicit with Madame Defarge's revelation of her personal stake in punishing the St. Evrémonde family.

Madame Defarge is the sister of the raped girl and murdered boy. Her whole involvement in the revolutionary cause has been fueled less by an abstract desire for justice and social progress than by a secret personal hatred, a craving toward private revenge. Madame Defarge is the reverse image of Darnay, just as she is of Lucie. Seeking to be just and to expunge the guilt of his class, Darnay is unaware of his own intimate involvement in a central, representative crime. By contrast, Madame Defarge's apparent concern for her class masks a private vendetta spurring her to public action. Ironically Madame Defarge, who has labored at bringing a specific destiny into being, dies "accidentally" by her own weapon when she struggles with Miss Pross in an effort to get at Lucie and her child. Dickens was fully conscious of the implicit moral balance he wished to achieve by this outcome, defending the use of accident in fiction generally, and specifically in the scene of Madame Defarge's death. "Where the accident is inseparable from the passion and action of the character; where it is strictly consistent with the entire design, and arises out of some culminating proceeding on the part of the individual which the whole story has led up to; it seems to me to become, as it were, an act of divine justice." Dickens adds that he purposely used the "half-comic intervention" of Miss Pross to emphasize the angry woman's failure and to contrast her mean death to a desperate but bold death in the streets. Madame Defarge's "mean death" is also opposed "to the dignity of Carton's."[7]

A Tale of Two Cities is a story of guilt and retribution, with retribution as its energizing core. While the narrative demonstrates that retribution operates at a historical as well as personal level, so that nations will eventually suffer for their crimes as individuals do, it must also denounce a retribution brought about by individuals motivated by hatred, vengeance, spite, and other unchristian emotions. The great grindstone used to sharpen the weapons of the revolutionaries provides one major symbol of the public nature of this bloody error. J. M. Rignall is wrong, I think, to assert that the grindstone scene demonstrates Dickens' impulse to solve violence with violence (579–80). The scene is very repulsive and surely Dickens intended it to evoke revulsion rather than gratification.

By incorporating fictional private histories, containing secrets to be disclosed through the narrative's progress within the larger historical, and thus known, story of the French Revolution—which contains no secrets about its development—the narrator can establish a tension between two ways of viewing justice in the universe in a manner that resembles the narrative strategy of Bleak House, where the more personal and private outlook is chiefly provided by Esther and the general and social by the third-person narrator. The great events that we describe as historical are governed by providence, or by fate, in the sense that implies inevitability. An unjust ruling class will inevitably suffer punishment for its conduct. At the personal level individuals are free to make crucial moral decisions that might bind them to or free them from "destiny," which is to say the evil consequences of bad acts. By choosing pardon, mercy, or forgiveness, individuals can break the chain of crime and revenge that leads to greater and greater suffering. If the grindstone is a symbol of the unthinking viciousness of rebellion, the guillotine is a symbol of its false justice. But even that symbol can be transformed. The positive power to transform symbols is at the heart of Sydney Carton's crowning act. Like all thoughtful human beings, Carton is something of a mystery to himself, and certainly he is a mystery to others, who cannot understand the waste he has made of his life. Carton is as he is partly because he can establish no clear identity for himself. He sinks his own identity into Stryver's work. He casually saves Darnay's life by calling attention to their apparent interchangeability. The one way he has of anchoring his nature is by the secret buried alive in his heart—his love for Lucie. But this, too, he shares with Darnay. Carton represents lack of initiative, whereas Darnay is all conscientious effort. But in the most dissipated among us, if only they have faith in some enduring belief or feeling, the power of transformation, or resurrection, as the language of the novel would have it, remains. He can *become* Charles Darnay. There is an oddly ceremonial quality to his rescue. The necessarily realistic change of clothes also resembles an investiture through which Carton assumes a phatic role among the condemned prisoners. By assuming Darnay's identity while retaining his own character, Carton divests himself of his worst self. His private secret of love for Lucie becomes the public secret of his disguise. The mystery of his nature becomes the sacrament of his act. As he mounts to the guillotine, this symbol of dreadful rage and revenge is transformed to a symbol of love. By Carton's act it comes to resemble Christ's cross; his death is an atonement reflecting the great Atonement that makes existence possible in a world complicated by evil destinies. Carton's act involves not only self-forgiveness but forgiveness for the violence that men do to one another. The great public crime of the Terror begets the great private sacrifice and redemption betokening love.[8]

If individuals can govern their own moral destinies, they are not therefore utterly free. National and personal histories not only resemble one another, they are inevitably intertwined, though not necessarily so melodramatically as in the case of Madame Defarge. The wood sawyer, as a figure associated both with the brutality of the French aristocracy and the violence of the revolutionaries, indicates that much human activity is thoughtless and habitual, easily guided by interested forces. To a degree, he represents the unalterable forces of destiny. But the very fact that such a destiny should be embodied in an individual human being suggests that deterministic forces are not inescapable after all. Roads are similarly important in this narrative. Like linear time, roads go from one locus to another. Lorry is carrying Lucie from Dover to Paris to accomplish a certain "destiny." But the very route that Lorry takes to enfranchise Dr. Manette later becomes the road that Charles Darnay takes toward freedom from revolutionary reprisal. The road of history may be reversed. The linear movement along a predetermined route may be altered and the new road may lead to freedom, not imprisonment.[9]

Another interesting feature of this novel emphasizes the role of analogous narratives embedded within the larger narrative. The narrator's task is to indicate the differences between historical and personal "fates," and to suggest how experience may be read to reveal the secrets of human destiny and to therefore change that destiny for the better. One way for the narrator to educate his characters and readers is to indicate by way of embedded narratives what might be expected in the main narrative, as Christ's parables illustrate his larger message. When Mr. Lorry meets Lucie at Dover to escort her to France, he tells her "the story of one of our customers" (20). This is an account of her unnamed father's circumstances, designed to prepare her for the revelation that he is alive. Dickens and other Victorian novelists frequently used this and similar devices, having characters break good or bad news gradually to their audiences, and so such an instance is not remarkable. Later an analogous tale prepares the reader for events to come in the same way that Lorry has prepared Lucie, though not so openly. Darnay recounts an anecdote about a prisoner in the Tower of London who had hidden a document in his cell that was later unearthed. Dr. Manette's response, and other clues, suggest that Dr. Manette knows of a similar case. Of course Darnay's anecdote, which does not mention the contents of the recovered documents, foreshadows Dr. Manette's hidden account, recovered by Defarge, describing the primal transgression that generates all of the events that follow. Dr. Manette's narrative is itself an analogue of the larger history of France—the suppression ('burying') of truth by the aristocracy to ensure the continuance of its own privileges.

This narrative device operates at a subordinate level as well. Thus in the embedded narrative about the historically real Foulon, the people are told that this rich speculator, supposed dead, has been found alive and brought back for execution. He had "caused himself to be represented as dead, and had a grand mock-funeral" to deceive the people whom he feared (212). This factual incident connects with the personal and fictional part of the narrative by preparing for the revelation about Roger Cly's false funeral. Revelation of Cly's ruse puts John Barsett in Carton's power, enabling him to carry out the rescue—the return to life—of the doomed Charles Darnay.

These narratives within the narrative and other anticipatory methods, such as the reiterated theme of approaching footsteps, create a predictive, proleptic effect very like that of statements in which the narrator openly anticipates the future. Such proleptic references seem to endorse a world of inevitable unfoldings where what will be is already existent, as though the future were foreknown and therefore already history. But these various forms of foreshadowing are transformed into a positive rather than pessimistically determinist version of anticipation when, at the conclusion of the novel, the narrator relates what Sydney Carton's words on his way to execution would have been ("and they were prophetic") if he had uttered them. Carton's conjectured story tells what the future will bring both for the individuals he loves and for England and France. The narrative that Carton projects into the future ends with Lucie's son telling Carton's story to his son. So the narrative we have just read becomes, at its conclusion, a story of a time gone by but made ever present by retelling, just as Carton's life, at the moment it ends, becomes an exemplary story worthy of being repeated.[10] Moreover, both Carton's story and Dickens' novel count on the instructive redundancy of frequent repetition to make memorable the errors of the past and the virtues of those who struggled against them. In letting Carton tell the story of the beneficent future, the narrator endorses his own task, for his novel is the calling to life of a communal memory, and its account of individuals who suffered intensely is designed to touch the heart and make it alive to injustice in its own day, much in the way the Christmas ghosts use the past and the future to revive Scrooge's heart. Only the wicked or foolish wish to forget. Even those like Clemency Newcome in *The Battle of Life*, who defend the maxim "Forgive and Forget" and Forget," do not really mean to obliterate memory, but to forget the injury. Memory of good and bad, as *The Haunted Man* makes clear, is necessary to our very humanity. Unresolved suffering or injustice must be recalled, faced, and transformed into strength in nations as in individual human beings. Narratives can help us to do this; they can capture in a memorable form the moral energies that help us to understand the secrets of the human heart, and those great rules by which Dickens believed mankind was governed, rules ensuring that, in time, retribution comes to all who transgress and victory to all who suffer. This was Dickens' great hope and the moral foundation for the stories he told.

NOTES

1. Charles Dickens, *A Tale of Two Cities* (New York: Oxford University Press, 1967), 55.

2. W. H. Auden "Spain" says "History to the defeated may say / Alas but cannot help or pardon" (*The Collected Poems of W. H. Auden* [New York: Random House, 1945], 185).

3. There has been a fair amount of discussion about the mystery of self in *A Tale of Two Cities*, but J. M. Rignall comments that, although the novel contains an unusual statement in the first person about the mystery of the self, in fact the characters in the novel prove to be quite knowable ("Dickens and the Catastrophic Continuum of History in *A Tale of Two Cities*," *ELH* 51, no. 3 [Fall 1984], 575–87). Subsequent references appear in the text. Rignall makes a good point but forgets that the characters in the novel are knowable to us as readers, not necessarily to the other characters, and that only because we have the advantage of an omniscient narrator to reveal them to us.

4. K. J. Fielding says of *A Tale of Two Cities* that its Christian symbols are "partly parasitical ... borrowed for a purpose not purely Christian," and that "what is holy in life is shown in terms of romantic love" (*Charles Dickens: A Critical Introduction* [Boston: Houghton Mifflin Co., 1965], 204). But it is Lucie's embodiment of Christian principles,

not merely her physical attractiveness, that makes her the object of interest both to Darnay and to Carton.

5. Steven Marcus calls attention to this powerful awareness of repression in *Barnaby Rudge*, where individuals and objects resemble vessels that are likely to explode. These images, he suggests, are drawn from Carlyle's *French Revolution*. For Marcus, Dickens' conception of the novel took shape "in various ideas and images of compression and repression, of fermentation and intoxication, of swellings and explosions and of corrosive anxiety and tenseness stretched to the breaking point. These images, developed in the course of the novel's action, are brought to their consummate expression in the eruption of the riots: in the breaking down of restraints, in drunkenness, fire and general explosive violence" (*Dickens: From Pickwick to Dombey* [New York: Basic Books, Inc., 1965], 206).

6. A. O. J. Cockshut, *The Imagination of Charles Dickens* (New York: New York University Press, 1962), 71.

7. John Forster, *The Life of Charles Dickens* (London: Chapman and Hall, Ltd., 1893), 565. Harvey Peter Sucksmith discusses this passage and the general issue of retribution in Dickens, in *The Narrative Art of Charles Dickens: The Rhetoric of Sympathy and Irony in his Novels* (Oxford: The Clarendon Press, 1970), 238ff.

8. Edgar Johnson says that "Carton's renunciation is a deed of purification and redemption that is at once the consummation of a deeper justice amid the excesses of vengeance called revolutionary justice and a triumphant assertion of the saving and creating power of love" (*Charles Dickens: His Tragedy and Triumph* [Boston: Little, Brown and Co., 1952], 2:981).

9. Andrew Sanders calls attention to the use of roads in this symbolic and almost allegorical manner in *Tale* and in *The French Revolution* in *The Companion to A Tale of Two Cities* (London: Unwin Hyman, 1988), 109. J. M. Rignall regards these parallel carriage scenes as signifying an escape from history and from fiction (578–79).

10. Garrett Stewart offers an exciting and, I feel, convincing reading of Carton's death. He credits the death scene as an extremely significant feature of Dickens' enterprise in the novel. "No novel," he states, "could fasten more surely the always tacit bond between mortality and communicable narration. Carton's dramatized and consummating death scene is displaced into an articulate exemplum discovered at the very moment of his death to be recoverable in the telling, time out of mind. And so the tale recounted by Lucie's son becomes, in short—and of course in its shortened form—the title scene of *The Tale* that earns its closure by foreseeing it" (*Death Sentences: Styles of Dying in British Fiction* [Cambridge: Harvard University Press, 1984], 93).

JOHN B. LAMB

Domesticating History:
Revolution and Moral Management
in A Tale of Two Cities

In *A Tale of Two Cities*, as Charles Darnay awaits the judgment of the Revolutionary Tribunal, Dickens' narrator speculates on what has drawn Darnay and men like him to the "wild infection" that is, for Dickens like Carlyle before him,[1] the madness of the French Revolution: "In seasons of pestilence, some of us will have a secret attraction to the disease—a terrible passing inclination to die of it. And all of us have like wonders hidden in our breasts, only needing circumstances to evoke them" (310). Dickens' novel is a story of "profound secret[s] and myster[ies]," of "buried" desires enclosed in the "Darkly clustered houses" (44) and hearts of his characters. After more than six years of marriage to Lucie Manette, Darnay, once the aristocrat and now the prosperous bourgeois, grows "restless" (267) and leaves the bliss of his English home and the respectability of his wife to court the fierce, passionate, and raging female, La Revolution, who is embodied in Thérèse Defarge and her bloodthirsty sisterhood, the women of St. Antoine. For while the looks of the men of the Revolution are "dark, repressed, and revengeful," it is on the features of the women that the frightful insanity and signs of social violation that are the French Revolution are most clearly written:

> The men were terrible ... but, the women were a sight to chill
> the boldest. From such household occupations as their bare

From *Dickens Studies Annual* 25 (1996): pp. 227–243. © 1996 by AMS Press.

> poverty yielded, from their children, from their aged and their
> sick crouching on the bare ground famished and naked, they ran
> out with streaming hair, urging one another, and themselves, to
> madness with the wildest cries and actions. (252)

This is the "disease" that Darnay has "an inclination to die of," a
transgressive and passionate energy that is both sexual and political. In *A
Tale of Two Cities*, female revolutionaries, like Madame Defarge, represent a
nexus of Victorian anxieties relating to gender and class, particularly those
related to sexual and political revolt. As Linda M. Shires suggests, in the
1830s and 1840s, "that which threatens the hegemonic status quo becomes
linked to the female who sexually stimulates others into a fascination with
horror or sublime exaltation" (148). The danger and power that those
revolutionary women possess is not only that they will violate the rules and
regulations of bourgeois society, particularly those inherent in Victorian
domestic ideology, but that they also will spread the madness of their revolt
to others, unleashing a carnal and civil carmagnole whose chaotic potential
is both threatening and boundless.

    Throughout the Victorian period there were long-standing anxieties
about female sexuality and working-class political revolt, both of which
were seen as a threat to middle-class life and property. Revolutionary desire
posed as big a threat as sexual desire, and the French Revolution served as a
convenient metaphor for social ruin as well as political upheaval. As Jeffrey
Weeks points out, "sexual collapse seemed the necessary path of social
revolution; sexual and family decorum a vital part of social stability" (27).
To an anxious middle-class population continually threatened by political
instability and economic uncertainty, the ideals and ideology of bourgeois
domesticity were seen as central to moral discipline; domesticity was the only
safe-haven from the horrors of a revolutionary world.[2] In fact, the middle-
class institutions of family and home were thought to have immunized
England against the very disease of Revolution like the one that had infected
France in 1789, and during the Victorian period, the discourse of revolution
"makes as its object, not the Bastille or the factory, but the home" (Shires
156). The revolutionary women immortalized in Carlyle's history and
translated nearly wholesale into *A Tale of Two Cities*, symbolize those socially
transgressive energies Victorian culture labeled as pathological. Insanity is
one of the most powerful models of pathology,[3] and during the nineteenth
century, it is coupled with sexual activity as signs of deviant behavior. Such
were the signs Dickens' friend John Conolly, the physician to the Middlesex
Lunatic Asylum at Hanwell, read in the histories of his working-class female
patients:

some of these were women of middle age, who had been handsome, and who possessed considerable acuteness of intellect, ingenuity and activity, but whose lives had been a sort of troubled romance. Profligate, intemperate, violent, regardless of domestic ties, their children abandoned to all the evils of homeless poverty, themselves by degrees given up to utter recklessness—they had been the cause of ruin and shame to their families and the history of their wild life had closed in madness. (*Treatment* 127)

As Lynda Nead suggests, revolution itself was equated with "*deviant femininity*" (6) (Dickens' France is a place without mothers or with mothers who abandon their children), and it was defined in relation to the standards and practices of domestic life. Like the sexualized female, the revolutionary was seen as a source of disease and corruption as well as political dissent, and like her working-class counterparts at Hanwell, she was "both eroticized and condemned" as an immoral pollutant (Mort 47).

Against such moral contaminants and the pathology that is revolution, Victorian culture pitted the forces of various practices of "moral treatment," complex systems of intervention and social control aimed at restoring the self-discipline and individual responsibility perceived to be at the heart of bourgeois ideology and conspicuously absent in the pathological individual. Under the rubric of morals and moral management were "subsumed a terrifying catalogue of barbarous habits," particularly the "collapse of family life" and "political sedition" (Mort 47). In *A Tale of Two Cities*, revolution is perceived as a social phenomena whose moral etiology (revolution = madness = sexual and political transgression) is marked by an ensemble of signs—restlessness, rage, passion, vehemence, etc.—which allow the reader to designate such behavior as pathological. Revolutionary energy and activity in Dickens' novel stands out as that which is lacking relative to the standards of domesticity, and the characteristics that define revolution and the revolutionary female are purely negative. In *A Tale of Two Cities*, as well as in bourgeois culture at large, the revolutionary is not just retarded in her socialization; she is also in a profound state of anomic crisis. She has not yet interiorized, or has rejected, the values by which patriarchal society thrives and maintains its own self-control. Like the middle-class Victorian home or the Victorian asylum, *A Tale of Two Cities* performs its own therapy of interiorization as Dickens seeks to define and manage transgressive political and sexual energy and to erase history by inscribing onto both the novel's content and its form the Victorian psychiatric practice known as "moral management."

II

During the first half of the nineteenth century, there was a long struggle to reform the treatment of the mentally ill, and Victorian medical psychology sought to reclaim the insane as moral subjects, subjects lacking control and self-restraint, who for various and often unknown reasons had failed to internalize the moral standards of the middle class. The most significant development in nineteenth-century psychiatric reform was the domestication of insanity; the violent therapeutic practices still used to "tame" the wildly asocial in the early part of the century were replaced by the "invisible" discipline of a facsimile of the bourgeois family life. The cornerstones of this new discipline, as Elaine Showalter points out, were moral insanity, moral management, and moral architecture:[4]

> "Moral insanity" redefined madness, not as a loss of reason, but as deviance from socially acceptable behavior. "Moral management" substituted close supervision and paternal concern for physical restraint and harsh treatment, in an attempt to re-educate the insane in habits of industry, self-control, moderation, and perseverance. "Moral architecture" constructed asylums planned as therapeutic environments in which lunatics could be controlled without the use of force. (29)

Writing in 1833, James Cowles Pritchard, the ethnologist and senior physician to the Bristol Infirmary, noted in *A Treatise on Insanity* that in cases of moral insanity the "moral and active principles of the mind are strangely perverted and depraved," and that the "power of self-government is lost or impaired" (15). Hence, he defined moral insanity as "madness consisting in a morbid perversion of the natural feelings, affections, inclinations, temper, habits, moral dispositions, and natural impulses" (16). Furthermore, Pritchard maintained that moral insanity, or "moral perversion" as he also referred to it, was marked by an "unusual prevalence of angry and malicious feelings" (26).

In a similar manner, John Conolly, who along with Samuel Tuke and John Gardiner Hill was one of the most notable British psychiatric reformers, argued that in mental disorders the "social feeling is lost and sympathy with others seems extinct." Insanity tears "away the conventionalities of life." Yet, while many of the insane were, according to Conolly, depraved and given over to evil tendencies, for some, virtues and kind feelings existed, "buried and obscured, but not lost" (*On Some of the Forms of Insanity* 7).

The concept of moral insanity, therefore, was socially constructed. It was a generalization that denoted the absence of those "conventionalities" and "feelings" that were the staples of middle-class Victorian life. "Insanity" designated any behavior that deviated from the norms of bourgeois domesticity. As a working term in the rhetoric of social distinction, it was, in most cases, an exaggeration of the attributes the middle class ascribed to the laboring population. As Michael Donelly suggests, moral insanity and the signs of madness it called into play emerged during the Victorian period "ideologically charged" (133), and madness was defined by moral standards inherent in the relations between both the classes and the sexes.

Moral management was *the* central component in a Victorian psychiatric strategy that attempted to neutralize and manipulate mental illness through a complex system of social control, and it offered the promise of a "cure" by non-medical means. Corresponding to the moral explanation of insanity, moral therapy involved, as Elizabeth Fee notes, the "Close supervision of patients, the control of behavior and especially sexual behavior, and the inculcation of work discipline." Deficient in self-control and self-discipline, the insane had to undergo "a personal re-evolution, to be re-brought up." Psychic equilibrium could only be achieved through a return to childhood, and since "the experience of childhood was the locus of formation of moral (and sexual) identity, the adult in search of cure must recover, re-create, and relive childhood" (640).

At the heart of moral management was the notion that without moral discipline the passions "acquire greater power, and a character is formed subject to caprice and to violent emotions" (Pritchard 131). Moral management sought to instill and reassert powers of self-control, and like other forms of social repression, it was authorized by the very threat of social anarchy it was said to identify and cure. But moral treatment was not based on an organic or psychic etiology. It was based instead on a moral symptomatology drawn from a middle-class perspective on mental health that found its fullest expression in the domestic order. As Robert Castel convincingly argues, in moral management there existed "less a medical theory of illness than a *social perception of health*, against which the pathological stands out as that which is *lacking* in relation to (the) normality characterized by orderliness of conduct, equilibrium between affectivity and intelligence, the capacity to adopt social roles without fail." Since it lacked the requirements of scientific rationality, moral management was "*permeable to non-medical norms*, and ready to reinterpret within the framework of an extramedical synthesis representations which have no theoretical relation to medically founded knowledge" ("Moral Treatment" 253, 251). These representations are, as Castel rightly notes, simply the values of the dominant class, particularly order, discipline, the sanctity of the family, work, and respect for authority.

Moral architecture, the construction and maintenance of a morally disciplined environment, was, therefore, a direct outgrowth of the politico-moral ideology of moral management. The new asylum was necessitated by the need to re-instate in the pathological individual exactly the same norms that reigned in bourgeois society, particularly work, the strict organization of time, and due respect for and submission to patriarchal authority. Hence, institutions like the York Retreat and Hanwell were conceived and at least partly constructed on the model of a middle-class home complete with surrogate family, and the "domesticated" asylum provided the controlled atmosphere for a "regression to infantile existence combined with a new moral upbringing" (Fee 640). By reconstructing the social discipline and structure of the family, these asylums aimed at reproducing a fictional domesticity that would encourage the interiorization of domestic values and revive, as Michel Foucault points out, the "prestige of patriarchy" (*Civilization and Madness* 253). There madness was controlled through the arrangement of space and through daily activities and routines. The insane lived within a comfortable but highly controlled domestic regime, and female patients were encouraged to participate in the patterns of middle-class domestic life by engaging in the "customary" female pursuits of sewing, knitting, crochet, and fancy work. The external organization and internal domestic economy of the asylum was thought to provide a special environment which embodied the very values and the order whose interiorization was the condition for cure. In the morally managed asylum, Conolly asserted, "Those even who came in a state of dangerous violence seemed so acted upon by the character of the house" that they became "composed," "orderly in habits," "active" and "useful" (*Treatment* 121).

III

Madame Defarge is the epitome of the "frightful moral disorder" (376) and the monstrous abuse of "all laws, forms, and ceremonies" (344) signified in revolutionary passion. With her rich, "dark hair" and her "supple freedom" (391) of movement, she has, Dickens' narrator claims, "a kind of beauty" (390); and like the nineteenth-century working-class women on which she is partly modeled, she is both eroticized and condemned. But Thérèse Defarge clearly suffers from moral insanity; her affections, habits, and moral attitudes have been perverted, and she is full of anger and malice. Her "moral perversion" has transformed her into a "furious" woman "absolutely without pity" (391), and her shadow falls "threatening and dark" (297) on both Lucie and her child. Furthermore, Madame Defarge's "register," "Knitted, in her own stitches and her own symbols" (202), is a ghastly semiotic impenetrable to the eyes of the State, which symbolizes male anxieties about the unknowable and uncontrollable nature of female sexuality. In pursuing the "family annihilation" (381) of the Darnays, Thérèse Defarge threatens not the aristocracy, but the bourgeois domicile, and it is no surprise that her madness is finally incarcerated and, indeed, erased in Lucie's Paris home.

But it is Sidney Carton's interiorization of the norms of bourgeois domesticity—especially self-discipline, self-denial, and self-sacrifice—invisibly imposed upon him in the "anchorage" of Lucie Manette's home, that most clearly indicates the success of moral management. For while Lucie saves both her father and husband "from the edge of the grave" (160), restoring her father to sanity and rescuing Darnay from the "terrible attraction" of the French Revolution, it is her "weaving the service of her happy influence" (240) through the wasted tissue of Carton's life, that crowns her success and the success of domestic discipline. For Carton, who begins the novel as the "idlest and must unpromising of men" (117), ends it as a man "who had wandered and struggled and got lost, but who had at length struck into his road and saw its end" (342).

Lucie is the novel's chief resurrectionist, and her recalling of Carton to middle-class respectability parallels the recalling to life of her father and husband. For Sidney Carton is more than just Charles Darnay's physical double. He is, Dickens' novel suggests, a man previously drawn to the "Loadstone Rock" of some secret sexual passion, some "fall" in which, like the Revolution, the qualities within Carton "good by nature" had become "warped and perverted" (307). Like Darnay, Carton has "lost" himself in a Paris of revolutionary fever, a Paris in which he is an "old student" (341). For Dickens' depiction of revolution, like Carlyle's includes comparing it and the revolutionary mob to the elemental forces of a rising, "remorseless," and uncontrollable sea: "The beach was a desert of heaps of sea and stones tumbling wildly about, and the sea did what it liked, and what it liked was destruction. It thundered at the town, and thundered at the cliffs, and brought the coast down, madly" (51). With "deep wounds" (238) in his heart, Carton is already a victim of revolution's transgressive energies; there are "waste forces within him, and a desert all around" (121). Carton epitomizes the individual infected with moral insanity, the "man of good abilities and good emotions, incapable of their directed exercise, incapable of his own help and his own happiness" (122). He is the antithesis of *A Tale of Two Cities*'s conventionally "sane" person, the "orderly and methodical" Jarvis Lorry, whose face is "habitually suppressed and quiet," drilled "to the composed and reserved expression of Tellson's Bank" (49). Lorry's house, Tellson's Bank, is Lucie's house writ large, a place where you can "meditate on your misspent life" (83), and like the asylum, it "imposes its restraints and its silences" (113).[5]

It is Lucie who cures Carton, who transforms him as she transformed her father into a man with "great firmness of purpose, strength of resolution, and vigour of action" (161). She "binds" him, as she has bound her father and husband, with the invisible strands of domestic discipline: "Ever busily winding the golden thread which bound her husband, and her father, and herself, and her old directress and companion, in a life of quiet bliss" (239). And the "Home" which she establishes in England and transplants to France are identically arranged. In both, everything has "its appointed place and its appointed time" (304). It is a place of rest and repose, a quiet "harbour from the raging streets" (123), and it duplicates the "Perfect order, perfect cleanliness, and great tranquility" (Conolly, *Treatment* 54) prevailing in the well-managed asylum. It is a place "more abundant" (242) than the revolutionary waste, where everything turns and revolves around Lucie. There she reigns, the model of feminine respectability; there her "duty," "faithful service," "affection," and "thrift" merge with obedience and proper submissiveness. Like the morally managed asylum, it is not a home, but a caricature of a home, not a place of freedom but a place of moral discipline and social control, as Carton's confession to Lucie betrays:

> I wish you to know that you have been the last dream of my soul. In my degradation I have not been so degraded but that the sight of you with your father, and of this house, made such a home by you, has stirred old shadows that I thought had died out of me. Since I knew you, I have been troubled by a remorse that I thought would never reproach me again, and have heard whispers from old voices impelling me upward, that I thought were silent forever. (181)

That "remorse" is the beginning of Carton's cure; his sacrifice is the end. Because "sacrifice" is at the heart of domestic ideology; it is the law of Tellson's house and Lucie's home. Carton must be cured so that Lucie's home and Tellson's house can be preserved, so that the domestic idyll that ends *A Tale of Two Cities* and saves the State can resist the transgressive forces of history that threaten it.

IV

But "sacrifice" is the law of the Revolution as well and reminds us that the maenadic Thérèse Defarge is Lucie's terrifying other. Sexual and political revolution or "restlessness," Dickens seems all too painfully aware, come not from without, but from within, perhaps even from skeletons hid in our own domestic closets.[6] We have all, like Dickens himself, "done and suffered" (29) what is depicted in the pages of the novel. In the history of every family lies a "buried" tale of transgression, and it is that history that *A Tale of Two Cities* first seeks to manage, but finally wishes to annul.

In this historical novel, then, Carton's restoration to the bourgeois fold, his interiorization of the norms of domestic ideology, signals, ironically, the death of history, for when Carton goes to the guillotine, "Memory" dies. The domestic realm in Dickens' novel is an atemporal space, a timeless utopia where Lucie follows Lucie in endless succession and where time is ordered, regulated, and finally erased in an endless series of occupations. As Louis Marin suggests, utopia knows nothing of time or change: "It is constituted by the representation of the identical, of the 'same' of repetitive indifference.... it is immobile representation and repetition compulsion" (xxiv). Such repetition works toward what Peter Brooks calls a "binding of textual energies that allows them to be mastered" (101); revolutionary desire is bound by the repetitive sameness of domesticity itself. The domestic is the space without history, particularly the history of a society's or an individual's madness. It is a lacuna of history that makes bourgeois culture possible, and hidden within domestic ideology is Victorian society's desire not to master memory, but to master forgetfulness, to make absent the political and sexual desires that threaten hegemony.

Domestic ideology defines subjectivity not only in terms of sexual identity, but, like moral management, in terms of rationality and morality as well. It rewrites the historical in terms of the psychological and reduces the collective nature of sexual and political revolutionary struggle to individual instances of moral pathology. As Nancy Armstrong suggests, domestic ideology and domestic fiction unfold "the operation of human desire as if they were independent of political history" in the creation of "a private domain of the individual outside and apart from social history" (9, 10). Domestic ideology turns history into case histories constitutive of personal identity and redirects political violence into the world of social relations where political rights are renounced in the pursuit of a model of mental health that encourages submission. But history, whether in the form of Chartist agitation, the Industrial Revolution, or the political disturbances on the Continent, constantly destabilizes existing gender and class relationships, reshaping and reorganizing subjectivity and the sexual division of labor on which domesticity thrives.

As Carlyle had taught Dickens, history *is* revolution, and in *A Tale of Two Cities* revolution is degradation and not the progressive fiction that the middle-class so wanted to believe. History as revolution is essentially transgressive and crosses not only the boundaries of established political and social practices, but also exposes the limits of those ideologies and discourses of social control (like moral management or domesticity) that define and delimit those practices. Moral insanity is inherently contradictory: buried beneath the surface of anti-social tendencies lie a host of bourgeois virtues. Hence, it is also revolutionary, always potentially "ruptural." Like moral management, domestic ideology must constantly reclassify the alterity it meets. It must dissolve the essentially contradictory nature of the revolutionary, "morally insane," individual and must control this rupture of transgressive energies by making a *tabula rasa* of the insane individual, erasing previous "historical" influences and rewriting the subject as morally consistent. Like all ideological practices, domesticity seeks to transform the individual "traversed and worked by social contradiction" into "a consistent subject in control of his [or her] own destiny." The power of the family as an institution of moral management, therefore, is its fusion of ideology and law. It not only "puts every individual in a place as a consistent [rational] subject," but "ensures that those who go wrong are judged in the name of this consistent [rational] subjectivity" (Coward and Ellis 75, 77). Because it is based on an imaginary etiology of insanity, moral management is, therefore, itself an imaginary resolution or "cure" of psychic contradictions, and domesticity "an ideological act in its own right with the function of inventing imaginary or formal 'solutions' to unresolvable social contradictions" (Jameson 79). But as the parallels to moral management should make clear, domestic ideology works, in fact, by a double invention: before it can "cure" the "wild infection" of revolution, it must first rewrite social contradiction in terms of a moral symptomatology and symbology of mental illness. It must create the very ensemble of signs which label social contradiction and revolutionary behavior as inherently pathological, as different from socially regulated modes of behavior. Such labelling authorizes domestic ideology itself; like moral management, it becomes the formal solution to a crisis only it is capable of perceiving.

The pathology of revolutionary change threatens the idea of progress central to the Victorians' conviction that their place in history was somehow unique, and the notion of progress was "imposed upon history to create the sense of order the Victorians craved" (Bowler 3). History in *A Tale of Two Cities* is not order but chaos; it is the carmagnole, that manifestation of collective insanity that blurs the boundaries of class and sexuality, the morally corrosive and deviant dance where "women danced together, men danced together, as hazard had brought them together" (307). History is the perversion of the once "innocent" past. Just as moral treatment must erase from the patient "all intrusions of history and spontaneity" (Castel, "Moral Treatment" 258), so, too, Dickens' novel must silence the "echoes" and wash away the "Headlong, mad, and dangerous footsteps" (243) that bring the threat of revolution into the Manette household and Victorian society. Domestic ideology is threatened by any suggestion that it is historical and subject to radical change, and written into the form and content of *A Tale of Two Cities*, it becomes the primary containment strategy by which Dickens attempts to morally manage and ultimately repudiate the forces of revolution.[7] While Lucre is a kind of domesticated Clio, whose golden thread unites her father "to a Past beyond his misery, and to a Present beyond his misery" (110), both past and present are, incarcerated in the same domestic space. Here, as in the recurrent patterns of asylum life, domestic synchrony replaces the diachrony of history.

Despite the Victorians' glorification of history and historical process, then, *A Tale of Two Cities*, like other nineteenth-century novels permeated by domestic ideology, betrays a societal anxiety about history, and it suggests that the bourgeois myth of history as progress is the saving fiction that attempts to mask a notion of history as the pathological, as *difference*, as domesticity's terrifying other. In *Tale of Two Cities*, Clio is really Thérèse Defarge and her lesson is, "Judge you! Is it likely that the trouble of one wife and mother would be much to us now?" (298).

V

Thomas Carlyle's solution for the pathology of revolution is nomination or what he called "right-Naming": "History, and indeed all human Speech and Reason does yet, what Father Adam began like by doing: strive to *name* the new Things it sees of Nature's producing.... Any approximation to the right Name as value; were the right Name itself once here, the Thing is known henceforth; the Thing is then ours, and can be dealt with" (333). As Michel de Certeau points out, historians, like doctors or exorcists, respond to social transgression "through a labor of naming" (246). Like the doctor, the novelist's task is also "one of nomination," which aims at categorizing the socially deviant and "confining them in a place circumscribed by [the novelist's] knowledge"; a knowledge that is "assumed to be capable of *naming*" (247). Following Certeau, we might also argue that the novelist of domestic fiction is opposed to the revolutionary female because through her "madness" she "betrays the very linguistic topography with which the social order can be organized" (247). Like the doctor of the insane, the novelist engages in defining who the revolutionary other is by placing him or her "in a topography of Proper names," (255) and that act of denomination is "intended to reclassify a protean uncanniness within an established language" (255–5). By labelling the revolutionary subject as morally insane, the novelist "assigns to [that] subject a locus in language and therefore 'secures' an order of socio-linguistic practice" (256), which is domestic ideology itself. Domestic fiction recodifies the "uncanniness" of gender and class by "designating a determinate name" (256) drawn from the nomenclature of bourgeois morality.

As D. A. Miller suggests, "the genre of the novel *belongs* to the disciplinary field it portrays" (21), which in the case of *A Tale of Two Cities* specifically, and nineteenth-century novels by middle-class writers generally, is moral management, because moral management as an ideological form of social control most clearly displays the linguistic practice indigenous to the bourgeois novel itself: the renomination of gender and class within the discourse of bourgeois value. Like discipline itself, the novel as a form of social control is both "a complex social function" and a "political tactic" which conceals the repressiveness and violence of the asylum behind a therapeutic model of family life (Foucault, *Discipline and Punish*); like moral management, it hides "the relationships of force under relationships of meaning" (Castel, *The Regulation of Madness* 170).

Moral management, as Robert Castel insists, is the "ideal model" and "paradigm of every authoritarian pedagogy," and as a metaphor for the novel's ideological process, it underscores the way in which the nineteenth-century novel, particularly domestic fiction, excludes the marginal, "morally insane" figure and preserves the social and ideological status quo:

> It is still a matter of deploying strategies for subjugation. It is the same armory of disciplinary techniques that is capable of both effecting the recovery of reason (i.e. a return to the predominant form of normality) and also of subduing the people (i.e. causing them to internalize the rules that ensure the reproduction of bourgeois order). (*The Regulation of Madness* 121)

The nineteenth-century novel becomes the site for the re-evolution and recovery not only of the characters, but of the reader as well. The novel is the locus for moral therapy, because like the asylum it provides an imaginary substitute for the social and familial environment. The novel as asylum seeks to re-educate its readers, to re-create correct patterns of thinking and to re-establish appropriate standards of behavior.

In *A Tale of Two Cities*, domestic space is no longer the opposite of the asylum, no longer the private home from which the insane individual is removed and to which he or she must return. It *is* the asylum, and as such, it is the specific location for the management of political and sexual transgression. It harbors the pathology that is history as its double, containing, controlling, and canceling it. And just as Lucie's home is the site for Carton's transformation, so too the nineteenth-century novel turns readers into what Foucault calls "docile bodies" that may be "subjected, used, transformed, and improved" (*Discipline and Punish* 131). In his engagement with the novel the reader is uprooted from his familiar historical environment—England in the late 1850s, the site of contemporary forces of sexual and political disruption—and relocated in a special environment whose internal economy, the triumph of domestic ideology over revolution, embodies the order whose repeated interiorization is the condition for his successful integration and "return" to the real world. Here, the reader is exposed to the fate of those like Madame Defarge who have failed to interiorize the values that order bourgeois society.

Novel reading, particularly the reading of serialized novels like *A Tale of Two Cities*, mimics the patterns of managed asylum life, redistributing time. It replaces the processive "history" of reading with a monthly exercise, with discrete and yet homogeneous experiences of the text's duration and its ideology. The privacy of novel reading isolates the reader from the outside world, from the uncontrollable and contradictory forces of history, which is the place where his disorder is produced, and transplants him into an imaginatively ordered space co-extensive with the domesticity itself. As Linda K. Hughes and Michael Lund suggest, "the virtues that sustain a home and the traits required of serial readers so often coincided" (16). In this ordered therapeutic space, the reader lives in the "lucidity of the law," a law he once more makes his own. In the world of the novel, as in the asylum, moral order is "reduced to its bare bones of law, obligations, and constraints," and the novel functions as the model of an ideal society, "in the sense of being ideally reduced to order" (Castel, *The Regulation of Madness* 75).

The imposition of ideal order by the novel is backed by the relationship of authority between the novelist and the reader. Similar to nineteenth-century psychiatric reformers, Dickens attacks the more violent forms of treatment of the insane, symbolized in Dr. Manette's incarceration in the Bastille, while instituting the "invisible" discipline of moral management and the managing function of the asylum in everyday life. *A Tale of Two Cities* is an elaborate case history of the diagnosis, treatment, and cure of the social body infected with the pathology of revolution. Dickens casts himself in the role of the attending physician or benevolent asylum head and his narrator evinces those qualities without which "no man can be personally successful in the moral treatment of the insane":

A faculty of seeing that which is passing in the minds of men
is the first requisite of moral power and discipline, whether in
asylums, schools, parishes, or elsewhere. Add to this a firm will,
the faculty of self-control, a sympathizing distress at moral pain, a
strong desire to remove it, and that biologizing power is elicited,
which enables men to domineer for good purposes over the
minds of others. (Bucknill and Tuke 489)

The "power" which allows the novelist to "domineer" for moral purposes
over the minds of his readers is clearly taxonomic, an ordering of signs. Like
the expert in moral treatment, Dickens carefully nominates, codifies, and
regulates the behavior of the characters in his novel in his attempt to "declare
the truth" about revolution.[8] The novelist, like the asylum physician, is
omnipotent, if not completely omniscient: "innermost personality," Dickens
admits, is ultimately "inscrutable" (44). His power lies, therefore, not in the
knowledge of the sexual or political secrets at the heart of social disorder
and individual pathology, but in his control over the signs which confirm
that such secrets must and do exist. The novelist is a specialist in the
symptomatology of social disorder, and Dickens "seeks the narratable in that
which deviates most markedly from the normal, in the criminal, the outside-
the-law, the unsocialized, and the ungoverned" (Brooks 153). Unable to
fathom the root causes of social anomie, he directs attention instead to
the signs or symptoms of social unrest, and those signs are simply those
which "distinguish pathological behavior from socially regulated modes
of conduct" (Castel, *The Regulation of Madness* 97). Such symptoms—like
Carton's lassitude or Madame Defarge's malice—signify a preponderance of
moral causes, particularly political and sexual transgression, which in turn
legitimize moral therapy (here, in the form of domestic ideology) as the only
means of treatment capable of eradicating the moral causes of pathology
and restoring the insane individual to rationality, to the regulated modes
of conduct that constitute the bourgeois, domestic norm. The relationship
of the novelist and his reader is, therefore, analogous to that between the
doctor and the patient; it is a relationship of authority that binds the novelist
to the reader "in the exercise of a power that [lacks] reciprocity" (Castel, *The
Regulation of Madness* 75), since it is only the novelist who can order the signs
that designate transgressive behavior. Such a relationship suggests that the
reader suffers from the disorder of moral insanity, from those "buried" but no
less transgressive energies that political events and social conflict, or history,
generate. The novel interpellates the reader/subject as "free" and responsible
for his own actions, as the point of origin of his own transgression and cure.
Although readers may aspire to the ideal of characters like Lucie Manette

or Jarvis Lorry, the determinate names the novel designates for them are "Thérèse Defarge" or "Sidney Carton." The novel as asylum is a "world constructed in the image of the rationality" (Castel, *The Regulation of Madness* 76) embodied by the novelist, and the novel multiplies his power, since the order of things that triumph in the novel—domesticity and rationality—come to life as a moral order backed by society itself. Thus, the diagnosis and judgment of pathology at the heart of the Victorian novel becomes for the reader a social reality. It is only when he has regained his rational autonomy, has interiorized domestic ideology, that the novel pronounces him cured. It is only when he puts down the novel that the novelist's power is ostensibly canceled.

That power, however, is never really canceled, since the novel and the world "outside" are constructed by the same ideology. The reader's return to the world of lived experience, therefore, merely attests to the "truth" of the novel and the novelist's disciplinary vision. For the discourse of the novel, like moral management, is constructed around a social perception of health, ordered by the same moral symptomatology and symbology, and permeated by the values of the middle class. Domestic ideology, moral management, and the nineteenth-century novel are all forms of authoritarian pedagogy, of a re-educational process that seeks to suppress the focuses of sexual and political revolt and to extinguish them at their source—the revolutionary, "morally insane," subject. But just as *A Tale of Two Cities* betrays a societal anxiety about the forces of history, it also betrays an anxiety about the doctor's or novelist's power to morally manage transgression and cure the pathological. For if revolution and madness are marked by "restlessness," so, too, is writing; and throughout the 1850s, a period of intense personal restlessness for Dickens, he equates that restlessness, and indeed madness, with novel production itself.[9] As Peter Brooks points out, "The plotted novel is a deviance from or transgression of the normal, a state of abnormality and error which alone in 'narratable'" (84–85). The "ferocious excitement" of writing that caused Dickens to run "wildly about and about" a new novel in his own creative carmagnole is a form of imbalance that Dickens appears powerless to cure and Dickens often appears in his letters to be as much writing's victim as its master.

Doctor Manette cannot save Madame Defarge's sister from her madness, from the "high fever of her brain" (331), a "frenzy" so great that he does not even unfasten the bandages that restrain her. Thus, Dickens' novel unconsciously draws a disturbing parallel between the State bonds that the brothers Evrémonde use to imprison Defarge's sister and the domestic bonds or "golden threads" that Lucie employs to save Carton and her husband from moral insanity and revolution. Lucie's threads, therefore,

are the "invisible" ideological counterpart to the Evrémondes' more brutal
and arbitrary forms of incarceration and disguise the violence at the heart of
domestic ideology. Rather than liberating the reader, rather than making him
a "free" and autonomous subject, the novel as asylum places him "within a
moral element where he will be in debate with himself and his surroundings:
to constitute for him a milieu where, far from being protected, he will be
kept in perpetual anxiety, ceaselessly threatened by Law and Transgression"
(Foucault, *Civilization and Madness* 245). The novel, like Tellson's bank,
is a place to "meditate on your misspent life," and attests to the truth of
the Marquis St. Evrémonde's observation, "Repression is the only lasting
philosophy" (153).

NOTES

1. For the relationship between Carlyle's *The French Revolution* and *A Tale of Two
Cities*, see Michael Goldberg's *Carlyle and Dickens*, pp. 100–28, as well as Baumgarten,
Timko, Vanden Bossche, and Gilbert.

2. Michael Timko makes a similar argument in reference to the importance of the
"symbol" of the family and "domestic tranquility" in *A Tale of Two Cities*: "Much of the
novel's emotional appeal, Dickens thought, would come from his readers' immediate
response to this picture of domestic bliss; they would recognise in it those moral and
ethical qualities nurtured in family life that would assure the survival of nations and of
mankind itself" (182).

3. As Sander Gilman notes, "Of all the models of pathology, one of the most powerful
is mental illness. For the most elementally frightening possibility is loss of control over
the self.... Often associated with violence ... the mad are perceived as the antithesis to the
control and reason that define the self" (23),

4. In addition to Showalter, see also Scull, Dorner, and Skultans.

5. As James M. Brown notes, "Tellson's functions as a social microcosm and the
description of Tellson's building works to suggest the operation of a complex and ominous
set of social forces beneath the prosperous middle-class surface" (120).

6. In a letter to Forster in 1856, Dickens attributes a "year of restlessness" to what
he calls the "skeleton in his domestic closet" (qtd. in Ackroyd 756, 763).

7. See Fredric Jameson's reading of the "Dickensian paradigm" and the relationship
between realism and revolutionary change in *The Political Unconscious*, pp. 188–94.

8. John Conolly maintains that the business of the asylum physician is "to declare the
truth." *On Some of the Forms of Insanity*, p. 85.

9. Writing to Forster in 1854 on the composition of *Hard Times*, Dickens declared,
"I am three parts mad, and the fourth, delirious, with perpetual rushing at Hard Times"
(qtd. in Johnson 799).

WORKS CITED

Ackroyd, Peter. *Dickens*. London: Sinclair and Stevenson, 1990.
Armstrong, Nancy. *Desire and Domestic Fiction*. New York: Oxford UP, 1987.
Baumgarten, Murray. "Writing Revolution." *Dickens Studies Annual* 12 (1984): 161–76.

Bowler, Peter J. *The Invention of Progress: The Victorians and the Past*. Oxford: Basil Blackwell, 1989.

Brooks. Peter. *Reading for the Plot*. New York: Knopf, 1984.

Brown, James M. *Dickens: Novelist in the Market Place*. Totowa, N.J.: Barnes &. Noble, 1982.

Bucknill, John Charles and Daniel H. Tuke. *A Manual of Psychological Medicine*. Philadelphia: 1858.

Carlyle. Thomas. *The French Revolution*. New York: Oxford UP, 1989.

Castel, Robert. "Moral Treatment: Mental Therapy and Social Control in the Nineteenth Century," *Social Control and the State*. Eds. Stanley Cohen and Andrew Scull. Oxford: Basil Blackwell, 1983.

———. *The Regulation of Madness*. Trans. W. D. Halls. Berkeley: U of California Press, 1988.

Conolly, John. *The Treatment of the Insane Without Mechanical Restraints*. London: 1856.

———. *On Some of the Forms of Insanity*. London: 1849.

Coward, Rosalind and John Ellis. *Language and Materialism*. New York: Routledge, 1977.

de Certeau, Michel. *The Writing of History*. trans. Tom Conley. New York: Columbia UP, 1988.

Dickens, Charles. *A Tale of Two Cities*. New York: Penguin, 1991.

Doerner, Klaus. *Madmen and the Bourgeoisie: A Social History of Insanity*. Trans. Joachim Neugroschel and Jean Steinberg. Oxford: Basil Blackwell, 1981. pp. 20–95.

Donelly, Michael. *Managing the Mind*. New York: Tavistock, 1983.

Fee, Elizabeth. "Psychology, Sexuality, and Social Control in Victorian England," *Social Science Quarterly* 58 (March 1978): 632–46.

Foucault, Michel. *Civilization and Madness*. Trans. Richard Howard. New York: Vintage, 1988.

———. *Discipline and Punish*. Trans. Alan Sheridan. New York: Vintage, 1977.

Gilbert, Elliot L. "'To Awake from History': Carlyle, Thackeray, and *Tale of Two Cities*." *Dickens Studies Annual* 12 (1984): 247–66.

Gilman, Sander R. *Differences and Pathology: Stereotypes of Sexuality, Race, and Madness*. Ithaca: Cornell UP, 1985.

Hughes, Linda K. and Michael Lund. *The Victorian Serial*. Charlottesville: UP of Virginia, 1991.

Jameson, Fredric. *The Political Unconscious*. Ithaca: Cornell UP, 1981.

Johnson, Edgar. *Charles Dickens: His Tragedy and Triumph*. New York: Simon and Schuster, 1959.

Marin, Louis. *Utopics: the Semiological Play of Textual Spaces*. Trans. Robert A. Vollrath. Atlantic Highlands, N.J.: Humanities P, 1990.

Miller, D. A. *The Novel and the Police*. Berkeley: U of California P, 1988.

Mort, Frank. *Dangerous Sexualities*. New York: Routledge, 1987.

Nead, Lynda. *Myths of Sexuality*. New York: Basil Blackwell, 1988.

Pritchard, James Cowles. *A Treatise on Insanity and Other Disorders Affecting the Mind*. Philadelphia: 1837.

Scull, Andrew. *Museums of Madness: The Social Organization of Insanity in Nineteenth-Century England*. London: Penguin, 1979.

———. "Moral Treatment Reconsidered: Some Sociological Comments on an Episode in the History of British Psychiatry." In *Madhouses, Mad-doctors, and Madmen*. Ed. Andrew Scull. Philadelphia: U. of Pennsylvania P, 1981. pp. 104–17.

———. The Domestication of Madness." *Medical History* 2 (1983): 233–48.

Shires, Linda M. "Of maenads, mothers, and feminized males: Victorian readings of
    the French Revolution," *Rewriting the Victorians: Theory, History and the Politics of
    Gender*. Ed. Linda M. Shires. New York: Routledge, 1992.
Skultans, Vida. *English Madness: Ideas on Insanity 1580–1890*. Boston: Routledge, 1979.
Timko, Michael. "Splendid Impressions and Picturesque Means: Dickens, Carlyle, and
    The French Revolution." *Dickens Studies Annual* 12 (1984): 177–96.
Vanden Bossche, Chris R. "Prophetic Closure and Disclosing Narrative: *The French
    Revolution* and *A Tale of Two Cities*." *Dickens Studies Annual* 12 (1984): 209–22.
Weeks, Jeffrey. *Sex, Politics and Society*. New York: Longman, 1981.

CATHERINE WATERS

A Tale of Two Cities

When he began writing the weekly parts of *A Tale of Two Cities* for his new journal, *All the Year Round*, in 1859, Dickens complained about 'the time and trouble of the incessant condensation' required by this form of publication.[1] His second attempt at 'historical fiction', the novel lacks the dense social atmosphere and proliferation of 'unnecessary' detail that characterise the 'big books' like *Bleak House* and *Little Dorrit*. But notwithstanding the relative tautness and economy of its narrative, *A Tale of Two Cities* shares the fascination with the family shown by the more expansive works. As Dickens explained in another letter recorded by Forster, part of his intention in the novel was to contrast the 'feudal cruelties' of the *ancien régime* with the 'new philosophy' espoused by Charles Darnay: 'With the slang of the new philosophy on the one side, it was surely not unreasonable or unallowable, on the other, to suppose a nobleman wedded to the old cruel ideas, and representing the time going out as his nephew represents the time coming in.'[2] This contrast involves the juxtaposition of two different conceptions of the family, as the Marquis's 'good breeding' (144) and concern for 'the power and honour of families' (145) are set against the Victorian middle-class domestic ideal to which his anglicised nephew is committed. Critical discussions of the family in the novel have often focussed upon the relationship between the Marquis

From *Dickens and the Politics of the Family*, pp. 122–149. © 1997 by Catherine Waters.

St Evrémonde and Charles Darnay as a version of the generational rivalry between fathers and sons that is evident elsewhere in the relations between Darnay and Doctor Manette, Carton and Stryver, and Young Jerry and his father. Albert D. Hutter has analysed the novel in these terms, arguing that 'As much as any other work of 1859, *A Tale of Two Cities* demonstrates the correlation between family and nation, and it uses the language of psychological conflict and psychological identification to portray social upheaval and the restoration of social order.'[3]

But rather than offering another psychoanalytic account of relationships between fathers and sons in the novel, my analysis focusses upon the way in which concepts of the family and female identity are invested in Dickens's appalled and yet fascinated response to the French Revolution. The novel uses gender difference—defined by the Victorian middle-class ideal of domesticity—to represent its political conflicts in a narrative strategy designed to universalise the horror of the crisis. Dickens characteristically rejects politics in favour of a personal, familial resolution; but the dissemination of the ideal of domesticity in his fiction that this narrative procedure entails has a normalising effect that is, nonetheless, politically significant. Dickens genders the Revolution, turning its overtly political conflicts into questions of sexual difference. Posing the political crisis as a threat to the values of the English middle-class family, the novel performs a larger cultural function by participating in the development of forms of knowledge and power based upon a model of sexual difference. In *A Tale of Two Cities*, this process is primarily shown in the sustained effort to identify the French Revolution with female deviance in the narrative.

Dickens's primary source for the novel was Carlyle's great narrative, *The French Revolution*. Like Carlyle, Dickens uses a prophetic voice to discover order in the apparent anarchy of the French Revolution. His narrator fashions a coherent account of events to explain the past and apprehend the truths of history. Carlyle's charting of the 'cycles and seasons' in the progress of the Revolution is an attempt to identify the ordering principles of history that resembles the providential design evident in *A Tale of Two Cities*—the pattern recognised by Charles Darnay according to which, he says, 'All things have worked together as they have fallen out' (413). Carlyle recognised the importance of the imagination in understanding the past: he sought to resuscitate dead facts into a living reality in a process that cast history as an act of imaginative projection and identification, and turned its writing into a work of literary creation. And to this end his personal pronouns and use of the present tense situate the reader in the midst of the revolutionary turmoil, as he focusses upon the role of heroic individuals in the course of the conflict.

Like Carlyle, Dickens attempts to provide an imaginative reconstruction of this historical conflict. But rather than finding a way out of revolutionary chaos through hero-worship, he relies upon the saving power of the middle-class family, conceived as an ideal transcending social and national differences. Dickens's moral aim is expressed in the novel by Charles Darnay in his determination to return to France that he may try 'to do something to stay bloodshed, and assert the claims of mercy and humanity' (297). The novel's apparent goal, suggested in the opening antitheses which mock attempts to define the age, is to universalise the action—to emphasise the commonality of human experience everywhere—and the representation of the family is central to this process, because the domestic ideal is invoked as a norm ostensibly beyond the contingency of historical difference. Dickens uses the idea of the family in an attempt to depoliticise and dehistoricise the events recorded in what one might expect to be the most overtly political and historical of his novels.

A number of commentators have criticised Dickens for posing private answers to the public problems of history and failing to provide an adequate analysis of the Revolution in *A Tale of Two Cities*. Lukács provided the most well known of these criticisms in his study of the historical novel, where he objects that Dickens uses the events of the French Revolution merely as a 'romantic background' to the lives of his fictional characters.[4] However, rather than betraying Dickens's failure to provide a satisfactory historical investigation of the revolutionary process, the novel's use of private lives to explore public conflicts should itself be seen as a historically significant strategy. In *A Tale of Two Cities*, the Victorian middle-class family appears to promise a haven of true love and humanity in the midst of the Revolution that transcends the turmoil of class conflict and national difference, and grounds identity in the locus of the domestic hearth. This account of the family provides another example of the representation of middle-class ascendancy.

The event which precipitates the major actions of the plot of *A Tale of Two Cities* is a crime against the domestic family. The younger of the Evrémonde brothers rapes a young peasant girl, the daughter of one of his tenants. Her young husband had previously been worked to death in a harness and her father's heart had 'burst' (403) at the news of her capture. When her brother, who recounts these events, attempts to punish the ravisher, he is mortally wounded. Only one member of the family escapes—a younger sister—who turns out to be Madame Defarge. In the account of this precipitating crime recorded by Doctor Manette, aristocratic *droit de seigneur* is defined as a violation of the family whose integrity and purity are identified with female chastity. Social exploitation and sexual violence are yoked together. The use of this figure of female/familial violation to characterise the *ancien régime* has important consequences for the portrayal of the Revolution in the novel, for if the aristocratic oppression of the French peasantry which leads to the Revolution is represented as a rivalry between men over the possession of a woman, in a process of signification which grounds itself in the apparent timelessness of gender arrangements beneath the vicissitudes of social conflict, the depiction of the Revolution itself also involves a displacement of class on to gender. The Revolution is represented as a kind of Amazonian 'misrule'. It is gendered, and set in opposition to the idealised domestic family in the narrative, enabling Dickens to offer an ostensibly apolitical analysis of his subject.

The gendering of the Revolution in *A Tale of Two Cities* is primarily brought about through the concentration of the narrative upon the figure of Madame Defarge, 'leader of the Saint Antoine women' (271). In the cover design created by Hablôt Browne for the part issues,[5] Madame Defarge is set in opposition to Lucie on the left-hand side of the page, clearly signalling their juxtaposition in the text. The symmetry of their pairing is part of a set of parallels drawn between England and France, designed to bridge national differences in the interests of rendering universal human nature. Other parallels included in this set are the 'Two Cities' of the title, the crowds in England and France, the trials of Darnay in each country, and the pairing of Stryver and the Marquis St Evrémonde through their respective relationships with Carton and Darnay. However, as the careful juxtapositioning of Madame Defarge with Lucie Manette in the novel shows, the universal human nature which Dickens is attempting to portray through these techniques of parallelism takes gender as the transhistorical constituent of identity, and yet, at the same time, grounds it in the ideology of the Victorian middle-class family. For the definition of female identity produced through the opposition between these two women hinges upon the wider formation of domestic ideology and the propagation of the values of home in Victorian middle-class culture. The fear of social disintegration generated by the hostility of class difference is apparently allayed through the commonality of a belief in shared familial values that define the activities of Madame Defarge as deviant. However, the family proves to be a problematic mechanism for easing bourgeois anxieties about the consequences of class conflict, since its use in the novel is informed by the very social differences it was supposed to transcend.

The characterisation of Madame Defarge carries strong echoes of the portrayal of her compatriot, Mademoiselle Hortense, from *Bleak House*. Hortense is described as 'a large-eyed brown woman with black hair; who would be handsome, but for a certain feline mouth, and general uncomfortable tightness of face, rendering the jaws too eager, and the skull too prominent' (143). Like the 'universal watchfulness' (302) that characterises the inhabitants of revolutionary France, Hortense has a 'watchful way of looking out of the corners of her eyes without turning her head, which could be pleasantly dispensed with—especially when she is in an ill-humour and near knives' (143). As a double for Lady Dedlock, she blends the threat of violence with the threat of female sexuality. When Mr Bucket informs her of his wife's part in her capture, Hortense, 'panting tigress-like', exclaims:

> 'I would like to kiss her!'...
> 'You'd bite her, I suspect,' says Mr Bucket.
> 'I would!' making her eyes very large. 'I would love to tear her, limb from limb.' (652)

Esther makes the connection with Madame Defarge even more directly when she remarks 'a lowering energy in [Mademoiselle Hortense's] face ... which seemed to bring visibly before me some woman from the streets of Paris in the reign of terror' (286).

However, Madame Defarge is distinguished from Hortense by her beguiling steadiness of demeanour. Until the moment for rebellion arrives, she remains outwardly calm and imperturbable. While Hortense cannot help betraying her passionate anger, Madame Defarge is remarkable for the success with which she conceals her rage. Indeed, it is the extraordinary tension between her hidden fury and her façade of equanimity that makes her so fascinating and formidable. The narrator refers repeatedly to her astonishing 'composure'. On her first appearance in Book the First, chapter V, she is described as 'a stout woman of about [30], with a watchful eye that seldom seemed to look at anything, a large hand heavily ringed, a steady face, strong features, and great composure of manner' (37). Clearly, her 'watchful eye' suggests a capacity for dissimulation that worries the narrator, whose cautious and tentative account of her behaviour conveys a sense of hidden menace. Her gipsy-like attire adds to the dubiousness of her moral status and suggestively casts her as something of an outlaw, as exotic and 'other'. Andrew Sanders notes that the manuscript of the novel reveals a change from the original paragraph in which Dickens had portrayed Madame Defarge as a 'little woman' intent on her needlework.[6] These assertions of Madame Defarge's freedom from the norms and restraints of English middle-class femininity sit oddly and ironically with the narrator's conventional reference to Monsieur Defarge as 'her lord'. The incongruity makes apparent the way in which the normalising discourse of Victorian domesticity underlines cultural difference here, and provides a means for evaluating and containing the revolutionary threat.

Much of the menace surrounding Madame Defarge in these early descriptions obviously comes from the ominousness of the narrator's inordinate attention to her every movement and expression. The most trivial details and innocent gestures—Madame's habit of picking her teeth, slight coughs, raising her eyebrows by nicely calculated degrees—are loaded with hidden meaning as they are repeatedly particularised and dwelt upon in the narrative. Of course, the knitting of Madame Defarge is the most famous of these secret codes. The threat posed by her knitting draws on the symbolism of the Three Fates which is made explicit at the end of Book the Second, chapter VII. When the Marquis attempts to make token reparation for running over the child of Gaspard by contemptuously flinging two gold coins to the bereft father, he is incensed to find the money thrown back into his carriage:

> 'Hold!' said Monsieur the Marquis. 'Hold the horses! Who threw that?'
>
> He looked to the spot where Defarge the vendor of wine had stood, a moment before; but the wretched father was grovelling on his face on the pavement in that spot, and the figure that stood beside him was the figure of a dark stout woman, knitting. (132)

The substitution of wife for husband at the side of Gaspard foreshadows the gender reversal which is used to represent the revolutionary threat in the narrative. After the child's body is taken away by its father, Madame Defarge remains by the fountain, knitting on 'with the steadfastness of Fate' (133).

Madame Defarge's knitting associates her with the notorious *tricoteuses*, the patriotic knitting-women of Paris, who are described in Carlyle's *The French Revolution*. She knits a register of all the oppressors belonging to the *ancien régime*, dooming them to destruction. Her knitting is an unalterable chronicle, a grim history which records the past in a mysterious female language that only she and her sister-knitters can decipher. It forms an analogue for omniscient narration in the novel, contrasting with Dickens's apparently more fluid and sympathetic handling of history.[7] But perhaps the most important thematic and ideological function of her inexorable knitting is its relevance to the representation of domesticity and the feminine ideal in the novel. The knitted register produces a shock in its implicit linkage of images and emotions normally opposed in Victorian middle-class ideology. The creativity, nurture and maternal affection, conventionally associated with knitting, are connected here with vengeance, violence and death.

The incongruity is given a darkly comic expression in a brief conversation witnessed by the 'mender of roads' during his excursion to Versailles with the Defarges. A bystander remarks on her knitting:

> 'You work hard, madame,' said a man near her.
> 'Yes,' answered Madame Defarge; 'I have a good deal to do.'
> 'What do you make, madame?'
> 'Many things.'
> 'For instance—'
> 'For instance,' returned Madame Defarge, composedly, 'shrouds.' (209)

The striking mixture of domestic activity and public violence involved in the knitted register finds its climax in the description of the *tricoteuses* who encircle the guillotine and sit 'knitting, knitting, counting dropping heads' (225). This overriding of the boundary between public and private realms in the deadly knitting of the patriotic women defies the Victorian middle-class ideals of femininity and domesticity. It shows not only Madame Defarge's failure to conform to the normal 'requirements' of her gender, but her strategic use or abuse of these requirements as a guise for her sinister activities. A related example is to be found in the rose which she pins in her head-dress as a warning-signal to her compatriots in Book the Second, chapter XVI. While the function of the rose as an emblem of England is relevant here, it is also significant that the aesthetics of feminine adornment are deployed in the service of the Revolution. Rather than observing the rules of fashion in an effort to attract the admiration of male onlookers, Madame Defarge uses the trappings of female finery as a code for political intrigue. The ritual expression of beauty and sexual attractiveness becomes a guise for the subversive activities of the revolutionaries.

The subversion of gender promoted by the knitting of Madame Defarge is extended in other aspects of her characterisation. Traits of masculinity are suggested in the narrator's observation of her 'large hand', 'steady face' and 'strong features' in Book the First, chapter V, and this impression is confirmed in the depiction of her relationship with Monsieur Defarge. There is more than a hint of the reversal in power-relations, shown elsewhere by such comic Dickensian partners as Mr and Mrs Snagsby, Joe and Mrs Joe, and Mr and Mrs Wilfer, in the portrayal of the Defarges, husband and wife. The circumspection shown by Madame in managing the trade of the wine-shop is not unlike the thriftiness and vigilance manifested by her fictional English counterparts, and Monsieur Defarge's reaction finds a similar parallel in the behaviour of their meek English husbands:

'All this while, Defarge, with his pipe in his mouth, walked up and down, complacently admiring, but never interfering; in which condition, indeed, as to the business and his domestic affairs, he walked up and down through life' (214–15). However, the masculine authority apparently assumed in these matters by Madame Defarge does not provide the only test to the limits of gender entailed in her characterisation. This scene in Book the Second, chapter XVI, draws upon Victorian ideals of wifely duty which enjoined a woman to comfort and counsel her partner, but does so only to show Madame Defarge abusing and undermining them. The counsel she gives her husband is to sustain his rage and discontent in secret, and the comfort she offers is the promise of vengeance and retribution. Her strategy in this discussion is to insinuate a charge of cowardice against her husband, and his 'weakness' is implicitly contrasted with her own courage and deadly determination. The scene recalls the dialogue between Lady Macbeth and her faltering husband in its questioning of the attributes of gender. Echoing something of the shock generated by Lady Macbeth's violent repudiation of maternity, Madame Defarge's routine actions, in knotting up into her handkerchief the small moneys taken in the shop, are seen as a series of executions. Her conversation with Monsieur Defarge is punctuated by narrative comments on her sinister delight in this occupation: 'She tied a knot with flashing eyes, as if it throttled a foe' (216). The discussion between husband and wife ends with Madame exhorting her partner to sustain himself without needing 'to see [his] victim and [his] opportunity': 'Madame enforced the conclusion of this piece of advice by striking her little counter with her chain of money as if she knocked its brains out, and then gathering the heavy handkerchief under her arm in a serene manner, and observing that it was time to go to bed' (217). The relish of imagined murder is incongruously combined with the routine preparation for bed, reinforcing the link with Lady Macbeth that is clear in the verbal echo here.[8] Madame Defarge is (appropriately) childless, and she admonishes her quailing husband, who characteristically 'stand[s] before her with his head a little bent, and his hands clasped at his back, like a docile and attentive pupil before his catechist' (216).

The reversal in the power-relations between husband and wife becomes more pronounced as the novel progresses. This subversion of gender differences signifies a breakdown in male authority—an overthrowing of social order—and it gathers momentum around the question of the respective fates of Lucie, Charles and Doctor Manette. When the marriage of Lucie and Charles is made known to the Defarges by Barsad in Book the Second, chapter XVI, Monsieur Defarge finds himself 'rather pleading with his wife to induce her to admit' the 'strangeness' of the fact that Lucie and her father should be proscribed under her hand after having been the objects of their sympathy. His 'pleading' proves to be ineffectual, and when this discussion recurs in Book the Third, chapter XII, Monsieur Defarge is reduced to feeble protests in the face of his wife's implacable wrath: 'Defarge, a weak minority, interposed a few words for the memory of the compassionate wife of the Marquis; but only elicited from his own wife a repetition of her last reply. "Tell the Wind and the Fire where to stop; not me!"' (421). The narrator's reference to Defarge as a 'minority' indicates not only a difference in the opinions of the husband and wife, but a change in the dynamics of the household and in its decision-making procedures. The male–female pairing ratified by marriage has apparently been cut across by new relationships and alliances formed in the pursuit of revolutionary goals. Madame Defarge's closest ally is no longer her husband, but a female friend who was introduced in Book the Second, chapter XXII, as one of Madame's 'sisterhood'—one who sits faithfully beside her, knitting, and who 'had already earned the complimentary name of The Vengeance' (271). The terms of endearment repeatedly exchanged between Madame and her lieutenant are given a ghoulish aspect by the murderous sentiments which are shown to prompt them. Madame's relishing assertion of her power over the fate of Lucie—'"Let me but lift my finger—!" She seemed to raise it ..., and to let it fall with a rattle on the ledge before her, as if the axe had dropped' (420)—provokes The Vengeance to embrace her Chief and cry 'She is an Angel!' In return, Madame Defarge acknowledges the devotion of her passionate friend by addressing her in a travesty of tenderness as 'my little Vengeance' (420).

The bond between these two women is shown to become more close and deadly as the Revolution gathers momentum. Madame Defarge holds 'darkly ominous council with The Vengeance and Jacques Three of the Revolutionary Jury' in Book the Third, chapter XIV, to plot the execution of Lucie and her child. The secret council measures the extent of the rupture between husband and wife, as Madame condemns his 'weaknesses', explains that she 'dare not confide to him the details of my projects' and announces her decision to act for herself (444). This transfer of confidence and loyalties from her husband to her revolutionary comrades is the most obvious sign of a fracture in the family. However, there is also something particularly sinister about the emphasis upon the alliance between the two women here. Jacques Three is full of praise for Madame and is said to vie with The Vengeance 'in their fervent protestations that she was the most admirable and marvellous of witnesses' (445). But his rivalling acclamations and gestures serve to underline the threat posed by the homosocial bond between the two women, who embrace one another with melodramatic fervour. The Vengeance is entrusted with the safe-keeping of the fatal register, and the blood-lust shared by the two women here represents perhaps the Revolution's most significant challenge to patriarchal authority and order. Both The Vengeance and the Juryman, looking after Madame Defarge as she walks away, are said to be 'highly appreciative of her fine figure, and her superb moral endowments' (447). Clearly, the narrator's irony emphasises the moral chaos implied by such an approving estimation of ruthlessness. But the equivalence of their admiration also disrupts the structuring of sexual relations associated with Victorian middle-class ideology. The relationships shown to obtain between these revolutionary citizens are not 'properly' refracted by gender. There is no differentiation between the underlying bonds of desire joining Madame Defarge to her male and female comrades. And this failure to preserve the difference between heterosexual and homosocial relationships represents a challenge to the patriarchal social structure that characterises not only the *ancien régime* in France, but the social order of Victorian England. Directed against an oppressive patriarchal system, the sisterly solidarity of Madame Defarge and The Vengeance is therefore especially threatening.

The Vengeance is characterised throughout the novel by an exhibition of extreme passion and violence bordering on insanity. When the lynching of Foulon commences in chapter XXII, she 'tears' from house to house, rousing the women, 'uttering terrific shrieks, and flinging her arms about her head like all the forty Furies at once' (272). She 'screeches' admiration for Monsieur Defarge in the midst of Darnay's trial, and when the President rings his bell, 'shrieks' defiance of his warning (392). She is equally vehement in her affection for her 'Chief', 'kissing her cheek' (447) and lavishing extravagant epithets of praise upon her. Madame Defarge is occasionally required to moderate the enthusiasm of The Vengeance—'"Peace, little Vengeance," said Madame Defarge, laying her hand with a slight frown on her lieutenant's lips, "hear me speak"' (443)—and these cautions emphasise the barely controlled madness in her behaviour. The crazed passion of The Vengeance betrays a fundamental loss of rationality that is part of the novel's feminisation of the Revolution, and that is suggested elsewhere in the imagery of natural disaster used to portray the rising of the people. Madame Defarge's reply to her husband's plea in Book the Third, chapter XII, 'Tell the Wind and the Fire where to stop; not me!' (371), invokes the resistless forces of nature to identify her implacability with the impulse of the Revolution, which is also described as the working-out of catastrophic natural history.[9] The coming of the Revolution and its intrusion into the lives of Lucie and Doctor Manette are heralded in the electrical storm which interrupts the family gathering seated beneath the plane-tree at the Doctor's lodgings in Soho in June 1780 (the fictional event coinciding with the timing of the

Gordon Riots), and the storming of the Bastille nine years later is described as an all-destroying ocean, the rising of a 'living sea' (263).

Dickens was drawing upon a well-established apocalyptic tradition for the imagery he used to portray the Revolution. But this representation of the Revolution in terms of catastrophic natural history is also part of the novel's exploitation of sexual difference to represent political conflict. The history of the concept of reason in Western philosophical thought has been characterised by the use of oppositional formulations in which men have been distinguished by their rational capacity and women have been defined as irrational and associated with the uncontrollable forces of nature.[10] In a similar way, the characterisation of the revolutionary mob in *A Tale of Two Cities* as an irresistible natural force locates its violent activity outside the realm of patriarchal culture and helps displace political conflict on to gender conflict. The description of the emblematic wrath of Saint Antoine as a relentless natural force in Book the Second, chapter XXI—a 'sea of black and threatening waters, and of destructive upheaving of wave against wave', containing 'faces hardened in the furnaces of suffering until the touch of pity could make no mark on them' (268)—is echoed in the later portrait of Madame Defarge as a figure 'absolutely without pity', and one whom 'the troubled time would have heaved ... up, under any circumstances' (447). As a movement that is mindlessly passionate and dangerously unpredictable, the Revolution suggests the chaos associated with the idea of female insubordination. As Dickens's sympathies shift from the revolutionaries to their victims in *A Tale of Two Cities*, the representation of the Revolution itself is increasingly shaped by the nature/culture dichotomy so prevalent in the Western philosophical and literary traditions, and embodied, for example, in *King Lear*, where Lear's relinquishment of his patriarchal power to his diabolical daughters is shown to issue in natural and civil disorder.

Dickens emphasises the role of the women in the French Revolution as evidence of a violation of the sexual hierarchy. Even that most notorious instrument of revolutionary justice—La Guillotine—is female. It is a 'devouring and insatiate' (459) monster, a rapacious woman whose appetite can never be satisfied: 'Lovely girls; bright women, brown-haired, black-haired, and grey; youths; stalwart men and old; gentle born and peasant born; all red wine for La Guillotine, all daily brought into light from the dark cellars of the loathsome prisons, and carried to her through the street to slake her devouring thirst' (338). Adding to this effect of 'unnatural' female blood-lust, the melodramatic vision of the revolutionaries' lynching of Foulon, given in Book the Second, chapter XXII, uses the transgression of gender norms to describe the social disorder:

[T]he women were a sight to chill the boldest. From such household occupations as their bare poverty yielded, from their children, from their aged and their sick crouching on the bare ground famished and naked, they ran out with streaming hair, urging one another, and themselves, to madness with the wildest cries and actions. Villain Foulon taken, my sister. Old Foulon taken, my mother. Miscreant Foulon taken, my daughter. Then, a score of others ran into the midst of these, beating their breasts, tearing their hair, and screaming, Foulon alive. (272)

In an effort to convey the horror of the mob, the narrator focusses upon the abandonment of domestic responsibilities, and the violence and madness that seem to possess the women. The mixture of free direct speech with narrative comment and description is used to convey the chaos of the scene. The passage draws upon historical accounts describing the Eumenides of the Revolution. In particular, it was the Parisian women in their march to Versailles to demand bread from the king and the National Assembly who were condemned by English observers as 'furies', 'harlots', and 'shrews'.[11] One of Dickens's sons later remembered his father naming

two scenes in literature which he regarded as being the most dramatic descriptions he could recall ... The first was the description of the Woman in White's appearance on the Hampstead Road after her escape from the asylum in Wilkie Collins's famous book *The Woman in White*. The other was the stirring account of the march of the women to Versailles in Carlyle's *French Revolution*.[12]

The violation of gender norms illustrated by the women who cry for the blood of Foulon is repeated in the description of two other set scenes of the Revolution: the Terror and the Carmagnole. Dickens encapsulates the Reign of Terror in the emblem of the blood-smeared grindstone in Book the Third, chapter II, which is turned by two men whose faces

were more horrible and cruel than the visages of the wildest savages in their most barbarous disguise. False eyebrows and false moustaches were stuck upon them, and their hideous countenances were all bloody and sweaty, and all awry with howling, and all staring and glaring with beastly excitement and want of sleep. As these ruffians turned and turned, their matted locks now flung forward over their eyes, now flung backward

over their necks, some women held wine to their mouths that
they might drink; and what with dropping blood, and what with
dropping wine, and what with the stream of sparks struck out
of the stone, all their wicked atmosphere seemed gore and fire.
(321)

Smeared with blood, the men who shoulder one another in an effort to get at
the grindstone are 'devilishly set off with spoils of women's lace and silk and
ribbon, with the stain dyeing all those trifles through and through'. As the
men work at the grindstone while the women supply them with drink, gender
differences appear to be preserved only in order to set off their obliteration
elsewhere in the indiscriminate frenzy of blood-lust. The revolutionaries are
characterised by their violence and passion, and the disgust of the narrator
is strikingly registered in the brutal frankness with which he intrudes at
the end of the passage, seeking to 'petrify' the 'frenzied eyes' of the mob
'with a well-directed gun' (322). Images of barbarism and sexual perversion
convey the horror of the scene. Instead of being portrayed as a cataclysmic
natural force—a living sea, raging fire or earthquake—the revolutionaries
are figured here as the members of a degenerate race. The gathering of the
throng is like a crazy primitive ritual, a carnal scene of blood, sweat, filth
and dissipation. Nineteenth-century depictions of revolution commonly
fantasised the conflict as a reversion to cannibalism,[13] and here the metaphor
of cannibalism is literalised in the syntax, which identifies the 'dropping
blood' with the 'dropping wine', bringing this scene together with the
earlier account of the spilt wine outside the shop of Monsieur Defarge (33).
But whereas the breaking of the wine cask is represented as an opportunity
for innocent conviviality, the activity around the grindstone is represented
as the work of degeneracy. The perversion of gender identity evident in
the ghastly appearance of the revolutionaries is an important part of this
critique. According to Andrew Sanders, there is no reference to the 'false
eyebrows and false moustaches' of the revolutionaries in any of Dickens's
likely sources for this section, and he attributes the description to Carlyle's
account of the murder of the Princess de Lamballe at La Force in 1789,
noting that Dickens does not seem to have read, or remembered, the original
French which appears to have been available to him.[14] In Mercier's account,
one of the assassins of the Princess cut off her pubic hair and made himself
moustaches of it. Whatever Dickens knew of this incident, the detail adds to
the promiscuous mixing of genders in the scene of carnality described. The
signs of parodic cross-dressing are yet another example of the way in which
a violation of the sexual hierarchy is used to represent the social upheaval of
the Revolution.

These images of the Terror anticipate the description of the Carmagnole in Book the Third, chapter V. Near the shop of the wood-sawyer on the outskirts of La Force, Lucie encounters a throng of people dancing, 'in the midst of whom was the wood-sawyer hand in hand with The Vengeance':

> Men and women danced together, women danced together, men danced together, as hazard had brought them together. At first, they were a mere storm of coarse red caps and coarse woollen rags; but, as they filled the place, and stopped to dance about Lucie, some ghastly apparition of a dance-figure gone raving mad arose among them. (342)

The description emphasises the incongruous mixture of organised ritual and violent anarchy evident in the fiery patriotic dance. A primitive patterning is evident in the recurrence of gestures, and the movements made in unison. But these signs of order are offset by the violence and overt sexuality of the performance: 'Such grace as was visible in it, made it the uglier, showing how warped and perverted all things good by nature were become,' says the narrator. Partnering in the dance ignores the rules of sexual difference, leaving the combinations to 'hazard', and the suggestion of promiscuity implicit in this defiance of convention is compounded by the stress upon the unrestrained energy and physicality of the dancers, who 'strike', 'clutch', 'tear', 'spin' and 'scream'. The Carmagnole is a 'fallen sport', a 'something, once innocent, delivered over to all devilry'. Social disorder is expressed through the loss of female purity shown by the 'baring' of 'maidenly bosoms', the 'distracting' of 'pretty' heads, and the 'mincing' of 'delicate feet' in 'this slough of blood and dirt'. The narrator is both appalled and fascinated by the sight. His description of the Carmagnole assumes the grounding of gender difference in 'nature' in order to distinguish the perversions of this 'disjointed time'. But in identifying the revolutionary turmoil with female deviance, and dwelling upon its description in such scenes of mob frenzy in the novel, the narrator also seems to reveal a repressed fascination with the horrors he so strenuously deplores.[15] It is as if he cannot evade the implications of the model of heterosexual desire upon which his representation of female subjectivity is founded. This sexual tension in the narrative recalls the ambiguous imaginative interest Dickens shows elsewhere in 'fallen' women like Edith Granger and Lady Dedlock, and is further evidence that his attitudes towards the middle-class ideals of femininity and family were never entirely straightforward.

The link between political violence and sexual anarchy in Dickens's representation of the Revolution was not new. Edmund Burke had used the image of the Furies to represent the political threat in his *Reflections on the Revolution in France* (1790).[16] Revolutionary activity in France and America provided feminists of the Enlightenment, like Mary Wollstonecraft, with encouragement in their call for equality between the sexes. The language of political libertarianism was adapted for the articulation of a feminist position, and it is no coincidence that in the midst of this exciting atmosphere of change women became more politicised. A number of female clubs and societies were formed in France which initiated women into public life and gave them a forum for discussing their demands for justice and education. So it is hardly surprising that Dickens should associate the overthrow of government there with female insubordination. Dickens's original for Madame Defarge was Théroigne de Méricourt, who was active as a feminist in the last years of the constitutional monarchy and a member of the 'Société fraternelle des patriotes des deux sexes'. She took part in the October 1789 march to Versailles, and is described by Carlyle's narrator as 'the brown-locked, light-behaved, fire-hearted Demoiselle Théroigne'.[17] Carlyle indicates the transgression of gender norms evident in the behaviour of Théroigne, and Dickens develops this suggestive combination of violence and sexual attraction in his portrayal of Thérèse Defarge. In pursuit of Lucie, she is described as a 'tigress', a woman 'absolutely without pity':

> Such a heart Madame Defarge carried under her rough robe. Carelessly worn, it was a becoming robe enough, in a certain weird way, and her dark hair looked rich under her coarse red cap. Lying hidden in her bosom, was a loaded pistol. Lying hidden at her waist, was a sharpened dagger. Thus accoutred, and walking with the confident tread of such a character, and with the supple freedom of a woman who had habitually walked in her girlhood, bare-foot and bare-legged, on the brown sea-sand, Madame Defarge took her way along the streets. (448)

Like Mademoiselle Hortense, Madame Defarge's perversion of female nature is predictably expressed in her identification with the wild animal which epitomised, for the Victorians, the greatest threat to be feared from the animal kingdom and from restive human subordinates: the tigress.[18] But what is most striking about this description is the way in which the danger represented by Madame Defarge is combined with hints of sexual fascination. Just as the accounts of the grindstone and Carmagnole reveal undercurrents of sexual horror and fascination, the characterisation of Madame Defarge shows a peculiar tension between feelings of attraction and repulsion in the narrator's stance. Given the informal censorship associated with the practice of 'family reading' amongst the Victorian middle classes and dominant assumptions about women's sexuality during the period, any description of the female body in Victorian domestic fiction treads on dangerous ground; and the portrait of Madame Defarge dwells upon bodily details that were specific sites of sexual signification in Victorian middle-class culture: her hair, bosom, waist and legs. There is something rather tantalising about the narrative emphasis given to the deadly weapons hidden in these erotogenic zones upon the body of Madame Defarge—the pistol secreted in her bosom, the dagger at her waist—despite their function as evidence of her 'unwomanly' activities. The emphasis given here to her 'confidence' and 'supple freedom' accords with the loud assertion of female independence that accompanied the Revolution. Mary Wollstonecraft's *A Vindication of the Rights of Woman* was published in the first year of the new Republic, and Madame Defarge's alliance with The Vengeance in the novel may well owe something to the reputation of Théroigne de Méricourt as a member of the 'Société fraternelle' and an advocate for the formation of a women's militia company in February 1792.[19]

Albert D. Hutter has noted an interesting change in the illustration of Madame Defarge since the novel's first publication in 1859. In the original 'Phiz' drawings, she is shown as a strong, young woman, with a beautiful but determined face, and dark hair. The illustrations set her in contrast with the blond-haired beauty of Lucie Manette. However, many subsequent versions of Madame Defarge in film and illustration have made her a witch. According to Hutter, the Harper and Row cover to *A Tale of Two Cities*, for example, 'shows a cadaverous old crone, gray-haired, hunched over her knitting, with wrinkles stitched across a tightened face'.[20] In the 1935 film, starring Ronald Colman, Madame Defarge is a rather haggard and plain-faced woman, with dark circles beneath her eyes, whose grim appearance contrasts with the fair complexion and rosy lips of the beautiful Lucie.

This change in the visual representation of Madame Defarge denotes a cultural shift in the construction of female subjectivity from the nineteenth to the twentieth century, and highlights Defarge's function in the novel. As a crucial part of the novel's effort to solve the problems posed by the Revolution, Madame Defarge serves as the monstrous female 'other' against which the norms of Victorian middle-class femininity and domesticity can be invoked. She is characterised as dangerously sexual and violent, oblivious of her wifely role and domestic responsibilities, lacking the feminine virtues of meekness, compassion and purity shown by Lucie and ominously intimate with like-minded women. All of these traits are informed by a Victorian middle-class conception of female subjectivity. Later representations showing Madame Defarge as a witch provide evidence of a historical change in the significance of femininity and domesticity as cultural norms. In order to continue serving as the 'other' woman, Madame Defarge is represented as old, ugly and deformed, because overt sexual attractiveness, assertiveness and freedom from convention have become attributes of the new twentieth-century heroine. These traits no longer function as signs of female deviance.

Madame Defarge's ruthless behaviour is shown to be driven by the vengeance she seeks for the original crime against her family perpetrated by the Evrémondes. But her defiance of gender norms is nevertheless condemned for its 'unnaturalness'. When her husband expresses sympathy for 'the compassionate wife of the Marquis' (421) in Book the Third, chapter XXII, Madame Defarge remains implacable in her revenge. Dickens juxtaposes the contrasting behaviour of two wives here: one is 'a good, compassionate lady' (409), according to the testimony of Doctor Manette, the other a pitiless 'wife of Lucifer' (452–3), in the words of Miss Pross. What redeems the wife of the Marquis St Evrémonde is her embodiment of the Victorian ideal of womanhood. Her class and connection with the *ancien régime* are overridden by her gender in the narrative. Doctor Manette's hidden diary provides the most direct portrait of the Marquise in the novel, and he describes her anguish at the cruelty of the Evrémonde brothers and her desire to comfort their victim: 'Her hope had been, she said in great distress, to show her, in secret, *a woman's sympathy*' (408, my emphasis). Learning that the girl is dead, the Marquise wants to make reparation by helping the young sister of the victim, and she therefore enjoins her son, Charles, to atone for the family's suffering:

> 'What I have left to call my own—it is little beyond the worth of a few jewels—I will make it the first charge of his life to bestow, with the compassion and lamenting of his dead mother, on this injured family, if the sister can be discovered.'
>
> She kissed the boy, and said, caressing him, 'It is for thine own dear sake. Thou wilt be faithful, little Charles?' The child answered her bravely, 'Yes!' I kissed her hand, and she took him in her arms, and went away caressing him. (409)

The Marquise's call upon her son to repair the injury done to the family fractured by the Evrémonde brothers, together with her display of maternal affection and devotion, shows her embodiment of the Victorian middle-class ideals of domesticity and womanhood. She indicates the novel's investment in the middle-class family and forms a foil for Madame Defarge, the very sister she had hoped to assist. For in contrast to the Marquise St Evrémonde, Madame Defarge is represented as a female who lacks femininity.

Even more important as a foil for the behaviour of Madame Defarge, however, is the devotion shown by Lucie Manette as daughter, wife and mother. One of the most obvious points of comparison is the contrast drawn between Madame Defarge's knitting in the service of the Revolution and Lucie's busy winding of 'the golden thread which bound her husband, and her father, and herself, and her old directress and companion, in a life of quiet bliss' (256). While the handiwork of one promotes violence and destruction, the other toils only to secure peace and domestic harmony. The significance of their juxtaposition for the novel's construction of female subjectivity is evident in the description of their encounter in Book the Third, chapter III. Madame Defarge accompanies her husband when he delivers a note to Lucie from her imprisoned husband. Thrown into a 'transport' by the tidings, Lucie's instinctive response is a 'womanly' one: 'she turned from Defarge to his wife, and kissed one of the hands that knitted. It was a passionate, loving, thankful, womanly action, but the hand made no response—dropped cold and heavy, and took to its knitting again' (327). Lucie assumes the existence of a fellow-feeling between herself and Madame Defarge, based on their common gender. She automatically expects Madame Defarge to identify with her joy *as a woman*. The realisation of her mistake strikes her with 'terror' and leads to the admission—'We are more afraid of you than of these others'—which Madame calmly receives as 'a compliment' (328). Notwithstanding the evidence of the fierce Frenchwoman's failure to conform to the womanly ideal she herself upholds, Lucie appeals once more for mercy, crying to Madame Defarge, 'O sister-woman, think of me. As a wife and mother!' (329). Lucie demonstrates an ardent faith in the overriding power of gender as the natural determinant of female identity. Her supreme appeal is to the sanctity of the Victorian middle-class family and to the status of women as relative creatures within it. Surely, implies Lucie, Madame Defarge is at one with her in her reverence for these fundamental truths; surely she has a woman's 'nature'.

Lucie's appeal to a shared belief in the value of familial roles as determinants of female identity is, of course, shown to be useless, and its failure confirms Madame Defarge's repudiation of the norms of femininity and domesticity. The worship of the middle-class hearth is shown to be of little importance to one who is bent upon reversing the hierarchies of a patrilineal order. Indeed, her motives are based upon a different notion of family altogether. Already subject to censure in the narrative for her violence, overt sexuality and sisterly solidarity, she is finally condemned by her ironic dedication to the sovereign power of genealogy for which the aristocracy of the *ancien régime* is overthrown. Madame Defarge is motivated by the blood-ties of a 'race'. When she explains to her comrades, in Book the Third, chapter XII, the reason for having 'this [Evrémonde] race a long time on my register, doomed to destruction and extermination', she repeats the secret previously disclosed to her husband:

> '[T]hat peasant family so injured by the two Evrémonde brothers, as that Bastille paper describes, is my family. Defarge, that sister of the mortally wounded boy upon the ground was my sister, that husband was my sister's husband, that unborn child was their child, that brother was my brother, that father was my father, those dead are my dead, and that summons to answer for those things descends to me!' (421)

Madame Defarge stresses the fact of kinship here, rather than the affective ties that one might expect to be uppermost in her memory of her lost 'loved ones'. Her inheritance of the 'summons' is determined by the very pattern of descent that she would seek to overthrow. Ironically, she now invokes the language of the law—that most patriarchal and aristocratic of institutions—to ratify her inheritance.

The reactionary stance implied in her ironic capitulation to the very principle of genealogy set up as a distinguishing trait of the aristocracy sits oddly with the more subversive activities undertaken by Thérèse Defarge, as a revolutionary worker and as a woman, in the novel. But such inconsistency only enhances her function as the monstrous example of female deviance with which the horror of the Revolution can be identified. As she is finally brought down in the text to be punished and eliminated, some of the threat posed by the alien realm of revolutionary France is symbolically diminished. And it is for this reason that the nemesis chosen for Madame Defarge is the otherwise unlikely figure of Miss Pross.

Miss Pross is described in terms which evoke the stereotypical Victorian old maid. She is a comic grotesque, 'A wild-looking woman, whom even in his agitation, Mr Lorry observed to be all of a red colour, and to have red hair' (30). Despite her masculine strength and her spinsterhood (and her red hair), Miss Pross represents no challenge to the norms of femininity and domesticity. On the contrary, she is assimilated into the family by her devotion as a surrogate mother to Lucie. But her wiry strength and characterisation as a decidedly *English* grotesque also make her a fit opponent for Madame Defarge. While Madame Defarge represents a repudiation of the ideals Miss Pross so vigilantly protects in the person of her 'Ladybird', it is primarily the national differences between the two women that determine their fateful encounter. As the two of them are set face to face in the narrative, other categories of difference—gender, generational and class difference—are ostensibly overridden by the opposition of nationalities. What distinguishes the struggle between Madame Defarge and Miss Pross is not its commonly proclaimed thematic function as 'a contest between the forces of hatred and love',[21] but its characterisation as a confrontation between France and England. The significance of Miss Pross's defence is expressed in her vow, 'you shall not get the better of me. I am an Englishwoman' (453). This proud assertion of national identity informs her behaviour throughout the episode. Each woman speaks in her own language—English, of course, being privileged in the narrative anyway—and Miss Pross's words have a peculiarly idiomatic flavour that complements Dickens's literal translation of French idioms into English in order to represent the speech of the francophones in the novel. For example, she responds to the unintelligible exclamations of Madame Defarge with a peculiarly English image of defiance: "'If those eyes of yours were bed-winches," returned Miss Pross, "and I was an English four-poster, they shouldn't loose a splinter of me. No, you wicked foreign woman; I am your match"' (453). And so she is. In spite of the novel's conscientious effort to condemn the revolutionaries' desire for revenge, Miss Pross's victory over Madame Defarge brings with it all the satisfaction of an exacted retribution. An unmistakable note of triumph informs the narrator's ironic adjurations to The Vengeance in the final chapter to 'cry louder' for the missing Thérèse at the site of La Guillotine (462).

With the defeat and death of Madame Defarge, the salvation of Lucie Manette and her family is secured. Their survival, together with the ideals they represent, is of course exactly what Miss Pross fights for. But while 'eccentric' figures like Miss Pross (and Sydney Carton) play such an important role in enabling the representative Victorian middle-class family to withstand the assault of the French Revolution, its initial formation is entrusted primarily to Lucie. Whether or not Lucie's description is based upon Ellen Ternan as Michael Slater suggests,[22] she has the 'short, slight, pretty figure', 'quantity of golden hair', and 'blue eyes', that typically distinguish those heroines who embody the feminine ideal in Dickens's fiction. More important than the details of her appearance, however, although in fact culturally inseparable from them, is her function as a home-maker. On visiting the Doctor's lodgings, Mr Lorry is charmed to detect evidence of Lucie's silent presence everywhere:

> The disposition of everything in the rooms, from the largest object to the least; the arrangement of colours, the elegant variety and contrast obtained by thrift in trifles, by delicate hands, clear eyes, and good sense; were at once so pleasant in themselves, and so expressive of their originator, that, as Mr Lorry stood looking

about him, the very chairs and tables seemed to ask him, with
something of that peculiar expression which he knew so well by
this time, whether he approved? (110–11)

This household bespeaks the loving superintendence of a model domestic
economist. Its objects are signs of the taste and 'good sense' of the woman
who cares for them—as if Lucie's identity were coterminous with the
domestic space she inhabits. Simple, reassuring, and, above all, utterly
familiar, Lucie's home is set up as a haven in contrast with the foreign turmoil
of revolutionary France. And like Ruskin's 'true wife' whose 'home is always
round her',[23] Lucie arranges the 'little household' in Paris, while Charles is
imprisoned, 'exactly as if her husband had been there': 'everything had its
appointed place and its appointed time' (338–9). Indeed, given her French
birth, Lucie seems to reconcile national differences in her own person. She
helps to define a norm of respectable femininity that supposedly cuts across
the conflicts generated by class and national differences.

Lucie's womanliness is shown to have rescued her father from the
psychological trauma induced by his imprisonment in the Bastille, and
she continues to fulfil this function in the wake of her marriage to Charles
Darnay, 'Ever busily winding the golden thread that bound them all
together, weaving the service of her happy influence through the tissue of all
their lives' (257). Her role at the centre of the home, winding the thread of
domestic harmony and cohesion, obviously sets her in contrast with Madame
Defarge, whose activities and attitudes fracture the family. However, while
the representation of the domestic ideal in Victorian culture depends upon
the supervision of the home exercised by the Angel at its centre, it also
requires the support of an appropriate personification of manhood, one
who will manifest the virtues of industry and self-reliance necessary for the
achievement of middle-class independence and respectability. As Leonore
Davidoff and Catherine Hall have shown, the concept of occupation became
an integral part of masculine identity in the nineteenth century, requiring
middle-class men to wrest economic independence and public status away
from the personal ties of dependency involved in the performance of service
for a patron.[24] The emerging concept of middle-class manhood was thus
implicated in the shift to a less paternalistic social order in which domesticity
would become the dominant definition of the family. In *A Tale of Two Cities*,
the ideal of domesticity Lucie embodies is thus appropriately complemented
by her marriage to a self-made man. Charles Darnay's subscription to the
values of middle-class self-making is clearly indicated in the description
of his employment as 'a higher teacher of the French language' (155) in
England. He shows 'great perseverance and untiring industry' (155), and as

a result, he prospers. Samuel Smiles's *Self-Help* was published in the same year as *A Tale of Two Cities*; and Charles Darnay embodies its ideal of the self-made man who achieves success through his diligence and thrift. He holds a 'new philosophy', one that is based upon a distaste for aristocratic privilege and a belief in individual effort. While his uncle preaches 'repression' as 'the only lasting philosophy' (146), Charles renounces his heritage and embraces England and the doctrine of middle-class self-making instead.

A *Tale of Two Cities* recalls another historical novel, Thackeray's *The History of Henry Esmond* (1852), in its record of a historical shift in the form of the family, from the portrait of a rakish French aristocratic 'race' to the emergence of an English middle-class domestic circle. Like Henry Esmond, who renounces his title once his identity as the legitimate heir of the Castlewoods is known, and marries the woman who has embodied the values of middle-class domesticity throughout the novel, Charles Darnay relinquishes the Marquisate, withdraws to England and marries a domestic Angel. When he returns temporarily to France in Book the Second, chapter IX, the remonstrance made to his uncle opposes bourgeois to aristocratic conceptions of the family. The Marquis St Evrémonde stands for the 'grandeur of the family' (146), receiving the 'dark deference of fear and slavery' deplored by his nephew as a compliment to its greatness. When Charles bitterly attributes his freedom to the disgrace which has kept his uncle from obtaining a 'letter *de cachet*', the Marquis excuses these notorious documents as 'little instruments of correction, ... gentle aids to the power and honour of families' (145).

In his analysis of the historical movement from a government *of* families to a government *through* the family in the development of social discipline during the eighteenth and the nineteenth centuries, Jacques Donzelot explains the role played by the practice of *lettres de cachet*. Under the *ancien régime*, he argues, social power was exercised through a collaboration between the state administration and families, thus effecting a direct insertion of the family into the political sphere:

> The notorious *lettres de cachet de famille* derived their significance from this regulated exchange of obligations and protections between the public agencies and family authority, playing alternately on the menace to public order constituted by an individual who had broken with religion and morality, and on the threat to the family interest posed by the disobedient acts of one of its members.[25]

The taking of the Bastille, where many of those detained through the procedure of *lettres de cachet* were confined, marks for Donzelot the symbolic

destruction *par excellence* of the old government of families.[26] It ushered in a
new form of family that was regulated internally by moral norms, providing a
more flexible organisation of ties and obligations than was available under the
old juridical regime. In other words, the outlawing of the practice of *lettres
de cachet* was an integral part of the historical transformation of the family
as a mechanism of social discipline. As a supporter of the system of *lettres
de cachet*—of the 'manner in which the family has sustained its grandeur'
(146)—the Marquis clings to an older form of family authority. But Charles's
conception of the 'honour' of the family is quite different:

> '[Death] has left me,' answered the nephew, 'bound to a system
> that is frightful to me, responsible for it, but powerless in it;
> seeking to execute the last request of my dear mother's lips, and
> obey the last look of my dear mother's eyes, which implored me
> to have mercy and to redress; and tortured by seeking assistance
> and power in vain.' (147–8)

Charles's dedication to discharging the sacred trust of the dead Marquise
expresses a middle-class worship of motherhood. The holiness of a woman's
function as mother was a central tenet of the ideology of domesticity, as the
thrashing delivered by the normally passive Oliver Twist to the cringing
Noah Claypole in chapter VI of *Oliver Twist* makes clear. Charles Darnay's
devotion to this middle-class ideal leads him to renounce France and the
Marquisate, to anglicise his name, and to practise the virtues of self-making
in his adopted country. His determination shows the shaping force of the
middle-class family already at work in the construction of gender in the
narrative, providing the norms against which aristocratic deviance and excess
can be evaluated. And of course it is precisely by assuming such ground that
the ascendancy of the middle classes is represented.

As a result of his mother's injunction to repair class conflict, Charles
Darnay forms a new middle-class family in England. But this form of family
is threatened when the Revolution breaks out by the many invasions and
public expositions of the private that are part of its progress. Doctor Manette
is put on show 'to a chosen few' by Monsieur Defarge (43), and Lucie is
later brought before Madame Defarge under the pretence that Madame
'wishes to see those whom she has the power to protect at [turbulent] times,
to the end that she may know them—that she may identify them' (327).
The Revolution is characterised by images of the gaze: Madame Defarge
always 'looks steadily', the Gorgon's Head surveys the château of Monsieur
the Marquis, and a 'universal watchfulness' encompasses Charles on his
return to France. Moreover, it is an ordinance of the Republic that on the

door of every house the names of its inmates must be inscribed (356). This exposure of the domestic and private to public gaze adds to the more explicit assaults upon the middle-class family made by the Revolution. A parody of the ideal of family unity is presented in the wood-sawyer's grim imitation of La Guillotine, cutting off the heads of 'All the family!' (341). Similarly, the judgment of the President overseeing the Paris Tribunal before which Charles is brought in Book the Third, chapter X, is a grotesque elevation of patriotic over paternal feeling. Fearful for the loss of his own head, he rules that Doctor Manette 'would doubtless feel a sacred glow and joy in making his daughter a widow and her child an orphan' in order to root out 'an obnoxious family of Aristocrats' (411).

The comment of the President brings into focus the opposition between the domestic and the genealogical family that constitutes Doctor Manette's dilemma. The personal history he writes and conceals in his Bastille cell provides the explanation of the events which drive the novel's plot, and it contains a solemn denunciation of the Evrémondes, 'them and their descendents, to the last of their race' (410). The memorial unwittingly implicates him in the dominance of the very regime he would seek to overthrow, by affirming the power of lineage. His obsession with the 'race' resembles Madame Defarge's capitulation to the metaphysics of blood. This surrender to the aristocratic principle of genealogy is brought into conflict with the wish to save his son-in-law in the narrative. Newly formed bonds of affection and devotedness are set against blood-ties, as the Doctor struggles to assert the value of the roles and relationships of the domestic family over the facts of consanguinity. He fails in this effort, and it is left to Sydney Carton to save Charles Darnay and defend the ideals of the middle-class family.

At first sight, Sydney Carton seems an unlikely figure to be associated with the defence of the middle-class family. In many ways, he stands outside the domestic sphere in the novel and calls it into question. His marginal position is suggested early on in Book the Second, chapter IV, when Carton remains aloof from the 'congratulatory' group gathered around the acquitted Darnay: 'Another person, who had not joined the group, or interchanged a word with any one of them, but who had been leaning against the wall where its shadow was darkest, had silently strolled out after the rest, and had looked on until the coach drove away' (94–5). His anonymity and association with the shadows here combine with Carton's subsequent characterisation as a 'self-flung away, wasted, drunken, poor creature of misuse' (181) to set him outside the domestic circle. While Lucie strives to use her influence to 'save' and 'recall' him 'to a better course', his 'fixed despair of himself' (181) defeats her. Revealing the limits to the redeeming power of the domestic

Angel, Carton embodies something of the transgressive desire that is evident elsewhere in Dickens's fascination with ambivalent figures like Steerforth or Eugene Wrayburn, who also pose a threat to the family. Physically similar to Charles Darnay, the two are opposed in terms of personality and character, and look forward to other pairings such as Pip and Orlick in *Great Expectations* or Wrayburn and Headstone in *Our Mutual Friend*.[27] Dickens's strong identification with the alienation and self-division that Carton represents is indicated by his passion for playing the role of Richard Wardour in the Wilkie Collins's play, *The Frozen Deep*, which gave him the 'main idea' for his story. As he writes in the Preface of this idea and its shaping: 'Throughout its execution, it has had the complete possession of me; I have so far verified what is done and suffered in these pages, as that I have certainly done and suffered it all myself' (xxvii). Richard Wardour is the rejected suitor who dies in the arms of the woman he still loves at the end of the play after saving the life of his rival. This moment of consummation is matched in the novel by the 'confidence' Carton reposes in Lucie on the single occasion when he opens his heart to her in Book the Second, chapter XII—a confidence that is not shared with her husband, but that is licensed by the impossibility of her ever returning Carton's love.

Carton's marginal relation to the middle-class family would seem to call its efficacy into question. While he acknowledges the good influence of Lucie's domestic devotion—'I have not been so degraded but that the sight of you with your father, and of this home made such a home by you, has stirred old shadows that I thought had died out of me'—his love for her remains ineffectual, described as a fire 'inseparable in its nature from myself, quickening nothing, lighting nothing, doing no service, idly burning away' (182). Not even the loving compassion of a domestic Angel is enough to restore his bitterly divided self. He asks the newly married Darnay for permission 'to come and go as a privileged person here; that I might be regarded as an useless ... piece of furniture, tolerated for its old service, and taken no notice of' (253) and he remains a disengaged observer throughout, despite the 'strange sympathy' Lucie's children have with him (258). While his final sacrifice asserts the transcendent value of his complete devotion to Lucie, it also expresses his profound alienation and his conviction, grimly put to Stryver in Book the Second, chapter XI, 'I have no business to be, at all, that I know of' (167). However, it is precisely because he *cannot* be domesticated that Carton is available to sacrifice himself and therefore ensure the survival of Darnay's family. Ironically, the triumph of the representative middle-class family is secured through an instance of its own failure.

Notwithstanding Carton's self-estrangement and alienation, however, he also assists in reaffirming the dominance of domestic ideology, for the fact that two such different men as Carton and Darnay, constituting opposed sides of a single ego, can take the same woman as their object of desire, demonstrates the unifying power of the domestic woman in Victorian culture. Nancy Armstrong has analysed the function of the domestic woman as a figure used to establish horizontal connections between the members of a heterogeneous economic group by embodying a norm—a figure used 'to generate the belief that there was such a thing as a middle class with clearly established affiliations before it actually existed'.[28] In *A Tale of Two Cities*, the rivalry between Carton and Darnay for the love of Lucie strengthens the authority of the ideal she represents by demonstrating its ability to attract and accommodate such diverse desiring subjects.

Furthermore, Carton's scheme of self-sacrifice stems from a notion of family and identity that depends upon the ideology of domesticity, rather than blood-relatedness—not simply because it is done for the love of Lucie, but because it is an endorsement of *surrogate* familial relationships. The genealogical family does not concern itself with the provision of substitute kin. Its interest is in blood-ties, rather than surrogate relationships. In contrast, the domestic ideal is preoccupied with the fulfilment of familial roles and duties, whether these coincide with the relations of consanguinity or not. According to this ideal, the provision of fatherly and motherly care, for example, is of far greater importance than the facts of blood-relatedness, and Carton's sacrifice ratifies this principle of familial substitution. The narrator's record of his final words offers a vision of a new kind of lineage based not on blood, but on commemoration of his devotion to Lucie and all that she represents. The name that is passed on to subsequent generations is the Christian name, rather than the patronymic, and the story that is told to the child who bears this name continues the translation of public into private history begun by Dickens's novel.

The sacrifice of Sydney Carton closes the narrative. Dickens would seem to have epitomised the progress of the French Revolution in the story of the Evrémondes and Defarges in order to draw the oft-quoted moral, which opens the concluding chapter, concerning the dire consequences of 'crush[ing] humanity out of shape' (459). History is shown to unfold causally in his narrative, and its effects are traced through the representation of the family. The novel finds an exemplary impetus for the Revolution in the practice of *droit de seigneur*. As the Evrémonde brothers violate the family of Madame Defarge, they sow the seeds of a violent harvest. In turn, the overthrow of the *ancien régime* threatens to fracture the family of Lucie and Charles.

Dickens manages the turmoil of the French Revolution by its gradual identification with the activity of Madame Defarge and her knitting sisters throughout the narrative. Revolutionary violence becomes an exhibition of female deviance. By constructing the desires of the revolutionaries as transgressive of gender, the novel apparently makes them 'other' and clears a safe space for the English middle-class subject. This strategy of displacement and denial is part of a normalising technique which enables the reproduction of respectable femininity and domesticity as the mutually authorising and dominant definitions of female identity and the family. However, at the same time, the use of a male omniscient narrator to gender the Revolution makes the instability of this rhetorical and ideological strategy apparent. The figures of female deviance with which the Revolution is identified threaten to exercise an allure that would undermine the project of narrative containment they ostensibly enable. The narrator's denunciation of the revolutionary mob remains haunted by a fascination with its frenzied forms of power. The feminisation of the French Revolution is thus not an unequivocal strategy of consolation, for this narrative gesture is inhabited by the kind of unruly desires it would seek to restrain and exclude.

NOTES

1. Quoted by Forster, *Life*, vol. II, p. 281.

2. *Ibid.*, p. 282.

3. Albert D. Hutter, 'Nation and Generation in *A Tale of Two Cities*', *PMLA* 93 (1978), 448.

4. Georg Lukács, *The Historical Novel*, trans. Hannah and Stanley Mitchell (London: Merlin, 1962), p. 243.

5. *A Tale of Two Cities* was serialised without illustrations in *All The Year Round* from April to November 1859, but appeared simultaneously in monthly numbers from June to December 1859, illustrated by Browne.

6. *A Tale of Two Cities*, ed. Andrew Sanders, The World's Classics (Oxford University Press, 1988), p. 481 n. 37.

7. For a discussion of Dickens's use of doubles to define the innocence of his own omniscient activity, see Catherine Gallagher's essay, 'The Duplicity of Doubling in *A Tale of Two Cities*', in *Dickens Studies Annual*, ed. Michael Timko, Fred Kaplan and Edward Guiliano, vol. xii (New York: AMS Press, 1983), pp. 125–145.

8. LADY MACBETH:

> I would while it was smiling in my face
> Have plucked my nipple from his boneless gums
> And dashed the brains out, had I so sworn as you
> Have done to this. (I. vii. 56–8)

9. For a discussion of the imagery of natural catastrophe in the novel, see Kurt Tetzeli Von Rosador, 'Metaphorical Representations of the French Revolution in Victorian Fiction', *Nineteenth-Century Literature* 43 (1988), 1–23.

10. For a classic study of the maleness of reason in philosophy, see Genevieve Lloyd, *The Man of Reason: 'Male' and 'Female' in Western Philosophy*, 2nd edn (London: Routledge, 1993).

11. Jane Rendall, *The Origins of Modern Feminism: Women in Britain, France and the United States 1780–1860*, Themes in Comparative History (London: Macmillan, 1985) p. 47.

12. Sir Henry Dickens, *The Recollections of Sir Henry Dickens, K.C.* (London, 1934), p. 54. Quoted in Martin Meisel, 'Miss Havisham Brought to Book', *PMLA* 81 (June 1966), 281.

13. Lee Sterrenburg, 'Psychoanalysis and the Iconography of Revolution', *Victorian Studies* 19 (1975), 241–64.

14. Sanders, ed., *A Tale of Two Cities*, p. 511 n. 321.

15. As John Carey has observed, 'Dickens, who saw himself as the great prophet of cosy, domestic virtue, purveyor of improving literature to the middle classes, never seems to have quite reconciled himself to the fact that violence and destruction were the most powerful stimulants to his imagination', *The Violent Effigy: A Study of Dickens' Imagination* (1973; London: Faber, 1979), p. 16.

16. For a psychoanalytic account of the links between erotic and political attitudes in the representation of the 1848 Revolution and the Commune, see Neil Hertz, 'Medusa's Head: Male Hysteria under Political Pressure', *Representations* 4 (1983), 27–54.

17. Thomas Carlyle, *The French Revolution: A History*, ed. J. Holland Rose, 3 vols. (1837; London: G. Bell and Sons, 1913), vol. 1, p. 160.

18. Harriet Ritvo, *The Animal Estate: The English and Other Creatures in the Victorian Age* (1987; Harmondsworth: Penguin, 1990), p. 28. The fascination of the British public with tiger attacks led the East India Company to put a mechanical model of a tiger eating an Englishman on display at its London offices in 1800, where it drew large crowds for several generations.

19. See Rendall's description of the activities of these eighteenth-century French feminists. Rendall, *Origins of Modern Feminism*, p. 49.

20. Hutter, 'Nation and Generation', 457.

21. George Woodcock, Introduction, *A Tale of Two Cities*, by Charles Dickens, Penguin English Library (1859; Harmondsworth: Penguin, 1970), p. 21.

22. Slater, *Dickens and Women*, pp. 210–11.

23. Ruskin, 'Of Queens' Gardens', p. 74.

24. Davidoff and Hall note that 'Male domestic servants were the last category of men to be enfranchised and were banished from organizations such as the Freemasons who were concerned to establish bases for independence as alternatives to paternalistic hierarchies.' Davidoff and Hall, *Family Fortunes*, p. 199.

25. Donzelot, *Policing of Families*, pp. 49–50.

26. *Ibid.*, p. 51.

27. See also Hutter, 'Nation and Generation'. Hutter has analysed the relationship between the rival lovers in *A Tale of Two Cities* in psychoanalytic terms, showing how Sydney Carton functions as a double for Charles Darnay by enacting one side of his character.

28. Armstrong, *Desire and Domestic Fiction*, p. 66.

BARBARA BLACK

A Sisterhood of Rage and Beauty: Dickens' Rosa Dartle, Miss Wade, and Madame Defarge

> But [Polly] was a good plain sample of a nature that is ever, in the mass,
> better, truer, higher, nobler, quicker to feel, and much more constant to
> retain, all tenderness and pity, self-denial and devotion, than the nature
> of men.
>
> —*Dombey and Son* (27)

Any discussion of Dickens and his female characters must confront the
great faith he places upon women in his novels. His interest in the domestic
sublime—that elevation of the home fundamental to the separate spheres
of Victorian gender configuration—leads consequently to an apotheosis
of women. As the genii of the hearth, women are ready moral agents
able to resurrect and repair the many men of their lives—father, brother,
employer—who journey out into the world and are tainted by it. Dickens'
belief in women's potential for good is evident in the characteristic statement
above from *Dombey and Son*. Here Dickens describes women as "better, truer,
higher, nobler, quicker to feel" than men. Dickensian women are virtuous
in their capacity for service to others, in their "self-denial and devotion." It
seems that Dickens' conceptions of femininity are hardly complex and offer
little challenge to the critical commonplace of the Victorian angel in the
house. For like his favorite child and favorite self, David, Dickens would wish
for every man an Agnes as the reward for life's arduous peregrinations.

From *Dickens Studies Annual* 26 (1998): pp. 91–106. © 1998 by AMS Press.

And yet alongside this feminine ideal lies an uneasy and unsettling connection between women and violence in Dickens' novels. Dickens depicts men violating women, women who do violence to others, and women who violate and mutilate themselves. Explicit violence exists often in the novel's periphery, in fleeting suggestions concerning tertiary characters such as the woman in the police station in *Our Mutual Friend* "who was banging herself with increased violence, and shrieking most terrifically for some other woman's liver" (67). An examination of female violence in the Dickens corpus, moreover, uncovers the rage that seethes beneath the surface of many of Dickens' most famous, mild heroines. Nascently violent, Florence Dombey represses the death-wishes she feels for her father; finally violated, she shuns her own breast branded by "the darkening mark of an angry hand" (680). In reading Little Dorrit's life, we come to understand the harsher implications of the equation above from *Dombey and Son*: For women, "devotion" and "self-denial" are synonymous. Amy's commitment to the ideal of service involves the affliction of unshod feet and the punishment of a malnutrition that verges on anorexia. Even Esther, whom many readers embrace as the genuine voice of a sincere discourse and who is saved from explicit violence by Hortense's function in the novel, speaks a language churning with rage:

> [H]ow often had I considered within myself that the deep traces of my illness, and the circumstances of my birth, were only new reasons why I should be busy, busy, busy.... So I went about the house, humming all the tunes I knew; and I sat working and working in a desperate manner, and I talked and talked, morning, noon, and night. (612, 686)

The rhythms of this passage suggest that Esther's function as a "pattern" is *for her* far less congenial than it is compulsive, debilitating, and "desperate." Although Edmund Wilson contrasts Esther, whom he calls the "sweet and submissive illegitimate daughter" with Miss Wade, the "embittered and perverse illegitimate daughter" (53), Esther shares with Miss Wade a peculiarly female rage. Her dutiful housewifery, symptomatic of the pain she feels in her own mutilated face, maps out a radically different pattern: Out of victimization emerges the potential for rage.

From the extensive ranks of Dickens' violent women, then, I have chosen to discuss three particularly resonant female characters in the Dickens ouevre: Rosa Dartle, Miss Wade, and Madame Defarge. They are intriguing, in part, because relatively little has been written about them.[1] In *The Triumph of the Novel*, for example, Albert Guerard discounts the significance of Miss Wade for "she occupies relatively few pages" (41). And Nina Auerbach's treatment of *David Copperfield* in *Woman and the Demon*, despite its promising title, focuses on the angelic Agnes, locating the demonic as the exclusive property of the utterly masculine Steerforth. But these characters further intrigue because they defy standard categorizing of Dickens' women into groups such as "heroines," "old maids," "shrews," "adventuresses," and "new women."[2] I have joined Rosa, Miss Wade, and Madame Defarge in a sisterhood because they share two qualities: rage and beauty. As enraged yet beautiful women, Rosa, Miss Wade, and Madame Defarge are doubly passionate and thus doubly threatening to Dickens, his narrators, and his novels. Their rage cannot be dismissed as geriatric like that of Mr. F's aunt in *Little Dorrit* and Mrs. Sparsit in *Hard Times* nor defused through caricature like that of Mrs. Joe in *Great Expectations* or Miss Nipper in *Dombey and Son* nor contained as lower-class like that of Hortense or Molly in *Great Expectations*. Instead, time and again, their characters are centers of attraction—and distraction—for Dickens' imagination;[3] and, thus, they risk becoming the unruly presence in the text, the fissure in the narrative that escapes narratorial control.

This study has been inspired by something I have long known: Rosa has an unforgettable face. When I last taught *David Copperfield*, Rosa monopolized the class's final discussions, for students felt duly haunted by a suspicion that Dickens, although the master of wrap-up endings, had far from mastered her. In similar fashion, Michael Slater writes of Miss Wade: she is a "vital creation, who stays in the reader's mind long after the minor role she plays in the novel's intricate plot has been forgotten" (269). Time and again, readers seem to sense what too many scholars have often neglected: the narrative gaze's relentless pursuit of these enraged beauties and the questions that pursuit raises—questions of gender, body, and voice or narrative. Striking as both physical and textual presences in their novels, Rosa, Miss Wade, and Madame Defarge represent what Peter Brooks in *Body Work* calls the "semioticization of body" and "somatization of story" central to nineteenth-century realism (xii). In these characters the body, the word, as well as the psyche intersect; here Dickens anticipates Freud's attempts to read the psychic as it is inscribed upon the body. Somatic voices, marked and signifying bodies—such inscriptions expose not only the buried lives of imagined women but also the psychic traces of a male authorial imagination. As we read, we realize that we do not forget these characters because Dickens cannot. The undocile sisters of Freud's Dora, Rosa, Miss Wade, and Madame Defarge challenge the mid-Victorian ideal of female passionlessness and look forward instead to fin de siecle representations of women, to the late-Victorian fascination with female monsters and monstrous femininity, and to Freud's explorations into hysteria and into the connections between repression and expression. As Peter Gay argues in his recent revisionist portrait of the nineteenth century, *The Cultivation of Hatred*, rage and aggression for the Victorians wore a familiar and attractive face.[4]

While few readers will deny these characters their rage, some indeed overlook their beauty. For example, Slater contrasts the "beautiful and spirited" Estella and Bella with Madame Defarge whom he groups with Miss Havisham as the "two grim older women" (277); however, Defarge is the same age as Rosa, thirty years old, and only slightly older than Miss Wade, who is twenty-six. To underscore their attractiveness Dickens introduces these characters in voyeuristic moments. In fact, rarely do we encounter Rosa, Miss Wade, and Madame Defarge without a voyeur present: Equipped with the feminine quality Laura Mulvey calls "to-be-looked-at-ness" (19), they function to be watched, and their scenes are intensely visual. For David, Rosa's mesmeric charm conjures up a sexual fantasy—"The air of wicked grace: of triumph, in which, strange to say, there was yet something feminine and alluring ... worthy of a cruel Princess in a Legend" (563). And in presenting Madame Defarge, Dickens repeatedly foregrounds her body, detailing her clothes and what lies underneath: the knife in her girdle, the heart under her "rough robe," the loaded pistol "lying hidden in her bosom," and the sharpened dagger "lying hidden at her waist." Lingering over her robe, the narrator observes, "Carelessly worn, it was a becoming robe enough, in a certain weird way, and her dark hair looked rich under her coarse red cap" (391). Dickens' striking choice of the word "weird" here is much like Freud's *unheimlich* as indicative of something alluring yet frightening, familiar yet strange and indefinable.[5] Here the eroticism of the strange upholds Barthes's sense of narrative as striptease, especially in the succeeding lines when the narrator imaginatively unwraps Madame Defarge's clothes and lays bare her Amazonian, primal fleshliness, "bare-foot and bare-legged, on the brown sea-sand" (391). Such description gives the lie to Slater's insistence on the "virtual absence in Dickens' fiction of any descriptions of female beauty below neck-level" (359).

Rosa and Miss Wade enter their respective texts in the act of mesmerizing Dickens' narrators. Here the sheer abundance of detail indicates the narrators' fascination; the dilatory description suggests the narrators' erotic surge:

> There was a second lady in the dining-room, of a slight short figure, dark, and not agreeable to look at, but with some appearance of good looks too, who attracted my attention: perhaps because I had not expected to see her; perhaps because I found myself sitting opposite to her; perhaps because of something really remarkable in her.... She was a little dilapidated—like a

house—with having been so long to let; yet had, as I have said, an appearance of good looks. (251)

The shadow in which she sat, falling like a gloomy veil over her forehead, accorded very well with the character of her beauty. One can hardly see the face, so still and scornful, set off by the arched dark eyebrows, and the folds of dark hair, without wondering what its expression would be if a change came over it. That it could soften or relent, appeared next to impossible. That it could deepen into anger or any extreme of defiance, and that it must change in that direction when it changed at all, would have been its peculiar impression upon most observers.... Although not an open face, there was no pretence in it. I am self-contained and self-reliant ... this it said plainly. It said so in the proud eyes, in the lifted nostril, in the handsome, but compressed and even cruel mouth. (23)

Both introductions present the image of sexualized femininity, its seizure by the "phallic gaze,"[6] and the heightened pleasure afforded the gazer when beauty is linked with pain. Throughout *Little Dorrit*, the narrative focus seems unable to relinquish the erotics of pain as it gazes upon Miss Wade, who, as the self-tormentor, is a body in pain explicitly and, later, doubly so through Tattycoram's mirroring of her: "It was wonderful to see the fury of the contest in the girl, and the bodily struggle she made as if she were rent by the Demons of old" (25). In *David Copperfield*, Rosa Dartle's scar keeps the observer ever aware of the presence of pain; from it, David "could not dissociate the idea of pain" (367). In short, David cannot stop talking about Rosa's disfigurement:

[A]nd [she] had a scar upon her lip. It was an old scar—I should rather call it, seam, for it was not discolored, and had healed years ago—which had once cut through her mouth, downward towards the chin, but was now barely visible across the table, except above and on her upper lip, the shape of which it had altered. (251)

In her passion, a passion "killing her by inches" (673), in what David calls "an eagerness that seemed enough to consume her like a fire" (367), a rage that "might tear her within" (606), Rosa's scar becomes enlarged and swollen: "I saw her face grow sharper and paler, and the marks of the old wound lengthen out until it cut through the disfigured lip, and deep into the nether lip, and slanted down the face" (366). Rosa's scar is a grotesque erogenous zone that is simultaneously the site of her pain. And, although David finds the wound horrifying—"There was something positively awful to me in this" (367)—the scar fascinates him—"I could not help glancing at the scar with a painful interest when we went in to tea" (253). As an image for the female genitalia, for a wounded sexuality or for a sexuality that is little else than pain, Rosa's scar attracts and repels male fascination. For David, Rosa seems "to pervade the whole house"; he is expectant of her approaching, crushing anatomy—"I heard her dress rustle ... I saw her face pass.... she closed her thin hand on my arm like a spring, to keep me back" (366).

Such spectacular, specular bodies in pain lead to the gazer's eventual stupefaction.[7] This surprising turn is apparent from the start when, in introducing Rosa, David betrays his own nervousness about the indefinability yet certainty of her appeal. Now the dilatory expression of Rosa's introduction seems more like stammering when David confesses that the sight of her is both agreeable and disagreeable; she is "perhaps" this, "perhaps" that, "perhaps," most truthfully, "remarkable." So too is Mr. Meagles captivated yet confused by Miss Wade. We are told "Mr. Meagles stared at her under a sort of fascination" (319), surveying this "handsome young Englishwoman" with a "puzzled look" and confessing "that you were a mystery to all of us.... I don't know what you are" (323)—a sentiment Clennam later echoes with "I know nothing of her" (523). The inscrutable and erotic most clearly merge in the details of Miss Wade's introduction: the shadow, the dark tresses, and especially Dickens' synecdochic use of the veil. When Dickens uses this motif again to describe Miss Wade's "composure itself (as a veil will suggest the form it covers) [intimating] the unquenchable passion of her own nature" (319), the narrative again turns striptease, energized by the erotics of concealment. Yet we have also confronted the incomprehensible femininity that threatens to disable the male gaze.

Rosa, Miss Wade, and Madame Defarge present an instability in the text because they are objects of the gaze that aspire to be themselves gazing subjects. Such a battle over the gaze ensues when, for example, David spends the night at Highgate only to find Rosa's likeness "looking eagerly at [him] from above the chimney-piece" in his room (255). Here her presence forces him to continue to look and submit to being looked at himself. Indeed, he is compelled to correct the painter's omission and to see the face as he must see it in life, with scar intact. Even in the darkness afforded by night and sleep, he knows that her gaze remains vigilant, chasing him in his dreams. As the novel progresses, David's chronic watching comes to resemble something more like hypnosis, and we wonder who, after all, is watching whom:

> But what I particularly observed, before I had been half-an-hour
> in the house, was the close and attentive watch Miss Dartle kept

upon me.... So surely as I looked towards her, did I see that eager visage, with its gaunt black eyes and searching brow, intent on mine.... In this lynx-like scrutiny she was so far from faltering when she saw I observed it, that ... I shrunk before her strange eyes, quite unable to endure their hungry lustre. (365–66)

And yet he suffers the sight of Rosa constantly; later in the same chapter we witness through David's eyes and ears Rosa's music-playing:

I don't know what it was, in her touch or voice, that made that song the most unearthly I have ever heard in my life, or can imagine. There was something fearful in the reality of it. It was as if it had never been written, or set to music, but sprung out of the passion within her; which found imperfect utterance in the low sounds of her voice ... I was dumb when she leaned beside the harp again. (369)

For David, Rosa's allure renders a crisis in meaning, evident in the phrases "I don't know" and "I was dumb," in the vague term "something," and in the use of the subjunctive in the third sentence.

It is curious that David's dreams at Highgate are dreams of language in which Rosa's voice seizes control of his tongue—"I found that I was uneasily asking all sorts of people in my dreams whether it really was or not—without knowing what I meant" (255). Both Rosa's dream-conjuring and harp-playing are only two of the numerous scenes of articulation in which these women use their rage to generate alternative voices of protest, voices that arrest the male eye and silence the dominant discourse. Bodily expressions of rage—Rosa's scar, Miss Wade's striking of her breast and seizure of Tattycoram—are the overt, anatomical manifestation of a psyche in pain; however, rage for these women also manifests itself as voice. Miss Wade's tale within the tale, her "History of a Self-Tormentor," is certainly a striking instance of rage grown articulate. Interrupting the novel with her own tale, Miss Wade shows how these characters, in body and in voice, repeatedly disrupt the narrative, taking it in new directions—not only in what they say (which I will turn to later) but also in how they say it, in the subversive ways they use language. For example, both Miss Wade and Rosa are deft at using irony to learn as well as to reproach. And Rosa's greatest rhetorical strategy is her use of indirection: "It appeared to me that she never said anything she wanted to say, outright; but hinted it, and made a great deal more of it by this practice" (251). Even to the disadvantage of his beloved Steerforth, David attributes to Rosa a sharpness, a cleverness: "Miss Dartle insinuated in the same way: sometimes, I could not conceal from myself, with great power, though in contradiction even of Steerforth" (252). Such an utterance as Rosa's "That sort of people.—Are they really animals and clods, and beings of another order?" underscores the dark ramifications of Steerforth's charms (252). Through sarcasm and irony, through being "all edge" and a "grindstone," Rosa offers an alternative voice critical of Steerforth, one that exposes his indifference and cruelty long before any other voice in the novel can—if, indeed, it ever can.[8]

As the wound that cuts through her mouth, Rosa's scar physicalizes the linguistic "edge" she wins through her tortured discourse of insinuation. So, too, in turn does Dickens' use of linguistic imagery to describe her scar reinforce the conflation of Rosa's passion, pain, and body with her language. The instrument of her speech is the locus of her pain is the space of her arousal:

> I observed that [the scar] was the most susceptible part of her face, and that, when she turned pale, that mark altered first, and became a dull, lead-colored streak, lengthening out to its full extent, like a mark in invisible ink brought to the fire.... I saw it start forth like the old writing on the wall. (253)

In fact, Rosa's entire body becomes a semiotic tissue:

> The mere vehemence of her words can convey, I am sensible, but a weak impression of the passion by which she was possessed, and which made itself *articulate* in her whole figure. (400, my emphasis)

Time and again, voice and body come together for Rosa, whether it be in the moment of playing harp music that appears to usher forth from her body rather than her instrument or when she seems to caress the very words of Littimer's report on Steerforth (564). Such an articulate body supports contemporary feminist theory's claim for the intimate connections between pain and women's discourse. Elaine Scarry in *The Body in Pain* argues more broadly that "the story of expressing physical pain eventually opens into the wider frame of invention" (22). And specifically about Brontë's *Villette*, Rachel Brownstein writes, "The language of Lucy Snowe [is] the language of the sensual self that has been denied expression and has acquired, in consequence, strange new energies that can transform conventional signs" (62).

Madame Defarge's knitted register, the creation of her ability to "transform conventional signs" into "her own stitches and her own symbols," is another image of voice, here expressing the counterforce of Revolution: "It would be easier for the weakest poltroon that lives, to erase himself from existence, than to erase one letter of his name or crimes from the knitted register of Madame Defarge" (202). Out of her clothes Madame Defarge constructs symbols, such as the "rose in her headdress" and the pattern she picks out on her sleeve. As other women join Defarge in her work, knitting becomes the novel's central image, symbolic of the Revolution in its inception: "So much was closing in about the women who sat knitting, knitting, that they their very selves were closing in around a structure yet unbuilt, where they were to sit knitting, knitting, counting dropping heads" (216). And this work comes from pain—"The fingers of the knitting women were vicious, with the experience that they could tear" (250–51); their knitting, we learn, is a displacement for their hunger (215). Always at work, Madame Defarge is an author of "shrouds," a maker of "portraits," and her masterpiece is a script concerned with the payment of old, aristocratic debts (imaged in the counting of money and tabulation of accounts).[9]

But it is her body and her gender themselves that make Madame Defarge the most eloquent figure in *A Tale of Two Cities*, contrary to Slater's following dismissal of her:

> Her vitality derives from one totally dominating passion.... We know all about her, once we have understood this, and never feel in the way she is presented that there is any transcending of the immediate requirements of the story. The figure of this implacable knitting woman does not come to seem symbolic of some aspect of human experience or the human condition. (291)

The embodiment of life under the Terror, Defarge is an image of political desire and class fear that horrifies because she provokes in Dickens and his narrator a more primal sexual desire and fear. Madame Defarge holds for the narrator the "terrible attraction" that Paris holds for Darnay. Identifying Madame Defarge's beauty as "that kind of beauty which not only seems to impart to its possessor firmness and animosity, but to strike into others an instinctive recognition of those qualities" (390–91), Dickens implies, first, that Defarge's beauty endows her with rage and, second, that the observer will instinctively see the intimacy of rage with beauty. From the bloody bosom of St. Antoine to the Guillotine—"that sharp female newly-born" (282), "the great sharp female" (307)—to the Gorgon's head that turns Monsieur the Marquis's chateau to stone to the Revolutionary "men devilishly set off with spoils of women's lace and silk and ribbon" (291), Dickens feminizes the Revolution (and masculinizes the aristocracy represented by Monseigneur).

Like Carlyle in his *French Revolution* (Dickens' historical source for *A Tale of Two Cities*), Dickens is fascinated with the revolutionary women, those Carlyle calls "Menads" in his seventh book, "The Insurrection of Women." "The men," writes Dickens, "were terrible ... but, the women were a sight to chill the boldest" (252). He makes us hear "the women passionately screeching" and witness their "frenzy" as they "whirled about, striking and tearing at their own friends until they dropped into a passionate swoon" (254, 252).

In "Orgasm, Generation, and the Politics of Reproductive Biology," Thomas Laqueur calls the Revolution "the argument made in blood that mankind in all its social and cultural relations could be remade" and argues it "engendered both a new feminism and a new fear of women" (18). Dickens fears Madame Defarge and her counterpart, La Guillotine, in their power to decapitate and its symbolic and psychological equivalency, to castrate, perhaps most directly acknowledged in the chapter title "The Gorgon's Head." Defarge's ability to mutilate transfixes the narrator and appropriately serves as subject matter for the novel's most violent moment:

> [T]here was but one quite steady figure, and that was a woman's ... [she] remained immovable close to him when the long-gathering rain of stabs and blows fell heavy; was so close to him when he dropped dead under it, that, suddenly animated, she put her foot upon his neck, and with her cruel knife—long ready—hewed off his head. (249)

Lucie's failed appeals to Madame Defarge as "wife," "mother," and "sister-woman" reveal how far removed she is from the Dickensian ideal of feminine service to others; her furiously knitting hand rests impassive to Lucie's womanly kiss. When Dickens describes the Carmagnole, his vocabulary reveals his horror: he calls the dance "a fallen sport—a something, once innocent, delivered over to all devilry"; formerly "healthy" now "angering" and "bewildering," now "warped" and "perverted"; the pastime of a time of "hazard," of a "disjointed time" (307–08). Seemingly, Dickens' faith in the renovating power of the female body leads easily into his fear of the uncontrollable fecundity produced by the female body as an image for the Revolution. Madame Defarge is necessarily childless, enabling her to engage in the new, demonic type of proliferation (replete poverty and plentiful death) for which the Guillotine is responsible.

Although *David Copperfield*, *Little Dorrit*, and *A Tale of Two Cities* seem widely divergent novels, all three are definitive nineteenth-century novels in their concern with the formation as well as the potential mis-formation of identity. While *David Copperfield* is the only traditional *Bildungsroman* of the three, *Little Dorrit* tells the tale of an arrested adult protagonist finally prepared to form(ulate) his identity, and *A Tale of Two Cities* depicts the growing pains and growing concerns of a developing British empire— allegorically coded in Carton's and Darnay's struggles. According to all three texts, one of the obstacles to healthy growth is misalliance, particularly the threat of aristocratic leanings and sympathies lurking in Steerforth's "tasteful easy negligence," Clennam's family secret that cancels out forgiveness, and the French aristocracy. Against such moneyed masculinity, then, rises enraged femininity as the retributive voice, as the punisher of such dangerous tendencies. An etiology of their pain reveals that all three enraged, beautiful women share origins in dependency and rejection and/or violence at the hands of privileged males. Madame Defarge's motive for violence, we discover, is avenging her servant-class family and violated sister—"imbued from her childhood with a brooding sense of wrong, and an inveterate hatred of a class, opportunity had developed her into a tigress" (391). Discarded by Steerforth and Gowan, Rosa and Miss Wade share similarly orphaned lives of social and monetary dependency. Their social uselessness—Rosa considers herself a "mere disfigured piece of furniture"—and impoverishment are stressed time and again. As if Rosa's scar were not a sufficiently eloquent expression of her neglect, Steerforth himself imparts to David Rosa's brief life-story:

> She was the motherless child of a sort of cousin of my father's. He died one day. My mother, who was then a widow, brought her here to be company to her. She has a couple of thousand pounds of her own, and saves the interest of it every year, to add to the principal. There's the history of Miss Rosa Dartle for you. (253)

Pancks's narrative of Miss Wade's life is all too similar:

> She is somebody's child—anybody's—nobody's. Put her in a room in London here with any six people old enough to be her parents, and her parents may be there for anything she knows.... She knows nothing about 'em. She knows nothing about any relative whatever.... [Mr. Casby] has long had money (not overmuch as I make out) in trust to dole out to her when she can't do without it. (524–25)

The slimness of their lives as narrated by others, however, does not capture the potency of Rosa's irony, Miss Wade's self-penned history, and

Madame Defarge's knitted register as subversive discourses: Rosa is able to implicate David in the Steerforth/Emily tragedy, Miss Wade sharpens the pangs of guilt Arthur feels in his breast, Madame Defarge can alter political structures. They mesmerize and rage and articulate in order to punish. Their identity is a rebuff, particularly to gender and class expectations. While Lucie comforts her six-year-old child, the very next page depicts Madame Defarge sporting a pistol, resisting submission to her husband for whom she plays the catechist in aggression, stern when his appetite for violence flags. Miss Wade challenges the currency of the word "gentleman" (516), and both she and Rosa interrogate what is "natural" for women (*Little Dorrit* 22, *David Copperfield* 367–68). The visual vocabulary that describes Miss Wade's home life—the bare garden, the London and Calais flats posted with "to let" signs—is shorthand certainly for her rejection of the conventional community afforded by bourgeois family life (she lives in a house that is home to no one) and possibly for what some readers interpret as her iconoclastic choice to lead a coded lesbian existence with Tattycoram. Neither nurturers nor comforters, these stern and unforgiving females are thus freed to assault privilege in its numerous manifestations. As Miss Wade asserts in *Little Dorrit*'s opening pages, a prisoner does not forgive his prison; and, indeed, she keeps returning, a sort of choric presence in the novel, like destiny to punish the wrongs of the past. She does not let the amnesiac Clennam forget; her incriminations that force Clennam into accountability facilitate one of Dickens' key purposes for the novel, clearly stated in the novel's former title, "Nobody's Fault." So too does Madame Defarge play the part of Fate, the Furies, or—much like her lieutenant—Vengeance. Although one of her taglines is "and she saw nothing," we quickly learn that she sees everything, including prophetically that which is "inaudible and invisible" (195). Miss Wade's tagline "I understood," much like Rosa's clever appeals "to know," underscores their similar abilities to acquire and possess information that will turn out to be central to the novel's resolution. Both are figures of curiosity, blackmailers of sorts who hunt down knowledge, for Rosa pays Littimer for his words just as Miss Wade rewards Blandois for information concerning Gowan. For all three, Miss Wade makes the claim, "I have the curse to have not been born a fool," and their erotic potency is matched only by this kind of authority. They pose the riddle and hold the answer. As Helena Michie claims, "If women's bodies are written transcriptions of cultural problems, they are also, consciously or not, repositories of secret knowledge that must be processed to be understood" (120).

Although Rosa, Miss Wade, and Madame Defarge protest in order to punish the protagonists for their dangerous connections, the battle between narrated and narrator takes a final turn when these retributive voices are themselves ultimately punished. Self-avowal eventually leads to disavowal, the somatic expression of which is, again, succinctly contained in Rosa's scar. As a mark of erasure, Rosa's scar invalidates her—WOMAN or WOMAN's MOUTH—she is present in the text only to be vanquished and disappear. So too Miss Wade's "The History of a Self-Tormentor"—in one way powerful in its refusal to be assimilated—also cancels itself out to remain at best an act of self-betrayal, harmless to others and defeating to the self. Dickens' working notes for *Little Dorrit* remind him to revise in order to isolate Miss Wade's narrative, to "change this to two chapters, getting the Self-Tormentor narrative by itself" (822). The writing, thus, resides in its chapter, socially and fictionally alienated, much like its author. Miss Wade's history, "From her own point of view," does not ultimately liberate her character nor does it rescue a feminine, buried discourse; rather it is an anatomy—"Dissect it," Dickens instructs—of a perspectival disease. What begins as a feminist revision of the word "hate"—"You don't know what I mean by hating"—concludes as Miss Wade's embarrassing, purposeless self-exposure to Arthur Clennam. "Unconsciously laying bare all her character" is Dickens' plan for "Miss Wade's story"; and the resulting confession drawn from her bosom, inscribed on the papers from her bureau's inner drawer, reveals a self guilty of her own torment, a clinically drawn case study of neurosis and repression.

One by one, these voices of protest expire. What should mark Rosa's long-awaited triumph, her confrontation with Emily in Martha's London room, is in fact the beginning of her demise. This scene is one of the novel's most intensely visual scenes with abundant, if unintentional, charged references to what characters can and cannot see. Although Rosa's incrimination of Emily takes on specular shape—"I have come to see James Steerforth's fancy"—it is actually David who visually steals the scene, strategically positioned, as he is, at an aperture afforded him by a special back door.[10] In what stands as the novel's voyeuristic climax, we watch David watch Rosa gaze upon Emily:[11]

> [Her tone's] mastered rage, presented her before me, as if I had seen her standing in the light. I saw the flashing black eyes, and the passion-wasted figure; and I saw the scar, with its white track cutting through her lips, quivering and throbbing as she spoke. (604)

When Rosa attempts to strike Emily, the gesture seems purposeless—"[t]he blow, which had no aim, fell upon the air" (606). Here and elsewhere, Dickens emphasizes the purposelessness of such rage. Rosa repeatedly strikes only her own wound, and Miss Wade continually places "that repressing hand upon her own bosom." In order to limit the scope of these women's influence even further, Dickens uses doubling or coupling, most evident in Miss Wade's and Tattycoram's alliance—here, appropriately, an object of Clennam's eye:

> As each of the two handsome faces looked at the other, Clennam felt how each of the two natures must be constantly tearing the other to pieces.... Arthur Clennam looked at them, standing a little distance asunder in the dull confined room, each proudly cherishing her own anger; each, with a fixed determination, torturing her own breast, and torturing the other's. (642, 643)

In each novel, the enraged women fall at the hands of a female tribunal (purging female rage with female rage). Rosa's punishment is to endure an eternal incarceration with Mrs. Steerforth—"Thus I leave them; thus I always find them; thus they wear their time away, from year to year" (735). Miss Wade is betrayed by Tattycoram who rededicates her love for the Meagleses and bears witness against Miss Wade: "I have had Miss Wade before me all this time, as if it was my own self grown ripe—turning everything the wrong way, and twisting all good into evil" (787). And Madame Defarge dies in battle with Miss Pross, branding her killer's face with "the marks of griping fingers" (398).

So too are Dickens' texts "branded" with marks remaining to tell the story the enraged, female body tries to tell. Such textual and somatic traces locate the rupture in the text wherein lies an unstable discursive space where body, pain, and expression intersect. Signifying parts of the body—Madame Defarge's knitting hand, Miss Wade's breast, and most vividly Rosa's scarred mouth—seem to confirm both what Helena Michie argues specifically about Esther Summerson, "The body and sexuality assert themselves ... through pain and scarring. In learning to read the scars we read desire" (29), and what Peter Gay writes in his opening line of *The Cultivation of Hatred*: "The scars that aggression has left on the face of past are indelible" (3). As I have argued, Rosa, Miss Wade, and Madame Defarge attract, repel, and even stand in for Dickens' own imaginative and psychic states even though the eventual eradication of these violent females, upon whom the gaze ultimately turns hostile, will ensure the triumph of good Dickensian heroines. After completing the novel's unpleasant task of denouncing Emily as the unpalatable female and thus diffusing the threat of a rekindled childhood love for David, Rosa ushers in Agnes. Tattycoram receives a new role model into her malleable life, Amy Dorrit. She is thus able to learn the womanly lesson, for as Mr. Meagles professes, "Yet I have heard tell, Tattycoram, that [Amy's] young life has been one of active resignation, goodness, and noble service" because she always focused upon "duty" (788). And, in *A Tale of Two Cities*, the "poor little seamstress," as a reworking of the image of Madame Defarge, is the unexpected heroine. In her "work-worn, hunger-worn young fingers" (384), we see Dickens' rescue of the images of sewing, work, gender, and body.[12] As a vocational, dutiful essence, she is "girlish," "patient," self-sacrificing ("I am not unwilling to die"), "uncomplaining," enduring, "constant." On the other side of Dickens' enraged, beautiful women stands this "poor little seamstress" ready to die so that her cousin might "profit" and have a better life by it.

NOTES

1. Or little that is positive. Long ago, Forster set the trend when he identified the "curiously unpleasant" Rosa Dartle as the single flaw in an otherwise perfect novel; and in similar impatience he called the "surface-painting" of both Miss Wade and Tattycoram "anything but attractive" (II: 132, 226).

2. These categories come from Merryn Williams's *Women in the English Novel, 1800–1900*; another set can be found in Patricia Ingham's *Dickens, Women, and Language*.

3. In his chapter "Women Passing By" in *From Copyright to Copperfield: The Identity of Dickens*, Alexander Welsh analyzes the ways in which *David Copperfield* "stresses 'woman'" (124), citing how "much energy in *Copperfield* is expended in positioning the hero with respect to the women in his life" (129). Welsh continues, "All this positioning in respect to women ... represents most of the work in plotting the novel; the men in this personal history, even Steerforth, fall more readily in and out of place." Of course, almost as provocative is the chapter's title itself, with its implied visual exchange; I disagree only with Welsh's sense that, as in the case of Emily and David, when women pass by in *David Copperfield* males "try ... **not** to look" (131).

4. A generation ago, John Carey catalogued Dickens' attraction to violence in "Dickens and Violence" from *The Violent Effigy*. When he moves from such violent forces as fire and cannibalism to the potential for human violence, however, Carey speaks exclusively of Dickens' violent men.

5. In her article "Victorian Women and Insanity," Elaine Showalter recounts Dickens' visit to St. Luke's Hospital where he found himself fascinated with the female inmates, particularly "one old-young woman, with her dishevelled long light hair, spare figure, and weird gentility" (157). Both visually and linguistically charged, this moment from Dickens' life appears to inform the fictionalized scene here.

6. This famous phrase indicates my debt to Luce Irigaray's *Speculum of the Other Woman*, even though I will go on to argue that these characters give challenge, if indeed temporarily so, to her claim that "[w]oman has no gaze, no discourse for her specific specularization" (224).

7. Of course, Freud's "The Medusa's Head" and the interpretation it has generated make such an irony far from unexpected. For example, Laura Mulvey writes, "Thus, the woman as icon, displayed for the gaze and enjoyment of men, the active controllers of the look, always threatens to evoke the anxiety it originally signified" (21).

8. Many generations of readers have noted David's love for Steerforth, which fuels his desire to identify with his affluent friend and even to become him. Yet Rosa's presence

admonishes David for such a desire, feminizing him, making him see what it is not to be the seducer but rather the seducer's victim.

9. It is not pushing the point too far to argue that these women are figures of the author. Given their way with words, given their familiarity with accounts of all kinds and, as I will later claim, accountability, Rosa, Miss Wade, and Madame Defarge are invested with the powers of authorship. Perhaps this is clearest in the case of Miss Wade, whose greatest act is the penning of an autobiographical novel in miniature, inserted in one of Dickens' own numerous autobiographically charged novels.

10. Precisely because David cannot actually see Rosa's attack but rather is able to conjure up the tableau based only on what he hears, this scene, as evident in the passage I quote, showcases his visual command of the moment. This scene is the first time in the novel that David watches Rosa without her knowledge of it or without her returning the gaze.

11. Although Welsh claims that David in this scene "stands idly by" (139), and Slater writes, "Worse still, [Dickens] determines, despite the great implausibility involved, to have David overhear the tremendous tongue-lashing that Rosa administers to Em'ly" (268), David's spectatorship here is far from idle or implausible and is, in fact, the scene's key element. As Slater later allows, this scene is for Dickens "irresistible," and such moments of irresistibility are precisely the focus of this article. In his essay "From Outrage to Rage: Dickens's Bruised Femininity," U.C. Knoepflmacher is drawn to this very scene as illustrative of Dickens' "orchestration of male and female anger," here veiling masculine anger "by displacing it onto the female" (85). Although my gloss of the precise nature of David's and Dickens' fascination for Rosa will differ from Knoepflmacher's biographical/ psychoanalytical focus on Dickens' hostility towards his mother, I relish Knoepflmacher's close examination of the subtleties of this scene.

12. A "cleansing" of the imagery is also apparent in Dickens' description of Lucie Manette as "the golden thread" in her father's life (110).

Works Cited

Auerbach, Nina. *Woman and the Demon*. Cambridge: Harvard UP, 1982.
Brooks, Peter. *Body Work*. Cambridge: Harvard UP, 1993.
Brownstein, Rachel. *Becoming a Heroine*. New York: Penguin, 1982.
Carey, John. *The Violent Effigy*. London: Faber and Faber, 1973.
Dickens, Charles. *Bleak House*. Introduction, Sir Osbert Sitwell. New York: Oxford UP, 1962.
———. *David Copperfield*. Ed. Jerome Buckley. New York: Norton, 1989.
. *Dombey and Son*. Introduction H. W. Garrod. New York: Oxford UP, 1960.
———. *Little Dorrit*. Ed. Harvey Peter Sucksmith. New York: Oxford at Clarendon P, 1979.
———. *Our Mutual Friend*. Ed. Stephen Gill. New York: Penguin, 1971.
———. *A Tale of Two Cities*. Ed. George Woodcock. New York: Penguin, 1970.
Forster, John. *The Life of Charles Dickens*. New York: Charles Scribner's Sons, 1899.
Gay, Peter. *The Cultivation of Hatred*. New York: Norton and Co., 1993.
Guerard, Albert. *The Triumph of the Novel: Dickens, Dostoevsky, Faulkner*. New York: Oxford UP, 1976.
Ingham, Patricia. *Dickens, Women, and Language*. Toronto: U of Toronto P, 1992.
Irigary, Luce. *The Speculum of the Other Woman*. Ithaca: Cornell UP, 1985.

Knoepflmacher, U.C. "From Outrage to Rage: Dickens's Bruised Femininity." *Dickens and Other Victorians*. Ed. Joanne Shattock. New York: St. Martin's, 1988. 75–96.

Laqueur, Thomas. "Orgasm, Generation, and the Politics of Reproductive Biology." *Representations* 14 (1986): 1–41.

Michie, Helena. *The Flesh Made Word*. New York: Oxford UP, 1987.

Mulvey, Laura. *Visual and Other Pleasures*. Bloomington: Indiana UP, 1989.

Scarry, Elaine. *The Body in Pain*. New York: Penguin, 1982.

Showalter, Elaine. "Victorian Women and Insanity." *Victorian Studies* 23. 2 (Winter 1980): 157–181.

Slater, Michael. *Dickens and Women*. Stanford: Stanford UP, 1983.

Welsh, Alexander. *From Copyright to Copperfield: The Identity of Dickens*. Cambridge: Harvard UP, 1987.

Williams, Merryn. *Women in the English Novel, 1800–1900*. New York: St. Martin's, 1984.

Wilson, Edmund. *The Wound and the Bow*. New York: Oxford UP, 1970.

BJØRN TYSDAHL

Europe Is Not the Other:
A Tale of Two Cities

I

Dickens's account of France in *Pictures from Italy* leaves readers in no doubt that the writer has learnt something about Englishness from eighteenth-century forerunners like Hogarth and Sterne:[1] adjectives like "strange" and "queer" run like a refrain through the first chapter, which describes his journey through France (6–18). These pages do not, of course, give the whole story about Dickens's attitudes, which were far from simple or stable.[2] What I am highlighting here is thus only one important element in a composite picture, one that can serve as an illuminating antithesis to what his novel about the Revolution says about the two countries.

The very title of *A Tale of Two Cities* invites us to believe that this will be another text concerned with contrasts, and as soon as readers realize that this is an historical novel about Paris and London before and during the French Revolution, they will of course expect the book to give descriptions of two entirely different urban societies and historical developments. Differences there are. Dickens, though no great historian, writes in such a way that the general reader will think of his account of political events as true. The Paris of the French Revolution, the worst excesses of which even Lady Bracknell remembered, *is* different from the British capital. London, as we meet it in the novel's account of the years from 1789–92, is relatively peaceful. It

From *Dickens Quarterly* 15, no. 2 (June 1998): pp. 111–122. © 1998 by the Dickens Society.

is interesting in this context to note that Dickens is entirely silent about Corresponding Societies and other kinds of organized political radicalism in England.

II

In "*A Tale of Two Cities*: A French View," Sylvère Monod reminds us that for the treatment of the French Revolution the "London scenes are indeed indispensable for purposes of preparation, contrast and warning" (33). To this list of significant nouns, I want to add the word "similarity." The contrast between the two cities is not allowed to reign unchallenged. The reader is alerted to this as early as in the structure of the very first chapter. After the initial paragraph about the period that will be treated, it compares England and France, but the central paragraphs, three to five, are not organized as the repeated see-saw we might expect: "on the one hand, and on the other." What happens is that paragraph three and paragraph five are about London, so that France, in paragraph four, is enveloped by England. That Dickens might have structured the chapter differently is seen in the short second paragraph which *is* organized in the balanced way that we associate with extended lists of differences. What is promised in these pages is, in other words, a novel which will not be a straightforward series of comparisons, but a narrative that allows descriptions of England to embrace France, and vice versa.

This nascent understanding of what we are going to get, suggested by the structure of the first chapter, is reinforced by the semantic and symbolic parallels between the two countries in the first pages. Superstition in London, in particular such as is concerned with prophecy, is paralleled by the systematic (as the narrator sees it) superstition represented by the Roman Catholic Church in France. And the gruesome account of the peasant on the road, who did not kneel to a holy procession and was tortured and burned to death for his criminal sin, leads on to descriptions of English roads where people meet death, too. It must be admitted that the style of highwaymen is different: they favour expedition rather than long drawn-out ritual. But the stress is on the similarity.

The similarity in the road incidents in Chapter 1 is the first example of a basic rule in what might be called Dickens's grammar of comparison in *A Tale of Two Cities*: nearly everything that happens in one city has its counterpart in the other. As they meet the eye, such pairs are far from being identical, but the events that are thus coupled share an underlying similarity.[3]

Many of the most memorable scenes in the book find their place within such a framework. The Carmagnole is being danced in the streets of

Paris, danced as street entertainment for the poor, as a chance for the mob to let social and political inhibitions go, as a hate-enhancing ritual, as an expression of revolutionary fellowship. Mass action can have a more definite purpose, too, as in the attack on the Bastille. The counterpart in London is the "funeral" of Roger Cly. It is cheap entertainment, it is an expression of a sudden joyful fellowship, it has an animus against the establishment of a kind that resembles the carnivalesque attitudes that Bakhtin analyses in *Rabelais and His World*.[4] Indeed, though this particular London mob riot spends itself in the course of an afternoon, and the concerted movement of the poor in Paris has the magnitude of world history, the similarities are being highlighted: it is the poor and oppressed that are given to this kind of action; the concrete trigger mechanism is often beyond the control of reason; the line between hilarious abandonment and violent outrage is thin; there is no knowing how far the people will go.

The wider symbolic and thematic networks these scenes are placed in strengthen these similarities. The attack on the Bastille will bring prisoners freedom, bring the living-dead back to life. When the poor mob carries Darnay home after his acquittal, he is brought back from the brink of death. The life and death motif is not absent in London either. There, the mob moves towards a funeral which is not averted, but Jerry Cruncher, the local Resurrectionist, will soon be at work. That Roger Cly has already "come back to life," has indeed never been in the coffin, is a further irony which enriches the scene. He is an example of a more general theme, given memorable expression both here and in *Little Dorrit*: though not (or not always) prisoners in a concrete sense, human beings cannot easily free themselves from their social and psychological bondage. In his way, Cly is also a prisoner.

Anny Sadrin has pointed to another link with *Little Dorrit*. Bleeding Heart Yard, in the middle of London, is not altogether different from the Paris of the Revolution. Pancks,

> snip[s] off "the sacred locks" [of Casby] with as much fierceness and alacrity as the "National Barber" will chop off the heads of aristocrats in revolutionary France.... Read in the light of Dickens's French Revolution novel, the popular uprising of the "Bleeding Hearts" appears as more dangerously subversive than its anecdotal and farcical character would at first seem to suggest. (88)[5]

Cly's "funeral" has much the same message: it shows the gentle reader how street violence can rise, and what it means. Most readers of *A Tale of Two*

Cities would have the Gordon Riots in mind (they might have been reminded
of them by *Barnaby Rudge*), and they all remembered the popular unrest in
England in the late 1840s. Though the London scene is presented in a comic
mode, the twofold political point is still made: mob rule is terrible, but it is
also understandable. Author and reader can see why it happens, in Paris and
in London, but in both countries the Establishment cannot or will not see
and understand.[6]

The logical structure—differences in which there is a basic similarity—
is seen in many other situations. The wine-shop of Defarge and his wife has
its opposite number in Tellson's Bank in London. The main difference is of
course that between a conservative and passive atmosphere in London and
a subversive and active group of citizens in Paris. But both are places where
"extremists" meet and loiter, both are places where news is exchanged,
both are secretive, and in both there is a great deal of emotional and moral
blindness to anything but the cause.

Tellson's Bank functions in another narrative construction, too: it is
the counterpart to the Bastille. The bank is situated next to the courts, and
has only recently been "released from the horror of being ogled through
the windows, by the heads exposed on Temple Bar" (60; book 2, ch. 1). We
remember similar practices in France (see e.g. 206–7; book 2, ch. 15). The
bank is "very small, very dark, very ugly, very incommodious" (59; book 2,
ch. 1), and, like *ancien régime* prisons, it takes lives:

> Thus, Tellson's, in its day, like greater places of business, its
> contemporaries, had taken so many lives, that, if the heads laid
> low before it had been ranged on Temple Bar instead of being
> privately disposed of, they would probably have excluded what
> little light the ground floor had, in a rather significant manner.
> (61; book 2, ch. 1)

Dr. Manette has been buried in the Bastille, Mr. Lorry has been buried in
Tellson's. In both places men are incarcerated; in both men are separated
from family life; in both men must bow to an authority that they cannot
parley with. The weaknesses and human costs of the estate-based system of
economy in France are paralleled by those of an economy for which the bank
is the proper symbol.

The grammar of narrative, as I have called it, in *A Tale of Two Cities*
creates networks in which the comedy of the novel spreads. Take for instance
the figure that we can call the observer of street life with a sharp eye for
death. In Paris it is Madame Defarge, in London Jerry Cruncher. Since they
share this function, we are invited to extend the "Dickensian" humor in the

portrait of Jerry the "Resurrection-Man" (196; book 2, ch. 14), or, as he says himself, an "Agricultooral character" (378; book 3, ch. 9), to the *tricoteuse* of Saint Antoine. She thus partakes of grotesque humor, but at one remove. And this suits the overall purpose of the novel: to have made her a character we laugh at in an outright way would have been to undermine her political function. Ridicule must approach her in more insidious ways, and her functional connection with the "agricultooral" Jerry is one important way in which her status is made more complex. It was, I think, necessary to establish her not only as a political agent, an historical force, but also as a creature from comedy and melodrama: without deft background work of this sort her death would not have given the reader the marvellous emotional uplift that it now provides.

The official trials in the novel—one in London and two in Paris—fit the pattern I have suggested. But they have been well analyzed by others, in particular by Andrew Sanders (ix–xii), and I shall therefore not spend time on them here.

An awareness of this narrative strategy makes *A Tale of Two Cities* a richer novel than it would otherwise be. It has been said to be deficient in humor compared with other Dickens novels,[7] but what is the case is that in a story with less space for expansive humorous characters like Mrs. Gamp or Mr. Micawber, a great deal of thoughtful chuckle is embedded in the parallels between the two settings. The pattern of similarity in differences also gives greater depth and power to indirect political commentary, not least that which examines the price paid in England for early capitalism.

III

Europe is not the Other. This idea cannot be explored without a consideration of Dickens's imagery.

A widespread and frequent kind of figurative language in the novel is that connected with the fluid, the boundless and the all-embracing. To take an example from a scene in a court room first. A court is a place where we would expect clear distinctions, both between the people present and in the application of the Law itself. But when Darnay is taken into the court in London, "all the human breath in the place, rolled at him, like a sea, or a wind, or a fire." And Jerry's ugly-smelling breath "mingle[s] with the waves of other beer, and gin, and tea, and coffee, and what not, that flowed at him [Darnay], and already broke upon the great windows behind him in an impure mist and rain" (71; book 2, ch, 2). Life—breath—cannot be contained in separate compartments. The imagery of sea, waves and wind unites mankind here, as did the wine flowing in the Saint Antoine street when we were first introduced to Paris (32–6; book 1, ch. 5). A wit among the poor writes "BLOOD" on a wall with the red wine—and we are reminded not only of the cry for blood which will soon be heard in the streets, but also of the way in which blood unites human beings, as did the spilt wine that young and old gathered to drink. There is a play on the sacramental here, not so as to bring a great deal of theology to bear on the scene, but enough to remind readers of the oneness of life stressed by Saint John's Gospel (e.g. 6:54–7).

The streets of Paris and those of London are united by water and sea imagery. When people gather to attack the Bastille, "the living sea rose, wave on wave, depth on depth, and overflowed the city to that point" (263; book 2, ch. 21). These images are repeated five pages later on—"the sea of black and threatening waters, and of destructive upheaving of wave against wave, whose depths were yet unfathomed" (268; book 2, ch. 21)—and here with Old Testament echoes that underline the evil ways of the mob (cf. II Samuel 22:17, Psalm 18:16, Psalm 69:15 and Psalm 124:4–5). In London, when the Old Bailey trial is over, "the crowd came pouring out" (91; book 2, ch. 3); and later Jerry Cruncher, "on his stool in Fleet Street ... sat watching the two streams" of people moving before him (185; book 2, ch. 14). Here, too, the flowing of people into the mouths of destruction is given added power by a reference to a classical source: Jerry sits there "like the heathen rustic who has for several centuries been on duty watching one stream—saving that Jerry has no expectation of their ever running dry."

The sea imagery tightens as we move from the second to the third book of *A Tale of Two Cities*. Chapter 22 is called "The Sea still rises," and Chapter 24 "Drawn to the Loadstone Rock." Here, since the story moves to France, it is Paris that the imagery centers on. In terms of geography, it is the Paris of the Revolution which is the Loadstone. But by now the basic point made in the imagery—we may call it the One Life idea—is so well established that Paris is no longer simply the French capital on the Seine, it is a stage where life is acted out, life as it is in Paris and may be in England, or Rome, or Birmingham. Reminders of these basic connections are embedded in the texture of this part of the story, too. The terrible grindstone scene, for instance, is rounded off in this way: "The great grindstone, Earth, had turned when Mr. Lorry looked out again, and the sun was red on the court-yard" (323; book 3, ch. 2). The "lesser grindstone" is red with blood; the sun that shines over us all, is also red. The general significance of what happens in France is brought out even more forcefully in the account of the *morituri*:

In the black prison of the Conciergerie, the doomed of the day awaited their fate. They were in number as the weeks of the year.

Fifty-two were to roll that afternoon on the life-tide of the city
to the boundless everlasting sea. Before their cells were quit of
them, new occupants were appointed; before their blood ran into
the blood spilled yesterday, the blood that was to mingle with
theirs tomorrow was already set apart. (428; book 3, ch. 13)

This memorable paragraph shows us—and this is another main point in my
discussion of figurative language—that the boundless is not only a spatial
concept. In *A Tale of Two Cities* powerful and pervasive clusters of imagery do
not only unite Paris and London; they also unite the past, the present and
the future.

Andrew Sanders's note on the first paragraph of the novel stresses the
way in which it "reminds us that this is a historical novel" and "also ... alert[s]
readers to the nineteenth-century's awareness of the distinctiveness of certain
historical periods" (474–5). True, from late eighteenth-century historians
(and not least those of the Scottish Enlightenment) later generations learned
something about the importance of stages in historical development.[8] But
there is another reading of the first paragraph which is at least equally
natural: "It was the best of times, it was the worst of times, ..."—this list of
opposites which goes on for eight lines highlights, it seems to me, the way
in which people have seen and still tend to see *all* historical periods in the
same terms. In the last lines of this paragraph, too, there is a reminder that
the inclination towards drama and simplification is always with us.

No reader of *A Tale of Two Cities* can, I suppose, forget the play on
echoes in the story. An echo connects two or more places—the initial source
of the sound and the vertical structure or structures from which it is returned
(and the place where the hearer is if she or he is not situated where the sound
originated). And since sound takes time, appreciable time, to move, an echo
will also combine the past with the present. The echoes that are heard in Dr.
Manette's quiet flat in London serve both purposes—they are reflections of
the busy town life outside the charmed circle, and of the past from which he
cannot completely free himself. The fact that two *or* three places are involved
reminds readers of the fact (an important one in the novel) that what comes
back may either be the results of the earlier actions of the hearer or of forces
that individuals cannot possibly control.

Sea imagery is modulated in similar ways. The sea moves, and it moves in
time. In Carton's dreamy impressions as he wakes up after having slept briefly
on the bank of the Seine, the nouns "tide," "stream," "eddy" and "sea," and
the verbs "carried," "glided," "floated" (389; book 3, ch. 9)—they are found
together in two short paragraphs—combine the spatial and the temporal, and
here particularly so as to stress temporal continuity and unity.

The frequency of journeys in the story has a similar effect. The very first chapter of the book sums up what happens in 1775 in the image of people being conducted "along the roads that lay before them" (4; book 1, ch. 1). A journey is a progress in time and space, and when this book, called *A Tale of Two Cities*, is in fact almost as much about journeys as about localities where characters stay put, the thematic force of connections is being underlined.

The imagery that expresses and creates unity of time and space in *A Tale of Two Cities* has a Romantic ring. We are reminded of the "One Life" theme that Robert Penn Warren finds in "The Rime of the Ancient Mariner" (see in particular 214 and 245–50). But Dickens's idea of the one life, though it is steeped in natural imagery, does not lead to a "sacramental vision;" it does not hail the great creative and unifying potential of existence, at least not in any simple or idyllic way. The heart of the author of this novel does not dance with the daffodils. Instead, we have the Carmagnole, described with such intensity that we are, so to speak, invited to join in the street dance for the moment. This one-life theme stresses the common humanity of the characters—a messy mixture of care, responsibility, political inertia, political violence, hardness of heart, anger, slovenliness, growth, decay, and romance. It is interesting to note that when a Wordsworth poem is echoed in the first line of Chapter 17, it is not "Tintern Abbey" but (appropriately for a novel about towns) the sonnet "Composed upon Westminster Bridge, September 3, 1802," a poem from a period in which the poet is beginning to query the "sense sublime" of a "spirit ... that rolls through all things" (134).

The non-transcendental nature of the imagery becomes very conspicuous in a comparison with the waves that wash and the rivers that run in the pages of *Dombey and Son*. A "swift river" bears little Paul into eternity at the end of chapter 16; and on the last page of the novel the waves speak to Mr. Dombey of his daughter, and he remembers "their ceaseless murmuring to her of the love, eternal and illimitable, extending still, beyond the sea, beyond the sky, to the invisible country far away." We might have expected waves and rivers to wet the much maligned paragraph in which Lucie's son dies (257; book 2, ch. 21),[9] but they are conspicuously absent. The boy's ascent to heaven is described in terms of a halo on the pillow, a divine order ("I am called, and I must go!"), and the biblical promise that he will see God face to face. There is scarcely a trace in this paragraph of the unifying imagery which is so strong elsewhere in this novel (such metaphors return in the very next paragraph, which moves towards the living).[10] In Carton's last moments Christianity is represented by a bare quotation from the Bible: the imagery is remarkable in that even at this stage it very powerfully, and almost exclusively, stresses *human* connections. Carton and the girl are "children of the Universal Mother"

(463; book 3, ch. 15); and fluid, boundless images are invoked in the description of the crowd's reaction to the execution.

Intriguing links between the past and the present are also found in the narrative act which gives us *A Tale of Two Cities*. The narrator implicates himself in the story he tells us. This is done with good-humored self-irony in the first chapter: he satirizes Mrs. Southcott, the famous prophetess, in the very same pages where he establishes himself as a man who knows the past, the present, and the future. He can see what trees the Woodman, Fate, marks for the framework of the future guillotine (2; book 1, ch. 1). In the first description of Paris, four chapters later, the narrator's knowledge of the future is stressed again (see in particular 34; book 1, ch. 5). Most often this kind of knowledge is hinged on the word "Fate" (for another example see 133; book 2, ch. 7), a vague concept which does not commit the narrator to a Christian interpretation of the future. One can see why: a consistent use of the prophetic language of the Bible might have smacked too much of Calvinism. The main business of this narrator who knows the future is not to compete with Mrs. Southcott but to stress certain ways in which human life—past, present and future; in Paris and London—coheres. In a recent discussion of Dickens as an historical novelist Ian Duncan argues, correctly I think, that "history does not appear as a category of dynamic process in his narratives," but when he goes on to suggest that history "signifies not even lives passing, but only a dark, blind, dead past" (16), both the narrative strategy and the imagery of *A Tale of Two Cities* can be mustered in protest. It is true that the concept of the past as a discrete category is weakened almost to extinction, but that which was there seventy years ago still exists as part of a biological and cultural web that also includes the present, an organic network which is alive, and over which both darkness and light play.

IV

Recent critical theory has given us a fair number of memorable slogans, such as Frederic Jameson's seductive "Always historicize!" (9). If on a smaller scale one might offer a generalization (self-defeating, I am afraid) in the imperative for Dickens studies, it must be "Never generalize!" The imagery in *A Tale of Two Cities*, in which I have highlighted elements that suggest a unifying force, provides other powerful patterns, too.[11] Throughout the story that which is sharp and stony presents an antidote to the boundless. The shooting in the first chapter, the killing of the child, the stone faces on the Evrémonde chateau, the shot that kills Madame Defarge, and finally the falling of the guillotine—this cluster of images and symbols tells another story inside the story, one that contrasts time and timelessness, and suggests a religious or proto-religious awareness quite different from the mild moral messages highlighted in *The Life of Our Lord*. But this is not a figurative constellation which undermines the view of England and France as essentially united in what the novel says about sublunary existence.

NOTES

1. Hogarth said about the French that they were characterized by "poverty, slavery and insolence, with an affectation of politeness" (quoted from MacWilliam, 114). His famous painting and engraving "The Gate of Calais" has the emaciated poor in one foreground corner and a starved Jacobite refugee in another. In the middle is a fat greedy monk; and a huge piece of English beef, probably on its way to the English tavern in the town, is carried by a meagre cook attended by an equally lean soldier. Dickens praises Hogarth for his robustness and dislike of bigotry. As old stereotypes go, these are English, not French, virtues. (See the *Pilgrim Letters*, 1: 408, and 2: 201.)

Sterne is hailed as an enemy of cant (*Pilgrim Letters*, 4: 305, and 1: 274, n). In this note to p. 274 the editors quote what Dickens said about *A Sentimental Journey* in *Household Words* (Extra Christmas Number, 1855) when he found the book at Holly-Tree Inn: "I knew every word ... already." Very many of the incidents in *A Sentimental Journey* play on the differences between England and France, though not, of course, with Hogarth's straightforward moral censure. A good example is found in the last chapter of Vol. 1, "The Rose. Paris" (51–2).

2. See e.g. Surveyer (46–56, 122–9, 197–201). Dickens's experience of himself as a citizen of Europe is brought out in "Our French Watering-Place": "But, to us, it is not the least pleasant feature of our French watering-place that a long and constant fusion of the two great nations there has taught each to like the other, and to learn from the other, and to rise superior to the absurd prejudices that have lingered among the weak and ignorant in both countries equally." *The Uncommercial Traveller* (412).

3. There are illuminating parallels both in semantics and phonetics to the "grammar" I am outlining. The memorable parallelisms in Dr. Johnson's style work on a similar principle. In a phrase like "this universal and incessant competition" (from *The Rambler*, No. 183) the adjectives are different and at the same time they share a basic semantic component (in this case that of the unlimited) which may be clear to the reader only at a second glance. W. K. Wimsatt, Jr.'s *The Prose Style of Samuel Johnson* gives a shrewd analysis of this play on differences and similarities (15–23).

A set of terms from phonetics can also serve as an illustration of Dickens's strategy. A phoneme, one of the basic significant units in speech, is often expressed as different allophones. Depending on context, a particular Japanese phoneme may for instance be heard as either [r] or [l]. Though clearly different in sound quality, the allophones have the same function.

4. See Ch. 4 "Popular-Festive Forms and Images in Rabelais," and in particular 207.

5. John Carey makes a similar point when he compares the mob violence in *Barnaby Rudge* to the burning of the Evrémonde chateau (13–4). See also Monod (34): "Dickens's ruthless analysis of the mechanism of violence shows his awareness that the very real danger of revolutionary incidents was by no means restricted to the Continent."

6. Cf. Earle Davis who says: "The thesis of the novel is: *Revolution can happen in England too!*" (253). An analysis of the similarities between England and France does not

disprove a general statement like this, but it brings out the way in which the same forces *are* in fact at work in both countries even through the revolution took place in France only.

7. See for instance John Gross (194–5); and Angus Wilson (267).

8. For a fine survey of this theory of history see Cyrus Vakil (404–18).

9. For an incisive example of the critical attitude, see Monod (25).

10. An important reason for the brevity with which Lucie's son is dispatched is found in its overall function in the story. The main point here is not to describe a deathbed, but to judge the father, Darnay, who in important matters has been so dilatory that he does not deserve the heroic stamp which male issue represents.

11. The imagery of *A Tale of Two Cities*, memorable as it is for its insistence both on the boundless and the sharp, does not, therefore, provide unequivocal support for Harald William Fawkner's view that "in its final form, then, Dickens's imaginative universe is a world of meaningful, not destructive, transformation: one of coherence and of harmony between the organic and the inorganic. Images of intergrowth and reciprocal exchange between the human and the non-human reflect a vision of this world as a place of ultimate oneness." (155)

WORKS CITED

Bakhtin, M. M. *Rabelais and His World*. Tr. H. Iswolsky. Bloomington: Indiana UP, 1984.

Carey, John. *The Violent Effigy: A Study of Dickens' Imagination*. 1973. London: Faber and Faber, 1991.

Davis, Earl. *The Flint and the Flame: The Artistry of Charles Dickens*. London: Gollancz, 1964.

Dickens, Charles. *Dombey and Son*. 1848. Ed. Peter Fairclough. Harmondsworth: Penguin, 1970.

———. *Pictures from Italy*. London: Bradbury and Evans, 1846.

———. *Pilgrim Letters*. Vol. 1. Ed. M. House and G. Storey. Oxford: The Clarendon Press, 1965.

———. *Pilgrim Letters*. Vol. 2. Ed. M. House and G. Storey. Oxford: The Clarendon Press, 1969.

———. *Pilgrim Letters*. Vol. 4. Ed. K. Tillotson. Oxford: The Clarendon Press, 1977.

———. *A Tale of Two Cities*. 1859. Ed. Andrew Sanders. Oxford: OUP, 1988.

———. *The Uncommercial Traveller*. 1861. Oxford, OUP, 1968.

Duncan, Ian. *Modern Romance and Transformations of the Novel: The Gothic, Scott, Dickens*. Cambridge: CUP, 1992.

Fawkner, Harald William. *Animation and Reification in Dickens's Vision of the Life-Denying Society*. Uppsala: Acta Universitatis Upsaliensis, 1977.

Gross, John. "*A Tale of Two Cities*." *Dickens and the Twentieth Century*. Ed. John Gross and G. Pearson. London: Routledge and Kegan Paul, 1962. 187–97.

Jameson, Frederic. *The Political Unconscious: Narrative As a Socially Symbolic Art*. London: Methuen, 1981.

MacWilliam, Neil. *Hogarth*. London: Studio Editions, 1993.

Monod, Sylvère. "*A Tale of Two Cities*: A French View." *Dickens Memorial Lectures 1970*. Supplement to *The Dickensian* (1970). 23–37.

Sadrin, Anny. *Parentage and Inheritance in the Novels of Charles Dickens*. Cambridge: CUP, 1994.

Sanders, Andrew. Introduction. *A Tale of Two Cities*. Oxford: OUP, 1988.

Sterne, Laurence. *A Sentimental Journey through France and Italy*. 1768. Ed. Tom Keymer. London: J. M. Dent, 1994.

Surveyer, Eduard Fabré. "Dickens in France." *The Dickensian* 28 (1932): 46–56, 122–9, 197–201.

Vakil, Cyrus. "Walter Scott and the Historicism of Scottish Enlightenment Philosophical History." *Scott in Carnival*. Ed. J. H. Alexander and David Hewitt. Aberdeen: Association for Scottish Literary Studies, 1993. 404–18.

Warren, Robert Penn. "A Poem of Pure Imagination: An Experiment in Reading." *Selected Essays*. New York: Random House, 1958. 198–305.

Wilson, Angus. *The World of Charles Dickens*. New York: The Viking Press, 1970.

Wimsatt, W. K. Jr. *The Prose Style of Samuel Johnson*. 1941. New Haven: Yale UP, 1963.

Wordsworth, William. "Tintern Abbey". *William Wordsworth*. Ed. Stephen Gill. Oxford: OUP, 1990. 131–5.

HILARY M. SCHOR

Hard Times *and* A Tale of Two Cities:
The Social Inheritance of Adultery

The early Dickens novel depends upon stories of identity: *Oliver Twist*, *Nicholas Nickleby*, and *Martin Chuzzlewit* all concentrate on the young hero's assumption of his patrimony and his personality—a process that comes to the fore in the autobiographical "favourite child," *David Copperfield*. In that light, "a daughter after all" seems a mere distraction—the literary equivalent of the "base coin" Florence Dombey's father thought her. How much more ephemeral seems the plot of the daughter's adulterous mother, or the daughter's own progress through the meanderings of the adultery plot. And yet, as Dickens moved from these novels of identity toward the wider screen of the social novel, it was the adultery plot that served him in better stead—that allowed him to move from stories of identity to those of social position; to question the connections between individuals and the forces of historical transformation.

One example from *David Copperfield* might suggest why this is so. Mid-novel, David meets Annie Strong, the young and beautiful wife of his teacher, Doctor Strong. While Doctor Strong adores Annie, calling her "the dear lady" and his "contract-bargain,"[1] Annie is flighty and nervous, and seemingly infatuated with her cousin, the bounder Jack Maldon. The young David is incapable of recognizing her wandering ways; the older, narrator David seems more cognizant:

From *Dickens and the Daughter of the House*, pp. 70–98. © 1999 by Cambridge University Press.

she was looking up at [her husband]. But with such a face as I
never saw. It was so beautiful in its form, it was so ashy pale, it was
so fixed in its abstraction, it was so full of a wild, sleep-walking,
dreamy horror of I don't know what. The eyes were wide open,
and her brown hair fell in two rich clusters on her shoulders, and
on her white dress, disordered by the want of the lost ribbon.
Distinctly as I recollect her look, I cannot say of what it was
expressive, I cannot even say of what it is expressive to me now,
rising again before my older judgement. Penitence, humiliation,
shame, pride, love and trustfulness—I see them all; and in them
all, I see that horror of I don't know what. (304)

The retrospective narrator David is here playing with the reader's sense
of the ignorance of the *character* David, for what we are meant to "see"
(what the young David cannot see—or more accurately, can see but cannot
"know") is the guilt of adultery.

But the narrator is being disingenuous here: the older David,
narrating, knows that Annie was never an adulteress, and in fact, her
shame comes from something quite different. By keeping that shame
a vague horror, he can manipulate the reader's desire to read for the
adulterous plot, a desire to *see* her fall, and still hold on to the didactic
efficacy of her alleged misprision—while never exactly telling the distinct
untruth, never saying directly that she was untrue to her husband.
Annie's secret is in fact not sexual but financial: what she fears is that her
husband will think she married him for his money, dreading "the mean
suspicion that my tenderness was bought—and sold to you, of all men,
on earth" (729). What Annie wants made clear is not that she is not an
adulteress, but that she is not a "contract-bargain". Annie's misery comes
from her husband's generosity and the financial demands of her family
(in particular her mother), for she is "unhappy in the mercenary shape
I was made to wear" (730). "Mercenary," in that sentence, takes the
place of "adulterous," and in similar fashion, David's ignorance must be
transformed from sexual blindness to economic mystery: what he (and the
Doctor) cannot know is the guilt of someone assumed to be nothing but
a commodity. What seems more important, at this moment, than David's
initiation into sexual wisdom, is the revelation of exchange relations: what
Annie Strong reflects on is her own status as property, and the narratives
spun around female ownership and material worth—in essence, her
legal status as property and as conveyor of property. Though the other
characters, David and Aunt Betsey in particular, think that Annie has
been using her husband's money to pay off her lover, this is a sign only

of their blindness: Annie *seems* to have been playing both a sexual and a property game, but in fact, she has been faithful and honest, a "contract-bargain" indeed.[2]

David, led in part by Annie's example, and by her words of warning, makes his way through the path of the false heart to perfect happiness and narratorial authority; Dickens, in the undoing of his marriage that took him through the 1850s, not only named his daughter Dora Annie, after the two wandering heroines of the novel, but found himself at the end explaining that his long-lived and many child-producing marriage was itself the mistake of an "undisciplined heart."[3] The Dickens novel, as it makes its way through the historical and social minefields of the same decade, has a less easy time of it. At the heart of the social novels, in particular *Hard Times* and *A Tale of Two Cities*, is a now familiar anxiety over the daughter's ability to signify truth—to stay true to their husbands, their fathers, the past. Repeatedly, as with Annie Strong, it is the male anxiety over female erotic wandering that is mistaken, a wandering off from the truth. But the plot of mistaken adultery provides not only a period of suspense for the reader, but a kind of suspension of meaning and of social coherence. In these two novels, anxieties over social coherence and the transmission of history—anxieties, in short, about authority and authorship—are tested through the plot of female disruption, and the daughter's adulterous plot turns out to be the key to the better ordering of society, and the proper uses of fiction.

Dickens returns in *Hard Times* to the central question of *Dombey and Son*: what use is the daughter? As in the earlier novel, he finds a variety of ways to test the daughter's true worth; and as in *Dombey and Son*, he allies the daughter's plot to the economic critique at the novel's core.[4] In *Hard Times*, Louisa Bounderby's plot is the one that most clearly parallels that of the workers, and her destiny seems to be worked out through theirs; she is also the character who comes closest to understanding and expressing the sense of impending revolt that the dangerous masses represent in the novel—however mild Dickens chooses to make their chief representative, Stephen Blackpool. But where Louisa and Stephen meet most fully is in their shared participation in the divorce plot, and it is in Louisa's sexual frustration, the anger she seems to inherit from Edith Dombey, that she most illustrates the forces the novel needs to contain. In this novel, the daughter is passionate, angry, and gains the most power by straying from the paths of narrative virtue.

Louisa herself makes the connection between her plight and that of the workers when she is told by her father, the Utilitarian Thomas Gradgrind, that she is sought by his friend, the blustery Josiah Bounderby for his wife.

Staring out at the "works," Louisa comments on how quiet they look in the evening; and yet, she says, "when the night comes, Fire bursts out."[5] The threat of her own fire, the passionate nature she suppresses, jostles the novel along far more compellingly than does the somewhat inadequate plot of workers' revolution, but even more striking is the connection Dickens makes between her sexual wandering and the "wonder" that is to suffuse the workers' blighted lives. In a sleight-of-hand metaphorical twist, Dickens aligns the workers, Louisa's bad marriage, and the faulty education of the Gradgrind children, all as a form of repression, an unnatural growth, ready to bear stunted and (were such a thing possible) violent fruit.[6]

The central evildoer in this fairy-tale would seem to be the children's father, Thomas Gradgrind, who gets his own fairy-tale introduction. When Louisa goes to meet her father in his study, we are told that "although Mr. Gradgrind did not take after Blue Beard, his room was quite a blue chamber in its abundance of blue books" (75).[7] The odd conjunction between fathers, daughters, and the Arabian Nights continues in an anecdote Sissy Jupe tells of her father and the days when she would read to him from "wrong books." She tells Louisa, whose capacity for "wonder" has been locked up by the domestic Blue Beard, that these books

> "kept him, many times from what did him real harm. And often and often of a night, he used to forget all his troubles in wondering whether the Sultan would let the lady go on with the story, or would have her head cut off before it was finished." (49)

Sissy's story does more than remind Louisa of what a truly affectionate father and daughter share: it suggests the power of fiction in a world of harsh (and harmful) reality. The intrusion of Scheherazade into the text suggests further the ways Dickens's sexual plot—and the readerly desire generated in particular by the adulterous plot—will immunize the reader against what might do "real harm." If Stephen Blackpool had read fairy-tales, he might not be tempted to threaten revolt; if Louisa Gradgrind had learned the narrative striptease Scheherazade practiced, she would neither have married the wrong man nor have been isolated from the lives of those who surround her.

The reader who follows Louisa's plight is drawn on through another fantasy altogether, that crafted by Mrs. Sparsit, Bounderby's housekeeper. Mrs. Sparsit's *ressentiment* (she is a down-on-her-luck gentlewoman, freed from the tyrannies of her mysteriously bed-ridden cousin Lady Scadgers only by the genteel employment granted her by Mr. Bounderby) turns to sexual resentment when the beautiful young Louisa comes into the house.

When Harthouse, one of the fact-party's minions, comes to town and is entranced by the young Louisa, Mrs. Sparsit makes it the "business" of her life to imagine Louisa's sexual fall, in an elaborate conceit that the narrator follows wholeheartedly:

> Now, Mrs. Sparsit was not a poetical woman; but she took an idea in the nature of an allegorical fancy, into her head. Much watching of Louisa, and much consequent observation of her impenetrable demeanour, which keenly whetted and sharpened Mrs. Sparsit's edge, must have given her as it were a lift, in the way of inspiration. She erected in her mind a mighty Staircase, with a dark pit of shame and ruin at the bottom; and down those stairs, from day to day and hour to hour, she saw Louisa coming. (150–151)

The passage is a curious mixture of authorial and characterological insight: Mrs. Sparsit's "observation" of Louisa's "impenetrable demeanour" echoes Harthouse, who, pondering Louisa, remarked that she "baffled all penetration"; at the same time, the capitalization of "Staircase" suggests that the narrator, at least briefly, looks with Mrs. Sparsit's eyes. She is granted a vision beyond her own, and we are asked to share it—and for all that her "allegory" eventually fails, it is our path through the novel.

Mrs. Sparsit's plot is compelling largely because it has generic coherence: it has a melodramatic sequence of events, and Louisa is patently a melodramatic heroine, heaving bosom, flashing eyes, and all. From the scene where her father proposed Bounderby, when she addressed the "Fire [that] bursts out" (78) at night, Louisa has seemed a sleeping-beauty heroine, waiting for erotic awakening. The progress that started when Sissy Jupe entered her home and introduced those dangerous Arabian Nights narratives to the fiction-starved children cries out for physical embodiment—which it will find, eventually, not in Louisa's successful sexual escape with James Harthouse, but in her collapse into the loving Sissy's arms. More than mere embodiment, it seems to cry out for physical violence: the first sign of Louisa's sexual nature came early, when Bounderby demands a kiss from her, and she submits in stony silence—only to rub the area red after he leaves, and tell her brother he could cut it out with a knife, and she wouldn't cry out. The violence of Mrs. Sparsit's imaginings of the fall satisfies the reader's sense of Louisa's masochism, and of the vivid (repressed) desires that underwrite it—here, as elsewhere, the novel carries out the narrator's initial pronouncement, that fantasy, repressed in one space, will grow in cramped and warped form in another.

But it is Dickens who needs Louisa's fall—or more accurately, her near-fall. Mrs. Sparsit, in her quest for Louisa's ruin and her own return to power in the Bounderby household, has used a metaphor near to Dickens's heart: "Eager to see [the descent] accomplished, and yet patient, she waited for the last fall, as for the ripeness and fulness of the harvest of her hopes" (153). So, too, does Louisa's descent seem to Dickens the *proper* harvest of her own hopes: when she collapses on Sissy's breast, Louisa cries out, "Forgive me, pity me, help me! Have compassion on my great need" (168). The words are almost exactly Dombey's, when he cries out to God and Florence, "Forgive me, for I need it very much." Only those who know they have nothing stand any chance of gaining anything in a Dickens world, and the adultery plot seems to work (unlike the workers' plot, which gives to those who have nothing even more of nothing) by this image of stores replenished by a heavenly (loving) reward. But Louisa's progress through the bad marriage plot, past the dangers of the adultery plot, and into the plot of daughterly redemption (the plot in which she is saved by her return to the father; and he by her return) has actually had to make its way as well through a plot of property, of dispossession, and of repossession. This, in turn, reflects back on the connection between the fiercely angry, hardhearted woman and the gentle, muddle-headed worker: the worker and the woman, it turns out, have in common that they are bodies that cannot possess themselves; they are subjects who can only uneasily become bodies of their own.

Images of violent disembodiment haunt the novel: the battered body of the woman worker; the fall of Stephen Blackpool down the Old Hell shaft; Louisa's collapse at her father's feet after she flees her husband and her would-be lover. Where these images coalesce is in the connections (of plot and of imagery) between Louisa's and Stephen's stories. Despite his representative status as "hand" in the novel, Stephen, far from being the most radical of the workers, has (nobly) refused to join his fellows in their strike, thereby allowing Dickens to avoid the direct representation of radical action and staying closer to the hearts (and hearths) of the workers. But this commitment to the domestic yields two important subplots, the first, Stephen's legal and moral bondage to his drunken, filthy wife; the second, the introduction of Rachael, the woman worker who offers a different version of the worker's miseries. Stephen's wife is the reason he visits Bounderby and meets Louisa in the first place; eventually, his inability to be freed from her will offer another point of connection for Louisa, chained to her marriage to Bounderby. While Bounderby's explanation of Stephen's obligation offers Dickens a brief moment of Chancery-like irony (Stephen is reminded, essentially, that divorce is cumbersome and marriage a moral obligation—except for wealthy people), Stephen's encounter with his wife offers the description of urban slime that is missing from Dickens's description of the workers. Dickens's Coketown is rather clean: there is virtually no ooze of the sort Engels, and novelists like Elizabeth Gaskell, depict—a primeval slime more familiar to us from *Bleak House* and *Our Mutual Friend*. Though Coketown seems to resonate with filth, the city is more often seen as a vague blotch on the horizon than as specific trails of grime: only James Harthouse seems to notice that it is an "extraordinarily black town," where the workers appear "to have been taking a shower-bath of something fluffy" (92).

All the dirt that does not exist in Coketown seems, conveniently enough, to have found its way onto Stephen's alcoholic wife, who represents in her person all the ills of industrial decay—even though there is no evidence she has been near a factory in recent years.

> Such a woman! A disabled, drunken creature, barely able to preserve her sitting posture by steadying herself with one begrimed hand on the floor, while the other was so purposeless in trying to push away her tangled hair from her face, that it only blinded her the more with the dirt upon it. A creature so foul to look at, in her tatters, stains and splashes, but so much fouler than that in her moral infamy, that it was a shameful thing even to see her. (55)

The foulness not only shames everyone who sees her, it contaminates even Stephen's apartment, "a room... as neat, at present, as such a room could be ..." in which "the furniture was decent and sufficient, and, though the atmosphere was tainted, the room was clean" (54–5). This description precedes Stephen's discovery of his wife in the corner, and seems initially a description of the foulness of the Coketown air—but in fact, the atmosphere turns out to be more susceptible to her drunken foulness than to any of the ills of industrial pollution; the foulness is both encapsulated in her body, and miasmically fluid: when she scrambles up, it is "dangling in one hand by the string, a dunghill-fragment of a bonnet," and when she falls asleep, Stephen, cowering with his eyes covered, gets up but once, "to throw a covering over her, as if his hands were not enough to hide her, even in the darkness" (55). This is a dirt stronger than hands, stronger than fabric, stronger than darkness itself.

Stephen is incapable of cleaning up his room, or his wife, just as he is incapable of taking on the ills of industrialization ("a' a muddle," as he describes the chaos of social change).[8] Only Rachael's gentle hands can restore the realm of female sanctity, replacing his wife's "disgraceful garments [which] were removed, and some of Rachael's were in the room"

(66). Indeed the whole room is restored to order: "everything was in its place and order as he had always kept it, the little fire was newly trimmed, and the hearth was freshly swept" (66). What Rachael cannot reorder is society, and she remains a voice of hopeless (and somewhat irresponsible) harmony: her requirement that Stephen pledge he will not join the striking workers leads to his social isolation ("You are the Hand they have sent to Coventry," says Bitzer, singling him out [110]) and, eventually, to his death in the tricky plot of Tom Gradgrind.

The vow he takes for Rachael suggests a further connection with Louisa Bounderby's plot, and offers another icon for the daughter's representative plight in the machinery of industrialization. Rachael has requested Stephen's oath that he abstain from political action (and here the illogic is Dickens's, and not my own) as a result of the tragic fate of her little sister. In a passage Dickens cut at a late stage in the publication of the novel, Stephen recalls Rachael's sister's dismemberment at the hands of the machinery:

> "Thou'st spokken o' thy little sisther. There agen! Wi' her child arm tore off afore thy face!" She turned her head aside, and put her hand up to her eyes. "Where dost thou ever hear or read o' *us*—the like o' *us*—as being otherwise than onreasonable and cause o' trouble? Yet think o' that...." (247)[9]

The violence directed against the sister here seems to indict, fatally, the system of factory labor that otherwise needs only to be "moderated" so that workers and masters can both continue to prosper—Stephen goes on to echo one of *Household Words'* own editorials on "rend[ing] and tear[ing] human creeturs to bits in a Chris'en country!" (247). But Dickens's excision of the violence against her not only (for socially minded readers) limits the "realism" of this venture into the arena of social fiction, it wreaks havoc with Dickens's conventional fictional skills: this scene explained Stephen's vow to Rachael that he would not enter into the strike against the masters, and without it, his obstinacy seems mere muddle-headedness. With the departure of the maimed sister from the text, Stephen is an even less effective speaker for the workers than he might be, and his refusal to join the strike seems more novelistic, and less credible, than ever.

Dickens wants to keep Stephen and Rachael clean, unsullied by the rebellious sludge (the "fluffy men") of Coketown, but he needs—without provoking revolution—to suggest the powers of those banked fires that Louisa imaginatively conjures. Stephen is protected from active rebellion; Louisa is kept from committing adultery; and yet, both suggest—perhaps in the very nobility of their nearing and then refusing an action that would embody their discontent—a revolutionary force that the novel cannot quite contain.[10] The connection between female rage and workers' resistance accomplishes some of this—and indeed, Bounderby himself makes such a connection when Louisa's father returns to ask her husband for patience in her unhappy state of mind:

> "I know the works of this town, and I know the chimneys of this town, and I know the smoke of this town, and I know the Hands of this town. I know 'em all pretty well. They're real. When a man tells me anything about imaginative qualities, I always tell that man, whoever he is, that I know what he means. He means turtle soup and venison, with a gold spoon, and that he wants to be set up with a coach and six. That's what your daughter wants."
> (179)

Bounderby is not entirely wrong. Louisa, like the workers, wants something she can't name—it is the same "wild escape into something visionary" (162) which betrays her in her marriage; that something which is "not an Ology at all" (149) which she missed in her education at home. She has been transformed into someone who feels the unspoken connection with others always at the heart of Dickens's social program—and, as is often the case in a Dickens novel, a changed heart seems to be the substitute for social transformation.

That is not, however, entirely true in Louisa Bounderby's case, nor does Dickens's critique stop with her transformation. He went to considerable trouble to set up the connections between Louisa and Stephen: not only the parallel miseries of their bad marriages, but the scenes in which they meet and talk, in which he explains the workers' disenfranchisement. The plot drags Stephen into the web of deceit practiced by Tom Gradgrind, but Stephen (we believe) instructs Louisa in the web of social connection that restores her to herself, beginning the work Sissy Jupe will finish when Louisa returns home. All this works to quiet social outrage and to promote the ideological work of social connection—like the introduction of Honoria Dedlock to Jo the crossing sweep, or Arthur Clennam to poor Little Dorrit, these cross-class meetings prove the deeper connections between us in the great weavings of time, and Dickens thought of them (as in the meeting of Nancy and Rose Maylie in *Oliver Twist*) as his best ideas.

Hard Times goes farther, for it suggests not only that Louisa must meet and understand the abused victims of society, but that she herself is one. In some sense, this is the work of the adultery plot, for Louisa becomes an element of social disruption, another strand in the unweaving of society.

Once the slime of industrial despair has been moved to Louisa, once she
is an element of adulteration, she can be cleaned up and society reordered
simply by removing from her the stain of adultery and restoring her to
sanctimony and moral cleanliness. As Mary Douglas famously wrote of dirt,
"if uncleanness is matter out of place, we must approach it through order.
Uncleanness or dirt is that which must not be included if a pattern is to be
maintained."[11] Culture needs dirt—in its own special place—in order to
exist, and in this novel, Louisa provides both the dirt and the spot of cleaning
up. This is accomplished through Mrs. Sparsit's hunting down Louisa on
what she thinks is the great night of adulterous passion. Mrs. Sparsit follows
Louisa into the garden, then into a train, and then back to Coketown,
expecting to catch her in the act of degradation, only to wind up herself an
ungodly mess:

> Wet through and through: with her feet squelching and squashing
> in her shoes whenever she moved; with a rash of rain upon her
> classical visage; with a bonnet like an over-ripe fig; with all
> her clothes spoiled; with damp impressions of every button,
> string, and hook-and-eye she wore, printed off upon her highly
> connected back; with a stagnant verdure on her general exterior,
> such as accumulates on an old park fence in a mouldy lane; Mrs.
> Sparsit had no resource but to burst into tears of bitterness and
> say, "I have lost her!" (160)

Louisa escapes both Mrs. Sparsit and the act of adultery—she has, to echo
that earlier phrase of James Harthouse's, baffled both the reader's penetration
and that of the characters nearest to her. But with all her moral ambiguity
"printed off upon [Mrs. Sparsit's] highly connected back," Louisa is freed
for the higher work of the plot, the industrial slime has been cleaned up and
modern society reframed through the body of the tragic daughter, and the
adultery novel seems to have contained all of the collective rage (workers;
torn bodies; angry daughters) of the novel.

   Louisa's abrupt rescue from the adultery plot returns us to the model
Annie Strong offered David Copperfield: that being an adulteress is no more
shameful than being called a mercenary. *Hard Times* encourages us to read
Louisa's plot not as sexual desire but as the discontent of a woman *owned*
by her husband. Louisa's flight is as much from the "contract-bargain" of
marriage as from the disgusting sexual advances of her husband, the "bully
of humility."

   Bounderby may not "buy" Louisa as directly as Dombey purchased
Edith Granger, but he certainly views her as an acquisition, another sign

that he has risen from poverty and can acquire trophies. He is fond of introducing her as "Tom Gradgrind's eldest daughter Loo," crammed with lots of "expensive knowledge" (98); their betrothal took on a "manufacturing aspect," in which "Love was made on these occasions in the form of bracelets ... Dresses were made, jewellery was made, cakes and gloves were made, settlements were made, and an extensive assortment of Facts did appropriate honour to the contract" (83). The wedding feast is an array of "imported and exported" objects, with "no nonsense" about any of it—in short, the marriage is a parody of the "party of Fact"'s pure materialism (83).

But so, also, is Louisa's affair, both in that she is the victim of Harthouse's tired seduction routine because she has no grounds but material grounds on which to make romantic choices, and in that the secret of her marriage, which Harthouse learns and uses to seduce her, is that she has sold herself into marriage not for her own improvement but for her brother's. Her father's system has left her viewing herself only as a commodity best exchanged for the good of others, in another dreadful parody of the maxim of the Utilitarians, the greatest good for the greatest number, and it is as a property plot that the adultery plot unfolds.

Louisa first reveals her sexual volatility to Harthouse through her devotion to her brother, "the whelp." Harthouse watches her brighten in response to her brother, and thinks, "it would be a new sensation, if the face which changed so beautifully for the whelp, would change for him" (126). In the overall coldness of Louisa's presence, her devotion to Tom is the only sign that she is at all penetrable. But the scenes in which Harthouse wins Louisa's sympathy, and begins to win her erotic attention through his own attention to her brother, center on her brother's siphoning off of her money, and her own dubious relationship to her property. Harthouse, insinuating his knowledge of the lack of affection between her brother and her husband, asks, "may there be a better confidence between yourself and me?" (129), asking not for sexual favors, but financial information:

"Tom has borrowed a considerable sum of you?"....

"When I married, I found that my brother was even at that time heavily in debt. Heavily for him, I mean. Heavily enough to oblige me to sell some trinkets. They were no sacrifice. I sold them very willingly. I attached no value to them. They were quite worthless to me."

Either she saw in his face that he knew, or she only feared in her conscience that he knew, that she spoke of some of her husband's gifts. She stopped, and reddened again. If he had not

known it before, he would have known it then, though he had
been a much duller man than he was.

"Since then, I have given my brother, at various times, *what
money I could spare: in short, what money I have had*." (129–30;
emphasis added)

What money Louisa could spare, which turns out to be all her money, must
be the money she is given by her husband, for she can have, we know, no
money of her own: similarly, she can sell her jewelry for him, for it is the only
part of her property that belongs expressly to her—and to sell it says clearly
to Harthouse that its "giver" is of no value to her. Harthouse's "penetration"
into Louisa's economic relationship with her brother automatically gives him
entrance into her economic relationship with her husband. As the whelp
complains, Bounderby will give him no money; his father "draw[s] what he
calls a line," and "here's my mother who never has anything of her own,
except her complaints. What *is* a fellow to do for money, and where *am* I to
look for it, if not to my sister?" (132). Looking to his sister involves describing
the sustained prostitution which is his sister's marriage to Bounderby:

"She could get it. It's of no use pretending to make a secret of
matters now, after what I have told you already; you know she
didn't marry old Bounderby for her own sake, or for his sake, but
for my sake. Then why doesn't she get what I want, out of him,
for my sake? She is not obliged to say what she is going to do
with it; she is sharp enough; she could manage to coax it out of
him, if she chose. Then why doesn't she choose, when I tell her
of what consequence it is? But no. There she sits in his company
like a stone, instead of making herself agreeable and getting it
easily. I don't know what you may call this, but *I* call it unnatural
conduct." (133)

This perverted sense of what is unnatural follows a description of the
interweaving of erotic energy and familial debt that is chilling, no less so is
the "confidence with her" that Harthouse has established "that absolutely
turned upon her indifference towards her husband, and the absence, now
and at all times, of any congeniality between them" (134). This financial
knowledge (and secret intimacy) seems as damning as sexual intimacy—but
it is through her "indifference" that the largely indifferent Harthouse intends
to trap Louisa.

That she escapes him suggests the way "mere" materialism will
not save her: Louisa must find another answer to her questions of "what

matters" than material goods. However, material goods—in the form of marital property—continue to follow her moral progress as her father and Bounderby negotiate over what turns out to be the return of Louisa—and her property—to her father's house. In some ways, she has never left it: Mrs. Sparsit, ever the reader's friend, helps us towards that reading by her inability to remember Louisa Bounderby's married name, calling her, variously, "Miss Gradgrind," "Mrs. Gradgrind," and—most tellingly—"Miss Bounderby" (145).[12] Gradgrind's attempts to impress Bounderby with Louisa's new self-knowledge ("I see reason to doubt whether we have ever quite understood Louisa" [178]) impress Bounderby only with Gradgrind's having been "brought low." In his version, there is "what people call some incompatibility between Loo Bounderby and myself," and he translates that immediately to mean "that your daughter don't properly know her husband's merits, and is not impressed with such a sense as would become her, by George! of the honour of his alliance" (179). Rejecting her father's plea that he "aid in trying to set her right," *he* responds by transforming the conversation immediately into one about property:

> "As to your daughter, whom I made Loo Bounderby and might have done better by leaving Loo Gradgrind, if she don't come home to-morrow, by twelve o'clock at noon, I shall understand that she prefers to stay away, and I shall send her wearing apparel and so forth over here, and you'll take charge of her for the future...."
>
> So Mr. Bounderby went home to his town house to bed. At five minutes past twelve o'clock next day, he directed Mrs. Bounderby's property to be carefully packed up and sent to Tom Gradgrind's; advertised his country retreat for sale by private contract; and resumed a bachelor life. (180–1)

The dissolution of the marriage, which ends the chapter, is marked not by romantic discussion, or even the erotic exchange suggested by Louisa's flight from her father's friend to her father's party-mate, but by the removal of her property (or that of her fictional legal self, "Mrs. Bounderby") and the sale of Bounderby's estate—his "private contract" here not marriage, but resale, and marital status not, as Gradgrind wished, an arrangement in "a friendly manner" (180) but merely a question of land ownership and rentals.

The novel's efforts focus on the attempt to avoid the accounting book model of marriage—indeed, of all human relationships—and Louisa's abrupt departure from her marriage is no exception. Bounderby remains committed to counting: his will calls for the founding of a house for orphans and the creation of twenty-five identical copies of himself; after Bounderby dies of a fit in the street, the will lingers in a Dickensian maze of "little service and much law," never yielding a result (218). Louisa returns to her father's house, leading a life of "not fantastic" duty, with "happy Sissy's happy children loving her," and with herself holding her course "simply as a duty to be done" (219). Louisa Bounderby, like Edith Dombey before her and Honoria Dedlock after, does not return to the happy ending, but is allowed a filial attachment. Her much-changed father, who clutched his favorite child to his bosom, only to hear her cry out "I shall die if you hold me! Let me fall upon the ground!" and see the "triumph of his system" lie an insensible heap at his feet (163), is now himself returned to sensibility, his system redeemed by her fall and her resurrection into a "gentler and a humbler" Louisa (218).

What Louisa Bounderby wanted from the world, her equivalent of "turtle soup and venison, with a gold spoon," is something more, what Bounderby calls with equal contempt, "imaginative qualities." From the book's beginning those qualities are summed up in the word "wonder," but from the time of Louisa's fall, we might rename them "wandering." What the novel wants is for people to learn to adulterate: to mix fact and fancy, to allow for the release of natural forces, to be "amuthed." "There is a love in the world, not all Thelf-interetht after all, but thomething very different" that "hath a way of ith own of calculating or not calculating" which is "hard to give a name to" (215). In *Dombey and Son*, of course, the only thing greater than money was the joy in another's destruction. In *Hard Times*, Dickens moves through a woman's joy in her own destruction to posit something like a moral awareness—only slightly undercutting it in the circus master Sleary's voice by aligning it to what dogs know. But in this novel, Dickens also imagines that the most imaginative and sensitive character in the industrial world, the woman who tries to imagine a destiny for herself beyond material interest, might fall short of her own imaginings; while her father is transformed, and her brother learns her value, and happy Sissy's happy children love her, Louisa Bounderby sits silent and alone by the cold hearth fire, an emblem for readerly rebirth, but unable herself to wander, to adulterate, to rejoin the plots of marriage and childbirth. She is left with no "fantastic vow, or bond, or brotherhood, or sisterhood, or pledge, or covenant, or fancy dress, or fancy fair; but simply ... a duty to be done" (219), and she does it, but despite her powers of prestidigitation by the fire, she sees no "blessing and happiness" for herself. The wandering daughter may be the road to social salvation, but for herself, at least in this novel, her only inheritance is the general good.

Readers of *A Tale of Two Cities* can only be amused by the extent to which it remains a "Dickens novel": it features a quiet, gentle daughter; an angry, passionate, dark woman; a father baffled by imprisonment and history; a husband, somewhat tamed and listless in the face of duty; and a dark, willful, charming, and dissolute lover, who must be forced (by love and destiny) to own up to his own inheritance and *act*. The novel, in effect, domesticates the French Revolution, and returns it to the key motifs we have been tracing: the daughter and her uncanny double, the heroine's perilous trek through the adultery plot, the maternal text from beyond the grave.[13] Indeed, revolution in *A Tale of Two Cities* is a plot carried out by fathers and daughters: Dickens self-consciously quotes the key-note of Thomas Carlyle, who, in characteristic fashion, referred to the guillotine as "Doctor Guillotin's daughter"; we can only note, in keeping with the pattern of doubling and daughters we have been stressing throughout, that this novel is patently "A Tale of Two Daughters" and of the daughter's duplicitous progress through history.[14]

The novel begins with the release from prison of Dr. Manette, the "good doctor of Beauvais," who has been in the Bastille for eighteen years, buried alive. He is reunited with the daughter he did not know he had, but whose image kept him alive all these years: she is 17, small, earnest, loving, with a head of golden hair, hair that will become, the narrator tells us, the "golden thread" that will lead Manette from prison, connect his present with his past, and serve as the narrative thread connecting the sections of the book.[15] In this way, Lucie (whose very name suggests the light of reason and memory she represents) will fulfill a familiar plot: the daughter's duty is to be the memory of her family, her father, her culture, the novel itself. And in a book obsessed with memory, restoration, connections—a book in which a character, Sydney Carton, is nicknamed "Memory Carton"—this is the central role, the melodramatic fulcrum of the novel.

But as the daughter's memory becomes the crisis-point of the novel, so she enters both the adultery plot and the plot of historical change. When the Manettes return to England, where Lucie has lived for many years, they become friends with a young French emigré known to them as Charles Darnay. He is tried for treason in England, and acquitted, in part because he is shown to have an uncanny double, Sydney Carton, who works for Darnay's lawyer. Carton, like Darnay, is soon in love with Lucie, whom he nonetheless describes with devastating accuracy as a "golden-haired doll."[16] Unlike Darnay, Carton is a wastrel, a drunkard, a ne'er-do-well and probably a rake; still, his love for Lucie is the one golden moment of his life, and (conveniently for the plot) he promises one day to do something to redeem his wasted life and "embrace any sacrifice for you and for those dear to you" (183). This seems a safe promise, but no sooner has Lucie married Darnay (despite some mysterious shrinking on the part of her father, Dr. Manette) than the French Revolution appears on the scene, drawing all the characters back to France and into their destiny. Darnay is arrested as an aristocrat and an emigré (a capital offence under the new regime); he is saved in a melodramatic trial scene by his father-in-law, whose status as a survivor of the Bastille carries considerable power in revolutionary France. The book could end here—except that Darnay is re-arrested, and charged with the past crimes of his family, crimes documented in a buried letter written by none other than Dr. Manette, and hidden by him in the Bastille.

The manuscript was recovered (and Darnay hunted down) by the book's most memorable character, Madame Defarge, wife of Manette's old servant, and (in the book's metaphorical scheme) the chief planner of the revolution, a tiger woman, who (pleasantly occupied in knitting throughout the whole novel) has been keeping within her needlework a secret register of those to be killed. "What do you knit?" a stranger has asked her; "many things," she replied; "For instance?" "For instance, shrouds" (203). Indeed, the narrative suggests, Madame Defarge has knit nothing less than the entire French Revolution, and as the book moves to its conclusion, the guillotine, under her watchful eye, carries out the deaths inscribed in her handiwork.

So far the novel's symbology seems carefully set up along conventional lines: Lucie Manette, the golden-haired doll, keeps a quiet home, filled with tactful French touches, though she has never lived in France. She has a worried little forehead, capable of a myriad expressions, and always at work—but *her* only work is to make a home for her father, choose the proper suitor to marry, and then reconcile her father to her marriage. Hers is an aggressively private life, calm and stable, the daughter's perfection of her domestic duty. Her opposite, in every way, is Madame Defarge, walking barefoot through the streets of France, a "tigress ... without pity" (391). It is Madame Defarge who keeps the spirit of the revolution: when her husband fears it will never come, that "we shall not see the triumph,"

> "We shall have helped it," returned madame, with her extended hand in strong action. "Nothing that we do, is done in vain. I believe, with all my soul, that we shall see the triumph. But even if not, even if I knew certainly not, show me the neck of an aristocrat and tyrant, and still I would—"
>
> Then madame, with her teeth set, tied a very terrible knot indeed. (208)

The "terrible knot" she is tying is the revolution, and specifically the executions that will follow; she "enforces" the conclusion of her advice to her husband by "striking her little counter with her chain of money as if she knocked its brains out" (208–209).

Madame Defarge is associated here, as elsewhere, with the violence of the guillotine and the spectacle of revolution: it is she who takes the humble "mender of roads" to see the royal family:

> "As to you," said she, "you would shout and shed tears for anything, if it made a show and a noise. Say! Would you not?"
>
> "Truly Madam, I think so. For the moment."
>
> "If you were shown a great heap of dolls, and were set upon them to pluck them to pieces and despoil them for your own advantage, you would pick out the richest and gayest. Say! Would you not?"
>
> "Truly, yes, Madam."
>
> "Yes. And if you were shown a flock of birds, unable to fly, and were set upon them to strip them of their feathers for your own advantage, you would set upon the birds of the finest feathers; would you not?"
>
> "It is true, Madam."
>
> "You have seen both dolls and birds today." (204)

It is the sheer unexpectedness of this passage—not only the violence, but the placidity of Madame Defarge's diction and its eerie resemblance to instruction, the deceptive gentleness of dolls and birds—that accentuates its viciousness: it is also the undoing of Madame Defarge's "womanly" character, and the uncanny invocation of Lucie Manette, called a "golden haired doll" by Sydney Carton and "Ladybird" by her servant, Miss Pross, in the specter of the "heaps of dolls" and "flock of birds" that are to be set upon, stripped, and despoiled. Madame Defarge's violence is an undoing of domesticity; the same violation of womanhood represented by the crowds of women on the streets, who break down the laws of public and private when they dance the Carmagnole; a "fallen sport—a something, once innocent, delivered over to all devilry—a healthy pastime changed into a means of angering the blood, bewildering the senses, and steeling the heart" (307). For Dickens, the terror of the dance was that it "perverted all things good by nature"—by which he means femininity: "The maidenly bosom bared to this, the pretty almost-child's head thus distracted, the delicate foot mincing in this slough of blood and dirt were types of the disjointed time" (307–308).

What Madame Defarge wants is precisely to disjoint that scene: to her and her henchman, Lucie, with her "pretty almost-child's head," is only a threat, the wife of the traitor Evrémonde and the mother of his daughter. In their view, all this only adds to the spectacle she will make before the guillotine:

> "She has a fine head for it," croaked Jacques Three. "I have seen blue eyes and golden hair there, and they looked charming when Samson held them up."
> Ogre that he was, he spoke like an epicure.
> Madame Defarge cast down her eyes, and reflected a little.
> "The child also," observed Jacques Three, with a meditative enjoyment of his words, "has golden hair and blue eyes. And we seldom have a child there. It is a pretty sight." (388)

This could stand not only as a representative conservative denunciation of revolution ("Look, they don't spare even women and children," as we might paraphrase it—or as Jerry Cruncher summarizes the revolution, "a goin' on dreadful round him, in the way of Subjects without heads" [337]), but as a representative icon for Dickens's art. Women, children, golden hair, and blue eyes: "a pretty sight" in the "way of Subjects" indeed.

But this is not all that links pretty, blonde, blue-eyed Lucie Manette to the spectacle of the French revolution, and Dickens begins to complicate the daughter's relationship to history. Lucie has also become part of the spectacle around her: while her husband has been imprisoned, she has been seen daily outside his prison, waving and kissing her hand to him, holding up their daughter to his eyes. In the revolution's breakdown of public and private spheres, Lucie's movements mark her as a spy, and the woodcutter whose hut she stands near is prepared to testify against her, for she has been "making signs and signals to Prisoners." Her devotion, Carton reports, will be read as "a prison plot, and ... it will involve her life—and perhaps her child's—and perhaps her father's ..." (373). Here Dickens's view of the interpenetration of domestic and political space anticipates Lynn Hunt's: "the other side of the rhetorical refusal of politics was the impulse to invest politics everywhere. Because politics did not take place in a defined sphere, it tended to invade everyday life instead." In what Hunt calls the "compulsive publicity" of the revolution, and what Dickens calls the "universal watchfulness," there is no private life left.[17]

Lucie is linked even more powerfully than through paranoia with the book's spectacle of political life, however: the central image of the novel (and the revolution) is apostrophized in terms uncannily like those that summon up our heroine. There was no more potent symbol of the revolution's power (and the terror it conjured) than the guillotine; and yet the guillotine, as imagined by Carlyle's *French Revolution*, is "the product of Guillotin's endeavors, gained not without meditation and reading; which product popular gratitude or levity christens by a feminine derivative name, as if it were his daughter: *La Guillotine!*"[18]. Dickens, as well, refers to the "sharp female newly-born" (283), the "sharp female called La Guillotine" (302), but in bringing together these two images (the sharp female, the dutiful daughter) he seems to be bringing together his own two opposite poles of femininity, Lucie Manette (whose father is called, by one character, "a doctor with a daughter" [156]) and Thérèse Defarge, whose sharpness is the terror of the novel.

The guillotine, that public spectacle, is at the center of daily life in the revolution—indeed, it is relentlessly domesticated by the novel. It was, the novel says,

> the popular theme for jests; it was the best cure for headache, it infallibly prevented the hair from turning grey, it imparted a particular delicacy to the complexion, it was the National Razor which shaved close: who kissed La Guillotine, looked through the little window and sneezed into the sack. (302)

A recent scholar has commented that Dickens, typically, has recorded virtually all the contemporary humour surrounding that "sharp female newly-born"[19]: in his account the blood is merely "red wine" for La Guillotine, "to slake her devouring thirst." The wood-sawyer who watches Lucie at the prison calls his saw "my Little Guillotine" or "Little Sainte Guillotine," for "the great sharp female was by that time popularly canonised" (305, 307). But that "canonization" is also Dickens's way of treating small, soft women, and the description invokes both heroines. The guillotine is a not an uncommon sign for male anxiety, but the anxiety reaches further into the culture: as Jacques Barzun wrote of Berlioz's generation, they were "as much haunted by the guillotine as we are by the death camps".[20] The images of the guillotine are poised between the gothic animation of the "sharp female," and the mechanization of death the guillotine represented: quick, impersonal death, meant to mimic the impersonality and equality of justice, emphasizing that government by the people is exclusive of all expressions of individual will; that, as Robespierre wrote, the virtue with which the people are imbued consists precisely in the "sublime sentiment [that] prefers the public to all private interest."[21] As Daniel Arasse summarizes it, the guillotine from this standpoint exemplified "the very principle of revolutionary democracy: it emphasized the individuality of each of its victims the better to annihilate it—more exactly, to deny this individuality by the mechanical process with which the victim was destroyed."[22]

It is not in the nature of novels to prefer the public to the private—indeed, the work of the novel seems the opposite of the very transparency of the private sphere the revolution called for, the rendering of each event public, political, momentous. The world of spies called forth by the Terror, one subtly invoked by Dickens, is one in which the most random gesture signifies a political stand—and it is a world in which citizens could be charged with not supporting the Revolution with enough enthusiasm; a world in which, Marat said, citizens could not be blamed for making false accusations against others, for their vehemence suggested their passion for the revolution; a world in which "twenty-one Girondins were dispatched in twenty-six minutes;" in which the skin of aristocrats was tanned, for its softness, and the hair of victims was turned into wigs; a world which, indeed, suggests a horror of impersonality we fear we live with; a world of spectacle gone awry, in which prisoners would practice their own guillotining, so as to make a noble show for themselves.[23]

But it is also a world of chummy violence, horror rendered (to return to our central terms) domestic: as one recent account has it, the guillotine "became a tourist attraction, inspired songs, was reproduced in fashion items (earrings, gowns *en guillotine*), and even appeared as a household appliance, in the form of a bread slicer."[24] This suggests the reverse of the process I have been charting, in which the revolution reveals the horror in the domestic; in this account, we might say, the revolution comes home.

Or perhaps, as Dickens's novel suggests, it *begins* at home. If gentle Lucie Manette, receptacle of cultural and paternal memory, is allied in unexpected ways to the guillotine, the force that cuts through the novel, she is thus allied to Thérèse Defarge, who seemed merely her evil double. The novel's doubleness is so powerful that it can be read in the opposite direction as well, for with the revelation of Thérèse's family history, with her movement back into the private sphere, the public revolution becomes more sympathetic, and her anger at "birds of the finest feather" moves closer to Lucie's fierce defense of home. Thérèse's sister was raped by Charles Darnay's uncle, and her father and brother were killed to conceal the crime—a crime revealed in Dr. Manette's prison narrative.[25] The real crime in the novel, the omission that the revolution must fill in, is Charles Darnay's inability to complete his mother's last request, for his mother had come to the doctor to see the girl, who is, alas, already dead: "Her hope had been, she said in great distress, to show her, in secret, a woman's sympathy" (360). Further, "she had reasons for believing that there was a young sister living, and her greatest desire was, to help that sister." In the doctor's presence she makes Charles, her "pretty boy," swear to "bestow, with the compassion and lamenting of his dead mother, [money little beyond the worth of a few jewels], on this injured family, if the sister can be discovered" (360). Charles has not pursued this search zealously enough: Madame Defarge has been under his (and our) gaze for the whole of the novel, and her "vengeance" (the Revolution) is her response:

> "I tell him, 'Defarge, I was brought up among the fisherman of the sea-shore, and that peasant family so injured by the two Evrémonde brothers, as that Bastille paper describes, is my family. Defarge, that sister of the mortally wounded boy upon the ground was my sister, that husband was my sister's husband, that unborn child was their child, that brother was my brother, that father was my father, those dead are my dead, and that summons to answer for those things descends to me!'" (370)

At that moment, with Thérèse Defarge's "answer," the Revolution and its terror become the daughter's revenge, the act of memory this novel seems to have been calling for: Lucie's story and Thérèse's have come together, and the Revolution has become a female narrative, born in a story of rape, violation, and filial memory.

In some compelling ways, adultery is the only outcome of this text, primarily because of the text's relentless doubling: not only are there two daughters, but (at various times) the novel becomes a tale of two cuisines (Miss Pross learns to cook dinners "half English and half French" [129]); two decorating styles (Lucie's London lodging "appeared to have innately derived from [the country of her birth] that ability to make much of little means" [124]); two banks (Tellson's London and Paris offices, which exchange the documents that generate the plot); and of course two languages (little Lucie speaks in "the tongues of the Two Cities" [240]). The novel worries constantly about the relationship between these doubles: are they truly separate; can they be merged in a happy marriage; can the two be reconciled in one historical narrative? But with the same force that Lucie Manette is haunted by Thérèse Defarge, twin daughters of history-swept fathers, so is her husband, Charles Darnay, mirrored by Sydney Carton, his physical double, and the tale of the two husbands proves more complicated, however much they are drawn together. After Carton saves Darnay's life the first time, he mockingly asks him, "Do you think I particularly like you?" (115). But the scene ended with Carton's muttering to himself in the mirror, "why should you particularly like

a man who resembles you? There is nothing in you to like; you know that"
(116). Different versions of "like" seem constantly at risk in this text, and
it is worth noting only the central characterological resemblance between
Darnay and Carton: both are sons of devout mothers, haunted by the image
of a mother who wants them to reform, and both imagine carrying out that
reformation through Lucie. Charles's mother, from whom he has taken his
English name, represents the force of historical restoration, the wrong never
righted that must somehow be avenged; Sydney Carton, whose body will
take the place of Charles's in that great historical righting of the wrong,
hopes in that action to appease his mother and fulfill the promise of what he
would have been had he followed her guidance. That promise is repeated in
the novel—specifically, and adulterously, to Lucie Manette, who proves (like
all good daughters) the stand-in for all mothers (historical, memorialized,
and in any way fetishized) in the novel.

     Carton's fantasy of maternal remembrance and fraternal resemblance
becomes explicitly sexualized as the novel goes on, and takes the specific
form of imagining himself as adulterous father to Lucie's children. The
scene in which he first does this is the climax of the book's middle, nominally
courtship, section: Lucie Manette has been pursued by three suitors, Darnay,
Carton, and Stryver, the self-impressed lawyer. These men may be courting
Lucie, but we never actually see any of them propose to her: Darnay speaks
to her father prior to an offstage proposal; Stryver discusses the matter with
Jarvis Lorry, who (also offstage) raises the question with the Manettes, and
returns to repeat his advice that Stryver not attempt a proposal; and Carton
begins his odd pursuit of Lucie by remarking that it is fortunate after all
that Lucie does *not* love him. This absence of propositional scenes serves to
throw attention not on Lucie and Darnay's dance of attraction (which is of
minimal interest at best) but rather on the relationship between Darnay and
Lucie's father: the tension of the middle of the book leads up to the scene
in which Darnay (again, offstage) reveals to Dr. Manette that he is the son
of the Marquis St Evrémonde; that his father and uncle raped the sister of
Thérèse Defarge and murdered her father, brother, and husband—and that
Dr. Manette is the only witness to their deed. This secret remains a secret
from the reader until the great trial scene of the third volume, but readers
are poised to be more curious about the secret meeting between bridegroom
and father than about anything that happens between Darnay and Lucie.

     Into this erotic void sidles Sydney Carton. Although his dissipation
is merely hinted at ("the life I lead," he says, "is not conducive to health"
[180]) his very posture singles him out as the erotic other in the novel: rather
than striding or standing erect, he "leans" (112, 132), he "lounges" (133),
he "wander[s]" (342), he walks aimlessly—he is, for the heroine, the guide

to the erotic wanderings that mark (off) the adulterous path. The scene in which he approaches Lucie comes after her engagement, at a moment when he is "thankful" that she cannot feel tenderness for, or return the love of "the man you see before you—self-flung away, wasted, drunken, poor creature of misuse as you know him to be" (180). The work of the novel is to remake that self-flinging into the heroic self-sacrifice Carton effects at the end, when he takes Darnay's place first in the prison, and then at the guillotine; its origins are in this scene of secret meeting, when he tells her "you have been the last dream of my soul"; that in her presence he has "heard whispers from old voices impelling me upward, that I thought were silent for ever"; that "with ... a sudden mastery you kindled me, heap of ashes that I am, into fire" (181). The scene, with its heightened, eroticized mixture of self-loathing and adoration, ends with two gestures on Carton's part: his request that "my name, and faults, and miseries [be] gently carried in your heart" (182); the second, his promise that

> "when the little picture of a happy father's face looks up in yours, when you see your own bright beauty springing up anew at your feet, think now and then that there is a man who would give his life, to keep a life you love beside you!" (183)

The burden of Carton's meeting is that the "last confidence" of his life be carried by her, and by her alone. That shared secret creates the twin progeny of the scene: his relationship to her children, and his mastery over her husband's life.

Carton's presence in the perfect domesticity of the Darnays is, as he wants it to be, that of a "useless ... piece of furniture" (237), or would be were it not for Lucie's imploring her husband to be gentle with the wanderer who carries "wounds" in his heart—and if not for her child's sympathy with him, for, the narrator assures the reader, "No man ever really loved a woman, lost her, and knew her with a blameless though an unchanged mind, when she was a wife and mother, but her children had a strange sympathy with him" (241). Carton is the "first stranger" to whom little Lucie holds out her chubby arms; he is the last ("almost at the last") person to whom the "little boy" speaks before death: "Poor Carton! Kiss him for me!" The adultery plot works itself out not only through Carton's sacrifice, and his continued presence—however furniture-like—in the Darnay menage, but in this displaced paternity: his ability, at his death, to invent still more children to remember and name him.

This fantasy matters so profoundly because questions of memory and proper naming (questions of inheritance and descent) are essential not only to the familial but to the historical plot of the novel. Indeed, the adultery plots register not only as part of a more general anxiety about male paternity and female fidelity, but an anxiety about the transmission of value: as the anthropologist Carol Delaney has argued, adultery disrupts the motions of transmission upon which orderly society depends, not only of paternity, but of honor and masculine identity. As Delaney summarizes it,

> Contrary to the evidence of the senses, paternity has meant the creative, life-giving role. Paternity is over-determined, and in proportion so too are the social measures constructed to ensure the legitimacy of paternity ...[26]

These measures are harsh to the degree that women are perceived as vulnerable—indeed, in an unexpected echoing of Lucie and Carton's secret meeting, Delaney reports that in Turkish village society, women are held to be so incapable of containing their own boundaries that if men and women are alone together for more than twenty minutes it is assumed they have had intercourse, and this constitutes grounds for divorce. "It is because women are thought to be so vulnerable, so open to persuasion, that they must be socially closed or covered";[27] it follows, then, that a man has access to social authority—to the legitimacy of paternity—only through a female property defined by its vulnerability.

In *A Tale of Two Cities*, that legitimacy takes the form of historical authority—the ability to inscribe not only views of the future, but visions of the past. Madame Defarge's memory, enhanced by her knitting (which includes names, dates, and faces) contends with the (loving) memory of the Darnay/Manette party, who bind people to themselves with affection and recollection. The most horrifying moment of the novel, and the one bit of suspense it maintains, is that it is Dr. Manette's own *written* text, one written to preserve the memory he feared was fading in the darkness of the Bastille, which will condemn Charles Darnay to death—just as, with similar irony, it is Darnay's attempt to honor his mother's memory, to enact her dying wish that he make amends to the Defarge family, that leads him to the Manettes in the first place; his loyalty to Gabelle, the estate's manager, that draws him back to the ruins of France, and his own probable death. The letter Gabelle sends to "Monsieur heretofore the Marquis" (270) is only one of many documents within the text inscribed to persons who are already ghosts.

To write to ghosts—or to expect ghosts to fulfill promises; or in any way to expect the future to "right" the past—is to impose an uneasy burden through inheritance and through memory. While the novel is in many ways on the side of history, the persistence of memory is synonymous with the

Terror itself: the "Ghosts" of La Force prison ("the ghost of beauty, the ghost of stateliness, the ghost of elegance, the ghost of pride ... all waiting their dismissal from the desolate shore" [285]) may be harmless "apparations" (286), but Madame Defarge's determination to extinguish the entire "race" (370) of Evrémondes suggests that one's family will write one's story forever, and one's individual deeds count as nothing. Not only individuals but the society will be unable to forget; all existence will become a haunting. *A Tale of Two Cities* shares its ambivalence about this inheritance with much of Dickens's later fiction, and registers a departure from some of the earlier work of good daughters like Florence Dombey, who claims she can never be made to forget. As the selfish but honest Fanny Dorrit cries out, to her obsessively memorial sister Amy, "are we never to be permitted to forget?" Amy Dorrit's insistence that it would be cruel to forget places where people have been kind to one takes on a nightmare twist in Thérèse Defarge's "Dickensian" repetition of the past: "that sister ... was my sister, that husband was my sister's husband, that unborn child was their child, that brother was my brother, that father was my father, those dead are my dead, and that summons to answer for those things descends to me!" (370). In the power of the "me" who answers is a "me" who is *never* permitted to forget, and out of whom will be born nothing of promise.

The problem of memory becomes not only one of proper transmission, but of when time is to have an end, of what thread is to bind the past to the present and the future, and whether that thread should run uncut. As in *The Old Curiosity Shop*, *Dombey and Son*, and *David Copperfield*, the key to memory is the daughter who, in her resemblance to her mother, *is* the thread that binds the generation—in that daughter, the mother lives again. Without the assurance of that connection, Dr. Manette would wander forever in the darkness of the Bastille; Darnay would leave no progeny; the book would end, one assumes, without hope. Nonetheless, when Lucie first appears to Dr. Manette, he is terrified, and Lucie is terrorized by her own guilt at somehow not having known that her father was alive all along. The terror is not that memory will fade but that it will perilously persist—it will be "buried alive."

If the daughter's memory in this novel holds real terror, much as Madame Defarge's memory provokes the Terror of the Revolution, one alternative form of memory is away from maternal or daughterly transmission, and through the illicit progress of the adultery plot. As in *Hard Times*, adultery suggests a possible reordering of narrative and the social order: here, it further suggests a profound ambivalence about historical descent. The way this novel ensures a future is not through Darnay, but through his wandering, dissolute, and seemingly sterile double, Carton,

whose evocation of future generations generates the end of the novel, and
suggests the power of history to continue.

When Carton is finally on his way to save Darnay, he walks the city
streets, and the narrator claims "It was the settled manner of a tired man,
who had wandered and struggled and got lost, but who at length struck
into his road and saw its end" (342). That passage suggests the end of the
adultery plot, the end of wandering and the substitution of a firm goal (the
road's end) for the dilatory travails he has indulged in so far. The road's end
is still clouded in secrecy for the reader: Carton arrives secretly ("who could
that be ... who must not be seen" [309]), plots secretly (he has "business... in
his secret mind" [327]), and, whatever is in his mind, he "never mentioned
Lucie's name" (373). He progresses in silence through the complicated plot
of substituting himself for Darnay and dying his death, but he nonetheless
transmits one message: he kisses the unconscious Lucie, and "The child, who
was nearest him, told them afterwards, and told her grandchildren when she
was a handsome old lady, that she heard him say, 'A life you love.'" (366).
She repeats, unknowingly, the promise he had made in his earlier scene with
Lucie, and it is the daughter who becomes the fulfillment of their secret
memory-pact.

But Carton is not satisfied with one child or one inheritance: his final
vision is of Lucie "with a child upon her bosom, who bears my name"; of
himself "hold[ing] a sanctuary in their hearts, and in the hearts of their
descendants, generations hence"; of "that child who lay upon her bosom
and who bore my name, a man winning his way up in that path of life which
once was mine" (404). And finally, Carton sees *that* child become a man
("foremost of just judges and honoured men") bringing "a boy of my name,
with a forehead that I know and golden hair, to this place—then fair to look
upon, with not a trace of this day's disfigurement." The figure he summons,
a child with his name and Lucie's face, the child of a child she doesn't have
yet, will repair the disfigurement: the child who is somehow theirs will not
only redeem the legal profession (no small feat in a Dickens novel) but
restore the beauty of history, making the hideous fair to look upon, as well as
justly judged. If Carton's final historical vision is to "see the evil of this time
and of the previous time of which this is the natural birth, gradually making
expiation for itself and wearing out," he must conjure up a rather unnatural
birth to carry out that redemption of France, the family, history itself.

This fantasy of male birth through adulterous passion is, however,
far from all-conclusive. Carton seems to capture all narrative authority
to himself through his heroic self-sacrifice and his posthumous narration,
even dictating his suicide note to the hapless and impotent Darnay, but
the text presents several important counter-arguments to his version of

history. Carton's final prophecies, his (the text's) closing words are variously imagined as passing through not masculine but feminine ventriloquism, and invoke again a literary authority slightly at odds with Dickens's intense overidentification with the adulterous, wasted, heroic ne'er do well and his theatrical end.[28] The conclusion of *A Tale of Two Cities* makes its way through a series of spectacular women, and invokes a literary inheritance far different from that of the lone hero facing his death and his possible erasure from history.

Carton's valedictory message is introduced by the narrator's invocation of the most famous scribbling woman who faced the guillotine, Madame Roland:

> One of the most remarkable sufferers by the same axe—a woman—had asked at the foot of the same scaffold, not long before, to be allowed to write down the thoughts that were inspiring her. If [Carton] had given an utterance to his, and they were prophetic, they would have been these.... (404)

What follows is a series of visions: "I see ... long ranks of the new oppressors who have risen on the destruction of the old perishing by this retributive instrument"; "I see the lives for which I lay down my life, peaceful, useful, prosperous and happy," "I see Her with a child upon her bosom, who bears my name ..." and so on (404). It is odd enough that these meditations are invoked in such a dreamy way, with the narrator's series of conditional clauses: there is no guarantee either that Carton had a vision or that it had the truth of prophecy.[29] What is more remarkable is that they are invoked through Madame Roland, whose prison memoir was one of the central documents of the revolution circulating in England. When Carton goes to "give utterance," he follows in the path of an unfinished manuscript by a woman writer—one whose last letter, interestingly enough, was to her daughter, and whose last note, in her memoir, was of her pleasure that her property would, upon her death, pass to that daughter. Not only the novelist's vision, but the vision of "a beautiful city" rising from the ashes is handed over, by extension, to a prophetic, propertied, "remarkable" woman.

The text dilutes still further Carton's closural authority—or rather, dilates it through the gaze of another prophetic woman. In the tumbril on his way to the guillotine, Carton meets a young seamstress who was in prison with Darnay, the one fellow-sufferer to recognize that Carton is someone else. She asks if he dies "for him"—"Yes," answers Carton, "and his wife and child," repeating again his earlier promise to Lucie (384). The seamstress's fate is more interesting: when he asks her what she is in prison for, she answers "Plots." "But," she goes on, "who would think of plotting with a poor little weak creature like me?" (384). The question opens up the novel once more: like the guillotine's specular display of the heads of small women and their beautiful children, the seamstress's plaintive cry comments on Dickens's own narrative as the spectacle of the suffering of "poor little weak creatures." But yet once more, it also suggests the ways that the revolution (with its blurring of public and private, familial and historical) *is* a plot by poor little weak creatures: in a world where Madame Defarge's knitting sends many to their deaths, what is so innocent about being a seamstress?

Most interesting of all, at the end of this rather reactionary novel of political change and upheaval, the seamstress unexpectedly gets one of the most radical statements the novel allows itself. As they ride to their deaths, she asks Carton a question:

> "I have a cousin, an only relative and an orphan like myself whom I love very dearly.... Poverty parted us, and she knows nothing of my fate—for I cannot write—and if I could, how should I tell her! It is better as it is.... If the Republic really does good to the poor, and they come to be less hungry, and in all ways to suffer less, she may live a long time: she may even live to be old.... Do you think ... that it will seem long to me, while I wait for her in the better land where I trust both you and I will be mercifully sheltered?" (403)

For the first time in many pages in the novel, someone reminds readers of why the revolution was necessary: the Republic could do good to the poor, and they could come to be less hungry. There was a brief, similar moment when Darnay is walked to La Force prison, and is suddenly invisible, for at this moment, that an aristocrat, "a man in good clothes should be going to prison, was no more remarkable than that a labourer in working clothes should be going to work" (283). When the seamstress turns to history she connects her own imminent death with the labor of Dr. Manette at his shoe-making and Jerry Cruncher at his "resurrection": for Dickens, the Revolution is in part the terror, and in part, the problem of social order and labor, much more in the vein of *Hard Times* (and of Thomas Carlyle's social writings) than of romantic historical fiction. Carton, characteristically, ignores that part of the seamstress's question, and assures her they are going to a place where "there is no Time ... and no trouble there." Like his final invocation of the "better rest" he goes to, his response gestures at a space outside narrative, history, memory, where all revolutions, including the normal revolutions of plot, will cease to matter—although, of course, his prophecy depends on the transmission of his historical message through Lucie's as-yet unborn children.

The *seamstress's* final invocation of vatic authorship, however, suggests something else: "for I cannot write—and if I could, how should I tell her!" Neither Lucie nor Madame Defarge, the text's twin "daughters of time," is allowed such a prophetic moment, and the novel ends by suggesting that the events of these dark days remain unreportable—in contrast to Sydney, the daughter is more hesitant to claim the authority over history, and as I have suggested, her inheritance is troubled by its affiliation with the other terrors of the novel. "That story," in the words of *Dombey and Son's* narrator, "never goes about": like the good daughter, it must here remain domesticated. But *A Tale of Two Cities* hints at something more: that not male prophecy but female property will go on to tell a different story, and that the daughter's hand will write another revolution. If she could write, this novel suggests, the daughter would have *much* to tell, and in a letter to another (even if unknown) woman, would open a different account book of history.

If the role of the adultery plot in all these novels has been to adjust the balances of social order, and return everyone to a rightful (righted, written) place within plot and history, the daughter's story has been the fulcrum of that balancing act, whether in the circus of *Hard Times* or the carnival of the French Revolution. In *Bleak House*, however, when the daughter claims a different "portion," and the mother bestows a different inheritance, female writing will offer another story, one that as yet cannot be told ("How should I tell?"), but will come to have its own revolutionary matrix.

NOTES

1. *David Copperfield* (Harmondsworth, Middlesex: Penguin Books, 1966), pp. 685, 335.

2. The importance of what David "sees" when he thinks he sees her adultery connects with the narrator's repetition of Aunt Betsey's quiet refrain "blind, blind, blind," the sign of his misunderstanding of his own "mistaken impulses" and "undisciplined heart," all of which lead him to marry Dora rather than Agnes; Annie Strong's speech is crucial to David's coming to clearer (for which, read adult) erotic sight. See Gwendolyn Needham, "The Undisciplined Heart of David Copperfield" (*Nineteenth-Century Fiction*, 9, 1954, pp. 81–107) for the classic exposition of these questions; see my Introduction for further discussion.

3. Alexander Welsh, in *Copyright to Copperfield: Dickens and Identity* (Cambridge, MA: Harvard University Press, 1988) makes this connection between the child's names. For accounts of the breakdown of Dickens's marriage, see, among others, Michael Slater, *Dickens and Women* (Stanford, CA: Stanford University Press, 1983).

4. There are several studies that attempt to connect various "personal" plots to political structures; see in particular Catherine Gallagher, "Relationship Remembered

against Relationship Forgot," in *The Industrial Reformation of English Fiction: Social Discourse and Narrative Form 1832–1867* (Chicago: The University of Chicago Press, 1985). Several of these studies raise questions of imagination and wonder; few connect them explicitly to sexual adventures.

5. *Hard Times*, edited by George Ford and Sylvère Monod (New York: Norton, 1990), p. 78.

6. At many points in the novel, Dickens seems to suggest industrialism might go on as it is, and only be softened by the relaxation of play-days: the "attributes" of Coketown that produce the "comforts of life" that make their way "all over the world" can continue; those aspects "which are voluntary" should be changed, to give some "physical relief" and "recognized holiday" to the workers, lest their craving for relief "inevitably go wrong" (pp. 22, 24). For a wonderful analysis of Dickens's "industrial" prose, see Nicholas Coles, "The Politics of *Hard Times*: Dickens the Novelist versus Dickens the Reformer," *Dickens Studies Annual*, Vol. 15, 1986, pp. 145–179; my favorite critique of the "let them have circuses" argument remains John Holloway's, in *Hard Times: A History and a Criticism*, edited by John Gross and Gabriel Pearson (Toronto: University of Toronto Press, 1962). Holloway takes on squarely the chief defense of the novel's "moral fable," that of F. R. Leavis (in *Dickens the Novelist* [New York: Pantheon, 1970]) and argues for Mrs. Sparsit's pursuit of Louisa as the liveliest part of the novel: The "passages in *Hard Times* where Dickens most shows his genius," he argues, come when he is least involved with what Leavis terms the "peculiarly insistent moral intention" (p. 174).

7. For a compelling feminist reading of the "Bluebeard" scene and *Mrs*. Gradgrind, see Jean Ferguson Carr, "Writing as a Woman: Dickens, *Hard Times* and Feminine Discourses," *Dickens Studies Annual*, Vol. 18, 1989, pp. 161–178.

8. Stephen uses this phrase so often that characters within the novel tease him for it—Rachael (54) and Bounderby (113) in particular. It is not really possible, given the inter-textual mockery, to believe that Dickens thought Stephen had an adequate response to the complexities of industrialism.

9. The passage appears in manuscript and in the corrected proof, where it is not cancelled, yet it did not appear in the *Household Words* publication of *Hard Times* or subsequent editions. See *Hard Times* (Norton Critical Edition), p. 247.

10. Nonetheless, the quiescence of both plots remains hard to accept—and it is interesting in that light that only Louisa escapes the worst of her fate. My colleague Barry Glassner has suggested to me that the difficulty in aligning the Louisa/Stephen plots lies in the absence of a specific political program for the working class in the 1850s; while Louisa's plot can be read through the debates over the married women's property laws, despite the widespread interest in the Preston Lockout, there was no comparable political debate in the 1850s over increased workers' representation.

11. Douglas, *Purity and Danger: An Analysis of the Concepts of Pollution and Taboo* (London: Routledge and Kegan Paul, 1966), p. 40.

12. Robert Newsom has noted that the "problem of identity" is "absent in any sustained way from *Hard Times*," but it seems to me where it comes up most powerfully is in Louisa's attempt to make the connection between her legal identity *as* Mrs. Bounderby, and her psychic identity as both Tom Gradgrind's daughter and her own, self-possessed self. That the parody of the quest for identity is Bounderby's repetition of himself in a multiplicity of renamed orphans comments again on the relationship between individual identity and legal, marital, reproductive identity. See Newsom, "'To Scatter Dust': Fancy and Authenticity in *Our Mutual Friend*," *Dickens Studies Annual*, Vol. 8, 1980, pp. 39–60.

13. There is a powerful body of work connecting the French Revolution to sexual anxiety: See in particular Neil Hertz, "Medusa's Head: Male Hysteria under Political Pressure" (*Representations* 4, 1983, reprinted in *The End of the Line: Essays on Psychoanalysis and the Sublime*, New York: Columbia University Press, 1985, 161–191). Catherine Gallagher's response in the same volume (pp. 194–196) suggestively relocates the site of anxiety, as I have tried to do, from male castration to female generativity. For further work along these lines, see Dorinda Outram, *The Body and the French Revolution: Sex, Class and Political Culture* (New Haven, CT: Yale University Press, 1989), and *The Family Romance of the French Revolution* (Berkeley: University of California Press, 1992); for general discussions of problems of representation and revolution, in particular the power of spectacle, see Lynn Hunt, *Politics, Culture, and Class in the French Revolution* (Berkeley: University of California Press, 1984).

14. Thomas Carlyle, *The French Revolution* (London: Everyman's Library, 1906, 1973), Vol. 1, p. 115. For a fine essay on doubling in *A Tale of Two Cities*, see Catherine Gallagher, "The Duplicity of Doubling in *A Tale of Two Cities*," in *Dickens Studies Annual*, Vol. 12, 1983, pp. 125–145.

15. The second of the novel's "Books" is called "The Golden Thread," suggesting the almost organic work that Lucie (or her symbolic embodiment, her hair) must do. This organicism is another of the things that links the novel to the historical work of Thomas Carlyle, to whose researches and thematic exposition Dickens was profoundly indebted in writing *A Tale of Two Cities*. This debt to Carlyle is too extensive to be explored here; Andrew Sanders has offered a compelling account of the more specific borrowings in "'Cartloads of Books': Some Sources for *A Tale of Two Cities*," in *Dickens and other Victorians: Essays in Honor of Philip Collins*, edited by Joanne Shattock (New York: St Martin's Press, 1988), pp. 37–52. Obviously, Carlyle's influence extends throughout the historical and social novels of the 1850s, as the dedication and the section titles for *Hard Times* ("Sowing," "Reaping," "Garnering") suggest; where it enters the adultery plot is both in the spectacularizing of the revolution in both novels, and in the faith in spiritual growth that centers both Louisa and Sydney Carton's "Dawn of knowledge of [their] immaterial self," to quote the working plans for *Hard Times*.

16. *A Tale of Two Cities*, edited by George Woodcock (Harmondsworth: Penguin, 1970), p. 121; all subsequent page references to the novel are included in the text.

17. Hunt, *Politics, Culture and Class*, p. 56. See her discussion of public life, pp. 33–46.

18. Carlyle, *The French Revolution*, ibid.

19. Daniel Gerould, in *Guillotine: Its Legends and Lore* (New York: Blast Books, 1992), p. 153.

20. Jacques Barzun, *Berlioz and the Romantic Century*, quoted in Gerould, *Guillotine* p. 85.

21. Robespierre, *Oeuvres completes*, X, p. 353 (February 5, 1794); quoted in Daniel Arasse, *The Guillotine and the Terror*, translated by Christopher Miller (London: Allen Lane The Penguin Press, 1989), p. 81.

22. Arasse, *The Guillotine and the Terror*, p. 83.

23. The passage from Marat reads in full: "It is essential that every justified denunciation should entitle the informer to public respect. Each unfounded denunciation, if made from patriotic motives, should not expose the informer to any penalty." Marat, *L'Ami du Peuple*, quoted in Peter Vansittart, *Voices of the Revolution* (London: Collins, 1989), p. 228. Vansittart also quoted a decree from the Paris Commune that no certificate of citizenship shall be issued to "those who, while in no ways hostile to the Revolution, have lifted no finger on behalf of it" (250); in *A Tale of Two Cities*, "Five were to be tried together, next, as enemies of the Republic, forasmuch as they had not assisted it by word

or deed" (314); they are condemned before Darnay who has been temporarily freed, has time to leave the building.

The count of dead Girondins comes from Arasse, *The Guillotine and the Terror*, p. 83; the tanning of aristocrats is given by Carlyle, as described by Montgaillard: "The skins of the men, he remarks, was superior in toughness (*consistance*) and quality to shamoy; that of the women was good for almost nothing, being so soft in texture!" (Carlyle, *French Revolution*, II: 328.) Gerould describes Frenchman appearing in Haiti with wallets of human skin; I have not found this detail elsewhere. The description of perukes is also Carlyle's: "O Reader, they are made from the Heads of Guillotined women! The locks of a Duchess, in this way, may come to cover the scalp of a Cordwainer; her blond German Frankism his black Gaelic poll, if it be bald. Or they may be worn affectionately, as relics; rendering one Suspect? Citizens use them, not without mockery; of rather a cannibal sort." (*The French Revolution*, II: 327).

24. Gerould, *Guillotine*, p. 5.

25. For a brilliant reading of rape and revolutionary politics as "generational" conflict, see Albert D. Hutter, "Nation and Generation in *A Tale of Two Cities*," PMLA, 93, 1978, pp. 448–462.

26. Carol Delaney "Seeds of Honor, Fields of Shame," in *Honor and Shame and the Concept of Mediterranean Unity*, edited by David Gilmore (Washington, D.C.: American Anthropological Society, 1987), pp. 35–48; extract p. 40.

27. Delaney, ibid, p. 41.

28. Dickens first conceived the hero's sacrificial plot in writing *The Frozen Deep* with Wilkie Collins; in initial performances, Dickens played the Carton figure, ending with his death, as the tears of the actress playing the heroine fell on his face. The sister of that actress was Ellen Ternan, herself a minor player in the drama, with whom Dickens was to carry on an affair for the rest of his life. Among the other details that link *Tale of Two Cities* to Dickens's adulterous passion, Michael Slater has noted that he gave Lucie Manette the wrinkled and expressive forehead of Ellen Ternan (Slater, *Dickens and Women*, pp. 210–11). In general, the novel's theatricality provides a continuing connection to Dickens's theatrical self-presentation and the end of his marriage.

29. Garrett Stewart gives a beautiful reading of this scene in *Death Sentences: Styles of Dying in British Fiction* (Cambridge, MA: Harvard University Press, 1984), pp. 83–97. But he reads Carton's last vision as "prophetically remembered," and seems to accept its veracity in ways I cannot.

CAROLYN DEVER

Psychoanalyzing Dickens

The point about both Dickens and Freud and why one likes to see the grand sweep of their lives is that they're both essentially heroic characters, Freud a hero of thought and Dickens a hero of literature. Moreover, both were aware that they were heroes, that they had heroic destinies and heroic mythological structures in their lives

—Steven Marcus[1]

Not only would the echoes die away, as though the steps had gone; but, echoes of other steps that never came would be heard in their stead, and would die away for good when they seemed close at hand.

—Charles Dickens[2]

Charles Dickens and Sigmund Freud were strangers, yet they seem to have known each other intimately. Joined in a uniquely humane agenda, they sought understanding of the spoken and unspoken desires of human beings in relation to one another, to an unknowable past, a haunted present, a mortgaged future. Dickens and Freud were observers of human life and crafters of bold narratives of character.

They were also both "Victorians." Psychoanalysis is an invention of the Victorian period. Dickens is too: as novelist, editor, and public speaker, Dickens had as much to do with the constitution of "the Victorian" as a

From *Palgrave Advances in Charles Dickens Studies*, edited by John Bowen and Robert L. Patten, pp. 216–233. © 2006 Palgrave Macmillan.

recognizable category as Freud, writing at the end of the century, had to do with its deconstruction. Taken together, Dickens and Freud are remarkably sympathetic figures, polar opposites yet sharing concerns, questions, conclusions, and even methodologies. Both Dickens and Freud are interested in children and childhood; in the expression of a self and the unknowability of that self to itself; in the unruliness of human erotic desire; and in the nuclear family, less as an ideal or a given but as something hard-fought and hard-won, as the repository for anxieties and pathologies as well as virtue, truth, and stability.

Though they have much in common, however, Dickens and Freud did not engage one another directly: Dickens died in 1870, when Sigmund Freud was just a fourteen-year-old boy in Austria. The name "Charles Dickens" appears in none of the indexes to the 24-volume *Standard Edition of the Complete Psychological Works of Sigmund Freud*, nor in the accompanying concordance. This is more of an anomaly than it might initially seem: the general editors of the *Standard Edition* have provided an "Index of Works of Art and Literature" that appear in Freud's writing. That list includes many British literary writers, among them Jane Austen, George Eliot, Rudyard Kipling, John Milton, William Shakespeare, Jonathan Swift, and Oscar Wilde.[3] Though Dickens himself is not on this list, Freudian psychoanalysis is shot through with Dickensian elements—ways of seeing; ways of describing people, conflicts, desire and sexuality, moral and ethical development; and, as I will argue here, narrative strategies.

As Freud's index suggests, psychoanalysis has always concerned itself with literature. And literature, in its exploration of the core psychoanalytic concerns of consciousness and desire, has concerned itself with the psyche. From its inception at the dawn of the twentieth century, psychoanalysis has drawn critics of literature toward new insights into the power of language and the transformative possibilities of literary texts. And of course literature has transformed psychoanalysis in turn: beginning with Sigmund Freud's interpretation of family dynamics through the lens of Sophocles' *Oedipus*, literary writers have often provided psychoanalysts with figures to describe the intricacies of the human psyche.

The history of psychoanalytic criticism of Dickens holds a mirror to the history of psychoanalytic criticism in general. Beginning in the early twentieth century as a mechanism for analyzing the author's inner conflicts, contradictions, and desires, psychoanalytic criticism has evolved into a means of understanding textual complexities, particularly those circulating around questions of gender and sexual identity. Psychoanalysis is often excoriated by feminist critics as a misogynist critical method: surely Freud, the figure who conceived of anatomy as destiny and who argued that women's bodies are castrated and women's minds are but pale and inadequate pretenders to the full flowering of phallic male glory, is guilty of perpetuating the most vile of patriarchal, misogynist oppressions. Yet more recently (and perhaps counterintuitively) psychoanalysis has been embraced by feminists and other theorists of sexuality as a valuable critical tool, instrumental in illuminating the remarkable perversities of human desire.[4]

As generations of critics have demonstrated, psychoanalysis is a methodology with considerable explanatory power for the analysis of Dickens's fiction.[5] I will suggest here, however, that the most profound of these critics was the very first: Dickens himself, a brilliant psychoanalytic thinker, *avant la lettre*. Indeed, I will suggest that so powerful a psychoanalytic thinker was Dickens that Dickens himself—not just the man but the entire repertoire of Dickensian observations and means of expression—haunted Freud, haunted nascent psychoanalysis, and continues to this day to haunt the ways in which human beings explain themselves to themselves and to others.

First, however, a word about how psychoanalytic theory may or may not work to illuminate the relationship between an author's life and his or her work. In its earliest days, psychoanalytic criticism of Dickens was largely focused on "diagnosing" certain aspects of Dickens's personality from evidence drawn from his fiction, and especially his "Autobiographical Fragment." Focusing on traumatic incidents in Dickens's childhood, particularly his boyhood employment in Warren's Blacking Warehouse, early psychoanalytic critics linked Dickens's representations of childhood innocence and betrayal directly to the failure of his own childhood family.

Though this was a compelling line of inquiry, it soon ran hard into its limits as an analytical technique: connecting the dots between biography and literary text did not get critics very far in terms of yielding new insights into Dickens, into his literary texts, or into psychoanalysis as a critical practice. In fact, psychoanalysis is most useful as an interpretive methodology less in its consideration of the rational, the real, and the known than as a means of access to what is unknown, or knowable only indirectly or by means of fantasy only loosely tethered to the historical "real." As Albert D. Hutter writes in 1976, "the most powerful diagnostic tool of psychoanalysis" is its "ability to derive unconscious and infantile meanings from a conscious, adult text. This reductive principle may ... lead to significant distortion, whereby all events begin to look the same when seen through the analyst's peculiar prism."[6] The problem, in Hutter's view, involves the discrepancy between what is known and unknown, knowable and unknowable, for Charles Dickens himself. Hutter explains: "Any autobiographical statement—whether written, nostalgically imagined, or recounted on an analyst's couch over a period of years—is a fabrication.

Facts are distorted, relationships colored, not necessarily to lie, or to persuade an audience, but rather because of the individual's desire to make sense out of the past as he understands it—and always incompletely understands it—in the present."[7] In other words, autobiographical statements, whether offered explicitly or through the veiled medium of literary representation, involve an alchemy of past and present and an agenda to make coherent retrospectively and retroactively the incoherences of personal history. Thus the critic who sees, for example, Dickens's representations of abandoned little children as a reference to his own status as an "abandoned" child privileges the past— Dickens's childhood—over the present—Dickens's conscious production, as an adult, of a coherent autobiographical identity for himself. The biographical reading also misses the opportunity to consider Dickens's labor as an artist: while he certainly works from what he knows, he also works, as any artist does, to transform the matter of everyday life according to his unique interpretive vision. It is interesting to read, say, Oliver Twist as the vulnerable young Charles Dickens. But to read the novel only biographically is to miss out on Oliver Twist as *Oliver Twist*, a work of art in which "meaning" is contingent on and, as in any work of art, irreducible to the rigid coordinates of a single or singular interpretation.[8]

There is no question that Dickens puts his personal history to use in his art. To borrow an insight that Freud and Dickens himself offer with equal emphasis, however, "personal history" is something to which an individual man or woman actually has very little access. For Dickens as for Freud, history resolutely refuses to stay in the past, instead inhabiting the present as the not-quite-visible, not-quite-knowable ghost in the machine of orderliness and reason. To be a subject is, for both authors, to live at once in the present and the past. Thus a progressive and stable society, as Dickens demonstrates in his most canonical historical novel, requires its subjects to find strategies for putting their ghosts to good use—for resisting the repetition, again and again, of history's conflicts.

A Tale of Two Cities is a haunted text. As Dickens explains in a letter to his friend and biographer John Forster, the novel is unique among his oeuvre. In writing *A Tale*, which was published in 1859 (serially in *All the Year Round*, in monthly parts, and in a single-volume edition), Dickens says:

> I set myself the little task of making a picturesque story, rising in every chapter with the characters true to nature, but whom the story itself should express, more than they should express themselves, by dialogue. I mean, in other words, that I fancied that a story of incident might be written, in place of the bestiality

["odious stuff"] that *is* written under that pretence, pounding the characters out of its own mortar, and beating their own interests out of them. If you could have read the story all at once, I hope you wouldn't have stopped halfway.[9]

Such a subordination of character to story is extremely unusual for Charles Dickens, novelist *sine qua non* of character. I want to suggest, however, that here Dickens puts the concept of "story" strategically to work because it allows him to open up a radical theory of character. In *A Tale of Two Cities* Dickens explores questions of agency, self-determination, and historical context. He suggests that individual characters are produced by histories both social and private—histories which those characters do not and cannot fully understand. Beholden to history's ghosts, the social agency of individual men and women is mediated, radically limited, by the story in which they find themselves inscribed.

A Tale of Two Cities might seem like a perverse text to choose to demonstrate Dickens's psychoanalytic intelligence. The novel is about the "real" events of history—yet I have just suggested that psychoanalysis is a methodology best turned to questions of the unreal, the unknowable, the unstable, the unaccounted. The novel also relegates the individual subject to second-order status, while psychoanalysis is the theory of modern, liberal individualism, which is concerned primarily with the etiologies of individual human development and relations—concerned, in short, with questions of character, its evolution and complexities. I would suggest, however, that *A Tale of Two Cities* is precisely the text in which Dickens's psychoanalytic intervention makes itself most vividly known because it addresses the contours of historical knowability in such complex ways. I would also suggest that *A Tale of Two Cities* reveals several assumptions that are important but underdeveloped within Freud's work. The novel's consideration of these assumptions—which concern the individual subject's relation to history and temporality and the desire to break patterns of historical repetition—enables new insights into the psychoanalytic method.

For Dickens the "story" in question is a big one, the French Revolution. If a historical novel takes up the panorama of social events, *A Tale of Two Cities* is one of two Dickens texts (the other is 1841's *Barnaby Rudge*) that sets its sights, hypothetically, on this, the grandest of horizons.[10] I describe this novel's genre and setting as *hypothetically* historical not in order to challenge its situation in the bloodied streets of revolutionary Paris but to suggest that its distinctiveness within the Dickens canon is a matter of degree, not kind. In fact every Dickens novel is about "history," about the situation of individual men, women, and children within a particular social fabric, and about the violence that ensues from the expression of individual human needs and desires within that milieu.

In the second sentence of *David Copperfield* (1849–50), for example, the eponymous narrator takes a historical stand: "To begin my life with the beginning of my life, I record that I was born (as I have been informed and believe) on a Friday, at twelve o'clock at night."[11] As David makes quite clear, to write "history" is necessarily to take a leap of faith into the unknowable. He has "been informed [about] and believe[s]" the day and time of his birth. As an unconscious infant at that liminal midnight moment, however, dependent on the testimony of other historical witnesses, David marks his story's beginning with a trope of instability. The ultimate unknowability of historical evidence, even autobiographical evidence, suggests that the self is unknowable even to itself. His multiple names alone—ranging from David Copperfield to Betsey Trotwood Copperfield and back—underscore the sense in which David cannot control either the "life" that "begins" poised at this liminal Friday (or is it Thursday? or Saturday?) midnight or its narration.

The gesture is characteristically Dickensian, at once historicizing the subject in question and destabilizing that subject's claim to historical knowledge and credibility. Again typically, Esther Summerson's narrative within *Bleak House* (1852–53) "begins" several chapters into the novel, in a chapter titled "A Progress," and with the confession that Esther knows nothing of her origins or her parentage. The novel's more formal beginning, offered at the head of the first chapter's first page by a third-person narrator, takes its history in a different register: "London. Michaelmas Term lately over, and the Lord Chancellor sitting in Lincoln's Inn Hall. Implacable November weather. As much mud in the streets as if the waters had but newly retired from the face of the earth, and it would not be wonderful to meet a Megalosaurus, forty feet long or so, waddling like an elephantine lizard up Holborn Hill."[12] Dickens establishes the novel's realism through the coordinates of place—"London"—and time—"Michaelmas Term lately over," "Implacable November weather." Then he immediately inscribes those topical coordinates within a much vaster, even geological, historical frame: with flood waters retiring, the elephantine Megalosaurus is perhaps surprised to find himself stuck in the traffic of modern-day Holborn.

The title of the first of the three books that constitutes *A Tale of Two Cities* is "Recalled to Life." Just as Holborn's Megalosaurus establishes ghostly inhabitation as a condition of modern life, social subjectivity, in Dickens's *Tale*, requires the constant navigation of modernity's historical relics. For Dickens as for Freud, present-day consciousness is composed of the endless repetition of unresolved psychic conflicts: the traumas and unspeakable, and thus unresolvable, desires are repressed from the aware, conscious mind (and therefore displaced to, and displayed by, the unruly, uncontrollable unconscious). In "Remembering, Repeating, and Working-Through," an important 1914 essay about psychoanalytic technique, Freud writes that "the patient does not *remember* anything of what he has forgotten and repressed, but *acts* it out. He reproduces it not as a memory but as an action; he *repeats* it, without, of course, knowing that he is repeating it."[13] Freud counsels psychoanalysts that their patients will repeat repressed events in the therapeutic relationship itself. Freud calls this "transference," and suggests that psychoanalysts can use patients' re-staging of old conflicts to help them to become conscious of, and thus work through, history's endless, repetitive loop:

> The main instrument ... for curbing the patient's compulsion to repeat and for turning it into a motive for remembering lies in the handling of the transference. We render the compulsion harmless, and indeed useful, by giving it the right to assert itself in a definite field. We admit it into the transference as a playground in which it is allowed to expand in almost complete freedom and in which it is expected to display to us everything in the way of pathogenic instincts that is hidden in the patient's mind ... The transference thus creates an intermediate region between illness and real life through which the transition from the one to the other is made.[14]

In the concept of "working through," Freud is concerned with prolepsis, with the possibility of making a turn from the past to the future. Such a transition requires a middle space (in this case the space of analysis and transference) in which compulsive repetition of the past can be shifted and adapted and put to use toward the production of future patterns which are different and, presumably, healthy. Like Freud, Dickens is deeply concerned with the need to put repetition—the echoes that make history inescapably current—to good use. *A Tale of Two Cities* is a novel of tragedy, but with a happy ending disjoined from and yet joined intimately to the text's tragedies. By means of what redemptive "intermediate region" is that ending produced? How then might we read *A Tale of Two Cities* as a parable of social discontinuity, as a novel of radical and ameliorative historical change in which the past is at least partially put to rest?

The novel, I argue, demonstrates Dickens's awareness of the compulsion to repeat, and also his investment in a process of exorcism, the process of flushing out and working through repressed traumas from the historical past. This novel, set in the late eighteenth century, gestures forcefully and optimistically toward a redemptive future located squarely in the heart of Victorian London. This requires the remembering, repeating, and working through of past violence and shame.

Several figures "recalled to life" in the novel's beginning reveal their traumatic and thus repressed associations over time; the present, Dickens seems to suggest, is always beholden to the past. Historical novels exist within at least two temporal frames of reference: the present moment of the text's exegesis and the present moment of its composition and publication. In writing *A Tale of Two Cities* as a historical novel, then, Dickens "recalls to life" events of the previous century, opening in 1775 and casting from that point to days both earlier—1757—and later—1794—in order to trace the developmental arc of French revolutionary sentiments and actions. Resuscitating this history, via Carlyle's monumental work of social criticism, *French Revolution* (1837), Dickens offers last-century Paris as contemporary London's Megalosaurus.

Consistent with the doubleness indexed in the novel's title, however, Dickens juxtaposes the Revolution's resuscitation with a case of private haunting; the two illuminate one another. Early in the novel's present-day action, banker Jarvis Lorry breaks difficult, if happy, news to Lucie Manette, a young French woman who has been raised in London since early girlhood, anal who believes herself to be an orphan. Lucie's father, Lorry tells her, has "'been found. He is alive. Greatly changed, it is too probable; almost a wreck, it is possible; though we will hope the best. Still, alive. Your father has been taken to the house of an old servant in Paris, and we are going there: I, to identify him if I can: you, to restore him to life, love, duty, rest, comfort'" (1:4, 29). For Lucie the restoration is quite literal: like Esther Summerson, she learns that a parent whom she believed dead actually lives, and like Esther Lucie also learns that her "orphaned" identity was the product of an early lie (in this case, on the part of her well-intentioned mother who did not want Lucie to know that her patriot father lived on, a victim of torture and unjust imprisonment, in the Bastille). However, not only is Dr. Manette restored to life and to Lucie, but Lucie herself, Mr. Lorry makes clear, is to be an agent of the "resurrection" process: the good daughter is to take charge of her shattered father and "'to restore him to life, love, duty, rest, comfort.'"

Having reprised in reverse their original journey from the Paris of Lucie's birth, Lucie and Lorry make their way to the Defarge household, where they find Dr. Manette ensconced in a dark top-floor garret, compulsively engaged in cobbling shoes. Manette is a ghost of his former self, his voice "like the last feeble echo of a sound made long and long ago. So entirely had it lost the life and resonance of the human voice, that it affected the senses like a once beautiful color faded away into a poor weak stain. So sunken and suppressed it was, that it was like a voice underground" (1:6, 46). Traumatized by decades of imprisonment and deprivation, Manette is but a fragment of his former self, his voice subterranean, evocative more of absence, loss, and negation than of a presence either physical or mental. The only identity the man has left to him is the signifier of his institutional identity as prisoner: "'Did you ask me for my name?' ... 'One Hundred and Five, North Tower'" (1:6, 49). The only activity the man remains capable of performing is the one that he used to soothe himself during his institutionalization. This tedious, repetitive labor of shoemaking exemplifies purposiveness without purpose. Manette toils over a lady's slipper that will never fit a foot or come in contact with the hard, irregular paving stones of a Paris in which starving women knit rather than dance, knit because they have no food to feed their dying children. Indeed, as Manette makes shoes, "All the women knitted. They knitted worthless things; but, the mechanical work was a mechanical substitute for eating and drinking; the hands moved for the jaws and the digestive apparatus: if the body fingers had been still, the stomachs would have been more famine-pinched" (2:16, 224).

Trauma has turned Manette and the women of Paris into machines, their bodies beholden to their minds' inability to fathom the predicament of their lives, to find a solution to the suffering in which they are imprisoned. Compulsive knitting and compulsive shoemaking are, for Dickens, physical signifiers of such mental suffering. This endless, endlessly alienated work tells a story that has nothing at all to do with woolens or shoes, and everything to do with the psychic pain of which the sufferers cannot speak but in which they nevertheless continue to dwell, a pain which they long to numb.[15] Jasper Lorry and the novel describe the trauma of origin as a "shock," and even Manette, nurtured toward recovery by his daughter Lucie, admits that traumatic associations may bring about a relapse into compulsive behavior. Speaking of himself in the third person, Manette says:

> "You see, ... it is very hard to explain, consistently, the innermost workings of this poor man's mind. He once yearned so frightfully for that occupation, and it was so welcome when it came; no doubt it relieved his pain so much, by substituting the perplexity of the fingers for the perplexity of the brain, and by substituting, as he became more practiced, the ingenuity of the hands, for the ingenuity of the mental torture; that he has never been able to bear the thought of putting it quite out of his reach." (2:19, 248)

What Manette calls substitution, Freud calls displacement: like the hysteric Dora of Freud's famous case-study, Manette's body, and the knitting fingers of the women of Paris, tell stories that remain unspoken, unspeakable in the novel's narrative. In drawing the reader's attention to the novel's unnarrated-because-unnarratable narrative, Dickens directs the reader in a psychoanalytic direction: to seek that which is signified by the body but which remains unspoken and unspeakable, the symptom of the story behind the story. It is by this means that Dickens establishes Manette and the novel's other characters as a focalizing device for the sweeping, epochal narrative of the French Revolution, a public story of private trauma. This is the logic of synecdoche, in which the individual part stands for the whole: the pain of Dr. Manette stands for the pain of the knitting women, which in turn stands for the pain of the crowds of men and women in whose actions and reactions the period's violent claim to liberty, equality, and fraternity, reposed. Dickens suggests that the story of Manette and other characters is gripping, that it is tragic, but also that it is common. Through the bodies of how many other mute Manettes and silenced Sydney Cartons might the tale of revolution be told? The narrator replies:

> A wonderful fact to reflect upon, that every human creature is constituted to be that profound secret and mystery to every other. A solemn consideration, when I enter a great city by night, that every one of those darkly clustered houses encloses its own secret; that every room in every one of them encloses its own secret; that every beating heart in the hundreds of thousands of breasts there, is, in some of its imaginings, a secret to the heart nearest it! (1:3, 12)

Social revolutions are composed of layer upon layer of such unspoken stories. Dickens goes to great lengths to suggest, however, that these stories are deeply imbedded in context. For Dickens as for Freud, "history" is a profoundly personal and psychic phenomenon. When Dickens wrote to Forster that story produces character in *A Tale of Two Cities*, he suggested that the novel explores the effects of their historical situation on the minds and hearts of the individual men and women imprisoned in a particular space and time: "One Hundred and Five, North Tower," "London. Michaelmas Term lately over." Here Dickens explores the dialectical process by which the particulars of history writ small (one imprisoned doctor, one knitting woman, one raped sister) and the particulars of history writ large (The French Revolution) conspire to constitute one another.

Dickens suggests that the agency of any particular traumatized doctor, blonde daughter, banker, alcoholic, or code-knitting wine-merchant's wife is constituted in relation not only to that person's private developmental trajectory but also in relation to the social circumstances—feast or famine— in which that individual finds himself or herself. In this effort Dickens might have had something to teach Freud, whose interest in the relationship between the individual and the social dramatically favors the individual. When Freud, for example, sources his theory of unconscious desire and its repression in a reading of Sophocles' *Oedipus Rex*, he concerns himself neither with the social circumstances attending the story of a particular baby left on a particular hillside, nor with the literary conventions of Greek drama. Rather, he suggests that the central conflict is universal rather than situated in a historical or even literary context. Similarly, in the case of Dora, Freud extrapolates from Dora's dreams and physical symptoms an account of her repressed sexuality; as many feminist critics have argued, however, Freud fails to consider the historical situation in which Dora finds herself, or his own countertransferential identification with the predatory and lecherous older men whose attentions Dora wishes to deflect.[16] Dickens uses *A Tale of Two Cities* to explore the volatile dialectic between historical and individual conflict, historical and individual development, while for Freud historical change is a phenomenon of private psychological development.

Famously, Freud collected archaeological artifacts: he placed them around his consulting room as metaphors for the psychoanalytic process. For Freud this suggested that the psychoanalyst, like the archaeologist, digs patiently through layer after layer of accumulated matter, probing the unconscious as an archaeologist probes in a dig. Historical artifacts, for the psychoanalyst, are buried deep in a person's unconscious. Like the archaeologist who happens upon a piece of evidence, the analyst works to interpret, and to extrapolate from whatever it is he or she unearths.[17] For a psychoanalyst, however, evidence comes in the form of symbols, which often emerge in the medium of language. Psychoanalysts interpret symbols and narratives: their methodologies have a great deal in common with those of literary authors and literary critics. Freud bases many theories on analyses of literary texts, and the most famous of these involves the Oedipal complex, which Freud describes first in *The Interpretation of Dreams*, his 1900 *tour de force* of linguistic exegesis.[18] For Freud, Sophocles's Oedipus story vividly portrays the socially taboo desires that lurk in the heart of every person; when those disturbing taboo desires are repressed into the unconscious, they surface elsewhere, displaced from their original source but expressed nonetheless (think of shoemaking hands expressing a pain so great that it cannot be spoken). Unless and until the Oedipus-figure works through and exorcises this repressed material, his (or presumably her) unconscious desires cannot be suppressed: they will come out somehow, somewhere, and thus liberated from conscious control, they can be violent and destructive. As Freud argues in "Remembering, Repeating, and Working-Through," the subject will endlessly repeat a repressed trauma, anxiety, or dynamic until the cycle is somehow broken. The breaking of the cycle, in the form of genuine, redemptive change, is extremely difficult to achieve; it is, however, what Dickens has in mind in *A Tale of Two Cities*.

Freud's interpretation of the *Oedipus* story attributes powerful unconscious desires to the hero's actions. He explicates the myth as follows: "Oedipus, son of Laïus, King of Thebes, and of Jocasta, was exposed as an infant because an oracle had warned Laïus that the still unborn child would be his father's murderer."[19] The oracle of course turns out to be correct: Laïus's preemptive actions notwithstanding, Oedipus not only kills his father but marries his mother, begets sibling-children by her, and having discovered the truth of his identity, "blinds himself and forsakes his home."[20] Our fascination with Oedipus's tragedy, Freud suggests, inheres in its expression of universal but unspeakable human desires:

> His destiny moves us because it might have been ours—because the oracle laid the same curse upon us before our birth as upon him. It is the fate of all of us, perhaps, to direct our first sexual impulse towards our mother and our first hatred and our first murderous wish against our father ... Like Oedipus, we live in ignorance of these wishes, repugnant to morality, which have been forced upon us by Nature, and after their revelation we may all of us well seek to close our eyes to the scenes of our childhood.[21]

Children's relationship with their parents is "Oedipal" in the sense that it engages two related forms of repressed desire: a sexual desire directed toward (but repressed away from) the mother; and a murderous desire, directed toward (but repressed away from) the potent father. Extrapolating from this, Freud suggests that human erotic desire is essentially linked with power, violence, and anxiety; and that in turn, power, violence, and desire are erotic. In the Oedipal theory, the mother represents the quintessential object of erotic desire for her child. The child's expression of that desire is prohibited by an incest taboo policed by the frightening, potent, violent figure of the castrating father. Fearing patriarchal retribution, the child represses desire for the mother and learns to identify with the potent, phallic father—but this identification, based on the repression of a powerful erotic urge, is unstable: the "phallus" that the child gains by identifying with the father is always vulnerable to "castration" if the truth comes out. Whence comes Oedipus, for whom it all went wrong: instead of repressing his desire for his mother, he acted upon it, however unwittingly; instead of repressing his murderous rage toward his abandoning, castrating father, he acted upon it. The punishment for his failure to repress these desires is, ultimately, castration: Oedipus's self-blinding and banishment are but a displacement upward and outward of the ultimate punishment. Freud argues that in describing Oedipus's failure to fully repress his desire and rage, Sophocles describes the universal history of the unconscious mind.

That history is one of misdirected sexual desire and its murderous consequences, of the bloody revolt against patriarchal power, and of tragedies that are destined to repeat themselves over and over again. It is a history of martyrdom. And it serves as an object-lesson to its readers. In a 1914 footnote added to *The Interpretation of Dreams*, Freud suggests the following: "Later studies have shown that the 'Oedipus complex', which was touched upon for the first time in the above paragraphs in the *Interpretation of Dreams*, throws a light of undreamt-of importance on the history of the human race and the evolution of religion and morality."[22] Social codes of morality, in other words, evolve historically: the meaning of goodness itself has developed over the centuries, and has developed by means of the institutionalization of the very repressive processes that failed so spectacularly in the case of Oedipus Rex.[23]

A Tale of Two Cities is a fiercely Oedipal text. The history of desire, rage, and displacement, Dickens's novel is a tale of misdirected sexual desire and its murderous consequences: would the bloodthirsty Madame Defarge be bloodthirsty at all if not for the tragic rape, suffering, and death of her beloved sister? What more vivid example exists of the bloody revolt against patriarchal power than the French Revolution in which Dickens sets his *Tale*? The novel is a story of generations locked in loops of tragic repetition, its hours of cobbling and days of knitting punctuated by the martyrdom of Sydney Carton on behalf of the woman he loves, Lucie Manette Darnay. And finally, it is, in theory, an object-lesson: the happy ending the novel imagines for Sydney Carton involves the birth, to Lucie and Charles Darnay, of an infant son, Sydney Darnay. That boy will channel his superabundance of patriarchal models into a good and true career, becoming a representative of justice—"foremost of just judges and honest men"—and fathering a golden-haired Sydney Darnay of his own. Carton's sacrifice serves a redemptive end by forecasting a blond, English boy two generations in the future—that is, a Victorian citizen—who will stand as an icon of moral virtue. That hypothetical child's hypothetical father will tell him the story of Carton's martyrdom, apostrophizing Carton himself in the novel's final words: "'It is a far, far better thing that I do, than I have ever done; it is a far, far better rest that I go to than I have ever known'" (3:15, 466).

In his dramatization of the range of Oedipal plot elements, Dickens performs a kind of historical archaeology that is quite similar to Freud's in *The Interpretation of Dreams* in particular, and in the psychoanalytic methodology that emerged from the *fin-de-siècle* dream-book. The violent figure at the novel's center is a castrating woman: "Above all, one hideous figure grew as familiar as if it had been before the general gaze from the foundations of the world—the figure of the sharp female called La Guillotine" (3:4, 336). The "sharp female," the "National Razor" (3:4, 336), performs her castrating work in service of a series of social ideals—liberty, equality, fraternity—that, in theory, redistribute power from the aristocracy to a fraternal democracy of the people. As Lynn Hunt has astutely observed,[24] the family metaphors of French social revolution situate the moment's politics squarely in a psychoanalytic context; Dickens's novel never hesitates to put the metaphorical vocabulary of domesticity and power to use. Thus in the Freudian interpretation, "La Guillotine" chops off an aristocratic, patriarchal phallus displaced upward, as Oedipus's self-castration was displaced upward to the eyes; Dickens's facility with this particular mode of displacement recalls the aptly-named Mr. Dick's preoccupation with the decapitation of King Charles I in *David Copperfield*. In *A Tale*, feminized violence extends seamlessly from the "sharp female" to Madame Defarge herself: Defarge and her band of knitting women eagerly, almost greedily, witness the guillotine's daily work, hailing each execution as one more act of revenge. Though Dickens is often associated with the sort of secular humanist, democratic ideals expressed in public discourses of the French Revolution, he does not, in *A Tale of Two Cities*, glamorize either the intentions or the practices of the revolutionaries themselves, especially the women, as he suggests in the novel's concluding executions of two figures of martyrdom, the little seamstress and the heroic, martyred Sydney Carton.

Dickens is a Freudian—or Freud, perhaps, is a Dickensian—in their shared privatization of social history. *A Tale of Two Cities* is a tale of a revolution told through the experiences of a couple of families, and within those families, of several key figures whose desires, suffering, and traumas constitute the novel's action. The novel suggests a synecdochal process by which cases of individual trauma first affect family histories and ripple from there to the social communities in which those individuals and families play out their material lives. "History," then, consists of the massing-together of such stories. The possibility of positive historical change inheres in healing processes that work through the personal.[25]

The novel's narrative structure implicitly establishes the French Revolution as the effect of one particular causal trauma, structurally endorsing Freud's theory of history's private origins even as it challenges that theory in other ways. Quite late in the narrative, Dickens recursively justifies the desperate, vengeful rage of Madame Defarge. In telling this story he identifies Madame Defarge not by name but only as an innocent child whose family was destroyed by the twin Evrémondes, father and uncle of the protagonist Charles Darnay; the little girl's older sister was raped and died delirious and pregnant, and her older brother, who tried to come to the sister's rescue, was brutally beaten, and died in pain. Though her brother safely spirited his little sister to safety, she was so well hidden that Darnay's well-intentioned mother, young Charles himself in tow, failed to find her and thus to make reparations. From the blood of her brother and sister, from the trauma of the abandoned little girl, the French Revolution springs.

Later, as a woman talking with her husband, that girl claims her history:

> "Defarge, I was brought up among the fishermen of the sea-shore, and that peasant family so injured by the two Evrémonde brothers, as that Bastille paper describes, is my family. Defarge, that sister of the mortally wounded boy upon the ground was my sister, that husband was my sister's husband, that unborn child was their child, that brother was my brother, that father was my father, those dead are my dead, and that summons to answer for those things descends to me!" (3:12, 420–1)

Dickens gives Madame Defarge, again and again, the possessive pronoun that twins her with her dead sister: "'My husband, my father, and my brother,'" rants the delirious sister (3:9, 397). My sister, my brother, echoes Madame Defarge—my father, my dead, my injuries at the hands of the despicable twin Evrémondes. With Madame Defarge's possession comes possession—of identification, rage, responsibility, and the thirst for revenge.

By rooting Madame Defarge's rage in the personal trauma of her sister's sexual exploitation, Dickens suggests that the class warfare at the heart of the French Revolution is not only personalized, not only feminized, but also a sexualized wound that perpetuates itself through identification. As in the case of Oedipus, whose reparation involves a form of self-castration, this novel's sexualized wound requires reparation by means both erotic and violent.

Though Madame Defarge's story explains and perhaps justifies her rage, the brutally pure spirit with which she enters into revenge only perpetuates the cycle of tragedy that the Evrémonde twins began. In the spirit of the novel's repetition compulsion, it takes another pair of male twins to redeem and break that vicious cycle. Through the bodies of these good male twins, Dickens locates ground for redemptive sexual possibility. As Carolyn Williams has suggested, Dickens splits and distributes an array of masculine qualities between two virtually identical male protagonists, the virtuous Darnay and the impetuous alcoholic Carton.[26] The trope of splitting, Williams argues, enables Dickens to reveal the processes by which goodness and vice are consolidated. Though both men love Lucie Manette, Darnay wins her hand. Yet in a stroke worthy of the moment at which Oedipus and his father Laïus meet at the fated crossroads, the good Darnay is his own father-in-law's worst nightmare: though Darnay has repudiated his past as a member of the French aristocratic Evrémonde family, Manette has already sworn a blood oath in perpetuity against that—and thus his own—family. The two men are on a collision course to tragedy when in steps Darnay's double, Carton, who lives (and dies) to serve Lucie, the forbidden object of his desire and devotion. Carton swaps identities with Darnay, is decapitated in his name, and begets by his proxy the child, Sydney Darnay.

The boy's creation story approximates a virgin birth. Doubly fathered, he shares with his mother Lucie his golden hair and distinctively blank forehead. Born both posthumously and in a future world detached from the novel's present moment, he redeems the infant who tragically died along with its mother, Madame Defarge's sister, killed at the hands of Darnay's twin brothers. He also redeems the dead toddler Charles Darnay, who dies before his father's impetuous return to Paris even while lisping his love to his friend Carton. By means of Sydney Darnay's subjunctive birth, Dickens posits a break to the cycle of revenge and tragedy—posits, indeed, a happy, healthy, golden, just, and quite distinctively Victorian future for the assimilated Carton-Darnays. In the words of Hilary Schor, the child will "restore the beauty of history."[27]

Decades before the events of *A Tale of Two Cities* commenced, the father of the girl who grew to become Madame Defarge told his children that "'it was a dreadful thing to bring a child into the world, and that what we should most pray for, was, that our women might be barren and our miserable race die out!'" (3:10, 401). In the end, though, it is not the race's demise but its future that two barren—or at least childless—women purchase. As Madame Defarge and Miss Pross fight to the death, Madame Defarge remains anchored firmly in the past as she seeks revenge for the suffering and death of her siblings. In contrast, Miss Pross strikes not for the dead but for the living, insuring the escape to safety of a loving, healthy, and—not inconsequentially—fertile nuclear family of husband, wife, and child. Dickens counters barrenness with fertility, death with birth. In the person of Sydney Darnay, Dickens creates a hybrid race that assimilates distinctions of nation, social class, and historical struggle under the smooth cover of a boy "with a forehead that I know and golden flair ... then fair to look upon, with not a trace of this day's disfigurement" (3:15, 465). The boy blossoms from the wasted pasts of his predecessors, and the novel fantasizes on behalf of Sydney Carton, standing before the guillotine, "a beautiful city and a brilliant people rising from this abyss, and, in their struggles to be truly free, in their triumphs and defeats, through long long years to come, I see the evil of this time and of the previous time of which this is the natural birth, gradually making expiation of itself and wearing out" (3:15, 465).

The novel, in short, imagines that Carton's death purchases serious, positive social change: the end of an era's violence, the beginning of a nineteenth century personated in a golden boy who stands for peace, for justice, and for "true freedom." In his footnote to *The Interpretation of Dreams*, Freud argues that society's repression of the Oedipal story—the primal story of lust and violence that is the starting-point of every human narrative—illuminates "the history of the human race and the evolution of religion and morality." Psychoanalysis provides a means of interpreting human history, of understanding the shifting meanings not only of religion and morality but of other ethical categories for the consideration of goodness and badness in their historical contexts. Yet as Freud suggests, events of the past, gone untended, are fated to repeat themselves *ad infinitum*. In the figure of the boy child Sydney Darnay, Dickens suggests that Victorian Britain has remembered, has repeated, and has ultimately, virtuously, worked through the trauma of shame and violence that is the Revolution's Victorian legacy. Contemporary moral justice, figured here through a virtuous patriarchal chain of loving fathers and golden, just sons, is the Eden of this new Genesis.

NOTES

1. Steven Marcus, "A Biographical Inclination," in Samuel H. Baron and Carl Pletsch, eds., *Introspection in Biography: The Biographer's Quest for Self-Awareness* (Hillsdale, NJ: The Analytic Press, 1985), p. 303.

2. Charles Dickens, *A Tale of Two Cities*, Andrew Sanders, ed., Oxford World's Classics (New York: Oxford University Press, 1998), 2:6, 116. All subsequent quotations refer to this edition and will be cited parenthetically in the text.

3. *Indexes and Bibliographies*, vol. 24 of *The Standard Edition of the Complete Psychological Works of Sigmund Freud*, James Strachey, ed. and trans. (London: Hogarth Press, 1974). All subsequent citations of Freud's work refer to the *Standard Edition* and

will by cited by volume and page number. Sigmund Freud, *Letters of Sigmund Freud*, Ernst L. Freud, ed., Tania and James Stern, trans. (New York: Basic Books, 1975). Freud was of course a reader of Dickens. According to his biographer, Ernest Jones, Freud wooed his future wife Martha with a copy of his favorite Dickens novel, *David Copperfield*. In contrast to his positive response to *Copperfield*, however, Freud cared for neither *Hard Times* nor *Bleak House*, criticizing both for their "hardness." For details see Ernest Jones, *The Life and Work of Sigmund Freud* (New York: Basic Books, 1953–57), pp. 104, 174.

4. For an account of feminism's volatile relationship to psychoanalysis, see "The Activist Unconscious: Feminism and Psychoanalysis," in my *Skeptical Feminism: Activist Theory, Activist Practice* (Minneapolis: University of Minnesota Press, 2004), pp. 52–90.

5. See, for example, Hutter (n. 6), Nina Auerbach, *Woman and the Demon: The Life of a Victorian Myth* (Cambridge, MA: Harvard University Press, 1982); Karen Chase, *Eros and Psyche: The Representation of Personality in Charlotte Brontë, Charles Dickens, and George Eliot* (New York: Methuen, 1984); Carolyn Dever, *Death and the Mother From Dickens to Freud: Victorian Fiction and the Anxiety of Origins* (Cambridge: Cambridge University Press, 1998); Lawrence Frank, *Charles Dickens and the Romantic Self* (Lincoln: University of Nebraska Press, 1984); Marianne Hirsch, *The Mother/Daughter Plot: Narrative, Psychoanalysis, Feminism* (Bloomington: Indiana University Press, 1989); John O. Jordan, "The Purloined Handkerchief," *Dickens Studies Annual* 18 (1989), 1–17; John Kucich, *Repression in Victorian Fiction: Charlotte Brontë, George Eliot, and Charles Dickens* (Berkeley: University of California Press, 1987); Ned Lukacher, *Primal Scenes: Literature, Philosophy, Psychoanalysis* (Ithaca: Cornell University Press, 1986); Steven Marcus, *Dickens: From Pickwick to Dombey* (New York: Basic Books, 1965); Jill Matus, *Unstable Bodies: Victorian Representations of Sexuality and Maternity* (Manchester: Manchester University Press, 1995); David Lee Miller, *Dreams of the Burning Child: Sacrificial Sons and the Father's Witness* (Ithaca: Cornell University Press, 2003); J. Hillis Miller, *Victorian Subjects* (Durham, NC: Duke University Press, 1991); Dianne F. Sadoff, *Monsters of Affection: Dickens, Eliot, and Brontë on Fatherhood* (Baltimore: Johns Hopkins University Press, 1982); Alexander Welsh, *From Copyright to Copperfield: The Identity of Dickens* (Cambridge, MA: Harvard University Press, 1987); Edmund Wilson, *The Wound and the Bow* (New York: Oxford University Press, 1947).

6. Albert D. Hutter, "Psychoanalysis and Biography: Dickens' Experience at Warren's Blacking," *University of Hartford Studies in Literature* 8 (1976): 23–37, 25–6.

7. Ibid., p. 23.

8. Hutter, trained as a psychoanalyst as well as a literary critic, gently but persuasively takes issue with those literary critics who would read Dickens's representations of childhood trauma as signifiers of his own childhood trauma. Considered developmentally, for example, Dickens's experience at the blacking factory coincided with the normative conflict required in and by early adolescence. Processing experience in the way that Dickens did quite arguably suggests not debilitating trauma but the normal reordering of life "common to adolescent development" (ibid., p. 33): "I have suggested that he used this experience to manage and resolve earlier crises, and that he continued to use his adult memory of Warren's to preserve a sense of his own boyishness, his own identity as a ... child—elements that say as much about the idiosyncratic nature of his personality and charm, as about neurosis ... We tend to forget that Warren's was not, as most biographers would have

us believe, the beginning; it partakes of that autobiographical reconstruction which characterizes so much of Dickens's fiction, and it is itself his first important piece of fiction" (ibid., pp. 33–4).

9. Charles Dickens to John Forster, 25 August 1859, in *The Letters of Charles Dickens*, ed. Madeline House, Graham Storey, et al., The Pilgrim/British Academy edition, 12 vols. (Oxford: Clarendon Press 1965–2002), 9:112–13.

10. See especially Georg Lukács, *The Historical Novel*, Hannah Mitchell and Stanley Mitchell, tans. (London: Merlin, 1982).

11. Charles Dickens, *David Copperfield*, Nina Burgis, ed. Oxford World's Classic (Oxford: Oxford University Press, 1992), ch. 1, p. 49.

12. Charles Dickens, *Bleak House*, Stephen Gill, ed., Oxford World's Classics (Oxford: Oxford University Press, 1998), ch. 1, p. 11.

13. Sigmund Freud, "Remembering, Repeating, and Working-Through: Further Recommendations on the Technique of Psycho-Analysis II," *Standard Edition* 12:150, emphasis in original.

14. Ibid., p. 154.

15. On trauma and history, see Cathy Caruth, *Unclaimed Experience: Trauma, Narrative, and History* (Baltimore: Johns Hopkins University Press, 1996).

16. Freud published the Dora case-study under the title "Fragment of An Analysis of a Case of Hysteria," *Standard Edition* 7, pp. 7–122. For provocative interpretations of Freud's theory of hysteria, see Charles Bernheimer and Claire Kahane, eds., In *Dora's Case: Freud—Hysteria—Feminism* (New York: Columbia University Press, 1985); and two books by Elaine Showalter, *Sexual Anarchy: Gender and Culture at the Fin-de-siècle* (New York: Viking, 1990), and *Hystories: Hysterical Epidemics and Modern Culture* (New York: Columbia University Press, 1997).

17. On Freud's display of Egyptian archaeological relics throughout his consulting room, see Peter Gay, *Freud: A Life For Our Time* (New York: Doubleday, 1989), pp. 170–3. The text in which Freud's interest in "primitive cultures" emerges most directly is *Totem and Taboo* (1913), *Standard Edition* 13, pp. 1–162; *Totem and Taboo* also vividly models Freud's theory of history as a private developmental phenomenon.

18. On Freud's relationship to the literary, see Marjorie Garber, *Shakespeare's Ghost Writers: Literature as Uncanny Causality* (New York: Methuen, 1987).

19. Freud, *The Interpretation of Dreams*, in *Standard Edition* 4, p. 261.

20. Ibid., p. 262.

21. Ibid., pp. 262–3.

22. Ibid., p. 263, n.2.

23. On the concept of the "repressive hypothesis" in nineteenth-century Europe, see Michel Foucault, *The History of Sexuality, Vol. I, An Introduction*, Robert Hurley, trans. (New York: Vintage Books, 1990). On the concept of "repression" in Victorian literature, see Kucich, *Repression in Victorian Fiction*.

24. Lynn Hunt, *The Family Romance of the French Revolution* (Berkeley: University of California Press, 1992).

25. For a wonderful reading of Dickens's "domestication," see Hilary Schor, "*Hard Times* and *A Tale of Two Cities*: The Social Inheritance of Adultery," in *Dickens and the Daughter of the House* (Cambridge: Cambridge University Press, 1999), especially pp. 89–95.

26. Carolyn Williams, "Prison Breaks," paper presented at the Dickens Universe, University of California, Santa Cruz, 1 August 2004.

27. Schor, "Social Inheritance of Adultery," p. 95.

FURTHER READING

For rich context concerning Victorian theories of psychology, see Jenny Bourne Taylor and Sally Shuttleworth, *Embodied Selves*, and Steven Marcus, *Freud and the Culture of Psychoanalysis: Literature and Psychoanalysis*, ed. Shoshana Felman, offers a variety of approaches to psychoanalytic literary theory, and Cathy Caruth's *Unclaimed Experience* provides a theory of trauma, narrative, and repetition. On issues of gender difference and psychoanalysis, see Jane Gallop's *The Daughter's Seduction*, and the introductions by Juliet Mitchell and Jacqueline Rose, respectively, to their edited volume *Feminine Sexuality*.

For psychoanalytically informed interpretations of Victorian fiction, see especially Christopher Lane, *The Burdens of Intimacy*, as well as Shuttleworth's *Charlotte Brontë and Victorian Psychology* and Taylor's *In the Secret Theatre of the Home*. On psychoanalysis in particular relation to Dickens and his work, see Peter Brooks, *Reading for the Plot*; Dever, *Death and the Mother From Dickens to Freud*; Lawrence Frank, *Charles Dickens and the Romantic Self*; John Glavin, ed., *Dickens on Screen*; John Kucich, *Repression in Victorian Fiction*; and Dianne Sadoff, *Monsters of Affection*.

Chronology

1812	Charles John Huffman Dickens is born on February 7 to John and Elizabeth Dickens, at Landport, Portsea. He is the second of eight children.
1824	John Dickens is arrested for debt and sent to Marshalsea Prison. Dickens works at Warren's Blacking Factory. Father is released three months later and Charles returns to school.
1824–1826	Attends Wellington House Academy, London.
1831	Becomes reporter for the *Mirror of Parliament*.
1832	Works as staff writer for the *True Sun*.
1833	First published piece, "A Dinner at Poplar Walk," is published in *Monthly Magazine* under pen name Boz.
1834	Works as staff writer on the *Morning Chronicle*.
1836	*Sketches by Boz* is published. *Pickwick Papers* begins to appear in monthly installments. In April, Dickens marries Catherine Hogarth, daughter of editor of the *Evening Chronicle*. Meets John Forster, who becomes lifelong friend and his biographer.
1837	First child, Charles Jr., is born. *Pickwick Papers* is published in book form. Catherine's sister, whom Dickens deeply loved, dies suddenly in his house. Dickens becomes editor of *Bentley's Monthly* and *Oliver Twist* begins to appear there.

1838	*Nicholas Nickleby* begins to appear in installments. Daughter Mary is born.
1839	Second daughter, Kate, is born. *Nickleby* appears in book form.
1840	Dickens edits *Master Humphrey's Clock*, a weekly periodical in which *The Old Curiosity Shop* appears in installments.
1841	Son Walter is born.
1842	Tours America with wife from January to June. Publishes *American Notes*.
1843	*Martin Chuzzlewit* begins to appear in installments. *A Christmas Carol* is published.
1844	Dickens moves to Italy. Christmas book, *The Chimes*, is published. Fifth child, Francis, is born.
1845	Returns to England. Son Alfred is born. Christmas book, *The Cricket on the Hearth*, is published.
1846	Moves to Switzerland. *Dombey and Sons* begins appearing in monthly installments. *The Battle of Life: A Love Story* is published.
1847	Lives in Lausanne; moves to Paris. Seventh child, Sydney, is born. Helps philanthropist Angela Burdett Coutts establish a residence for homeless women and continues to help for the next 10 years. Begins to manage a theatrical company.
1848	Sister Fanny dies. *The Haunted Man* is published.
1849	*David Copperfield* begins appearing in installments. Son Henry is born.
1850	Editor of new weekly periodical, *Household Words*. Third daughter, Dora, is born and dies within a year.
1851	*A Child's History of England* is published in *Household Words*.
1852	*Bleak House* begins appearing in monthly installments. First bound volume of *A Child's History of England* appears. Son Edward is born.
1853	Gives public readings from his Christmas books.
1854	*Hard Times* begins to be published in *Household Words* and appears in book form.
1855	*Little Dorrit* begins to appear in monthly installments. The Dickens family travels to Paris.
1856	Purchases Gad's Hill Place, and family returns to London.
1857	Meets young actress Ellen Ternan, who shortly becomes his companion.

1858	Dickens separates from his wife.
1859	Concludes *Household Words* and establishes new weekly, *All the Year Round*. *A Tale of Two Cities* begins to be published there and is published in book form in December.
1860	*Great Expectations* appears in weekly installments.
1862	Gives many public readings and travels to Paris.
1863	Continues readings in Paris and London. Mother Elizabeth dies.
1864	*Our Mutual Friend* begins monthly installments.
1865	Suffers a stroke that leaves him disabled. Dickens is also in train accident. Though he is unhurt, he decides to change the ending of *Our Mutual Friend*, which soon appears in book form.
1866	Gives 30 public readings in the English provinces.
1867	Continues provincial readings, then travels to America and reads there.
1868	In April, Dickens returns to England, where he continues to tour.
1869	Stops reading tour on doctors' advice.
1870	Gives 12 readings in London. Six parts of *The Mystery of Edwin Drood* appear from April to September. On June 9 Charles Dickens dies. He is buried in the Poets' Corner, Westminster Abbey.

Contributors

HAROLD BLOOM is Sterling Professor of the Humanities at Yale University. He is the author of 30 books, including *Shelley's Mythmaking*, *The Visionary Company*, *Blake's Apocalypse*, *Yeats*, *A Map of Misreading*, *Kabbalah and Criticism*, *Agon: Toward a Theory of Revisionism*, *The American Religion*, *The Western Canon*, and *Omens of Millennium: The Gnosis of Angels, Dreams, and Resurrection*. *The Anxiety of Influence* sets forth Professor Bloom's provocative theory of the literary relationships between the great writers and their predecessors. His most recent books include *Shakespeare: The Invention of the Human*, a 1998 National Book Award finalist, *How to Read and Why*, *Genius: A Mosaic of One Hundred Exemplary Creative Minds*, *Hamlet: Poem Unlimited*, *Where Shall Wisdom Be Found?*, and *Jesus and Yahweh: The Names Divine*. In 1999, Professor Bloom received the prestigious American Academy of Arts and Letters Gold Medal for Criticism. He has also received the International Prize of Catalonia, the Alfonso Reyes Prize of Mexico, and the Hans Christian Andersen Bicentennial Prize of Denmark.

J.M. RIGNALL teaches in the Department of English at the University of Warwick. Among his publications are *Realist Fiction and the Strolling Spectator*, *George Eliot and Europe*, and the *Oxford Reader's Companion to George Eliot*.

LISA ROBSON is Associate Professor of English at Brandon University.

TOM LLOYD teaches at Southern Georgia Technical College. His published work includes studies of Dickens and Carlyle and *Crisis of Realism: Representing Experience in the British Novel, 1816–1910*.

JOHN R. REED is Distinguished Professor of English at Wayne State University. He has published several titles, including *Victorian Conventions*, *Victorian Will*, and *Perception and Design in Tennyson's Idylls of the King*.

JOHN B. LAMB is Associate Professor of English at West Virginia University and the editor of *Victorian Poetry*. His essays have been published in *Victorian Literature and Culture*, *Victorians Institute Journal*, *Victorian Newslettter*, and *Nineteenth-Century Literature*.

CATHERINE WATERS is Senior Lecturer in English at the University of New England, New South Wales, Australia. She is the author of *Dickens and the Politics of the Family* and the managing editor of the *Australasian Victorian Studies Journal*.

BARBARA BLACK has been an associate professor of English at Skidmore College. She is the author of *On Exhibit: Victorians and Their Museums*. Her essays and reviews have appeared in *Victorian Poetry*, *Nineteenth-Century Contexts*, and *The Grolier Encyclopedia of the Victorian Era*.

BJØRN TYSDAHL is a Professor Emeritus at the Institute for British and American Studies at the University of Oslo. His publications include *Joyce and Ibsen* and *William Godwin as a Novelist*, a book on the rise of Norwegian fiction, and articles on English and Scandinavian literature. He also is the author of the first biography of James Joyce to be written in Norwegian.

HILARY M. SCHOR is Professor of English at the University of Southern California. She is the editor of *Hard Times: A Cultural Edition* and author of *Scheherezade in the Marketplace: Elizabeth Gaskell and the Victorian Novel*. She has been on the editorial board of *Dickens Studies Annual*.

CAROLYN DEVER is Professor of English and Women's and Gender Studies at Vanderbilt University, where she also serves as Associate Dean of Vanderbilt's College of Arts and Science. Her books include *Death and the Mother from Dickens to Freud* and *Skeptical Feminism*. She is involved in ongoing research on perversity and Victorian domesticity.

Bibliography

Allingham, Philip. "*A Tale of Two Cities*: A Model of the Integration of History and Literature." *BCETA Professional Journal* (July 1991): 35–43.

Ayres, Brenda. *Dissenting Women in Dickens' Novels: The Subversion of Domestic Ideology*. Westport, Conn.: Greenwood Press, 1998.

Baldridge, Cates. "Alternatives to Bourgeois Individualism in *A Tale of Two Cities*." *SEL: Studies in English Literature, 1500-1900* 30, no. 4 (Autumn 1990): 633–654.

Bloom, Harold, ed. *Charles Dickens*. Philadelphia: Chelsea House Publishers, 2003.

Bowen, John and Robert L. Patten, eds. *Palgrave Advances in Charles Dickens Studies*. Basingstoke, England; New York: Palgrave Macmillan, 2006.

Britton, Wesley. "Carlyle, Clemens, and Dickens: Mark Twain's Francophobia, the French Revolution, and Determinism." *Studies in American Fiction* 20, no. 2 (Autumn 1992): 197–204.

Cotsell, Michael A. *Critical Essays on Charles Dickens's* A Tale of Two Cities. New York: G.K. Hall; London: Prentice Hall International, 1998.

Court, Franklin E. "*A Tale of Two Cities*: Dickens, Revolution, and the 'Other' C--D--." *Victorian Newsletter* 80 (Fall 1991): 14–18.

Davis, Paul B. *Critical Companion to Charles Dickens*. New York, N.Y.: Facts On File, 2007.

Foor, Sheila M. *Dickens' Rhetoric*. New York: P. Lang, 1993.

Glancy, Ruth F. *Student Companion to Charles Dickens*. Westport, Conn.: Greenwood Press, 1999.

————. A Tale of Two Cities: *Dickens's Revolutionary Novel*. Boston: Twayne Publishers, 1991.

Hobsbaum, Philip. *A Reader's Guide to Charles Dickens*. Syracuse, N.Y.: Syracuse University Press, 1998.

Houston, Gail Turley. *Consuming Fictions: Gender, Class, and Hunger in Dickens's Novels*. Carbondale: Southern Illinois University Press, 1994.

Ingham, Patricia. *Dickens, Women, and Language*. Toronto; Buffalo: University of Toronto Press, 1992.

Jacobson, Wendy. "The Redemption of 'All Sorrows': King Lear, The Old Curiosity Shop, and A Tale of Two Cities. *Shakespeare in Southern Africa: Journal of the Shakespeare Society of Southern Africa* 5 (1992): 13–32.

————. "'The World within Us': Jung and Dr. Manette's Daughter." *Dickensian* 93, no. 2 (Summer 1997): 95–108.

Jordan, John O., ed. *The Cambridge Companion to Charles Dickens*. London; New York: Cambridge University Press, 2001.

Kemper, Beth. "The 'Night Shadows' Passage in *A Tale of Two Cities*: Narrative Anxiety and Conscious Fiction-Building." *Kentucky Philological Review* 10 (1995): 22–26.

Maglavera, Soultana. *Time Patterns in Later Dickens: A Study of the Thematic Implications of the Temporal Organization of* Bleak House, Hard Times, Little Dorrit, A Tale of Two Cities, Great Expectations *and* Our Mutual Friend. Amsterdam; Atlanta, Ga.: Rodopi, 1994.

McKnight, Natalie. *Idiots, Madmen, and Other Prisoners in Dickens*. New York: St. Martin's Press, 1993.

Myers, Richard M. "Politics of Hatred in *A Tale of Two Cities*." In *Poets, Princes, and Private Citizens: Literary Alternatives to Postmodern Politics*, edited by Joseph M. Knippenberg and Peter Augustine Lawler, 63–74. Lanham, Md.: Rowman & Littlefield, 1996.

Nardo, Don, ed. *Readings on* A Tale of Two Cities. San Diego, Calif.: Greenhaven Press, 1997.

Newlin, George. *Understanding* A Tale of Two Cities: *A Student Casebook to Issues, Sources, and Historical Documents*. Westport, Conn.: Greenwood Press, 1998.

Petch, Simon. "The Business of the Barrister in *A Tale of Two Cities*." *Criticism: A Quarterly for Literature and the Arts* 44, no. 1 (Winter 2002): 27–42.

Rosen, David. "A Tale of Two Cities: Theology of Revolution." *Dickens Studies Annual: Essays on Victorian Fiction* 27 (1998): 171–185.

Sanders, Andrew. *Charles Dickens*. Oxford; New York: Oxford University Press, 2003.

Schlicke, Paul, ed. *Oxford Reader's Companion to Dickens*. Oxford; New York: Oxford University Press, 1999.

Schor, Hilary. "Novels of the 1850s: *Hard Times, Little Dorrit,* and *A Tale of Two Cities.*" In *The Cambridge Companion to Charles Dickens*, edited by John O. Jordan. Cambridge, England: Cambridge University Press, 2001.

Slater, Michael. *An Intelligent Person's Guide to Dickens*. London: Duckworth, 1999.

Sroka, Kenneth M. "A Tale of Two Gospels: Dickens and John." *Dickens Studies Annual: Essays on Victorian Fiction* 27 (1998): 145–169.

Swisher, Clarice. *Readings on Charles Dickens*. San Diego, Calif.: Greenhaven Press, 1998.

Tambling, Jeremy. *Dickens, Violence, and the Modern State: Dreams of the Scaffold*. New York: St. Martin's Press, 1995.

Acknowledgments

"Dickens and the Catastrophic Continuum of History in *A Tale of Two Cities*" by J.M. Rignall. From *ELH* 51, no. 3 (Autumn 1984): pp. 575–587. © 1984 by the Johns Hopkins University Press. Reprinted by permission of the Johns Hopkins University Press.

"The 'Angels' in Dickens's House: Representation of Women in *A Tale of Two Cities*" by Lisa Robson. From *Dalhousie Review* 72, no. 3 (Fall 1992): 311–333. © 1993 by *Dalhousie Review*. Reprinted by permission.

"Language, Love and Identity: *A Tale of Two Cities*" by Tom Lloyd. From *The Dickensian* 88, no. 428, part 3 (Autumn 1992): 154–170. © 1992 by Tom Lloyd. Reprinted by permission.

From the book *Dickens and Thackeray: Punishment and Forgiveness* by John R. Reed. Reprinted with permission of Ohio University Press, Athens, Ohio.

From Stanley Friedman, et al., eds., *Dickens Studies Annual: Essays on Victorian Fiction*, Vol. 25 (1996), 227–243. Copyright © 1996, AMS Press, Inc. Used with permission.

"*A Tale of Two Cities*" by Catherine Waters. From *Dickens and the Politics of the Family*: 122–149. © 1997 by Catherine Waters. Reprinted by permission of Cambridge University Press.

From Stanley Friedman, et al., eds., *Dickens Studies Annual: Essays on Victorian Fiction*, Vol. 26 (1998), 91–106. Copyright © 1998, AMS Press, Inc. Used with permission.

"Europe Is Not the Other: *A Tale of Two Cities*" by Bjørn Tysdahl. From *Dickens Quarterly* 15, no. 2 (June 1998): 111–122. © 1998 by the Dickens Society. Reprinted by permission.

"*Hard Times* and *A Tale of Two Cities*: The Social Inheritance of Adultery" by Hilary M. Schor. From *Dickens and the Daughter of the House*: 70–98. © 1999 by Cambridge University Press. Reprinted by permission of Cambridge University Press.

"Psychoanalyzing Dickens" by Carolyn Dever. From *Palgrave Advances in Charles Dickens Studies*, edited by John Bowen and Robert L. Patten: 216–233. © 2006 Palgrave Macmillan. Reprinted by permission of Palgrave Macmillan.

Every effort has been made to contact the owners of copyrighted material and secure copyright permission. Articles appearing in this volume generally appear much as they did in their original publication with few or no editorial changes. In some cases foreign language text has been removed from the original essay. Those interested in locating the original source will find bibliographic information in the bibliography and acknowledgments sections of this volume.

Index

Accuracy, value of, 2–3
Adultery
   birth and, 184–185
   disruption of society and, 182
   history and, 183–184
   Louisa Bounderby and, 168–170
   mistaken, 161
   social structure and, 187
   victimization and, 167–168
Aesthetic Education of Man (Schiller), 53
Alienation, Sydney Carton and, 20, 125–126
Altruism, sacrifice and, 22
Anarchy, rituals and, 114–115
Androgyny, 41–42
Angel, femininity and, 28
Angels
   Miss Pross as, 30–31
   repression and, 28–29
   virtue and, 33–34, 45
Animality, Madame Defarge and, 39
Antoinette, Marie, 40
Anxiety, guillotines and, 177–178
Apocalypse, 14, 110
Archaeology, historical, 204
Aristocracy
   exploitation and, 33
   guilt of, 74–75

language and, 50, 52–53
Medusa and, 43
violence and, 39
Artifacts, Freud and, 201–202
Artificiality, as criticism, 49
Asylum, novels as, 94–98
Authority, historical, 182–183
Autobiographical statements, psychoanalysis and, 193–194
Awareness, imagery and, 155–156

Barnaby Rudge (Dickens), 76, 195
Bastille, 122–123, 124
Beasts, women as, 40–42
Beauty, rage and, 131, 132, 137
Belief, Sydney Carton and, 57–62
Benjamin, parallels with, 14, 23–24
Births, Freud and, 206
Bleak House (Dickens), 1, 104–105, 196–197
Bonaparte, Napoleon, 41
Bondage, freedom from, 149–150
Bounderby, Louisa
   desires of, 172
   gender roles and, 161–163
   sexuality and, 168–170
   transformation of, 167–168
Boundlessness, 150–154
Burials, 150

Cannibalism, 113
Caricatures, 2–3, 19
Carlyle, Thomas
  French Revolution and, 36–37
  guillotines and, 177
  knowledge of work of, 5–6
  repetition in history and, 198
  right-Naming and, 93
  romantic irony and, 49–50
  as source, 102–103, 173
  transcendental experience and,
    59–60
  violence and, 53
  women of, 84–85
Carlyle and Dickens (Goldberg),
  36–37, 40
Carmagnole, 41–42, 92–93, 114–
  116, 138, 154
Carton, Sydney
  adultery and, 184–185
  ambiguous prophecy of, 49–50,
    62–64
  imagery and, 154–155
  middle class values and, 124–126
  moral management and, 89
  mystery of identity and, 78–79
  redemption and, 21–23, 51–53,
    57–62, 203–204
  self-recovery of, 74
  sexuality and, 89–90, 180–181
  significance of final scene and,
    14
  as victim, 20–21
  weakness of representation of, 7
Castration, 203
Categorization, naming and, 93–94
Change, 91, 92–93
Chaos, history as, 92–93
Characterization
  ambiguity of, 63
  ignorance of, 160
  subordination of, 195

Charles. *See* Darnay, Charles
Childbirth, 206
Childhood, 59, 202–204
A Christmas Carol (Dickens),
  popularity of, 5
Classes, Medusa and, 43
Class relations
  families and, 104
  guilt and, 74–76
  Miss Pross and, 28, 31–32
  moral insanity and, 86–87
  representation of women and,
    34–45
  women and, 44–45
Cleanliness, 168
Collins, Wilkie, 125
Conolly, John, 84–85, 86
Contrasts, 147–148
Conventionality, lack of in female
  characters, 28
Corday, Charlotte, 40

Dance, 41–42
Darnay, Charles
  arrest of, 174
  crime of, 178–179
  Everyman and, 20
  ghosts and, 56–57
  guilt and, 77
  middle class and, 121–122, 123
  morality and, 103
  repression and, 53–54
  weakness of representation of, 7
Darnay, Sydney, 206–207
Dartle, Rosa
  allure of, 135–136
  beauty of, 131
  rage of, 135–136
  sexuality and, 133–134
  vengeance and, 141–142
  violence and, 130–131
Daughters, 161–162, 183–184

David Copperfield (Dickens), 131,
139, 159–160, 196
Deaths
  guilt and, 75–76
  history and, 91
  mystery of identity and, 71
  resurrection and, 60–62
  significance of, 16–17
  similarities and, 150
  social change and, 207
Defarge (Madame)
  beauty of, 131, 132
  destiny and, 70–71
  eloquence of, 136–137
  families and, 119
  as force of nature, 54
  gendering of revolution and,
    104–105
  intensity of, 7–11
  moral disorder and, 88–89
  negativity of, 73
  non-verbal communication and,
    55–56
  physical traits of, 116–117
  radical statements of, 186
  rage and, 105–108
  as representation of France, 28,
    104
  restrictions on women and,
    37–39
  sexuality and, 205–206
  vengeance and, 18
  violence and, 130–131, 139–140,
    174–175
Determinism, 13–15, 79
Deviant femininity, 85
*Dickens and Carlyle: The Question of
  Influence* (Oddie), 36–37
Dionysus, Maenads and, 43
Discontinuity, 16
Displacement, substitution and,
  200

Divine power, justice and, 69–70
Dombey, Florence, violence and,
  130
Dombey and Son (Dickens), 71,
  129–130
Domestic ideology. *See also*
  Victorian ideals
  as asylum, 95
  Dickens and, 129–130
  knitting and, 106–108
  moral management and, 96
  naming and, 93–94
  subjectivity and, 90–93
  Sydney Carton and, 125–126,
    181–182
  violence and, 178–179
Domesticity, redemption and,
  29–30
Dreams, 135, 201–202
Drum-Taps (Whitman), Henry
  James on, 1

Echoes, 153–154
Effort, Charles Darnay and, 79
Ego, splitting of, 11
Eliot, T.S., on characters of
  Dickens, 4–5
Embedded narratives, 79–81
England
  abuses in, 75
  imagery and, 150–151
  immunity of to revolution, 84
  Lucie Manette as representation
    of, 28, 104
  similarities of to France, 148–
    151
Eroticism, 132–134, 170, 180–181,
  202–204
Eumenides of the Revolution, 112
Everyman, Charles Darnay and,
  20
Exploitation, rape and, 33

Fagin, as Shylock, 4
Faith, language and, 59–60
Falstaff, 4
Families. *See also* Domestic
  ideology
    crimes against, 103–104
    fascination with, 101–102
    government and, 122–123
    Lucie Manette and, 118–119
    Madame Defarge and, 119
    Marquis de St. Evrémonde and,
      122
    Miss Pross and, 119–120
    salvation of, 120–121
    saving-power of, 103
    sexuality and, 204
Fatalism, Sydney Carton and,
  21–23
Fate, 70–71, 106–107
Faust (Goethe), 58
Femininity
  angels and, 28
  deviant, 85
  Dickens and, 129–130, 175–176
  French Revolution and, 43–44
  Lucie Manette and, 28–30, 121
  Madame Defarge and, 138
  Miss Pross and, 30–31
  psychoanalysis and, 192–193
  sexuality and, 132–134
Figurative language, 151–155
Forgiveness, redemption and,
  70–71
Foucault, Michel, 88
France
  abuse of aristocracy and, 74–75
  imagery and, 150–151
  Madame Defarge as
    representation of, 28, 104
  similarities of to England,
    148–151
Freedom, 149–150

French Revolution
  apocalypse and, 110
  complexity of women's roles in,
    34–41
  denunciation of, 176
  domestication of, 173
  feminine nature of, 43–44
  gendering of, 104, 106–107
  gender roles and, 111–113
  guilt and, 78–79
  history as, 91–92
  knitting and, 174
  lack of true understanding of,
    103
  Lucie Manette and, 176–177,
    205
  Madame Defarge and, 126–127,
    178–179
  as metaphor for social ruin, 84
  perception of, 85–86
  psychoanalysis and, 195–197
  reasons for attraction to, 83–84
  reasons for necessity of,
    186–187
  sacrifice and, 90–93
  sexuality and, 84
  Thomas Carlyle and, 5–6
  violence and, 178
  women and, 102–103
The French Revolution (Carlyle)
  historical frames of reference in,
    198
  knitting and, 106–107
  language and, 50–51
  as source, 102–103
  violence and, 53
Freud, Sigmund, 191–192, 201–204
The Frozen Deep (Collins), 125

Gazing, 134–135
Gender roles
  French Revolution and, 111–113

Hard Times (Dickens) and, 161–162
narration and, 127
political conflicts and, 102–103
revolution and, 106–107
subversion of, 107–109
Victorian ideals and, 39–40
Ghosts
Dr. Manette as, 198–199
Freud and, 196–197
language and, 56–57
promises and, 182–183
Goldberg, Michael, 36–37, 40
Golden thread
harmony and, 38
Lucie Manette as, 20, 29–30, 118
Gorgon's spell, 43
Gouges, Olympe de, 40
Government, families and, 122–123
Gradgrind, Thomas, 162
Great Expectations (Dickens), 131
La Guillotine, 43–44
Guillotines
fate and, 70
knitting and, 107
Lucie Manette and, 178
Madame Defarge and, 175
symbolism of, 56–57, 78
Thomas Carlyle and, 173, 177–178
Guilt, 77, 78–79

Hard Times (Dickens)
childhood and, 59
gender roles and, 161–162
ownership and, 168–169
rage and, 131
truth and, 161
Harmony, golden thread and, 38
Hill, John Gardiner, 86
History. *See also* French Revolution
authority and, 182–183

death of, 91
determinism and, 13–15
emotions driving, 18–19
guilt and, 74–75
language and, 55
links to, 155
naming and, 93–94
narration and, 196–197
ordering principles of, 102
privatization of social, 204–205
psychoanalysis and, 195–196
reading and, 95
repetition in, 197–198
resistance to catastrophic continuum of, 18
as revolution, 91–92
secrets and, 72–73
sexuality and, 203–205
women and, 200–201
The History of Henry Esmond (Thackeray), 122
History of the French Revolution (Carlyle), 5–6
Hortense (*Bleak House*), 104–105
Humanity, 154, 199
Hutter, Albert D., 34

Idealism, 59, 90–93, 94–97
Identity
early Dickens novels and, 159
formation of, 139
fragmentation of self and, 50
language and, 50–51
mystery of, 71, 78–79
Imagery, use of, 151–155
Imprisonment, language and, 52–53
Individuality, 15–16, 20–21
Industrialization, gender roles and, 166, 172
Inferno (Dante), 56
Initiative, Sydney Carton and, 79

Insanity, 84–85. *See also* moral
  management
Intensity, Madame Defarge and,
  7–11
The Interpretation of Dreams
  (Freud), 201–202, 203, 204, 207

James, Henry, 1–2
Jameson, Frederic, 155
Judgement Day, 74–75
Justice, 69–70, 78

Kelly, Linda, 40
Knitting
  French Revolution and, 174
  golden thread and, 29–30
  as metaphor for storytelling, 7
  rage and, 106
  sexuality and, 89
  suffering and, 199–200

Language
  figurative, 151–155
  guillotines and, 56–57
  identity and, 50–51
  imprisonment and, 52–53
  love and, 55–56
  Madame Defarge and, 136–137
  Miss Wade and, 140
  moral management and, 94–95
  naming and, 94
  narratives and, 150–151
  non-verbal communication and,
    55–56
  rage and, 135–136
  resurrection and, 51–53
  revivification of, 59–60
  transcendental experience and,
    59–60
  value of, 49–50
  vengeance and, 54–55
Lesbianism, Bloom on, 11

Letters, 51, 174
Literature, psychoanalysis and,
  192–193
Little Dorrit (Dickens)
  freedom from bondage and,
    149–150
  Henry James on, 1
  identity and, 139
  rage and, 131
Lorry, Jarvis, language and, 52
Love, Lucie Manette and, 58–59,
  73
Lucie. *See* Manette, Lucie

Maenads, 43
Manette (Dr.)
  dehumanization of, 50–51
  dilemma of, 124
  displacement and, 200
  as ghost, 198–199
  oppression and, 73
  reasons for imprisonment of, 33
Manette, Lucie
  angels and, 29–30
  family values of, 118–119,
    120–121
  French Revolution and, 176–
    177, 205
  as golden thread, 20, 29–30, 73
  guillotines and, 178
  love and, 58–59
  as representation of England,
    28, 104
  resurrection and, 89–90
  weakness of representation of, 7
Marquis de St. Evrémonde. *See* St.
  Evrémonde (Marquis de)
Marriage, 161, 168–171
Martin Chuzzlewit (Dickens),
  identity and, 159
Materialism, 170–171
Medusa, aristocracy and, 43

Memory
    crisis of, 173
    daughters and, 183–184
    guilt and, 75–76
    repetition and, 197–198
    transmission and, 182–183
    value of, 71–72
Mental illness. *See* moral
    management
Mercenaries, adulterers vs., 168
Méricourt, Théroigne de, 40, 116
Metaphors, knitting as metaphor
    for, 7
Middlemarch (Eliot), 63
Mobs
    flight from, 17–18
    symbolism of, 149
    treatment of, 76, 112
Monsters, Madame Defarge as, 39
Moral architecture, 88
Moral crisis, Sydney Carton and,
    57–62
Moral insanity, Madame Defarge
    and, 88–89
Moral management
    legitimization of, 96
    moral insanity and, 86–88
    social control and, 94–95
    Sydney Carton and, 89
    Victorian ideals and, 85

Naming, history and, 93–94
Napoleon, 41
Narration
    credibility of, 196–197
    gender roles and, 127
    grammar of, 150–151
    horror of mobs and, 112
    ignorance of character and, 160
Narratives, embedded analagous,
    79–81
Nationality, 34–45, 102

Nature, denial of, 53–54
Necessity, revolution and, 186–187
Nicholas Nickleby (Dickens), identity
    and, 159
"Night Shadows" meditation, 16,
    21
Nihilism, prophecy and, 62–64
Novels, 94–98, 101–102

Oddie, William, 36–37
"Ode: Intimations of Immortality"
    (Wordsworth), 59
Oedipus (Sophocles), 201–203, 207
Oliver Twist (Dickens), identity and,
    159
Oppression, Dr. Manette as, 73
Our Mutual Friend (Dickens), 1–2,
    130
Ownership, *Hard Times* (Dickens)
    and, 168–169

Parallels, 104, 148–151, 179–180
Parenting, Freud and, 202–204
Past, links to present, 155
Pathology, sexuality and, 84–85
Patriarchies
    dependence of women and,
        34–35
    identity and, 159
    indictment of, 34
    Marquis and, 43
    prestige of, 88
    thematics of suppression and,
        32–33
Patterns, imagery and, 155–156
Perception, moral insanity and, 87
Perversion. *See* moral management
Phallic gaze, 133
Pictures from Italy (Dickens), 147
Pollock, Johnathan Frederick, 19
Popularity, Bloom on, 4–5
Power, 96, 107–109

Price, Martin, comparison of
    Dickens to Johnathan Swift by,
    3–4
Pritchard, James Cowell, 86
Privatization of social history,
    204–205
Progress, history as, 93
Prolepses, 80–81, 197
Prophecy, ambiguity of,
    49–50
Pross (Miss)
    class and, 28, 31–32
    families and, 119–120
    language and, 55–56
    satire and, 30–31
Psychiatric treatment. See moral
    management
Psychoanalysis
    Dickens and, 191–192
    Freud and, 191–192
    literature and, 192–193
    memory and, 197
    theory of, 193–194

Rage
    beauty and, 131, 132, 137
    expressions of, 135–136
    language and, 135–136
    Madame Defarge and, 105–108
    violence of women and, 130,
        142–143
Rape, 33–34, 103–104, 178
Rasselas (Johnson), 52–53
Redemption
    domesticity and, 29–30
    Sydney Carton and, 21–23,
        51–53, 57–62, 203–204
    women and, 41
Repetition
    imagery and, 153–154
    sexuality and, 203–204
    use of, 80–81, 197–198

Repression
    angels and, 28–29
    dangers of, 74
    St. Evrémonde case and, 53–54,
        77
Resistance, Sydney Carton and, 24
Ressentiment, 162
Resurrection
    death and, 60–62
    forgiveness, redemption and,
        70–71
    language and, 51–53
    Lucie Manette and, 29–30,
        89–90
Retribution. See vengeance
Revenge. See vengeance
Revivification, of language, 59–60
Revolution. See French Revolution
Revolutionaries, 37, 40–41
Right-Naming, 93
The Rights of Women and the Citizen
    (Gouges), 40
"Rime of the Ancient Mariner",
    154
Rituals, anarchy and, 114–115
Roland (Madame), 60–62
Romantic irony, influence of, 49
Romanticism, imagery and, 154
Rosa. See Dartle, Rosa
Roses, 107
Ruskin, John, 2–3

Sacrifice
    altruism and, 22
    as law of revolution, 90–93
    Sydney Carton and, 126
    violence and, 34
St. Evrémonde (Marquis de), 54,
    74–75, 77, 122
Salvation, families and, 103, 120–121
Satire, Miss Pross and, 30–31,
    119–120

Saviors, women as, 32–33, 34–35
Scars, 133–134, 141
Schiller, Friedrich, 53–54, 61–62
Sea imagery, 151–153, 154–155
Secrecy, suffering and, 71–73
Self
    fragmentation of, 50
    mystery of, 71
    renunciation of, 61–62
    understanding of, 171
Self-Help (Smiles), 122
Semioticization of body, 131
Sexuality
    angels and, 28–29
    Bloom on, 11
    blurring of, 41–42
    femininity and, 132–134
    gender roles and, 161–163
    history and, 203–205
    knitting and, 89
    Louisa Bounderby and, 168–170
    Madame Defarge and, 205–206
    political conflicts and, 111,
        114–115
    revolution and, 84
    Sydney Carton and, 89–90,
        180–181
    violence and, 204
    wisdom and, 160–161
Shakespeare, William, Bloom on,
    4–5, 9
Shylock, 4
Similarities between France and
    England, 148–151
Slogans, 155–156
Smethurst, Thomas, 19
Smiles, Samuel, 122
Social circumstances, trauma and,
    201
Social position, *David Copperfield*
    (Dickens) and, 159–160
Social structure, 86–87, 187, 207

Society of Revolutionary
    Republican Women, 40–41
Somatization of story, 131
Sparsit (Mrs.), 162–163
"Stage fire", 3–5, 7
Stephen, James Fitzjames, reviews
    by, 5–6
Storytelling, knitting as metaphor
    for, 7
Stryver (Mr.)
    as caricature, 19
    energy and values of, 20–21
    language and, 52
Stuart, Maria, 61–62
Substitution, displacement and, 200
Suffering, 71–73, 199–200
Superficiality, Henry James on, 1–2
Superstition, 148–149
Suppression, thematics of, 32
Suspension of disbelief, 49
Swift, Johnathan, comparison to,
    3–4
Sydney. *See* Carton, Sydney
Symbolism, guillotines and, 56–57

Taxation populaire, 36
Tellson's Bank, 150
Theroigne, Sybil, 54
Three Fates, 106
Tower of London, 51
Tragedy, Friedrich Schiller and,
    61–62
Transcendental experience, 59–60,
    63 64
Transmission, memory and,
    182–183
Trauma, 199–200, 201
A Treatise on Insanity (Pritchard),
    86
Tribunals, 142
Truth, 77, 161
Tuke, Samuel, 86

Ulysses (Tennyson), 57
Understanding, lack of, 103
Utopias, change and, 91

Vengeance
    communication and, 54–55
    Dr. Manette and, 51
    guillotines and, 56–57
    guilt and, 78–79
    knitting needles and, 38
    Madame Defarge and, 18, 37–38
    rage and, 140
    suffering and, 72–73
The Vengeance, violence and,
    109–110
Victimization, adultery and, 167–
168
Victorian ideals. See also domestic
    ideology
    angels and, 28–29
    families and, 101–102, 103
    gender roles and, 39–40
    moral management and, 86–88
    revolutionary change and, 92–93
    sexuality and, 84
A Vindication of the Rights of Women
    (Wollstonecraft), 116
Violence
    anarchy and, 114–115
    domestic ideology and, 178–179
    The French Revolution and, 53
    gender roles and, 166
    injustice and, 76
    lack of control and, 14–15
    Madame Defarge and, 38–39,
        174–175
    overwhelming nature of, 17–18
    persistence of, 19, 23
    reaction to, 19–20
    reasons for, 139–140

revolution and, 178
sexuality and, 114–115, 204
The Vengeance and, 109–110
women and, 130–131
Virgin birth, 206
Virtue, angels and, 33–34, 45

Wade (Miss)
    beauty of, 131, 134
    rage of, 135
    vengeance and, 140, 141–142
    violence and, 130–131, 139–140
Water imagery, 151–153, 154–155
Weakness, Bloom on, 7
Weariness, ending of novel and,
    23–24
Welsh, Alexander, on Dickens' use
    of angels, 28
Wilson, Edmund, 130
Wollstonecraft, Mary, 116
Women. See also patriarchies, rape
    class relations and, 44–45
    Dickens and, 138
    faith placed in, 129–130
    French Revolution and, 34–41,
        83–84, 102–103
    history and, 200–201
    lack of conventionality and,
        28–29
    redemption and, 29–30, 41
    representation of, 27–28, 58–59
    social transgressive energies and,
        84–85
    violation of, 104
    violence and, 130–131
Women of the French Revolution
    (Kelly), 40
Wordsworth, William, 59
Writing of novel, fascination with
    family and, 101–102

URBANMAN

URBANMAN

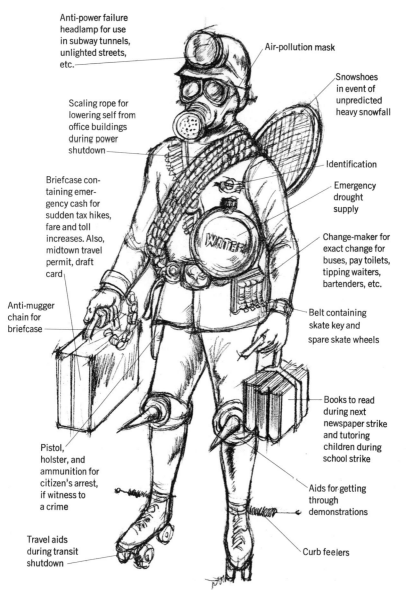

Anti-power failure headlamp for use in subway tunnels, unlighted streets, etc.

Air-pollution mask

Snowshoes in event of unpredicted heavy snowfall

Scaling rope for lowering self from office buildings during power shutdown

Identification

Emergency drought supply

Briefcase containing emergency cash for sudden tax hikes, fare and toll increases. Also, midtown travel permit, draft card

Change-maker for exact change for buses, pay toilets, tipping waiters, bartenders, etc.

Anti-mugger chain for briefcase

Belt containing skate key and spare skate wheels

Books to read during next newspaper strike and tutoring children during school strike

Pistol, holster, and ammunition for citizen's arrest, if witness to a crime

Aids for getting through demonstrations

Travel aids during transit shutdown

Curb feelers

URBANMAN

The Psychology of Urban Survival

Edited by **JOHN HELMER,** Harvard University, and **NEIL A. EDDINGTON**

The Free Press
New York
Collier-Macmillan Publishers
London

Contents

Introduction, vii
  John Helmer

1. The Experience of Living in Cities: A Psychological Analysis, 1
  Stanley Milgram

2. Driving to Work, 23
  Anthony F. C. Wallace

3. Learning to Live with Lines, 42
  Leon Mann

4. Bystander "Apathy," 62
  Bibb Latané and *John M. Darley*

5. Fear and the House-As-Haven in the Lower Class, 92
  Lee Rainwater

6. Architecture, Interaction, and Social Control: The Case of a
  Large-Scale Public Housing Project, 107
  William L. Yancey

7. The Social Psychology of Privacy, 123
    Barry Schwartz

8. Opening Conversations, 142
    Emanuel A. Schegloff

9. Rapping in the Black Ghetto, 170
    Thomas Kochman

10. The Human Choice: Individuation, Reason and Order Vs.
    Deindividuation, Impulse and Chaos, 196
    Philip G. Zimbardo

11. The City as a Mechanism for Sustaining Human Contact, 239
    Christopher Alexander

Introduction

John Helmer

This book is about the experiences of urbanman (collective noun, no sex differentiation, men and women together). It is about the ways in which urbanman organizes his behavior to deal with the problematical nature of his daily life—getting to work; waiting in line for goods and services; avoiding stress, threat, physical danger, and disease; communicating with others; preserving privacy, intimate contacts, and peace.

Of course, these are needs and goals which are shared by most people, not merely by those who happen to live in cities. But, as our cities have grown progressively larger and more complex, and as the total of demands placed on urban facilities—from the air we breathe to the spaces we work and live in—exceeds their capacity for supply or satisfaction, so urbanman has come to experience as problematical in his daily life what to others, living in richer, less overloaded environments, is routinely available and so unproblematic as to be taken for granted. The dynamics of simple economic exchanges, of mutual trust, of joking, of meaning what you say, as in ordinary conversation, and of elementary physical security on the street and in the home—these and many other commonplace transactions, events, and experiences are cause for continuous and fateful decision-making on urbanman's part.

This is because he cannot assume an order in other people's behavior which lends predictability and regularity to the flow of events in which he himself is an active participant and from which he draws consequences that are vital to his own plans and well-being. Thus we say that urbanman's activities become *fateful* when their accomplishment is problematic, in the sense of their being unpredictable, even doubtful, and when their consequences are important enough to spill over into other realms of activity and are noticeable enough to affect his experience of life.[1] This book, then, is about many of urbanman's activities, which, in other environments or at other times, are routine, commonplace, conventional, but which are for him, now, chronically fateful.

The experience of fatefulness in everyday urban life has produced in recent years a lot of talk about the crisis in the quality of urban life, though the fateful experience that is the focus of greatest public concern—the threat of violence against the person—is more commonly a vicarious experience, suffered by a relatively limited few, yet felt by many who are considerably removed, in fact and in likelihood, from threat or harm. However, for a large part of the city's population, the problematics of survival are as old as it can remember. This is the urban under-class, the poor (black, white, old, immigrant) for whom the fatefulness of daily living is and always has been chronic, without alleviation or respite.

There is nothing new in their experience, unless it has gotten worse. What prompts new-found concern for this experience is not the discovery of urban poverty or the culture of poverty, these being social phenomena which are always being rediscovered. Rather, the prompter is that the problematical nature of urban living, the fatefulness of urbanman's daily activity, has become a new experience for the urban *middle classes*—large sections of the metropolitan population who may or may not live within the city limits, but who regularly travel in and use it, and who, in some way, regard themselves as members of and belonging to the city.

The novelty of this experience for middle-class urbanites has prompted most of the recent discussion concerning law and order, personal survival, and security. If it means anything, the law-and-order label refers to social situations of high regularity and predictability, in which problematic choice is minimized and the necessity for fateful decisions all but eliminated. (Individuals and groups aiming at this degree of conventionality still keep a place for fatefulness in sports—that includes sex—gambling and war.) And it is from the middle-class experience of the fatefulness of urban disorder that the greatest pressures have emerged to develop new public and individual policies for the use of urban space. Urban psychology and much behaviorally founded urban design are highly responsive to these pressures, and this book represents a sample of some of the initial responses to this novel situation.

Chapters 5 and 6 are intended, however, to serve as points of comparison between the kinds of problems which the lower-class urbanman must continue to deal with—for example, rats, poisons, fire, trash, or insufficiently guarded heights—and the kinds of problematic experiences which are most salient in the consciousness of middle-class urbanman. But it has not been the intention of the editors to provide a thorough-going guide to urbanman's consciousness any more than it has been our intention to document differences in consciousness among the social classes of the city.

The aim has been more limited: to draw the reader's attention to those elementary, commonplace activities—walking, queueing, driving, talking, joking, shopping—the experience of which has come to be seen as increasingly more problematical and fateful in recent times, and which, to an important degree, is our most sensitive indicator of the current quality of urban life.

In part, this book is intended to help the reader to consider his own experience of the city in a more systematic way, enabling him to turn vague impressions and inferences from personal observation into more widely testable hypotheses, and these into solidly based findings about the psychological impact of the urban environment.

In part also, this book is designed to deal with some of the most urgently felt problems of urbanites. When will people come to the help of others? Why will they often fail to come to others' assistance (Chapter 4)? What accounts for the violence of city life—vandalism, assaults, and wanton destructiveness (Chapter 10)? What are the effects of city space and city living on mental health, individual sense of well-being, happiness (Chapters 1, 7, and 11)? How can urban planning make a significant impact, not merely on the physical layout of the city, but also on the dispositions and behavior of its inhabitants (Chapter 11)?

In part too, the book is designed to provide a guide to the

methodological means which are currently being devised or used towards answering these questions and for study and policy-making in this area.

Driving to work is analyzed in ethnoscientific terms, as a measure of the cognitive complexity of urbanman's universe, by Anthony Wallace, an anthropologist. Two chapters are concerned with the games people play with words. In Chapter 8, Schegloff looks at deceptively simple telephone and intercom conversations from the ethnomethodological perspective, which is a kind of syntax and sociology combined. In Chapter 9, Kochman draws on recent ethnographic approaches to communication so as to analyze the intricate powerplays of the rap. The largest part of the book, Chapters 1, 3, 4, 7, and 10 provide illustrations of current psychological and social psychological approaches to the analysis of urban experience—some laboratory manipulations, some in-the-field or "natural" experiments, and some participant observation.

To the urbanite, the data described in the chapters of this book are not likely to be news, and many of the findings reported may strike few readers as provocatively novel. Urbanman's practical knowledge of his environment is clearly not identical with the social science of urban life, but neither is it easy to say whether the former lags a couple of steps behind the awareness reached by the latter, or vice versa. Notwithstanding what urbanman may himself know about city life, however, planning decisions are being put into effect all the time to reshape the physical environment of the city, on the basis of assumptions about urbanman's behavior which are manifestly not shared by all urbanites.

Some of these assumptions are long-established, and jealously preserved by guilds of architects, builders, and city planners. But as both Rainwater (Chapter 5) and Yancey (Chapter 6) attest, there are many classic monuments to lack of behavioral knowledge or orientation in these professions. In general, we might add, the Modern Movement in architecture has created some very distinguished behavioral sinks, where architectural theory has had catastrophic effects on large groups of people forced to live out the theory. But also, to be quite fair, *some* psychological and sociological research as a basis for urban design may not be *enough,* and where inadequate, has had equally catastrophic effects. One writer, reviewing the impact of social science on public architecture in England, recently decried the search for a "scientific basis" for public urban design as "sociological baloney," as hopeless, he argued, as looking for the Philosopher's Stone.[2] Christopher Alexander offers more hope than this, and his chapter (11) is a rare and brilliant attempt at synthesizing the best of our knowledge and the most urgent of our needs with a practical design plan, which the reader can see for himself and use as a measuring stick against his own neighborhood—or the one he dreams about.

Before the design and planning professions can usefully or even safely adopt behavioral criteria in the shaping of city space, we need to be much clearer than we are at present about what is known and what yet remains to be learned about urbanman's behavior, the interaction between it and the existing urban environment, and the likely consequences of planned change. It is important that we be modest on this point: The knowledge vitally needed for managing the urban environment to effectively deal with its behavioral problems does not appear to exist at present.[3] Yet we still continue to regulate or reproduce these environments on the basis of plans of action whose human consequences are either now known to be harmful (whatever the cause) or remain unknown.

One lesson of the book is this: that however sophisticated urbanman's common sense and accumulated everyday knowledge may be— and the pressure of fatefulness encourages in him greater sophistication and self-consciousness all the time—he remains impotent to significantly change the human environment of the city to suit himself. But the present generation of urban and environmental decision-makers— architects, engineers, builders, natural resource managers, etc.—are not much better informed.[4] Indeed, they can differ so markedly in their comprehension of the urban environment from the resident urbanites or the institutional clients for their services, that their decisions and practice may avoid or contradict the social and psychological goals sought after by urbanman, who must then endure the consequences.

A final role for this book to play is one of assisting designers and planners—indeed, all who participate in determining the future course of the city—to compile an inventory of the current state of our knowledge about urbanman. One selection (Chapter 3) has not appeared before in print; the remainder have been published in widely scattered sources, not all of them readily available. By gathering them in this format, the editors have sought to accomplish the several purposes already mentioned, and to stimulate the reader toward making his own judgment of how best to promote the survival of urbanman and to enhance the quality of urban life.

NOTES

1. This terminology is drawn from Erving Goffman's usage, in a somewhat different context, in the essay, "Where the Action Is," *Interaction Ritual* (Garden City, N.Y.: Doubleday, 1967), pp. 152–53.
2. Martin Pawley, "Architects and the Philosopher's Stone," *New Society*, April 29, 1971, p. 720. For a review of the American situation, see Kenneth H. Craik, "The Environmental Dispositions of Environmental Decision-Makers," *The Annals*, Volume 389, May 1970 (Special Issue: Society and Its Physical Environment), pp. 87–94.
3. See, for example, Steven Zlutnick and Irwin Altman, "Crowding and Human Behavior," J. F. Wohlwill and D. H. Carson, eds., in *Behavioral Science and the Problems of our Environment* (Washington, D.C.: American Psychological Association, 1971).
4. Alan Lipman, "The Architectural Belief System and Social Behavior," *British Journal of Sociology*, Volume 20, June 1969, pp. 190–204.

URBANMAN

1

The Experience of Living in Cities:
A Psychological Analysis

Stanley Milgram

"When I first came to New York it seemed like a nightmare. As soon as I got off the train at Grand Central I was caught up in pushing, shoving crowds on 42nd Street. Sometimes people bumped into me without apology; what really frightened me was to see two people literally engaged in combat for possession of a cab. Why were they so rushed? Even drunks on the street were bypassed without a glance. People didn't seem to care about each other at all."

This statement represents a common reaction to a great city, but it does not tell the whole story. Obviously cities have great appeal because of their variety, eventfulness, possibility of choice, and the stimulation of an intense atmosphere that many individuals find a desirable background to their lives. Where face-to-face contacts are important, the city offers unparalleled possibilities. It has been calculated by the Regional Plan Association[1] that in Nassau County, a suburb of New York City, an individual can meet 11,000 others

"The Experience of Living in Cities: A Psychological Analysis," Stanley Milgram, *Science*, Vol. 167 (March 13, 1970), pp. 1461–68. Copyright © 1970 by the American Association for the Advancement of Science. Reprinted by permission of the author and *Science*.

within a 10-minute radius of his office by foot or car. In Newark, a moderate-sized city, he can meet more than 20,000 persons within this radius. But in midtown Manhattan he can meet fully 220,000. So there is an order-of-magnitude increment in the communication possibilities offered by a great city. That is one of the bases of its appeal and, indeed, of its functional necessity. The city provides options that no other social arrangement permits. But there is a negative side also, as we shall see.

Granted that cities are indispensable in complex society, we may still ask what contribution psychology can make to understand the experience of living in them. What theories are relevant? How can we extend our knowledge of the psychological aspects of life in cities through empirical inquiry? If empirical inquiry is possible, along what lines should it proceed? In short, where do we start in constructing urban theory and in laying out lines of research?

Observation is the indispensable starting point. Any observer in the streets of midtown Manhattan will see (i) large numbers of people, (ii) a high population density, and (iii) heterogeneity of population. These three factors need to be at the root of any sociopsychological theory of city life, for they condition all aspects of our experience in the metropolis. Louis Wirth,[2] if not the first to point to these factors, is nontheless the sociologist who relied most heavily on them in his analysis of the city. Yet, for a psychologist, there is something unsatisfactory about Wirth's theoretical variables. Numbers, density, and heterogeneity are demographic facts but they are not yet psychological facts. They are external to the individual. Psychology needs an idea that links the individual's *experience* to the demographic circumstances of urban life.

One link is provided by the concept of overload. This term, drawn from systems analysis, refers to a system's inability to process inputs from the environment because there are too many inputs for the system to cope with, or because successive inputs come so fast that input *A* cannot be processed when input *B* is presented. When overload is present, adaptations occur. The system must set priorities and make choices. *A* may be processed first while *B* is kept in abeyance, or one input may be sacrificed altogether. City life, as we experience it, constitutes a continuous set of encounters with overload, and of resultant adaptations. Overload characteristically deforms daily life on several levels, impinging on role performance, the evolution of social norms, cognitive functioning, and the use of facilities.

The concept has been implicit in several theories of urban experience. In 1903 George Simmel[3] pointed out that, since urban dwellers come into contact with vast numbers of people each day, they conserve psychic energy by becoming acquainted with a far smaller proportion of people than their rural counterparts do, and by maintaining more superficial relationships even with these acquaintances. Wirth[4] points specifically to "the superficiality, the anonymity, and the transitory character of urban social relations."

One adaptive response to overload, therefore, is the allocation of less time to each input. A second adaptive mechanism is disregard of low-priority inputs. Principles of selectivity are formulated such that investment of time and energy are reserved for carefully defined inputs (the urbanite disregards the drunk sick on the street as he purposefully navigates through the crowd). Third, boundaries are redrawn in certain social transactions so that the overloaded system can shift the burden to the other party in the exchange; thus, harried New York bus drivers once made change for customers, but now this responsibility has been shifted to the client, who must have the exact fare ready. Fourth, reception is blocked off prior to entrance into a system; city dwellers increasingly use unlisted telephone numbers to prevent individuals from calling them, and a small but growing number resort to keeping the telephone off the hook to prevent incoming calls. More subtly, a city dweller blocks inputs by assuming an unfriendly countenance, which discourages others from initiating contact. Additionally, social screening devices are interposed between the individual and environmental inputs (in a town of 5000 anyone can drop in to chat with the mayor, but in the metropolis organizational screening devices deflect inputs to other destinations). Fifth, the intensity of inputs is diminished by filtering devices, so that only weak and relatively superficial forms of involvement with others are allowed. Sixth, specialized institutions are created to absorb inputs that would otherwise swamp the individual (welfare departments handle the financial needs of a million individuals in New York City, who would otherwise create an army of mendicants continuously importuning the pedestrian). The interposition of institutions between the individual and the social world, a characteristic of all modern society, and most notably of the large metropolis, has its negative side. It deprives the individual of a sense of direct contact and spontaneous integration in the life around him. It simultaneously protects and estranges the individual from his social environment.

Many of these adaptive mechanisms apply not only to individuals but to institutional systems as well, as Meier[5] has so brilliantly shown in connection with the library and the stock exchange.

In sum, the observed behavior of the urbanite in a wide range of situations appears to be determined largely by a variety of adaptations to overload. I now deal with several specific consequences of responses to overload, which make for differences in the tone of city and town.

SOCIAL RESPONSIBILITY

The principal point of interest for a social psychology of the city is that moral and social involvement with individuals is necessarily restricted. This is a direct and necessary function of excess of input over capacity to process. Such restriction of involvement runs a broad spectrum from refusal to become involved in the needs of another person, even when the person desperately needs assistance, through refusal to do favors, to the simple withdrawal of courtesies (such as offering a lady a seat, or saying "sorry" when a pedestrian collision occurs). In any transaction more and more details need to be dropped as the total number of units to be processed increases and assaults an instrument of limited processing capacity.

The ultimate adaptation to an over-loaded social environment is to totally disregard the needs, interests, and demands of those whom one does not define as relevant to the satisfaction of personal needs, and to develop highly efficient perceptual means of determining whether an individual falls into the category of friend or stranger. The disparity in the treatment of friends and strangers ought to be greater in cities than in towns; the time allotment and willingness to become involved with those who have no personal claim on one's time is likely to be less in cities than in towns.

BYSTANDER INTERVENTION IN CRISES

The most striking deficiencies in social responsibility in cities in crisis situations, such as the Genovese murder in Queens. In 1964, Catherine Genovese, coming home from a night job in the early hours of an April morning, was stabbed repeatedly, over an extended period of time. Thirty-eight residents of a respectable New

York City neighborhood admit to having witnessed at least a part of the attack, but none went to her aid or called the police until after she was dead. Milgram and Hollander, writing in *The Nation*,[6] analyzed the event in these terms:

> Urban friendships and associations are not primarily formed on the basis of physical proximity. A person with numerous close friends in different parts of the city may not know the occupant of an adjacent apartment. This does not mean that a city dweller has fewer friends than does a villager, or knows fewer persons who will come to his aid; however, it does mean that his allies are not constantly at hand. Miss Genovese required immediate aid from those physically present. There is no evidence that the city had deprived Miss Genovese of human associations, but the friends who might have rushed to her side were miles from the scene of her tragedy.
>
> Further, it is known that her cries for help were not directed to a specific person; they were general. But only individuals can act, and as the cries were not specifically directed, no particular person felt a special responsibility. The crime and the failure of community response seem absurd to us. At the time, it may well have seemed equally absurd to the Kew Gardens residents that not one of the neighbors would have called the police. A collective paralysis may have developed from the belief of each of the witnesses that someone else must surely have taken that obvious step.

Gaertner and Bickman[7] of The City University of New York have extended the bystander studies to an examination of help across ethnic lines. Blacks and whites, with clearly identifiable accents, called strangers (through what the caller represented as an error in telephone dialing), gave them a plausible story of being stranded on an outlying highway without more dimes, and asked the stranger to call a garage. The experimenters found that the white callers had a significantly better chance of obtaining assistance than the black callers. This suggests that ethnic allegiance may well be another means of coping with overload: the city dweller can reduce excessive demands and screen out urban heterogeneity by responding along ethnic lines; overload is made more manageable by limiting the "span of sympathy."

In any quantitative characterization of the social texture of city life, a necessary first step is the application of such experimental methods as these to field situations in large cities and small towns. Theorists argue that the indifference shown in the Genovese case would not be found in a small town, but in the absence of solid experimental evidence the question remains an open one.

More than just callousness prevents bystanders from participating in altercations between people. A rule of urban life is respect for other people's emotional and social privacy, perhaps because physical privacy is so hard to achieve. And in situations for which the standards are heterogeneous, it is much harder to know whether taking an active role is unwarranted meddling or an appropriate response to a critical situation. If a husband and wife are quarreling in public, at what point should a bystander step in? On the one hand, the heterogeneity of the city produces substantially greater tolerance about behavior, dress, and codes of ethics than is generally found in the small town, but this diversity also encourages people to withhold aid for fear of antagonizing the participants or crossing an inappropriate and difficult-to-define line.

Moreover, the frequency of demands present in the city gives rise to norms of noninvolvement. There are practical limitations to the Samaritan impulse in a major city. If a citizen attended to every needy person, if he were sensitive to and acted on every altruistic impulse that was evoked in the city, he could scarcely keep his own affairs in order.

WILLINGNESS TO TRUST AND ASSIST STRANGERS

We now move away from crisis situations to less urgent examples of social responsibility. For it is not only in situations of dramatic need but in the ordinary, everyday willingness to lend a hand that the city dweller is said to be deficient relative to his small-town cousin. The comparative method must be used in any empirical examination of this question. A commonplace social situation is staged in an urban setting and in a small town—a situation to which a subject can respond by either extending help or withholding it. The responses in town and city are compared.

One factor in the purported unwillingness of urbanites to be helpful to strangers may well be their heightened sense of physical (and emotional) vulnerability—a feeling that is supported by urban crime statistics. A key test for distinguishing between city and town behavior, therefore, is determining how city dwellers compare with town dwellers in offering aid that increases their personal vulnerability and requires some trust of strangers. Altman, Levine, Nadien, and

TABLE 1

Percentage of Entries Achieved by Investigators
for City and Town Dwellings (see text).

	ENTRIES ACHIEVED (%)	
Experimenter	*City**	*Small town†*
Male		
No. 1	16	40
No. 2	12	60
Female		
No. 3	40	87
No. 4	40	100

* Number of requests for entry, 100.
† Number of requests for entry, 60.

Villena[8] of The City University of New York devised a study to compare the behaviors of city and town dwellers in this respect. The criterion used in this study was the willingness of householders to allow strangers to enter their home to use the telephone. The student investigators individually rang doorbells, explained that they had misplaced the address of a friend nearby, and asked to use the phone. The investigators (two males and two females) made 100 requests for entry into homes in the city and 60 requests in the small towns. The results for middle-income housing developments in Manhattan were compared with data for several small towns (Stony Point, Spring Valley, Ramapo, Nyack, New City, and West Clarkstown) in Rockland County, outside of New York City. As Table 1 shows, in all cases there was a sharp increase in the proportion of entries achieved by an experimenter when he moved from the city to a small town. In the most extreme case the experimenter was five times as likely to gain admission to homes in a small town as to homes in Manhattan. Although the female experimenters had notably greater success both in cities and in towns than the male experimenters had, each of the four students did at least twice as well in towns as in cities. This suggests that the city-town distinction overrides even the predictably greater fear of male strangers than of female ones.

The lower level of helpfulness by city dwellers seems due in part to recognition of the dangers of living in Manhattan, rather than to mere indifference or coldness. It is significant that 75 percent of all the city respondents received and answered messages by shouting through closed doors and by peering out through peepholes; in the towns, by contrast, about 75 percent of the respondents opened the door.

Supporting the experimenters' quantitative results was their general observation that the town dwellers were noticeably more friendly and less suspicious than the city dwellers. In seeking to explain the reasons for the greater sense of psychological vulnerability city dwellers feel, above and beyond the differences in crime statistics, Villena points out that, if a crime is committed in a village, a resident of a neighboring village may not perceive the crime as personally relevant though the geographic distance may be small, whereas a criminal act committed anywhere in the city, though miles from the city-dweller's home is still verbally located within the city; thus, Villena says, "the inhabitant of the city possesses a larger vulnerable space."

CIVILITIES

Even at the most superficial level of involvement—the exercise of everyday civilities—urbanites are reputedly deficient. People bump into each other and often do not apologize. They knock over another person's packages and, as often as not, proceed on their way with a grumpy exclamation instead of an offer of assistance. Such behavior, which many visitors to great cities find distasteful, is less common, we are told, in smaller communities, where traditional courtesies are more likely to be observed.

In some instances it is not simply that, in the city, traditional courtesies are violated; rather, the cities develop new norms of non-involvement. These are so well defined and so deeply a part of city life that *they* constitute the norms people are reluctant to violate. Men are actually embarrassed to give up a seat on the subway to an old woman; they mumble "I was getting off anyway," instead of making the gesture in a straightforward and gracious way. These norms develop because everyone realizes that, in situations of high population density, people cannot implicate themselves in each other's affairs, for to do so would create conditions of continual distraction which would frustrate purposeful action.

In discussing the effects of overload I do not imply that at every instant the city dweller is bombarded with an unmanageable number of inputs, and that his responses are determined by the excess of input at any given instant. Rather, adaptation occurs in the form of gradual evolution of norms of behavior. Norms are evolved in response to frequent discrete experiences of overload; they persist and become generalized modes of responding.

OVERLOAD ON COGNITIVE CAPACITIES: ANONYMITY

That we respond differently toward those whom we know and those who are strangers to us is a truism. An eager patron aggressively cuts in front of someone in a long movie line to save time only to confront a friend; he then behaves sheepishly. A man is involved in an automobile accident caused by another driver, emerges from his car shouting in rage, then moderates his behavior on discovering a friend driving the other car. The city dweller, when walking through the midtown streets, is in a state of continual anonymity vis-à-vis the other pedestrians.

Anonymity is part of a continuous spectrum ranging from total anonymity to full acquaintance, and it may well be that measurement of the precise degrees of anonymity in cities and towns would help to explain important distinctions between the quality of life in each. Conditions of full acquaintance, for example, offer security and familiarity, but they may also be stifling, because the individual is caught in a web of established relationships. Conditions of complete anonymity, by contrast, provide freedom from routinized social ties, but they may also create feelings of alienation and detachment.

Empirically one could investigate the proportion of activities in which the city dweller or the town dweller is known by others at given times in his daily life, and the proportion of activities in the course of which he interacts with individuals who know him. At his job, for instance, the city dweller may be known to as many people as his rural counterpart. However, when he is not fulfilling his occupational role—say, when merely traveling about the city—the urbanite is doubtless more anonymous than his rural counterpart.

Another direction for empirical study is investigation of the beneficial effects of anonymity. The impersonality of city life breeds its own tolerance for the private lives of the inhabitants. Individuality and even eccentricity, we may assume, can flourish more readily in the metropolis than in the small town. Stigmatized persons may find it easier to lead comfortable lives in the city, free of the constant scrutiny of neighbors. To what degree can this assumed difference between city and town be shown empirically? Judith Waters,[9] at The City University of New York, hypothesized that avowed homosexuals would be more likely to be accepted as tenants in a large city than in small towns, and she dispatched letters from homosexuals and from normal individuals to real estate agents in cities and towns across the country. The results of her study were inconclusive. But the general idea of examining the protective benefits of city life to the stigmatized ought to be pursued.

ROLE BEHAVIOR IN CITIES AND TOWNS

Another product of urban overload is the adjustment in roles made by urbanites in daily interactions. As Wirth has said: "Urbanites meet one another in highly segmental roles. . . . They are less dependent upon particular persons, and their dependence upon others is confined to a highly fractionalized aspect of the other's round of activity."[10] This tendency is particularly noticeable in transactions between customers and individuals offering professional or sales services. The owner of a country store has time to become well acquainted with his dozen-or-so daily customers, but the girl at the checkout counter of a busy A & P, serving hundreds of customers a day, barely has time to toss the green stamps into one customer's shopping bag before the next customer confronts her with his pile of groceries.

Meier, in his stimulating analysis of the city,[11] discusses several adaptations a system may make when confronted by inputs that exceed its capacity to process them. Meier argues that, according to the principle of competition for scarce resources, the scope and time of the transaction shrink as customer volume and daily turnover rise. This, in fact, is what is meant by the "brusque" quality of city life. New standards have developed in cities concerning what levels of services are appropriate in business transactions (see Fig. 1).

McKenna and Morgenthau,[12] in a seminar at The City University of New York, devised a study (i) to compare the willingness of city dwellers and small-town dwellers to do favors for strangers that entailed expenditure of a small amount of time and slight inconvenience but no personal vulnerability, and (ii) to determine whether the more compartmentalized, transitory relationships of the city would make urban salesgirls less likely than small-town salesgirls to carry out, for strangers, tasks not related to their customary roles.

To test for differences between city dwellers and small-town dwellers, a simple experiment was devised in which persons from both settings were asked (by telephone) to perform increasingly onerous favors for anonymous strangers.

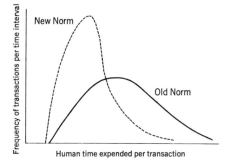

FIGURE 1. Changes in the demand for time for a given task when the overall transaction frequency increases in a social system. (Reprinted with permission from R. L. Meier, *A Communications Theory of Urban Growth,* 1962. Copyright 1962 by the MIT Press.)

Within the cities (Chicago, New York, and Philadelphia), half the calls were to housewives and the other half to salesgirls in women's apparel shops; the division was the same for the 37 small towns of the study, which were in the same states as the cities. Each experimenter represented herself as a long-distance caller who had, through error, been connected with the respondent by the operator. The experimenter began by asking for simple information about the weather for purposes of travel. Next the experimenter excused herself on some pretext (asking the respondent to "please hold on"), put the phone down for almost a full minute, and then picked it up again and asked the respondent to provide the phone number of a hotel or motel in her vicinity at which the experimenter might stay during a forthcoming visit. Scores were assigned the subjects on the basis of how helpful they had been. McKenna summarizes her results in this manner:

> People in the city, whether they are engaged in a specific job or not, are less helpful and informative than people in small towns; . . . People at home, regardless of where they live, are less helpful and informative than people working in shops.

However, the absolute level of cooperativeness for urban subjects was found to be quite high, and does not accord with the stereotype of the urbanite as aloof, self-centered, and unwilling to help strangers. The quantitative differences obtained by McKenna and Morgenthau are less great than one might have expected. This again points up the need for extensive empirical research in rural-urban differences, research that goes far beyond that provided in the few illustrative pilot studies presented here. At this point we have very limited objective evidence on differences in the quality of social encounters in city and small town.

But the research needs to be guided by unifying theoretical concepts. As I have tried to demonstrate, the concept of overload helps to explain a wide variety of contrasts between city behavior and town behavior: (i) the differences in role enactment (the tendency of urban dwellers to deal with one another in highly segmented, functional terms, and of urban sales personnel to devote limited time and attention to their customers); (ii) the evolution of urban norms quite different from traditional town values (such as the acceptance of noninvolvement, impersonality, and aloofness in urban life); (iii) the adaptation of the urban dweller's cognitive processes (his inability to identify most of the people he sees daily, his screening of sensory stimuli, his development of blasé attitudes toward deviant or bizarre behavior, and his selectivity in responding to human demands); and (iv) the competition for scarce facilities in the city (the subway rush; the fight for taxis; traffic jams; standing in line to await services). I suggest that contrasts between city and rural behavior probably reflects the responses of similar people to very different situations, rather than intrinsic differences in the personalities of rural and city dwellers. The city is a situation to which individuals respond adaptively.

FURTHER ASPECTS OF URBAN EXPERIENCE

Some features of urban experience do not fit neatly into the system of analysis presented thus far. They are no less important for that reason. The issues raised next are difficult to treat in quantitative fashion. Yet I prefer discussing them in a loose way to excluding them because appropriate language and data have not yet been developed. My aim is to suggest how phenomena such as "urban atmosphere" can be pinned down through techniques of measurement.

The "Atmosphere" of Great Cities

The contrast in the behavior of city and town dwellers has been a natural starting point for urban social scientists. But even among great cities there are marked differences in "atmosphere." The tone, pacing, and texture of social encounters are different in London and New York, and many persons willingly make financial sacrifices for the privilege of living within a specific urban atmosphere which they find pleasing or stimulating. A second perspective in the study of cities, therefore, is to define exactly what is meant by the atmosphere of a city and to pinpoint the factors that give rise to it. It may seem that urban atmosphere is too evanescent a quality to be reduced to a set of measurable variables, but I do not believe the matter can be judged before substantial effort has been made in this direction. It is obvious that any such approach must be comparative. It makes no sense at all to say that New York is "vibrant" and "frenetic" unless one has some specific city in mind as a basis of comparison.

In an undergraduate tutorial that I conducted at Harvard University some years ago, New York, London, and Paris were selected as reference points for attempts to measure urban atmosphere. We began with a simple question: Does any consensus exist about the qualities that typify given cities? To answer this question one could undertake a content analysis of travelbook, literary, and journalistic accounts of cities. A second approach, which we adopted, is to ask people to characterize (with descriptive terms and accounts if typical experiences) cities they have lived in or visited. In advertisements placed in the *New York Times* and the *Harvard Crimson* we asked people to give us accounts of specific incidents in London, Paris, or New York that best illuminated the character of that particular city. Questionnaires were then developed, and administered to persons who were familiar with at least two of the three cities.

Some distinctive patterns emerged.[13] The distinguishing themes concerning New York, for example, dealt with its diversity, its great size, its pace and level of activity, its cultural and entertainment opportunities, and the heterogeneity and segmentation ("ghettoization") of its population. New York elicited more descriptions in terms of physical qualities, pace, and emotional impact than Paris or London did, a fact which suggests that these are particularly important aspects of New York's ambiance.

A contrasting profile emerges for London; in this case respondents placed far greater emphasis on their interactions with the inhabitants than on physical surroundings. There was near unanimity on certain themts: those dealing with the tolerance and courtesy of London's inhabitants. One respondent said:

When I was 12, my grandfather took me to the British Museum . . . one day by tube and recited the *Aeneid* in Latin for my benefit. . . . He is rather deaf, speaks very loudly and it embarrassed the hell out of me, until I realized that nobody was paying any attention. Londoners are extremely worldly and tolerant.

In contrast, respondents who described New Yorkers as aloof, cold, and rude referred to such incidents as the following:

I saw a boy of 19 passing out anti-war leaflets to passersby. When he stopped at a corner, a man dressed in a business suit walked by him at a brisk pace, hit the boy's arm, and scattered the leaflets all over the street. The man kept walking at the same pace down the block.

We need to obtain many more such descriptions of incidents, using careful methods of sampling. By the application of factor-analytic techniques, relevant dimensions for each city can be discerned.

The responses for Paris were about equally divided between responses concerning its inhabitants and those regarding its physical and sensory attributes. Cafés and parks were often mentioned as contributing to the sense that Paris is a city of amenities, but many respondents complained that Parisians were inhospitable, nasty, and cold.

We cannot be certain, of course, to what degree these statements reflect actual characteristics of the cities in question and to what degree they simply tap the respondents' knowledge of widely held preconceptions. Indeed, one may point to three factors, apart from the actual atmospheres of the cities, that determine the subjects' responses.

1) A person's impression of a given city depends on his implicit standard of comparison. A New Yorker who visits Paris may well describe that city as "leisurely," whereas a compatriot from Richmond, Virginia, may consider Paris too "hectic." Obtaining reciprocal judgment, in which New Yorkers judge Londoners, and Londoners judge New Yorkers, seems a useful way to take into account not only the city being judged but also the home city that serves as the visitor's base line.

2) Perceptions of a city are also affected by whether the observer is a tourist, a newcomer, or a longer-term resident. First, a tourist will be exposed to features of the city different from those familiar to a long-time resident. Second, a prerequisite for adapting to continuing life in a given city seems to be the filtering out of many

observations about the city that the newcomer or tourist finds particularly arresting; this selective process seems to be part of the long-term resident's mechanism for coping with overload. In the interest of psychic economy, the resident simply learns to tune out many aspects of daily life. One method for studying the specific impact of adaptation on perception of the city is to ask several pairs of newcomers and old-timers (one newcomer and one old-timer to a pair) to walk down certain city blocks and then report separately what each has observed.

Additionally, many persons have noted that when travelers return to New York from an extended sojourn abroad they often feel themselves confronted with "brutal ugliness"[14] and a distinctive, frenetic atmosphere whose contributing details are, for a few hours or days, remarkably sharp and clear. This period of fresh perception should receive special attention in the study of city atmosphere. For, in a few days, details which are initially arresting become less easy to specify. They are assimilated into an increasingly familiar background atmosphere which, though important in setting the tone of things, is difficult to analyze. There is no better point at which to begin the study of city atmosphere than at the moment when a traveler returns from abroad.

3) The popular myths and expectations each visitor brings to the city will also affect the way in which he perceives it.[15] Sometimes a person's preconceptions about a city are relatively accurate distillations of its character, but preconceptions may also reinforce myths by filtering the visitor's perceptions to conform with his expectations. Preconceptions affect not only a person's perceptions of a city but what he reports about it.

The influence of a person's urban base line on his perceptions of a given city, the differences between the observations of the long-time inhabitant and those of the newcomer, and the filtering effect of personal expectations and stereotypes raise serious questions about the validity of travelers' reports. Moreover, no social psychologist wants to rely exclusively on verbal accounts if he is attempting to obtain an accurate and objective description of the cities' social texture, pace, and general atmosphere. What he needs to do is to devise means of embedding objective experimental measures in the daily flux of city life, measures that can accurately index the qualities of a given urban atmosphere.

EXPERIMENTAL COMPARISONS OF BEHAVIOR

Roy Feldman[16] incorporated these principles in a comparative study of behavior toward compatriots and foreigners in Paris, Athens, and Boston. Feldman wanted to see (i) whether absolute levels and patterns of helpfulness varied significantly from city to city, and (ii) whether inhabitants in each city tended to treat compatriots differently from foreigners. He examined five concrete behavioral episodes, each carried out by a team of native experimenters and a team of American experimenters in the three cities. The episides involved (i) asking natives of the city for street directions; (ii) asking natives to mail a letter for the experimenter; (iii) asking natives if they had just dropped a dollar bill (or the Greek or French equivalent) when the money actually belonged to the experimenter himself; (iv) deliberately overpaying for goods in a store to see if the cashier would correct the mistake and return the excess money; and (v) determining whether taxicab drivers overcharged strangers and whether they took the most direct route available.

Feldman's results suggest some interesting contrasts in the profiles of the three cities. In Paris, for instance, certain stereotypes were borne out. Parisian cab drivers overcharged foreigners significantly more often than they overcharged compatriots. But other aspects of the Parisians' behavior were not in accord with American preconceptions: in mailing a letter for a stranger, Parisians treated foreigners significantly better than Athenians or Bostonians did, and, when asked to mail letters that were already stamped, Parisians actually treated foreigners better than they treated compatriots. Similarly, Parisians were significantly more honest than Athenians or Bostonians in resisting the temptation to claim money that was not theirs, and Parisians were the only citizens who were more honest with foreigners than with compatriots in this experiment.

Feldman's studies not only begin to quantify some of the variables that give a city its distinctive texture but they also provide a methodological model for other comparative research. His most important contribution is his successful application of objective, experimental measures to everyday situations, a mode of study which provides conclusions about urban life that are more pertinent than those achieved through laboratory experiments.

TEMPO AND PACE

Another important component of a city's atmosphere is its tempo or pace, an attribute frequently remarked on but less often studied. Does a city have a frenetic, hectic quality, or is it easygoing and leisurely? In any empirical treatment of this question, it is best to start in a very simple way. Walking speeds of pedestrians in different cities and in cities and towns should be measured and compared. William Berkowitz[17] of Lafayette College has undertaken an extensive series of studies of walking speeds in Philadelphia, New York, and Boston, as well as in small and moderate-sized towns. Berkowitz writes that "there does appear to be a significant linear relation between walking speed and size of municipality, but the absolute size of the difference varies by less than ten percent."

Perhaps the feeling of rapid tempo is due not so much to absolute pedestrian speeds as to the constant need to dodge others in a large city to avoid collisions with other pedestrians. (One basis for computing the adjustments needed to avoid collisions is to hypothesize a set of mechanical manikins sent walking along a city street and to calculate the number of collisions when no adjustments are made. Clearly, the higher the density of manikins the greater the number of collisions per unit of time, or, conversely, the greater the frequency of adjustments needed in higher population densities to avoid collisions.)

Patterns of automobile traffic contribute to a city's tempo. Driving an automobile provides a direct means of translating feelings about tempo into measurable acceleration, and a city's pace should be particularly evident in vehicular velocities, patterns of acceleration, and latency of response to traffic signals. The inexorable tempo of New York is expressed, further, in the manner in which pedestrians stand at busy intersections, impatiently awaiting a change in traffic light, making tentative excursions into the intersection, and frequently surging into the street even before the green light appears.

VISUAL COMPONENTS

Hall has remarked[18] that the physical layout of the city also affects its atmosphere. A gridiron pattern of streets gives the visitor a feeling of rationality, orderliness, and predictability but is sometimes monotonous. Winding lanes or streets branching off at strange angles, with many forks (as in Paris or Greenwich Village), create feelings of surprise and esthetic pleasure, while forcing greater decision-making in plotting one's course. Some would argue that the visual component is all-important—that the "look" of Paris or New York can almost be equated with its atmosphere. To investigate this hypothesis, we might conduct studies in which only blind, or at least blindfolded, respondents were used. We would no doubt discover that each city has a distinctive texture even when the visual component is eliminated.

SOURCES OF AMBIANCE

Thus far we have tried to pinpoint and measure some of the factors that contribute to the distinctive atmosphere of a great city. But we may also ask, Why do differences in urban atmosphere exist? How did they come about, and are they in any way related to the factors of density, large numbers, and heterogeneity discussed above?

First, there is the obvious factor that, even among great cities, populations and densities differ. The metropolitan areas of New York, London, and Paris, for example, contain 15 million, 12 million, and 8 million persons, respectively. London has average densities of 43 persons per acre, while Paris is more congested, with average densities of 114 persons per acre.[19] Whatever characteristics are specifically attributable to density are more likely to be pronounced in Paris than in London.

A second factor affecting the atmosphere of cities is the source from which the populations are drawn.[20] It is a characteristic of great cities that they do not reproduce their own populations, but that their numbers are constantly maintained and augmented by the influx of residents from other parts of the country. This can have a determining effect on the city's atmosphere. For example, Oslo is a city in which almost all of the residents are only one or two generations removed from a purely rural existence, and this contributes to its almost agricultural norms.

A third source of atmosphere is the general national culture. Paris combines adaptations to the demography of cities *and* certain values specific to French culture. New York is an admixture of

American values and values that arise as a result of extraordinarily high density and large population.

Finally, one could speculate that the atmosphere of a great city is traceable to the specific historical conditions under which adaptations to urban overload occurred. For example, a city which acquired its mass and density during a period of commercial expansion will respond to new demographic conditions by adaptations designed to serve purely commercial needs. Thus, Chicago, which grew and became a great city under a purely commercial stimulus, adapted in a manner that emphasizes business needs. European capitals, on the other hand, incorporate many of the adaptations which were appropriate to the period of their increasing numbers and density. Because aristocratic values were prevalent at the time of the growth of these cities, the mechanisms developed for coping with over-load were based on considerations other than pure efficiency. Thus, the manners, norms, and facilities of Paris and Vienna continue to reflect esthetic values and the idealization of leisure.

COGNITIVE MAPS OF CITIES

When we speak of "behavioral comparisons" among cities, we must specify which parts of the city are most relevant for sampling purposes. In a sampling of "New Yorkers," should we include residents of Bay Ridge or Flatbush as well as inhabitants of Manhattan? And, if so, how should we weight our sample distribution? One approach to defining relevant boundaries in sampling is to determine which areas form the psychological or cognitive core of the city. We weight our samples most heavily in the areas considered by most people to represent the "essence" of the city.

The psychologist is less interested in the geographic layout of a city or in its political boundaries than in the cognitive representation of the city. Hans Blumenfeld[21] points out that the perceptual structure of a modern city can be expressed by the "silhouette" of the group of skyscrapers at its center and that of smaller groups of office buildings at its "subcenters" but that urban areas can no longer, because of their vast extent, be experienced as fully articulated sets of streets, squares, and space.

In *The Image of the City*,[22] Kevin Lynch created a cognitive map of Boston by interviewing Bostonians. Perhaps his most significant finding was that, while certain landmarks, such as Paul Revere's house and the Boston Common, as well as the paths linking them, are known to almost all Bostonians, vast areas of the city are simply unknown to its inhabitants.

Using Lynch's technique, Donald Hooper[23] created a psychological map of New York from the answers to the study questionnaire on Paris, London, and New York. Hooper's results were similar to those of Lynch: New York appears to have a dense core of well-known landmarks in midtown Manhattan, surrounded by the vast unknown reaches of Queens, Brooklyn, and the Bronx. Times Square, Rockefeller Center, and the Fifth Avenue department stores alone comprise half the places specifically cited by respondents as the haunts in which they spent most of their time. However, outside the midtown area, only scattered landmarks were recognized. Another interesting pattern is evident: even the best-known symbols of New York are relatively self-contained, and the pathways joining them appear to be insignificant on the map.

The psychological map can be used for more than just sampling techniques. Lynch argues, for instance, that a good city is highly "imageable," having many known symbols joined by widely known pathways, whereas dull cities are gray and nondescript. We might test the relative "imagibility" of several cities by determining the proportion of residents who recognize sampled geographic points and their accompanying pathways.

If we wanted to be even more precise we could construct a cognitive map that would not only show the symbols of the city but would measure the precise degree of cognitive significance of any given point in the city relative to any other. By applying a pattern of points to a map of New York City, for example, and taking photographs from each point, we could determine what proportion of a sample of the city's inhabitants could identify the locale specified by each point (see Fig. 2). We might even take the subjects blindfolded to a point represented on the map, then remove the blindfold and ask them to identify their location from the view around them.

One might also use psychological maps to gain insight into the differing perceptions of a given city that are held by members of its cultural subgroups, and into the manner in which their perceptions may change. In the earlier stages of life, whites and Negroes alike probably have only a limited view of the city, centering on the immediate neighborhood in which they are raised. In adolescence,

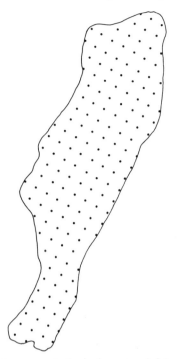

FIGURE 2. To create a psychological map of Manhattan, geographic points are sampled, and, from photographs, the subjects attempt to identify the location of each point. To each point a numerical index is assigned indicating the proportion of persons able to identify its location.

however, the field of knowledge of the white teen-ager probably undergoes rapid enlargement; he learns of opportunities in midtown and outlying sections and comes to see himself as functioning in a larger urban field. But the process of ghettoization, to which the black teen-ager is subjected, may well hamper the expansion of his sense of the city. These are speculative notions, but they are readily subject to precise test. . . .

NOTES

1. *New York Times* (June 15, 1969).
2. L. Wirth, *American Journal of Sociology*, Vol. 44, No. 1 (1938). Wirth's ideas have come under heavy criticism by contemporary city planners, who

point out that the city is broken down into neighborhoods, which fulfill many of the functions of small towns. See, for example, H. J. Gans, *People and Plans: Essays on Urban Problems and Solutions* (New York: Basic Books, 1968); J. Jacobs, *The Death and Life of Great American Cities* (New York: Random House, 1961); G. D. Suttles, *The Social Order of the Slum* (Chicago: The University of Chicago Press, 1968).

3. G. Simmel, *The Sociology of Georg Simmel*, K. H. Wolff, ed. (New York: Macmillan, 1950). [English translation of G. Simmel, *Die Grossstadte und das Geistesleben Die Grossstadt* (Dresden: Jansch, 1903).]
4. L. Wirth, *American Journal of Sociology*.
5. R. L. Meier, *A Communications Theory of Urban Growth* (Cambridge, Mass.: M.I.T. Press, 1962).
6. S. Milgram and P. Hollander, *Nation*, Vol. 25, No. 602 (1964).
7. S. Gaertner and L. Bickman (Graduate Center, The City University of New York), unpublished research.
8. D. Altman, N. Levine, M. Nadien, J. Villena (Graduate Center, The City University of New York), unpublished research.
9. J. Waters (Graduate Center, The City University of New York), unpublished research.
10. L. Wirth, *American Journal of Sociology*.
11. R. L. Meier, *A Communications Theory of Urban Growth*.
12. (Graduate Center, The City University of New York), unpublished research.
13. N. Abuza (Harvard University), "The Paris-London-New York Questionnaires," unpublished.
14. P. Abelson, *Science*, Vol. 165, No. 853 (1969).
15. N. Abuza (Harvard University), "The Paris-London-New York Questionnaires," unpublished.
16. R. E. Feldman, *Journal of Personality and Social Psychology*, Vol. 10, No. 202 (1968).
17. W. Berkowitz, personal communication.
18. E. T. Hall, *The Hidden Dimension* (New York: Doubleday, 1966).
19. P. Hall, *The World Cities* (New York: McGraw-Hill, 1966).
20. R. E. Park, E. W. Burgess, R. D. McKenzie, *The City* (Chicago: The University of Chicago Press, 1967), pp. 1–45.
21. H. Blumenfeld, in *The Quality of Urban Life* (Beverly Hills, Calif.: Sage, 1969).
22. K. Lynch, *The Image of the City* (Cambridge, Mass.: M.I.T. Press and Harvard University Press, 1960).
23. D. Hooper (Harvard University), unpublished research.
* Barbara Bengen worked closely with me in preparing the present version of this article. I thank Dr. Gary Winkel, editor of *Environment and Behavior*, for useful suggestions and advice.

2

Driving to Work

Anthony F. C. Wallace

INTRODUCTION

It was A. I. Hallowell who pointed out to me, when I was a student of his, that cognitive maps were an interesting object of study for an anthropologist. He spoke of "the self" as an object of human awareness, developing along with man's moral capacity in the long reaches of human evolution, and of the unique "behavioral environment" that in each culture man has created for himself by a process of selective attention to his total environment. These ideas were of importance to me in developing the concept of "mazeway," by which I mean the sum of all the cognitive maps which at any moment a person maintains, of self, of behavioral environment, and of those valued experiences or states of being which attract or repel him.

This paper is devoted to an effort to describe in some detail one segment of the mazeway of one individual in one culture. The tech-

"Driving to Work," Anthony F. C. Wallace, in Melford E. Spiro, *Context and Meaning in Cultural Anthropology* (New York: The Free Press, 1965), pp. 277–92. Copyright © 1965 by The Free Press, a Division of The Macmillan Company. Reprinted by permission of the publisher.

nical background for the train of thought represented here may be found in several of the writer's publications (see Wallace: 1961a, 1961b, 1962). But for the documentation of the empirical data to be presented, no informant, no authority can be cited beyond the writer himself. This paper is simply an introspective account in which the anthropologist uses himself as his own informant. In it, the informant-anthropologist seeks to describe the cognitive operations he carries out in performing a task which, in a sense, is "required" by the culture in which he lives: driving an automobile from home to work.

For the anthropologist to act as his own informant presents some interesting methodological problems. At first glance, it would appear that the issue is simply one of "introspection" versus objective description of behavior by an "outsider" observer. Introspection, indeed, has little or no value as a source of information about certain sorts of psychological processes, or even about the finer details of processes for which it has some value as an initial method of observation. But, nonetheless, it is unavoidable, and the anthropologist derives a large proportion of his information by the simple procedure of asking an informant to introspect: to say, or write, what he is thinking about a certain subject. Thus for the anthropologist to record, by writing or by dictating, his own thoughts about his own culturally relevant behavior involves only a minor difference in method from standard procedure. And, as in this case, when the technique is used as a means of approach to certain theoretical problems, it has the advantage of permitting a high degree of thoroughness of inquiry and of directness of approach to "psychological reality."

But, one may legitimately inquire, would not the faithfulness of recall of a task like driving to work be improved by lessening the time span between actual behavior and introspective recall of that behavior? Would it not be better, for instance, to have the informant dictate to a portable tape recorder while he is carrying out the task? There are two strong reasons why this would be, in balance, positively undesirable. First of all, the purpose of the investigation is not to describe one day's experience, but the mental pattern, the cognitive map, or mazeway, which is the ever-changing product of many days' experiences. Since not all of that mazeway will be evoked by the circumstances of one day, it is evident that only an introspective process can approach the complexity of the mazeway as it exists even on a single day. And second, requiring the informant to "inform" while he is carrying out the task would change the very psychological processes which are the object of description. Memory, for all its well-known fallibility, is at least *a* record of the actual experience; requiring the informant to record data while he is supposedly doing something else would change the experience itself. We have here another instance of the awkward principle of behavioral complementarity, akin to the principle of complementarity in physics, which may be more serious for the behavioral sciences than for the physical.

Thus, the description of the process of driving to work will depend upon the introspective consultation of memory by an anthropologist-informant, sitting at his writing table, recalling patterns of experience in specific activity which he has personally experienced approximately five hundred times.

THE ROUTE

The route to work—or at least certain features of it—is displayed in brief in Fig. 1. The map shows the general compass orientation of the roadway, the turns at intersections or choice points (but not all intersections where the route continues straight ahead), the location of all stop signs and traffic lights, certain environmental landmarks (including origin and destination), and the names of several major roads and highways which are followed for part of the way. The map was drawn from memory on September 15, 1963.[1] The total driving distance is about 17 miles. Any section of it (i.e., any stretch between any pair of turns, stop signs, lights, or landmarks) can be "blown up," in memory, into sufficient detail to characterize the major type of construction, minor landmarks, road surface, and miscellaneous features of approximately 100-foot units of distance. Thus, for instance, the stretch between the first and second traffic lights is a distance of about 300 yards (see Fig. 2). Although from memory it is not possible for me to list and describe in order every building and every intersecting alley or road, nevertheless the character of the area, its major type of construction, its traffic and parking pattern, and the pedestrian activity to be expected are generally available to recall. Effort to recall this detail mobilizes dozens of specific memories of particular incidents: stopping at the drug store (on the way home) to ask for directions; parking along the highway to let a child off at the school; visiting the shoe store and the bowling alley; stopping for gas at the second gas station; being held up in traffic at the second light behind a car with a torn fan belt, and so on to less vivid, more selective images of past impressions. The possible maximum speed in this area is about 40 miles per hour; the legal limit is 35; one must watch out for children at the drug store and the school, and for cars entering and leaving the shopping area. The pavement is concrete, traffic markings are apt to be arbitrary (cross-walks are now painted Kelly green, for instance, no doubt by an overly zealous police department), and the surface may be slippery when wet—it is an old, smooth, concrete road. Traffic is single lane, although the pavement is wide enough for two lanes in each direction, because of cars and trucks parking or stopping on the right, and because the highway has not been painted for two-lane traffic, thus encouraging drivers to wander slowly between the curb and the center line. This strip is somewhat over-patrolled by police: I was arrested once (going the

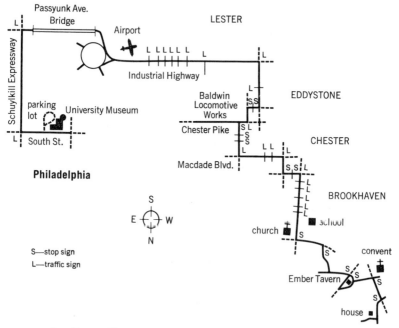

FIGURE 1. Route Plan.

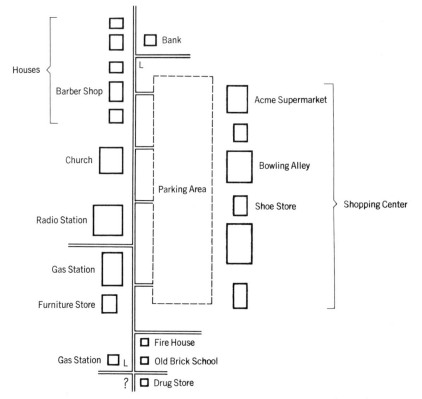

FIGURE 2.   Route Plan section between first and second traffic lights.

other way) for passing on the right, but discharged by the magistrate because the traffic markings and signs were misleading; foot-police control traffic at market rush hours. The town has a curfew for teenagers. In general, the atmosphere is one of disorganization in the face of suburban inundation by a neighboring industrial city, with local authorities attempting to control the tide, including traffic, by heavy police coverage. All this dictates cautious driving.

The number of times I have driven this route is on the order of five hundred, spread out over a three-year period. The length of time varies between forty-five minutes, as a minimum, and an hour (barring unusual mishaps, such as car trouble or a traffic jam), as a maximum. Usually the drive is made in the morning, leaving the house between eight-thirty and nine-o'clock, and arriving at work between nine-thirty and ten. Earlier travel tends to run into heavy traffic on the industrial highway when it is crowded by workmen hurrying to get to their plants by eight or eight-thirty. By now, I feel, as the saying goes, that I could drive this road in my sleep.

DRIVING RULES

There are a number of standard driving rules (what in military jargon used to be called "standard operating procedure" or "SOP") which constitutes a set of instructions for what to do under various circumstances. The rules to which I refer are *my* rules, which may or may not conform to the legal regulations for driving; in general, however, these rules are intended to effect a reasonable compromise between, on the one hand, considerations intended to maximize speed and comfort while driving and, on the other hand, considerations intended to minimize the likelihood of accident or arrest by police. These rules govern the following major matters: the pattern of spatial distance between my car and other objects; speed; and response to signals and written instructions on, or at the side of the road. The rules are as follows:

Rule 1: Aim car along route, keeping to right side of road and changing direction as required by Route Plan in order to keep car moving along route toward goal, and go as fast as possible consistent with Rule 2.

Rule 2: Do not exceed posted legal speed limits by more than ten miles per hour except in an emergency (e.g., in order to avoid collision, or in order to get a sick person to a hospital).

Rule 3: Obey all traffic signals and written instructions (e.g., traffic lights, stop signs, painted guide lines on road surface, instructions to slow down, emergency slowdown blinkers at obstructions, etc.).

Rule 4: Reduce speed when visibility is poor, road surface is slippery, traffic is heavy, road bends, or in general whenever current speed is greater than that permitting safe driving.

Rule 5: Maintain visual pattern characterized by safe distance between own car and cars proceeding and following, and equal distance between own car and the lane (especially opposing traffic lane) on left and road shoulders (or lane marker) on right.

Rule 6: Pass vehicles proceeding ahead in same direction as own car but more slowly than own car by turning out to left of these vehicles and accelerating; return to original lane when passing is complete.

Rule 7: Use turn signals to indicate major changes in direction of own car.

Rule 8: At all times be able to control the vehicle and to monitor relevant information; if control and information monitoring functions are seen to be nearing a limit of minimal adequacy, slow down and if necessary stop.

Rule 9: Under all circumstances and by any means, including means which violate any of the other rules except Rule 8, avoid collision between own car and other cars, pedestrians, and large objects or obstructions; this implies automatically giving other vehicles the right of way whenever a collision is liable to occur if both own and other vehicle continue in present course.

While each of the terms included in these nine rules can be given further definition, to spell out the meaning of all terms would be a long and tedious task and will not be attempted here. Suffice it to say that there are criteria for judging whether or not visibility is "poor," traffic is "heavy," etc. (Rule 4); whether a distance is "safe" (Rule 5); whether, because of speed, the condition of the car, or whatever, one is approaching a point of no control of the vehicle (Rule 8); whether, in general, a specific operation must be performed in order to follow the route plan and to remain in compliance with the rules.

OPERATIONS

In order to travel along the route from home to work, and to follow the driving rules, I must perform various operations. These involve, in general, two kinds of activity: moving various parts of the car in order to control its motion; and moving various parts of the car, or my own position in the car, in order to maintain myself in a comfortable condition for driving.

CONTROL OF DIRECTION AND SPEED OF THE AUTOMOBILE

The automobile which I am describing is a 1962 Volkswagen. It has twelve mechanical controls which must be adjusted in order to direct the car safely, legally, and efficiently in a given direction, at the appropriate acceleration, and at the optimal velocity, in conformity with the Driving Rules. These controls are: the ignition switch; the steering wheel; the clutch pedal; the brake pedal; the accelerator pedal; the gearshift; the horn; the emergency brake; the headlight switch; the headlight beam control; the turn signal; and the windshield wiper. The ignition switch starts and stops the motor. It is managed by the left hand and turns "on" clockwise a quarter turn; if the car stalls, the switch must be turned counterclockwise first, and then clockwise, in order to start again. The steering wheel, which faces the seated driver at chest height, is normally grasped by both hands; turning it clockwise turns the car right, turning it counter-clockwise turns the car to the left; in a central position the car moves straight ahead. It can normally be turned, or held steady, by one hand. The "settings" are not marked and the correct position must be judged by the directional movement of the car. The steering wheel must be held in the correct position by one or both hands at all times, and minor adjustments in its position must be made almost continuously—at least once every second or two on the average—in order to correct drift caused by wind, irregularities in the road sur-face, or slight error in the previous wheel setting. Major movements, involving turns of the wheel of 90% amplitude or more, in order to avoid obstacles and follow turns in the route, generally require the use of both hands. The accelerator pedal is pressed down with the right foot in order to make the motor go faster; when the foot is off the pedal, or resting so lightly that the pedal is not depressed, the motor idles at a minimum speed. The speed of the car can be in-creased by stepping on the accelerator pedal; it can be decreased, at a low negative acceleration, by reducing the pressure on the accelera-tor pedal. The brake pedal is also controlled by the right foot; it slows down the car, when in motion, and prevents it from moving when it is stopped. Because both the accelerator and the brake are managed by the right foot, it is not possible (without an awkward movement of the left foot) to operate so as to increase motor speed and to brake the car at the same time. The clutch pedal is managed by the left foot; when it is depressed, it is possible to operate the gear shift so as to connect the rear wheels with the motor in one or another gear position. The gear shift is operated by the right hand. There are six positions: neutral, in which the motor does not drive the wheels; reverse, in which the motor drives the car backward; and four forward-driving positions, within approximate velocity ranges: respectively, 0–20, 10–30, 20–50, and 30 to the maximum speed of about 85 miles per hour. The gear shift can be moved from any position to any other, provided the clutch pedal is depressed and the velocity of the car is within shifting range. The horn ring is located inside the circumference of the steering wheel and sounds when pressed by either hand. The emergency brake, for use when the foot brake fails or (more usually) to hold the car when it is stopped or parked, is operated by the right hand; pulling up the lever from a horizontal position sets the brake, letting it drop releases the brake. In order to let the lever drop, a button in the end must be pressed by the thumb. A switch on the instrument panel controls the outside lights. It is managed by the right hand; pulling it out one notch lights the front and rear parking lights (used, actually, most often for driving in twilight); the second notch sets the headlights on, for driving at night; and rotating the knob brightens or dims the light on the instrument panel. The button on the floor near the left foot sets the headlights to high-beam or low-beam; stepping on it shifts the beam from high to low or low to high, depending on where the beam is set at the moment. The outside turn signals are turned on to indicate a right or left turn by moving a lever on the steering column, below the wheel, with the left hand; clockwise a few degrees for a right turn, counterclockwise for a left turn. Finally, the windshield wiper, for driving in rain, snow, or mist, is located on the instrument panel and is operated by pulling by the right hand.

The twelve major controls are thus managed by four limbs. The steering wheel and the horn are managed by both hands, or either one. Of the other nine, two are managed by the left foot (clutch and headlight beam button); two by the right foot (accelerator and brake); two by the left hand (ignition switch and turn signal); and four by the right hand (gearshift, lights, windshield wiper, emergency brake). Evidently the right limbs are given both more, and more responsible, assignments than the left; the three controls of critical importance to safety are all handled, optionally or exclusively, by the right side of the body (steering wheel, brake, and accelerator).

Control of Comfort and Convenience

In addition to the twelve critical direction-and-speed control devices, there are thirteen others (or rather, thirteen classes of others) which the driver operates to maximize his comfort and convenience while driving. These do not require the continuous high-priority attention given to the first twelve; they are apt to be adjusted before, or in the early part of the trip, and then are given occasional attention during relaxed stretches when critical decisions are occurring with minimal frequency. These comfort-and-convenience devices are: the sun visors (two); the rear-view mirrors (two: one inside and one outside); the window open-shut controls (four); seat position levers (two); dome light switch (one switch with three positions); the heater valve handle (a wheel); the ventilator controls (four); cigarette lighter; radio (six); clock (one wheel control); and antifogging cloth. Of these twenty-five discrete devices, nineteen can be managed by the driver while driving: one by the left foot; five by the left hand; and thirteen by the right hand. These controls in general can be said to be important, without being critical, because they enable the driver to maintain an uninterrupted flow of information via windows, mirrors, sun visors, and antifogging cloth; keep him from being too hot or too cold (ventilators and heat valve); permit him to select the least fatiguing posture (seat position); and make it easier and safer to light cigarettes (electric lighter).

The controls in both groups, with a few exceptions, operate by simple motions: pushing, pulling, releasing, and rotating. The electric controls tend to be a binary, on-off type; the mechanical controls tend to have continuous settings, so that the precise position has to be selected by estimation and corrected from feed-back information. None permit, or require, heavy muscular effort except, occasionally, the brakes. And no more than three, in addition to the steering wheel, can be manipulated at the same time.

MONITORING

I make decisions as to which control to operate, and how, in order to follow the Route Plan in conformity with the Driving Rules, on the basis of a continuous influx of information. This information is gathered via many sensory modalities: sight, sound, smell, temperature, pressure (measuring acceleration and deceleration), equilibrium (measuring angular momentum and slope), internal situations of various kinds. In general, for routine decisions, sight is the principal modality and sound a somewhat distant second; but in extreme emergency, or in case of trouble with the car itself, sound and the other modalities may become as important as sight. We may classify the data monitored into three regions of origin: the space outside the car; the car itself; and the driver.

THE SPACE OUTSIDE THE CAR

From outside the car, by sight and sound, I acquire a great deal of information which is relevant to decisions concerning the operation of the vehicle. Most obviously, of course, I keep my eye on the road almost all of the time, matching its course with the configurations of the cognitive map of the route, and turning, slowing down, speeding up, and so forth, as I recognize successive points for which standard instructions are provided by the map itself. I constantly check the road for vehicles: vehicles ahead, vehicles behind, vehicles approaching on the other lane, vehicles which may be entering my traffic lane, vehicles parked beside the lane. I check for bicyclists, for pedestrians, for animals, and for obstructions like slow-moving vehicles, excavations, accidents, and so on; for traffic lights, official instructions in signs, flares, and painted road markings. I monitor the state of the road with respect to its width, the condition of the surface (dry, wet, snow, ice, leaves), its physical smoothness (ripples, pot-holes, etc.), the condition of the shoulders, its composition (concrete, asphalt of various kinds, gravel, wind, etc.), its grade. I note the wind conditions and I monitor the efficiency of the monitoring itself, noting the lighting conditions outside (dawn, dark, bright, cloudy, foggy, rainy, snowy), the clearness of vision through the windows, the noise level from wind, air turbulence, machinery, and other sources.

THE CAR ITSELF

Within the car, there are certain instruments which must be checked from time to time, changes in the reading of which indicate the need for control operation. These include the speedometer, the gasoline gauge, the oil pressure light (which shines green when pressure is low), the generator light (which shines red when the generator is not charging the battery), the clock, and the odometer (mileage indicator). Any variation in the sound of the motor from the expected pattern; the smell of gasoline, of burning rubber, of burning electrical insulation or cloth; unusual vibration in the body; a constant pulling or swaying of the car unaccountable by wind or road conditions: all of these indicate probable trouble with motor, gasoline supply, brakes, or tires. And, of course, I must monitor the current setting of the control devices in order to know what action to take in response to information.

THE DRIVER

I, the driver, must also monitor my own state. I must recognize sleepiness, undue fatigue, slow reaction time, distracting pain or discomfort, any difficulty with any of my own sensory equipment, and any motivational state which is prompting me to such behavior as excessive speed, excessive caution, irritability, competitiveness with other drivers, or inattention, any one of which may interfere with efficient driving.

ATTENTION CONTROL

The nature of the monitoring activity in general seems to me to involve several principles in the control of attention which are, insofar as they are applied to driving, the product of experience rather than of explicit instruction. One of these principles is the control of the angle of the cone of visual attention. When driving routinely, the attention is scattered over a wide visual field, shaped like a cone with perhaps 120° of arc from side to side, and covering a considerable distance ahead of the car—where visibility is unhampered, perhaps a quarter of a mile. When, however, data are available to indicate that a decision has to be made on the basis of further information as the situation develops, an "alert" instruction is invoked and the cone of attention is narrowed to an acute angle of perhaps 10° of arc, so that the other data are relegated to the periphery of consciousness. Such a condition will occur if, for instance, a car suddenly appears at a side street, a hundred yards ahead. Will it stop? Attention focuses on that car, in order to glean all possible data relevant to the decision on whether or not to slow down, turn, stop, or sound horn.

Another feature of attention control is the way in which it is distributed over the various control devices inside the car, and over the various regions and types of data monitored. Some parts of the system function almost autonomously and will continue to function satisfactorily even when conscious attention is directed elsewhere. This is particularly true with respect to the subsystem of visual extravehicular data, responsive control of the steering wheel, and maintenance of all other controls at "steady." This system can, as it were, be forgotten and, as long as no disturbance of routine driving occurs, be left to operate by itself while attention is devoted to other monitoring data and controls, or to thinking about other matters: a paper one is writing, a problem at home or at the office, or whatever. Furthermore, most of the stream of monitored data, although it is being received and processed, leads to no executive action at all; the process of sensory intake and semantic evaluation of the data occurs without consciousness. Only when its nature suddenly invokes an executive responsibility does one become conscious of it. Thus the sound of the motor is constantly being funneled into the ear; but only when the motor begins to miss, or clank, or whine, or whatever, does conscious attention suddenly focus on it. The process is similar to that in the well-trained radio operator who can sleep soundly beside his open receiver, ignoring all the radio traffic until his own call letters are transmitted; he wakes up suddenly and completely as soon as these come over the air.

A third feature of attention control might be referred to as a cyclical ranging of conscious attention. "Every so often" I check the speed by glancing at the speedometer rather than by simply assessing the revolutions per second of the motor from its sound; I check the rear-view mirror for following traffic, and look to the left for cars on the left, particularly in the blind spot over the left shoulder; I note the time; check the gasoline gauge. This flickering passage of conscious attention over various types of monitored data supplements the nonconscious readiness to respond to certain cues by directing attention to these sources of data which cannot be judged accurately without conscious attention, which require additional data, or which fall outside the cone of visual observation. The rate of this ranging would be difficult to estimate; I would guess that every second or two, for a fraction of a second, conscious attention shifts from a stream of conscious thinking or talking about nondriving matters to monitor some datum or other, and among these flickers of attention, every twenty or thirty seconds, the ranging process turns on.

ORGANIZATION

The simplest model of how this total process operates is to consider the driver as a cybernetic machine. Diagrammatically, one might represent the system as follows (see Fig. 3):

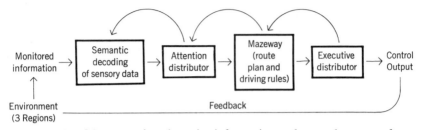

FIGURE 3. Mazeway functions in information-and-control system for driving.

This diagram does not, of course, adequately reflect the complexity of the system of information and control. Some minimum estimate of this complexity is implicit in the simple enumeration of the classes of monitored data which must be meshed with the classes of control responses. At any choice point in the route—such as a traffic light—data from all three regions of information must be screened. The observed combination defines the current situation as one of several types, corresponding to which is one combination of the several possible control responses. That one response combination must be the output. The control responses, which are fewer in number, may be analyzed first.

Let us assume that at route choice points, only major responses involving one or more of the twelve primary controls are allowed. The recognition that the situation involves a route choice point may be regarded as Phase 1. The initial response to this recognition is an alerting function, in which Mazeway instructs Attention Distributor to scan for data relevant to major response. Phase 2 involves the selective scanning of the monitored data, according to a setting of the Attention Distributor; the recognition of the situation as belonging to situation type such-and-such (defined according to criteria selected for attention) by Mazeway; and the selection of response type so-and-so, onto which the situation type maps according to instructions from Mazeway.

With respect to route choice points, data concerning the interior state of the car and the condition of the driver must be considered temporarily irrelevant. Certain aspects of the space outside the car are relevant, however. Let us say that the immediate dimension of importance, and the one which alerted the driver, is approach to a traffic light. The outside-of-car dimensions and values listed in Table 1 are relevant and must be scanned consciously:

TABLE 1
Outside-of-Car Dimensions

DIMENSION	VALUES
A. Traffic light	a_1 red; a_2 yellow; a_3 green
B. Route direction	b_1 turns right; b_2 straight; b_3 turns left
C. Traffic (preceding)	c_1 no car in front; c_2 car in front too close; c_3 car in front distance safe
D. Traffic (following)	d_1 no car following; d_2 car following too close; d_3 car following distance safe
E. Road surface	e_1 slippery; e_2 normal
F. Cross traffic	f_1 object entering from right; f_2 no object entering from right
G. Closeness of light	g_1 within stopping distance at current speed; g_2 not within stopping distance at current speed

The matrix of possible states of the system resulting from the combination of these criteria contains $3 \times 3 \times 3 \times 2 \times 2$, or 216 cells. The possible combinations of action at such a choice point, however, are more limited. Ignition switch, clutch pedal, gearshift, emergency brake, headlight switch, turn signal, and windshield wiper may be considered temporarily irrelevant. The control operations listed in Table 2—again defined as dimensions and values—are relevant:

TABLE 2
Control Operations

DIMENSION	VALUES
V. Steering wheel	v_1 turn left; v_2 hold steady; v_3 turn right
W. Accelerator	w_1 press; w_2 release
X. Brake	x_1 press; x_2 release
Y. Horn	y_1 press; y_2 do not press
Z. Clutch	z_1 press; z_2 do not press

There are, thus, no more than $3 \times 2 \times 2 \times 2 \times 2$ or 48 combinations of actions each to be considered as a unitary response. But, as a matter of fact, there are fewer than this, because the combination $w_1 \ x_2$ is impossible (not absolutely impossible, but nearly so, for the left foot has standing instructions not to touch the brake) so that the number reduces to 24.

Now we can see that the large matrix of situations, under the alerting rubric *traffic light,* which is on the order of 216, is mapped onto a much smaller matrix of outputs, on the order of 24. But we also must recognize that the defining of the situation must be performed repeatedly, at intervals of time considerably less than a second, because the situation changes as a result of the motion of the car, the (possibly) changing setting of the traffic light, movement of traffic and the action of the driver on the controls.

Now a sequence of events comparable to the one just illustrated is initiated whenever the monitoring system receives a signal which means "choice to be made." The map of route (Fig. 1) illustrates major classes of choice points: traffic lights; stop signs; turns from one road or street onto another; start of journey; end of journey. The foregoing list of classes of data to be monitored includes as a minimum some 29 dimensions of relevance to the 24-cell accelerate-slow-down-stop matrix previously listed. But the complexity of the whole system—whose measure reaches very large numbers indeed, when one includes all the second-order dimensions relevant to comfort, convenience, and the maintenance of the car itself—is made manageable by two factors: first, its division into a hierarchical, branching taxonomy of situations and responses, governed by the Driving Rules; and second, by the serial invocation of parts of the taxonomy according to the actual situation revealed by the monitoring process. Thus the actual behavior sequence, following the general TOTE model of Miller, Galanter, and Pribram (1960) (where T represents the information input selected by the attention distributor and O the control response output), must resemble the following (in which we add the symbol A for the Alert Signal to invoke a particular subsection of the monitoring matrix):

A_1	O_1					T_2					
a_1	v_2	w_2	x_2	y_1	z_2	a_1	b_2	c_1	d_2	e_2	f_2	g_1
T_2							O_3				
a_1	b_2	c_1	d_2	e_2	f_2	g_1	v_2	w_2	x_1	y_1	z_1
T_n							O_n				A_2
a_1	b_2	c_1	d_2	e_2	f_2	g_1	v_2	w_2	x_1	y_1	z_1	a_3

From this standpoint, indeed, it would appear that what I have been referring to as "The Mazeway" can in part be regarded as an extremely large system of related monitoring and operation taxonomies, matching portions of which are invoked serially (and to a lesser extent simultaneously, where several systems are operating at the same time) at fraction-of-a-second intervals. Higher order codings, such as the alerting and motivational or value signals, are contained in the Route Plan and Driving Rules, and serve to "switch on" or "alert" the portion of the taxonomy relevant to the task at hand. The magnitude of the total logical net is, of course, very large indeed; but the size of the monitoring and operational segments in use at any one time is very much smaller.

The possibility, of course, does exist that situations can develop whose relevant defining matrices are extremely large, too large for convenient and rapid matching with the appropriate response matrices, and the result in such cases should be confusion, indecision, and possibly disaster. As we all know, such disasters do occur.

CONCLUSION

In the foregoing passages, I have attempted to delineate in some detail the system of cognitive maps—or portion of mazeway—which I, as one informant, use in driving to work. It is a minimal description, in the sense that not only are there, probably, additional categories to be added at the level of analysis which I have been using, but also other categories, both more abstract cover categories and less abstract subordinate categories, which have not been mentioned. Nonetheless, this statement does describe, with reasonable adequacy I feel, a portion of mazeway of a kind which it is necessary for a person now in my society to learn, maintain, and use in order to drive himself to work. Thus I have been describing also a piece of culture.

I have also been interested in questions of the magnitude of the logical complexity of culturally institutionalized tasks (see Wallace: 1961b). The exploration of this one technical operation, which involves only a moderate degree of skill and experience for its successful performance, suggests that there is a class of technical tasks in which the complexity of definitions of the situation exceeds the complexity of the available response repertoire. In the case used for illustration, for instance, we can observe a scale of complexity somewhat as follows (see Table 3):

TABLE 3

Orders of Complexity

CATEGORY	COMPLEXITY
Matrix of sensory input	Maximal
Matrix of sensory input attended to	
Matrix of conscious attention	
Matrix of definition of situation	
Matrix of available responses	Minimal

The matrix of responses made available under the particular alerting signal used in the illustration is well within the 2^6 rule discussed in an earlier paper (Wallace: 1961b), but the matrix of definitions of the situation is much larger, on the order of 2^{10}. While obviously arithmetic observations based only on a single example intended to illustrate the probable form of a general process cannot be offered as quantitative evidence, they may be of interest in suggesting that the human organism is more restricted in the complexity of its pattern of output of meaningful behavior than in the complexity of the pattern of meaningful perception. This is certainly true of individual neurons, which can receive and discriminate within a complex pattern of stimuli, but can only respond dichotomously, by firing or not firing. Perhaps a similar process occurs in mazeway and, therefore, in culture, namely, that far more subtle perceptions of situations are possible for men than their available neurological, muscular, and technical apparatus can permit them to recognize in response.

Finally, it may be suggested that the model employed for describing this mazeway segment may be more generally useful in formulating psychologically real, cultural descriptions of technological tasks. The model for driving to work involves five categories of descriptions and analysis: Route Plan (the specification of the origin state, destination state, and intervening transitional states at which instrumental choices must be made); Driving Rules (the specification of general rules for making choices among alternative actions); Control Operations (the specification of the minimal behavioral responses available to the actor); Monitored Information (the specification of the types of data relevant to choice of response); and Organization (the pattern of interpretation employed in relating data to action). Those categories may, more generally, be labeled as Action Plan; Action Rules; Control Operations; Monitored Information; and Organization. This model should be adequate to describe such technical tasks (including physical action) as transportation, manufacture, hunting, warfare, and the like. Whether a homologous frame of analysis would be applicable to behavior in social organization remains to be seen.

NOTES

1. I checked the Route Plan for accuracy after drawing it from memory. Two too few lights were inserted in the industrial highway sequence; one too many in the Brookhaven segment.

REFERENCES

G. A. Miller, E. Galanter, and K. H. Pribram, *Plans and the Structure of Behavior* (New York: Holt, 1960).

A. F. C. Wallace, *Culture and Personality* (New York: Random House, 1961a).

———, "On Being Just Complicated Enough," *Proceedings of National Academy of Sciences,* **47,** 1961b, 458–464.

———, "Culture and Cognition," *Science,* **135,** 1962, 351–357.

3

Learning to Live with Lines

Leon Mann

Chances are that today you spent a few frustrating minutes standing in line to get a seat in a cafeteria, to buy a train ticket, or to get tickets for a popular movie. If you did not actually stand while waiting for service you probably were in your car waiting to get through the tollbooths, off the freeway, and into the crowded parking lot near your university. Perhaps you queued to make a telephone call or waited in line at the check-out counter of the library. With the growth of large cities and the growing demand for all kinds of services, queues have become commonplace, unavoidable, and for some, a way of life. For some years mathematicians in the field of queuing theory have been describing queues in terms of their causes, the special form they take and the interesting way they build up and shrink (see Liebowitz, 1968). Operations researchers concerned more with the problem of shortening queues have tried to control them with an eye to improving economy and efficiency of service. And social scientists, always interested in the way in which man adapts to his changing environment, have begun to investigate how city dwellers learn to live with them (Mann, 1969, 1970).

"Learning to Live with Lines," appears for the first time in this book.

FOUR KINDS OF QUEUES

The common or garden variety of queue, *a single line with a single server,* can be found in almost every cafeteria, greasy spoon, and airport. Its strength lies in the sense of camaraderie which sometimes develops between adjacent queuers as they complain about the slow service. For the cafeteria owner, its advantage lies in the customer with the big eyes and the "smorgasbord" appetite. Restauranteurs believe the big line-up will eventually disappear; the hungry customer will punch a series of buttons, the orders will be dispensed automatically and will be ready and waiting by the time he manages to find his wallet. It is possible, of course. to have queues for which there is no actual service. For example, in waiting lines for washrooms and water fountains "self-service" is the rule.

A variation on the single line-single server theme is to be found in large supermarkets, airport check-in counters, and small-town banks, where a *series of lines* are routed to a number of different servers. This system can produce a great deal of frustration. The real loser is the unwary customer who has yet to recognize the slow tellers in the bank and the tortoises at the check-ins and check-outs. People in other lines come and go while the checker searches for his supply of nickels, or tries to figure out where he left his pencil. This system is at its worst when the person up front produces a piggy bank full of pennies or the lady at the head of the line suddenly drops a dozen eggs on the check-out conveyor belt. Then there is nothing you can do except fume while people in other lines smirk at your misfortune. But there is some advantage in a system which includes a diversified series of lines. It permits the setting up of one or two express lines which provide quick service to customers who are fortunate enough to have only a few items to check out.

The frustrations of the multiple line–multiple server system can be combatted by the more efficient *one line–multiple server* system. This system already exists in barbershops with four chairs, British banks, and their larger Manhattan counterparts. There is a single "feeder" line which branches at the service counter to each of four or five clerks. As each clerk finishes serving a customer he cries "next please!" and the next one in the "feeder" line steps up to take his turn. The basic system is sometimes elaborated by installation of a "Take-A-Check" of a "Take-A-Tab" number dispenser. On arriving at the store the customer takes a number, takes a seat, and waits patiently until his number is called. The system works well in the Eastern Airlines office in San Francisco, but poorly at the photography supplies counter of the Harvard Coop (it seems that Coop clerks abhor numbers). The system can also be a little tough on the worst barber in the barbershop; if his hoarse cry of "next please!" evokes no visible response from customers waiting for a hair cut, his future in the shop is very uncertain.

Exotic *station-to-station* lines, sometimes called "interconnected" queues, are to be found in most hospitals and some Moscow stores. The customer moves from one line to the next in an ever mounting crescendo of impatience and frustration. For example, a shopper for pickled herring in *Gastronom,* the Moscow food store, must work her way through a queue to the counter where they sell herring. A clerk tells her the price, and she walks across the store to the appropriate cashier's window, tells the cashier she wants herring, pays for it, and receives a receipt slip. Then back to the counter, receipt in hand, all set to pick up the wrapped herring, praying that they have not sold out.

Patients at Manhattan's Metropolitan Hospital are constantly exposed to the rigors of station-to-station queueing. This is what happened to Mason Roberts when he appeared at the Metropolitan's out-patient clinic one afternoon in March, 1969, and complained of stomach pains (*New York Times,* March 26, 1969). First he lined up at the central registration window to get forms for the window 6 line, which permitted him to join the chest x-ray line, which set up a wait for the doctor. Somewhere along the line he also queued to pay his bill and to make another appointment. The six different lines took over an hour; the visit with the doctor—who told Roberts he was eating too many spicy foods—took exactly 9 seconds. Roberts' experience is fairly typical of what happens in most large city hospitals. Much worse queues can be found both inside and outside the welfare centers of large cities. On a normal day a welfare applicant or recipient can expect to wait in a series of lines for at least two hours before getting to see a case-worker at Manhattan's Grammercy Welfare Center (*New York Times,* April 25, 1970).

NEW YORK, CITY OF QUEUES

Beyond a shadow of doubt, New York is the uncrowned queueing capital of the U.S. Over the years there have been some memorable lines on Broadway, outside the Met Opera and the Metropolitan Museum, at Madison Square Garden, and outside Yankee Stadium.

New Yorkers turn out in force when there is an astronaut to be greeted or a hero to be farewelled. During the twenty-four hours when the body of Senator Robert Kennedy lay in St. Patrick's Cathedral (June, 1968), thousands of New Yorkers in lines over one mile long waited patiently to file past the casket. The average wait in line was seven hours, but many who could stay only the one hour of their lunch break, and knew they had no chance of viewing the casket, stood in line as a mark of respect for the slain leader.

On February 7, 1963, despite rain, slush, and bone-chilling cold, a crowd of 23,872 New Yorkers queued up at the Metropolitan Museum of Art to get a glimpse of the *Mona Lisa*. The lines that day stretched over three city blocks. During its three and one-half week sojourn at the Metropolitan, half a million people passed in front of the *Mona Lisa*. When *I am Curious (Yellow)* opened at the Rendezvous theater on West 57th Street on March 10, 1969, it quickly drew large crowds and long queues; people were queuing six deep for one and a half blocks for the evening sessions and lines for the 10:00 AM session were forming at 7:00 o'clock in the morning. Waiting lines for Broadway hit shows are often themselves smash hits. *South Pacific, My Fair Lady,* and *Hello Dolly* drew remarkably long lines during their record runs. When the box office for the musical *Coco* opened on November 3, 1969, the line stretched along 51st Street, turned the corner onto Broadway, headed uptown, and finally came to an end half way up 52nd Street.

It would appear that theater owners have caught onto the idea that a long line of customers in front of their movie house can be good for business. In *Esquire* magazine (December, 1969), movie critic Jacob Brackman observed that many Manhattan movie houses, especially the ones screening "art" movies, were deliberately creating lines on the sidewalk out front, although half the seats inside were still empty. In this age of popular causes a long visible line of eager customers is undeniable evidence of success and provides a free advertisement to any passerby. Even if the movie line is somewhat out in the suburbs, well-removed from the public eye, a shrewd distributor can bring it to the public's attention. The ad for the movie *Monterey Pop,* when it was running on Long Island, featured a large, compact photograph of three bulging lines of teenagers standing outside the theater.

How does the interminable wait to get inside affect the long-suffering moviegoer? Here too the theater owners have modern psychology on their side. Several years ago Leon Festinger (1957), a Stanford social psychologist, carried out a series of studies to test his theory of cognitive dissonance. Festinger and his colleagues found that people who become entangled in a dull, boring task, and for no good reason, tend to reduce their feelings of dysphoria (called "cognitive dissonance") by rationalizing that the task was really quite interesting. This can be applied to the customer who has waited for two hours in a long, cold movie line only to find himself viewing a dull, boring movie. Unless he decides to ask for his money back, the best way to throw off a painful bout of cognitive dissonance is to start believing that the movie really was rich in hidden meanings and stunning in its visual effects. If the customer can enlist some social support for his marathon wait by convincing friends and neighbors about the greatness of the movie, cognitive dissonance can be reduced even further.

Not everyone is sensitive to cognitive dissonance, and those who are do not always attempt to reduce it in a way which drums up business for the theater. Even then, a long wait on the sidewalk need not be harmful for business. For some customers, the relief of getting out of the cold and finding a seat is well worth the price of a ticket.

THE OPTIMISTIC QUEUER

Why do people stand in line when their chances of getting to see a hit play or movie range from poor to hopeless? This puzzle is of more than academic interest for it involves a strange quirk of human behavior. When *My Fair Lady* opened at the Mark Hellinger Theater in 1956, a line would appear nightly outside the theater to wait for the box office to open at 10 o'clock in the morning. Then thirty standing-room tickets for that night's performance would go on sale. But invariably at dawn, four hours before the opening of the ticket box, there would be many more people in line than tickets available. For some peculiar reason the hopeful failed to appreciate that their chances were really hopeless.

Together with Keith Taylor, a psychologist at the University of Melbourne, I decided to investigate why latecomers in long queues are optimistic about their chances of success (Mann and Taylor, 1969).

Our first study involved twenty-two queues of football fans outside the Melbourne Football Stadium, in August, 1966. Going on the official notices about the number of tickets on sale, only the first 140 in each queue were likely to get tickets. But, in some of the lines, there were well over 200 people. We decided to interview every tenth person and ask each one to estimate how many people stood ahead of him in line. People in the very first part of the line, as we expected, estimated the length of the queue and their chances of success quite accurately. Then, after the thirtieth person in line, there was a consistent tendency to *over*estimate the number in front, and this occurred all the way up to person 130, almost exactly the point at which the supply of tickets was likely to run out. After the "critical point" the mood of the queuers began to change; people consistently *under*estimated the size of the crowd in front. In other words, they started getting optimistic precisely at the point where they should have given up and gone home. The latecomers' unwarranted optimism seemed to us like a desperate subconscious maneuver to justify standing in line, a case of unintentionally deluding oneself that the line is shorter than it really is. We called this interpretation of the latecomers' optimism, the wish fulfilment hypothesis.

We decided to investigate whether this same phenomenon could be found in very long and very short lines. Observation of a single queue at the Collingwood Football Ground several weeks later showed that the point at which the supply of tickets was likely to run out—position 500—again marked the point at which unjustified optimism began. Next we interviewed 66 small boys in a line for free Batman shirts, outside a movie house in downtown Melbourne. To attract a large juvenile audience the management had announced that 25 Batman shirts would be given away to the first 25 queuers at the morning matinee. Once again, queuers after the critical point tended to underestimate their position in line.

An alternate explanation for this unbridled optimism is the self-selection interpretation. It holds that a difference might exist between the kinds of people who are found in queues before and after the critical point. Early comers are by nature cautious and pessimistic, while late-comers are adventurous and optimistic. A frivolous variant of the self-selection hypothesis is that the people who join a line after a critical point must be either myopic or psychotic, since normal people give up and go home.

For our final foray into the psychology of latecomers we arranged to take over a high school for a morning and form the 521 students into two parallel lines. This feat was managed with the cooperation of the Principal and Staff of Wattle Park High School, Victoria, Australia. Both lines were told that the experiment was a study of attitudes toward queueing, but our hidden purpose was much more devious. We wanted to create an "experimental" line, in which all of the members knew that a valued commodity (chocolate bars) would be distributed to the first half of the line, and a "control" line, in which the members had no idea that chocolate, indeed any commodity, would be made available. We reasoned that if the wish-fulfilment hypothesis is the correct explanation for the latecomers' optimism, then any tendency to give optimistic estimates should be confined almost entirely to the experimental line, and only after the critical point. While there was a tendency for "latecomers" in the chocolate line to underestimate numbers in front, our findings were not nearly so impressive as in the earlier studies.

But we were not inclined to feel pessimistic about this turn of events. We concluded that "latecomers" in the chocolate line do not experience much pressure to justify standing in line since, in the first place, they were coerced into this hopeless cause by a pair of psychologists. Moreover, in comparison to football tickets and Batman T-shirts, a ten-cent chocolate bar is not quite the stuff delusional fantasies are made of. . . . When the study was over, we fully debriefed the school about the real purpose of our experiment, and for good measure treated every student to a well-earned chocolate bar.

SERVING TIME IN QUEUES

First-come first-served, the basic principle of queueing, is an example of what George Homans (1961), a Harvard sociologist, calls the rule of distributive justice. If a person is willing to invest large amounts of time and suffering in an activity, people who believe there should be an appropriate fit between effort and reward will respect his right to priority. In most queues there is a direct correspondence between inputs (time spent waiting) and outcomes (preferential service). The rule of distributive justice is modified in marathon queues, however, because the queuers need to absent themselves from the line from time to time. Continuous residence in a long, overnight line would impose terrible hardship on the queuers, and so they come to an informal understanding about the minimum inputs of time they must spend to validate occupancy of a position. From our observations of football queues in Melbourne, and from anecdotal evidence, it is clear that rules regarding the serving of time constitute the core of queue culture.

Every August in Melbourne, thousands of football fans form mammoth lines outside the Melbourne Stadium to buy tickets for the equivalent of the "World Series" of Australian rules football. Over the past few years, the social psychology students of the University of Melbourne have descended on the lines to make observations and ask questions. From our interviews and observations we have learned that although arrangements made to control behavior in the queue are informal, they are clearly identifiable. Brief "time outs" or leaves of absence from the queue are accomplished by two universally recognized procedures. One technique is the "shift" system, in which the person joins the queue as part of a small group and takes his turn in spending one hour "on" to every three hours "off." The second technique is designed specially for people who come alone and who for various reasons need to leave the line briefly. They "stake a claim" by leaving some item of personal property such as a labeled box, folding chair, or sleeping bag. The rule in leaving position markers is that one must not be absent for longer than periods of two to three hours. If the norm is broken the person cannot gain re-entry into the queue, and many return to find their property smashed or thrown aside. This actually happened in August, 1966, when irate latecomers noticed that many people in the middle of the queue had not made an appearance for most of the day, and spontaneously seized their boxes and burnt them.

In some marathon queues, "time-outs" are regulated by an ingenious roll call system. The weekly line for tickets at the Metropolitan Opera House in New York is notable for this kind of arrangement. According to a story in the *New Yorker* (January 14, 1967), the lines begin to form the day before the box office opens. The first person in line is the unofficial "keeper of the list," who registers applicants in order of arrival and assigns numbers. Ordinarily, queuers are required to report for "roll call" every two hours thoughout the day and night, although the keeper of the list can and does vary this requirement. Otherwise they are free to wander about or go home. Anyone who misses a roll call has his name struck off the list and must start again from the end of the line. Although the Metropolitan security men keep an eye on the proceedings, it is the "keeper of the list" who keeps order, calls off names, pushes people into place, and hands out numbered tags which are recognized at the ticket office. Nobody seems to know how one gets to be appointed "keeper of the list," or if they know they are not saying. Apparently the system works well, because most people know the rules and there are very few attempts to jump the queue.

For the 1968 season the Metropolitan people decided to do away with the overnight part of the queue (as a precaution against the possibility of nocturnal violence and robbery), and the system was modified to cut the amount of time actually spent in line while an increase was made in the frequency of the roll calls. The new system, as described by one of my students (a devoted opera buff), consisted of a series of weekend queue reunions. "People check in on Friday night and their names are taken and they are given numbers. They come back on Saturday and check in again with the head of the line. On Sunday the people meet in a park across the street from Lincoln Center at about 7:00 A.M. and check in again. At 8:00 they cross the street to the Met and wait there until 9:00 when the Met hands out its own tags. Then everyone breaks for breakfast and comes back sometime before 11:00 to wait for the box office to open." . . . In 1969, much to the sorrow of opera buffs and queue addicts, there was no Metropolitan Opera season and no opera queues.

The Metropolitan Opera line is a good example of the principle of keeping the queue "honest" by ensuring that only the dedicated, determined few who are prepared to sacrifice sleep and comfort qualify for the privilege of buying tickets. The imposition of hardship ensures that the casual passerby or the less devoted opera fan cannot claim priority on the basis of order of arrival alone, and so cannot gain an advantage over the genuine opera buff. The "roll call" system illustrates the basic principle that a place in line must be "earned," and to earn it inputs of time and effort are necessary.

Japanese queues for the purchase of home sites provide another example of the roll call system at work. In Tokyo, where home sites are in chronic short supply, mammoth lines form outside real estate company offices whenever it is announced that a parcel of land is about to go on sale. These lines, numbering hundreds of people, will sometimes last for more than two weeks. The *Melbourne Age* (November 11, 1969) has described how the Japanese organize a roll call system. Soon after they arrive the queuers elect a committee from among their numbers. This committee acts as a kind of Queue Self Government Association which compiles a list of people in order of their arrival and fixes the number of roll calls to be held each day. The president of the Queue Association calls the roll—sometimes three times, occasionally seven times a day. Anyone who misses the roll call loses his place. Similar arrangements for regulating time spent in and out of line are to be found in marathon queues in many large cities.

PRE-QUEUES

But mammoth queues which last for a week or two tend to be frowned upon by city authorities. Such queues tend to clutter sidewalks, pose a health hazard, and sometimes require continual surveillance by police and officials to prevent outbreaks of violence.

In the Melbourne football queues of 1965, thousands of people waited for tickets, some of them for over a week, in mud and drizzling rain. Queuers erected a shanty town of tents and caravans and conditions rapidly became squalid and unhygienic. The following year, to prevent a recurrence of the shanty town, the mayor of Melbourne banned queues outside the stadium until twenty hours before ticket sales started. But football fans, anxious to be sure of getting tickets, spontaneously formed an unofficial pre-queue several hundred yards away from the stadium many hours before the official line was allowed to start. When the barricades were lowered by officials and queueing began, people folded their camp chairs and, keeping the line intact, filed in perfect order to the ticket windows to commence the official twenty-hour wait. The formation of a pre-queue meant that people did not have to converge on the ticket boxes all at the same time, thus preventing chaos and the possibility of violence.

In Havana, lines at the post office, outside ice cream parlors, and in front of restaurants are commonplace. Sometimes the police will not allow a line to form too much in advance in order to keep the sidewalks clear. The Cubans meet this challenge by forming a pre-queue. They station themselves across the street or down the block from the ice cream parlor and check as they arrive as to who preceded them. When formal lining up becomes permitted, the underground line emerges and takes up its official wait.

Pre-queues represent an ingenious solution to the problem of how to maintain order when a large throng gathers before the official starting time.

QUEUE JUMPING

One of the biggest headaches associated with life in a queue is safe-guarding it against the activities of would be queue jumpers.

Before we discuss how people actually deal with queue jumpers, try answering this question, an item from the Allport test of Ascendance-Submission:

> "Someone tries to push ahead of you in line. You have been waiting for some time, and can't wait much longer. Suppose the intruder is the same sex as yourself; do you usually
>
> • remonstrate with the intruder. . . . . ?
> • "look daggers" at the intruder or make clearly audible comments to your neighbor . . . . . ?
> • decide not to wait and go away . . . . ?
> • do nothing . . . . . ?"

The word "remonstrate" sounds a little archaic these days, but in 1928, when Gordon Allport devised the Ascendance-Submission test, it was a perfectly fashionable word. Scores on the A-S scale enabled Allport to decide whether a person was ascendant or submissive, whether he would try to control or dominate a situation, or prefer to yield the right of way.

Several years ago the Ascendance-Submission test was given to 60 Harvard men and a similar number of male students at the University of Melbourne, Australia. Responses to the item about the queue jumper make for some interesting comparisons.

> • 42% of Harvards and 55% of Melburnians said they would "remonstrate"
> • 32% of Harvards and 27% of Melburnians said they would "look daggers"
> • 2% of Harvards and 1% of Melburnians said they would be inclined to "go away"

· and 3% of both Harvards and Melburnians said they would probably "do nothing"

It is apparent that the Harvard and the Melbourne response is rather passive. What emerges from responses to the test items is evidence perhaps that many young people prefer Gandhian non-violence over physical aggression as a *modus vivendi* in waiting lines.

Interviews we have carried out with students from colleges in the Boston area tend to support this preference for non-violence in dealing with queue jumpers. In November 1969, we spent a morning at Boston Garden surveying the line for tickets to a Rolling Stones concert. There were about 600 long-haired, bearded, and beaded college students waiting for tickets to go on sale at 10 A.M. One of the questions we asked was, "What would you do if someone tried to push in front of you?" The answers that morning spoke mainly of peace. "If they want it that bad, let them get in front of me." But some of the queuers seemed ambivalent in their attitudes. One Tufts student, trying to be magnanimous, asserted, "I would tell him to leave, and make it sound serious enough so he wouldn't want to stand around . . . but if he didn't leave, I'd let him stay, because then he'd be spiting himself. But knowing myself, I might just push him out."

Generations of psychologists have long agonized over the apparent discrepancy between people's statements of what they think they will do in a situation and what they actually do. Nowhere is this discrepancy more apparent than in the football waiting line. When quizzed about their preferred ways of handling queue jumpers, football fans, unlike college students, almost always vow they would resort to physical violence to throw out the intruder. But when the queue jumper actually makes his move, it is painfully obvious that the offended victim is more inclined to do nothing.

Why do queuers fail to act together to kick out the queue jumper? The answer to this knotty question lies partially in the varying interests and characteristics of people in different parts of the queue. Naturally, people at the front don't care much about the people who push in behind them, unless queue jumping is so widespread that the entire line becomes vulnerable. For others there is the thought that the intruder might be so desperate that a struggle might bring about injury and damage. There is the fear, too, that if everyone resorts to physical violence, the illusion that the queue is for the most part well-controlled and orderly is quickly shattered; once this happens, there is a danger of complete disintegration.

But, if queuers are reluctant to use physical force to discourage intruders, they have other techniques available for guarding their positions. A barricade of strategically placed barriers, camp cots, and boxes can be effective protection. Keeping close interpersonal distance helps keep people warm and also serves to maintain the "territory" against would-be infiltrators. At times of maximum danger, and in the few moments before the ticket box opens, there is always a visible bunching together, or shrinkage, in the length of a line—literally a closing of the ranks. At the head of the line suspicious-looking outsiders are intimidated by loud catcalls and jeering. Ordinarily this works best during daylight; the sight and sound of fifty jeering people usually inhibits even the boldest queue jumper. But in the dark, when the queue relaxes its vigilance, social pressure tends to be less effective.

It seems puzzling but it is a fact that the favorite hunting ground for the queue jumper lies somewhere near the tail of the queue. If someone is going to risk pushing in, why not try at the front, where the rewards are greater and the wait is shorter? Here we must bear in mind that the people at the front almost always belong to a strong, well-knit clique and are ready for police action, either because they came together at the outset, or because they have had time to establish a strong sense of community. The latecomers at the end, alienated and disorganized, are far less able to defend themselves against predators. Then, again, the queue jumper risks a lot less toward the end of the line, as fewer people are put out by the violation.

Another reason for the high incidence of queue crashing toward the back is the difficulty the latecomers have in spotting an illegal act of entry from the somewhat more acceptable act of *place keeping*. It is always hard to decide whether a person who marches confidently into a line is attempting to crash the queue, or is merely joining his group. Thus, latecomers are usually reluctant to challenge anyone who walks into a line, unless a furtive manner and a pair of shifty eyes mark the person as a nervous, inexperienced queue jumper. Then the queue rarely acts together to expel the violator, but the onus for kicking him out falls squarely on the shoulders of the person who "let him in"; those further back may jeer, catcall, and whistle, but the immediate victim is expected to get rid of the crasher. The reasoning seems to be that the victim was careless in guarding his territory, so it is up to him to handle the situation, quietly and efficiently.

QUEUE BUSINESSES

Whenever demand exceeds supply, it is almost inevitable that businesses associated with ticket speculation will crop up and flourish both inside and outside the queue.

Two major kinds of professional activity can be observed in queues for hard-to-get tickets. Big-time operators are super-efficient entrepreneurs who hire dozens of people to buy up tickets for the black market. This kind of business has been going on for a long time. When Charles Dickens toured America in 1842 to read from his works, enterprising speculators made a fortune scalping tickets to an insatiable public. Speculators engaged teams of up to fifty people to take places in the $2 ticket queue; then, having bought up the choice tickets, resold them for as much as $26 each. Small-time operators, the amateur scalpers, are often university students who resell their two or three tickets to the highest bidder before a football game. A wealthy patron who neglects to buy his seat through regular channels sometimes commissions a small-time operator to stand in line for tickets. Speculation in the physical position itself, rather than in tickets, has been known to occur in waiting lines for Broadway hit shows. For example, in the overnight lines for *My Fair Lady* in 1956, some people made a business of getting in line early in order to sell their advanced positions to latecomers for as much as $20.

In mammoth football queues, another kind of business, queue counting, tends to flourish. Concerned at the number of tickets left, some people want to know where they stand in line. Queue counters are boys who run up and down the length of the line at regular intervals; for a fee (usually 10¢) they give customers up-to-date information on the numbers ahead and behind, as well as topical news and gossip.

As far as we know, there are no records of professional placekeepers, people who *mind* places in queues for a fee, but the existence of such a business would not be surprising in the least.

QUEUES INTERNATIONAL

How widespread is queue culture, and how typical are the kinds of behavior observed in New York opera lines, Tokyo real estate lines, and Melbourne football queues? Although lines for sporting events tend to be unique in their atmosphere and makeup, queues for all kinds of services in practically every country have a great deal in common. In most queues, there is a concern with the problem of safeguarding order, a desire to keep the queue "honest," and the emergence of ingenious systems to balance hardship and "time out." The anthropologist E. T. Hall (1959), in *The Silent Language,* has suggested that a cultural value of egalitarianism is responsible for the manner in which queues and queueing are treated with deference in Western society. In his book, *The Human Dimension,* Hall (1964) asserts that respect for queues can also be attributed to a cultural value of orderliness. Presumably the English are high on both egalitarianism and orderliness, because in England democratic queueing is a way of life.

A friend living in England told me she was once waiting for a London bus at a rarely used stop. Since there was only one other person waiting, an elderly lady, she felt no need to bother about a line. Much to my friend's surprise, the matron began to mutter darkly and, unable to contain herself any longer, snapped out "Can't you read the sign? You're supposed to get into a queue!"

Queuing is a traditional part of the Soviet way of life. Commenting on Soviet lines, fifty years after the Revolution, I. Korzhinevsky, head of the consumption department at the Ukranian Institute of Trade Research, was moved to observe: "We have simply resigned ourselves to the existence of lines." When he visited Russia in the summer of 1954, Henri Cartier-Bresson, the French photographer, was enchanted by the ubiquitous Moscow lines. His camera recorded lines in front of fruit stores, bookshops, groceries, and butcher shops. He was impressed with the orderliness of the long lines outside Lenin's mausoleum and the patience of shoppers in GUM, the large department store. If Cartier-Bresson were to revisit Moscow today, he would probably find that very little has changed. Moscow, like New York, is still a city of queues.

Of course every large city, and a few not so large ones, are plagued by queues, but it is interesting to note what people are queuing for, since this tells us something about their everyday needs and how cities are failing to cope with them. Outside Havana's ice cream parlors, called *coppelias,* Cubans stand in line for two hours for a dish of six-flavor ice cream, while in Mexico City, committees wait patiently in line to catch a *pesero,* a shared, fixed-route taxicab. In Tokyo, people wait in lines outside real estate development offices for as long as two weeks hoping to buy a block of land for a home site. Queues of shoppers form at dawn in Rangoon, Burma to buy rice, bread, and soap at the "People's Store." And somewhere in Nigeria, long lines of Biafrans wait patiently for a turn to wash their clothes at a primitive outdoor laundry.

Queuing is a truly international phenomenon and, in most countries, a culture of the waiting line has developed to regulate order and to control such matters as time outs and place-keeping.

LEARNING TO LOVE QUEUES

One of the most disconcerting findings in our research on football queues is that people are beginning to accept them, almost as a kind of cherished tradition or ritual. During the regular football season, although it is possible to get choice seats two hours before the start of most Saturday games, long queues form outside stadiums on Friday afternoons. The new attitude is exemplified by a woman who was heard to say, outside the Melbourne stadium, "People are always knocking queues—what I would like to know is what people like myself would do without them?" In 1966, on a mild afternoon before the World Series football tickets went on sale, we interviewed 122 queuers and discovered that 47 per cent were happy with the queue system. In 1967, after a dreadfully cold, wet night, we interviewed the all-nighters and found that even then 26 per cent reported satisfaction.

Perhaps these statistics should not be regarded as surprising since life in a mammoth queue can be in many ways quite pleasant and relaxing, even though time consuming. The enterprising queuers of Melbourne have learned to cope with the harsh environment outside their stadium by tying tarpaulins to the side of barricades, sleeping on stretchers, and consuming large quantities of liquor. In August 1966, when we went down to Collingwood, a working-class suburb of Melbourne, to interview the football queuers, we were impressed with the successful adjustment they had made to queue living. The first three families in line, numbering approximately thirty men, women and children, pitched a tent on the sidewalk fronting the ticket box and

settled down to a six-day wait around a blazing campfire. Some enthusiasts moved out of their homes and took up formal residence in
the queue. Five days before tickets went on sale the general secretary
of Collingwood Football Club, Gordon Carlyon, received a letter addressed to "Mr. Alfred McDougall, c/o Queue outside Collingwood
Football Ground, Collingwood, 3066." The Melbourne *Herald* reported that Mr. Carlyon threaded his way through beds and tents on
the sidewalk outside the stadium to deliver the letter.

It would appear, then, that urban man with his remarkable capacity
to put up with continual delays and irritations is not only learning to
adapt to queues but is actually beginning to value them as social
occasions. The social value of queues is borne out by George Nash,
a sociologist at Columbia University, who has carried out surveys of
people in movie lines on New York's East Side. He has found that
73 percent of those who wait in movie lines are under thirty and that
these young people, rather than complaining about the waste of time
(the wait to get in is frequently between one and two hours) regard
it as a very rewarding experience. The *New York Times* (April 25,
1970), in reporting Nash's findings, made the following observations:

> Noticing—and getting noticed—is what makes waiting to see a popular
> "in" movie not just another deadening urban plague to be endured but
> instead a tolerable and, for many, even pleasurable pastime in itself.
> The longer the line, the younger, more modish it is likely to be, and
> the more bemused—and thus not bored—by itself. Almost invariably
> the predominant conversational gambit has to do with similar evenings
> at the movies: not remembered great films, but remembered great lines.

In our survey of ticket lines for the Rolling Stones concert at Boston Garden, we obtained further evidence of the social function of
queues. When we arrived at the Garden to conduct our interviews,
there were approximately 600 college students communing together on
blankets and sleeping bags. The sweet smell of marijuana hung in the
air. During the night, many of the kids had met up with old friends
or made new ones. To one of our questions, "How do you feel about
having to wait in line?" a Radcliffe girl answered, "I'm really excited.
It's a kind of social event." A Boston University student told us, "It's
a groovy way to meet people." These were fairly typical responses.
The evidence suggests that queues for concerts, movies, and sporting
events have emerged as occasions for socializing and as opportunities
for sociability.

GETTING RID OF QUEUES

But queues at airports, and in banks, hospitals, and stores are rarely treated as an occasion for meeting people and conducting sociability. The emotional cost of waiting in such lines is formidable (consider the frustrations, fights, and aggravation generated by a long, tiring wait). And their economic cost is incalculable (consider the waste in man-hours and loss of goodwill for the store).

With the proliferation of queues and queuing, it has become increasingly important to formulate measures to reduce the number and length of lines, to reduce the cost in boredom and misery, and to eliminate, wherever possible, their attendant friction and hostility. What can be done about reducing the number and length of lines?

The application of the computer to ticket selling is one possible solution. Only recently two companies, *Ticketron* and *Computicket,* began to offer instant ticketing to scores of sporting and theatrical events. The system is engagingly simple. The buyer goes to a ticket sales outlet in a department store, railroad station, or supermarket, and tells the clerk the events he wants to see and when. The clerk pushes buttons on a computer console and quizzes a regional memory bank about the best seats available at the preferred price. From its bank of data, the computer provides an instant reading of the best seats at each price level. If the customer decides to buy, the clerk pushes another button and the computer instantaneously delivers a printed ticket for the show.

With the advent of the jumbo 747 jets, computers are being used to speed up airline reservation systems. At the Eastern Airlines terminal in New York passengers check in baggage and receive their seat numbers in a single quick transaction, without having to wait in long lines during the loading of the aircraft. But even though it is not always economical to install a computer ticketing system, it is still possible to introduce more efficient methods of organization to curtail needless waiting.

We all have experienced interminable delays caused by organizational negligence and inefficiency. My pet story stems from a visit to Mexico in the summer of 1969. We wanted to take a bus from Mexico City to Taxco, a journey of 130 miles. Although there were only twenty people ahead of us in line, it was over ninety minutes before we were served. The clerk required five minutes to locate the bus log book, write the destination, date, time of departure and seat number of each ticket, enter the traveler's name and address in another book, and finally exchange the ticket for money. Since the bus company refused to make return reservations in advance, we had to go through the same ordeal the next day in Taxco. In case the manager of the bus company is reading this, here is some (unsolicited) advice. Introduce pre-stamped tickets (it will reduce service time by one-half); hire a second clerk to help out at peak hours (i.e., always); have the two clerks work from a single common queue (both will be occupied constantly and no customer will complain about belonging to a slower line); and finally, put on more buses.

What about friction and fighting in lines caused by queue jumping, disputes about rightful position, and so on? A line which is vaguely defined or poorly regulated is extremely stressful for its members. In such lines the responsibility for safeguarding his place falls entirely on the person. He must remain constantly vigilant and therefore cannot relax for a moment. If a dispute arises, and it is inevitable that one will, he must choose to settle it by force, which is unpleasant, or back down, which is humiliating.

Often these problems arise because the seller neglects to decide where and how people should queue, and there are no police or other officials on the scene to adjudicate. Understandably, the seller is reluctant to intercede in disputes about priority of service. But such disputes need not arise if there is a recognized system for registering order of arrival, such as a *Take-A-Check* or *Take-A-Tab* dispenser. A number system of this kind helps reduce tension in the queue, because if a dispute erupts the victimized person can appeal directly to the authority of the number. Number dispensers are not always feasible, but even then, the strategic erection of barriers to force customers into a single line on arrival (as in the rambling, serpentine lines at Disneyland) can help prevent bitterness and bloodshed. Of course, no method of protecting the line is foolproof. The only way to discourage queue jumping (short of making it a capital offence) is to improve speed and certainty of service.

Finally, what can be done to reduce the boredom, tension, and weariness associated with waiting in lines? A look at recent World's Fairs is instructive. Queues were a common sight during New York's World Fair of 1964, but Fair officials solved the problem outside Michelangelo's *Pieta* by putting visitors on three tiers of conveyor belts and drawing them slowly past the sculpture. Expo '67, the

World's Fair in Montreal, came up with some novel ideas. Twenty-four computerized electronic signboards flashed facts about the most crowded exhibits and restaurants, and urged fairgoers to visit the less-crowded sites. A typical message read: "Lots of room and no waiting at the Cuban pavilion; why not go there now?" Inevitably there were long delays outside the most popular pavilions (at Labyrinth, the wait was sometimes as long as eight hours, rarely less than three hours). To cope with boredom and irritation, strolling troubadors, jazz combos, clowns, and even ice-skaters on a movable rink were dispatched to entertain the longest queues. Then someone decided it would be better to draw crowds away from the congested areas, not to them, and so the entertainers were directed to perform outside the less-popular exhibits.

That is all very well for World Fairs, but what about the typical large city and its labyrinth of waiting lines? We can see it even now. Strolling troubadours, jazz combos, and clowns entertaining the folks waiting to be seen in hospitals, unemployment agencies, and welfare centers. Meantime, joining an urban queue can be a long, boring, and frustrating experience unless, of course, the queue happens to be for football or cinema tickets.

REFERENCES

L. Festinger, *A Theory of Cognitive Dissonance* (New York: Harper & Row, 1957).

E. T. Hall, *The Silent Language* (New York: Doubleday, 1959).

————, *The Hidden Dimension* (New York: Doubleday, 1964).

G. C. Homans, *Social Behavior: Its Elementary Forms* (New York: Harcourt, 1961).

M. A. Liebowitz, "Queues," *Scientific American*, Vol. 219 (1968), pp. 96–103.

L. Mann, "Queue Culture: The Waiting Line as a Social System," *American Journal of Sociology*, Vol. 75 (1969), pp. 340–54.

————, "The Social Psychology of Waiting Lines," *American Scientist*, Vol. 58 (1970), pp. 390–98.

————, and K. F. Taylor, "Queue Counting: The Effect of Motives upon Estimates of Numbers in Waiting Lines," *Journal of Personality and Social Psychology*, Vol. 12 (1969), pp. 95–103.

4

Bystander "Apathy"

Bibb Latané and John M. Darley

> *Do the work that's nearest*
> *Though it's dull at whiles,*
> *Helping, when you meet them,*
> *Lame dogs over stiles.*

In the century since it was written, this minor bit of exhortatory doggerel has become sheer camp. We have become too sophisticated to appreciate the style—many believe that we have become too cynical to appreciate the moral. Working at dull tasks is now taken as a sign of dullness, and helping lame dogs is no longer much in vogue. At least, that is the impression we get from the newspapers.

On a March night in 1964, Kitty Genovese was set upon by a maniac as she came home from work at 3 A.M. Thirty-eight of her Kew Gardens neighbors came to their windows when she cried out in terror—none came to her assistance. Even though her assailant took over half an hour to murder her, no one even so much as called the police.

This story became the journalistic sensation of the decade.

"Bystander 'Apathy,' " Bibb Latané and John M. Darley, *American Scientist,* Vol. 57 (1969), pp. 244–68. Reprinted by permission, *American Scientist,* journal of The Society of the Sigma Xi.

"Apathy," cried the newspapers. "Indifference," said the columnists and commentators. "Moral callousness," "dehumanization," "loss of concern for our fellow man," added preachers, professors, and other sermonizers. Movies, television specials, plays, and books explored this incident and many more like it. Americans became concerned about their lack of concern.

But can these epithets be correct? We think not. Although it is unquestionably true that witnesses in such emergencies have often done nothing to save the victims, "apathy," "indifference," and "unconcern" are not entirely accurate descriptions of their reactions. The thirty-eight witnesses to Kitty Genovese's murder did not merely look at the scene once and then ignore it. Instead they continued to stare out their windows at what was going on. Caught, fascinated, distressed, unwilling to act but unable to turn away, their behavior was neither helpful nor heroic; but it was not indifferent or apathetic either.

Actually, it was like crowd behavior in many other emergency situations; car accidents, drownings, fires, and attempted suicides all attract substantial numbers of people who watch the drama in helpless fascination without getting directly involved in the action. Are these people alienated and indifferent? Are the rest of us? Obviously not. It seems only yesterday we were being called overconforming. But why, then, don't we act?

There are certainly strong forces leading us to act. Empathy or sympathy, innate or learned, may cause us to share, at least in part, a victim's distress. If intervention were easy, most of us would be willing to relieve our own discomfort by alleviating another's suffering. As Charles Darwin put it some years ago, "As man is a social animal it is almost certain that . . . he would, from an inherited tendency, be willing to defend, in concert with others, his fellow men; and be ready to aid them in any way, which did not interfere too greatly with his own welfare or his own strong desires."

Even if empathy or sympathy were not strong enough to lead us to help in emergencies, there are a variety of social norms which suggest that each of us has a responsibility to each other, and that help is the proper thing to do. "Do unto others as you would have them do unto you," we hear from our earliest years. Although norms such as these may not have much influence on our behavior in specific situations, they may imbue us with a general predisposition to try to help others.

Indeed, in many non-emergency situations, people seem surprisingly willing to share their time and money with others. According to the

Internal Revenue Service, Americans contribute staggering sums to a great variety of charitable organizations each year. Even when tax deductions don't fan the urge to help, people still help others. When Columbia students asked 2,500 people on the streets of New York for 10¢ or 20¢, over half of these people gave it.

If people are so willing to help in non-emergency situations, they should be even more willing to help in emergencies when the need is so much greater. Or should they? Emergencies differ in many ways from other types of situations in which people need help, and these differences may be important. The very nature of an emergency implies certain psychological consequences.

CHARACTERISTICS OF EMERGENCIES

Perhaps the most distinctive characteristic of an emergency is that it involves threat or harm. Life, well-being, or property is in danger. Even if an emergency is successfully dealt with, nobody is better off afterwards than before. Except in rare circumstances, the best that can be hoped for if an emergency occurs is a return to the status quo. Consequently, there are few positive rewards for successful action in an emergency. At worst, an emergency can claim the lives not only of those people who were initially involved in it, but also of anybody who intervenes in the situation. This fact puts pressures on individuals to ignore a potential emergency, to distort their perceptions of it, or to underestimate their responsibility for coping with it.

The second important feature of an emergency is that it is an unusual and rare event. Fortunately. although he may read about them in newspapers, or watch fictionalized accounts on television, the average person probably will encounter fewer than half a dozen serious emergencies in his lifetime. Unfortunately when he does encounter one, he will have had little direct personal experience in handling such a situation. Unlike the stereotyped patterns of his every-day behavior, an individual facing an emergency is untrained and unrehearsed.

In addition to being rare, emergencies differ widely, one from another. There are few common requirements for action between a drowning, a fire, or an automobile accident. Each emergency presents a different problem, and each requires a different type of action. Consequently, unlike other rare events, our culture provides us with little secondhand wisdom about how to deal with emergencies. An individual may cope with the rare event of a formal dinner party by using manners gleaned from late night Fred Astaire movies, but the stereotypes that the late movies provide for dealing with emergencies are much less accurate. "Charge!" "Women and children first!" "Quick, get lots of hot water and towels." This is about the extent of the advice offered for dealing with emergencies and it is singularly inappropriate in most specific real emergency situations.

The fourth basic characteristic of emergencies is that they are unforseen. They "emerge," suddenly and without warning. Being unexpected, emergencies must be handled without the benefit of forethought and planning and an individual does not have the opportunity to think through in advance what course of action he should take when faced with an emergency. He must do his thinking in the immediacy of the situation, and has no opportunity to consult others as to the best course of action or to alert others who are especially equipped to deal with emergencies. The individual confronted with an emergency is thrown on his own resources. We have already seen that he does not have much in the way of practiced responses or cultural stereotypes to fall back upon.

A final characteristic of an emergency is that it requires instant action. It represents a pressing necessity. If the emergency is not dealt with immediately, the situation will deteriorate. The threat will transform itself into damage; the harm will continue or spread. There are urgent pressures to deal with the situation at once. The requirement for immediate action prevents the individual confronted with an emergency from leisurely considering the possible courses of action open to him. It forces him to come to a decision before he has had time to consider his alternatives. It places him in a condition of stress.

The picture we have drawn is a rather grim one. Faced with a situation in which there is no benefit to be gained for himself, unable to rely on past experience, on the experience of others, or on forethought and planning, denied the opportunity to consider carefully his course of action, the bystander to an emergency is in an unenviable position. It is perhaps surprising that anyone should intervene at all.

A MODEL OF THE INTERVENTION PROCESS

If an individual is to intervene in an emergency, he must make, not just one, but a *series* of decisions. Only one particular set of choices will lead him to take action in the situation. Let us now consider the behavioral and cognitive processes that go on in an individual who is in the vicinity of an emergency. What must he do and decide before he actually intervenes? These may have important implications for predicting whether an individual will act.

Let us suppose that an emergency is actually taking place. A middle-aged man, walking down the street, has a heart attack. He stops short, clutches his chest, and staggers to the nearest building wall, where he slowly slumps to the sidewalk in a sitting position. What is the likelihood with which a passerby will come to his assistance? First, the bystander has to *notice* that something is happening. The external event has to break into his thinking and intrude itself on his conscious mind. He must tear himself away from his private thoughts or from the legs of the pretty girl walking down the street ahead of him and pay attention to this unusual event.

Once the person is aware of the event as something to be explained, it is necessary that he *interpret* the event. Specifically, he must decide that there is something wrong, that this ambiguous event is an emergency. It may be that the man slumped on the sidewalk is only a drunk, beyond any assistance that the passerby can give him. If the bystander decided that something is indeed wrong, he must next decide that he has a *responsibility* to act. Perhaps help is on the way or perhaps someone else might be better qualified to help. Even in an emergency, it is not clear that everybody should immediately intrude himself into the situation.

If the person does decide that he should help, he must decide what *form of assistance* he can give. Should he rush in directly and try to help the victim or should he detour by calling a doctor or the police? Finally, of course, he must decide how to *implement* his choice and form of intervention. Where is the nearest telephone? Is there a hospital nearby? At this point, the person may finally begin to act in the situation. The socially responsible act is the end point of a series of decisions that the person makes.

Obviously, this model is too rational. It seems unlikely that a bystander will run through the series of choice points in a strictly logical and sequential order. Instead, he may consider two or three of them simultaneously and "try on" various decisions and their consequences before he finally arrives at his overall assessment of the situation. Since he has no commitment to any intermediary decision until he has taken final action, he may cycle back and forth through the decision series until he comes up with a set which serves both his needs and the needs of "reality."

Second, the bystander in an emergency is not a detached and objective observer. His decisions have consequences for himself just as much as for the victim. Unfortunately, however, the rewards and penalties for action and inaction are biased in favor of inaction. All the bystander has to gain from intervention is a feeling of pride and the chance to be a hero. On the other hand, he can be made to appear a fool, sued, or even attacked and wounded. By leaving the situation, he has little to lose but his self-respect. There are strong pressures against deciding that an event is an emergency.

Intervention, then, requires choosing a single course of action through a rather complex matrix of possible actions. The failure to intervene may result from failing to notice an event, failing to realize that the event is an emergency, failing to feel personally responsible for dealing with the emergency, or failing to have sufficient skill to intervene.

SOCIAL DETERMINANTS OF BYSTANDER INTERVENTION, I

Most emergencies are, or at least begin as, ambiguous events. A quarrel in the street may erupt into violence, but it may be simply a family argument. A man staggering about may be suffering a coronary or an onset of diabetes; he may simply be drunk. Smoke pouring from a building may signal a fire; on the other hand, it may be simply steam or airconditioner vapor. Before a bystander is likely to take action in such ambiguous situations, he must first define the event as an emergency and decide that intervention is the proper course of action.

In the course of making these decisions, it is likely that an individual bystander will be considerably influenced by the decisions he perceives other bystanders to be taking. If everyone else in a group of onlookers seems to regard an event as nonserious and the proper course of action as non-intervention, this consensus may strongly affect the perceptions of any single individual and inhibit his potential intervention.

The definitions that other people hold may be discovered by discussing the situation with them, but they may also be inferred from their facial expressions or their behavior. A whistling man with his hands in his pockets obviously does not believe he is in the midst of a crisis. A bystander who does not respond to smoke obviously does not attribute it to fire. An individual, seeing the inaction of others, will judge the situation as less serious than he would if alone.

But why should the others be inactive? Unless there were some force inhibiting responses on the part of others, the kind of social influence process described would, by itself, only lead to a convergence of attitudes within a group. If each individual expressed his true feelings, then, even if each member of the group were entirely guided by the reactions of the others, the group should still respond with a likelihood equal to the average of the individuals.

An additional factor is involved, however. Each member of a group may watch the others, but he is also aware that others are watching him. They are an audience to his own reactions. Among American males, it is considered desirable to appear poised and collected in times of stress. Being exposed to the public view may constrain the actions and expressions of emotion of any individual as he tries to avoid possible ridicule and embarrassment. Even though he may be truly concerned and upset about the plight of a victim, until he decides what to do, he may maintain a calm demeanor.

The constraints involved with being in public might in themselves tend to inhibit action by individuals in a group, but in conjunction with the social influence process described above, they may be expected to have even more powerful effects. If each member of a group is, at the same time, trying to appear calm and also looking around at the other members to gauge their reactions, all members may be led (or misled) by each other to define the situation as less critical than they would if alone. Until someone acts, each person sees only other non-responding bystanders, and is likely to be influenced not to act himself. A state of "pluralistic ignorance" may develop.

It has often been recognized (Brown, 1954, 1965) that a crowd can cause contagion of panic, leading each person in the crowd to over-react to an emergency to the detriment of everyone's welfare. What we suggest here is that a crowd can also force inaction on its members. It can suggest, implicitly but strongly, by its passive behavior that an event is not to be reacted to as an emergency, and it can make any individual uncomfortably aware of what a fool he will look for behaving as if it is.

This line of thought suggests that individuals may be less likely to intervene in an emergency if they witness it in the presence of other people than if they see it alone. It suggests that the presence of other people may lead each person to interpret the situation as less serious, and less demanding of action than he would if alone. The presence of other people may alter each bystander's perceptions and interpretations of the situation. We suspect that the presence of other people may also affect each individual's assessment of the rewards and costs involved in taking action, and indeed we will discuss this possibility in some detail later. First, however, let us look at evidence relevant to this initial process. The experiments reported below were designed to test the line of thought presented above.

EXPERIMENT 1. WHERE THERE'S SMOKE, THERE'S (SOMETIMES) FIRE[1]

In this experiment we presented an emergency to individuals either alone, in the presence of two passive others (confederates of the experimenter who were instructed to notice the emergency but remain indifferent to it), or in groups of three. It was our expectation that individuals faced with the passive reactions of the confederates would be influenced by them and thus less likely to take action than single subjects. We also predicted that the constraints on behavior in public combined with social influence processes would lessen the likelihood that members of three-person groups would act to cope with the emergency.

Male Columbia students living in campus residences were invited to an interview to discuss "some of the problems involved in life at an urban university." As they sat in a small room waiting to be called for the interview and filling out a preliminary questionnaire, they faced an ambiguous but potentially dangerous situation as a stream of smoke began to puff into the room through a wall vent. Some subjects filled out the questionnaire and were exposed to this potentially critical situation while alone. Others were part of three-person groups consisting of one subject and two confederates acting the part of naive subjects. The confederates attempted to avoid conversation as much as possible. Once the smoke had been introduced, they stared at it briefly, made no comment, but simply shrugged their shoulders, returned to the questionnaires and continued to fill them out, occasionally waving away the smoke to do so. If addressed, they attempted to be as uncommunicative as possible and to show apparent indifference to the smoke. "I dunno," they said, and no subject persisted in talking. In a final condition, three naive subjects were tested together. In general, these subjects did not know each other, although in two groups, subjects reported a nodding acquaintance with another subject. Since subjects arrived at slightly different times and since they each had individual questionnaires to work on, they did not introduce themselves to each other, or attempt anything but the most rudimentary conversation.

As soon as the subjects had completed two pages of their questionnaires, the experimenter began to introduce the smoke through a small vent in the wall. The "smoke" was finely divided titanium dioxide produced in a stoppered bottle and delivered under slight air pressure through the vent. It formed a moderately fine-textured but clearly visible stream of whitish smoke. For the entire experimental period, the smoke continued to jet into the room in irregular puffs. By the end of the experimental period, vision was obscured in the room by the amount of smoke present.

All behavior and conversation was observed and coded from behind a one-way window (largely disguised on the subject's side by a large sign giving preliminary instructions). When and if the subject left the experimental room and reported the smoke, he was told that the situation "would be taken care of." If the subject had not reported the smoke within six minutes of the time he first noticed it, the experiment was terminated.

The typical subject, when tested alone, behaved very reasonably. Usually, shortly after the smoke appeared, he would glance up from his questionnaire, notice the smoke, show a slight but distinct startle reaction, and then undergo a brief period of indecision, and perhaps return briefly to his questionnaire before again staring at the smoke. Soon, most subjects would get up from their chairs, walk over to the vent, and investigate it closely, sniffing the smoke, waving their hands in it, feeling its temperature, etc. The usual Alone subject would hesitate again, but finally walk out of the room, look around outside, and, finding somebody there, calmly report the presence of the smoke. No subject showed any sign of panic; most simply said, "There's something strange going on in there, there seems to be some sort of smoke coming through the wall. . . ." The median subject in the Alone condition had reported the smoke within two minutes of first noticing it. Three-quarters of the 24 people run in this condition reported the smoke before the experimental period was terminated.

The behavior of subjects run with two passive confederates was dramatically different; of ten people run in this condition, only one reported the smoke. The other nine stayed in the waiting room as it filled up with smoke, doggedly working on their questionnaires and waving the fumes away from their faces. They coughed, rubbed their eyes, and opened the window—but they did not report the smoke. The difference between the response rate of 75% in the Alone condition and 10% in the Two Passive Confederates condition is highly significant ($p < .002$ by Fisher's Exact test, two-tailed).

Because there are three subjects present and available to report the smoke in the Three Naive Bystander condition as compared to only one subject at a time in the Alone condition, a simple comparison between the two conditions is not appropriate. On the one hand, we cannot compare speeds in the Alone condition with the average speed of the three subjects in a group, since, once one subject in a group had reported the smoke, the pressures on the other two disappeared. They legitimately could feel that the emergency had been handled, and that any action on their part would be redundant and potentially confusing. Therefore, we used the speed of the *first* subject in a group to report the smoke as our dependent variable. However, since there were three times as many people available to respond in this condition as in the Alone condition, we would expect an increased likelihood that at least one person would report the smoke by chance alone. Therefore, we mathematically created "groups" of three scores from the Alone condition to serve as a baseline.[2]

In contrast to the complexity of this procedure, the results were quite simple. Subjects in the Three Naive Bystander condition were markedly inhibited from reporting the smoke. Since 75% of the Alone subjects reported the smoke, we would expect over 98% of the three-person groups to include at least one reporter. In fact, in only 38% of the eight groups in this condition did even one person report ($p < .01$). Of the twenty-four people run in these eight groups, only one person reported the smoke within the first four minutes before the room got noticeably unpleasant. Only three people reported the smoke within the entire experimental period. Social inhibition of reporting was so strong that the smoke was reported quicker when only one person saw it than when groups of three were present ($p < .01$).

Subjects who had reported the smoke were relatively consistent in later describing their reactions to it. They thought the smoke looked somewhat "strange," they were not sure exactly what it was or whether it was dangerous, but they felt it was unusual enough to justify some examination. "I wasn't sure whether it was a fire, but it looked like something was wrong." "I thought it might be steam, but it seemed like a good idea to check it out."

Subjects who had not reported the smoke also were unsure about exactly what it was, but they uniformly said that they had rejected the idea that it was a fire. Instead, they hit upon an astonishing variety of alternative explanations, all sharing the common characteristic of interpreting the smoke as a nondangerous event. Many thought the smoke was either steam or airconditioning vapors, several thought it was smog, purposely introduced to simulate an urban environment, and two (from different groups) actually suggested that the smoke was a "truth gas" filtered into the room to induce them to answer the questionnaire accurately (surprisingly, they were not disturbed by this conviction). Predictably, some decided that "it must be some sort of experiment" and stoically endured the discomfort of the room rather than overreact.

Despite the obvious and powerful report-inhibiting effect of other bystanders, subjects almost invariably claimed that they had paid little or no attention to the reactions of the other people in the room. Although the presence of other people actually had a strong and pervasive effect on the subjects' reactions, they were either unaware of this or unwilling to admit it.

The results of this study clearly support the predictions. Individuals exposed to a room filling with smoke in the presence of passive others themselves remained passive, and groups of three naive subjects were less likely to report the smoke than solitary bystanders. Our predictions were confirmed—but this does not necessarily mean that our explanation for these results is the correct one. As a matter of fact several alternatives are available.

Two alternative explanations stem from the fact that the smoke represented a possible danger to the subject himself as well as to others in the building. Subjects' behavior might have reflected their fear of fire, with subjects in groups feeling less threatened by the fire than single subjects and thus less concerned to act. It has been demonstrated in studies with human beings (Schachter, 1959) and with rats (Latané, 1969; Latané and Glass, 1968) that togetherness reduces fear, even in situations where it does not reduce danger. In addition, subjects may have felt that the presence of others increased their ability to cope with fire. For both these reasons, subjects in groups may have been less afraid of fire and thus less likely to report the smoke than solitary subjects.

A similar explanation might emphasize, not fearfulness, but the desire to hide fear. To the extent that bravery or stoicism in the face of danger or discomfort is a socially desirable trait (as it appears to be for American male undergraduates), we might expect individuals to attempt to appear more brave or more stoic when others are watching than when they are alone. It is possible that subjects in the Group condition saw themselves as engaged in a game of "Chicken," and thus did not react.

Although both of these explanations are plausible, we do not think that they provide an accurate account of subjects' thinking. In the post-experimental interviews, subjects claimed, *not* that they were unworried by the fire or that they were unwilling to endure the danger; but rather that they had decided that there was no fire at all and the smoke was caused by something else. They failed to act because they thought there was no reason to act. Their "apathetic" behavior was reasonable—given their interpretation of the circumstances.

EXPERIMENT 2. A LADY IN DISTRESS[3]

Although it seems unlikely that the group inhibition of bystander intervention observed in Experiment 1 can be attributed entirely to the fact that smoke represents a danger to the individual bystander, it is certainly possible that this is so. Experiment 2 was designed to see whether similar group inhibition effects could be observed in situations where there is no danger to the individual himself for not acting. In addition, a new variable was included: whether the bystanders knew each other.

Male Columbia undergraduates waited either alone, with a friend, or with a stranger to participate in a market research study. As they waited, they heard someone fall and apparently injure herself in the room next door. Whether they tried to help, and how long they took to do so, were the main dependent variables of the study. Subjects were telephoned and offered $2 to participate in a survey of game and puzzle preferences conducted at Columbia by the Consumer Testing Bureau (CTB), a market research organization. Each person contacted was asked to find a friend who would also be interested in participating. Only those students who recommended friends, and the friends they suggested, were used as subjects.

Subjects were met at the door by the market research representative, an attractive young woman, and taken to the testing room. On the way, they passed the CTB office and through its open door they were able to see a desk and bookcases piled high with papers and filing cabinets. They entered the adjacent testing room which contained a table and chairs and a variety of games, and they were given a preliminary background information and game preference questionnaire to fill out. The representative told subjects that she would be working next door in her office for about 10 minutes while they completed the questionnaires, and left by opening the collapsible curtain which divided the two rooms. She made sure that subjects were aware that the curtain was unlocked and easily opened and that it provided a means of entry to her office. The representative stayed in her office, shuffling papers, opening drawers, and making enough noise to remind the subjects of her presence. Four minutes after leaving the testing area, she turned on a high fidelity stereophonic tape recorder.

The emergency: If the subject listened carefully, he heard the representative climb up on a chair to reach for a stack of papers on the bookcase. Even if he were not listening carefully, he heard a loud crash and a scream as the chair collapsed and she fell to the floor. "Oh, my God, my foot . . . I . . . can't move . . . it. Oh . . . my ankle," the representative moaned. "I . . . can't get this . . . thing . . . off me." She cried and moaned for about a minute longer, but the cries gradually got more subdued and controlled. Finally, she muttered something about getting outside, knocked over the chair as she pulled herself up, and thumped to the door, closing it behind her as she left. The entire incident took 130 seconds.

The main dependent variable of the study, of course, was whether the subjects took action to help the victim and how long it took him to do so. There were actually several modes of intervention possible: a subject could open the screen dividing the two rooms, leave the testing room and enter the CTB office by the door, find someone else, or, most simply, call out to see if the representative needed help. Four experimental conditions were run. In one condition (Alone, $n = 26$) each subject was by himself in the testing room while he filled out the questionnaire and heard the fall. In a second condition (Stooge, $n = 14$), a stranger, actually a confederate of the experimenter, was also present. The confederate had instructions to be as passive as possible and to answer questions put to him by the subjects with a brief gesture or remark. During the emergency, he looked up, shrugged his shoulders, and continued working on his questionnaire. Subjects in the third condition (Strangers, $n = 20$ pairs) were placed in the testing room in pairs. Each subject in the pair was unacquainted with the other before entering the room and they were not introduced. Only one subject in this condition spontaneously introduced himself to the other. In a final condition (Friends, $n = 20$ pairs), pairs of friends overheard the incident together.

Mode of intervention: Across all experimental groups, the majority of subjects who intervened did so by pulling back the room divider and coming into the CTB office (61%). Few subjects came the round-about way through the door to offer their assistance (14%), and a surprisingly small number (24%) chose the easy solution of calling out to offer help. No one tried to find someone else to whom to report the accident. Since experimental conditions did not differ in the proportions choosing various modes of intervention, the comparisons below will deal only with the total proportions of subjects offering help.

Alone vs. Stooge conditions: Seventy percent of all subjects who heard the accident while alone in the waiting room offered to help the victim before she left the room. By contrast the presence of a non-responsive bystander markedly inhibited helping. Only 7% of subjects in the Stooge condition intervened. These subjects seemed upset and confused during the emergency and frequently glanced at the passive confederate who continued working on his questionnaire. The difference between the Alone and Stooge response rates is, of course, highly significant ($p < .001$).

Alone vs. Two Strangers: Since 70% of Alone subjects intervened, we should expect that at least one person in 91% of all two-person groups would offer help if members of a pair had no influence upon each other. In fact, members did influence each other. In only 40% of the groups did even one person offer help to the injured woman. Only 8 subjects of the 40 who were run in this condition intervened. This response rate is significantly below the hypothetical baseline ($p < .001$). Social inhibition of helping was so strong, that the victim was actually aided more quickly when only one person heard her distress than when two did ($p < .01$).

Strangers vs. Stooge: The response rate in the Two Strangers condition appears to be somewhat higher than the 7% rate in the

Stooge condition. Making a correction similar to that used for the Alone scores, the expected response rate based on the Stooge condition is 13%. This is significantly lower than the response rate in the Strangers condition ($p < .05$).

Alone vs. Two Friends: Pairs of friends often talked about the questionnaire before the accident, and sometimes discussed a course of action after the fall. Even so, in only 70% of the pairs did even one person intervene. While, superficially, this appears as high as the Alone condition, there must again be a correction for the fact that twice as many people are free to act. When compared to the 91% hypothetical base rate, friends do inhibit each other from intervening ($p < .10$). They were also slower to intervene than would be expected from the Alone condition ($p < .05$).

Friends vs. Strangers: Although pairs of friends were inhibited from helping when compared to the Alone condition, they were significantly faster to intervene than were pairs of strangers ($p < .01$). The median latency of the first response from pairs of friends was 36 seconds; the median pair of strangers did not respond at all within the arbitrary 130-second duration of the emergency.

Subjects who intervened usually claimed that they did so either because the fall sounded very serious or because they were uncertain what had occurred and felt they should investigate. Many talked about intervention as the "right thing to do" and asserted they would help again in any situation.

Many of the non-interveners also claimed that they were unsure what had happened (59%), but had decided that it was not too serious (46%). A number of subjects reported that they thought other people would or could help (25%), and three said they refrained out of concern for the victim—they did not want to embarrass her. Whether to accept these explanations as reasons or rationalizations is moot—they certainly do not explain the differences among conditions. The important thing to note is that non-interveners did not seem to feel that they had behaved callously or immorally. Their behavior was generally consistent with their interpretation of the situation. Subjects almost uniformly claimed that, in a "real" emergency, they would be among the first to help the victim.

Interestingly, when subjects were asked whether they had been influenced by the presence of action of their coworkers, they were either unwilling or unable to report that they had. Subjects in the passive confederate condition reported, on the average, that they were "very little" influenced by the stooge. Subjects in the Two Strangers condition claimed to have been only "a little bit" influenced by each other, and friends admitted to "moderate" influence. Put another way, only 14%, 30%, and 70% of the subjects in these three conditions admitted to at least a "moderate" degree of influence. These claims, of course, run directly counter to the experimental results, in which friends were the least inhibited and subjects in the Stooge condition most inhibited by the other's actions.

These results strongly replicate the findings of the Smoke study. In both experiments, subjects were less likely to take action if they were in the presence of passive confederates than if they were alone, and in both studies, this effect showed up even when groups of naive subjects were tested together. This congruence of findings from different experimental settings supports the validity and generality of the phenomenon: it also helps rule out a variety of alternative explanations suitable to either situation alone. For example, the possibility that smoke may have represented a threat to the subject's personal safety and that subjects in groups may have had a greater concern to appear "brave" than single subjects does not apply to the present experiment. In the present experiment, non-intervention cannot signify bravery! Comparison of the two experiments also suggests that the absolute number of non-responsive bystanders may not be a critical factor in producing social inhibition of intervention. One passive confederate in the present experiment was as effective as two in the smoke study; pairs of strangers in the present study inhibited each other as much as did trios in the former study.

How can we account for the differential social inhibition caused by friends and strangers? It may be that people are less likely to fear possible embarrassment in front of friends than before strangers, and that friends are less likely to misinterpret each other's inaction than are strangers. If so, social influence should be less likely to lead friends to decide there is no emergency than strangers. When strangers overheard the accident, they seemed noticeably concerned but confused. Attempting to interpret what they had heard and to decide upon a course of action, they often glanced furtively at one another, apparently anxious to discover the other's reaction yet unwilling to meet eyes and betray their own concern. Friends, on the other hand, seemed better able to convey their concern nonverbally, and often discussed the incident and arrived at a mutual plan of action. Although these observations are admittedly impressionistic, they are consistent with other data. During the emergency, a record was kept of whether the bystanders engaged in conversation. Unfortunately, no attempt was made to code the amount or content of what was said, but it is possible to determine if there was any talking at all. Only 29% of subjects attempted any conversation with the stooge; while 60% of the pairs of strangers engaged in some conversation, it was mostly desultory and often unrelated to the accident. Although the latter rate seems higher than the former, it really is not, since there are two people free to initiate a conversation rather than just one. Friends, on the other hand, were somewhat more likely to talk than strangers—85% of the pairs did so. Friends, then, may show less mutual inhibition than strangers because they are less likely to develop a state of "pluralistic ignorance."

These first experiments show that in two, widely different types of emergency settings, the presence of other people inhibits intervention. Subjects were less likely to report a possible fire when together than alone, and they were less likely to go to the aid of the victim of an accident when others were present. Is this a general effect? Will it apply to all types of emergency? Are there situations in which the presence of other people might actually facilitate bystander intervention? One possible set of circumstances in which we might expect social facilitation of intervention is when an emergency is caused by a villain. People who fail to intervene in real emergencies sometimes claim they were afraid of the consequences of intervention —afraid of direct attack, afraid of later retribution, afraid of having to go to court. In situations involving a villain, even if one person is afraid to take action, the presence of other people as potential risk-sharing allies might embolden him to intervene. Under these circumstances, there might actually be a group facilitation of intervention. To test this possibility, two Columbia undergraduates, Paul Bonnarigo and Malcolm Ross, turned to a life of crime.

EXPERIMENT 3. THE CASE OF THE STOLEN BEER

The Nu-Way Beverage Center in Suffern, New York, is a discount beer store. It sells beer and soda by the case, often to New Jerseyans who cross the state line to find both lowered prices and a lowered legal drinking age. During the spring of 1968 it was the scene of a minor crime wave—within one two-week period, it was robbed 96 times. The robbers followed much the same *modus operandi* on each occasion. Singly or in a pair, they would enter the store and ask the cashier at the checkout counter, "What is the most expensive imported beer that you carry?" The cashier, in cahoots with the robbers, would reply "Lowenbrau. I'll go back and check how much we have." Leaving the robbers in the front of the store, the cashier would disappear into the rear to look for the Lowenbrau. After waiting for a minute, the robbers would pick up a case of beer near the front of the store, remark to nobody in particular, "They'll never miss this," walk out of the front door, put the beer in their car, and drive off. On 46 occasions, one robber carried off the theft; on 46 occasions, two robbers were present.

The robberies were always staged when there were either one or two people in the store, and the timing was arranged so that the one or both customers would be at the checkout counter at the time when the robbers entered. On 46 occasions, one customer was at the checkout counter during the theft; on 46 occasions, two customers were present. Although occasionally the two customers had come in together, more usually they were strangers to each other. Sixty-one percent of the customers were male, 39% female. Since the checkout counter was about 20 feet from the front door, since the theft itself took less than a minute, and since the robbers were both husky young men, nobody tried directly to prevent the theft. There were, however, other courses of intervention available.

When the cashier returned from the rear of the store, he went to the checkout counter and resumed waiting on the customers there. After a minute, if nobody had spontaneously mentioned the theft, he casually inquired, "Hey, what happened to that man (those men) who was (were) in here? Did you see him (them) leave?" At this point the customer could either report the theft, say merely that he had seen the man or men leave, or disclaim any knowledge of the event whatsoever. Overall, 20% of the subjects reported the theft spontaneously, and 51% of the remainder reported it upon prompting. Since the results from each criterion followed an identical pattern, we shall indicate only the total proportion of subjects in each condition who reported the theft, whether spontaneously or not.

Results: Whether there were one or two robbers present made little difference. Customers were somewhat but not significantly more likely to report the theft if there were two robbers (69%) than if there was only one (52%). Sex also made no difference; females were as likely to report as males. The number of customers, on the other hand, made a big difference. Thirty-one of the 48 single customers, or 65%, mentioned the theft. From this, we would expect that 87% of the two-person groups would include at least one reporter. In fact, in only 56% of the two-person groups did even one person report the theft ($p < .01$). Social inhibition of reporting was so strong that the theft was actually somewhat (though not significantly) less likely to be reported when two people saw it than when only one did.

In three widely differing situations the same effect has been observed. People are less likely to take a socially responsible action if other people are present than if they are alone. This effect has occurred in a situation involving general danger, in a situation where someone has been the victim of an accident, and in a situation involving one or more villains. The effect holds in real life as well as in the laboratory, and for members of the general population as well as college students. The results of each of these three experiments clearly support the line of theoretical argument advanced earlier. When bystanders to an emergency can see the reactions of other people, and when other people can see their own reactions, each individual may, through a process of social influence, be led to interpret the situation as less serious than he would if he were alone, and consequently be less likely to take action.

SOCIAL DETERMINANTS OF BYSTANDER INTERVENTION, II

So far we have devoted our attention exclusively to one stage of our hypothesized model of the intervention process: noticing the situation and interpreting it. Once an individual has noticed an emergency and interpreted it as being serious, he still has to decide what, if anything, he will do about it. He must decide that he has a responsibility to help, and that there is some form of assistance that he is in a position to give. He is faced with the choice of whether he himself will intervene. His decision will presumably be made in terms of the rewards and costs of the various alternative courses of action open to him.

In addition to affecting the interpretations that he places on a situation, the presence of other people can also alter the rewards and costs facing an individual bystander. Perhaps most importantly, the presence of other people can alter the cost of not acting. If only one bystander is present at an emergency, he carries all of the responsibility for dealing with it; he will feel all of the guilt for not acting; he will bear all of any blame others may level for non-intervention. If others are present, the onus of responsibility is diffused, and the individual may be more likely to resolve his conflict between intervening and not intervening in favor of the latter alternative.

When only one bystander is present at an emergency, if help is to come it must be from him. Although he may choose to ignore them (out of concern for his personal safety, or desire "not to get involved"), any pressures to intervene focus uniquely on him. When there are several observers present, however, the pressures to intervene do not focus on any one of the observers; instead the responsibility for intervention is shared among all the onlookers and is not unique to any one. As a result, each may be less likely to help.

Potential blame may also be diffused. However much we wish to think that an individual's moral behavior is divorced from considerations of personal punishment or reward, there is both theory and evidence to the contrary. It is perfectly reasonable to assume that, under circumstances of group responsibility for a punishable act, the punishment or blame that accrues to any one individual is often slight or nonexistent.

Finally, if others are known to be present, but their behavior cannot be closely observed, any one bystander may assume that one of the other observers is already taking action to end the emergency. If so, his own intervention would only be redundant—perhaps harmfully or confusingly so. Thus, given the presence of other onlookers whose behavior cannot be observed, any given bystander can rationalize his own inaction by convincing himself that "somebody else must be doing something."

These considerations suggest that, even when bystanders to an emergency cannot see or be influenced by each other, the more bystanders who are present, the less likely any one bystander would be to intervene and provide aid. To test this suggestion, it would be necessary to create an emergency situation in which each subject is blocked from communicating with others to prevent his getting information about their behavior during the emergency. Experiment 4 attempted to fulfill this requirement.

EXPERIMENT 4. A FIT TO BE TRIED[5]

Procedure: Thirteen male and 104 female students in introductory psychology courses at New York University were recruited to take part in an unspecified experiment as part of their class requirement. When a subject arrived in the laboratory, he was ushered into an individual room from which a communication system would enable him to talk to the other participants (who were actually figments of the tape recorder). Over the intercom, the subject was told that the experimenter was concerned with the kinds of personal problems faced by normal college students in a high-pressure, urban environment, and that he would be asked to participate in a discussion about these problems. To avoid possible embarrassment about discussing personal problems with strangers, the experimenter said, several precautions would be taken. First, subjects would remain anonymous, which was why they had been placed in individual rooms rather than face-to-face. Second, the experimenter would not listen to the initial discussion himself, but would only get the subjects' reactions later by questionnaire.

The plan for the discussion was that each person would talk in turn for two minutes, presenting his problems to the group. Next, each person in turn would comment on what others had said, and finally there would be a free discussion. A mechanical switching device regulated the discussion, switching on only one microphone at a time.

The emergency: The discussion started with the future victim speaking first. He said he found it difficult to get adjusted to New York and to his studies. Very hesitantly and with obvious embarrassment, he mentioned that he was prone to seizures, particularly when studying hard or taking exams: The other people, including the one real subject, took their turns and discussed similar problems (minus the proneness to seizures). The naive subject talked last in the series, after the last prerecorded voice.

When it was again the victim's turn to talk, he made a few relatively calm comments, and then, growing increasingly loud and incoherent, he continued:

> I er um I think I I need er if if could er er somebody er er er er er er er give me a little er give me a little help here because er I er I'm er

er h-h-having a a a a real problem er right now and I er if somebody could help me out it would it would er er s-s-sure be sure be good . . . because er there er er a cause I er I uh I've got a a one of the er sei ——er er things coming on and and and I could really er use some help so if somebody would er give me a little h-help uh er-er-er-er-er c-could somebody er er help er uh uh (choking sounds) . . . I'm gonna die er er I'm . . . gonna die er help er er seizure er (chokes, then quiet).

The major independent variable of the study was the number of people the subject believed also heard the fit. The subject was led to believe that the discussion group was one of three sizes: a two-person group consisting of himself and the victim; a three-person group consisting of himself, the victim and one other person; or a six-person group consisting of himself, the victim, and four other persons.

Varying the kind of bystanders present at an emergency as well as the number of bystanders should also vary the amount of responsibility felt by any single bystander. To test this, several variations of the three-person group were run. In one three-person condition, the other bystander was a female; in another, a male; and in a third, a male who said that he was a premedical student who occasionally worked in the emergency wards at Bellevue Hospital.

Subjects in the above conditions were female college students. To test whether there are sex differences in the likelihood of helping, males drawn from the same subject pool were tested in the three-person, female bystander condition.

Two final experimental variations concerned acquaintanceship relationships between the subject and other bystanders and between the subject and the victim. In one of these conditions, female subjects were tested in the three-person condition, but were tested with a friend that they had been asked to bring with them to the laboratory. In another, subjects were given prior contact with the victim before being run in the six-person group. Subjects underwent a very brief "accidental" encounter with an experimental confederate posing as the future victim. The two met for about a minute in the hall before the experiment began. During this time, they chatted about topics having nothing to do with the experiment.

The major dependent variable of the experiment was the time elapsed from the start of the victim's seizure until the subject left her experimental cubicle. When the subject left her room, she saw the experiment's assistant seated at the end of the hall, and invariably went to the assistant to report the seizure. If six minutes elapsed without the subject's having emerged from her room, the experiment was terminated.

Ninety-five percent of all the subjects who ever responded did so within the first half of the time available to them. No subject who had not reported within three minutes after the fit ever did so. This suggests that even had the experiment been allowed to run for a considerably longer period of time, few additional subjects would have responded.

Eighty-five percent of the subjects who thought they alone knew of the victim's plight reported the seizure before the victim was cut off; only 31% of those who thought four other bystanders were present did so. Every one of the subjects in the two-person condition, but only 62% of the subjects in the six-person condition ever reported the emergency. To do a more detailed analysis of the results, each subject's time score was transformed into a "speed" score by taking the reciprocal of the response time in seconds and multiplying by 100. Analysis of variance of these speed scores indicates that the effect of group size was highly significant ($p < .01$), and all three groups differed significantly one from another ($p < .05$).

Effect of group composition and sex of the subject: Several variations of the three-person group were run. In one pair of variations, the female subject thought the other bystander was either male or female, in another, she thought the other bystander was a premedical student who worked in the emergency ward at Bellevue Hospital. These variations in the sex and medical competence of the other bystander had no important or detectable effect on speed of response. Subjects responded equally frequently and fast whether the other bystander was female, male, or medically experienced.

Coping with emergencies is often thought to be the duty of males, especially when there are females present, but there was no evidence that this is the case in this study. Male subjects responded to the emergency with almost exactly the same speed as did females.

Effects of friendship and prior acquaintance: Friends responded considerably differently from strangers in the three-person condition. When two friends were each aware of the victim's distress, even though they could not see or be seen by each other, they responded significantly faster than subjects in the other three-person groups. In fact, the average speed of response by subjects who thought their friend was also present was not noticeably different from the average speed of response in the two-person condition, where subjects believed that they alone were aware of the emergency. This suggests that responsibility does not diffuse across friends.

The effects of prior acquaintance with the victim were also strong. Subjects who had met the victim, even though only for less than a minute, were significantly faster to report his distress than other subjects in the six-person condition. Subjects in this condition later discussed their reactions to the situation. Unlike subjects in any other group, some of those who had accidentally met the victim-to-be later reported that they had actually *pictured* him in the grip of the seizure. Apparently, the ability to *visualize* a specific, concrete, distressed individual increases the likelihood of helping that person.

Subjects, whether or not they intervened, believed the fit to be genuine and serious. "My God, he's having a fit," many subjects said to themselves (and we overheard via their microphones). Others gasped or simply said, "Oh." Several of the male subjects swore. One subject said to herself, "It's just my kind of luck, something has to happen to me!" Several subjects spoke aloud of their confusion about what course of action to take: "Oh, God, what should I do?"

When those subjects who intervened stepped out of their rooms, they found the experiment's assistant down the hall. With some uncertainty but without panic, they reported the situation. "Hey, I think Number 1 is very sick. He's having a fit or something." After ostensibly checking on the situation, the experimenter returned to report that "everything is under control." The subjects accepted these assurances with obvious relief.

Subjects who failed to report the emergency showed few signs of the apathy and indifference thought to characterize "unresponsive bystanders." When the experimenter entered her room to terminate the situation, the subject often asked if the victim were all right. "Is he being taken care of?" "He's all right, isn't he?" Many of these subjects showed physical signs of nervousness; they often had trembling hands and sweating palms. If anything, they seemed more emotionally aroused than did the subjects who reported the emergency.

Why, then, didn't they respond? It is not our impression that they had decided *not* to respond. Rather, they were still in a state of inde-cision and conflict concerning whether to respond or not. The emo-tional behavior of these non-responding subjects was a sign of their continuing conflict; a conflict that other subjects resolved by responding.

The fit created a conflict situation of the avoidance-avoidance type. On the one hand, subjects worried about the guilt and shame they would feel if they did not help the person in distress. On the other hand, they were concerned not to make fools of themselves by overreacting, not to ruin the ongoing experiment by leaving their intercoms and not to destroy the anonymous nature of the situation, which the experimenter had earlier stressed as important. For sub-jects in the two-person condition, the obvious distress of the victim and his need for help were so important that their conflict was easily resolved. For the subjects who knew that there were other by-standers present, the cost of not helping was reduced and the con-flict they were in was more acute. Caught between the two negative alternatives of letting the victim continue to suffer, or the costs of rushing in to help, the non-responding bystanders vacillated between them rather than choosing not to respond. This distinction may be academic for the victim, since he got no help in either case, but it is an extremely important one for understanding the causes of by-standers' failures to help.

Although the subjects experienced stress and conflict during the emergency, their general reactions to it were highly positive. On a questionnaire administered after the experimenter had discussed the nature and purpose of the experiment, every single subject found the experiment either "interesting" or "very interesting" and was willing to participate in similar experiments in the future. All subjects felt they understood what the experiment was all about and indicated they thought the deceptions were necessary and justified. All but one felt they were better informed about the nature of psychological research in general.

We asked all subjects whether the presence or absence of other bystanders had entered their minds during the time that they were hearing the seizure. We asked the question every way we knew how: subtly, directly, tactfully, bluntly, and the answer was always the same. Subjects had been aware of the presence of other bystanders in the appropriate conditions, but they did not feel that they had been influenced in any way by their presence. As in our previous experiments, this denial occurred in the face of results showing that the presence of others did affect helping.

SOCIAL DETERMINANTS OF BYSTANDER INTERVENTION, III

We have suggested two distinct processes which might lead people to be less likely to intervene in an emergency if there are other people present than if they are alone. On the one hand, we have suggested that the presence of other people may affect the interpretations each bystander puts on an ambiguous emergency situation. If other people are present at an emergency, each bystander will be guided by their apparent reactions in formulating his own impressions. Unfortunately, their apparent reactions may not be a good indication of their true feelings. It is possible for a state of "pluralistic ignorance" to develop, in which each bystander is led by the *apparent* lack of concern of the others to interpret the situation as being less serious than he would if alone. To the extent that he does not feel the situation is an emergency, of course, he will be unlikely to take any helpful action.

Even if an individual does decide that an emergency is actually in process and that something ought to be done, he still is faced with the choice of whether he himself will intervene. Here again, the presence of other people may influence him—by reducing the costs associated with non-intervention. If a number of people witness the same event, the responsibility for action is diffused, and each may feel less necessity to help.

Both the "social influence" and the "diffusion of responsibility" explanations seem valid, and there is no reason why both should not be jointly operative. Neither alone can account for all the data. For example, the diffusion explanation cannot account for the significant difference in response rate between the Strangers and Stooge conditions in Experiment 2. There should be equal diffusion in either case. This difference can more plausibly be attributed to the fact that strangers typically did not show such complete indifference to the accident as did the stooge. The diffusion process also does not seem applicable to the results of Experiment 1. Responsibility for protecting oneself from fire should not diffuse. On the other hand, "social influence" processes cannot account for results in Experiment 4. Subjects in that experiment could not communicate with each other and thus could not be influenced by each other's reactions.

Although both processes probably operate, they may not do so at the same time. To the extent that social influence leads an individual to define the situation as non-serious and not requiring action, his responsibility is eliminated, making diffusion unnecessary. Only if social influence is unavailable or unsuccessful in leading subjects to misinterpret a situation, should diffusion play a role. Indirect evidence supporting this analysis comes from observation of non-intervening subjects in the various emergency settings. In settings involving face-to-face contact, as in Experiments 1 and 2, non-interveners typically redefined the situation and did not see it as a serious emergency. Consequently, they avoided the moral choice of whether or not to take action. During the post-experimental interviews, subjects in these experiments seemed relaxed and assured. They felt they had behaved reasonably and properly. In Experiment 4, on the other hand, face-to-face contact was prevented, social influence could not help subjects define the situation as non-serious, and they were faced with the moral dilemma of whether to intervene. Although the imagined presence of other people led many subjects to delay intervention, their conflict was exhibited in the post-experimental interviews. If anything, subjects who did not intervene seemed more emotionally aroused than did subjects who reported the emergency.

The results of these experiments suggest that social inhibition effects may be rather general over a wide variety of emergency situations. In four different experiments, bystanders have been less likely to intervene if other bystanders are present. The nature of the other bystander seems to be important: a non-reactive confederate provides the most inhibition, a stranger provides a moderate amount, and a friend, the least. Overall, the results are consistent with a multiprocess model of intervention; the effect of other people seems to be mediated both through the interpretations that bystanders place on the situation, and through the decisions they make once they have come up with an interpretation.

"There's safety in numbers," according to an old adage, and modern city dwellers seem to believe it. They shun deserted streets, empty subway cars, and lonely walks in dark parks, preferring instead to go where others are or to stay at home. When faced with stress, most individuals seem less afraid when they are in the presence of others than when they are alone. Dogs are less likely to yelp when they face a strange situation with other dogs; even rats are less likely to defecate and freeze when they are placed in a frightening open field with other rats.

A feeling so widely shared should have some basis in reality. Is there safety in numbers? If so, why? Two reasons are often suggested: Individuals are less likely to find themselves in trouble if there are others about, and even if they do find themselves in trouble, others are likely to help them deal with it. While it is certainly true that a victim is unlikely to receive help if nobody knows of his plight, the experiments above cast doubt on the suggestion that he will be more likely to receive help if more people are present. In fact, the opposite seems to be true. A victim may be more likely to get help, or an emergency be reported, the fewer people who are available to take action.

Although the results of these studies may shake our faith in "safety in numbers," they also may help us begin to understand a number of frightening incidents where crowds have listened to, but not answered, a call for help. Newspapers have tagged these incidents with the label "apathy." We have become indifferent, they say, callous to the fate of suffering others. Our society has become "dehumanized" as it has become urbanized. These glib phrases may contain some truth, since startling cases such as the Genovese murder often seem to occur in our large cities, but such terms may also be misleading. Our studies suggest a different conclusion. They suggest that situational factors, specifically factors involving the immediate social environment, may be of greater importance in determining an individual's reaction to an emergency than such vague cultural or personality concepts as "apathy" or "alienation due to urbanization." They suggest that the failure to intervene may be better understood by knowing the relationship among bystanders rather than that between a bystander and the victim.

Our results may explain why the failure to intervene seems to be more characteristic of large cities than rural areas. Bystanders to urban emergencies are more likely to be, or at least to think they are, in the presence of other bystanders than witnesses of non-urban emergencies. Bystanders to urban emergencies are less likely to know each other or to know the victim than are witnesses of non-urban emergencies. When an emergency occurs in a large city, a crowd is likely to gather; the crowd members are likely to be strangers; and it is likely that no one will be acquainted with the victim. These are exactly the conditions that made the helping response least likely in our experiments.

In a less sophisticated era, Rudyard Kipling prayed "That we, with Thee, may walk uncowed by fear or favor of the crowd; that, under Thee, we may possess man's strength to comfort man's distress." It appears that the latter hope may depend to a surprising extent upon the former.

NOTES

1. A more detailed report of this experiment is given in: B. Latané and J. M. Darley "Group Inhibition of Bystander Intervention in Emergencies," *Journal of Personality and Social Psychology*, 10 (1968), 215–21.
2. The formula for calculating the expected proportion of groups in which at least one person will have acted by a given time is $1-(1-p)^n$ where p is the proportion of single individuals who act by that time and n is the number of persons in the group.
3. A more detailed description of this experiment is given in: B. Latané and J. A. Rodin, "Lady in Distress: Inhibiting Effects of Friends and Strangers on Bystander Intervention," *Journal of Experimental Social Psychology*, 5 (1969), 189–202.
4. Portions of these results have been reported in J. M. Darley and B. Latané, "Bystander Intervention in Emergencies: Diffusion of Responsibility," *Journal of Personality and Social Psychology*, 8 (1968), 377–83.
* The experiments reported in this paper were supported by National Science Foundation grants GS1238 and GS1239 and were conducted while the authors were at Columbia University and New York University, respectively. Their forthcoming book on this research (Latané and Darley, *The Unresponsive Bystander*, New York: Appleton-Century-Crofts, 1970) won the 1968 Socio-Psychological Prize awarded by the American Association for the Advancement of Science and the Century Psychology Prize for 1968.

REFERENCES

R. W. Brown, "Mass Phenomena," in G. Lindzey, Ed., *Handbook of Social Psychology*, Vol. 2 (Cambridge, Mass.: Addison-Wesley, 1954).

———, *Social Psychology* (New York: Free Press, 1965).

J. M. Darley and B. Latané, "Bystander Intervention in Emergencies: Diffusion of Responsibility," *Journal of Personality and Social Psychology*, Vol. 8 (1968), pp. 377–83.

B. Latané, "Gregariousness and Fear in Laboratory Rats," *Journal of Experimental Social Psychology,* Vol. 5 (1969), pp. 61–69.

———— and J. M. Darley, "Group Inhibition of Bystander Intervention in Emergencies," *Journal of Personality and Social Psychology,* Vol. 10 (1968), pp. 215–21.

———— and D. C. Glass, "Social and Non-social Attraction in Rats," *Journal of Personality and Social Psychology,* Vol. 9 (1969), pp. 142–46.

———— and J. Rodin, "A Lady in Distress: Inhibiting Effects of Friends and Strangers on Bystander Intervention," *Journal of Experimental Social Psychology,* in press.

S. Schachter, *The Psychology of Affiliation* (Stanford: Stanford University Press, 1959).

5

Fear and the House-As-Haven
in the Lower Class

Lee Rainwater

Men live in a world which presents them with many threats to
their security as well as with opportunities for gratification of their
needs. The cultures that men create represent ways of adapting to
these threats to security as well as maximizing the opportunities for
certain kinds of gratifications. Housing as an element of material
culture has as its prime purpose the provision of shelter, which is
protection from potentially damaging or unpleasant trauma or other
stimuli. The most primitive level of evaluation of housing, therefore,
has to do with the question of how adequately it shelters the individuals who abide in it from threats in their environment. Because
the house is a refuge from noxious elements in the outside world, it
serves people as a locale where they can regroup their energies for

"Fear and the House-as-Haven in the Lower Class," Lee Rainwater, *Journal of
the American Institute of Planners,* Vol. 32, No. 1 (January 1966), pp. 23–31.
Reprinted by permission of the *Journal of the American Institute of Planners.*
This paper is based in part on research aided by a grant from the National
Institute of Mental Health, Grant No. MH–09189, "Social and Community Problems in Public Housing Areas," Many of the ideas presented from discussions with
the senior members of the Pruitt-Igoe Research Staff—Alvin W. Gouldner, David
J. Pittman, and Jules Henry—and with the research associates and assistants on
the project.

interaction with that outside world. There is in our culture a long history of the development of the house as a place of safety from both nonhuman and human threats, a history which culminates in guaranteeing the house, a man's castle, against unreasonable search and seizure. The house becomes the place of maximum exercise of individual autonomy, minimum conformity to the formal and complex rules of public demeanor. The house acquires a sacred character from its complex intertwining with the self and from the symbolic character it has as a representation of the family.[1]

These conceptions of the house are readily generalized to the area around it, to the neighborhood. This fact is most readily perceived in the romanticized views people have about suburban living.[2] The suburb, just as the village or the farm homestead, can be conceptualized as one large protecting and gratifying home. But the same can also be said of the city neighborhood, at least as a potentiality and as a wish, tenuously held in some situations, firmly established in others.[3] Indeed, the physical barriers between inside and outside are not maintained when people talk of their attitudes and desires with respect to housing. Rather, they talk of the outside as an inevitable extension of the inside and of the inside as deeply affected by what goes on immediately outside.

When, as in the middle class, the battle to make the home a safe place has long been won, the home then has more central to its definition other functions which have to do with self-expression and self-realization. There is an elaboration of both the material culture within the home and of interpersonal relationships in the form of more complex rituals of behavior and more variegated kinds of interaction. Studies of the relationship between social class status and both numbers of friends and acquaintances as well as kinds of entertaining in the home indicate that as social status increases the home becomes a locale for a wider range of interactions. Whether the ritualized behavior be the informality of the lower middle class family room, or the formality of the upper middle class cocktail party and buffet, the requisite housing standards of the middle class reflect a more complex and varied set of demands on the physical structure and its equipment.

The poverty and cultural milieu of the lower class make the prime concern that of the home as a place of security, and the accomplishment of this goal is generally a very tenuous and incomplete one. (I use the term "lower class" here to refer to the bottom 15 to 20 percent

of the population in terms of social status. This is the group characterized by unskilled occupations, a high frequency of unstable work
histories, slum dwellings, and the like. I refer to the group of more
stable blue-collar workers which in status stands just above this lower
class as the "working class" to avoid the awkwardness of terms like
"lower-lower" and "upper-lower" class.) In the established working
class there is generally a somewhat greater degree of confidence in
the house as providing shelter and security, although the hangovers
of concern with a threatening lower class environment often are still
operating in the ways working class people think about housing.[4]

In Table 1, I have summarized the main differences in three orien-
tations toward housing standards that are characteristic of three
different consumer groups within the lower and working classes. I will
elaborate below on the attitudes of the first group, the slum dwellers,
whose primary focus in housing standards seem to be on the house as
a shelter from both external and internal threat.

ATTITUDES TOWARD HOUSING

As context for this, however, let us look briefly at some of the characteristics of two working class groups. These observations come from
a series of studies of the working class carried out by Social Research,
Inc. over the past ten years. The studies have involved some 2,000
open-ended conversational interviews with working class men and
women dealing with various life style areas from child rearing to
religion, food habits to furniture preferences. In all of this work, the
importance of the home and its location has appeared as a constant
theme. These studies, while not based on nationally representative
samples, have been carried out in such a way as to represent the
geographical range of the country, including such cities as Seattle,
Camden, Louisville, Chicago, Atlanta, as well as a balanced distribution of central city and suburban dwellers, apartment renters, and
home owners. In these studies, one central focus concerned the feelings working class people have about their present homes, their plans
for changes in housing, their attitudes toward their neighborhoods,
and the relation of these to personal and familial goals. In addition,
because the interviews were open-ended and conversational, much
information of relevance to housing appeared in the context of other
discussions because of the importance of housing to so many other

areas of living.[5] In our studies and in those of Herbert Gans and others of Boston's West End, we find one type of working class life style where families are content with much about their housing—even though it is "below standard" in the eyes of housing professionals—if the housing does provide security against the most blatant of threats.[6] This traditional working class is likely to want to economize on housing in order to have money available to pursue other interests and needs. There will be efforts at the maintenance of the house or apartment, but not much interest in improvement of housing level. Instead there is an effort to create a pleasant and cozy home, where housework can be carried out conveniently. Thus, families in this group tend to acquire a good many of the major appliances, to center their social life in the kitchen, to be relatively unconcerned with add-

TABLE 1

Variations in Housing Standards Within The Lower And Working Classes

Focus of Housing Standard	Core Consumer Group	MOST PRESSING NEEDS IN HOUSING	
		Inside the House	*Outside Environs*
Shelter	Slum Dwellers	Enough room Absence of noxious or dangerous elements	Absence of external threats Availability of minimum community services
Expressive elaboration	Traditional working class	Creating a pleasant, cozy home with major conveniences	Availability of a satisfying peer group society and a "respectable enough" neighborhood
All-American affluence	Modern working class	Elaboration of the above along the line of a more complex material culture	Construction of the all-American leisure style in terms of "outdoor living" "Good" community services

ing taste in furnishings to comfort. With respect to the immediate outside world the main emphasis is on a concern with the availability of a satisfying peer group life, with having neighbors who are similar, and with maintaining an easy access back and forth among people who are very well known. There is also a concern that the neighborhood be respectable enough—with respectability defined mainly in the negative, by the absence of "crumbs and bums." An emphasis on comfort and contentment ties together meanings having to do with both the inside and the outside.

Out of the increasing prosperity of the working class has grown a different orientation toward housing on the part of the second group which we can characterize as modern instead of traditional. Here there is a great emphasis on owning one's home rather than enriching a landlord. Along with the acquisition of a home and yard goes an elaboration of the inside of the house in such a way as not only to further develop the idea of a pleasant and cozy home, but also to add new elements with emphasis on having a nicely decorated living room or family room, a home which more closely approximates a standard of all-American affluence. Similarly there is a greater emphasis on maintenance of the yard outside and on the use of the yard as a place where both adults and children can relax and enjoy themselves. With this can come also the development of a more intense pattern of neighborhood socializing. In these suburbs the demand grows for good community services as opposed to simply adequate ones, so that there tends to be greater involvement in the schools than is the case with traditional working class men and women. One of the dominant themes of the modern working class life style is that of having arrived in the mainstream of American life, of no longer being simply "poor-but-honest" workers. It is in the service of this goal that we find these elaborations in the meaning of the house and its environs.

In both working class groups, as the interior of the home more closely approximates notions of a decent standard, we find a decline in concerns expressed by inhabitants with sources of threat from within and a shift toward concerns about a threatening outside world —a desire to make the neighborhood secure against the incursions of lower class people who might rob or perpetrate violence of one kind or another.

As we shift our focus from the stable working class to the lower class, the currently popular poor, we find a very different picture. In addition to the large and growing literature, I will draw on data from three studies of this group with which I have been involved. Two studies deal with family attitudes and family planning behavior on the part of lower class, in contrast to working class couples. In these studies, based on some 450 intensive conversational interviews with men and women living in Chicago, Cincinnati, and Oklahoma City housing was not a subject of direct inquiry. Nevertheless we gained considerable insight into the ways lower class people think about their physical and social environment, and their anxieties, goals, and coping mechanisms that operate in connection with their housing arrangements.[7]

The third study involves a five-year investigation of social and community problems in the Pruitt-Igoe Project of St. Louis. This public housing project consists of 33 11-story buildings near downtown St. Louis. The project was opened in 1954, has 2,762 apartments, of which only some 2,000 are currently occupied, and has as tenants a very high proportion (over 50 percent) of female-headed households on one kind or another of public assistance. Though originally integrated, the project is now all Negro. The project community is plagued by petty crimes, vandalism, much destruction of the physical plant, and a very bad reputation in both the Negro and white communities.[8] (In 1972 the project was closed and the buildings razed to the ground.) For the past two years a staff of ten research assistants has been carrying out participant observation and conversational interviewing among project residents. In order to obtain a comparative focus on problems of living in public housing, we have also interviewed in projects in Chicago (Stateway Gardens), New York (St. Nicholas), and San Francisco (Yerba Buena Plaza and Westside Courts). Many of the concrete examples which follow come from these interviews, since in the course of observation and interviewing with project tenants we have had the opportunity to learn a great deal about both their experiences in the projects and about the private slum housing in which they previously lived. While our interviews in St. Louis provide us with insight into what it is like to live in one of the most disorganized public housing communities in the United States, the interviews in the other cities provide the contrast of much more average public housing experiences.[9] Similarly, the retrospective accounts that respondents in different cities give of their previous private housing experience provides a wide sampling in the slum communities of four different cities.

In the lower class we find a great many very real threats to security, although these threats often do seem to be somewhat exaggerated by lower class women. The threatening world of the lower class comes to be absorbed into a world view which generalizes the belief that the environment is threatening more than it is rewarding—that rewards reflect the infrequent working of good luck and that danger is endemic.[10] Any close acquaintance with the ongoing life of lower class people impresses one with their anxious alienation from the larger world, from the middle class to be sure, but from the majority of their peers as well. Lower class people often seem isolated and to have but tenuous participation in a community of known and valued peers. They are ever aware of the presence of strangers who tend to be seen as potentially dangerous. While they do seek to create a gratifying peer group society, these groups tend to be unstable and readily fragmented. Even the heavy reliance on relatives as the core of a personal community does not do away with the dangers which others may bring. As Walter Miller has perceptively noted, "trouble" is one of the major focal concerns in the lower class world view.[11] A home to which one could retreat from such an insecure world would be of great value, but our data indicate that for lower class people such a home is not easy to come by. In part, this is due to the fact that one's own family members themselves often make trouble or bring it into the home, but even more important it is because it seems very difficult to create a home and an immediate environment that actually does shut out danger.[12]

DANGERS IN THE ENVIRONMENT

From our data it is possible to abstract a great many dangers that have some relation to housing and its location. The location or the immediate environment is as important as the house itself, since lower class people are aware that life inside is much affected by the life just outside.

In Table 2, I have summarized the main kinds of danger which seem to be related to housing one way or another. It is apparent that these dangers have two immediate sources, human and non-human, and that the consequences that are feared from these sources usually represent a complex amalgam of physical, interpersonal, and mortal damage to the individual and his family. Let us look first at the various sources of danger and then at the overlapping consequences feared from these dangers.

There is nothing unfamiliar about the non-human sources of danger.

They represent a sad catalogue of threats apparent in any journalist's account of slum living.[13] That we become used to the catalogue, however, should not obscure the fact that these dangers are very real to many lower class families. Rats and other vermin are ever present companions in most big city slums. From the sense of relief which residents in public housing often experience on this score, it is apparent that slum dwellers are not indifferent to the presence of rats in their homes. Poisons may be a danger, sometimes from lead-base paints used on surfaces which slum toddlers may chew. Fires in slum areas are not uncommon, and even in a supposedly well designed public housing project children may repeatedly burn themselves on uncovered steampipe risers. In slums where the tenant supplies his own heating there is always the possibility of a very cold apartment because of no money, or, indeed, of freezing to death (as we were told by one respondent whose friend fell into an alcoholic sleep without turning on the heater). Insufficiently protected heights, as in one public housing project, may lead to deaths when children fall out of windows or adults fall down elevator shafts. Thin walls in the apartment may expose a family to more of its neighbor's goings-on than is comfortable to hear. Finally, the very cost of the dwelling itself can represent a danger in that it leaves too little money for other things needed to keep body and soul together.

That lower class people grow up in a world like this and live in it

TABLE 2

A Taxonomy of Dangers in the Lower Class Home and Environs: Each of These Can Involve Physical, Interpersonal, and Moral Consequences

SOURCE OF DANGER

Non-Human	*Human*
Rats and other vermin	Violence to self and possessions
Poisons	Assault
Fire and burning	Fighting and beating
Freezing and cold	Rape
Poor plumbing	Objects thrown or dropped
Dangerous electrical wiring	Stealing
Trash (broken glass, cans, etc.)	Verbal Hostility, Shaming, Exploitation
Insufficiently protected heights	Own family
Other aspects of poorly designed	Neighbors
or deteriorated structures	Caretakers
(e.g. thin walls)	Outsiders
Cost of dwelling	Attractive alternatives that wean
	oneself or valued others away
	from a stable life

does not mean that they are indifferent to it—nor that its toll is only that of possible physical damage in injury, illness, incapacity, or death. Because these potentialities and events are interpreted and take on symbolic significance, and because lower class people make some efforts to cope with them, inevitably there are also effects on their interpersonal relationships and on their moral conceptions of themselves and their worlds.

The most obvious human source of danger has to do with violence directed by others against oneself and one's possessions. Lower class people are concerned with being assaulted, being damaged, being drawn into fights, being beaten, being raped. In public housing projects in particular, it is always possible for juveniles to throw or drop things from windows which can hurt or kill, and if this pattern takes hold it is a constant source of potential danger. Similarly, people may rob anywhere—apartment, laundry room, corridor.

Aside from this kind of direct violence, there is the more pervasive ever-present potentiality for symbolic violence to the self and that which is identified with the self—by verbal hostility, the shaming and exploitation expressed by the others who make up one's world. A source of such violence, shaming, or exploitation may be within one's own family—from children, spouse, siblings, parents—and often is. It seems very likely that crowding tends to encourage such symbolic violence to the self but certainly crowding is not the only factor since we also find this kind of threat in uncrowded public housing quarters.[14] Most real and immediate to lower class people, however, seems to be the potentiality for symbolic destructiveness by their neighbors. Lower class people seem ever on guard toward their neighbors, even ones with whom they become well-acquainted and would count as their friends. This suspiciousness is directed often at juveniles and young adults whom older people tend to regard as almost uncontrollable. It is important to note that while one may and does engage in this kind of behavior oneself, this is no guarantee that the individual does not fear and condemn the behavior when engaged in by others. For example, one woman whose family was evicted from a public housing project because her children were troublemakers thought, before she knew that her family was included among the twenty families thus evicted, that the evictions were a good thing because there were too many people around who cause trouble.

Symbolic violence on the part of caretakers (all those whose occupations bring them into contact with lower class people as purveyors of some private or public service) seems also endemic in slum and public housing areas. Students of the interactions between caretakers and their lower class clients have suggested that there is a great deal of punitiveness and shaming commonly expressed by the caretakers in an effort to control and direct the activities of their clients.[15]

The defense of the client is generally one of avoidance, or sullenness and feigned stupidity, when contact cannot be avoided. As David Caplovitz has shown so well, lower class people are subjected to considerable exploitation by the commercial services with which they deal, and exploitation for money, sexual favors, and sadistic impulses is not unknown on the part of public servants either.[16]

Finally, outsiders present in two ways the dangers of symbolic violence as well as of physical violence. Using the anonymity of geographical mobility, outsiders may come into slum areas to con and exploit for their own ends and, by virtue of the attitudes they maintain toward slum dwellers or public housing residents, they may demean and derogate them. Here we would have to include also the mass media which can and do behave in irresponsibly punitive ways toward people who live in lower class areas, a fact most dramatically illustrated in the customary treatment of the Pruitt-Igoe Project in St. Louis. From the point of view of the residents, the unusual interest shown in their world by a research team can also fit into this pattern.

Finally, the lower class person's world contains many attractive alternatives to the pursuit of a stable life. He can fear for himself that he will be caught up in these attractive alternatives and thus damage his life chances, and he may fear even more that those whom he values, particularly in his family, will be seduced away from him. Thus, wives fear their husbands will be attracted to the life outside the family, husbands fear the same of their wives, and parents always fear that their children will somehow turn out badly. Again, the fact that you may yourself be involved in such seductive pursuits does not lessen the fear that these valued others will be won away while your back is turned. In short, both the push and the pull of the human world in which lower class people live can be seen as a source of danger.

Having looked at the sources of danger, let us look at the consequences which lower class people fear from these dangers. The physical consequences are fairly obvious in connection with the nonhuman threats and the threats of violence from others. They are real and they are ever present: One can become the victim of injury, incapacitation, illness, and death from both nonhuman and human sources. Even the physical consequences of the symbolic violence of hostility, shaming, and exploitation, to say nothing of seduction, can be great if they lead one to retaliate in a physical way and in turn be damaged. Similarly there are physical consequences to being caught up in alternatives such as participation in alcohol and drug subcultures.

There are three interrelated interpersonal consequences of living in a world characterized by these human and nonhuman sources of danger. The first relates to the need to form satisfying interpersonal relationships, the second to the need to exercise responsibility as a family member, and the third to the need to formulate an explanation for the unpleasant state of affairs in your world.

The consequences which endanger the need to maintain satisfying interpersonal relations flow primarily from the human sources of danger. That is, to the extent that the world seems made up of dangerous others, at a very basic level the choice of friends carries risks. There is always the possibility that a friend may turn out to be an enemy or that his friends will. The result is a generalized watchfulness and touchiness in interpersonal relationships. Because other individuals represent not only themselves but also their families, the matter is further complicated since interactions with, let us say, neighbors' children, can have repercussions on the relationship with the neighbor. Because there are human agents behind most of the nonhuman dangers, one's relationships with others—family members, neighbors, caretakers—are subject to potential disruptions because of those others' involvement in creating trash, throwing objects, causing fires, or carrying on within thin walls.

With respect to the exercise of responsibility, we find that parents feel they must bring their children safely through childhood in a world which both poses great physical and moral dangers, and which seeks constantly to seduce them into a way of life which the parent wishes them to avoid. Thus, childrearing becomes an anxious and uncertain process. Two of the most common results are a pervasive repressiveness in child discipline and training, and, when that seems to fail or is no longer possible, a fatalistic abdication of efforts to protect the children. From the child's point of view, because his parents are not able to protect him from many unpleasantnesses and even from himself, he loses faith in them and comes to regard them as persons of relatively little consequence.

The third area of effect on interpersonal relations has to do with the search for causes of the prevalence of threat and violence in their world. We have suggested that to lower class people the major causes stem from the nature of their own peers. Thus, a great deal of blaming others goes on and reinforces the process of isolation, suspiciousness, and touchiness about blame and shaming. Similarly, landlords and tenants tend to develop patterns of mutual recrimination and blaming, making it very difficult for them to cooperate with each other in doing something about either the human or nonhuman sources of difficulty.

Finally, the consequences for conceptions of the moral order of one's world, of one's self, and of others, are very great. Although lower class people may not adhere in action to many middle class values about neatness, cleanliness, order, and proper decorum, it is apparent that they are often aware of their deviance, wishing that their world could be a nicer place, physically and socially. The presence of nonhuman threats conveys in devastating terms a sense that they live in an immoral and uncontrolled world. The physical evidence of trash, poor plumbing and the stink that goes with it, rats and other vermin, deepens their feeling of being moral outcasts. Their physical world is telling them they are inferior and bad just as effectively perhaps as do their human interactions. Their inability to control the depredation of rats, hot steam pipes, balky stoves, and poorly fused electrical circuits tells them that they are failures as autonomous individuals. The physical and social disorder of their world presents a constant temptation to give up or retaliate in kind. And when lower class people try to do something about some of these dangers, they are generally exposed in their interactions with caretakers and outsiders to further moral punitiveness by being told that their troubles are their own fault.

IMPLICATIONS FOR HOUSING DESIGN

It would be asking too much to insist that design *per se* can solve or even seriously mitigate these threats. On the other hand, it is obvious that almost all the nonhuman threats can be pretty well done away with where the resources are available to design decent housing for lower class people. No matter what criticisms are made of public housing projects, there is no doubt that the structures themselves are infinitely preferable to slum housing. In our interviews in public housing projects we have found very few people who complain about design aspects of the insides of their apartments. Though they may not see their apartments as perfect, there is a dramatic drop in anxiety about nonhuman threats within. Similarly, reasonable foresight in the design of other elements can eliminate the threat of falling from windows or into elevator shafts, and can provide adequate outside toilet facilities for children at play. Money and a reasonable exercise of architectural skill go a long way toward providing lower class families with the really safe place of retreat from the outside world that they desire.

There is no such straightforward design solution to the potentiality of human threat. However, to the extent that lower class people do have a place they can go that is not so dangerous as the typical slum dwelling, there is at least the gain of a haven. Thus, at the cost perhaps of increased isolation, lower class people in public housing sometimes place a great deal of value on privacy and on living a quiet life behind the locked doors of their apartments. When the apartment itself seems safe it allows the family to begin to elaborate a home to maximize coziness, comfortable enclosure, and lack of exposure. Where, as in St. Louis, the laundry rooms seem unsafe places, tenants tend to prefer to do their laundry in their homes, sacrificing the possibility of neighborly interactions to gain a greater sense of security of person and property.

Once the home can be seen as a relatively safe place, lower class men and women express a desire to push out the boundaries of safety further into the larger world. There is the constantly expressed desire for a little bit of outside space that is one's own or at least semiprivate. Buildings that have galleries are much preferred by their tenants to those that have no such immediate access to the outside. Where, as in the New York public housing we studied, it was possible to lock the outside doors of the buildings at night, tenants felt more secure.

A measured degree of publicness within buildings can also contribute to a greater sense of security. In buildings where there are several families whose doors open onto a common hallway there is a greater sense of the availability of help should trouble come than there is in buildings where only two or three apartments open onto a small hallway in a stairwell. While tenants do not necessarily develop close neighborly relations when more neighbors are available, they can develop a sense of making common cause in dealing with common problems. And they feel less at the mercy of gangs or individuals intent on doing them harm.

As with the most immediate outside, lower class people express the desire to have their immediate neighborhood or the housing project grounds a more controlled and safe place. In public housing projects, for example, tenants want project police who function efficiently and quickly; they would like some play areas supervised so that children are not allowed to prey on each other; they want to be able to move about freely themselves and at the same time discourage outsiders who might come to exploit.

A real complication is that the very control which these desires imply can seem a threat to the lower class resident. To the extent that caretakers seem to demand and damn more than they help, this cure to the problem of human threat seems worse than the disease. The crux of the caretaking task in connection with lower class people is to provide and encourage security and order within the lower class world without at the same time extracting from it a heavy price in self-esteem, dignity, and autonomy.

NOTES

1. Lord Raglan, *The Temple and the House* (London: Routledge & Kegan Paul, 1964).
2. Bennett M. Berger, *Working-Class Suburb* (Berkeley: University of California Press, 1960), and Herbert Gans, "Effect of the Move From the City to Suburb," in Leonard J. Duhl, Ed., *The Urban Condition* (New York: Free Press, 1963).
3. Anselm L. Strauss, *Images of the American City* (New York: Free Press, 1961).
4. In this paper I am pulling together observations from a number of different studies. What I have to say about working class attitudes toward housing comes primarily from studies of working class life style carried out in collaboration with Richard Coleman, Gerald Handel, W. Lloyd Warner, and Burleigh Gardner. What I have to say about lower class life comes from two more recent studies dealing with family life and family planning in the lower class and a study currently in progress of social life in a large public housing project in St. Louis (being conducted in collaboration with Alvin W. Gouldner and David J. Pittman).
5. These studies are reported in the following unpublished Social Research, Inc. reports: *Prosperity and Changing Working Class Life Style* (1960), and *Urban Working Class Identity and World View* (1965). The following publications are based on this series of studies: Lee Rainwater, Richard P. Coleman, and Gerald Handel, *Workingman's Wife: Her Personality, World and Life Style* (New York: Oceana Publications, 1959); Gerald Handel and Lee Rainwater, "Persistence and Change in Working Class Life Style," and Lee Rainwater and Gerald Handel, "Changing Family Roles in the

Working Class," both in Arthur B. Shostak and William Gomberg, *Blue-Collar World* (New York: Prentice-Hall, 1964).

6. Marc Fried, "Grieving for a Lost Home," and Edward J. Ryan, "Personal Identity in an Urban Slum," in Leonard J. Duhl, Ed., *The Urban Condition* (New York: Free Press, 1963); and Herbert Gans, *Urban Villagers* (New York: Free Press of Glencoe, Inc., 1962).

7. Lee Rainwater, *And the Poor Get Children* (Chicago: Quadrangle Books, 1960), and Lee Rainwater, *Family Design: Marital Sexuality, Family Size and Family Planning* (Chicago: Aldine, 1964).

8. Nicholas J. Demerath, "St. Louis Public Housing Study Sets Off Community Development to Meet Social Needs," *Journal of Housing,* XIX (October, 1962).

9. See, D. M. Wilner *et al., The Housing Environment and Family Life* (Baltimore: Johns Hopkins University Press, 1962).

10. Allison Davis, *Social Class Influences on Learning* (Cambridge: Harvard University Press, 1948).

11. Walter Miller, "Lower Class Culture as a Generating Milieu of Gang Delinquency," in Marvin E. Wolfgang, Leonard Savitz, and Norman Johnson, Eds., *The Sociology of Crime and Delinquency* (New York: John Wiley, 1962).

12. Alvin W. Schorr, *Slums and Social Insecurity* (Washington, D.C.: Department of Health, Education and Welfare, 1963).

13. Michael Harrington, *The Other America* (New York: Macmillan, 1962).

14. Edward S. Deevey, "The Hare and the Haruspex: A Cautionary Tale," in Eric and Mary Josephson, *Man Alone* (New York: Dell, 1962).

15. A. B. Hollinghead and L. H. Rogler, "Attitudes Toward Slums and Private Housing in Puerto Rico," in Leonard J. Duhl, *The Urban Condition* (New York: Free Press, 1963).

16. David Caplovitz, *The Poor Pay More* (New York: Free Press of Glencoe, 1963).

6

Architecture, Interaction and Social Control: The Case of a Large-Scale Public Housing Project

William L. Yancey

In this paper we will argue that the architectural design of the Pruitt-Igoe Project, located in St. Louis, Missouri, has had an atomizing effect on the informal social networks frequently found in lower- and working-class neighborhoods. Without the provision of semi-public space and facilities around which informal networks might develop, families living in Pruitt-Igoe have retreated into the internal structures of their apartments and do not have the social support, protection, and informal social control found in other lower- and working-class neighborhoods.

It is clear that social and economic factors, particularly the level

"Architecture, Interaction, and Social Control: The Case of a Large-Scale Public Housing Project," William L. Yancey, *Environment and Behavior,* Vol. 3, No. 1 (March 1971), pp. 3–21. Reprinted by permission of the author and the Publisher, Sage Publications. This paper is based in part on research supported by grants from the National Institute of Mental Health, Grant No. MH–09189, "Social and Community Problems in Public Housing Areas," and from the Urban and Regional Development Center, Vanderbilt University. Many of the ideas presented stem from discussions with the directors of the Pruitt-Igoe research—Alvin W. Gouldner and Lee Rainwater. This paper was presented at a Symposium on Environmental Perception at the meetings of the American Psychological Association at Miami Beach, Florida, on September 5, 1970.

and stability of incomes and occupations, are major determinants of the life styles of the poor. Yet there is also evidence which indicates that the physical environment in which families live, in particular the design and condition of dwelling units, has an effect on the manner in which they live (Schoor, 1963; Wilner *et al.,* 1962).

Among the effects of architectural design which have been identified by previous research is that of the physical proximity of dwelling units on the development of informal relationships between families. Gans (1963) has pointed out that the effects of proximity on informal relationships is somewhat contingent on differences in life styles exhibited by various groups. Gans' research indicates that it cannot be assumed that a particular architectural design will have the same effect on all social groups. The presence or absence of a particular design should have a variant effect on the total social life of a particular group, depending on the interdependence of the architecturally related behavior to other dimensions of the group's life. More specifically, we should find that the architectural relationships between dwellings and the effects of such spatial relationships on the social relationships that develop between families will have varying degrees of significance, depending on the importance of informal neighboring relationships in a particular social group.

In this paper, we will argue that informal networks among neighbors are an important means by which the urban lower and working classes cope with poverty and deprivation and that these networks are at least in part dependent on the semi-public space and facilities that are present in many working- and lower-class neighborhoods. Finally, we will review results of an ethnographic study of the Pruitt-Igoe Housing Project which indicate the nature of the consequences stemming, in part, from the absence of such space and facilities and the networks that might otherwise have developed.

SOCIAL CLASS AND INFORMAL NETWORKS

There is some ambiguity in the sociological literature concerning the importance of informal networks among different social classes. On the one hand, there are authors who argue that the frequency of neighboring and sociability is particularly prevalent in upper- and middle-class suburbs (Whyte, 1956; Bell and Boat, 1957; Fava, 1957). On the other hand, studies of the urban working and lower classes have shown rather strong interpersonal networks of neighbors and strong attachment to neighborhoods (Bott, 1957; Young and Wilmott, 1957; Gans, 1962; Fried and Gleicher, 1961; Fried, 1963; Suttles, 1968).

Careful reviews of these studies indicate that there is a difference in the character of social relationships with neighbors found in the middle class as compared to the working and lower classes. While neighboring is found to be frequent in both areas, "the intensity of social interaction tends to decrease as one moves from working class areas to upper income bracket residential suburbs" (Herberle, 1960: 279).

Illustrative of this debate are the results of a survey directed by John McCarthy and myself in Nashville and Philadelphia. The survey was taken in what were principally lower- and working-class neighborhoods in the two cities, with a smaller proportion of what might be considered lower-middle-class respondents. A total of 1,178 interviews were completed, 712 in Nashville, and 466 in Philadelphia. Approximately equal numbers of these were with black households (576) and white households (602). Samples were systematic, rather than random, and were not designed so as to be representative of either city.

Using a scale developed by Wallin (1953), we found no relationship between casual neighboring relationships and social status.[1] In contrast to these results were those obtained when we asked our respondents to tell us how far away their closest friends lived. In this case, lower-status respondents were more likely to have friends living nearby than were those of higher status.[2]

These results conform to statements by Alan Blum (1964) and Rudolf Herberle (1969), suggesting that once the distinction is made between casual acquaintances and relatively high levels of interdependence, lower-class respondents are more closely tied to their neighbors. Among the lower class, friends are more likely to be neighbors. While, among the middle class, one might be friendly with his neighbors, friendships are more likely to be based on common interests, rather than upon physical proximity[3] (see Gans, 1961).

There is also considerable literature suggestive of the functions of informal networks for the lower and working class. Marc Fried's (1963) research on the depressing effects of urban renewal and relocation, particularly for families who had strong personal ties to the Boston West End, is illustrative. Gerald Suttles' recent research in Chicago's Adams area documents the manner in which the development of neighborhood networks based on physical proximity, age, sex, and ethnicity provided social and moral norms, as well as a means of integration into the larger groups. He writes

> Within each small, localized peer group, continuing face-to-face relations can eventually provide a personalistic order. Once these groups are established, a single personal relation between them can extend the range of such an order. With the acceptance of age grading and territorial usufruct, it becomes possible for slum neighborhoods to work out a moral order that includes most of their residents [Suttles, 1968: 8].

A recent study of an all-white slum neighborhood in St. Louis found similar informal networks. Of particular interest here, and complementing the work of Suttles (1968), is the finding that the level of personal integration into networks was strongly related to the perception of human dangers in the environment. Persons who were not integrated into such networks were more likely to express concern over allowing their children out of the house, felt that they were vulnerable to strangers entering the neighborhood, felt unsafe on the street at night, and felt that children in the neighborhood were out of control (Wolfe *et al.*, 1968).

There are also some indications that the presence of ecologically local networks is more important to lower- and working-class urban dwellers than to their middle-class counterparts. Herbert Gans has noted that the move to suburban areas by middle-class families results in part in having more privacy from neighbors than they had in inner-city apartments. Gans' research suggests that, for the middle class, the move to suburban areas results in few changes in life style that were not intended. He writes: "They are effects, not of suburban life, but of the larger cultural milieu in which people form their aspirations" (Gans, 1963: 192).

The limited consequences of moving to suburbs by middle-class families stand in sharp contrast to those reported by Marris (1962) and Young and Wilmott (1957). These studies of the relocation of lower- and working-class communities indicate that the move to suburbia resulted in significant and unintended changes in their life styles. No longer available in the suburban housing estates were the amenities of the slum—the close proximity to work, the pub, and to friends and relatives. They changed their way of life and began focusing energies more sharply on their homes and jointly pursued family lives, and much less on separate activities by husband and wife participating in sex-segregated peer groups.

In addition to the ethnographic evidence on the relative importance of ecologically local informal networks, there is considerable research indicating that, much to the dismay of urban renewers, lower- and working-class populations are as satisfied with their neighborhoods as are members of the middle class (Foote *et al.,* 1960; Fried, 1963). Our recent survey in Nashville and Philadelphia indicated that there was no relationship between social status and neighborhood satisfaction. Over sixty percent of our respondents were satisfied with their neighborhoods, no matter what their social and economic status.

The works of Fried (1963), Gans (1962), and Foote et al. (1960) also indicate that among the lower and working classes, neighborhood satisfaction is rather closely tied to the presence of informal networks of friends and relatives. Results from our survey support this proposition. Without social class controls, we found no relationship between the proximity of friends and neighborhood satisfaction. When we controlled on the social class, we found that neighborhood satisfaction was related to the proximity of friends in the lower socioeconomic group, while there was no relationship in the higher-status respondents.[4]

These survey data suggest that, not only are the existence and integration into ecologically local, informal social networks significant for the lower and working classes, but our results go slightly beyond the earlier studies in that they are suggestive of the relative importance of such networks for different social and economic levels. While social and economic factors are the principal variables that determine the life styles of the poor, they have developed ways of coping with and adapting to poverty, thus making the condition less oppressive. We have argued that among these adaptations is the development of ecologically local informal neighborhood relationships. When these are disrupted, or a community is designed which makes their devolpment almost impossible, we should expect to see their importance made manifest by other differences that emerge in the life styles of a particular group. The Pruitt-Igoe Housing Project community is illustrative of one such group.

THE CASE OF PRUITT-IGOE

The Pruitt-Igoe Housing Project consists of 43 eleven-story buildings near downtown St. Louis, Missouri. The project was opened in 1954, had 2,762 apartments, and had as tenants a high proportion of female-headed households, on one form or another of public assistance. Though originally containing a large population of white families, the project has been all-Negro for the past several years. The project community is plagued by petty crimes, vandalism, much destruction to the physical plant, and has a rather widespread reputation as being an extreme example of the pathologies associated with lower-class life (Demerath, 1962; Rainwater, 1966a, the preceding chapter).

Pruitt-Igoe represents, in its architectural design, an extreme example of a national housing policy whose single goal is the provision of housing for individual families, with little knowledge about or concern for the development of a community and neighborhood. Unlike normal slums, with their cluttered streets and alleys, Pruitt-Igoe provides no semi-private space and facilities around which neighboring relationships might develop. There is a minimum of what is often considered "wasted space"—space within buildings that is outside of individual family dwelling units. An early review of the project's design (Architectural Forum, 1951) praised the designers for their individualistic design and the absence of such wasted space between dwelling units.

Walking into the project, one is struck by the mosaic of glass that covers what were grassy areas and playgrounds. The barren dirt, or mud when it rains, is constantly tracked into the apartments. Windows, particularly those on the lower floors, are broken out. The cost of replacing glass in vacant apartments led the Housing Authority to cover many with plywood. Streets and parking lots are littered with trash, bottles, and tin cans. Derelict cars provide an attractive source of entertainment for children. Fences around "tot lots" are torn; swings, sliding boards, and merry-go-rounds are noticeably unpainted, rusted, and broken.

Within the buildings themselves, the neglect is more apparent. Entering the buildings via one of the three stairwells, one is struck with the stale air and the stench of urine, trash, and garbage on the floors. One is also struck by the unfinished construction—the unpainted cinderblocks and cement. These unfinished walls in the stairwells are decorated with colorful graffiti.

The alternative route into the building is the single elevator. The elevator is used as a public restroom, as well as a means of transportation into the buildings. Even though it is mopped every morning, the smell of urine is noticeable throughout the day. Many individual

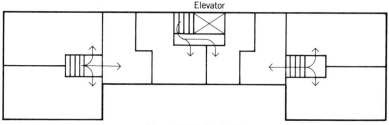

Floors: 2, 3, 5, 6, 8, 9, 11

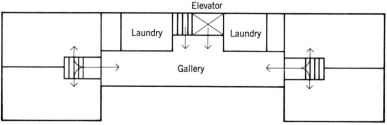

Floors: 1, 4, 7, 10

FIGURE 1.   Pruitt-Igoe typical floor plan.

building elevators are without handrails and in need of painting; all have the reputation of breaking down between floors.

On the fourth, seventh, and tenth floors, there is an open gallery, or hall, the only level public space within the building, one side of which is lined with broken windows and steel gratings. Next to the incinerator, open garbage is often found on the floor. The laundry rooms, located off the gallery, are sometimes used as lavatories. We observed residents and officials urinating in them.

The physical danger and detorioration of Pruitt-Igoe is but a reflection of the more pressing human dangers. Residents of Pruitt-Igoe continually expressed concern with being assaulted, beaten, or raped. We were frequently warned of such dangers and told that we should never enter buildings alone and should stay out of the elevators, especially after dark. We were told stories of people being cut by bottles thrown from the buildings and warned never to stand immediately outside of a building. In addition to the physical violence, there was also the danger to one's self—the verbal hostility, the shaming and exploitation from children, neighbors, and outsiders (see Rainwater, 1966a).

One of the first things pointed out by the residents of Pruitt-Igoe was the distinction between "private" space within apartments and the "public" space and facilities. In our early interviews with families, we asked what they liked about living in the housing project. Almost without exception, what they liked was limited to the physical space and amenities within the family unit. Characteristic of these interviews is the following exchange:

> Interviewer: How do you like living here in Pruitt-Igoe?
> Respondent: I like living here better than I like living on O'Fallon Street [in a private housing slum] where we had a first floor, but did not have heat provided in the winter and windows were broken out. We did have an inside toilet, but no modern plumbing—we had no water. I like living here because it's convenient.
> Interviewer: What do you mean by "convenient?"
> Respondent: The apartment itself—it's easier to take care of and to clean. Although the paint on these walls holds dirt badly, the Housing Authority does furnish the paint. We don't have a choice of what kind of paint, but I painted the walls. It's real convenient here, especially in the wintertime. It's always so nice and warm here, and I only have one rent to pay. I don't have to pay for gas and electricity and all that. I just pay once. I like that. I like this apartment, it's good for the kids. Here we have separate rooms.
> Interviewer: Each child has a separate room?
> Respondent: No, but this way the children have a bedroom and the parents have a bedroom. It gives them and us more freedom.

When the interviewer changed the focus of the interview by asking, "How do you feel about this building?" the character of the interview changed.

> Respondent: Well, I don't like being upstairs like this. The problem is that I can't see the kids. They're just too far away. If one of them gets hurt, needs to go to the bathroom, or anything, it's just too far away. And you can't get outside. We don't have any porches.
> And there are too many different kids around here. Some of them have parents, some do not. There are just a variety of families. Some have husbands, some not.
> If it weren't for the project police, the teen-agers would take over. I've got some children that are teen-agers, but I still think they are the most dangerous group.

This pattern of responses repeats itself throughout our research. The results of a survey taken in the housing project indicate that 78% of the residents were satisfied with their apartments, while only

49% were satisfied with living in the project. This pattern of satisfaction and dissatisfaction with one's dwelling unit as compared to one's neighborhood is exactly the opposite of that found in most studies of housing and neighborhood satisfaction. In contrast with Pruitt-Igoe, slum dwellers generally are dissatisfied with their specific dwellings, while satisfied with their neighborhoods.[5] In Pruitt-Igoe, the familiar aspects of slum living, such as fires and burning, freezing and cold, poor plumbing, dangerous electrical wiring, thin walls, and overcrowding of children and parents into single rooms are somewhat abated. *Yet the amenities of lower-class neighborhoods are apparently lost.*

Complementing the pattern of satisfaction with apartment and neighborhood, and again in sharp contrast to the research reviewed above, informal social networks did not form in the corridors and stairwells of Pruitt-Igoe. Residents of the projects had a similar number of friends as in other lower-class populations, yet these friendships bore little or no relationship to the physical proximity of families to each other.

In Pruitt-Igoe, relationships with neighbors ranged from occasional friendship and helping patterns to (more frequently found) open hostility or isolation. As one woman explained when we asked about troubles in the project:

> I think people bring trouble on themselves, but like the kids—see, the kids get fighting and the parents they get into it too. Now us, we mind our own business. I say little to the people across the hall. We don't have any friends in the building. Most of our friends are from work. Some of them we have known for a long time.

Still another replied, when asked about her neighbors:

> They are selfish. I've got no friends here. There's none of this door-to-door coffee business of being friends here or anything like that. Down here, if you are sick you just go to the hospital. There are no friends to help you. I don't think my neighbors would help me and I wouldn't ask them to anyway. I don't have trouble with my neighbors because I never visit them. The rule of the game down here is *go for yourself.*

THE CONSEQUENCES OF ATOMIZATION

Gerald Suttles notes that in the Adams area in Chicago, conflict between residents in the area results in the reinforcement of the small informal group. He writes (1968: 228):

Individuals in the Adams area achieve a positive association with co-residents of the same age, sex and ethnicity primarily because conflict with other persons forces them together into small face-to-face groupings. Otherwise, people might remain almost wholly isolated, associate indiscriminately, and be dependent on such dyadic relations as they could form.

Of particular interest here is his discussion of the sequence through which such groups develop. New residents of the area restrict their children's movement to the areas immediately around or close by their homes. As a result, small and continuous face-to-face associations develop around the immediate proximity of the home. They provide means of controlling children and provide "assurances that relieve their apprehension." Conflict with persons outside these small groups forces the residents to "throw their lot in with a definite group of people" (Suttles, 1968: 228).

In a similar manner, mothers in Pruitt-Igoe attempt to keep their children in close proximity to their apartments. Yet in contrast to the slum, the architectural design of the project is such that as soon as a child leaves an apartment he is out of his mother's sight and direct control. There are no areas within buildings, except the galleries (which cannot be seen from the apartments and which are shared by some twenty families) in which children can play. As one mother explained:

> I find that I can't keep up with the children when they leave the house to play. When they go out they play with just anybody; there are some people in the project who raise their children and some who don't. I want to have control over who they play with and when so many people live in one place you just can't choose your kid's playmates. If we were in a house I could keep them in a yard and see who they play with.

Mothers fear the early introduction and socialization of their children into sex and other troubles. They also see the adults in the housing project as being irresponsible, deviant, and beyond control. Said one:

> They tell their children one thing and go out and do the very opposite. They see kids in a fight and rather than break it up, will get into it themselves.

Yet attempts to control children who are members of unknown families frequently resulted in conflict between adults. Thus one woman reported:

I used to watch the kids in this building. In the beginning I tried to discipline them. I'd tell them every time I found them doing something mischievous what was wrong and what was right. But kids don't like that; their parents don't like it. They don't want somebody else to discipline their children. They put the blame on you. Watching children is dangerous.

Another explained that after she had "made one of the neighbor's boys do right," his mother came and said she was going to bring a gun.

The conflict is further escalated when one of the two adults calls the police. As one woman explained, after she was told the police had been called because her son had gotten into a fight:

Well, I'm not going to get shook because the police are coming. They always come to this house and tell me how bad my children are. It's too bad the parents had to call the police and could never take the time to come up and talk to me first.

Apparently without the informal networks, informal social control that might otherwise be based on the small social group is not strong enough to resolve such conflicts. Thus, as a means of resolving what might otherwise have been a relatively small complaint, a more powerful authority—the policeman—is called upon. This, in turn, further exacerbates the atomization that exists.

Our interviews and observations with families in the housing project contain many references to the police. A sample survey of the Pruitt-Igoe Housing Project showed that over 90% of the residents of the project indicated that there should be more policemen patrolling the area. As one lady explained:

In other projects they have enough policemen, but not here. You put lights in and they take them out, or the police never turn them on. They have policemen but they don't do any good. They are not here long enough. They used to have auxiliary policemen down here. But as soon as they took them away there was all kinds of raping and stealing all over the project. It has turned into a jungle.

Other features of the architecture, apart from the lack of semi-public space and facilities, have contributed to the fears that characterize the community. The design of the stairwells is such that they represent almost completely uncontrolled space. They are public in the sense that anyone can enter them without being challenged, yet they are private in that no one is likely to be held accountable for his behavior in the stairwell. This lack of accountability is particularly prevalent in the center stairwell, where a small anteroom separates the individual apartments from the stairwell. This room creates a buffer zone between the totally private apartment and the stairwell. Pruitt-Igoens fear this stairwell more than the others, and it is said to be used by teen-agers as a relatively private place in which they can engage in sexual intercourse. As one teen-ager explained, "All you have to do is knock out the light on the landings above and below you. Then when someone comes, if they are not afraid of the dark, they stumble around and you can hear them in time to get out."

The isolation, the lack of accountability for entry into the stairwells, and the fears that are centered around them are somewhat interdependent with the lack of informal networks. Given the number of families who have rights to this space, it should not be surprising that strangers can enter it without being challenged. While interviewing in lower- and working-class neighborhoods, one often encounters persons on the street who question you as to where you are going. After an introduction, such persons often give interviewers instructions as to where a family can be found, when they will return home, or how to get through an alley to an apartment. Later, when such an interviewer returns and introduces himself, he often gets a response such as, "Oh yes, you were here earlier." During our three years of intensive research in Pruitt-Igoe, such an experience never occurred. The presence of outsiders was noticed by the residents, but they were never challenged.

Absent from the architectural design of Pruitt-Igoe is what has sometimes been referred to as wasted space. We choose to call it "defensible space." In lower- and working-class slums, the littered and often trash-filled alleys, streets, and backyards provide the ecological basis around which informal networks of friends and relatives may develop. Without such semi-public space and facilities, the development of such networks is retarded; the resulting atomization of the community can be seen in the frequent and escalating conflict between neighbors, fears of and vlunerability to the human dangers in the environment, and, finally, withdrawal to the last line of defense—into the single-family dwelling unit. The sense of security and control that is found in other working- and lower-class neighborhoods is not present.

There are at least two alternative hypotheses which might be used to explain the atomized nature of the Pruitt-Igoe community. The first of these stems from the research and literature on social stratification, which rather clearly show that the level of interpersonal trust is lower in the lower class than in any other segment of the population. Thus it is argued that Pruitt-Igoe, being representative of the lowest class, is therefore a community of people none of whom trust one another. A comparison of Pruitt-Igoe's residents' responses to questionnaire items measuring the level of trust indicates that, while they are less trustful than are persons of higher status, they are not different from other lower-class populations (see Rainwater and Schwarts, 1965).

Perhaps a more credible hypothesis, one which might be termed the "police state" theory, stems from the public nature of life in public housing. Over fifty percent of the residents are on some form of welfare assistance. Welfare workers and housing authority officials maintain a rather close scrutiny of their clients who might otherwise break one of the many rules governing residence in the project. Under such a "police state," residents of the project may fear that becoming friendly with neighbors will result in their being turned in to the authorities. We observed neighbors calling the police about one another, as discussed above, and some families complained that neighbors had reported them to the housing authority or welfare office for an infraction of one of their rules.

Without a comparative study of Pruitt-Igoe with another housing project with a similar population, similar reputation, and similar administration by caretakers, it is difficult to adequately judge the effects of architecture per se. David Wilner's study of public housing in Baltimore shows, in contrast with Pruitt-Igoe, that with an architectural design which facilitated interpersonal interaction by the provision of common space and facilities, an increased amount of neighboring, visiting, and mutual aid was found among persons moving from a slum into a public housing project (Wilner et al., 1962: 161).

We obviously believe that architecture does have an effect on the manner in which the poor cope with poverty. And we further suggest that designers of housing for the poor, rather than viewing the space between dwelling units as something to be avoided or reduced as far as possible, should provide semi-public space and facilities around which smaller identifiable units of residence can organize their sense of "turf." Designers should minimize space that belongs to no one and maximize the informal control over the space required to get from one dwelling to another. In a word, if housing must be designed for the ghetto—if we must reconcile ourselves to not being able to change the social forces which produce the world of danger that lower-class families experience—the architect can make some small contribution by facilitating the constructive adaptations that have emerged as a means of defense against the world of the lower class.

NOTES

1. When status was measured by education, we found a positive, although weak, relationship. When status was measured by income, we obtained the opposite results.
   Neighboring and Social Status. Percentage of each status group scoring "high" on neighboring items:

EDUCATION COMPLETED			WEEKLY INCOME		
0–7 yrs	25.2	(306)	00–$59	41.2	(240)
8–11 yrs	33.8	(409)	60–129	29.9	(421)
12 yrs	33.8	(225)	$130 +	28.6	(318)
College	30.7	(192)			

2. *Friends' Distance and Social Status.* Percentage with first friend living on same block:

EDUCATION COMPLETED			WEEKLY INCOME		
0–7 yrs	43.7	(300)	00–$59	40.7	(231)
8–11 yrs	31.6	(415)	60–129	29.3	(413)
12 yrs	26.8	(220)	$130 +	19.9	(311)
College	14.5	(186)			
Probability	.0074		.0027		

   Similar results were obtained with each of three friends.
3. We also found that higher-status persons are more likely to have friends whose occupations are similar to their own, in level of prestige, than are members of the lower and working classes.
4. *Neighborhood Satisfaction and Proximity of First Friend by Social Status.* Percentage satisfied with neighborhood:

		DISTANCE IN BLOCKS		
		0–4	*5–25*	*26 +*
Total Sample		72.9(541)	69.4(264)	70.0(240)
Education completed				
0–8 yrs	LO	74.8(262)	76.0 (71)	71.0 (60)
9–12 yrs	MD	70.0(203)	61.9(126)	63.2 (87)
College	HI	77.3 (66)	67.3 (61)	78.2 (78)

As these data reveal, without social and economic controls there is little or no relationship between friends' distance and neighborhood satisfaction. Yet when we control on the level of education, we find that there is a relationship in the lower class, but not in the middle class.

Similar results were obtained with the second- and third-friend responses and when social status was measured by income and occupation. The levels of significance, beyond the .05 level, are not always achieved, but in every case the pattern of a stronger relationship between the proximity of friends and satisfaction with neighborhood is found in the lower-status groups.

5. A survey taken in the private slum neighborhood directly adjacent to Pruitt-Igoe found the more usual pattern of satisfaction with housing and neighborhood. The results of this and a survey taken in Pruitt-Igoe are presented below.

PERCENTAGE SATISFIED

	Pruitt-Igoe	*Adjacent Slum*
with apartment	78	55
with project living	49	
with neighborhood	53	74
	(n = 154)	(n = 69)

In more recent years, vandalism and lack of maintenance have resulted in the deterioration of the plumbing and heating of the building. Thus these data, if gathered more recently, would probably not be found to be as striking as they were when this study was done in 1965.

REFERENCES

"Slum Surgery in St. Louis," *Architectural Forum* (April 1951), pp. 128–36.

W. Bell and M. Boat, "Urban Neighborhoods and Informal Social Relations," *American Journal of Sociology,* Vol. 62 (January 1957), pp. 391–98.

A. F. Blum, "Social Structure, Social Class, and Participation in Primary Relationships," in A. B. Shostak and W. Gomberg, Eds., *Blue Collar World* (Englewood Cliffs, N.J.: Prentice-Hall, 1964).

E. Bott, *Family and Social Networks* (London: Tavistock, 1957).

N. J. Demerath, "St. Louis Public Housing Study Sets Off Community Development to Meet Social Needs," *Journal of Housing,* Vol. 19 (1962), pp. 472–78.

S. F. Fava, "Contrasts in Neighboring New York City and a Suburban County," in R. L. Warren, Ed., *Perspective on the American Community* (Chicago: Rand McNally, 1957).

L. Festinger, S. Schacter, and K. Back, *Social Pressures in Informal Groups* (New York: Harper & Row, 1950).

N. N. Foote, J. Abu-Lughod, M. M. Foley, and L. Winnick, *Housing Choices and Housing Constraints* (New York: McGraw-Hill, 1960).

M. Fried, "Grieving for a Lost Home," in L. J. Duhl, Ed., *The Urban Condition* (New York: Basic Books, 1963), pp. 151–71.

———— and P. Gleicher, "Some Sources of Residential Satisfaction in an Urban Slum," *Journal of American Institute of Planners,* No. 4 (1961), pp. 305–15.

———— and J. Levin, "Some Social Functions of the Urban Slum," in B. Friedman and R. Morris, Eds., *Urban Planning and Social Policy* (New York: Basic Books, 1968), pp. 60–83.

H. Gans, "Effect of the Move from City to Suburb," in L. J. Duhl, Ed., *The Urban Condition* (New York: Basic Books, 1963), pp. 184–98.

————, *The Urban Villagers* (New York: Free Press, 1962).

————, "Planning and Social Life: Friendship and Neighbor Relations in Suburban Communities," *Journal of American Institute of Planners,* Vol. 27, No. 2 (1961), pp. 135–39.

R. Herberle, "The Normative Element in Neighborhood Relations," *Pacific Sociological Review,* Vol. 3, No. 1 (1960), pp. 3–11.

P. Marris, *Family and Social Change in an African City* (Evanston, Ill.: Northwestern University Press, 1962).

L. Rainwater (1966a), "Crucible of Identity: The Negro Lower-class Family," *Daedalus,* Vol. 91, No. 1, pp. 172–216.

———— and M. J. Schwarts (1965), "Identity, World View, Social Relations, and Family Behavior in Magazines," Social Research, Inc.

A. L. Schorr, *Slums and Social Insecurity* (Washington, D.C.: Government Printing Office, 1963).

G. D. Suttles, *The Social Order of the Slum* (Chicago: University of Chicago Press, 1968).

P. Wallin, "A Guttman Scale for Measuring Women's Neighboring," *American Journal of Sociology,* Vol. 59 (November), pp. 243–46.

W. H. Whyte, *The Organization Man* (Garden City, N.Y.: Doubleday, 1956).

D. M. Wilner, R. P. Walkley, T. C. Pinkerton, and M. Tayback, *The Housing Environment and Family Life* (Baltimore, Md.: Johns Hopkins University Press, 1962).

A. Wolfe, B. Lex, and W. Yancey, *The Soulard Area: Adaptations by Urban White Families to Poverty* (St. Louis: Social Science Institute of Washington University, 1968).

M. Young and P. Wilmott, *Family and Kinship in East London* (Glencoe. Free Press, 1957).

7

The Social Psychology of Privacy

Barry Schwartz

Patterns of coming and staying together imply counterpatterns[1] of withdrawal and disaffiliation which, as modalities of action, are worthy of analysis in their own right. Simmel makes the identical point in his essay, "Brücke und Tür": "Usually we only perceive as bound that which we have first isolated in some way. If things are to be joined they must first be separated. Practically as well as logically it would be nonsense to speak of binding that which is not separate in its own sense. . . . Directly as well as symbolically, bodily as well as spiritually, we are continually separating our bonds and binding our separations."[2] Simmel, however, ignores the question of how separation subserves integration—of how men are bound by taking leave of one another as well as by their coming together. One sociologically relevant approach to this problem is through the analysis of privacy, which is a highly institutionalized mode of withdrawal.

"The Social Psychology of Privacy," Barry Schwartz, *American Journal of Sociology,* Vol. 73, No. 6 (1967–68), pp. 741–52. Copyright © 1968 by the University of Chicago. Reprinted by permission of the author and the Publisher, The University of Chicago Press.

THE GROUP-PRESERVING FUNCTIONS OF PRIVACY

Withdrawal into privacy is often a means of making life with an unbearable (or sporadically unbearable) person possible. If the distraction and relief of privacy were not available in such a case, the relationship would have to be terminated if conflict were to be avoided. Excessive contact is the condition under which Freud's principle of ambivalence most clearly exercises itself, when intimacy is most likely to produce open hostility as well as affection.[3] Issue must therefore be taken with Homans' proposition, "Persons who interact frequently with one another tend to like one another" (providing the relationship is not obligatory).[4] The statement holds generally, but misses the essential point that there is a threshold beyond which interaction is unendurable for both parties. It is because people frequently take leave of one another that the interaction-liking proposition maintains itself.

Guarantees of privacy, that is, rules as to who may and who may not observe or reveal information about whom, must be established in any stable social system. If these assurances do not prevail—if there is normlessness with respect to privacy—every withdrawal from visibility may be accompanied by a measure of espionage, for without rules to the contrary persons are naturally given to intrude upon invisibility. "Secrecy sets barriers between men," writes Simmel, "but at the same time offers the seductive temptations to break through the barriers."[5] Such an inclination is embodied in the spy, the Peeping Tom, the eavesdropper, and the like, who have become its symbols.

"Surveillance" is the term which is generally applied to institutionalized intrusions into privacy. And social systems are characterizable in terms of the tension that exists between surveillant and anti-surveillant modes. Much of our literature on the anti-utopia, George Orwell's *1984* for example, which depicts the dis-eases of excessive surveillance, is directed against the former mode. But dangers of internal disorder reside in unconditional guarantees of invisibility against which many administrative arms of justice have aligned themselves. On the other hand, surveillance may itself create the disorder which it seeks to prevent. Where there are few structural provisions for privacy, social withdrawal is equivalent to "hiding." For Simmel, "This is the crudest and, externally, most radical manner of concealment."[6] Where privacy is prohibited, man can only imagine separateness as an act of stealth.[7]

Since some provisions for taking leave of one another and for removing oneself from social observation are built into every establishment, an individual withdrawal into privacy and the allowance of such a withdrawal by other parties reflects and maintains the code that both sides adhere to. Leave taking, then, contains as many ritualistic demands as the act of coming together. Durkheim, like Homans, is not altogether correct in his insistence that the periodic gatherings of the group are its main sources of unity.[8] After a certain point the presence of others becomes irritating and leave taking, which is a mutual agreement to part company, is no less a binding agent than the ritual of meeting. In both cases individual needs (for gregariousness and isolation) are expressed and fulfilled in collectively endorsed manners. The dissociation ritual presupposes (and sustains) the social relation. Rules governing privacy, then, if accepted by all parties, constitute a common bond providing for periodic suspensions of interaction.

If privacy presupposes the existence of established social relations its employment may be considered as an index of solidarity. Weak social relationships, or relationships in the formative stage, cannot endure the strain of dissociation. By contrast, members of a stable social structure feel that it is not endangered by the maintenance of interpersonal boundaries. This point is of course well reflected in the Frostian dictum, "Good fences make good neighbors."

PRIVACY HELPS MAINTAIN STATUS DIVISIONS

It is also well known that privacy both reflects and helps to maintain the status divisions of a group. In the armed forces, for example, the non-commissioned officer may reside in the same building as the dormitoried enlisted man but he will maintain a separate room. The officer of higher rank will live apart from the non-commissioned, but on the same base, often in an apartment building; but officers of highest status are more likely to have private quarters away from the military establishment.

In organizational life the privacy of the upper rank is insured structurally; it is necessary to proceed through the lieutenant stratum if the top level is to be reached. In contrast, the lower rank, enjoying less control over those who may have access to it, find their privacy more easily invaded. Even in domestic life persons of the lower stratum lack "the butler" by means of whom the rich exercise tight control over their accessibility to others.

Privacy is an object of exchange. It is bought and sold in hospitals, transportation facilities, hotels, theaters, and, most conspicuously, in public restrooms where a dime will purchase a toilet, and a quarter, a toilet, sink and mirror. In some public lavatories a free toilet is provided—without a door.

Privacy has always been a luxury. Essayist Phyllis McGinley writes: "The poor might have to huddle together in cities for need's sake, and the frontiersman cling to his neighbor for the sake of protection. But in each civilization, as it advanced, those who could afford it chose the luxury of a withdrawing place. Egyptians planned vine-hung gardens, the Greeks had their porticos and seaside villas, the Romans put enclosures around their patios. . . . Privacy was considered as worth striving for as hallmarked silver or linen sheets for one's bed."[9] In this same respect Goffman comments upon the lack of front and back region differentiation in contemporary lower-class residences.[10]

The ability to invade privacy is also reflective of status. The physician's high social rank, for instance, derives perhaps not only from his technical skill but also from his authority to ignore barriers of privacy. However, this prerogative is not limited to those of high status. We must not forget the "non-person" who lacks the ability to challenge the selfhood of his superiors. Goffman cites Mrs. Frances Trollope: "I had indeed frequent opportunities of observing this habitual indifference to the presence of their slaves. They talk to them, of their condition, of their faculties, of their conduct exactly as if they were incapable of hearing. . . . A young lady displaying modesty before white gentlemen was found lacing her stays with the most perfect composure before a Negro footman."[11] In general society the assumption of the social invisibility of another is looked upon as indecency, that is, as a failure to erect a barrier of privacy between self and other under prescribed conditions.

The general rule that is deducible from all of this is that outside of the kinship group an extreme rank is conferred upon those for whom privacy shields are voluntarily removed. The prestige afforded the physician is exaggerated in order to protect the self from the shame which ordinarily accompanies a revelation of the body to a stranger, particularly if he is of the opposite sex. Likewise, the de-statusing of the servant is necessary if he is to be utilized for purposes of bathing, dressing, etc.

Persons of either high or low rank who have access to the private concerns of their clients are subject to definite obligations regarding both the manner in which secret knowledge is to be obtained and, most importantly, the way in which it is treated once it has been obtained. Explicit or implicit guarantees of confidentiality neutralize the transfer of power which would otherwise accompany the bestowal of private information. Both the possession of an extreme rank and the assurance of confidentiality thus legitimize the "need to know" and the intrusions which it makes possible.

PRIVACY AND DEVIATION

Up to this point we have tried to indicate privacy's stabilizing effect upon two dimensions of social order. Withdrawal subserves horizontal order by providing a release from social relations when they have become sufficiently intense as to be irritating. Privacy is also a scarce social commodity; as such, its possession reflects and clarifies status divisions, thus dramatizing (and thereby stabilizing) the vertical order. But we must recognize that privacy also opens up opportunities for such forms of deviance as might undermine its stabilizing effects. However, privacy admits of *invisible* transgression and therefore serves to maintain intact those rules which would be subverted by the public disobedience that might occur in its absence.

Moore and Tumin, in their discussion of the function of ignorance, stated: "All social groups . . . require some quotient of ignorance to preserve *esprit de corps*."[12] And Goffman has made it clear that every establishment provides "involvement shields" for its members wherein "role releases" may take place, particularly deviant ones.[13] As Merton puts it:

> Resistance to full visibility of one's behavior appears, rather, to result from structural properties of group life. Some measure of leeway in conforming to role expectations is presupposed in all groups. To have to meet the strict requirements of a role at all times, without some degree of deviation, is to experience insufficient allowances for individual differences in capacity and training and for situational exigencies which make strict conformity extremely difficult. This is one of the

sources of what has been elsewhere noted in this book as socially patterned, or even institutionalized, evasions of institutional rules.[14]

Thus, each group has its own "band of institutionalized evasion" which expands and contracts as conditions change. Rose L. Coser, in this connection, has considered observability in terms of the social status of the observer. She indicates that persons of high rank tend to voluntarily deprive themselves of visibility by signaling their intrusion with a prior announcement.[15] The deviation band, then, is normally condoned by both the upper and lower strata.

Moore and Tumin stress the importance of preventing deviation from being known to the group as a whole.[16] No doubt, a publication of all of the sins, crimes, and errors that take place in a social unit would jeopardize its stability. The preoccupation of the press with sensational deviations from norms might be considered from this point of view. Similarly, the more one person involves himself with another on an emotional basis the more both will need private facilities to conceal nasty habits and self-defaming information from each other. If the child, for instance, became suddenly aware of all the non-public performances of his father, and if the latter were aware of all the perversions that are privately enacted by his offspring, a father-son relationship characterized by mutual admiration would be impossible. This same point is illustrated in well-adjusted marriages which depend not only upon mutually acceptable role playing but also upon the ability of both parties to conceal "indecent" performances. This presupposes a modicum of physical distance between husband and wife. Simmel, in addition, adds that a complete abandon of one's self-information to another "paralyzes the vitality of relations and lets their continuation really appear pointless."[17]

Privacy enables secret consumption. We observe, for example, the adolescent practices of smoking or drinking in their locked rooms. Similarly, "women may leave *Saturday Evening Post* on their living room table but keep a copy of *True Romance* ('something the cleaning woman must have left around') concealed in their bedroom."[18] However, some modes of secret consumption have come into the public light. The erotic "girlie magazines," for example, no longer need be employed privately by the middle-class male since the advent of the *Playboy* magazine. As some activities emerge from secrecy others go underground. Thus, the person who nowadays finds pleasure in the Bible will most likely partake of it in private rather than in a public place or conveyance. These new properties are perhaps specific instances of a general rule set down by Simmel, that "what is originally open becomes secret, and what was originally concealed throws off its mystery. Thus we might arrive at the paradoxical idea that, under otherwise like circumstances, human associations require a definite ratio of secrecy which merely changes its objects; letting go of one it seizes another, and in the course of this exchange it keeps its quantum unvaried."[19]

Incidentally, just as the person must employ proper language for the public situations in which he finds himself, he is required to maintain an appropriate body language as well. Differing postures must be assumed in his public encounters. But public postures do not exhaust the many positions of which the human body is capable. Anyone who has maintained a single position over a long period of time knows that the body demands consistent postural variation if it is to remain comfortable and capable of good role performance. Privacy enables the person to enact a variety of non-public postures and thus prepares him physically for public life.

It should be stressed that the absence of visibility does not guarantee privacy. The hypertrophied super-ego certainly makes impossible the use of solitude for deviant objectives. The person who is constantly in view of an internalized father, mother, or God leads a different kind of private life than those possessed by a less demanding conscience. This reveals an interesting paradox. Privacy surely provides for some measure of autonomy, of freedom from public expectation; but as Durkheim so persistently reminded us, the consequences of leaving the general normative order are moral instability and social rootlessness. (It is for this reason that secret societies compensate for the moral anarchy inherent in pure autonomy by means of ritual.)[20] Is it then possible that through privacy the ego escapes the dominion of the public order only to subordinate itself to a new authority: the super-ego? In some measure this is certainly the case, but one may also venture the suggestion that the super-ego, like the social structure whose demands it incorporates, has its own "band of institutionalized evasion." The super-ego cannot be totally unyielding, for if every deviation of the ego called into play its punitive reaction the consequences for the self would be most severe.

PRIVACY AND ESTABLISHMENTS

It was earlier noted that rules or guarantees of privacy subserve horizontal and vertical order. Such rules are embodied in the physical structure of social establishments. Lindesmith and Strauss, for instance, have noted that proprieties concerning interpersonal contact and withdrawal are institutionalized in the architecture of buildings by means of a series of concentric circles. Specific regulations permit or forbid entry into the various parts of this structure, with a particular view to protecting the sacred "inner circle."[21] A more specific instance of the physical institutionalization of norms is found in the case of the bathroom, whose variation in size and design is limited by the requirement that body cleansing and elimination be performed privately.[22] This norm is reinforced by the architectural arrangements in which it is incorporated. The fact that the bathroom is only built for one literally guarantees that the performances which it accommodates will be solos. However, this normative-physical restriction admits of more complicated, secondary proprieties. Bossard and Boll write:

> The fact that the middle-class family rises almost together, and has few bathrooms, has resulted in a problem for it, which has been resolved by a very narrowly prescribed ritual for many of them—a bathroom ritual. They have developed set rules and regulations which define who goes first (according to who must leave the house first), how long one may stay in, what are the penalties for overtime, and under what conditions there may be a certain overlapping of personnel.[23]

The very physical arrangement of social establishments thus opens and shuts off certain possibilities for interaction and withdrawal and creates a background of sometimes complex ritual in support of a foreground of necessary proprieties. Needless to say, the form taken by such ritual is always subject to modification by architectural means.

Charles Madge also urges the architect to take explicit account in his designs of the ambivalences of social life. Men, for example, are given to both withdrawal and self-display. This duality, notes Madge, requires an "intermediate area" in housing projects, such as a backyard or garden which separates the home or inner circle from the "common green."[24] But it is one thing to so divide our physical living space as to insure ourselves of interactional options; it is another to regulate the interactional patterns that the division of space imposes upon us. The latter task is most efficiently met by the door.

DOORS

McGinley has referred to the door as a human event of significance equal to the discovery of fire.[25] The door must surely have had its origin among those whose sense of selfhood had already developed to the extent that they could feel the oppression of others and experience the need for protection against their presence. Continued use of the door very probably heightened that feeling of separateness to which it owed its creation. Doors, therefore, not only stimulate one's sense of self-integrity, they are required precisely because one has such a sense.

The very act of placing a barrier between oneself and others is self-defining, for withdrawal entails a separation from a role and, tacitly, from an identity imposed upon oneself by others via that role. Therefore, to waive the protection of the door is to forsake that sense of individuality which it guarantees. As Simmel points out, some measure of de-selfing is characteristic of everything social.[26]

I would like now to discuss various kinds of doors, including horizontal sliding doors (drawers) and transparent doors (windows). I shall also treat of walls, as relative impermeable interpersonal barriers, in contrast to doors, which are selectively permeable.

Doors provide boundaries between ourselves (i.e., our property, behavior, and appearance) and others. Violation of such boundaries imply a violation of selfhood. Trespassing or housebreaking, for example, is unbearable for some not only because of the property damage that might result but also because they represent proof that the self has lost control of its audience; it can no longer regulate who may and who may not have access to the property and information that index its depths.[27] The victim of a Peeping Tom is thus outraged not only at having been observed naked but also for having lost control of the number and type of people who may possess information about her body. To prove this we note that no nakedness need be observed to make Peeping Tomism intolerable.

"Alone, the visual feeling of the window," writes Simmel, "goes almost exclusively from inward to outward: it is there for looking out, not for seeing in."[28] This interdiction insures that the inhabitants of an establishment may have the outside world at their visual disposal, and at the same time it provides for control over their accessibility to this world. But, whereas the shade or curtain may be employed to regulate accessibility between the private and public spheres of action, situational proprieties are depended upon for protection in public. One such norm is that of "civil inattention" which has been elaborated by Goffman.[29]

Unlike the window, "the door with an in and out announces an entire distinction of intention."[30] There must be very clear rules as to who may open what doors at what times and under what conditions. The front and back doors are normally the only doors that any member of a family may enter at any time and under any circumstances. A parent may enter a child's room at any time and may inspect and replenish drawers, but visiting friends may not. But the parent must learn that some private doors (drawers) may not be opened (although they may be to friends); if they are, new receptacles for ego-indexes will be found, for example, the area between mattress and spring. The child, however, must never inspect the contents of the drawers of his parents nor enter their room at night. Thus the right of intrusion is seen to be an essential element of authority, whose legitimacy is affected by the degree to which it is exercised. Correspondingly, authority is dependent upon immunity against intrusion. Cooley notes that "authority, especially if it covers intrinsic personal weakness, has always a tendency to surround itself with forms and artificial mystery, whose object is to prevent familiar contact and so give the imagination a chance to idealize . . . self concealment serves, among other purposes, that of preserving a sort of ascendency over the unsophisticated."[31] In this same connection, Riesman writes:

> As compared with the one room house of the peasant or the "long house" of many primitive tribes, he (the inner directed child) grows up within walls that are physical symbols of the privacy of parental dominance. Walls separate parents from children, offices from home, and make it hard if not impossible for the child to criticize the parents' injunctions by an "undress" view of the parents or of other parents. What the parents say becomes more real in many cases than what they do. . . .[32]

Moreover, it is possible to map personal relations in terms of mutual expectations regarding intrusion. The invasion of various degrees of privacy may be a duty, a privilege, or a transgression, depending upon the nature of the interpersonal bond. And, clearly, expectations regarding such impositions may not be mutually agreed to.

Parental obligations concerning the care of a child override the child's rights to seclusion and place him in a position of social nakedness wherein he has no control over his appearance to others. However, to be subject to limitless intrusion is to exist in a state of dishonor, as implied in the rule against "coming too close." This point is made in Simmel's discussion of "discretion" as a quality which the person-in-private has a right to demand of another who is in a position to invade his seclusion.[33] Compromises between child and parent are therefore necessary and generally employed by the manipulation of the door. For example, the bedroom door may be kept half open while the child sleeps, its position symbolic of the parents' respect for the youngster's selfhood. Furthermore, a general temporal pattern might emerge if a large number of cases were examined. During infancy the door to self is generally fully open;[34] it closes perhaps halfway as a recognition of self development during childhood, it shuts but is left ajar at pre-puberty, and closes entirely—and perhaps even locks—at the pubertal and adolescent stages when meditation, grooming, and body examination become imperative. Parents at this time are often fully denied the spectatorship to which they may feel entitled and are kept at a distance by means of the privacy that a locked door insures.

There are also certain situations wherein husband and wife must remain separate from one another. A spouse, for example, must generally knock before entering a bathroom if the other is occupying it. This is a token of deference not to nudity but to the right of the other party to determine the way he or she wishes to present the self to the other. This rule insures that the self and its appearance will remain a controllable factor, independent of the whims of others, and it contributes to self-consciousness as well. This is seen most clearly in total institutions like the armed forces where open rows of toilets are used first with some measure of mortification and later with a complete absence of consciousness of self. In such doorless worlds we find a blurring of the distinction between "front and back regions," between those quarters where the self is put on and taken off and those in which it is presented.[35] In conventional society those who confuse these two areas are charged with vulgarity.

In contrast to the door, the wall symbolizes "separation" rather than "separateness' and denies the possibility of the encounter and withdrawal of social exchange. It strips away that element of freedom which is so clearly embodied in the door. "It is essential," notes Simmel, "that a person be able to set boundaries for himself, but freely, so that he can raise the boundaries again and remove himself from them."[36] In privacy, continues Simmel, "A piece of space is bound with himself and he is separated from the entire world."[37] But in enforced isolation man is bound *to* space. While the door separates outside from inside, the wall annihilates the outside. The door closes out; the wall encloses. Yet doors are converted into walls routinely, as is seen in the popular practice of "sending a child to his room" for misdeeds and the like. In this sense, many homes contain private dungeons or, rather, provisions for transforming the child's room into a cell—which forces upon us the distinction between formal and informal imprisonment.

Privacy is not dependent upon the availability of lockable doors. Goffman, for example, discusses "free places" in the institution where inmates may, free of surveillance, "be one's own man . . . in marked contrast to the sense of uneasiness prevailing on some wards."[38] In addition there is "personal territory" established by each inmate: for one a particular corner; for another a place near a window, etc. "In some wards, a few patients would carry their blankets around with them during the day and, in an act thought to highly regressive, each would curl up on the floor with his blanket completely covering him; within the covered space each had some margin of control."[39] Thus do men withdraw from others to be at one with themselves and to create a world over which they reign with more complete authority, recalling Simmel's observation that "the person who erects a refuge demonstrates, like the first pathfinder, the typically human hegemony over nature, as he cuts a particle of space from continuity and eternity."[40]

In summary, islands of privacy exist in all establishments and throughout even the most intimate household. These islands are protected by an intricate set of rules. When these rules are violated secret places are sought after, discovered, and employed as facilities for secret action. These places and their permeability constitute one type of map, as it were, of interpersonal relationships and reveal the nature of the selves participating in them.

PRIVACY, PROPERTY, AND SELF

Implied in any reference to a private place is its contents, personal property. One perhaps more often than not withdraws into privacy in order to observe and manipulate his property in some way, property which includes, of course, body and non-body objects.

There are two types of objects: those which may be observed by the public (and which may be termed personal objects) and those which are not available to public view (private property). Private property, as we are using the term, may be further delineated in terms of those intimate others who may have access to it in terms of visibility or use. Some private objectifications of self may be observed by family members, but some may be observed by *no one except the self*. There is no doubt that these latter objects have a very special meaning for identity; some of these are sacred and must not be contaminated by exposing them to observation by others; some are profane, and exposure will produce shame, but both are special and represent an essential aspect of self and, from the possessor's point of view, must not be tampered with.

It is because persons invest so much of their selves in private and personal things that total institutions require separation of self and material objects. When individualism must be minimized private ownership is always a vice worthy of constant surveillance. In such situations the acquisition and storage of personal things persist in the form of the "stash," which might be anything from a long sock to the cuff of one's pants.[41]

It follows that those who have direct or indirect access to the belongings of others or to articles which have been employed by them in private ways enjoy a certain amount of power which, if judiciously employed, may serve their interests well. Hughes observes:

> It is by the garbage that the janitor judges, and, as it were, gets power over the tenants who high-hat him. Janitors know about hidden love affairs by bits of torn-up letter paper; of impending financial disaster or of financial four-flushing by the presence of many unopened letters in the waste. Or they may stall off demands for immediate service by an unreasonable woman of whom they know from the garbage that she, as the janitors put it, "has the rag on." The garbage gives the janitor the makings of a kind of magical power over that pretentious villain, the tenant. I say a kind of magical power, for there appears to be no thought of betraying any individual and thus turning his knowledge into overt power.[42]

But, certainly, power need not be exercised to be effective. The mere knowledge that another "knows" invokes in the treatment of that other certain amount of humility and deference.

DEPRIVATIZATION

We have attempted to show that the possibility of withdrawal into well-equipped worlds which are inaccessible to others is that which makes intense group affiliations bearable. But we have also seen that men are not always successful in protecting their invisibility. Accidental leakages of information as well as the diverse modes of espionage threaten the information control that privacy is intended to maintain. But information control also consists of purposeful information leakage and even of the renunciation of secrecy. Just as men demand respite from public encounter they need periodically to escape themselves, for a privacy which lacks frequent remissions is maddening. The over-privatized man is he who is relieved of public demand only to become a burden to himself: He becomes his own audience to performances which are bound for tedium. Self-entertainment is thus a most exhausting business, requiring the simultaneous performance of two roles: actor and spectator. Both tire quickly of one another. When privacy thereby exhausts itself new and public audiences (and audienceships) are sought.

Moreover, we are led to relinquish our private information and activities by the expediencies and reciprocities routinely called for in daily life. We all know, for example, that in order to employ others as resources it is necessary to reveal to them something of ourselves, at least that part of ourselves which for some reason needs reinforcement. When this occurs (providing support is forthcoming), two things happen. First, we achieve some degree of gratification; second, and most important, our alter (or resource) reveals to us information which was heretofore withheld, for self-revelation is imbued with reciprocal power: It calls out in others something similar to that which we give ourselves. There is both mutual revelation and mutual gratification. It is easy to see that when stress or need is prolonged this process may become institutionalized: Intimacy is then no longer an alternative; it is enforced, and private activity becomes clandestine and punishable. The deprivation process approaches completion when we are not only penalized for our withdrawals but feel guilty about them. A housewife who had probably undergone the deprivatization process confided to Whyte: "I've promised myself to make it up to them. I was feeling bad that day and just plain didn't make the effort to ask them in for coffee. I don't blame them, really, for reacting the way they did. I'll make it up to them somehow."[43]

But loss of privacy among conventional folk is free of many of the pains of social nakedness which are suffered by inmates and by others undergoing total surveillance. The civilian voluntarily subjects himself to publicity and is relatively free of the contamination of unwanted contacts. His unmaskings are selective and subject to careful forethought. The intruder is chosen rather than suffered; indeed, his resourcefulness depends upon his ability to "know" his client-neighbor. Therefore, in civil life, we find valid rationalization for our self-revelations. The demand that we "be sociable" is too compelling and too rewarding to be ignored by any of us.

But a substantial self-sacrifice is made by those who actually believe themselves to be what they present to public view. An awareness of the masquerades and deceptions that are part of good role performance is necessary to recall ourselves to our *own* selfhood and to our opposition to that of others. We must indeed deceive others to be true to ourselves. In this particular sense privacy prevents the ego from identifying itself too closely with or losing itself in (public) roles. Daily life is therefore sparked by a constant tension between sincerity and guile, between self-release and self-containment, between the impulse to embrace that which is public and the drive to escape the discomfort of group demands. Accordingly, our identities are maintained by our ability to hold back as well as to affiliate. Thus Goffman writes:

When we closely observe what goes on in a special role, a spate of sociable interaction, a special establishment—or in any other unit of social organization—embracement of the unit is not all that we see. We always find the individual employing methods to keep some distance, some elbow room, between himself and that with which others assume he should be identified.

Our sense of being a person can come from being drawn into a wider social unit; our sense of selfhood can arise through the little ways in which we resist the pull. Our status is backed by the solid buildings of the world, while our sense of personal identity often resides in the cracks.[44]

For Goffman, privacy is one of "the little ways in which we resist the pull" of group commitments and reinforce our selfhood.

NOTES

1. The initiation of a social contact generally entails a withdrawal from a preceding one. Therefore, men may withdraw into new social circles as well as into seclusion. In this particular sense it would be most exact to employ the term "contact-withdrawal," as opposed to a single term for engagement and another for disengagement. However, this distinction does not apply to movements into privacy.
2. Georg Simmel, "Brücke und Tür," in *Brücke und Tür* (Stuttgart: K. F. Koehler, 1957), p. 1.
3. Sigmund Freud, *Group Psychology and the Analysis of the Ego* (New York: Bantam Books, Inc., 1960), pp. 41–42.
4. George C. Homans, *The Human Group* (New York: Harcourt, Brace & Co., 1950), p. 111.
5. Georg Simmel, "The Secret and the Secret Society," in Kurt Wolff, Ed., *The Sociology of George Simmel* (New York: Free Press, 1964), p. 334.
6. *Ibid.,* p. 364.
7. *Ibid.*
8. Émile Durkheim, *The Elementary Forms of the Religious Life* (Glencoe, Ill.: Free Press, 1947), pp. 214–19.
9. Phyllis McGinley, "A Lost Privilege," in *Province of the Heart* (New York: Viking Press, 1959), p. 56.
10. Erving Goffman, *The Presentation of Self in Everyday Life* (Edinburgh: University of Edinburgh, 1958), p. 123.
11. *Ibid.,* p. 95.
12. Wilbur E. Moore and Melvin M. Tumin, "Some Social Functions of Ignorance," *American Sociological Review,* XIV (December, 1949), 792. See also Barney Glaser and Anselm Strauss, "Awareness Contexts and Social Interaction," *American Sociological Review,* XXIX (October, 1964), 669–79, in social interaction is discussed in terms of "what each interactant in a situation knows about the identity of the other and his own identity in the eyes of the other" (p. 670). A change in "awareness context" accompanies acquisitions of knowledge, provisions of false knowledge, concealment of information, etc.
13. The "involvement shield" and Everett C. Hughes' concept of "role release" are elaborated in Erving Goffman's *Behavior in Public Places* (New York: Free Press, 1963), pp. 38–39.
14. Robert K. Merton, *Social Theory and Social Structure* (New York: Free Press, 1964), p. 343.
15. Rose L. Coser, "Insulation from Observability and Types of Social Conformity," *American Sociological Review,* 26 (February, 1961), 28–39.
16. Moore and Tumin, *op. cit.* (see n. 12 above), 793.
17. Simmel, "The Secret and the Secret Society," *op. cit.* (see n. 5 above), p. 329.

18. Goffman, *The Presentation of Self in Everyday Life, op. cit.* (see n. 10 above), p. 26. Needless to say, many instances of the employment of privacy for "secret production" could be given.

19. Simmel, "The Secret and the Secret Society," *op. cit.* (see n. 5 above), pp. 335–36.

20. *Ibid.,* pp. 360–61.

21. Alfred R. Lindesmith and Anselm L. Strauss, *Social Psychology* (New York: Henry Holt & Co., 1956), p. 435. However, in an interesting statement, McGinley announces the death of the very idea of the "inner-circle": "It isn't considered sporting to object to being a goldfish. On the same public plan we build our dwelling places. Where, in many a modern house, can one hide? (And every being, cat, dog, parakeet, or man, wants a hermitage now and then.) We discard partitions and put up dividers. Utility rooms take the place of parlors. Picture windows look not onto seas or mountains or even shrubberies but into the picture windows of the neighbors. Hedges come down, gardens go unwalled; and we have nearly forgotten that the inventor of that door which first shut against intrusion was as much mankind's benefactor as he who discovered fire. I suspect that, in a majority of the bungalows sprouting across the country like toadstools after a rain, the only apartment left for a citadel is the bathroom"(*op. cit.* [see n. 9 above], pp. 55–56).

   In contrast, Edward T. Hall observes: "Public and private buildings in Germany often have double doors for soundproofing, as do many hotel rooms. In addition, the door is taken very seriously by Germans. Those Germans who come to America feel that our doors are flimsy and light. The meanings of the open door and the closed door are quite different in the two countries. In offices, Americans keep doors open; Germans keep doors closed. In Germany, the closed door does not mean that the man behind it wants to be alone or undisturbed, or that he is doing something he doesn't want someone else to see. It's simply that Germans think that open doors are sloppy and disorderly. To close the door preserves the integrity of the room and provides a protective boundary between people. Otherwise, they get too involved with each other. One of my German subjects commented, 'If our family hadn't had doors, we would have had to change our way of life. Without doors we would have had many, many more fights. . . . When you can't talk, you retreat behind a door. . . . If there hadn't been doors, I would always have been within reach of my mother' " (*The Hidden Dimension* [Garden City: Doubleday & Co., 1966], p. 127. For a discussion of the norms regulating privacy among the English, French, Arab, and Japanese, see pp. 129–53).

22. Alexander Kira, *The Bathroom* (New York: Bantam Books, Inc., 1967), pp. 178–84. The requirement of complete privacy for personal hygiene is only a recent phenomenon (see pp. 1–8).

23. J. H. S. Bossard and E. S. Boll, *Ritual in Family Living* (Philadelphia: University of Pennsylvania Press, 1950), pp. 113–14 (cited by Kira, *op. cit.* [see n. 22 above], pp. 177–78).

24. Charles Madge, "Private and Public Places," *Human Relations,* 3 (1950), 187–99. F. S. Chapin (in "Some Housing Factors Related to Mental

Hygiene," *Journal of Social Issues,* VII [1951], 165) emphasizes that the need for relief from irritating public contact must be consciously and carefully met by the architect. On the other hand, Kira writes: "There are problems which cannot be resolved by architects and industrial designers alone, however; they also pose a challenge to the social scientists and to the medical and public health professions. This is an area in which the stakes are enormous and in which little or no direct work has been done." (*Op. cit.* [see n. 22 above], p. 192.)

25. See n. 21 above.
26. Simmel, "The Secret and the Secret Society," *op. cit.* (see n. 5 above) p. 373.
27. The law recognizes the psychological effect of such criminal acts and provides additional penal sanction for them. Wolfgang and Sellin report that "the chain store is more outraged by theft from a warehouse, where the offender has no business, than from the store where his presence is legal during store hours." Moreover, "the victim of a house burglary is usually very disturbed by the fact that the offender had the effrontery to enter the house illegally. . . . For these and similar reasons, breaking and entering as well as burglary carry more severe sanctions in the law" (Marvin E. Wolfgang and Thorsten Sellin, *The Measurement of Delinquincy* [New York: John Wiley & Sons, 1964], pp. 219–20).
28. Simmel, "Brücke und Tür," *op. cit.* (see n. 2 above), p. 5.
29. Goffman, *Behavior in Public Places, op. cit.* (see n. 13 above), pp. 83–88.
30. Simmel, "Brücke und Tür," *op. cit.* (see n. 2 above), p. 4.
31. Charles Horton Cooley, *Human Nature and the Social Order* (New York: Schocken Books, Inc., 1964), p. 351.
32. David Riesman, *The Lonely Crowd* (Garden City: Doubleday & Co., 1953), p. 61. Another characterologist, William H. Whyte, suggests that "doors inside houses . . . marked the birth of the middle class" (*The Organization Man* [Garden City, N.Y.: Doubleday & Co., 1956], p. 389).
33. Simmel, "The Secret and the Secret Society," *op. cit.* (see n. 5 above), pp. 320–24. Similarly, Erving Goffman writes, "There is an inescapable opposition between showing a desire to include an individual and showing respect for his privacy. As an implication of this dilemma, we must see that social intercourse involves a constant dialectic between presentational rituals and avoidance rituals. A peculiar tension must be maintained, for these opposing requirements of conduct must somehow be held apart from one another and yet realized together in the same interaction; the gestures which carry an actor to a recipient must also signify that things will not be carried too far" ("The Nature of Deference and Demeanor," *American Anthropologist,* 55 [June, 1956], 488).
34. The absence of ability among infants and children to regulate the appearance and disappearance of their audience does not mean that privacy or separateness is not an important feature of their development; the privacy need is simply expressed differently. The infant, for example, can sometimes remove himself from the field of stimulation by going to sleep or wriggling away from the adult who holds him. This is probably why pathology resulting from overcontact is less likely than that due to under-

contact, for the former is far more easily regulated by the infant than the latter. At a later stage of development, the infant learns that he can hold back and let go in reference not only to sphincters but to facial expressions and general dispositions as well. He comes to view himself as a casual agent as he inherits the power of voluntary reserve. When the child is locomoting he first confronts privacy imposed against him by others and begins to define himself in terms of where he may and may not go. On the other hand, his ambulatory ability gives him enormous control over his audience, a power in which he delights by "hiding." Espionage is practiced as well and suspected in others—whereby the condition of shame begins to acquire meaning for the child. These incomplete comments suffice to illustrate the point that the privacy impulse is not at all inactive in infancy and childhood. They further suggest that each stage of development has its own mode of privacy, which may be defined in terms of the ego's relationship to those from whom privacy is sought and the manner in which withdrawal is accomplished.

35. Goffman, *The Presentation of Self in Everyday Life, op. cit.* (see n. 10 above), pp. 66–86.

36. Simmel, "Brücke und Tür," *op. cit.* (see n. 2 above), p. 4.

37. *Ibid.,* p. 3.

38. Erving Goffman, "The Underlife of a Public Institution," in *Asylums* (Garden City, N.Y.: Doubleday & Co., 1961), p. 231.

39. *Ibid.,* p. 246. For more on norms regulating territorial conduct in face-to-face encounters, see Nancy Felipe and Robert Sommer, "Invasions of Personal Space," *Social Problems,* 14 (May, 1966), 206–14; and Robert Sommer, "Sociofugal Space," *American Journal of Sociology,* 72 (May, 1967), 654–60.

40. Simmel, "Brücke und Tür," *op. cit.* (see n. 2 above), p. 3.

41. Goffman, *Asylums, op. cit.* (see n. 38 above), pp. 248–54.

42. Everett C. Hughes, *Men and Their Work* (Glencoe, Ill.: Free Press, 1958), p. 51.

43. Whyte, *op. cit.* (see n. 32 above), p. 390.

44. Goffman, *Asylums, op. cit.* (see n. 38 above), pp. 319–20.

8

Opening Conversations

Emanuel A. Schegloff

INTRODUCTION

I use "conversation" in an inclusive way. I do not intend to restrict its reference to the "civilized art of talk" or to "cultured inter-
change" as in the usages of Oakeshott (1959) or Priestly (1926),
to insist on its casual character thereby excluding service contacts
(as in Landis and Burtt, 1924), or to require that it be sociable,
joint action, identity related, etc. (as in Watson and Potter, 1962).
"Dialogue," while being a kind of conversation, has special implications derived from its use in Plato, psychiatric theorizing, Buber,
and others, which limits its usefulness as a general term. I mean to
include chats as well as service contacts, therapy sessions as well
as asking for and getting the time of day, press conferences as well
as exchanged whispers of "sweet nothings." I have used "conversation" with this general reference in mind, occasionally borrowing
the still more general term "state of talk" from Erving Goffman.

"Opening Conversations," from "Sequencing in Conversational Openings," Emanuel
A. Schegloff, *American Anthropologist,* Vol. 70, No. 6 (1968), pp. 1075–95. Re-
printed, with editorial changes, by permission of the author and the American
Anthropological Association.

It is an easily noticed fact about two-party conversations that their sequencing is alternating. That is to say, conversation sequence can be described by the formula *ababab,* where "a" and "b" are the parties to the conversation. . . . The *abab* formula is a specification, for two-party conversations, of the basic rule for conversation: *one party at a time.* The strength of this rule can be seen in the fact that in a multi-party setting (more precisely, where there are four or more), if more than one person is talking, it can be claimed not that rule has been violated, but that more than one conversation is going on. Thus Bales can write:

> The conversation generally proceeded so that one person talked at a time, and all members in the particular group were attending the *same conversation.* In this sense, these groups might be said to have a "single focus," that is, they did not involve a number of conversations proceeding at the same time [Bales *et al.,* 1951:461].

When combined with an analytic conception of an utterance, the *abab* specification has a variety of other interesting consequences, such as allowing us to see how persons can come to say "X is silent," when no person in the scene is talking. (For a psychiatric usage, see Bergler, 1938.)

The problem I wish to address is the following: the *abab* formula describes the sequencing of a two-party conversation already underway. It does not provide for the allocation of the roles "a" and "b" (where "a" is a first speaker and "b" is a second speaker) between the two persons engaged in the conversation. Without such an allocation, no ready means is available for determining the first speaker of the convention. The *abab* sequence makes each successive turn sequentially dependent upon the previous one; it provides no resources when who the first speaker might be is treated problematically. I should like to examine the ways in which coordinated entry by two parties into an orderly sequence of conversational turns is managed. (This general area has been considered from a somewhat different perspective in Goffman 1953: chap. 14; see also Goffman, 1965: 88–95).

Notice that I do not mean to identify a "turn" necessarily with any syntactic or grammatical unit or combination of units, nor with any activity. In the former case, it should be clear that a turn may contain anything from a single "mm" (or less) to a string of complex sentences. In the latter, it is crucial to distinguish a single turn in which two activities are accomplished from two turns by the same party without an intervening turn of the other. An example of the latter occurs when a question must be repeated before it is heard or answered; an example of the former is the line, following the inquiry "How are you," "Oh I'm fine. How are you." A "turn," as I am using the term, is thus not the same as what Goffman refers to as a "natural message," which he describes as "the sign behavior of a sender during the whole period of time through which a focus of attention is continuously directed at him" (Goffman, 1953:165). There are, of course, other views of the matter, such as using a period of silence or "appreciable pause" to mark a boundary (as in Stephen and Mishler [1952:600] or Steinzor [1949:109]). But unanalyzed pauses and silences are ambiguous (theoretically) as to whether they mark the boundary of a unit or are included in it (as the very term "pause" suggests).

TELEPHONE CONVERSATION:
THE DISTRIBUTION RULE

A first rule of telephone conversation, which might be called a "distribution rule for first utterances," is: *the answerer speaks first.* Whether the utterance be "hello," "yeah," "Macy's," "shoe department," "Dr. Brown's office," "Plaza 1–5000," or whatever, it is the one who picks up the ringing phone who speaks it.

This rule seems to hold in spite of a gap in the informational resources of the answerer. While the caller knows both his own identity, and, typically, that of his intended interlocutor (whether a specific person or an organization is being phoned), the answerer, at least in most cases, knows only who he is and not specifically who the caller is. That is not to say that no basis for inference might exist, as, for example, that provided by time of day, the history of a relationship, agreed upon signaling arrangements, etc. To the question, "Whom are you calling?" a caller may give a definitive answer, but to the question, "Who's calling?" the answerer, before picking up the phone, can give only a speculative answer.

Without developing a full analysis here, the import of the gap in the answerer's information ought to be noted. If, in this society, persons uniformly used a single standardized item to open a conversation without respect to the identity of the other party or the relationship between the two, then the informational lack would have no apparent import, at least for the opening. This, however, is not the case. A variety of terms may be used to begin conversation and their propriety is geared to the identity, purposes, and relationships of either or both parties. Intercom calls, for example, are typically answered by a "yeah" or "yes" while incoming outside calls are seldom answered in that way (In citations of data in which the police receive the call, "D" refers to the police "dispatcher" and "C" refers to the caller.):

#68
D: Yeah.
C: Tell 85 to take that crane in the west entrance. That's the only entrance that they can get in.
D: O.K. Will do.
C: Yeah.

#88
D: Yes.
C: Uh Officer Novelada.
D: Yes, speaking.
C: Why uh this is Sergeant ———,
D: Yes Sergeant.
C: And uh I just talked to [etc.]

#123
D: Yeah.
C: If you can get a hold of car 83, go'm tell him to go to [etc.]

It may help to gain insight into the working of the distribution rule to consider, speculatively, what might be involved in its violation. One possible violation would involve the following: The distribution rule provides that the answerer normally talks first, immediately upon picking up the receiver. To violate the rule and attempt to have the other person-treated as the one who was called, he would not talk, but would remain silent until the caller spoke first. Suppose after some time the caller says "Hello?" This might be heard as an attempt by the caller to check out the acoustic intactness of the connection. In doing so, the caller employs a lexical item, and perhaps an intonation, that is standardly used by called parties in answering their home phones. This would provide the violator (i.e., the answerer acting as a caller) with a resource. Given the identity of the lexical items used by persons to check out and to answer in this case, the violator may now treat the checking out "hello" as an answering "hello." Continuing the role reversal, he would be required to offer a caller's first remark.

We may note that, without respect to the detailed substance of their remarks, it is a property of their respective utterances that the answerer typically says just "hello," whereas the caller, if he says "hello," typically then adds a continuation, e.g., "this is Harry." Our hypothetical violator, in having to make a caller's first remark to achieve the role reversal, must then say "hello" with a continuation.

To be sure, a caller might say only "hello," so as to invite the called person to recognize who is calling. This is a common attempt to establish or confirm the intimacy or familiarity of a relationship. To cite one instance from our data, in which a police complaint clerk calls his father:

```
#497
Other: Hello
Police: Hello
Other: Hello, the letter, you forgot that letter
Police: Yeah but listen to me, the ——— just blew up, [etc.]
```

The "intimacy ploy," however, is available only to a "genuine" caller, and not to the hypothetical violator under consideration. If the violator says it, the genuine caller might hear it as a correct answerer's first remark that was delayed. The attempted violation would thereupon be frustrated.

In saying "hello" with a continuation, however, the would-be violator would encounter trouble. While trying to behave as a caller, he does not have the information a genuine caller would have. In having to add to the "hello" to play the caller's part, the choice of an appropriate item depends on his knowing (as a genuine caller would know) to whom he is speaking. We may give three examples of what this bind might consist of:

(1). One common addition to a caller's "hello" involves the use of a term of address, for example: Answerer: "Hello?"; Caller:

"Hello, Bill." Not knowing to whom he is speaking, the violator can obviously not employ such an addition.

(2). Another frequent addition is some self-identification appended to the "hello." Self-identification involves two parts; (a) a frame and (b) a term of identification. By "frame" is meant such things as "this is ————," "my name is ————," or "I am ————."[1] Terms of identification include among others, first names, nicknames, or title plus last name. We may note that the choice both of appropriate frames and appropriate self-identification terms varies with the identity and relationship of the two parties. For example, the frame, "My name is ————" is normally used only in identifying oneself to a stranger. Similarly, whether one refers to oneself as Bill or Mr. Smith depends upon the relationship between the two parties. Our imagined violator would not have the information requisite to making a choice with respect to either determination. Although these two examples are not exhaustive of the variety of caller's continuations, a great many calls proceed by use of one or more of them, and in each case a masquerading caller, not having the simple information a genuine caller would have, would have trouble in using such a continuation.

(3). An alternative continuation for a caller, whether used in combination with one of the foregoing continuations or as the caller's next turn suggests another rule of opening conversations: the caller provides the first "topic" of conversation. This rule would confront a violator with the problem of formulating a topic of conversation that could serve appropriately without respect to whom he is speaking. Whether there are such topics is unclear. A promising candidate as a general first topic might seem to be the ritual inquiry "How are you?" or some common variant thereof. This inquiry is usable for a very wide range of conversational others, but not for all conversational others. For example, telephone solicitors or callers from the Chamber of Commerce would not be typically greeted in this way. As formulated here, the rule "The caller provides the first 'topic' " is not nearly as general as the distribution rule. There are obvious occasions where it is not descriptive, as when the "caller" is "returning a call." A formulation that would hold more generally might be "The initiator of a contact provides the first topic." But this alternative is no better in providing a continuation to "hello" that is usable for all conversational others. (It may be noted here that much of the analysis in this section will be superceded below.)

145

148 | *Emanuel A. Schegloff*

Other violations of the distribution rule are readily imaginable, and need not be enumerated here. My interest is chiefly in exploring the operation and constraints provided by the distribution rule, as well as the resources it provides for keeping track of the developing course of a conversation. I found, in attempting to imagine violations, that without the proper operation of the simple distribution rule, it was difficult to keep track of who was who, who the genuine caller and who the violator, the order of events, what remarks were proper for whom, etc. Although I have attempted to describe the hypothetical violation clearly, I fear, and trust, that the reader will have been sore pressed to follow the "play-by-play" account and keep the "players" straight. It may be noted, then, that not only does the distribution rule seem to be routinely followed in the actual practice of telephone conversationalists, but that it provides a format by which observers maintain a grasp of the developing activity.

SUMMONS-ANSWER SEQUENCES

Originally we spoke of two parties to a telephone interaction, a caller and an answerer. The distribution rule held that the answerer spoke first. One of the activities in the material under examination seems to be "answering," and it is appropriate to ask what kind of answering activity is involved and what its properties are.

Let us consider for a moment what kinds of things are "answered." The most common item that is answered is a question, and a standardized exchange is question-answer. At first glance, however, it seems incorrect to regard the "called" party as answering a question. What would be the question? A telephone ring does not intuitively seem to have that status. Other items that are answered include challenges, letters, roll calls, and summonses. It seems that we could well regard the telephone ring as a summons. Let us consider the structure of summons-answer sequences.

It can be noted at the outset that a summons—often called an "attention-getting device"—is not a telephone-specific occurrence. Other classes besides mechanical devices, such as telephone rings, include:

(1) terms of address (e.g., "John?" "Dr.," "Mr. Jones?," "waiter," etc.)
(2) courtesy phrases (e.g., "Pardon me," when approaching a stranger to get his attention)

(3) Physical devices (e.g., a tap on the shoulder, waves of a hand, raising of a hand by an audience member, etc.).

It is to be noted that a summons occurs as the first part of a two-part sequence. Just as there are various items that can be used as summonses, so are there various items that are appropriately used as answers, e.g., "Yes?," "What?," "Uh huh?," turning of the eyes or of the body to face the beckoner, etc. Some typical summons-answer sequences are: telephone ring—"hello"; "Johnny?"—"yes"; "Excuse me"—"Yes"; "Bill?"—looks up.

The various items that may be used as summonses are also used in other ways. "Hello," for example, may be used as a greeting; "Excuse me" may be used as an apology; a name may be used as a term of address only, not requiring an answer. How might we differentiate between the summons uses of such terms and other uses? Taking as an example items whose other use is as terms of address, it seems that the following are ways of differentiating their uses:

(1) When addressing, the positioning of a term of address is restricted. It may occur at the beginning of an utterance ("Jim, where do you want to go?"), at the end of an utterance ("What do you think, Mary?") or between clauses or phrases in an utterance ("Tell me, John, how's Bill?"). As summons items, however, terms of address are positionally free within an utterance. . . . As a mere address term, an item cannot occur between a preposition and its object, but as a summons it may, as in the following telephone call from the data:

#398
C: Try to get out t'—Joe?
D: Yeah?
C: Try to get ahold of [etc.]

(2) Summons items may have a distinctive rising terminal juncture, a raising of the voice pitch in a quasi-interrogative fashion. This seems to be typically the case when a summons occurs after a sentence has already begun, as in the above datum. It need not be the case when the summons stands alone, as in "Jim," when trying to attract Jim's attention.

(3) A term of address is "inserted" in an utterance. By that I mean that after the term of address is introduced, the utterance continues with no break in its grammatical continuity; e.g., "Tell me, Jim, what did you think of. . . ." When a summons occurs in the

course of an utterance, it is followed by a "recycling" to the beginning of the utterance. The utterance is begun again, as in the datum cited in point 1 above. Although in that datum the original utterance is altered when started again, alteration is not intrinsic to what is intended by the term "recycling."

It is an important feature of summonses and answers that, like questions and answers, they are sequentially used. This being so, the unit of our analysis is a sequence of summons and answer, which shall henceforth be abbreviated as "SA" sequence. Question-answer sequences shall be referred to as "QA." We now turn to an examination of two major and several subsidiary properties of SA sequences.

Nonterminality of SA Sequences

By nonterminality I mean that a completed SA sequence cannot properly stand as the final exchange of a conversation. It is a specific feature of SA sequences that they are preambles, preliminaries, or prefaces to some further conversational or bodily activity. They are both done with that purpose, as signaling devices to further actions, and are heard as having that character. This is most readily noticed in that very common answer to a summons "What is it?" Nonterminality indicates that not only must something follow, but that SA sequences are specifically preliminary to something that follows.

Is the continuation upon the completion of an SA sequence constrained in any way, e.g., in which party produces it? The very property of nonterminality is furnished by the obligation of the summoner to talk again upon the completion (by the summoned) of the SA sequence. It is he who has done the summoning and by making a summons incurs the obligation to talk again. With exceedingly rare exceptions, some of which will be noted below, the summoner fulfills this obligation and talks again. It is the fact of the routine fulfillment of the obligation to talk again that produces data in which every conversation beginning with an SA sequence does not terminate there.

It may be noted in passing that the structure of SA sequences is more constraining than the structure of QA sequences. It seems to be a property of many QA sequences that the asker of a question has the *right* to talk again, but not an obligation to do so. SA sentences more forcefully constrain both contributors to them. One way to see the constraining character of nonterminality as a normative property of an SA sequence is by observing what regularly occurs when the summoner, for whatever reason, does not wish to engage in whatever activity the SA sequence he originated may have been preliminary to. Here we characteristically find some variant of the sequence: "Sam?" "Yeah?" "Oh, never mind." Note that in the very attempt to appropriately withdraw from the obligation to continue after a completed SA sequence, an original summoner must in fact conform to it and not simply be silent. Even in telephone conversations between strangers, where maintaining the intactness of some relationship would not seem to be at issue, the obligation to continue talk upon an SA sequence has been observed to hold. For example, in calling an establishment to learn if it is open, that fact may sometimes be established positively when the ringing phone (summons) is lifted and "hello" or an establishment name is heard. Rather than hang up, having obtained the required information, many persons will continue with the self-evidently answered question "Are you still open?" (although note here the common tendency to append to it a more reasonable inquiry, one not rendered superfluous by the very act, as "How late are you open?" even though that might not, on the given occasion, be of interest). The limited rule, "the caller supplies the first topic," advanced earlier may be seen to be one partial application of the obligation of a summoner to talk again.

A property directly related to the nonterminality of SA sequences is their nonrepeatability. Once a summons has been answered, the summoner may not begin another SA sequence. A contrast is suggested with QA sequences where a questioner, having a *right* to talk again after an answer is given, may fill his slot with another question. Although a questioner may sometimes be constrained against asking the same question again (e.g., in two-person interaction: A: "How are you?" B: "Fine." A: "How are you?"), he may choose some question to fill the next slot. A summoner is not only barred from using the same summons again but from doing any more summoning (of the same "other"). If, as occurs on occasion, a summoner does not hear the answer of the other, and repeats the summons, should the answerer hear both summonses he will treat the second one as over-insistent. This is most likely to occur in those situations where physical barriers make it difficult for the summoned person to indicate his having received the summons and having initiated a course of answering. Continued knocking on the door is often met with the complaint as the answerer is on his way, "I'm coming, I'm coming." To sum up, the summoner's obligation to talk again cannot be satisfied by initiating another SA sequence to the same other. This does not mean, however, that one might not have, in a transcript of the opening of a conversation, two SA sequences back-to-back. As we shall shortly see, if the nonterminality property is not met, i.e., should the summoner not fulfill his obligation to talk again, the answerer of the first SA sequence may, in turn, start another with a summons of his own, as in the first line below (E has called M—the initial S):

> M: MacNamara (pause). Hello? (A#S)
> E: Yeah uh John? (A . . .)
> M: Yeah.
> E: I uh just trying to do some uh intercom here in my own set up and get ahold of you at the same time.

Nonterminality is an outcome of the obligation of the summoner to talk again. Corollary to that obligation is the obligation of the answerer, having answered the summons, to listen further. Just as the summoner, by virtue of his summons, obligates himself for further interaction, so the answerer, by virtue of his answer, commits himself to staying with the encounter. Compare, for example, two ways in which a mother may seek to call her child to dinner from a play area. One way would involve the use of his name as a term of address with the request that he return home, e.g., "Johnny, come home. It's time for dinner." It is not an anomalous experience in this culture that such calls may elicit no response from the parties to whom they are directed. It may be claimed, upon complaint about this nonresponse, that the call was not heard. Contrast with this, however, a sequence in which the child is summoned prior to a statement of the summoner's intention. If the child answers the summons, he is stopped from ignoring what follows it, e.g., "Johnny," "Yes?" "Come home for dinner." Children may resist answering the summons, knowing what may follow it, and realizing that to answer the summons commits them to hearing what they do not want to hear. Although they may nonetheless not obey the commandment, claiming they have not heard, it is more difficult if they have answered the summons.

It is to be noted that the nonterminality of an SA sequence and the obligations that produce it are mutually oriented to by the parties to the interaction and may affect the very choice of an answer to the original summons. A prospective answerer of a summons is attuned to the obligation of the summoner to respect the nonterminality of the sequence (i.e., to continue the interaction, either by talk or bodily activity) once the answer is delivered. He is likewise attuned to his obligation, having answered, to be prepared to attend the summoner's obligated next behavior. Should he not be in a position to fulfill this listener's obligation, he may provide for that fact by answering the summons with a "motion to defer," e.g., "John?" "Just a minute, I'll be right there." Of course, such deferrals may, in fact, serve to cancel the interaction, as when a "just a minute" either intendedly or unwittingly exhausts the span of control of the summons.

We now turn to a consideration of another property of SA sequences, one that will allow us to examine not only the relationship between completed SA sequences and their sequels, but the internal structure of the sequences themselves.

CONDITIONAL RELEVANCE IN SA SEQUENCES

The property of conditional relevance is formulated to address two problems. (The term and some elements of the idea of "conditional relevance" were suggested by Sacks [1972].) The first of these is: How can we rigorously talk about two items as a sequenced pair of items, rather than as two separate units, one of which might happen to follow the other? The second problem is: How can we, in a sociologically meaningful and rigorous way, talk about the "absence" of an item; numerous things are not present at any point in a conversation, yet only some have a relevance that would allow them to be seen as "absent." Some items are, so to speak, "officially absent." It is to address these problems that the notion of conditional relevance is introduced. By conditional relevance of one item on another we mean: given the first, the second is expectable; upon its occurrence it can be seen to be a second item to the first; upon its nonoccurrence it can be seen to be officially absent—all this provided by the occurrence of the first item.

We may begin to explicate conditional relevance in SA sequences by employing it to clarify further some materials already discussed. The property of "nonterminality" may be reformulated by saying that further talk is conditionally relevant on a completed SA sequence. In such a formulation we treat the SA sequence as a unit; it has the status of a first item in a sequence for which further talk becomes the second item, expectable upon the occurrence of the first. As noted, the specific focus of this expectation is upon the summoner who must supply the beginning of the further talk. Within this reformulation, if he fails to do so, that fact is officially noticeable and further talk is officially absent. It is by orienting to these facts that an answerer may find further talk coming fast upon him and, if unprepared to fulfill his obligation to attend to it, may seek to defer it by answering "Just a minute," as was noted above.

My main interest in conditional relevance at this point does not, however, have to do with that of further talk upon a completed SA sequence, but with the internal workings of the sequence itself. Simply said, *A is conditionally relevant on the occurrence of S.*

We can see the conditional relevance of A on S most clearly in the following sort of circumstance. If one party issues an S and no A occurs, that provides the occasion for repetition of the S. That is to say, the nonoccurrence of the A is seen by the summoner as its official absence and its official absence provides him with adequate grounds for repetition of the S. We say "adequate grounds" in light of the rule, previously formulated, that the summoner may *not* repeat the S if the sequence has been completed. As long as the sequence is not completed, however, the S may be repeated.

Two qualifications must be introduced at this point, one dealing with the extendability of repetitions of S, the other with the temporal organization of those repetitions relative to the initial S. To take the second point first: In order to find that an A is absent, the summoner need not wait for posterity. In principle, unless some limitation is introduced, the occurrence of S might be the occasion for an indefinite waiting period at some point in which an A might occur. This is not the case. In noting this fact, a subsidiary property of the conditional relevance of A on S may be formulated—the property of immediate juxtaposition.

The following observations seem to hold: In QA sequences, if one asks a question, a considerable amount of silence may pass before the other speaks. Nonetheless, if certain constraints on the content of his remarks (having to do with the relation of their substantive content to the substantive content of the question) are met, then the other's remark may be heard as an answer to the question. Secondly, even if the intervening time is filled not with silence but with talk, within certain constraints some later utterance may be heard as the answer to the question (e.g., *X:* "Have you seen Jim yet?" *Y:* "Oh is he in town?" *X:* "Yeah, he got in yesterday." *Y:* "No, I haven't seen him yet.").

By contrast with this possible organization of QA sequences, the following may be noted about SA sequences. The conditional relevance of an A on an S must be satisfied within a constraint of *immediate juxtaposition*. That is to say, an item that may be used as an answer to a summons will not be heard to constitute an answer to a summons if it occurs separated from the summons. While this point may seem to imply that temporal ordering is involved, it is far from clear that "time" or "elapsed time" is the relevant matter. An alternative, suggested by Harvey Sacks, would make reference to "nextness" plus some conception of "pacing" or of units of activity of finer or coarser grain by reference to which "nextness" would be located.

We may now note the relevance of this constraint to the formulation of the absence of an A. When we say that upon A's absence S may be repeated, we intend to note that A's absence may be found if its occurrence does not immediately follow an S. The phenomenon is encountered when examining occurrences in a series such as S-short pause-S-short pause, or "Dick" . . . no answer . . . "Dick" . . . , etc. In this mechanical age it may be of interest to note that the very construction and operation of the mechanical ring is built on these principles. If each ring of the phone be considered a summons, then the phone is built to ring, wait for an answer, if none occurs, to ring again, wait for an answer, ring again, etc. And indeed, some persons, polite even when interacting with a machine, will not interrupt a phone, but wait for the completion of a ring before picking up the receiver.

The other qualification concerning the repeatability of an S upon the official absence of an A concerns a *terminating rule*. It is empirically observable that S's are not repeated without limitation, until an A is actually returned. There is, then, some terminating rule used by members of the society to limit the number of repetitions of an S. I cannot at this point give a firm formulation of such a terminating rule, except to note my impression that S's are not strung out beyond three to five repetitions at the most. However, that some terminating rule is normally used by adult members of the society can be noted by observing their annoyance at the behavior of children who do not employ it. Despite the formulation in numerical terms, a similar reservation must be entered here as was entered with respect to time above. It is not likely that "number" or "counting" is the relevant matter. Aside from contextual circumstances (e.g., location), the requirement of "immediate juxtaposition" discussed above may be related to the terminating rule(s). It may be by virtue of a telephone caller's assumption of the priority or "nextness" of a response, given the ring of the phone, that the telephone company finds it necessary to use the phone book to advise callers to allow at least ten rings to permit prospective answerers time to maneuver their way to the phone.

While I am unable to formulate a terminating rule for repetitions of S when no A occurs, it is clear that we have a terminating rule when an A does occur: *A terminates the sequence.* As noted, upon the completion of the SA sequence, the original summoner cannot summon again. The operation of this terminating rule, however, depends upon the clear recognition that an A has occurred. This recognition normally is untroubled. However, trouble sometimes occurs by virtue of the fact that some lexical items, e.g., "Hello," may be used both as summonses and as answers. Under some circumstances it may be impossible to tell whether such a term has been used as summons or as answer. Thus, for example, when acoustic difficulties arise in a telephone connection, both parties may attempt to confirm their mutual availability to one another. Each one may then employ the term "Hello?" as a summons to the other. For each of them, however, it may be unclear whether what he hears in the earpiece is an answer to his check, or the other's summons for him to answer. One may, under such circumstances, hear a conversation in which a sequence of some length is constituted by nothing but alternatively and simultaneously offered "hellos." Such "verbal dodging" is typically resolved by the use, by one party, of an item on which a second is conditionally relevant, where that second is unambiguously a second part of a two-part sequence. Most typically this is a question, and the question "Can you hear me?" or one of its common lexical variants, regularly occurs. . . .

The power of the conditional relevance of A on S is such that a variety of strong inferences can be made by persons on the basis of it, and we now turn to consider some of them. We may first note that not only does conditional relevance operate "forwards," the occurrence of an S providing the expectability of an A, but it works in "reverse" as well. If, after a period of conversational lapse, one person in a multi-person setting (and particularly when persons are not physically present but within easily recallable range) should produce an item that may function as an A to an S, such as "What?," or "Yes?," then another person in that environment may hear in that utterance that an unspoken summons was heard. He may then reply "I didn't call you." (This, then, is another sort of circumstance in which we find an immediately graspable error, such as was remarked on earlier.) The connection between a summons and an answer provides both prospective and retrospective inferences.

A further inferential structure attached to the conditional relevance of A on S can lead us to see that this property has the status of what Durkheim (1950) intended by the term social fact; i.e., the property is both "external" and "constraining." When we say that an answer is conditionally relevant upon a summons, it is to be understood that the behaviors referred to are not "casual options" for the persons involved. A member of the society may not "naively choose" not to answer a summons. The culture provides that a variety of "strong inferences" can be drawn from the fact of the official absence of an answer, and any member who does not answer does so at the peril of one of those inferences being made. . . .

What sorts of inferences are involved? A first inference is "no answer–no person." When a person dials a number on the telephone, if the receiver on the other end is not picked up, he may say as a matter of course "there is no one home"; he does not typically announce "they decided not to answer." A person returning home seeking to find out if anyone else is already there may call out the name of his wife, for example, and upon not receiving an answer, may typically take it that she is not home or, while physically home, is not interactionally "in play" (e.g., she may be asleep. The term is from Goffman, 1965). If one person sees another lying on a couch or a bed with eyes closed and calls their name and receives no answer, he takes it that that person is asleep or feigning sleep. He does not take it that the person is simply disregarding the summons. Or, to use a more classical dramatic example, when Tosca, thinking that her lover has been only apparently and not really executed, calls his name, she realizes by the absence of his answer that he is not only apparently dead but really so. She does not take it that he is merely continuing the masquerade.

It is this very structure of inferences that a summoner can make from the official absence of an answer that provides a resource for members of the society who seek to do a variety of insolent and quasi-insolent activities. The resource consists in this: the inference from official absence of an answer is the physical or interactional absence of the prospective answerer. Persons who want to engage in such activities as "giving the cold shoulder," "sulking," "insulting," "looking down their noses at," etc., may employ the fact that such inferences will be made from "no answer" but will be controverted by their very physical presence and being interactionally in play (they are neither asleep nor unconscious). So, although members can, indeed, "choose" not to answer a summons, they cannot do so naively; i.e., they know that if the inference of physical or inter-actional absence cannot be made, then some other inference will, e.g., they are cold shouldering, insulting, etc.

We may note what is a corollary of the inferential structure we have been describing. The very inferences that may be made from the fact of the official absence of an answer may then stand as accounts of the "no answer." So, not only does one infer that "no one is home," but, also "no one is home" accounts for the fact of no answer. Not only may one see in the no answer that "he is mad at me," but one can account for it by that fact. More generally then, we may say that the conditional relevance of A on S entails not only that the nonoccur-rence of A is its official absence, but also that that absence is "ac-countable." Furthermore, where an inference is readily available from the absence of an answer, that inference stands as its account.

However, where no ready inference is available, then no ready account is available and the search for one may be undertaken. Something of this sort would seem to be involved in an incident such as the following: A husband and wife are in an upstairs room when a knock on the door occurs; the wife goes to answer it; after several minutes the husband comes to the head of the stairs and calls the wife's name; there is no answer and the husband runs down the stairs. If the foregoing analysis is correct, we might say that he does so in search of that which would provide an account for the absence of the wife's answer. The point made here does not follow logically, but empirically. From the relationship of the avail-ability of an inference to its use as an account, it does not logically follow that the absence of an inference entails the absence of an account and the legitimacy of a search. An account may not be needed even if absent. It happens, however, that that is so although not logically entailed.

We have now introduced as many of the features of conditional relevance as are required for our further discussion. While the discussion of conditional relevance in this section has focused on the relations between A and S, these features are intrinsic to conditional relevance generally, and apply as well to the relations between completed SA sequences, as a unit, and further talk. If a called person's first remark is treated as an answer to the phone ring's summons, it completes the SA sequence, and provides the proper occasion for talk by the caller. If the conditional relevance of further talk on a completed SA sequence is not satisfied, we find the same sequel as is found when an A is not returned to an S repetition or chaining. In our data:

#86
D. Police Desk (pause). Police Desk (pause). Hello, police desk (longer pause). Hello. (A#AA#A)
C: Hello. (S)
D: Hello (pause). Police Desk? (A#A)
C: Pardon?
D: Do you want the Police Desk?

We turn now to a consideration of the problem of the availability to talk that provides the theoretical importance of SA sequences and opening sequences in general.

THE AVAILABILITY TO TALK

Many activities seem to require some minimum number of participants. For thinking or playing solitaire, only one is required; for dialogue, at least two. When an activity has as one of its properties a requirement of a minimal number of parties, then the same behavior done without that "quota" being met is subject to being seen as an instance of some other activity (with a different minimum requirement, perhaps), or as "random" behavior casting doubt on the competence or normality of its performer. (This is so where the required number of parties is two or more; it would appear for any activity to get done, one party at least must be available.) Thus, one person playing the piano while another is present may be seen to be performing, while in the absence of another he may be seen to be practicing. Persons finding themselves waving to no one in particular by mistake may have to provide for the sense of their hand movement as having been only the first part of a convoluted attempt to scratch their head.

Conversation, at least for adults in this society, seems to be an activity with a minimal requirement of two participants. This may be illustrated by the following observations.

Buses in Manhattan have as their last tier of seats one long bench. On one occasion two persons were observed sitting on this last bench next to one another but in no way indicating that they were, to use Goffman's term (1965:102–103), "with each other." Neither turned his head in the direction of the other and for a long period of time, neither spoke. At one point, one of them began speaking without, however, turning his head in the direction of the other. It was immediately observed that other passengers within whose visual range this "couple" were located, scanned the back area of the bus to find to whom that talk was addressed. It turned out, of course, that the talk was addressed to the one the speaker was "with." What is of interest to us, however, is that the others present in the scene immediately undertook a search for a conversational other. On other occasions, however, similar in all respects but one to the preceding, a different sequel occurred. The dissimilarity was that the talker was not "with" anyone and, when each observer scanned the environment for the conversational other, no candidate for that position, including each scanner himself, could be located. The observers then took it that the talker was "talking to himself" and the passengers exchanged "knowing glances." The issue here could be seen to involve what Bales (1951:87–90) has called "targeting," and, to be sure, that is what the persons in the scene appear to have been attending to. It is to be noted, however, that it is by reference to the character of conversation as a minimally two-party activity that the relevance of seeking the target is established in the first place. In this connection, it may be remarked that such phenomena as "talking to the air" (Goffman, 1953:159) or glossing one's behavior by "talking to oneself," are best understood not as exceptions to the minimal two-party character of conversation, but as special ways of talking to others while not addressing them, of which other examples are given in Bales (1951:89–90).

On another occasion, two persons were observed walking toward one another on a college campus, each of them walking normally. Suddenly one of them began an extremely pronounced and angular walk in which the trunk of his body was exaggeratedly lowered with each step and raised with the next. The one encountering him took such a walk to be a communicative act and immediately turned around to search the environment for the recipient of the communication. In the background a girl was approaching. The two males continued on their respective paths and after some fifteen to twenty paces the one looked back again to see if, indeed, it was to the girl in the background that the gesture was directed.

We have said that conversation is a "minimally two-party" activity. The initial problem of coordination in a two-party activity is the problem of availability; that is, a person who seeks to engage in an activity that requires the collaborative work of two parties must first establish, via some interactional procedure, that another party is available to collaborate. It is clear that a treatment of members' solutions to the problem of availability might, at the same time, stand as a description of how coordinated entry into an interactive course of action is accomplished. Our task is to show that SA sequences are, indeed, germane to the problems both of availability and coordinated entry, and how they provide solutions to both these problems simultaneously.

We must show how the working and properties of SA sequences *establish* the availability of the two parties to a forthcoming two-party interaction (and, in the absence of a completed sequence, foreclose the possibility of the activity) and how they, furthermore, ensure that availability, both at the beginning and in the continuing course of the interaction. We noted before that the absence of an answer to a summons led strongly to the inference of the absence of a party or claimed the other's unavailability to interact. Conversely, the presence of an answer is taken to establish the availability of the answerer; his availability involves, as we have seen, his obligation to listen to the further talk that is conditionally relevant upon the completion of the sequence. In sum, the completion of a sequence establishes the mutual availability of the parties and allows the activity to continue, and failure to complete the sequence establishes or claims the unavailability of at least one of them and perhaps undercuts the possibility of furthering that course of action. . . .

Those who can remember their adolescence may recall occurrences such as the following in their high schools. In the morning, quite often as a first piece of official business, the teacher would "call the roll." In that case, a student, when his name was called, would respond by answering "present" or by raising his hand. Neither party then expected that further interaction between them would occur. Mere presence was being established. If they went to a "proper" high school they may have been required to respond to a teacher's calling of their name in a recitation period by jumping to their feet, and awaiting some further behavior by the teacher. In that situation, their presence already established, they were being summoned to be available for some interaction, typically some examination. Teachers who saw a student physically present but not attentive to the official environment might make that fact observable to the public there assembled by calling a student's name and allowing all to see that he did not answer by standing up and establishing his availability. In that way then, the properties of a summons-answer sequence could be employed not only to establish availability or unavailability but to proclaim it to all who could see.

In telephone interactions, the lifting of a receiver without further ado serves to establish the presence of a person at the called number. It does not, however, establish the availability of that person for further conversation. In this age, in which social critics complain about the replacement of men by machines, this small corner of the social world has not been uninvaded. It is possible, nowadays, to hear the phone you are calling picked up and hear a human voice answer, but nevertheless not be talking to a human. However small its measure of consolation, we may note that even machines such as the automatic answering device are constructed on social, and not only mechanical, principles. The machine's magnetic voice will not only answer the caller's ring but will also inform him when its ears will be available to receive his message, and warns him both to wait for the beep and confine his interests to fifteen seconds. Thereby both $ab\widehat{ab}$ and the properties of SA sequences are preserved.

While the machine's answer to a summoning incoming call is specifically constructed to allow the delivery of the message by the summoner, and is mechanically constructed with a slot for its receipt, the fact that it is a machine gives callers more of an option either to answer or not than they have when the voice emanates from a larynx and not a loudspeaker. One thing that is specifically clear and differentiated between a human and mechanical answerer is that although both may provide a slot for the caller to talk again, the human answerer will then talk again himself whereas currently available machines will not. We have previously provided for the obligation of the answerer to listen to that talk, but we have not yet provided for the possibility that the answerer may then talk again, and it is to that we now turn.

One hitherto unnoticed and important fact about answers to summonses is that they routinely either are, or borrow some properties of, questions. This is most obviously so in the case of "what?" but seems equally so of "yeah?," and "yes?," which three terms, together with glances of the eyes and bodily alignments, constitute the most frequently used answer items. The sheer status of these items as questions, and the particular kinds of questions that they are, allow us to deepen the previous analysis of the obligation of the summoner to talk again upon the completion of the sequence, the obligation of the answer to listen, and what may follow the talk he listens to.

The obligation of the summoner to talk again is not merely a distinctive property of SA sequences. In many activities similar to the SA sequence, where, for example, someone's name may also be called, the caller of it need not talk again to the person called. Such activities as indicating someone's "turn to go," as in a discussion or game, share with "signaling" by rings of the telephone the fact that they are prearranged or invoke some shared orders of priority and relevance. Such activities much more directly can be seen to be pure signaling devices and not summoning devices. That an activity starting, for example, with the enunciation of a name, is a summons, is provided by its assembly over its course. The obligation of the summoner to talk again is, therefore, not merely "the obligation of a summoner to talk again"; it is the obligation of a member of the society to answer a question if he has been asked one. The activity of summoning, is, therefore, not intrinsic to any of the items that compose it; it is an assembled product whose efficacious properties are cooperatively yielded by the interactive work of both summoner and answerer. The signaling devices accomplish different outcomes. By not including questions as their second items, they do not constrain the utterers of their first items to talk again. Rather, they invoke prearrangements, priorities, and shared relevances as matters to which the addressed party must now direct his attention.

We now see that the summons is a particularly powerful way of generating a conversational interaction. We have seen that it requires, in a strong way, that an answer be returned to it. By "in a strong way" we intend that the strong set of inferences we described before attend the absence of an answer, e.g., physical absence, social absence (being asleep or unconscious), or purposeful ignoring. Moreover, it seems to be the case that the answer returned to it has the character of a question. The consequence of this is two-fold: (1) that the summoner now has, by virtue of the question he has elicited, the obligation to produce an answer to it, and (2) the person who asked the question thereby assumes an obligation to listen to the talk he has obligated the other to produce. Thus, sheerly by virtue of this two-part sequence, two parties have been brought together; each has acted; each by his action has produced and assumed further obligations; each is then available; and a pair of roles has been invoked and aligned. To review these observations with specific reference to the two steps that are their locus:

> Summoner: Bill? [A summons item; obligates other to answer under penalty of being found absent, insane, insolent, condescending, etc. Moreover, by virtue of orientation to properties of answer items, i.e., their character as questions, provides for user's future obligation to answer, and thereby to have another turn to talk. Thus, preliminary or prefatory character, establishing and ensuring availability of other to interact.]

> Summoned: What? [Answers summons, thereby establishing availability to interact further. Ensures there will be further interaction by employing a question item, which demands further talk or activity by summoner.]

We may notice that in relating our observations to the first two steps of the sequence we have dealt not only with two steps but with the third as well. We may now show that the span of control of the first two items extends further still. Not only is it the case that a question demands an answer and thereby provides for the third slot to be filled by the summoner, but also one who asks a question, as we noted above, has the right to talk again. The consequence of this is that after the summoner has talked for the second time, this talk will have amounted to the answer to the answerer (of the summons), and the latter will have a right to take another turn. This provides for the possibility of four initial steps following from the use of a summons, which thus emerges as an extraordinarily powerful social item. We have not yet exhausted its power.

We may note that the item the summons elicits in the second slot is not adequately described as merely "a question." It is a question of a very special sort. Its special characteristic may become observable by contrast with other kinds of questions. One not unusual type of question has the property that its asker knows the specific content of the answer that must be returned to it. So, for example, radio interviewers acquainted with the person they are interviewing and perhaps long and intimate friends of theirs, may nonetheless ask such a question as was heard posed to one musician by another who doubles as a disc jockey: "Tell me, Jim, how did you first break into the music?" In a second type of question, while the asker does not know the specific content of the answer, he knows, if we may use a mathematical analogy, the general parameters that will describe it. So, for example, while the doctor in an initial interview may not know specifically what will be answered to his "What seems to be the trouble?" he very readily takes it that the answer will include references to some physical or phychic troubles.

The character of the question that is returned to a summons differs sharply from either of these. Its specific feature seems to be that the asker of "what?" may have little notion of what an accomplished answer may look like, both with respect to its substantive content and with respect to the amount of time that may be necessary for its delivery. This property—the specific ambiguity of what would constitute an answer—is clearly seen in the use that is often made of it by those persons in the society who may have restricted rights to talk. Thus, we may understand the elegance involved in a standardized way in which children often begin conversations with adults. A phrase such as "You know what, Mommy?," inviting a "what?" as its return, allows the child to talk by virtue of the obligation thereby imposed upon him to answer a question while retaining a certain freedom in his response by virtue of the adult's inability to know in advance what would have been an adequate, complete, satisfactory or otherwise socially acceptable answer.

Such an open-ended question does not expand what can be said beyond the constraints of the categorical relationship of the parties. But as compared with other kinds of answers to summonses, it does not introduce additional constraints. Additional constraints may of course be introduced by modifications on "what?," such as intonation or addition (e.g., "what now?"). (Other lexical items used as answers are [on the telephone] "hello" or some self-identification [e.g.

"Macy's"]. For a discussion of the ways the latter items impose additional constraints, see Schegloff [1967: chap. 4].)

In other words, there are constraints on the "contents" of a speaker's remarks once a conversational course is entered into and some conversational "line" is already present to be coordinated to. At the beginning of a conversation, however, no such "line" is already present and the open-endedness of the answer that "what?" allows is a reflection of that fact and the requirement that if there is to be a conversation it must be about something. The fact of open-endedness, however, does not necessarily imply the absence of all constraint. How much constraint is to be put, or can be put, on the content of some opening substantive remark may depend strongly on the relationship of the parties to one another, and that includes not only their relationship as it may turn out to be formulated, but their relationship as it develops from moment to moment. While two parties who are about to be joined by an interaction medium may later be properly categorized as father and son, for them, as the phone rings, and indeed when it is picked up and the "hello" is uttered, they may be strangers. Their relationship to one another may have to be "discovered" while interactional work must precede the "discovery." Under such a circumstance, given that strangers have restricted rights to talk to one another and restricted topics about which they may talk, then a completely open-ended "what" may be a "hazardous" opening for a phone conversation in which, at the moment of its utterance, the other may be a stranger. The consequences of such matters for the infrequence of answers such as "what" or "yes" on the phone, and for the alternatives that may be employed in their stead, are matters that cannot be gone into here.

To conclude the present discussion, it may be noted that provision is made by an SA sequence not only for the coordinated entry into a conversation but also for its continued orderliness. First, we may note, that in the very doing of the two items that constitute SA sequences, and in the two turns these items specifically provide for, the first two alternations of *abab* are produced and that sequence is established as a patterned rule for the interaction that follows.

Insofar as the answerer of the summons does not use his right to talk again to introduce an extended utterance, the work of SA sequences may be seen to extend over a yet larger span of conversation. By "not introducing an extended utterance," I mean that he simply employs one of what might be called the "assent terms" of the society, such as "mmhmm" or "yes" or "yeah," or "uh huh." Under that circumstance the following may be the case: as the initial response to the summons establishes the answerer's availability and commits him to attend the next utterance of the summoner (that is, ensures his continued availability for the next remark), this obligation to listen and this ensurance that he will, may be renewable. Each subsequent "uh huh" or "yes" then indicates the continuing availability of its speaker and recommits him to hear the utterance that may follow. Availability may, in this way, be "chained," and, in fact, speakers with extended things to say may routinely leave slots open for the other to insert an "uh huh," thereby recalling them to and recommitting them to the continuing course of the activity.

It was remarked earlier that conversation is a "minimally two-party" activity. That requirement is not satisfied by the mere copresence of two persons, one of whom is talking. It requires that there be both a "speaker" and a "hearer." To behave as a "speaker" or as a "hearer" when the other is not observably available is to subject oneself to a review of one's competence and "normality." Speakers without hearers can be seen to be "talking to themselves." Hearers without speakers "hear voices." SA sequences establish and align the roles of speaker and hearer, providing a summoner with evidence of the availability or unavailability of a hearer, and a prospective hearer with notice of a prospective speaker. The sequence constitutes a coordinated entry into the activity, allowing each party occasion to demonstrate his coordination with the other, a coordination that may then be sustained by the parties demonstrating continued speakership or hearership. It is by way of the status of items such as "uh huh" and "mmhmm" as demonstrations of continued, coordinated hearership that we may appreciate the fact that they are among the items that can be spoken while another is speaking without being heard as "an interruption."

NOTES

* The research on which the present discussion is based was supported in part by the Advanced Research Projects Agency, Department of Defense, through the Air Force Office of Scientific Research under Contact number AF 49 (638)–1761. I want to acknowledge, as well, the assistance of the

168 | *Emanuel A. Schegloff*

Bureau of Applied Social Research, Columbia University, and its director, Allen Barton. For much of the general approach taken here I am indebted to Harold Garfinkel and Harvey Sacks, and for specific suggestions, doubts, critical remarks, and suggestive additions I am grateful to Erving Goffman, Alan Blum, Michael Moerman, and especially to David Sudnow and Harvey Sacks. Responsibility is, of course, entirely mine.

This discussion is a shortened and modified version of chapters two and three of the author's Ph.D. dissertation (Schegloff, 1967). It is based on the analysis of tape-recorded phone calls to and from the complaint desk of a police department in a middle-sized Midwestern city. References to the "data" in the text should be understood as references to this corpus of materials. Names have been changed to preserve anonymity; numbers preceding citations of data identify calls within the corpus. I wish to thank the Disaster Research Center, Department of Sociology, The Ohio State University, for the use of this recorded material, which was obtained in connection with studies of organizational functioning under stress, especially disaster conditions. The views expressed and the interpretations of the data, of course are those of the author and not necessarily those of the Center.

REFERENCES

R. F. Bales, *Interaction Process Analysis* (Cambridge, Mass.: Addison-Wesley, 1951).
——— *et al.,* "Channels of Communication in Small Group Interaction," *American Sociological Review,* Vol. 25 (1951), pp. 461–68.
E. Bergler, "On the Resistance Situation: The Patient Is Silent," *Psychoanalytic Review,* Vol. 25 (1938), pp. 170–86.
Emile Durkheim, *The Rules of Sociological Method,* Sarah A. Solovay and John H. Mueller, trans., George E. G. Catlin, ed. (Glencoe: Free Press, 1950).
Erving Goffman, "Communication Conduct in an Island Community," Ph.D. dissertation, Department of Sociology, University of Chicago, 1953.
———, *Behavior in Public Places* (Glencoe: Free Press, 1965).
John J. Gumperz and Dell Hymes, eds., "The Ethnography of Communication," *American Anthropologist,* Vol. 66, No. 6 (1964), Part 2.
M. H. Landis and H. E. Burtt, "A Study of Conversations," *Journal of Comparative Psychology,* Vol. 4 (1924), pp. 81–89.
M. Oakeshott, *The Voice of Poetry in the Conversation of Mankind* (London: Bowes and Bowes, 1959).
Charles Perelman, *The Idea of Justice and the Problem of Argument* (London: Routledge and Kegan Paul, 1963).
J. B. Priestly, *Talking* (New York and London: Harper, 1926).
Harvey Sacks, "The Diagnosis of Depression," in David Sudnow, ed., *Studies in Interaction* (New York: Free Press, 1972).

Emanuel A. Schegloff, "The First Five Seconds: The Order of Conversational Openings," Ph.D. dissertation, Deparment of Sociology, University of California, Berkeley, 1967.

B. Steinzor, "The Development and Evaluation of a Measure of Social Interaction," *Human Relations,* Vol. 2 (1949), pp. 103–22, 319–47.

F. F. Stephen and E. Y. Mishler, "The Distribution of Participation in Small Groups: An Exponential Approximation," *American Sociological Review,* Vol. 17 (1952), pp. 598–608.

J. Watson and R. Potter, "An Analytical Unit for the Study of Interaction," *Human Relations,* Vol. 15 (1962), pp. 245–63.

9

Rapping in the Black Ghetto

Thomas Kochman

In the black idiom of Chicago and elsewhere, there are several words that refer to talking; *rapping, shucking, jiving, running it down, gripping, copping a plea, signifying,* and *sounding.* Led by the assumption that these terms, as used by the speakers, referred to different kinds of verbal behavior, this writer has attempted to discover which features of form, style, and function distinguish one type of talk from the other. In this pursuit, we would hope to be able to identify the variable threads of the communication situation: speaker, setting and audience, and how they influence the use of language within the social context of the black community. We also expect that some light would be shed on the black perspective behind a speech event, on those orientating values and attitudes of the speaker that cause him to behave or perform in one way as opposed to another.

Originally published as "Toward an Ethnography of Black American Speech Behavior" and reprinted with permission of the Macmillan Company from *Afro-American Anthropology: Contemporary Perspectives,* edited by Norman E. Whitten, Jr. and John F. Szwed. Copyright © 1970 by The Free Press, a Division of The Macmillan Company. A shorter version of this essay, entitled "'Rapping' in the Black Ghetto," appeared in *Transaction,* Vol. 6, No. 4 (February 1969), pp. 26–34.

The guidelines and descriptive framework for the type of approach used here have been articulated most ably by Hymes in his introduction to the publication, *The Ethnography of Communication* (Gumperz and Hymes, 1964:2ff.), from which I quote:

> In short, "ethnography of communication" implies two characteristics that an adequate approach to the problems of language which engage anthropologists must have. Firstly, such an approach cannot simply take results from linguistics, psychology, sociology, ethnology, as given, and seek to correlate them, however partially useful such work is. It must call attention to the need for fresh kinds of data, to the need to investigate directly the use of language in contexts of situation so as to discern patterns proper to speech activity, patterns which escape separate studies of grammar, of personality, of religion, of kinship and the like, each abstracting from the patterning of speech activity as such into some other frame of reference. Secondly, such an approach cannot take linguistic form, a given code, or speech itself, as frame of reference. It must take as context a community, investigating its communicative habits as a whole, so that any given use of channel and code takes its place as but part of the resources upon which the members of the community draw.
>
> It is not that linguistics does not have a vital role. Well analyzed linguistic materials are indispensable, and the logic of linguistic methodology is a principal influence in the ethnographic perspective of the approach. It is rather that it is not linguistics, but ethnography—not language, but communication—which must provide the frame of reference within which the place of language in culture and society is to be described.

The following description and analysis is developed from information supplied mainly by blacks living within the inner city of Chicago. Their knowledge of the above terms, their ability to recognize and categorize the language behavior of others (e.g., "Man, stop shucking!"), and on occasion, to give examples themselves, established them as reliable informants. Although a general attempt has been made here to illustrate the different types of language behavior from field sources, I have had, on occasion, to rely on published material to provide better examples, such as the writings of Malcolm X, Robert Conot, Iceberg Slim, and others. Each example cited from these authors, however, is regarded as authentic by my informants. In my own attempts at classification and analysis I have sought confirmation from the same group.

Rapping, while used synonymously to mean ordinary conversation, is distinctively a fluent and lively way of talking which is always characterized by a high degree of personal narration, a colorful rundown of some past event. A recorded example of this type of rap follows, an answer from a Chicago gang member to a youth worker who asked how his group became organized.

Now I'm goin tell you how the jive really started. I'm goin tell you how the club got this big. 'Bout 1956 there used to be a time when the Jackson Park show was open and the Stony show was open. Sixty-six street, Jeff, Gene, all of 'em, little bitty dudes, little bitty. . . . Gene wasn't with 'em then. Gene was cribbin (living) over here. Jeff, all of 'em, real little bitty dudes, you dig? All of us were little.

Sixty-six (the gang on sixty sixth street), they wouldn't allow us in the Jackson Park show. That was when the parky (?) was headin it. Everybody say, If we want to go to the show, we go! One day, who was it? Carl Robinson. He went up to the show . . . and Jeff fired on him. He came back and all this was swelled up 'bout yay big, you know. He come back over to the hood (neighbourhood). He told (name unclear) and them dudes went up there. That was when mostly all the main sixty-six boys was over here like Bett Riley. All of 'em was over here. People that quit gang-bangin [fighting, especially as a group], Marvell Gates, people like that.

They went on up there, John, Roy and Skeeter went in there. And they start humbuggin (fighting) in there. That's how it all started. Sixty-six found out they couldn't beat us, at *that* time. They couldn't *whup* seven-o (70). Am I right Leroy? You was cribbin over here then. Am I right? We were dynamite! Used to be a time, you ain't have a passport, Man, you couldn't walk through here. And if didn't nobody know you it was worse than that. . . .

Rapping to a woman is a colorful way of "asking for some pussy." "One needs to throw a lively rap when he is 'putting the make' on a broad" (Horton, 1967:6).

According to one informant the woman is usually someone he had seen or just met, looks good, and might be willing to have sexual intercourse with him. My informant remarked that the term would not be descriptive of talk between a couple "who have had a relationship over any length of time." Rapping then, is used by the speaker at the beginning of a relationship to create a favorable impression and be persuasive at the same time. The man who has the reputation for excelling at this is the pimp, or mack man. Both terms describe a person of considerable status in the street hierarchy, who, by his lively and persuasive rapping (*macking* is also used in this context), has acquired a stable of girls to hustle for him and give him money. For most street men and many teenagers he is the model whom they try to emulate. Thus, within the community you have a pimp walk, pimp style boots and clothes, and perhaps most of all "pimp talk." A colorful literary example of a telephone rap, which one of my informants regards as extreme, but agrees that it illustrates the language, style, and technique of rapping, is set forth in Iceberg Slim's book, *Pimp: The Story of My Life* (© 1967 Holloway House, Los Angeles; used by permission), p. 179. "Blood" is rapping to an ex-whore named Christine in an effort to trap her into his stable.

> Now try to control yourself baby. I'm the tall stud with the dreamy bedroom eyes across the hall in four-twenty. I'm the guy with the pretty towel wrapped around his sexy hips. I got the same hips on now that you x-rayed. Remember that hump of sugar your peepers feasted on?
>
> She said, "Maybe, but you shouldn't call me. I don't want an incident. What do you want? A lady doesn't accept phone calls from strangers."
>
> I said, "A million dollars and a trip to the moon with a bored, trapped, beautiful bitch, you dig? I'm no stranger. I've been popping the elastic in your panties ever since you saw me in the hall. . . ."

Field examples of this kind of rapping were difficult to obtain primarily because talk of this nature generally occurs in private, and when occurring in public places such as parties and taverns, it is carried on in an undertone. However, the first line of a rap, which might be regarded as introductory, is often overheard. What follows are several such lines collected by two of my students in and around the south and west side of Chicago:

> "Say pretty, I kin tell you need lovin' by the way you wiggle your ass when you walk—and I'm jus' the guy what' kin put out yo' fire."
> "Let me rock you mamma, I kin satisfy your soul."
> "Say, baby, give me the key to your pad. I want to play with your cat."
> "Baby, you're fine enough to make me spend my rent money."
> "Baby, I sho' dig your mellow action."

Rapping between men and women often is competitive and leads to a lively repartee, with the woman becoming as adept as the men. An example follows:

A man coming from the bathroom forgot to zip his pants. An unescorted party of women kept watching him and laughing among themselves. The man's friends "hip" [inform] him to what's going on. He approaches one woman—"Hey baby, did you see that big black Cadillac with the full tires ready to roll in action just for you?" She answers—"No mother-fucker, but I saw a little gray Volkswagen with two flat tires."

Everybody laughs. His rap was *capped* (excelled, topped).

When "whupping the game" on a "trick" or "lame" (trying to get goods or services from someone who looks like he can be swindled), rapping is often descriptive of the highly stylized verbal part of the maneuver. In well-established "con games" the verbal component is carefully prepared and used with great skill in directing the course of the transaction. An excellent illustration of this kind of "rap" came from an adept hustler who was playing the "murphy" game on a white trick. The maneuvers in the "murphy" game are designed to get the *trick* to give his money to the hustler, who in this instance poses as a "steerer" (one who directs or steers customers to a brothel), to keep the whore from stealing it. The hustler then skips with the money (Iceberg Slim, 1967:38).

> Look Buddy, I know a fabulous house not more than two blocks away. Brother you ain't never seen more beautiful, freakier broads than are in that house. One of them, the prettiest one, can do more with a swipe than a monkey can with a banana. She's like a rubber doll; she can take a hundred positions.
> At this point the sucker is wild to get to this place of pure joy. He entreats the con player to take him there, not just direct him to it.
> The "murphy" player will prat him (pretend rejection) to enhance his desire. He will say, "Man, don't be offended, but Aunt Kate, that runs the house don't have nothing but highclass white men coming to her place. . . . you know, doctors, lawyers, big-shot politicians. You look like a clean-cut white man, but you ain't in that league are you?"

After a few more exchanges of the "murphy" dialogue, "the mark is separated from his scratch."

An analysis of rapping indicates a number of things. For instance, it is revealing that one raps *to* rather than *with* a person, supporting the impression that rapping is to be regarded more as a performance than a verbal exchange. As with other performances, rapping projects the personality, physical appearance, and style of the performer. In each of the examples given above, in greater or lesser degree, the intrusive "I" of the speaker was instrumental in contributing to the total impression of the rap.

The relative degree of the personality-style component of rapping is generally highest when "asking for some pussy" (rapping 2) and lower when "whupping the game" on someone (rapping 3) or "running something down" (rapping 1). In each instance, however, the personality style component is higher than any other in producing the total effect on the listener.

In asking "for some pussy," for example, where personality and style might be projected through non-verbal means (stance, clothing, walking, looking), one can speak of a "silent rap" when the woman is won without the use of words, or rather, with the words being implied that would generally accompany the non-verbal components.

As a lively way of "running it down" the verbal element consists of two parts: the personality-style component and the information component. Someone *reading* my example of the gang member's narration might get the impression that the information component would be more influential in directing the audience response—that the youth worker would say "So that's how the gang got so big," in which case he would be responding to the information component, instead of saying "Man, that gang member is *bad* (strong, brave)," in which instance he would be responding to the personality-style component of the rap. However, if the reader would *listen* to the gang member on tape or could have been present (*watching-listening*) when the gang-member spoke, he more likely would have reacted more to the personality-style component, as my informants did.

Supporting this hypothesis is the fact that in attendance with the youth worker were members of the gang who *already knew* how the gang got started (e.g., "Am I right, Leroy? You was cribbin over there then"), and for whom the information component by itself would have little interest. Their attention was held by the *way* the information was presented—i.e., directed toward the personality-style component.

The verbal element in "whupping the game" on someone, in the above illustration, was an integral part of an overall deception in which the information component and the personality-style component were skillfully manipulated to control the "trick's" response. But again, greater weight must be given to the personality-style component. In the "murphy game," for example, it was this element which got the trick to *trust* the hustler and to leave his money with him for "safekeeping."

The function of rapping in each of the forms discussed above is *expressive*. By this I mean that the speaker raps to project his personality onto the scene or to evoke a generally favorable response from another person or group. In addition, when rapping is used to "ask for some pussy" (rapping 2) or to "whup the game" on someone (rapping 3), its function is *directive*. By this I mean that rapping here becomes the instrument used to manipulate and control people to get them to give up or do something. The difference between rapping to a *fox* (pretty girl) for the purpose of "getting inside her pants" and rapping to a *lame* to get something from him is operational rather than functional. The latter rap contains a concealed motivation whereas the former does not. A statement made by one of my high school informants illustrates this distinction. "If I wanted something from a guy I would try to *trick* him out of it. If I wanted something from a girl I would try to *talk* her out of it (emphasis mine)."

Shucking, shucking it, shucking and jiving, S-ing and J-ing or just *jiving*, are terms that refer to one form of language behavior practiced by the black when interacting with "the Man" (the white man, the establishment, or *any* authority figure), and to another form of language behavior practiced by blacks when interacting with each other on the peer group level.

When referring to the black's dealings with the white man and the power structure, the above terms are descriptive of the talk and accompanying physical movements of the black that are appropriate to some momentary guise, posture, or facade.

Originally in the South, and later in the North, the black learned that American society had assigned to him a restrictive role and status. Among whites his behavior had to conform to this imposed station and he was constantly reminded to "keep his place." He learned that before white people it was not acceptable to show feelings of indignation, frustration, discontent, pride, ambition, or desire; that real feelings had to be concealed behind a mask of innocence, ignorance, childishness, obedience, humility, and deference. The terms used by the black to describe the role he played before white folks in the South was "tomming" or "jeffing." Failure to accommodate the white southerner in this respect was almost certain to invite psychological and often physical brutality. The following description by black psychiatrist Alvin F. Poussaint (1967:53) is typical and revealing:

Once last year as I was leaving my office in Jackson, Miss., with my Negro secretary, a white policeman yelled, "Hey, boy! Come here!" Somewhat bothered, I retorted: "I'm no boy!" He then rushed at me, inflamed and stood towering over me, snorting "What d'ja say, boy?" Quickly he frisked me and demanded, "What's your name, boy?" Frightened, I replied, "Dr. Poussaint, I'm a physician." He angrily chuckled and hissed, "What's your first name, boy?" When I hesitated he assumed a threatening stance and clenched his fists. As my heart palpitated, I muttered in profound humiliation, "Alvin."

He continued his psychological brutality, bellowing, "Alvin, the next time I call you, you come right away, you hear? You hear?" I hesitated. "You hear me, boy?" My voice trembling with helplessness, but *following my instincts of self-preservation,* I murmured, "Yes, sir." *Now fully satisfied that I had performed and acquiesced to my "boy" status,* he dismissed me with, "Now boy, go on and get out of here or next time we'll take you for a little ride down to the station house! (emphasis mine)."

In northern cities the black encountered authority figures equivalent to the southern "crackers": policemen, judges, probation officers, truant officers, teachers, and "Mr. Charlies" (bosses), and soon learned that the way to get by and avoid difficulty was to *shuck.* Thus, he learned to accommodate "the Man," to use the total orchestration of speech, intonation, gesture, and facial expression to produce whatever appearance would be acceptable. It was a technique and ability that was developed from fear, a respect for power, and a will to survive. This type of accommodation is exemplified by the "Yes sir, Mr. Charlie," or "Anything you say, Mr. Charlie," "Uncle Tom" type "Negro" of the North. The language and behavior of accommodation was the prototype out of which other slightly modified forms of shucking evolved.

Through accommodation, many blacks became adept at concealing and controlling their emotions and at assuming a variety of postures. They became competent actors in the process. Many developed a keen perception of what affected, motivated, appeased, or satisfied the authority figures with whom they came into contact. What became an accomplished and effective coping mechanism for many blacks to "stay out of trouble" became for others a useful artifice for avoiding arrest or "getting out of trouble" when apprehended. *Shucking it* with a judge, for example, would be to feign repentance in the hope of receiving a lighter or suspended sentence, with a probation officer to give the impression of being serious and responsible so that if you violate probation, you would not be sent back to jail. Robert Conot reports an example of the latter in his book (1967:333):

> Joe was found guilty of possession of narcotics. But he did an excellent job of shucking it with the probation officer.

The probation officer interceded for Joe with the judge as follows:

> His own attitude toward the present offense appears to be serious and responsible and it is believed that the defendant is an excellent subject for probation.

Some field illustrations of *shucking* to get out of trouble after having been caught come from some seventh grade children from an inner city school in Chicago. The children were asked to "talk their way out of" a troublesome situation. Examples of the situation and their impromptu responses follow:

> Situation: You're cursing at this old man and your mother comes walking down the stairs. She hears you. Response to "talk your way out of this," "I'd tell her that I was studying a scene in school for a play."
>
> Situation: What if you were in a store and were stealing something and the manager caught you. Responses: "I would tell him that I was used to putting things in my pocket and then going to pay for them and show the cashier."
>
> "I'd tell him that some of my friends was outside and they wanted some candy so I was goin to put it in my pocket to see if it would fit before I bought it."
>
> "I would start stuttering. Then I would say, 'Oh, Oh, I forgot. Here the money is'."
>
> Situation: What do you do when you ditch school and you go to the beach and a truant officer walks up and says, "Are you having fun?" and you say, "Yeah," and you don't know he is a truant officer and then he says, "I'm a truant officer, what are you doing out of school?" Responses: "I'd tell him that I had been expelled from school, that I wasn't supposed to go back to school for seven days."
>
> "I'd tell him that I had to go to the doctor to get a checkup and that my mother said I might as well stay out of school the whole day and so I came over here."
>
> Situation: You're at the beach and they've got posted signs all over the beach and floating on the water and you go past the swimming mark and the sign says "Don't go past the mark!" How do you talk your way out of this to the lifeguard? Responses: "I'd tell him that I was having so much fun in the water that I didn't pay attention to the

sign." "I'd say that I was swimming under water and when I came back up I was behind the sign."

One literary and one field example of shucking to avoid arrest follow. The literary example of shucking comes from Iceberg Slim's autobiography, already cited above (1967:294). Iceberg, a pimp, shucks before "two red-faced Swede rollers (detectives)" who catch him in a motel room with his whore. My underlining identifies which elements of the passage constitute the shuck.

> I put my shaking hands into the pajama pockets. . . . *I hoped I was keeping the fear out of my face. I gave them a wide toothy smile.* They came in and stood in the middle of the room. Their eyes were racing about the room. Stacy was open mouthed in the bed.
>
> I said, *"Yes gentlemen, what can I do for you?"* Lanky said, "We wanta see your I. D."
>
> I went to the closet and got the phony John Cato Fredrickson I. D. I put it in his palm. I felt cold sweat running down my back. They looked at it, then looked at each other.
>
> Lanky said, "You are in violation of the law. You signed the motel register improperly. Why didn't you sign your full name? What are you trying to hide? What are you doing here in town? It says here you're a dancer. We don't have a club in town that books entertainers."
>
> I said, *Officers, my professional name is Johnny Cato. I've got nothing to hide. My full name had always been too long for the marquees. I've fallen into the habit of using the shorter version. My legs went out last year. I don't dance anymore. My wife and I decided to go into business. We are making a tour of this part of the country. We think that in your town we've found the ideal site for a southern fried chicken shack. My wife has a secret recipe that should make us rich here.*

The following example from the field was related to me by one of my colleagues. One Negro gang member was coming down the stairway from the club room with seven guns on him and encountered some policemen coming up the same stairs. If they stopped and frisked him, he and others would have been arrested. A paraphrase of his shuck follows: "Man, I gotta get away from up there. There's gonna be some trouble and I don't want no part of it." This shuck worked on the minds of the policemen. It anticipated their questions as to why he was leaving the club room, and why he would be in a hurry. He also gave *them* a reason for wanting to get up to the room fast.

It ought to be mentioned at this point that there was no uniform agreement among my informants in characterizing the above examples as shucking. One informant used shucking only in the sense in which it is used among the black peer group—viz., bullshitting—and characterized the above examples as *jiving or whupping game*. Others, however, identified the above examples as shucking and reserved *jiving and whupping game* for more offensive maneuvers. In fact, one of the apparent criterial features of shucking is that the posture of the black when interacting with members of the establishment be a *defensive* one. Some of my informants, for example, regarded the example of a domestic who changed into older clothing than she could afford before going to work in a white household as shucking, provided that she were doing it to keep her job. On the other hand, if she would be doing it to get a raise in pay, they regarded the example as *whupping the game*. Since the same guise and set of maneuvers are brought into play in working on the mind and feeling of the domestic's boss, the difference would seem to be whether the reason behind the pose were to protect oneself or to gain some advantage. Since this distinction is not always so clearly drawn, opinions are often divided. The following example is clearly ambiguous in this respect. Frederick Douglass (1968:57), in telling of how he taught himself to read, would challenge a white boy with whom he was playing by saying that he could write as well as the white boy, whereupon he would write down all the letters he knew. The white boy would then write down more letters than Douglass did. In this way, Douglass eventually learned all the letters of the alphabet. Some of my informants regarded the example as whupping game. Others regarded it as shucking. The former were perhaps focusing on the maneuver rather than the language used. The latter may have felt that any maneuvers designed to learn to read were justifiably defensive. One of my informants said Douglass was "shucking *in order to* whup the game." This latter response seems to be the most revealing. Just as one can *rap* to whup the game on someone, so one can *shuck* or *jive* for the same purpose —i.e., assume a guise or posture or perform some action in a certain way that is designed to work on someone's mind to get him to give up something. The following examples from Malcolm X (1965:87) illustrate the use of *shucking* and *jiving* in this context, though *jive* is the term used. Today, *whupping game* might also be the term used to describe the operation.

> Whites who came at night got a better reception; the several Harlem nightclubs they patronized were geared to entertain and *jive* (flatter, cajole) the night white crowd to get their money.

The maneuvers involved here are clearly designed to obtain some benefit or advantage.

> Freddy got on the stand and went to work on his own shoes. Brush, liquid polish, brush, paste wax, shine rag, lacquer sole dressing . . . step by step, Freddie showed me what to do.
>
> "But you got to get a whole lot faster. You can't waste time!" Freddie showed me how fast on my own shoes. Then because business was tapering off, he had time to give me a demonstration of how to make the shine rag pop like a firecracker. "Dig the action?" he asked. He did it in slow motion. I got down and tried it on his shoes. I had the principle of it. "Just got to do it faster," Freddie said. "*It's a jive noise, that's all. Cats tip better, they figure you're knocking yourself out!*" (Malcolm X, 1965:48, emphasis mine).

I was involved in a field example in which an eight-year-old boy whupped the game on me as follows:

> My colleague and I were sitting in a room listening to a tape. The door to the room was open and outside was a soda machine. Two boys came up in the elevator, stopped at the soda machine, and then came into the room and asked: "Do you have a dime for two nickels?" Presumably, the soda machine would not accept nickels. I took out the change in my pocket, found a dime and gave it to the boy for two nickels. After accepting the dime, he looked at the change in my hand and asked, "Can I have two cents? I need carfare to get home." I gave him the two cents.

At first I assumed the verbal component of the maneuver was the rather weak, transparently false reason for wanting the two cents. Actually, as was pointed out to me later, the maneuver began with the first question, which was designed to get me to show my money. He could then ask me for something that he knew I had, making my refusal more difficult. He apparently felt that the reason need not be more than plausible because the amount he wanted was small. Were the amount larger, he would no doubt have elaborated on the verbal element of the game. The form of the verbal element could be directed toward *rapping* or *shucking and jiving*. If he were to rap, the eight-year-old might say, "Man, you know a cat needs to have a little bread to keep the girls in line." Were he to shuck and jive he might make the reason for needing the money more compelling: look hungry, or something similar.

The function of shucking and jiving as it refers to transactions involving confrontation between blacks and "the Man" is both expressive and directive. It is language behavior designed to work on the mind and emotions of the authority figure to get him to feel a certain way or give up something that will be to the other's advantage. When viewed in its entirety, shucking must be regarded as a performance. Words and gestures become the instruments for promoting a certain image, or posture. In the absence of words, shucking would be descriptive of the *actions* which constitute the deception, as in the above example from Malcolm X, where the movement of the shine rag in creating the "jive noise" was the deceptive element. Similarly, in another example, a seventh grade boy recognized the value of stuttering before saying, "Oh, I forgot. Here the money is," knowing that stuttering would be an invaluable aid in presenting a picture of innocent intent. Iceberg showed a "toothy smile" which said to the detective, "I'm glad to see you" and "Would I be glad to see you if I had something to hide?" When the maneuvers seem to be defensive, most of my informants regarded the language behavior as shucking. When the maneuvers were offensive, my informants tended to regard the behavior as "whupping the game." The difference in perception is culturally significant.

Also significant is the fact that the first form of shucking which I have described above, which developed out of accommodation, is becoming less frequently used today by many blacks, as a result of a new found self-assertiveness and pride, challenging the system "that is so brutally and unstintingly suppressive of self-assertion" (Poussaint 1967:52). The willingness on the part of many blacks to accept the psychological and physical brutality and general social consequences of not "keeping one's place" is indicative of the changing self-concept of the black man. Ironically, the shocked reaction of the white power structure to the present militancy of the black is partly due to the fact that the black has been so successful at "putting whitey on" via shucking in the past—i.e., compelling a belief in whatever posture the black chose to assume. The extent to which this attitude has penetrated the black community can be seen from a conversation I recently had with a shoeshine attendant at O'Hare airport in Chicago.

I was having my shoes shined and the black attendant was using a polishing machine instead of the rag that was generally used in the past. I asked whether the machine made his work any easier. He did not answer me until about ten seconds had passed and then responded in a loud voice that he "never had a job that was easy, that he would give me one hundred dollars for any *easy* job I could offer him, that the machine made his job 'faster' but not 'easier.' " I was startled at the response because it was so unexpected and I realized that here was a new "breed of cat" who was not going to *shuck* for a big tip or ingratiate himself with "whitey" anymore. A few years ago his response would have been different.

The contrast between this shoeshine scene and the one illustrated earlier from Malcom X's autobiography, when "shucking whitey" was the common practice, is striking.

Shucking, jiving, shucking and jiving, or *S-ing and J-ing,* when referring to language behavior practiced by blacks when interacting with one another on the peer group level, is descriptive of the talk and gestures that are appropriate to "putting someone on" by creating a false impression, conveying false information, and the like. The terms seem to cover a range from simply telling a lie, to bull-shitting, to subtly playing with someone's mind. An important difference between this form of shucking and that described earlier is that the same talk and gestures that are deceptive to "the Man" are often transparent to those members of one's own group who are able practitioners at shucking themselves. As Robert Conot has pointed out (1967:161), "The Negro who often fools the white officer by 'shucking it' is much less likely to be successful with another Negro. . . ." Also, S-ing and J-ing within the group often has play overtones in which the person being "put on" is aware of the attempts being made and goes along with it for the enjoyment of it or in appreciation of the style involved. An example from Iceberg Slim illustrates this latter point (1967:162):

> He said, "Ain't you the little shit ball I chased outta the Roost?"
> I said, "Yeah, I'm one and the same. I want to beg your pardon for making you salty (angry) that night. Maybe I coulda gotten a pass if I had told you I'm your pal's nephew. I ain't got no sense, Mr. Jones. I took after my idiot father."

Mr. Jones, perceiving Iceberg's shuck, says,

> "Top, this punk ain't hopeless. He's silly as a bitch grinning all the time, but dig how he butters the con to keep his balls outta the fire."

Other citations showing the use of *shucking* and *jiving* to mean simply *lying* follow:

> "It is a *jive* (false) tip but there were a lot of cats up there on humbles (framed up charges)" (Brown, 1965:142).
> How would you like to have half a "G" ($500) in your slide (pocket)?
> I said, "All right, give me the poison and take me to the baby."

He said, "I ain't *shucking* (lying). It's creampuff work" (Iceberg Slim, 1967:68).

Running it down is the term used by ghetto dwellers when they intend to communicate information, either in the form of an explanation, narrative, giving advice, and the like. The information component in the field example cited under rapping (1) would constitute the "run down." In the following literary example, Sweet Mac is "running this Edith broad down" to his friends (King, 1965:24):

> Edith is the "saved" broad who can't marry out of her religion . . . or do anything else out of her religion for that matter, especially what I wanted her to do. A bogue religion, man! So dig, for the last couple weeks I been quoting the Good Book and all that stuff to her; telling her I am now saved myself, you dig.

The following citation from Claude Brown (1965:390) uses the term with the additional sense of giving advice:

> If I saw him (Claude's brother) hanging out with cats I knew were weak, who might be using drugs sooner or later, I'd *run it down* to him.

Iceberg Slim (1967:79) asks a bartender regarding a prospective whore:

> Sugar, *run her down* to me. Is the bitch qualified? Is she a whore? Does she have a man?

It seems clear that running it down has simply an informative function, telling somebody something that he doesn't already know.

Gripping is of fairly recent vintage, used by black high school students in Chicago to refer to the talk and facial expression that accompanies a *partial* loss of face or selfpossession, or displaying of fear. Its appearance alongside *copping a plea,* which refers to a total loss of face, in which one begs one's adversary for mercy, is a significant new perception. Linking it with the street code which acclaims the ability to "look tough and inviolate, fearless, secure, 'cool' " (Horton, 1967:11) suggests that even the slightest weakening of this posture will be held up to ridicule and contempt. There are always contemptuous overtones attached to the use of the term when applied to others' behavior. One is tempted to link it further with the degree of violence and level of toughness that is required to survive on the street. The intensity of both seems to be increasing. As one of my informants noted, "Today, you're *lucky* if you end up in the hospital" (i.e., are not killed).

Both *gripping* and *copping a plea* refer to behavior that stems from fear and a respect for superior power. An example of gripping comes from the record *Street and Gangland Rhythms* (Band 4, Dumb boy). Lennie meets Calvin and asks him what happened to his lip. Calvin tells Lennie that a boy named Pierre hit him for copping off him in school. Lennie, pretending to be Calvin's brother, goes to confront Pierre. Their dialogue follows:

> Lennie: "Hey you! What you hit my little brother for?"
> Pierre: "Did he tell you what happen man?"
> Lennie: "Yeah, he told me what happen."
> Pierre: "But you . . . but you . . . but you should tell your people to teach him to go to school, man. (Pause) I . . . I know . . . I know I didn't have a right to hit him."

Pierre, anticipating a fight with Lennie if he continued to justify his hitting of Calvin, tried to avoid it by "gripping" with the last line.

Copping a plea, originally used to mean "to plead guilty to a lesser charge to save the state the cost of a trial" (Wentworth and Flexner, 1960:123) (with the hope of receiving a lesser or suspended sentence), but is now generally used to mean "to beg, plead for mercy," as in the example "Please cop, don't hit me. I give" (*Street and Gangland Rhythms,* Band 1, Gang fight). This change of meaning can be seen from its use by Piri Thomas (1967:316) in *Down These Mean Streets*.

> The night before my hearing, I decided to make a prayer. It had to be on my knees, cause if I was gonna *cop a plea* to God, I couldn't play it cheap.

For the original meaning, Thomas (1967:245) uses "deal for a lower plea."

> I was three or four months in the Tombs, waiting for a trial, going to court, waiting for adjournments, trying to *deal for a lower plea,* and what not.

The function of gripping and copping a plea is obviously expressive. One evinces noticeable feelings of fear and insecurity which result in a loss of status among one's peers. At the same time one may arouse in one's adversary feelings of contempt.

An interesting point to consider with respect to copping a plea is whether the superficial features of the form may be borrowed to mitigate one's punishment, in which case it would have the same directive function as shucking, and would be used to arouse feelings of pity, mercy, and the like. The question whether one can arouse such feelings among one's street peers by copping a plea is unclear. In the example cited above from the record *Street and Gangland Rhythms,* which records the improvisations of eleven- and twelve-year-old boys, one of the boys convincingly *acts out* the form of language behavior, which was identified by all my informants as "copping a plea" with the police officer: "Please cop, don't hit me. I give." In this example it was clearly an artifice with a directive function and here we have the familiar dynamic opposition of black vs. authority figure discussed under shucking.

"Signifying" is the term used to describe the language behavior that, as Abrahams has defined it, attempts to "imply, goad, beg, boast by indirect verbal or gestural means" (1964:267). In Chicago it is also used as a synonym to describe a form of language behavior which is more generally known as "sounding" elsewhere and will be discussed under the latter heading below.

Some excellent examples of signifying as well as of other forms of language behavior discussed above come from the well known "toast" (narrative form) "The signifying monkey and the lion" which was collected by Abrahams from black street corner bards in Philadelphia. In the above toast the monkey is trying to get the lion involved in a fight with the elephant (Abrahams, 1964:150 ff.):

> Now the lion came through the jungle one peaceful day,
> When the signifying monkey stopped him, and that is what he started to say:
> He said, "Mr. Lion," he said, "A bad-assed motherfucker down your way,"
> He said, "Yeah! The way he talks about your folks is a certain shame.
> "I've even heard him curse when he mentioned your grandmother's name."
> The lion's tail shot back like a forty-four
> When he went down the jungle in all uproar.

Thus the monkey has goaded the lion into a fight with the elephant by "signifying," indicating that the elephant has been "sounding on" (insulting) the lion. When the lion comes back, thoroughly beaten up, the monkey again "signifies" by making fun of the lion:

... a lion came back through the jungle more dead than alive,
When the monkey started some more of that signifying jive.
He said, "Damn, Mr. Lion, you went through here yesterday, the jungle rung.
"Now you come back today, damn near hung."

The monkey, of course, is delivering this taunt from a safe distance away on the limb of a tree when his foot slips and he falls to the ground, at which point

Like a bolt of lightning, a stripe of white heat,
The lion was on the monkey with all four feet.

In desperation the monkey quickly resorts to "copping a plea":

The monkey looked up with a tear in his eyes.
He said, "Please, Mr. Lion, I apologize."

His "plea," however, fails to move the lion to any show of pity or mercy so the monkey tries another verbal ruse: "shucking":

He said, "You lemme get my head out of the sand
Ass out of the grass, I'll fight you like a natural man."

In this he is more successful as

The lion jumped back and squared for a fight.
The motherfucking monkey jumped clear out of sight.

A safe distance away again, the monkey returns to "signifying":

He said, "Yeah, you had me down, you had me at last.
But you left me free, now you can still kiss my ass."

The above example illustrates the methods of provocation, goading, and taunting as artfully practiced by the signifier. Interestingly, when the *function* of signifying is *directive,* the *tactic* which is employed is one of *indirection*—i.e., the signifier reports or repeats what someone else has said about the listener; the "report" is couched in plausible language designed to compel belief and arouse feelings of anger and hostility. There is also implication that if the listener fails to do anything about it—what has to be "done" is usually quite clear—his status will be seriously compromised. Thus the lion is compelled to vindicate the honor of his family by fighting or else leave the impression that he is afraid, and that he is not "king" of the jungle. When used to direct action, "signifying" is like "shucking" in also being deceptive and subtle in approach and depending for success on the naivete or gullibility of the person being "put on."

When the function of signifying is only expressive (i.e., to arouse feelings of embarrassment, shame, frustration or futility, for the purpose of diminishing someone's status, but without directive implication), the tactic employed is direct in the form of a taunt, as in the above example where the monkey is making fun of the lion. Signifying frequently occurs when things are dull and someone wishes to generate some excitement and interest within the group. This is shown in another version of the above toast:

> There hadn't been no disturbin in the jungle for quite a bit,
> For up jumped the monkey in the tree one day and laughed, "I guess I'll start some shit."

Sounding is the term which is today most widely known for the game of verbal insult known in the past as "playing the dozens," "the dirty dozens," or just "the dozens." Other current names for the game have regional distribution: *signifying* or "sigging" (Chicago), *joning* (Washington, D.C.), *screaming* (Harrisburg), and so on. In Chicago, the term "sounding" would be descriptive of the initial remarks which are designed to "sound" out the other person to see whether he will play the game. The verbal insult is also subdivided, the term "signifying" applying to insults which are hurled directly at the person and the "dozens" applying to insults which are hurled directly at the person and the "dozens" applying to insults hurled at your opponent's family, especially, the mother.

Sounding is often catalyzed by "signifying" remarks referred to earlier, such as "Are you going to let him say that about your mama?" in order to spur on an exchange between two (or more) other members of the group. It is begun on a relatively low key and built up by means of verbal exchanges.

Abrahams (1962b:208–10) describes the game:

> One insults a member of another's family; others in the group make disapproving sounds to spur on the coming exchange. The one who has been insulted feels at this point that he must reply with a slur on the protagonist's family which is clever enough to defend his honor (and therefore that of his family). This, of course, leads the other (once again, more due to pressure from the crowd than actual insult) to make further jabs. This can proceed until everyone is bored with the whole affair, until one hits the other (fairly rare), or until some

other subject comes up that interrupts the proceedings (the usual state of affairs).

McCormick (1960:8) describes the dozens as a verbal contest

... in which the players strive to bury one another with vituperation. In the play, the opponent's mother is especially slandered ... then, in turn fathers are identified as queer and syphilitic. Sisters are whores, brothers are defective, cousins are "funny" and the opponent is himself diseased.

An example of the "game" collected by one of my students goes as follows:

Frank looked up and saw Leroy enter the Outpost. Leroy walked past the room where Quinton, "Nap," "Pretty Black," "Cunny," Richard, Haywood, "Bull," and Reese sat playing cards. As Leroy neared the T.V. room, Frank shouted to him.

Frank: "Hey, Leroy, your mama—calling you man."

Leroy turned and walked toward the room where the sound came from. He stood in the door and looked at Frank.

Leroy: "Look motherfuckers, I don't play that shit."

Frank, signifying: "Man, I told you cats 'bout that mama jive" (as if he were concerned about how Leroy felt).

Leroy: "That's all right Frank; you don't have to tell those funky motherfuckers nothing; I'll fuck me up somebody yet."

Frank's face lit up as if he were ready to burst his side laughing. "Cunny" became pissed at Leroy.

Cunny: "Leroy, you stupid bastard, you let Frank make a fool of you. *He* said that 'bout your mama."

"Pretty Black": "Aw, fat ass head, 'Cunny' shut up."

"Cunny": "Ain't that some shit. This black slick head motor flicker got nerve 'nough to call somebody 'fathead.' Boy, you so black, you sweat super Permalube Oil."

This eased the tension of the group as they burst into loud laughter.

"Pretty Black": "What 'chu laughing 'bout 'Nap,' with your funky mouth smelling like dog shit."

Even Leroy laughed at this.

"Nap": "Your mama motherfucker."

"Pretty Black": "Your funky mama too."

"Nap" strongly: "It takes twelve barrels of water to make a steamboat run; it takes an elephant's dick to make your Grandmammy come; she been elephant fucked, camel fucked and hit side the head with your Grandpappy's nuts."

Reese: "Goddor damn; go on and rap motherfucker."

Reese began slapping each boy in his hand, giving his positive approval of "Nap's" comment. "Pretty Black," in an effort not to be outdone but directing his verbal play elsewhere, stated:

"Pretty Black": "Reese, what you laughing 'bout? You so square you shit bricked shit."

Frank: "Whooooowee!"

Reese sounded back: "Square huh, what about your nappy ass hair before it was stewed; that shit was so bad till, when you went to bed at night, it would leave your head and go on the corner and meddle."

The boys slapped each other in the hand and cracked up.

"Pretty Black": "On the streets meddling, bet Dinky didn't offer me no pussy and I turned it down."

Frank: "Reese scared of pussy."

"Pretty Black": "Hell yeah; the greasy mother rather fuck old, ugly, funky cock Sue Willie than get a piece of ass from a decent broad."

Frank: "Goddor damn! Not Sue Willie."

"Pretty Black": "Yeah ol' meat beating Reese rather screw that cross-eyed, clapsy bitch, who when she cry, tears drip down her ass."

Haywood: "Don't be so mean, Black."

Reese: "Aw shut up, you half-white bastard."

Frank: "Wait man, Haywood ain't gonna hear much more of that half-white shit; he's a brother too."

Reese: "Brother, my black ass; that white ass landlord gotta be this motherfucker's paw."

"Cunny": "Man, you better stop foolin with Haywood; he's turning red."

Haywood: "Fuck yall" (as he withdrew from the "sig" game).

Frank: "Yeah, fuck yall; let's go to the stick hall."

The above example of "sounding" is an excellent illustration of the "game" as played by fifteen-, sixteen-, and seventeen-year-old Negro boys, some of whom have already acquired the verbal skill which for them is often the basis for having a high "rep." Abrahams (1964:62) observed that ". . . the ability with words is as highly valued as physical strength." In the sense that the status of one of the participants in the game is diminished if he has to resort to fighting to answer a verbal attack, verbal ability may be even more highly regarded than physical ability. However, age within the peer group may be a factor in determining the relative value placed on verbal vis-à-vis physical ability.

Nevertheless, the relatively high value placed on verbal ability must be clear to most black boys at an early age in their cognitive development. Abrahams (1964:53) is probably correct in linking "sounding" to the taunt which is learned and practiced as a child and is part of "signifying," which has its origins in childlike behavior. The taunts of the "Signifying Monkey," illustrated above, are good examples of this.

Most boys begin their activity in "sounding" by compiling a repertoire of "one liners." When the game is played among this age group the one who has the greatest number of such remarks wins. Here are some examples of "one liners" collected from fifth and sixth grade black boys in Chicago:

> Yo mama is so bowlegged, she looks like the bite out of a donut.
> You mama sent her picture to the lonely hearts club, and they sent it back and said "We ain't that lonely"!
> Your family is so poor the rats and roaches eat lunch out.
> Your house is so small the roaches walk single file.
> I walked in your house and your family was running around the table. I said, "Why you doin that?" Your mama say, "First one drops, we eat."

Real proficiency in the game comes to only a small percentage of those who play it, as might be expected. These players have the special skill in being able to turn what their opponents have said and attack them with it. Thus, when someone indifferently said "fuck you" to Concho, his retort was immediate and devastating: "Man, you haven't even kissed me yet."

The "best talkers" from this group often become the successful street-corner, barber shop, and pool hall story tellers who deliver the long, rhymed, witty narrative stories called "toasts." A portion of the toast "The Signifying Monkey and the Lion" was given above. However, it has also produced entertainers, such as Dick Gregory and Redd Foxx, who are virtuosos at repartee, and preachers, whose verbal power has been traditionally esteemed.

The function of the "dozens" or "sounding" is invariably self-assertive. The speaker borrows status from his opponent through an exercise of verbal power. The opponent feels compelled to regain his status by "sounding" back on the speaker or some other member of the group whom he regards as more vulnerable. The social interaction of the group at the Outpost, for example, demonstrated less an extended verbal barrage between two people than a "pecking order." Frank "sounds" on Leroy; "Cunny" "signifies" on Leroy; "Pretty Black" "sounds" on "Cunny"; "Cunny" "sounds" back on "Pretty Black" who (losing) turns on "Nap"; "Nap" "sounds" (winning) back on "Pretty Black"; "Pretty Black" finally borrows back his status by "sounding" on Reese. Reese "sounds" back on "Pretty Black" but gets the worst of the exchange and so borrows back his status from Haywood. "Cunny" also "sounds" on Haywood. Haywood defaults. Perhaps by being "half-white," Haywood feels himself to be the most vulnerable.

The presence of a group seems to be especially important in controlling the game. First of all, one does not "play" with just anyone since the subject matter is concerned with things that in reality one is quite sensitive about. It is precisely *because* "Pretty Black" has a "black slick head" that makes him vulnerable to "Cunny's" barb, especially now when the Afro-American "natural" hair style is in vogue. It is precisely *because* Reese's girl-friend *is* ugly that makes him vulnerable to "Pretty Black's" jibe that Reese can't get a "piece of ass from a decent broad." It is *because* the living conditions are so poor and intolerable that they can be used as subject matter for "sounding." Without the control of the group "sounding" will frequently lead to a fight. This was illustrated by a tragic epilogue concerning Haywood; when Haywood was being "sounded" on in the presence of two girls by his best friend (other members of the group were absent), he refused to tolerate it. He went home, got a rifle, came back, and shot and killed his friend. In the classroom from about the fourth grade on fights among black boys invariably are caused by someone "sounding" on the other person's mother.

Significantly, the subject matter of "sounding" is changing with the changing self-concept of the black with regard to those physical characteristics that are characteristically "Negro," and which in the past were vulnerable points in the black psyche: blackness and "nappy" hair.

They still occur, as in the above example: from the Outpost, and the change in the above illustration is notably more by what has been added than subtracted—viz., the attack on black *slick* hair and half-white color. With regard to the latter, however, it ought to be said that for many blacks, blackness was always highly esteemed and it might be more accurate to regard the present sentiment of the black community toward skin color as reflecting a shifted attitude for only a *portion* of the black community. This suggests that "sounding" on someone's light skin color is not new. Nevertheless, one can regard the previously favorable attitude toward light skin color and "good hair" as the prevailing one. "Other things being equal, the more closely a woman approached her white counterpart, the more attractive she was considered to be, by both men and women alike. 'Good hair' (hair that is long and soft) and light skin were the chief criteria" (Liebow, 1966:138). Also, children's rhymes which before "black power" were

> If you like black
> Keep your black ass back
>
> and
>
> If you like white
> You're all right

have respectively changed to

> If you like black
> You have a Cadillac
>
> and
>
> If you like white
> You're looking for a fight.

Both Abrahams and McCormick link the "dozens" to the over-all psychosocial growth of the black male. McCormick has stated that a "single round of a dozen or so exchanges frees more pent-up aggressions than will a dose of sodium pentothal." The fact that one permits a kind of abuse within the rules of the game and within the confines of the group which would otherwise not be tolerated is filled with psychological importance, and this aspect is rather fully discussed by Abrahams. It also seems important, however, to view its function from the perspective of the non-participating members of the group. Its function for them may be directive: i.e., they incite and prod individual members of the group to combat for the purpose of energizing the elements, of simply relieving the boredom of just "hanging around" and the malaise of living in a static and restrictive environment. One of my informants remarked that he and other members of the group used to feed insults to one member to hurl back at another if they felt that the contest was too uneven, "to keep the game going." In my above illustration from the Outpost, for example, Frank seemed to be the precipitating agent as well as chorus for what was going on and "Bull" did not directly participate at all. For them the "dozens" may have had the social function of "having a little fun," or as Loubee said to Josh of just "passing the time" (Shorris, 1966: 65).

A summary analysis of the different forms of language behavior which have been discussed permit the following generalizations.

The prestige norms which influence black speech behavior are those which have been successful in manipulating and controlling people and situations. The function of all of the forms of language behavior discussed above, with the exception of "running it down," was either expressive or expressive-directive. Specifically, this means that language was used to project personality, assert oneself, or arouse emotion, frequently with the additional purpose of getting the person to give up or do something which will be of some benefit to the speaker. Only "running it down" has as its primary function to communicate information and often here, too, the personality and style of the speaker in the form of "rapping" is projected along with the information.

The purpose for which language is used suggests that the speaker views the social situations into which he moves as essentially agonistic, by which I mean that he sees his environment as consisting of a series of transactions which require that he be continually ready to take advantage of a person or situation or defend himself against being victimized. He has absorbed what Horton (1967:8) has called "street rationality." As one of Horton's respondents put it: "The good hustler . . . conditions his mind and must never put his guard down too far, to relax, or he'll be taken."

I have carefully avoided, throughout this paper, delimiting the group within the black community of whom the language behavior and perspective of their environment is characteristic. While I have no doubt that it is true of those who are generally called "street people" I am not certain of the extent to which it is also true of a much larger portion of the black community, especially the male segment. My informants consisted of street people, high school students, and blacks, who by their occupation as community and youth workers possess what has been described as a "sharp sense of the streets." Yet it is difficult to find a black male in the community who has *not* witnessed or participated in the "dozens" or heard of "signifying," or "rapping," or "shucking and jiving" at some time while he was growing up. It would be equally difficult to imagine a high school student in a Chicago inner city school not being touched by what is generally regarded a "street culture" in some way.

In conclusion, by blending style and verbal power, through "rapping," "sounding," and "running it down," the black in the ghetto establishes his personality; through "shucking," "gripping," and "copping a plea" he shows his respect for power; through "jiving" and "signifying" he stirs up excitement. With all of the above, he hopes to manipulate and control people and situations to give himself a winning edge.

REFERENCES

Roger D. Abrahams, "Playing the Dozens," *Journal of American Folklore*, Vol. 75 (1962), pp. 209–20.

————, *Deep Down in the Jungle . . . Negro Narrative Folklore from the Streets of Philadelphia* (Hatboro, Pa.: Folklore Associated, 1964).

Claude Brown, *Manchild in the Promised Land* (New York: Macmillan, 1965).

Robert Conot, *Rivers of Blood, Years of Darkness* (New York: Bantam, 1967).

Frederick Douglass, *Narrative of the Life of an American Slave* (New York: New American Library, 1968).

John J. Gumpera and Dell Hymes, eds. "The Ethnography of Communication," *American Anthropologist*, Vol. 66, No. 6 (1964), Part 2.

John Horton, "Time and Cool People," *Trans-action*, Vol. 4 (1967), pp. 5–12.

Woodie King, Jr., "The Game," *Liberator*, Vol. 5 (1965), pp. 20–25.

Elliot Liebow, *Tally's Corner: A Study of Negro Streetcorner Men* (Boston: Little, Brown, 1966).

Mack McCormick, "The Dirty Dozens: The Unexpurgated Folksongs of Men," Arhoolie record album.

Malcolm X, *The Autobiography of Malcolm X* (New York: Grove Press, 1965).

Alvin F. Poussaint, "A Negro Psychiatrist Explains the Negro Psyche," *The New York Times* (August 20, 1967), Section 6, pp. 52ff.

Earl Shorris, *Ofay* (New York: Dell, 1966).

Iceberg Slim, *Pimp: The Story of My Life* (Los Angeles: Holloway House, 1967).

Piri Thomas, *Down These Mean Streets* (New York: Knopf, 1967).

Harold Wentworth and Stuart Berg Flexner, *Dictionary of American Slang* (New York: Crowell, 1960).

10

The Human Choice:
Individuation, Reason and Order
Vs. Deindividuation, Impulse and Chaos

Philip G. Zimbardo

CONSISTENCY, RATIONALITY, AND RESPONSIBILITY

It is frequently necessary to strive for consistency because consistency between action and self-knowledge, between word and deed, is so prized in our culture that to be inconsistent is to be abnormal. If one's behavior is not comparable to that of people whom he uses for reference, then he must establish the rationality of his behavioral commitment. He must first convince his observing, critical self (who stands in for society) that his commitment follows *rationally* from an analysis of the stimulus conditions. It is irrational to expose oneself to a series of shocks previously experienced and known to be painful, especially when one is given little justification for doing so, as well as an explicit option to refuse (cf. Zimbardo, Cohen, Weisenberg, Dworkin, and Firestone, 1966). This psycho-logical self-deception

"The Human Choice: Individuation, Reason and Order vs. Deindividuation, Impulse and Chaos," Philip G. Zimbardo, from the Nebraska Symposium on Motivation, March 1969. Copyright © 1969 by the University of Nebraska Press. Reprinted by permission of the author and the University of Nebraska Press.

induces motivational changes which lower the drive state to match the behavioral commitment.

The psychological homeostasis posited by such a consistency principle is not an end in itself, but rather a means toward minimizing dependency on the environment and maximizing control over it. This is achieved not by accepting the environment as given but by modifying it to effect a "rational" fit after the commitment. The response then comes to determine the nature of the stimulus, rather than the opposite. It has been said:

> On a more primitive, personal level, consistency is a safeguard against chaos, it is the ordering aspect of rationality that is in constant struggle with the irrational forces within and outside the individual. Thus, consistency becomes a self-imposed principle in order for the individual to maintain a conception of himself as a normal member of society who, in behaving as others expect him to, gains their social recognition (the most potent of all reinforcers) as a rational decision-maker, whose decisions help him to control his environment. [Zimbardo, 1969, p. 280]

Volition, commitment, and responsibility fuse to form the core of one pole of the basic human choice[1] we shall be considering in this chapter. The act of freely making a commitment for which one assumes responsibility *individuates* the decision-maker. By this readiness to enter into a contractual agreement which has consequences for which he must be liable, man sets himself in opposition to all those who refuse to act individually, and thus separates himself from tribal ties to undifferentiated (safer) group action.

If the reader will be indulgent enough to sustain another flight of rhetoric, we can say that one way of conceptualizing the research we have done on the cognitive control of motivation is in terms of freedom. Through utilizing cognitive controls (of virtually limitless potential) man gains freedom from the behavioral prescriptions imposed by his history, physiology, and ecology. Indeed, thinking and believing can make it so!

ALL CONTROL BE DAMNED

"The eyes of chaos shining through the veil of order."—R. Rolland

While we were myopically uncovering the many implications of this approach and were demonstrating in the laboratory the remarkably fine degree of control which man had at his disposal, all hell was breaking loose outside in the real world. All about us—from the mass media, from our everyday observations, from reliable anecdotes—the evidence overwhelmingly points to a very different conception of the human organism. Reason, premeditation, the acceptance of personal responsibility, the feeling of obligation, the rational defense of commitments, appear to be losing ground to an impulse-dominated hedonism bent on anarchy.

Perhaps after surveying a portion of this evidence thrust upon our sensibilities, we can draw some inferences about the processes involved which may help clarify the nature of the other, darker side of the Human Choice we are considering.

1. SELF-DESTRUCTION

For each of the one thousand suicides committed every day, the UN's World Health Organization estimates (in its booklet *Prevention of Suicide,* 1968) that another seven attempts at self-destruction are unsuccessful. The means vary across countries—hanging in Nigeria, poison in Brazil, gas in Great Britain, guns for American men and asphyxiation for American women. There appear, however, to be some common causes which bridge national boundaries, notably social isolation from family or friends and a break with one's routine or habitual life pattern. Self-mutilation can also come under other guises, as seen in a report from two villages in Manila where hundreds of Filipinos "flogged themselves in processions behind masked men dragging crosses. They beat themselves until blood streamed down their backs" (*New York Times,* April 12, 1967). See also Mexico's *flagelantes* (*Look,* September 3, 1968). Young boys dying from sniffing hair spray in plastic bags and similar gruesome tales are constant reminders of how many of us are bent on self-destruction. (Cf. Schneidman, 1967.) One of the more extreme cases of a "mod" mode of destroying our bodies and minds was observed recently at the Haight-Ashbury Medical Clinic: A twenty-two-year-old boy had injected himself 37,000 times in the last four years with every conceivable drug he could put into his needle.

2. DESTRUCTION OF OTHERS

In America approximately 760,000 persons have been murdered by gunfire since the turn of the century. In 1967 alone there were (according to FBI statistics) 7,700 homicides with guns. This figure increased 16 percent in the first quarter of 1968, with rape up 19 percent and aggravated assault with a deadly weapon also soaring by 13 percent. Surveys across the nation reveal that only about 15 percent of murderers were strangers to their victims, two-thirds of the rape victims knew their attackers, and most victims of felonious assault were also acquainted with their assailants.

The public slaying of nationally known figures such as Medgar Evers, Martin Luther King, Malcolm X, John and Robert Kennedy, as well as Lee Harvey Oswald and George Lincoln Rockwell can be regarded as a catalyst for the recent flurry of mass murders by Charles Whitman (14 shot to death and 33 injured from his tower at the University of Texas), Richard Speck (8 nurses strangled and stabbed to death), and Robert Smith (5 women and 2 children arranged in a cartwheel formation and shot through the head). Although the nation is horrified by these crimes, nevertheless a Gallup poll of February, 1968, showed that 70 percent of the respondents wanted to continue bombing Vietnam in order to "improve our chances for meaningful peace talks."

Sometimes the murder is planned and systematic, as with Rio de Janeiro's "Death Squad" (a self-appointed group to help curb crime), which left their 150 victims in one month "bullet-ridden and tortured beyond recognition" (*San Francisco Chronicle,* January 28, 1969). In other cases, it is the result of an insignificant dispute over a parking space, a seat in a bar, or a lost wager, but more frequently it occurs for no apparent reason other than that one person wants to kill another—for the feel of it.

The hypocrisy which underscores this assault on humanity is seen in society's demand for revenge over one crime while ignoring a second and participating in a third. One cannot help but be horrified by the brutal rape-murder of young Ann Jiminez in San Francisco (*Chronicle,* December 26, 1968) witnessed by perhaps 25 other teenagers, who watched or participated in her being abused, sexually violated, kicked, and left to die in an alley with obscenities scrawled on her body with lipstick. The reason? She allegedly stole a friend's pair of motorcycle boots. The citizens of Zurich were likewise outraged at the merciless beating to death of a young girl by religious fanatics who claimed to be exorcising the devil from her (*Newsweek,* February 14, 1969). However, where was the concern for human values, for revenge, when the new superintendent of the Arkansas

State Penitentiary discovered that torture and killing of prisoners (over 200 inmates reported "missing") had been a common occurrence (*New York Times,* January 28, 1968)? He was removed from the position, and the "politically delicate situation" was quickly covered up. A congressional hearing into abuse of prisoners was conducted by Senator Dodd (D-Conn.) early this year. The thousands of complaints which forced this inquiry were substantiated by numerous statements such as the following: "I have seen them [boys no more than 12 years old] raped with a blanket around their head to muffle screams, forced into prostitution, bought and sold and even used for security in a loan or gambling debt" (*San Francisco Chronicle,* March 29, 1969).

But how many of us can afford righteous indignation at any inhumane crime when we are told that at least 700 children are killed each year in the United States at the hands of their parents, and that up to 40,000 more youngsters suffer serious injury by beatings and tortures from their parents and siblings. In their somber appraisal of the "battered child syndrome," Helfer and Kempe (1968) report some of the reasons given by parents who were incited to murder their child: "baby was fussy," "cried too much," "soiled diapers," "would not eat," "drinking sibling's bottle," "needed love and attention." One survey reported in this volume makes it clear that there is a community conspiracy of silence against the abused child, since it is estimated that about 3 million adults personally knew families in which there was child abuse. Only rarely did this knowledge ever result in intervention of any kind.

We are now also witnessing a new use of an age-old destructive technique, the "Dear John" letter. Not only has there been an apparent increase in the incidence of these letters to American servicemen fighting in Vietnam (compared to the Second World War), but their format is also predictably different than in the past. Dr. Emanuel Tanay, who has been studying this problem, reports that "some [wives and girl friends] send photographs of themselves with other men in compromising positions. Some send tape recordings of intimate exchanges with another man." No longer is the blow softened by the guilt experienced by the women or by their feelings of empathy; rather there is resentment at being abandoned, unwillingness to delay gratification, and direct expression of hatred toward the perceived cause of their frustration.

3. Riots and Mob Violence

The past five years have witnessed an unprecedented eruption of mass action against the government, war, industries, and "the establishment" as it exists in colleges and elsewhere. According to a report prepared by the National Commission on the Causes and Prevention of Violence there have occurred during this time: 230 violent urban outbursts resulting in 191 deaths and 8,000 injuries, as well as millions of dollars in property damage; 370 civil rights demonstrations and 80 counter-demonstrations with more than a million participants; hundreds of seizures and destruction of university buildings with injury to students, faculty, and police; and a large number of antiwar marches and protests, some of which have resulted in widespread injuries to participants from counter-demonstrators.

We have witnessed "police riots" of the Tactical Squad called in during the night to evacuate student rebels from occupied buildings at Columbia University in the spring of 1968, and the savage abuse displayed by the police at last year's Democratic Convention in Chicago.

> The ones who actually got arrested seemed to have gotten caught up among the police, like a kind of human medicine ball, being shoved and knocked back and forth from one cop to the next with what was obviously *mounting* fury. And this was a phenomenon somewhat unexpected, which we were to observe consistently throughout the days of violence—that rage seemed to engender rage; the bloodier and more brutal the cops were, the more their fury increased.

This account by writer Terry Southern ("Grooving in Chicago," *Esquire,* November, 1968) squares with a statement by a group of University of California Admissions Office clerks who accused police of the bloody beating of students, staff, and reporters without provocation. Their letter (quoted in the *San Francisco Chronicle,* February 29, 1969) alleges that a student being beaten as he was dragged down the stairs, screamed, " 'Please don't hit me any more! Won't someone help me?' . . . *The more he begged, the more they hit.*" It is also reminiscent of the account of an American sergeant who was part of an army intelligence unit interrogating (and torturing) Vietcong prisoners:

> First you strike to get mad, then you strike because you are mad, and in the end you strike because of the sheer pleasure of it. This is the

gruesome aspect of it which has haunted me ever since I came back from Viet Nam. [*Toronto Star,* November 24, 1967]

Mob violence doesn't require confrontations between ideologies—it can, under the right circumstances, be triggered by almost any event. Recently a crowd of about 100 teenagers in New York, angered when a girl was hit by a light panel truck, assaulted the driver, overturned his truck, set it ablaze, and hurled bricks and bottles at firemen attempting to douse the fire. A false rumor that a friend had been beaten by white girls sent a group of 15 black girls on a rampage through Lincoln High School in San Francisco (*San Francisco Chronicle,* February 27, 1969). "More than 300 persons were killed and about 500 injured in events that followed an unpopular ruling by the referee in a soccer match between Peru and Argentina" (*New York Times,* May 25, 1964). This tragedy was replayed last year when a stampede at a soccer stadium in Argentina killed 71 and injured 130 spectators (June 24, 1968).

4. Loss of the Value of Life

A crowd of 200 students at the University of Oklahoma gathered to watch a mentally disturbed fellow student who threatened to jump from a tower. Their chanting of "Jump, jump" in unison and taunting of him may have contributed to his subsequent jump and death. [UPI release, September 23, 1967]

Several years prior to this incident, an Albany, New York, man was saved from a similar suicide leap by the coaxing of his seven-year-old nephew while onlookers jeered, "Jump! Jump! Jump!" Among the curious crowd of about 4,000 were people challenging him to jump, "C'mon, you're chicken," "You're yellow," and betting whether he would or not. Instructive is the comment by one well-dressed man, "I hope he jumps on this side. We couldn't see him if he jumped over there" (*New York Times,* April 14, 1964).

The value we place on human life is in part reflected in our attitudes and treatment of the aged and the dead. Recently at a home for the aged in San Francisco (Laguna Honda), one man died of a heart attack shortly after being taunted by a roving band of teenagers, while another elderly resident collapsed after being lassoed by them.

One of the commodities which our affluence has been able to purchase is nursing homes in which many American children can now dump their aged parents. We have about 30,000 institutions offering long-term care for the aged, and regardless of the quality of care they dispense, being sent to one "is rather like condemning old cars to the scrap heap" (according to Charles Boucher, senior medical officer in the British Ministry of Health). Gerontologists have pointed out that many of these "homes" can strip a person's will to live by enforcing inactivity (keeping the patients bedridden makes them easier to deal with and less of an insurance risk); over-sedating the patients (to control them); disregarding their privacy (since they are only objects to be managed); depriving them of small conveniences; and serving minimally adequate diets (only 94 cents per patient per day is the average food cost—according to probably overestimated figures supplied by the homes to welfare agencies). Finally, the newest insult to the patient's humanity is the notorious "life-care contract." By making the institution his life insurance beneficiary in return for guaranteed bed and board for the patient, an insidious situation is created in which "the unconscious resentment of a guest who is 'overdue' cannot fail to have its effect" (cf. R. E. Burger, "Who Cares for the Aged?," *Saturday Review,* January 25, 1969).

In Atlanta, Georgia, a mortician has built a *drive-in* mortuary. "The deceased will be lying in a lighted window, sort of tilted to the front so they can conveniently be seen," said the mortician. This way busy people "who just don't have the time . . . can drive by and just keep on going." Another feature of this innovation, according to its originator, is that "the people won't have to dress up to view the remains" (*San Francisco Chronicle,* March 14, 1968).

5. Loss of Behavior Control

When an individual or collection of individuals loses control of the mechanisms which regulate behavior and make responses sensitive to feedback, then any of these phenomena can become common occurrences:

a) A teenage boy was beaten nearly to death during a junior high school fraternity initiation. When the boy refused to cry—the signal which would have terminated his being pounded by the fists of his fraternity brothers—"they lost their heads" and beat him until he lost consciousness. His father did not press charges because he said the boys liked his son, they had no grudge against him, but merely "got carried away" (*New York Post,* April 7, 1964).

b) From time to time certain automobile drivers experience episodes of violence and use their car as a weapon against other cars and their drivers, "almost certainly contributing to a significant number of automobile crashes" (according to a government advisory committee report, *New York Times,* February 29, 1968).

c) A resident surgeon who had an argument with his girl friend, a woman physician working with him at Methodist Hospital in Brooklyn, stabbed her 25 to 30 times (*New York Times,* December 26, 1967). This uncontrolled aggression, and the inability to terminate it after a "reasonable" time, reminds one of Albert Camus' stranger, who unloads the full chamber of his gun into his Arab adversary because once he pulls the trigger it is easier to do it again and again than it is to stop.

Recently, as soon as Montreal's police left their jobs in a wage dispute, the reaction of the professional criminals was immediate and predictable—they knocked off ten banks in short order. What was unexpected was the "national disgrace" created by "just plain people" doing their own inner thing once formalized social controls were lifted. Roving groups of "citizens" smashed store windows, looted, set fires, disrupted traffic, and ran amok until finally reinhibited by the return of the police and the presence of the Canadian army (*Time,* October 20, 1969).

THE TIMES THEY ARE A-CHANGING

This brief chronicle of American life in the latter part of this decade represents, I believe, a fundamental change in the quality of individual and mass hostility, aggression, and inhumanity from what it has been in our lifetime. Less than ten years ago, Anatol Rapaport (1961) was able to state with authority, "The mob has disappeared from the American scene and has carried with it into seeming oblivion the phenomenon of overt mob violence" (pp. 50–51).

But our concern should not be limited to the new forms of violence. Much more is happening which, though less dramatic, is equally significant. Audiences of the Living Theater are stripping off their clothes and marching naked through staid, old, blue New Haven. Wordy psychoanalysis is being pushed aside by encounter groups, implosive therapy, "touchies" and "feelies," and non-cognitive therapies. While the over-thirty crowd is getting divorced at a faster rate than ever before, getting turned on by topless and/or bottomless waitresses and public showings of pornographic films, their children are swinging in Free Sex League activities, becoming "groupies" (girls who sleep with all or most members of rock bands, cf. *Time,* February 28, 1969), entering communal marriages, and rapidly increasing the tide of illegitimate births and the cases of V.D. "Fly now, pay later" has become "Fly now, maybe later won't ever come, or if it does, you'll be too stoned to care."

What we are observing all about us, then, is a sudden change in the restraints which normally control the expression of our drives, impulses, and emotions. For better or for worse, we have here the emergence of a kind of freedom different from that made possible through use of the cognitive control mechanisms we described earlier. It is the freedom to act, to be spontaneous, to shed the straitjacket of cogitation, rumination, and excessive concern with "ought" and "should." Behavior is freed from obligations, liabilities, and the restrictions imposed by guilt, shame, and fear.

DIONYSUS REVISITED?

What we are setting up as protagonists are not simply Cognition and Action, but more basically the Forces of Individuation versus those of Deindividuation. These forces are hardly new to each other; their antagonism can be traced back through all recorded history, as an integral part of the myth and ritual of peoples everywhere.

If the reader recoils at the motiveless murders, senseless destruction, and uncontrolled mob violence we've just described, he might alter his sense of wisdom, justice, and propriety by considering Nietzsche's analysis of the similar Apollonian view of Dionysiac forces:

> In order to comprehend this total emancipation of all the symbolic powers, one must have reached the same measure of inner freedom those powers themselves were making manifest; which is to say that the votary of Dionysus could not be understood except by his own kind. It is not difficult to imagine the awed surprise with which the Apollonian Greek must have looked on him. And that surprise would be further increased as the latter realized, with a shudder, that all this was not so alien to him after all, that his Apollonian consciousness was but a thin veil hiding him from the whole Dionysiac realm. [P. 28]

Nietzsche goes on to note:

Throughout the range of ancient civilization . . . we find evidence of Dionysiac celebrations. . . . The central concern of such celebrations was, almost universally, a complete sexual promiscuity overriding every form of established tribal law; all the savage urges of the mind were unleashed on those occasions until they reached that paroxysm of lust and cruelty which has always struck me as the "witches' cauldron" *par excellence*. [Pp. 25–26]

Schopenhauer has described for us the tremendous awe which seizes man when he suddenly begins to doubt the cognitive modes of experience, in other words, when in a given instance the law of causation seems to suspend itself. If we add to this awe the glorious transport which arises in man, even from the very depths of nature, at the shattering of the *principium individuationis*, then we are in a position to apprehend the essence of Dionysiac rapture, whose closest analogy is furnished by physical intoxication. Dionysiac stirrings arise either through the influence of those narcotic potions of which all primitive races speak in their hymns, or through the powerful approach of spring, which penetrates with joy the whole frame of nature. So stirred, the individual forgets himself completely. [P. 22]

Mythically, deindividuation is the ageless life force, the cycle of nature, the blood ties, the tribe, the female principle, the irrational, the impulsive, the anonymous chorus, the vengeful furies. To be singular, to stand apart from other men, to aspire to Godhead, to honor social contracts and man-made commitments above family bonds, is to be individuated (as in Agamemnon's choice to sacrifice his daughter for his role as leader of men).

THE PSYCHOLOGY OF DEINDIVIDUATION

One might suppose that social scientists have long been concerned with a process which claims to underlie all human social organization and forms the very basis of human tragedy. Hardly. There appear to be only two experiments and one conceptual article explicitly dealing with these phenomena. Festinger, Pepitone, and Newcomb (1952) describe a state of affairs in which there is a "reduction in inner restraints" toward expression of counter-norm behavior when individuals are "submerged in a group." Their correlational study tends to show that groups in which there is more public expression of hostility toward parents (the experimental anti-social task response) are perceived by their members to be more attractive, and that these members notice less which others made specific negative remarks.

It took more than a decade before a second study was done by Singer, Brush, and Lublin (1965). They emphasize the loss of self-consciousness and the reduction in feelings of distinctiveness as essential to deindividuation. On the response side, this inferred construct should lead to engaging in a usually undesirable act and feeling greater attraction to the group which allows such behavior. Under manipulated conditions of identification (dressed in best clothes versus dressed in old clothes and baggy lab coats), differences in the use of obscene language were found. More groups given the Low Identifiability manipulation used obscenity than those given the High Identifiability treatment, and these groups were found to be more attractive.

Ziller's analysis (1964) of deindividuation centers more on the concepts of ego identity and individual assimilation into large organizations. Individuation is viewed as a subjective differentiation of self from other social objects in the field; "the greater the number of bits of information required to locate the person, the greater the degree of deindividuation" (p. 345). Ziller's proposal that "individuation is desirable within a supportive social climate, but deindividuation is sought as a defense against a threatening environment" (p. 344) certainly deserves to be put to empirical test, and will receive indirect support from our subsequent analysis of big-city vandalism.

Although Golding's *Lord of the Flies* is not a formal piece of social science research, it is perhaps the best available source of observations on and insights into the antecedents and range of consequences of deindividuation in emerging groups.[2]

DEINDIVIDUATION UNMASKED

The remainder of this chapter (which should be viewed only as a working paper in the process of developing a comprehensive model of deindividuation) will: a) define how the term *deindividuation* will be used; b) specify a set of antecedent variables and characteristic consequences; c) evaluate in field observations and in a simple field experiment conclusions derived from the laboratory studies; d) suggest new directions in which our research is headed; and e) distinguish dehumanization from deindividuation, as well as voluntary and involuntary forms of the latter.

Deindividuation is a complex, hypothesized process in which a series of antecedent social conditions lead to changes in perception of self and others, and thereby to a lowered threshold of normally restrained behavior. Under appropriate conditions what results is the "release" of behavior in violation of established norms of appropriateness.

Such conditions permit overt expression of antisocial behavior, characterized as selfish, greedy, power-seeking, hostile, lustful, and destructive. However, they also allow a range of "positive" behaviors which we normally do not express overtly, such as intense feelings of happiness or sorrow, and open love for others. Thus emotions and impulses usually under cognitive control are more likely to be expressed when the input conditions minimize self-observation and evaluation as well as concern over evaluation by others.

We may speak loosely of: conditions of deindividuation (conditions stimulating it), the feelings or state of deindividuation (the experiential aspect of the input variables together with the inferred subjective changes), and deindividuated behaviors (characterized by several specific output behaviors). Deindividuation refers to the entire process and only then becomes a unique psychological construct.

The major variables in the process are summarized in the descriptive model outlined in Table 1. At this primitive stage in formulating a theory to organize our diverse set of observations and to guide our future data-gathering, this schematic model is but a starting point to focus attention on some relevant variables and testable relationships. For the present argument, it must suffice to elaborate only briefly upon the reasoning (and intuition) which generated this categorization. Before examining each antecedent and consequence of deindividuation, let us mention two models to account for the control mechanism of this process.

A SOCIAL LEARNING OR ENERGY-FORM CORE MECHANISM

Our starting point may be either a mundane motivational assumption or a farfetched symbolic-mythical one. The first states that many behaviors which would be inherently pleasurable to manifest are denied expression because they conflict with norms of

TABLE 1
Representation of the Deindividuation Process

INPUT VARIABLES →	INFERRED SUBJECTIVE CHANGES →	OUTPUT BEHAVIORS
A Anonymity	Minimization of: 1. Self-observation-evaluation 2. Concern for social evaluation	a. Behavior emitted is emotional, impulsive, irrational, regressive, with high intensity
B Responsibility: shared, diffused, given up	→	b. Not under the controlling influence of usual external discriminative stimuli
C Group size, activity		c. Behavior is self-reinforcing and is intensified, amplified with repeated expressions of it
D Altered temporal perspective: present expanded, future and past distanced	Weakening of controls based upon guilt, shame, fear, and commitment	d. Difficult to terminate
E Arousal	→	e. Possible memory impairments; some amnesia for act
F Sensory input overload		f. Perceptual distortion—insensitive to incidental stimuli and to relating actions to other actors
G Physical involvement in the act	Lowered threshold for expressing inhibited behaviors	g. Hyper-responsiveness—"contagious plasticity" to behavior of proximal, active others
H Reliance upon noncognitive interactions and feedback		h. Unresponsiveness to distal reference groups
I Novel or unstructured situation		i. Greater liking for group or situation associated with "released" behavior
J Altered states of consciousness, drugs, alcohol, sleep, etc.		j. At extreme levels, the group dissolves as its members become autistic in their impulse gratification
		k. Destruction of traditional forms and structures

social appropriateness. The affect associated with these inhibited behaviors mounts over time, but is held in check by a learned concern for how others would react to the expression of this behavior, as well as by the self-observing aspect of conscience. Conditions which minimize the use of these twin inhibitors—looking outward for normative controls and inward for internalized controls —should lead to disinhibition, or to a release of the presumably gratifying behavior. By definition, expression of such pleasurable behavior is self-reinforcing; therefore, once initiated, it should be self-maintaining and perpetuating until a marked change occurs in the state of the organism or in environmental conditions.

Consider for a moment a very different core mechanism. Start by assuming that life represents the conversion of matter into energy; that initially this energy is undifferentiated and uncontrolled in its onset, direction, intensity, and terminal properties. Such a force is dangerous to the individual organism because it could be turned in on itself and become self-consuming and destructive. Likewise, it is dangerous for society because it makes every member potentially subject to the transient (demonic) impulses of all others. To contain this energy from destroying the substance which creates it or the environment which nourishes it, forms, structures, and institutionalized systems of control have evolved. The most basic of these is "ego identity"—the imposition of a unique form on this energy of nature which differentiates it, brings it into contact with social and physical reality. Although this reason-conferring form is essential for man to survive, evolve, and develop into the supremely intelligent being he is, nevertheless it is "as though nature were bemoaning the fact of her fragmentation, her decomposition into separate individuals" (Nietzsche, p. 27). In each of us, therefore, resides a fascination with the confrontation of natural energy and imposed human structure; an attraction toward the irrational and the impulsive; Caligula's arbitrary use of power; and a morbid curiosity about danger, destruction, and death. We admire the matador and intellectually want him to win, but our visceral side with the bull and emotionally we identify with the force of his untamed power.

We must then posit a "universal need" to shatter all formal controls, albeit temporarily, as occurs in every person through dreaming. This fact is the basis of society's institutionalization of revelous behavior—harvest festivals in agrarian societies and carnivals in religious ones—where an "unproductive waste of energy" is encouraged. Functionally such festivals serve to siphon off destructive energy, prevent unpredictable, individually initiated release of impulses, and enable the deindividuated reveller to experience both the pleasure of his revels and the satisfaction of becoming *reindividuated* following their termination. Since "ego identity" alone is not enough to thoroughly contain this energy, concepts of time, history, logic, law, and religion were developed to distill it further.

The human imposition of a temporal ordering on experienced events is the most interesting of these systems of control. Time can be thought of as a function of the ego which gives it a (spurious) continuity in the face of the timelessness of the unconscious and its instinctual demands.

> The concept of time is used among other methods as a defense against the too massive impact of the outer world. By breaking experience up into measured time units the mass of reality itself is broken into small bits which the eye can "taste." [Dooley, 1941]

Our insistence on preparing for the future makes our desires for immediate gratification seem infantile. The present becomes negated, according to Heidegger, since it is but "the no longer past and the not yet future." History and logic similarly force us to perceive continuity and rational consistency; legal systems impose future responsibility and liability, while religion denies the corporeal substance of this energy, except as sin to be obliterated. Behavior, then, usually succumbs to the control of these "cognitive" systems which guarantee the existence of self and society by fostering individuation.

COMPONENT ANALYSIS OF OUR MODEL

Since such talk is upsetting to many psychologists, let us rather pursue the more reasonable assumptions underlying the deindividuation process that we outlined previously (Table 1). How can we generate spontaneous, impulsive behavior—behavior which is "unusual" in the individual's life experience? Or put more personally, can you remember a time when you were completely spontaneous, where action precluded thought and you experienced total freedom of expression? If so, what conditions surrounded this unlikely event?

The output behaviors described above should become more likely as the individual feels more *anonymous*. If others can't identify or single you out, they can't evaluate, criticize, judge, or punish you;

thus, there need be no concern for social evaluation. Another type of anonymity derives from feeling alienated from others and from aspects of the self. Karl Marx distinguishes between estrangement from others (*Entfremdung*), loss of control over the products of one's labors (*Entaussurung*), and being made to feel one is only an object, a thing (*Verdinglichungen*). The loss of identifiability can be conferred by being "submerged in a crowd," disguised, masked, or dressed in a uniform like everyone else, or by darkness. Social conditions can also encourage anonymity, but we will hold our discussion of that until later. The most prevalent fantasy of children which illustrates the appeal of anonymity is wanting to be "the invisible man." That this loss of identifiability is also frightening can be seen from the ambivalent reaction of many children toward wearing masks or seeing other people in masks. Marcel Marceau's pantomime of a clown hopelessly struggling to remove his smiling mask is an eloquent expression of this ambivalence.

The *responsibility* one feels for the consequences of having engaged in antisocial behavior (here broadly defined) may be made insignificant by situations in which it is shared by others, by conditions which obscure the relationship between an action and its effects, or by a leader's willingness to assume all of it. The presence of others facilitates the first of these techniques. After the 1964 slaying of the civil rights workers (Schwerner, Chaney, and Goodman) in Mississippi, it is reported by Huie (1965) that the Klansmen passed the murder weapon from hand to hand, so that all shared equally the responsibility, or so that no one was individually responsible. Similarly, in modern electrocution chambers in American prisons there are often three executioners, each of whom pulls a switch simultaneously—only one of which is operative. In firing squads, one gun is loaded with blanks so that each man may believe he personally was not responsible. Compliance with the demands of a role limits perceived responsibility, as argued by Adolph Eichmann at his war crimes trial. Group and national leaders often trade assumption of responsibility for power: the masses yield their power to the fascist dictator in return for his willingness to relieve them of responsibility for many kinds of action. It is, of course, also likely that inadequate socialization can fail to develop a sense of responsibility in an individual, but we are here focusing primarily upon initially "responsible" persons.

Although the presence of a *group* (and its size) is an aid to member anonymity and shared responsibility, it can serve additional functions by providing models for action, generating physical activity which itself is arousing, or serving as a catalyst by triggering behavior in a given direction or toward a given object. It should be clear, however, that although deindividuation can be influenced by group phenomena, it is presented here as an intra-individual process. As such, it is also equally sensitive to the other antecedent variables and states outlined in Table 1 (items B through E).

Elicitation of any behavior at time t_1 should become more probable as the subject's *temporal perspective* is changed so that time t_1 is expanded and assumes greater significance than prior or subsequent time. Colloquially, such a person "lives for the moment," and his behavioral freedom is not trapped between past obligations and future accountings and liabilities.

A generalized state of *arousal* also increases the likelihood that gross, "agitated" behavior will be released, and that cues in the situation which might inhibit responding will not be noticed. Extreme arousal appears to be a necessary condition for achieving a true state of "ecstasy"—literally, a stepping out of one's self. In many societies, facilitative arousal techniques which have proved effective in inducing such states are institutionalized as preparatory rites for war, self-sacrifice, initiation, and rites of intensification.

The prototype of this preparatory arousal is, of course, the war dance (cf. Radcliffe-Brown, 1948, on the war dance of the Andaman Islanders). Loud repetitive music which is dominated by simple but powerful rhythms, group dancing for hours or days on end, singing, chanting, shouting, symbolic enactment of the anticipated confrontation with the enemy and with death, all merge to create a collective state of arousal which is then channeled into directions prescribed by tribal demands.

Preparatory arousal was also used in World War II by Japanese kamikaze pilots, whose individuation had to be sacrificed for the needs of the nation. Among cannibals, like the Cenis or certain Maori and Nigerian tribes, the activity of the ritual bonfire dance which precedes eating the flesh of another human being is always more prolonged and intense when the victim is to be eaten alive or uncooked (cf. Kilman, 1959; and Hogg, 1966). It is sometimes equally true that cannibalism facilitates arousal for war, just as the excitement of war facilitates battleground cannibalism.

Many cultures have rites which signify changes in status, where one's interaction with the society as a whole is to be intensified. Dance, physical torture, and exhaustion are the primary sources of preinitiation arousal, often for both the initiate and his initiators. Among the Buryats of Siberia, when a young girl is to be initiated as a shaman her seminude body is repeatedly massaged and stimulated and then "the older women bend over her and suck her breasts and belly with such force that bleed spurts out" (Eliade, 1964). After additional arousal is achieved by all participants, the older women mix their blood with hers.

The end state which extreme facilitatory arousal may achieve is perhaps best illustrated by the rite of intensification in some districts of southern Nigeria when a boy is permitted to join the men in his first antelope hunt. The excitement becomes so great that he is able to lose self-awareness to the point that he has intercourse with the first antelope he kills while the corpse is still warm (Talbot, 1927).

Cognitive-verbal-intellectual activities are anathema to the spontaneous, behavioral release (disinhibition) we are talking about. Therefore, they must be overwhelmed by intense *sensory stimulation* (the psychedelic light-show phenomenon), or the person must get *absorbed in the action* itself—in the way that children do when playing certain games—where the only meaning of the act is inherent in its performance and lacks further implications or goals. Related to this, a *noncognitive feedback* system must be operative, which does not rely on memory, logic, or association. Rather, it is influenced directly by proprioceptive feedback from one's own action as well as the activity of coacting others. This feedback becomes an auxiliary input to a closed-loop system which results in a spiralling intensity whose terminal state cannot be predicted from knowledge of the initial boundary conditions (cf. J. Durkin's analysis of "encountering," Christie and Geis, 1969).

When one is in a *novel* or *unstructured situation,* behavior is less constrained by learned situation-bound cues. There is more opportunity to act than merely to continue to react, to project what is being experienced internally rather than to accept external physical and social reality as personal reality. When a lower-class neighborhood is razed and replaced with better public housing, an unfamiliar environment replaces the familiar one. Neighborhood cohesiveness with its controlling influences is lost when such a novel environment is created. Our voluntary geographical mobility also puts many Americans into unfamiliar living situations, making us a nation of strangers, separated from our families and from ties to people and places we think of as our own. The American Institute of Real Estate Appraisers reported at their annual (1969) meeting that the total tenant turnover in the San Francisco Bay Area was 81 percent, while it was 85 percent in the Los Angeles area. Another way of looking at our national rootlessness comes from a survey by Srole and his associates of mental health in Manhattan. Of 1,660 respondents living in the Yorkville section of New York City in 1954, two-thirds were not born there (36 percent foreign-born and 28 percent migrants from other cities).

Cognitive controls can be directly undermined by *altering states of consciousness*. Drugs like LSD and mescaline shatter the ordering principles imposed on thought and action by our learned perceptions. Agitated, acting-out, impulsive behavior is characteristic of chronic amphetamine users due to that drug's action as a behavioral stimulant. Under the influence of alcohol, reality testing decreases and is impaired. In sleep all mechanisms of censorship control are abandoned and in the "behavior of dreaming" there is an abrogation of chronicity, consistency, meaningful ordering, and arrangement, and also of social altruism, the golden rule, and the Ten Commandments.

DEINDIVIDUATED BEHAVIORS

Now we turn to what comes out at the other end. Deindividuation can claim uniqueness as a theoretical construct only if we can show that its occurrence is characterized by a pattern of behavior not shared equally by existing related concepts such as contagion, extreme aggression, disinhibition of specific responses, etc.

Virtually by definition, deindividuated behavior must have the property of being a high-intensity manifestation of behavior which observers would agree is emotional, impulsive, irrational, regressive, or atypical for the person in the given situation. But that is not enough. In addition, the behavior must not be under discriminative stimulus control. It must be unresponsive to features of the situation, the target, the victim, or the states of self which normally evoke a given level of response or a competing response. This is due to the combined effects of arousal, involvement in the act, and the direct pleasure derived from action-feedback, without regard for associated conditions which sanction or justify the action.

Under individuating circumstances, the individual is normally responsive to many sources of feedback. With deindividuating ones, however, there is a gating or screening effect in which the only source of feedback allowed into the system is affective-proprioceptive. It is not diluted or contaminated by other feedback channels, and therefore is more intense. Since such feedback is assumed to be pleasurable, a self-reinforcing amplification process is generated. Once begun, each subsequent response should have progressively shorter latencies, coupled with greater vigor.

Evidence for this phenomenon comes from three sources: the undersea-explorer Jacques Cousteau, black racer snakes, and Yoko Ono. One of the most terrifying of all sights, according to Cousteau, is the "dance of death" by sharks when they surround a passive victim. After a dozen or so killer sharks circled an injured baby whale for several hours with no sign of attack, suddenly one bit into its flesh. Within moments pandemonium broke loose; the sharks tore and ripped flesh, leaped over each other, attacked again and again until soon only blood and bones remained.

Jim Myers, a psychologist at Johns Hopkins University, reported a similar phenomenon in his study of the effects of length of food deprivation on the eating behavior of snakes. He has consistently observed that when snakes are placed in a cage with live mice, their initial attack latency is unrelated to length of deprivation. However, once they strike the first mouse, there is an almost linear decrease in latency of subsequent strikes until all or most (five or six) are killed. The attack itself appears to provide a self-excitation feedback which stimulates more attack.

Human animals exhibit similar behaviors, only one example of which will be offered here. Yoko Ono originated an audience-participation act called "Cut Piece." "She sat in her best dress and invited the audience to cut it up with a pair of scissors. At first, there was an awful silence. Then—well—it was terrible. Once they started, they couldn't stop. They went wild. She was left naked, of course" (art critic's report, *Look,* March 18, 1969).

That the behavior will be difficult to terminate follows from the previous discussion of its self-reinforcing aspect and its lack of control by external stimuli. This provides a direct test of the assumed loss of concern for social evaluation, since the behavior ought not to cease even when confronted by verbal instructions to do so from a prestigious, powerful source. However, it may be that when the deindividuated behavior is still at a relatively low level of intensity, as in a mob getting worked up, it is easy to stop it and disperse the "mindless" mob by firm, unequivocal reason-restoring action. On the other hand, at some point of intensity, any agent of termination will be intolerable, and will be attacked and destroyed by the deindividuated mass.

Before explaining why the other behaviors listed in Table 1 are possible correlates of a state of deindividuation, it may be valuable to some readers first to recast our thinking about the initial set of behaviors just described. Two concepts borrowed from operant conditioning appear to be particularly useful: *drl* (differential reinforcement for *low* rates of responding) and *drh* (differential reinforcement for *high* rates of responding). The drl schedule generates a very low rate of responding by reinforcing responses only after a given inter-response time (IRT). "Gradually, the differential reinforcement of IRT's brings responding under the control of the temporal stimuli present when a response is reinforced" (Reynolds, 1968). Stable *drl* performance eventually results because of the equilibrium between the opposing functions of reinforcement: reinforcing responses increases their rate, but reinforcing responses in the presence of stimuli associated with long IRTs decreases their rate.

This schedule is of interest to us because it is the basic social reinforcement schedule underlying most social interaction. To be socially appropriate, behavior must not be at a high rate of output, but spaced. There must not be too much (even of a good thing) all at once. The individual must learn to bide his time and not be effusive even in making responses which are affectively positive. He learns that responding must be paced and consistent, and also that time is a key variable which relates his behavior to certain events. If our time sense is altered by manipulating the input variables, and the feedback from the response is its own continually increasing reinforcement, then social behavior is no longer under *drl* control, and responding shifts to a *drh* schedule. Delay between response and reinforcement and between successive reinforcements becomes minimized, and thus immediate gratification, great activity, and physical involvement are "locked in" by virtue of the demanding response rate. As *drl* schedules typify individuated social behavior, *drh* schedules reflect deindividuated asocial behavior.

The reader may be wondering how such behavior is ever terminated, once initiated in the ways we have described and maintained by the process postulated. Think back to the story mentioned earlier of the resident surgeon stabbing his girl friend over and over, 25 to 30 times, or Camus' Stranger repeatedly pulling the trigger of his gun. This behavior may be terminated by: a) a change in state of the person, such as fatigue or loss of consciousness; b) a marked change in state of the target object or victim, if there is one; or c) a total change in state of an instrument of action or of the environment, such as the gun being emptied. Following the act, amnesia or "blacking out" might occur as part of the termination sequence, or in reaction to the return of self and social awareness in the face of the action just completed (especially if it has been a very ego-alien one).

Arousal and emotion should reduce cue utilization as Easterbrook (1959) has shown (Simon Klevansky, Spencer Sherman, Alan Schiffenbauer, and I are currently studying this phenomenon across a variety of induced drives of high intensity). If one is not concerned with evaluating others or being evaluated by them, it follows that he ought to be unable to relate the deindividuated behaviors to specific participants in the action. This is the major conclusion of the study by Festinger, Pepitone, and Newcomb (1952), although it should be replicated.

Behavioral items g through j in Table 1 are relevant only when a group is present. The situation they describe is one in which deindividuation is not simply conforming behavior in response to perception of a new norm of what is acceptable. The presence of other actors stimulates contagious behavior which is not mediated by cognitive awareness of pressures toward group uniformity, but by sensory awareness of behaving others who are within one's personal distance space (as used by E. T. Hall, 1966). At the same time there is a total loss of conformity to relevant norms of any reference groups not physically present—this is the antisocial feature of the behavior.

If release of the behavior is pleasurable, then stimuli associated with it (such as the group itself) ought to become conditioned reinforcers and be perceived as more attractive. The concept of a group implies that individuals are interacting and influencing each other's behavior. However, attraction to the group and group inter-action break down once the divergent feedback control has reached a high level, because then each member is in a sense autistically responding only to himself and his own actions, and all others cease to exist for him.

Before I present the research done to test some of these relationships, we cannot omit mention of the behavior that would be derived from the "Jungian primitive energy-form model" advanced earlier. Forms, structures, and institutions which represent order, reason, and individuality ought to be likely targets for destruction. And given enough time and high levels of deindividuation, formed entities should be rendered into a formless mass by people in a deindividuated state.

ANONYMITY AND DESTRUCTION IN THE REAL WORLD

Now we must return to our starting point in the real world to demonstrate that the aggression observed under our contrived laboratory conditions of anonymity or unidentifiability is really a genuine phenomenon of the human condition. It should follow, from what we have described thus far, that where social conditions of life destroy individual identity by making people feel anonymous, then what will follow is the deindividuated types of behaviors outlined previously. Assaultive aggression, senseless acts of destruction, motiveless murders, great expenditure of energy and effort directed toward shattering traditional forms and institutionalized structures become our dependent variables. Vandalism is the prototype of this behavior and represents a social problem which will soon reach epidemic proportions. How serious is the problem now? Can it be understood in terms of our analysis of deindividuation?

VANDALISM

The extent and intensity of the mindless, wanton destruction of property and the expenditure of effort on the part of vandals may be extracted from the following sampling of individual cases and summary statistics. Following a Halloween celebration (October 31, 1967), a mob of teenagers began overturning gravestones in Montefiore Cemetery in Queens, New York, and throwing rocks at passing cars. Public School 26 in Brooklyn was broken into 15 times and 700 panels of glass broken in a two-month period (April to June, 1968).

The principal reported that vandals threw library books and catalog cards all over the floor and covered them with glue. Vandalism was also a major problem at the recent New York World's Fair. The Ford Company's cars, which conveyed visitors into a Disney-designed "past" and "future," were also reminders of the reality of the present. The exhibit supervisor remarked that vandals "tear things apart. They carve up the upholstery and pull some of the components out of the dash board. One Thunderbird came back with every wire ripped out."

"God is dead" may be a provocative intellectual issue of debate for theologians, but for kids in the Southeast Bronx (my primal neighborhood), its truth is reflected much more concretely; within a recent six-month period, 47 Christian churches and 20 synagogues were vandalized. One of them was the Netzach Israel Synagogue, where children broke the Torah scrolls, ripped curtains and prayer books, splashed paint on the walls, threw rocks through the stained-glass window, and finally tore the Star of David down from the roof. Anti-Semitism? That assumes motivation and purpose. The rector of the famed St. Mark's in the Bowery Episcopalian Church has threatened to close it down unless similar acts of theft and vandalism in his church are halted. During the past year the church has been broken into about a dozen times and graves in the adjoining church-yard have been desecrated.

While major cities provide a conducive setting for the appearance of vandalism, it is by no means solely an urban phenomenon. In Union Township, New Jersey, roving vandals damaged more than 250 autos parked on streets (March 21, 1968) by ramming them and breaking their windows. Across the country in Richmond, California, a small city near San Francisco, vandals stormed through six schools one weekend (February 25, 1969) causing $30,000 worth of damage. Equipment and furniture were overturned, windows were smashed, food was thrown on the floor and ink squirted on the walls and on library books. Vandals recently destroyed an irreplaceable arbor of beautiful trees in San Francisco's Golden Gate Park, to the puzzlement of all who couldn't understand why anyone would commit such a senseless act.

The incidence of vandalism can be appreciated by reference to the following statistics obtained from the relevant public and private agencies in a single city—New York City.

a) *Schools:* In 1967 there were 202,712 window panes broken (replacement cost over $1 million); there were 2,359 unlawful entries (causing $787,000 damage); there were 199 fires (costing $154,000 in destruction, but not including the loss of one entire school, P.S. 5 in Queens). The January, 1968 bulletin of the Board of Education's Division of Maintenance, noting that these figures do not include costs from defaced desks, walls, fixtures, etc., concludes, "It is almost impossible to estimate the costs of these items, but it is a huge amount." Even without a complete accounting of the havoc wrought on the free public education system in New York City, the bulletin indicates that the nearly $2 million cost of repairs in 1967 was up 21 percent from 1966, and preliminary 1969 reports reveal that the vandalism has continued its spiraling rise.

b) *Public Transportation:* Well over $100,000 was spent in 1967 to repair the damage caused by vandals to buses and subways.

c) *Public Parks:* The $650,000 damage to benches, rest rooms, playgrounds, lights, trees, and fences in 1967 represented an increase of more than 11 percent from the previous year, and it, too, continues to climb. In Brooklyn alone, there were 35 fires set in park buildings, mostly comfort stations.

d) *Public Telephones:* The convenience provided by the city's 100,000 pay phones is rapidly being undermined by hordes of vandals who wreck an average of 35,000 of them *monthly*. At least 25 percent of the sidewalk phones are out of service all the time, and it is a rarity to find a subway station phone in operation. Recently I tried 15 phone booths in the Times Square Station before I could find one whose metal-encased wires were not severed, dial ripped off, mouthpiece dismantled, change slots clogged, or money containers ripped out. The New York Telephone Company estimates that last year it lost nearly $1 million in stolen coins and spent another $4 million to repair vandalized phones.

e) *Automobiles:* The Sanitation Department reports that over 31,500 abandoned cars had to be removed from New York's streets last year (an increase of 5,000 from the previous year). These are cars which either had been stolen or were abandoned by their owners because they were no longer in good running condition. What is interesting is that most of them are stripped of usuable parts and then battered and smashed almost beyond recognition. During the past several years I have been systematically observing this new phenomenon of ritual destruction of the automobile—the symbol of America's affluence, technology, and mobility, as well as the symbol of its owner's independence, status, and (according to motivation researchers) sexual fantasies. In a single day, on a 20-mile route from my home in Brooklyn to the campus of New York University in the Bronx, I recorded 218 such vandalized cars.

Repeated observations of the transformation of a typical car lead me to conclude that there are six distinct stages involved. First, the car must provide some "releaser" stimuli to call attention to itself, such as lack of license plates, hood or trunk open, or a tire removed. However, there are also less obvious cues, such as a flat tire not repaired within a day or two, or simply a car which has not been moved from one place for several days. In a city that is always on the go, anything static must be dead, and it becomes public domain if no one calls for the body. Older boys and men are attracted by the lure of usable or salable parts, and so the car is stripped of all items of possible value. Either late in this stage or after it is completed (depending on implicit neighborhood norms), younger children begin to smash the front and rear windows. Then all easily broken, ripped, or bent parts are attacked. Next, the remainder of the car is smashed with rocks, pipes, and hammers. Sometimes it is set on fire, and sometimes even the body metal is torn off. Finally, and most ignominiously, the last stage in the metamorphosis occurs when people in the neighborhood (and even Sanitation Department clean-up men) use it as a big garbage can, dumping their refuse into it.

A FIELD EXPERIMENT ON "AUTO-SHAPING"

In order to observe in a more systematic fashion who are the vandals and what are the conditions associated with their acts of vandalism, Scott Fraser and I bought a car and left it on a street across from the Bronx campus of New York University, where it was observed continuously for 64 hours. At the same time, we repeated this procedure in Palo Alto, California, on a street near the Stanford University campus. The license plates of both cars were removed and the hoods opened to provide the necessary releaser signals.

What happened in New York was unbelievable! Within ten minutes the 1959 Oldsmobile received its first auto strippers—a father, mother, and eight-year-old son. The mother appeared to be a lookout, while the son aided the father's search of the trunk, glove compartment, and motor. He handed his father the tools necessary to remove the battery and radiator. Total time of destructive contact: seven minutes.

By the end of the first 26 hours, a steady parade of vandals had removed the battery, radiator, air cleaner, radio antenna, windshield wipers, right-hand-side chrome strip, hubcaps, a set of jumper cables, a gas can, a can of car wax, and the left rear tire (the other tires were too worn to be interesting). Nine hours later, random destruction began when two laughing teenagers tore off the rearview mirror and began throwing it at the headlights and front windshield. Eventually, five eight-year-olds claimed the car as their private playground, crawling in and out of it and smashing the windows. One of the last visitors was a middle-aged man in a camel's hair coat and matching hat, pushing a baby in a carriage. He stopped, rummaged through the trunk, took out an unidentifiable part, put it in the baby carriage and wheeled off. [As reported in *Time* magazine, February 28, 1969]

In less than three days what remained was a battered, useless hulk of metal, the result of 23 incidents of destructive contact. The vandalism was almost always observed by one or more other passersby, who occasionally stopped to chat with the looters. Most of the destruction was done in the daylight hours and not at night (as we had anticipated), and the adults' stealing clearly preceded the window-breaking, tire-slashing fun of the youngsters. The adults were all well-dressed, clean-cut whites who would under other circumstances be mistaken for mature, responsible citizens demanding more law and order. The one optimistic note to emerge from this study is that the number of people who came into contact with the car but did not steal or damage it was twice as large as the number of actual vandals.

In startling contrast, the Palo Alto car not only emerged untouched, but when it began to rain, one passerby lowered the hood so that the motor would not get wet!

VANDALISM IS ALIVE, THOUGH SLEEPING, IN STANFORD

Next, this car was abandoned on the Stanford University campus for over a week without incident. It was obvious that the releaser cues which were sufficient in New York were not adequate here. I expected that vandalism needed to be primed where it did not occur with a higher "natural" frequency. To do so, two of my graduate students (Mike Bond and Ebbe Ebbesen) and I decided to provide a better model for destruction by taking a sledge hammer to the car ourselves and then seeing if others would follow suit.

Several observations are noteworthy. First of all, there is considerable reluctance to take that first blow, to smash through the windshields and initiate the destruction of a form. But it feels so good after the first smack that the next one comes more easily, with more force, and feels even better. Although everyone knew the sequence was being filmed, the students got carried away temporarily. Once one person had begun to wield the sledge hammer, it was difficult to get him to stop and pass it to the next pair of eager hands. Finally they all attacked simultaneously. One student jumped on the roof and began stomping it in, two were pulling the door from its hinges, another hammered away at the hood and motor, while the last one broke all the glass he could find. They later reported that feeling the metal or glass give way under the force of their blows was stimulating and pleasurable. Observers of this action, who were shouting out to hit it harder and to smash it, finally joined in and turned the car completely over on its back, whacking at the underside. There seemed little hope to expect spontaneous vandalism of this car since it was already wrecked so badly. However, that night at 12:30 A.M. three young men with pipes and bars began pounding away at the carcass so intensely that dormitory residents (a block away) shouted out for them to stop.

We might conclude from these preliminary studies that to *initiate* such acts of destructive vandalism, the necessary ingredients are the acquired feelings of anonymity provided by the life in a city like New York, along with some minimal releaser cues. Where social anonymity is not a "given" of one's everyday life, it is necessary to have more extreme releaser cues, more explicit models for destruction and aggression, and physical anonymity—a large crowd or the darkness of the night. A heightened state of preparatory general arousal would serve to make the action go, with less direct priming. To maintain and intensify the action, the ideal conditions occur where the physical act is a gross one involving a great deal of energy, thus producing considerable noncognitive feedback. It is pleasurable to behave at a purely sensual, physical, unthinking level —regardless of whether the act is making love or making war.

It is only proper to conclude this section with two final, recently gathered anecdotes. 1) A tank, which was part of an army convoy traveling through the Bronx, developed trouble and had to be left in the street while a mechanic was dispatched. He arrived a few hours later to find it totally stripped of all removable parts (which earned it the *Esquire* Dubious Prize of the Year, 1968). 2) A motorist pulled his car off a highway in Queens, New York, to fix a flat tire. He jacked his car up and, while removing the flat tire, was startled to see his hood being opened and a stranger starting to pull out the battery. The stranger tried to mollify his assumed car-stripping colleague by telling him, "Take it easy, buddy, you can have the tires; all I want is the battery!"

What is being destroyed here is not simply a car, but the basic fabric of social norms which must regulate all communal life. The horrible scene from *Zorba the Greek* in which the old townswomen begin to strip the home of the dying Bubbalina before she is yet dead is symbolically enacted many times every day in cities like New York where young and old, poor and affluent strip, steal, and vandalize cars, schools, churches, and almost all symbols of social order.

It is for the sociologist to discover the specific roots of this induced anonymity,[3] but Hall (1966) sees the type of behaviors we have discussed as one consequence of squeezing man into too small a space and limiting his personal distance (the study of proxemics).

> The animal studies also teach us that crowding *per se* is neither good nor bad, but rather that overstimulation and disruptions of social relationships as a consequence of overlapping personal distances lead to population collapse. [P. 175]

LIVING FOR THE MOMENT, FOR THE KICKS NOW

One approach to studying the psychological process of deindividuation involves isolating theoretically relevant antecedent conditions and observing their effects, while a second approach starts with dramatic natural occurrences of the behavior and then traces back their causes. Our current research is utilizing both strategies—the first one to study the consequences of hypnotically induced alterations of time perspective, and the second to discover the psychological causes of the violent behavior attributed to "speed freaks," chronic amphetamine users.

TIME OUT OF TIME

Our model predicts that impulsive behavior is more likely to occur if a "here and now" time orientation is adopted, one which attenuates the controls imposed by past concerns, guilt, and commitments as well as by future anxieties and responsibilities. Aaronson (1967) has been using hypnosis as a technique to induce altered time sense. Simply suggesting to trained hypnotic subjects that their present will be expanded was sufficient to create marked changes in mood and behavior. As a subject under the skillful training of Dr. Paul Sacerdote, I experienced the "expanded present" suggestion as a state filled with sensations, simultaneous awareness of all one's senses, physical well-being, and a desire to run, jump, play, or do anything, but not sit still. My thoughts and perceptions were focused only on things in my immediate sensory field. Everything else seemed not to matter much, or else seemed too far away to merit any attention.

At Stanford, Gary Marshall, Christina Maslach, and I are currently working on this exciting phenomenon with a group of a dozen hypnotic subjects (drawn from my introductory psychology course). The subjective reactions I had were experienced similarly by all of our subjects. One girl reported she felt so good that she wanted to scream and shout, and then began to do so. Soon the other two subjects in her group were doing likewise. In another group, the eruptive laughter and joking of one "expanded present" subject infected a second one, and they went on in near hysteria for 15 minutes until stopped. When one boy got angry over not finding a name in a phone book (he was told he would not be able to), he began ripping out the pages in the book. The other subjects immediately followed suit with phone books we provided them. Suddenly pages were flying everywhere. In minutes the books were ripped to shreds, and paper missiles were fired at each other and at the researchers until we (somewhat frightened at this loss of control) gave the instruction to return immediately to a deep level of hypnotic relaxation. This is clearly a beautiful technique for studying emotional and behavioral contagion, and we are now working on developing appropriate tasks and response measures, as well as delineating the necessary control groups and procedures.

One of our "expanded present" female subjects has already provided us with a provocative lead into the relationship between time sense, physical identity, and responsibility.

I'm melted. I am so thin, I cover practically everything. In fact, I am sort of falling into everything because I am so thin, and I can hear all the little things vibrating, and I can taste all the different things, like wood and the carpet, and the floor and the chairs. I really can't see any more, though, I mean it's all different colors, but it's so big you can hardly see it, everything is very confusing, but I've just sort of melted into everything. . . . I'm unresponsible! . . . I'm everything! I can keep going. . . . I'm not a thing anymore, I'm everything so I can't do anything. There's nobody there, nobody who says to me, "Hey, Everything, you have to do this."

"ACID" BLOWS MINDS, BUT "SPEED" KILLS SOCIETY

We need look no further than the innumerable drug subcultures of our nation to find the embodiment of acting upon impulses for immediate gratification—the total immersion in the moment, in today's trip, in the high in the sky. However, it is only recently that violence and the senseless crimes mentioned in the introduction to this paper have become part of the drug scene. This change is most obvious in San Francisco's Haight-Ashbury district, where there have been 17 murders in a recent two-month period, innumerable assaults, muggings, rapes, torture orgies, and other crimes of violence. The director of the free medical clinic there, Dr. David Smith,[4] is convinced that the change from a "flower-peace" culture to one of violence can be traced to a transition from use of LSD ("acid") to methamphetamines ("speed"). The pseudo-religious, self-analytic, creative, transcendental, nonviolent "acid heads" have been replaced by a new generation of young, white, middle-class teenagers and adults who become hyperactive, irrational, paranoid, and violent. These are the reactions caused by excessive reliance upon speed. After the initial exhilaration of the injected speed and the well-being of the ride up comes an acute anxiety reaction on the ride down. To avoid this, speed users go on a speed "ride," "shooting up" again and again, up to ten times a day for several days, or in some cases a week or two. "Speed freaks" develop paranoid reactions (maybe as a side effect of prolonged sleep deprivation) which make them suspicious of and hostile toward everyone. The combination of agitation, anxiety, irritability, and paranoia experienced in the threatening environment of such a subculture makes violence a common, prepotent reaction to any type of real or imagined provocation.

A DIFFERENT FACE OF DEINDIVIDUATION: DEHUMANIZATION

We have just been talking about youths in desperate trouble—begging, stealing, and prostituting for drug money; living in fear of hepatitis, the police, and the underworld—as "speed freaks" or "acid heads." The mere use of such categorical labelling makes it difficult for you to empathize with the person, the human being who is just like you, huddled in a mass behind such labels. To exterminate Jews, the Nazis did not have to become deindividuated in the sense in which we have used the concept; they merely had to dehumanize their victims. By perceiving them as inferior forms of animal life, they could destroy them just as you would crush a mosquito, an ant, or even a harmless spider. Similarly, KKK lynch mobs in the South often posed for pictures next to the "strange fruit" of their labor, obviously not seeking anonymity.

This phenomenon is even more pervasive than its kindred spirit of deindividuation. There are four classes of situations which lead most people to treat others as if they were not human beings, as if they had no personal identity. Once that perception is adopted, there is no limit to the outrage one man can bring against his former "fellow man."

1) Dehumanization is more probable whenever a numerically large, continuous flow of people has to be managed efficiently and "processed." In such cases people get IBMized (a cause of the first Berkeley student riots), get stuffed into crowded subways by New York and Tokyo Transit employees hired as "packers," don't get listened to at the welfare bureau when they have justified complaints, etc. We plan to study the development of cynicism and loss of empathy among idealistic college students working in welfare in urban ghettos, as well as to employ an analogue of the phenomenon in a laboratory manipulation.

2) The "institutional sergeant" syndrome emerges when the individual is exposed to others (e.g., the mental patient, the mother on welfare) whose plight arouses extreme empathy. After repeated exposure, with improvement slow or not apparent, the individual feels helpless to effect any change and views such people as emotional burdens, to be serviced without personal involvement. Mental

patients at New Jersey's largest asylum in Trenton were recently discovered being used in a prostitution ring run by the psychiatric attendants. Women and even little girls were smuggled out of the hospital for prostitution and sexual abuse. The attendants received ten dollars for each set-up; the patients got a piece of candy.

3) Special training in dehumanization is required when an individual is called upon to perform a role which violates a social taboo. Surgeons represent the best illustration of this principle. Even though their goal is desirable, in practice they are violating the integrity of the human body. To be effective, they must learn to perceive not a person under their scalpel, but an organ or part. Their language clues us into this immediately, as illustrated in a recent medical report of a clinic patient which stated, "The *body* awoke approximately 18 hours later and complained of hunger and depression."

Another form of this dehumanization is the rigidly prescribed role which the doctor forces upon the patient. Recently when I was being given emergency treatment for an eye laceration, the resident surgeon abruptly terminated his conversation with me as soon as I lay down on the operating table. Although I had had no sedative or anesthesia, he acted as if I were no longer conscious, directing all his questions to a friend of mine—questions such as, What's his name?, What occupation is he in?, Is he a real doctor?, etc. As I lay there, these two men were speaking about me as if I were not there at all. The moment I got off the table and was no longer a cut to be stitched, the surgeon resumed his conversation with me, and existence was conferred upon me again.

How do medical schools train their students to be emotionally inoculated to cutting up their first cadaver? Would more students be unable to do so if they began with the face or eyes—where it is harder to deny the humanity of the object being operated upon? What characterizes medical students who do become eye surgeons or pathologists and coroners? How do gynecologists learn to inhibit their sexual arousal? We will also study issues like these in our future research, as well as what techniques are most effective in training soldiers to kill.

4) When a person wants to engage in a behavior solely for self-gratification and doesn't want to take into consideration the mutual needs of the other interacting person, he can best achieve that end by dehumanizing the other. Prostitution flourishes precisely because

it satisfies this aspect of absorption in self-gratification to the exclusion of giving of the self to another, or recognizing anything but the temporary instrumental function the other serves. Payment to a prostitute (especially by married men who are not sexually deprived) is for the privilege of dehumanizing her, which enables the buyer to indulge his fantasies without the constraints normally imposed by awareness of the woman's feelings of shame, or of future contact. This response is not limited to such men, but is part of the way most men learn to perceive almost all women. Women who are ugly are "beasts" or "dogs," promiscuous ones are "pigs," fertile ones are "cows." Or the part comes to stand for the whole person, as witnessed by expressions such as "a piece of ass." In short, the dehumanization of women by men is the only way many of them can come to react to women at a sexual level at all. They must render them into objects, perceiving them as little more than semen receptacles. Romance individuates, lust deindividuates.

But men do not have an exclusive on this process, nor is it limited to sexual expression. Most readers surely can fill in other areas of application personally known to them.

DEINDIVIDUATION: IMPOSED OR CHOSEN

Control—it is perfectly obvious—they have brought this whole mass of human beings to the point where they are one, out of their skulls, one psyche, and they have utter control over them—but they don't know what in the hell to do with it, they haven't the first idea, and they will lose it . . . suddenly ghhhhhhwooooooooowwwwwww, it is like the whole thing has snapped, and the whole front section of the arena becomes a writhing, seething mass of little girls waving their arms in the air, this mass of pink arms, it is all you can see, it is like a single colonial animal with a thousand waving pink tentacles;—vibrating poison madness and filling the universe with the teeny agony torn out of them . . . it is *one being*. They have been transformed into one being. [Tom Wolfe's description of the teeny-boppers' reaction to the Beatles' appearance at the Cow Palace, San Francisco, 1966, in *The Electric Kool-Aid Acid Test* (New York: Farrar, Straus, Giroux, 1968), p. 205]

Before concluding this chapter, we must distinguish between social situations which appear to have some of the characteristics of deindividuation but may either result in antisocial behavior, with a loss of control, or extreme conformity to social norms and even altruistic behavior. Two variables may explain much of the seeming confusion which arises when we think of orgies, the Mardi Gras, riots, the behavior of uniformed priests and nuns, the conformity of soldiers, etc., as all being instances of deindividuation. In the 2 x 2 matrix in Figure 1, the locus of deindividuation (internally generated needs versus ones externally imposed by another person or group) is orthogonal to the degree of voluntary exposure to group situations where anonymity, shared responsibility, and other deindividuating operations are likely to be experienced.

An individual may have high choice to enter the group, the decision being voluntary, rational, premeditated, and with certain outcomes anticipated. Or the decision may be a low-choice one, where entry into the group is involuntary or forced by circumstance. The locus of the need to become deindividuated may be internal, as when the individual uses the situation to satisfy his own needs which, to the extent that they are exclusively self-satisfying, must be antisocial. On the other hand, a deindividuation-like process may become institutionalized and used as a technique for achieving the leader's or group's goals. Here idiosyncrasy must give way to conformity, and whether the end is antisocial or not depends upon the norms of the group.

1) *High Choice: Internal Locus*—The individual chooses to enter a group or situation that holds promise of fulfilling his needs for expressing impulsive or taboo behavior. Leaders are not necessary, nor is it required that identifiability be reduced to in-group members, but only to outsiders.

2) *Low Choice: Internal Locus*—By chance or necessity, individuals find themselves in a situation in which their personal needs can be expressed and where there is no superordinate group goal to which such individual needs must be subjugated. Here a small minority can effectively steer a large group. This cell comes closest to what we have been talking about as deindividuation.

3) *High Choice: External Locus*—Externally imposed processes of deindividuation may also occur in groups which are voluntarily chosen. However, here the individual joins the group not for the purpose of being deindividuated, but rather because he values some norm of the group. For such a person, the demand of the group to minimize individual differences is not a major consideration. He

Entry Choice

	High: Voluntary	Low: Voluntary	
		Behavioral Contagion, Riots, Gang Rape	Norms of Social Appropriateness Are Violated
Internally Generated	Mardi Gras, Vandalism	2	
	1		
		3	4
			Consequences May Be Either Prosocial or Antisocial
Externally Imposed	Volunteer Army, Taking Holy Orders, Formal Dress Ball	Conscripted Army, Prisoners	

Locus of Needs

FIGURE 7. Examples of social phenomena, in which the choice of entering a group or situation and the locus of needs for anonymity result in different types of conformity and deindividuation.

recognizes that personal anonymity is a means rather than an end. In this manner, the priest assists in the deindividuation process demanded by his order because he recognizes it as a device for achieving the denial of egocentricity, which leads to the goal of freeing him from worldly preoccupations.

4) *Low Choice: External Locus*—Where group membership is involuntary, as in a conscripted army, loss of individuality is induced by rigid requirements of dress and behavior and by severe penalties for nonconformity. Although within such a group individuals may maintain singularity, their actions as a collective, identifiable unit demand the loss of each member's individuality in the eyes of the out-group.

The use of a distinctive uniform is a characteristic method for getting people to conform; the uniform becomes the visible symbol of that abstraction, the group, in which individuality is dissolved. In *Mein Kampf*, Hitler describes in detail this method of gaining control over usually unpredictable masses: dress them alike and variability in their behavior will be eliminated. When the American GI's in Charlie Company entered the Vietnamese village of Song My (or "Pinkville") on March 16, 1968, they proceeded to commit such atrocities that American eyewitnesses couldn't believe what they were seeing. Some soldiers "went crazy" and slaughtered wounded villagers, women and children. Others murdered perhaps hundreds of civilians in "business-like" fashion, firing M-79 grenade launchers as well as machine-gunning clumps of "gooks." Most of Charlie Company did kill . . . "everyone in the village, animals, and everything" (*San Francisco Examiner-Chronicle*, November 23, 1969).

In religious orders, monks, nuns, and priests are required to wear a habit. Dressing alike also encourages behavioral conformity to a code of group behavior, yet obviously, such behavior is not antisocial in the sense in which we usually employ this term. However, if we examine this group behavior we find that it is antisocial in a different, very special sense. The priest denies the impulses of his material nature; he takes himself out of the material flow of life (to the preservation of which society is dedicated) and enters a "community of souls." His dress and the code of behavior of the group to which he belongs are designed to help free him from his individuation.

In all of these examples, uniformity of appearance results in the perception by out-group members of a distinctive group within which individual members are not differentiated. The in-group member foregoes individual recognition from the out-group to achieve the greater recognition that accrues to him from his membership in the group. Although members may have personal identity within the group, the group's strength and impact depend upon the members' belief that all of them are equally valid representatives of the group's norms. Since the group gains in its power to the extent that its members sacrifice their individuation to the distinction of the group as a whole, it must demand from its members extreme conformity to its norms. To preserve its collective identity, the group can allow no individual deviation.

CONCLUSIONS

Although we have covered a lot of ground in this chapter, we have only treated this complex problem at a rather superficial level. Nevertheless, it becomes apparent that the human choice we have been considering is fundamental to understanding a wide range of human behavior. The study of deindividuation links social psychology not only to other social sciences but to the basic themes in Western literature, mythology, and religion. The model rather crudely outlined here is but a heuristic device for generating further ideas and pointing to relationships and areas of inquiry with which psychologists have not before been concerned. It needs to be refined, and much research must be done to firm it up or expose its inadequacies.

At the level where social scientists become involved with social issues, our discussion of deindividuation leads to the following suggestions. Police must be retrained to cope with the emergence of the "new" kind of crime and criminal depicted in this paper. The policeman must be individuated in the perception of those he must deal with, and must feel so, in order for him to maintain his individual integrity (they should wear their names on their uniforms as athletes do). Also, the current theory of ever-increasing deterrents against crime (more police patrols, search and seizure, aggressive police action) is based upon outmoded concepts of the criminal. When a dehumanized person has become an object, then it may be that the only means he can use to get anyone to take him seriously and respond to him in an individuated way is through violence. A knife at someone's throat forces the victim to acknowledge the power of the attacker and his control. In one sense, violence and destruction transform a passive, controlled object into an active, controlling person. When driven to the wall by forces of deindividuation, the individual must assert his own force or become indistinguishable from the wall. Conditions which foster deindividuation make each of us a potential assassin.

We might also venture the suggestion that what is wrong with American society is that currently it neither promotes individuation nor allows for deindividuation. There are a myriad of social forces which make anonymity prevalent while diminishing individual uniqueness, singularity, and personal pride. At the same time, there is a breakdown of tribal communal ties, as well as a weakening of the extended family due to our extreme geographical mobility. The concurrent breakdown of the nuclear family through divorce results in a loss of being related to the soil or the blood cycle of nature— the primitive (positive) deindividuated experience. What we will begin to see more and more is young people attempting to regain these lost ties through new forms of group marriages and communal families.

Viewed in another sense, what is wrong is that there are no institutionalized forms of release of antisocial impulses within a prescribed time period and other boundary conditions. Individuals who normally live controlled lives need such revels so that they can experience both the pleasure derived directly from such expression and the greater pleasure of becoming *reindividuated* following a period of abandon or running amok.

Although on special occasions the society must provide such opportunity for release, at all other times we must insist on greater individuation in all aspects of our lives.[5] For example, we should not give up our names for more efficient numbers, and should resist urban planning which nurtures sterile, drab sameness and wipes out neighborhoods where people are recognized by others and are concerned about the social evaluation of those others.

Furthermore, there must be provision for socialization training in which mild forms of aggression can be expressed. Megargee (1966) has found that the problem with extremely assaultive criminal offenders is not that they are uncontrolled, impulsive types. To the contrary, they are so over-controlled that they can never allow any release of aggression. Anything which threatens or breaks down this rigid control system can lead to unimagined acts of violence in response to minimal direct provocation. Many of the mass murders and senseless homicides which we examined earlier developed from just such a background.

In the eternal struggle between order and chaos, we openly hope for individuation to triumph, but secretly plot mutiny with the forces within, drawn by the irresistible lure of deindividuation.

> Even as on an immense, raging sea, assailed by huge wave crests, a man sits in a little rowboat trusting his frail craft, so, amidst the furious torments of this world, the individual sits tranquilly, supported by the *principium individuatonis* and relying on it.
>
> —Schopenhauer

NOTES

1. Under Italian law, a woman was arrested recently (in Caserta, Italy) for keeping her boyfriend a prisoner for five months. She was charged with the rare crime of *plagio*—reducing somebody to psychological slavery by eliminating his faculties of choice, criticism, and will.

   One way in which the Japanese avoid personal responsibility for their action is through the use of the passive-causative verb tense. This linguistic device characterizes the speaker as having been made to do something by someone else or some external force, as in "I don't want to be made to drink too much tonight because I must drive." The American counterpart appears in the old song, "You made me love you, I didn't want to do it. . . ."

2. Other fascinating aspects of the process of deindividuation and dehumanization (which will be treated later in this chapter) can be found in the novels of Anthony Burgess (*A Clockwork Orange* [New York: Ballantine, 1965]), George Bataille (*The Story of the Eye* [North Hollywood, Calif.: Brandon House, 1968]), and Pauline Réage (*Story of O* [New York: Grove Press, 1967]). The interested reader is also referred to the classic study *The Crowd* by LeBon (New York: Ballantine, 1969; first published 1895), Smelser's sociological *Theory of Collective Behavior* (New York: Free Press, 1962), and Canetti's *Crowds and Power* (New York: Viking Press, 1963).

3. One social indicator of urban anonymity is the failure of people living in tenement houses to display their name on their mailbox, at their downstairs doorbell, or on their door. In a survey I conducted of 100 tenements, the apartments of only 24 percent of the occupants could be located from their name plates on the ground-floor bells or mailboxes.

4. See Smith, D. E., "Changing Drug Patterns in Haight-Ashbury," *California Medicine,* Vol. 110, No. 10 (February, 1969) pp. 151–54.

5. An intriguing experimental situation involves placing a person in a small group in which the other members are all accomplices of the researcher. Their task and the experimental procedure are designed to deny the indi-

vidual any uniqueness. They wear masks which look like him, their voices are changed to be like his, they mimic his speech, gestures, posture, habits. They role play having identical attitudes, values, and goals. In short, there is nothing he is that they are not. Will this similarity be pleasing? Or will it motivate the person to demonstrate what he believes is unique about himself? But suppose he shows his cards and they also share that trait, ability, or whatever; then maybe it's better to keep it concealed and as long as *he* knows he has it, it's enough. Or is it? This raises the provocative question, What keeps you from becoming someone else, or someone else from becoming you?

REFERENCES

B. S. Aaronson, "Hypnotic Alterations of Space and Time." Presented at International Conference on Hypnosis: Drugs and Psi Induction, 1967.

R. Christie, and F. L. Geis, *Studies in Machiavellianism* (New York: Academic Press, 1969).

L. Dooley, "The Concept of Time in Defense of Ego Integrity," *Psychiatry*, Vol. 4 (1941), pp. 13–23.

J. A. Easterbrook, "The Effect of Emotion on Cue Utilization and the Organization of Behavior," *Psychological Review*, Vol. 66 (1959), pp. 183–201.

M. Eliade, *Shamanism: Archaic Techniques of Ecstasy* (New York: Princeton University Press, 1964).

L. Festinger, A. Pepitone, and T. Newcomb, "Some Consequences of Deindividuation in a Group," *Journal of Abnormal Social Psychology*, Vol. 47 (1952), pp. 382–89.

W. Golding, *Lord of the Flies* (New York: Capricorn Books, 1959).

E. T. Hall, *Hidden Dimensions* (New York: Doubleday, 1966).

R. E. Helfer and G. H. Kemper, *The Battered Child* (Chicago: University of Chicago Press, 1968).

G. Hogg, *Cannibalism and Human Sacrifice* (New York: Citadel Press, 1966).

W. B. Huie, *Three Lives for Mississippi* (New York: WCC Books, 1965).

E. Kilman, *Cannibal Coast* (San Antonio, Texas: Naylor, 1959).

E. I. Megargee, "Undercontrolled and Overcontrolled Personality Types in Extreme Anti-social Aggression," *Psychological Monographs*, Vol. 80 (1966), whole No. 11.

S. Milgram, "Some Conditions of Obedience and Disobedience to Authority," in I. D. Steiner and M. Fishbein, Eds., *Current Studies in Social Psychology* (New York: Holt, Rinehart, Winston, 1965), pp. 243–62.

F. Nietzsche, *The Birth of Tragedy* (New York: Doubleday, 1956).

A. R. Radcliffe-Brown, *The Andaman Islanders* (Glencoe, Illinois: The Free Press, 1948).

A. Rapaport, *Fights, Games, and Debates* (Ann Arbor, Mich.: University of Michigan Press, 1961).

G. Reynolds, *A Primer of Operant Conditioning* (Glenview, Ill.: Scott, Foresman, 1968).

E. S. Schneidman, Ed., *Essays in Self-Destruction* (New York: Science House, 1967).

J. E. Singer, C. A. Brush, and S. C. Lublin, "Some Aspects of Deindividuation: Identification and Conformity," *Journal of Experimental Social Psychology,* Vol. 1 (1965), pp. 356–78.

L. Srole, T. S. Langner, S. T. Michael, M. Opler, and T. A. Rennie, *Mental Health in the Metropolis: The Midtown Manhattan Study* (New York: McGraw-Hill, 1962).

J. Talbot, *Some Nigerian Fertility Rites* (Oxford: Oxford University Press, 1927).

L. Wheeler, "Toward a Theory of Behavioral Contagion," *Psychological Bulletin,* Vol. 73 (1966), pp. 179–92.

R. C. Ziller, "Individuation and Socialization," *Human Relations,* Vol. 17 (1964), pp. 341–60.

P. G. Zimbardo, *The Cognitive Control of Motivation* (Glenview, Ill.: Scott, Foresman, 1969).

———, A. R. Cohen, M. Weisenberg, L. Dworkin, and I. Firestone, "Control of Pain Motivation by Cognitive Dissonance," *Science,* Vol. 151 (1966), pp. 217–19.

11

The City as a Mechanism
for Sustaining Human Contact

Christopher Alexander

People come to cities for contact. That's what cities are—meeting places. Yet the people who live in cities are often contactless and alienated. A few of them are physically lonely: almost all of them live in a state of endless inner loneliness. They have thousands of contacts, but the contacts are empty and unsatisfying.

What physical organization must an urban area have, to function as a mechanism for sustaining deeper contacts?

Before we can answer this question, we must first define exactly what we mean by "contact" and we must try to understand just what it is about existing cities that prevents the deepest contacts from maturing. Once we have done that, we can define a set of

"The City as a Mechanism for Sustaining Human Contact," Christopher Alexander, from William R. Ewald, Jr., ed., *Environment for Man: The Next Fifty Years* (Bloomington: Indiana University Press, 1967), pp. 60–102, 292–96. Copyright © 1967 by Indiana University Press. Reprinted by permission of the author and the publisher.

characteristics which an urban area requires to sustain the contacts. This chapter therefore has four parts:

In the first part I shall define the most basic and most urgently needed kind of contact, *intimate contact.*

In the second part, I shall present a body of evidence which strongly suggests that the social pathologies associated with urban areas—delinquency and mental disorder—follow inevitably from the lack of intimate contact.

In the third part, I shall describe the interplay of phenomena which causes the lack of intimate contact in urban areas today. These phenomena are facets of a single complex syndrome: *the autonomy-withdrawal syndrome.* I shall try to show that this syndrome is an inevitable by-product of urbanization, and that society can recreate intimate contacts among its members only if they overcome this syndrome.

In the fourth part, I shall show that in order to overcome the autonomy-withdrawal syndrome a city's housing must have twelve specific geometric characteristics, and I shall describe an arrangement of houses which has these characteristics.

1. INTIMATE CONTACT

Modern urban society has more contact and communication in it than any other society in human history. People who would never have been in contact in a preindustrial society are in contact today. There are more contacts per person, and there are more kinds of contact. Individuals are in touch with a larger world than they ever were before. As metropolitan areas grow, society will become even more differentiated, and the number and variety of contacts will increase even more. This is something that has never happened before, in the whole of human history, and it is very beautiful: Durkheim said so long ago in the *Division of Labor in Society.*[1] Melvin Webber and Marshall McLuhan and Richard Meier are saying it eloquently today.[2]

But as the individual's world expands, the number of contacts increases, and the quality of contact goes down. A person has only twenty-four hours in his day. As the total number of his contacts increases, his contacts with any one given person become shorter, and less frequent, and less deep. In the end, from a human point of view, they become altogether trivial. It is not surprising that in just those urban centers where the greatest expansion of human contacts has taken place men have begun to feel their alienation and aloneness more sharply than in any preindustrial society. People who live in cities may think that they have lots of friends; but the word friend has changed its meaning. Compared with friendships of the past, most of these new friendships are trivial.

Intimate contact in the deepest sense is very rare. *Intimate contact is that close contact between two individuals in which they reveal themselves in all their weakness, without fear.* It is a relationship in which the barriers which normally surround the self are down. It is the relationship which characterizes the best marriages, and all true friendships. We often call it love. It is hard to give an operational definition of this kind of intimate contact: but we can make it reasonably concrete, by naming two essential preconditions without which it can't mature.

These conditions are: (1) The people concerned must see each other very often, almost every day, though not necessarily for very long at a time. (2) They must see each other under informal conditions, without the special overlay of role or situation which they usually wear in public.

In more detail: (1) If people don't meet almost every day— even if they meet once a week, say—they never get around to showing themselves; there are too many other things to talk about: the latest news, the war, the taxes, what mutual acquaintances have been doing lately. These things can easily fill an evening once a week. Unless people meet more often, they never have a chance to peel the outer layers of the self away, and show what lies inside. (2) Many people meet every day at work. But here the specific role relationship provides clear rules about the kinds of things they talk about, and also defines the bounds of the relationship—again there is little chance that the people will penetrate each other, or reveal themselves. The same thing is true if they meet under "social" circumstances, where the rules of what is proper make deep contact impossible.

These two conditions are not sufficient—they do not guarantee intimate contact—but they are necessary. If these conditions are not met, intimate contact can't mature.[3]

It may help to keep in mind an even more concrete criterion of intimacy. If two people are in intimate contact, then we can be sure that they sometimes talk about the ultimate meaning of one another's lives; and if two people do sometimes talk about the ultimate meaning of their lives, then we are fairly safe in calling their contact an intimate contact. If they do not talk about these things, then they are not really reaching each other, and their contact is superficial.

By this definition, it is clear that most so-called "friendly" contacts are not intimate. Indeed, it is obvious that the most common "friendly" occasions provide no opportunity for this kind of contact to mature. Friends who come around to dinner once a month ("Honey, why don't we have them round to dinner sometime?"), or the acquaintances who meet for an occasional drink together, clearly do not satisfy the two conditions which I have defined. At these occasions people neither reach each other, nor do they reveal themselves. Let us, therefore, begin by asking what social mechanism is required to make contacts intimate.

In preindustrial society, intimate contacts were sustained by primary groups. "A primary group is a small group of people characterised by intimate face to face association and cooperation."[4] The three most universal primary groups are the family, the neighborhood group of elders, and the children's play-group. These three primary groups have existed in virtually every human society, and they have been primary in forming the social nature and ideals of the individual. It is clear that the contacts which these primary groups created do meet the two conditions I have named. The members of a primary group meet often—almost daily; and they meet under unspecialized conditions, where behavior is not prescribed by role, so that they meet as individuals, man to man. It is therefore clear that in a society where primary groups exist, the primary groups do serve as mechanisms which sustain intimate contact.

Because intimacy is so important, and because primary groups have, so far, always been the vehicles for intimate contact, many anthropologists and sociologists have taken the view that man cannot live without the primary groups.[5]

Here are two typical statements: First Homans, writing in 1950:

> In the old society, man was linked to man; in the new agglomeration—it cannot be called a society—he is alone. . . . All the evidence of psychiatry shows that membership in a group sustains a man, enables him to maintain his equilibrium under the ordinary shocks of life, and helps him to bring up children who will in turn be

happy and resilient. If his group is shattered around him, if he leaves a group in which he was a valued member, and if, above all, he finds no new group to which he can relate himself, he will, under stress, develop disorders of thought, feeling, and behavior. His thinking will be obsessive, elaborated without sufficient reference to reality; he will be anxious or angry, destructive to himself or to others; his behavior will be compulsive, not controlled; and, if the process of education that makes a man easily able to relate himself to others is itself social, he will, as a lonely man, bring up children who have a lowered social capacity. The cycle is vicious; loss of group membership in one generation may make men less capable of group membership in the next. The civilization that, by its very process of growth, shatters small group life will leave men and women lonely and unhappy.[6]

Second—Linton:

> Although the disintegration of local groups in our society may progress even further than it has, the author is inclined to regard it as a transitory phenomenon. The sudden rise of the machine and of applied science has shattered Western civilization and reduced Western society to something approaching chaos. However, unless all past experience is at fault, the society will once more reduce itself to order. What the new order will be no one can forecast, but the potentialities of the local group, both for the control of individuals and for the satisfaction of their psychological needs are so great that it seems unlikely that this unit will be dispensed with.[7]

Linton wrote those words in 1936. In the years since then, many architects and planners have tried to recreate the local primary group artificially, by means of the neighborhood idea. They have hoped that if people would only live in small physical groups, round modern village greens, the social groups would follow the same pattern; and that these artificial groups would then once more provide the intimate contact which is in such short supply in urban areas today.[8] But this idea of recreating primary groups by artificial means is unrealistic and reactionary: it fails to recognize the truth about the open society. The open society is no longer centered around place-based groups; and the very slight acquaintances that do form round an artificial neighborhood are once again trivial: they are not based on genuine desire.[9] Though these pseudogroups may serve certain ancillary purposes (neighbors may look after one another's houses while they are away), there is no possible hope that they could sustain truly intimate contact, as I have defined it.

The only vestige of the primary groups which still remains is the nuclear family. The family still functions as a mechanism for sustaining intimate contact. But where the extended family of pre-industrial society contained many adults, and gave them many opportunities for intimate contact, the modern nuclear family contains only two adults. This means that each of these adults has at most *one* intimate contact within his family. (Although the contact between parent and child is, in a colloquial sense, an intimate one, it is not the kind of contact which I am discussing here; it is essentially one-sided; there can be no mutual revealing of the self between adults and children.) Furthermore, one-third of all households in urban areas contain only one adult (either unmarried, widowed or divorced[10]). These adults have *no* intimate contacts at all, at home.

As ways of providing intimate contact, it seems that primary groups are doomed. Modern urban social structure is chiefly based on secondary contacts—contacts in which people are related by a single role relationship: buyer and seller, disc-jockey and fan, lawyer and client.[11] Not surprisingly, the people who find themselves in this dismal condition try madly to make friends. Urban Americans are world-famous as an outgoing, friendly people. They are able to make friends very fast; and they join associations more than almost any other people. It is not hard to see that this is an inevitable consequence of urbanization and mobility, and will ultimately happen everywhere, as urban society spreads around the world. In a society where people move about a lot, the individuals who are moving must learn to strike up acquaintances quickly—it is essential for them, since they very often find themselves in situations where they don't know anybody. By the same token, since deep-seated, old, associations are uncommon, people rush to join new associations and affiliations, to fill the gap they feel. Instant friendship is well adapted to the circumstances which the average American urban dweller faces. But the very life stuff of social organization—true participation among people who learn to penetrate each other—is missing. Outward friendliness adds nothing to the need for deeper contact; it trivializes contact.

People may not be ready to admit that most of their contacts are trivial; but they admit it by implication, in their widespread nostalgia for college days, and for army days. What is it that makes the college reunions so powerful? Why do grown men and women at reunions pretend to be boys and girls again? Because at college, they had an experience which many of them never have again: they had many intimate friends; intimate contact was commonplace. The same is true of army days. However grisly war may be, it is a fact that the vast majority of men never forget their army days. They remember the close comradeship, the feelings of mutual dependence, and they regret that later life never quite recreates this wonderful experience again.

All the recent studies of dissatisfaction when slum dwellers are forced to move say essentially the same.[12] So far these studies have been used to demonstrate the poor quality of new towns and urban renewal; but this is really incidental. No one has been bold enough to face the larger fact. These people are moving from a traditional place-based society into the larger urban society where place-based community means nothing. When they make the move they lose their intimate contacts. This is not because the places they go to are badly designed in some obvious sense which could be easily improved. Nor is it because they are temporarily uprooted, and have only to wait for the roots of community to grow again. The awful fact is that modern urban society, as a whole, has found no way of sustaining intimate contacts.

Some people believe that this view is nothing but nostalgia for an imaginary past, and that what looks like alienation is really just the pain of parting from traditional society, and the birth pang of a new society.[13]

I do not believe it. I believe that intimate contacts are essential for human survival, and, indeed, that each person requires not one, but several intimate contacts at any given time. I believe that the primary groups which sustained intimate contact were an essential functional part of traditional social systems, and that since they are now obsolete, it is essential that we invent new social mechanisms, consistent with the direction that society is taking, and yet able to sustain the intimate contacts which we need.

Expressed in formal terms, this belief becomes a fundamental hypothesis about man and society:

An individual can be healthy and happy only when his life contains three or four intimate contacts. A society can be a healthy one only if each of its individual members has three or four intimate contacts at every stage of his existence.[14]

Every society known to man, except our own, has provided conditions which allow people to sustain three or four intimate contacts.

Western industrial society is the first society in human history where man is being forced to live without them. If the hypothesis is correct, the very roots of our society are threatened. Let us therefore examine the evidence for the hypothesis.

2. EVIDENCE

Unfortunately, the only available evidence is very indirect. Individual health is hard to define; social health is even harder. We have no indices for low-grade misery or sickness: we have no indices for fading social vitality. In the same way, the relative intimacy of different contacts is hard to define and has never explicitly been studied. The evidence we really need, showing a correlation between the intimacy of people's contacts and the general health and happiness of their individual and social lives, does not exist.

In a strictly scientific sense, it is therefore possible only to examine a very extreme version of the hypothesis: namely, that *extreme* lack of contact causes *extreme* and well-defined social pathologies like schizophrenia and delinquency. Several large-scale studies do support this extreme form of the hypothesis.

Faris and Dunham studied the distribution of mental disorders in Chicago in the 1930's. They found that paranoid and hebephrenic schizophrenias have their highest rates of incidence among hotel residents and lodgers, and among the people who live in the rooming house districts of the city. They are highest, in other words, among those people who are most alone.[15]

Faris and Dunham also found that the incidence of schizophrenia among whites was highest among those whites living in predominantly Negro areas, and that the incidence for Negroes was highest among those Negroes living in predominantly non-Negro areas.[16] Here again, the incidence is highest among those who are isolated.

Alexander Leighton and his collaborators have spent ten years in Stirling County, Nova Scotia, studying the effect of social disintegration on mental disorders.[17] To stress the fact that people in a disintegrated society exist as isolated individuals, without any kind of emotional bonds between them, he calls the disintegrated society a collection. In a collection there are numbers of individuals occupying the same geographical area, having nonpatterned encounters with each other. They have no personal contacts of any sort; they have no voluntary associations with one another—let alone any kind of intimate contact between households.[18] They are suspicious about making friends, and try to keep clear of all involvements with people.[19] These people have substantially higher rates of psycho-physiological, psychoneurotic, and sociopathic disorders than people who live in a closely knit traditional community.[20]

Langner and Michael, studying the incidence of mental disorders in Manhattan, find that people who report fewer than four friends have a substantially higher chance of mental disorder than those who report more than four friends.[21] What is more, their findings suggest that this effect may even be partly responsible for the well-known correlation between low socio-economic status and high rates of mental disorder and delinquency.[22] Langner and Michael find that people in the lowest socioeconomic groups tend to have fewer friends than the people in the highest socioeconomic groups. Thus in the lowest group, 12.7 per cent report no friends; in the highest group, only 1.8 per cent report no friends.[23] This may seem surprising to those readers who have an image of the lower socioeconomic groups as urban villagers, with widespread webs of friendship and kinship. Although the people who live in depressed areas of cities do occasionally still have such a traditional society, and many friends, most of them live in conditions of extreme social disorganization. They do lack intimate friends; and it is very possible that this lack of intimate friends plays a substantial part in the correlation between poverty and mental disorder. Langner and Michael show, finally, that membership in formal organizations and clubs, and contact with neighbors, have relatively slight effect on mental health—thus supporting the idea the contacts must be intimate before they do much good.[24]

Many minor studies support the same conclusion. Most important among them are the widely known correlations between age and mental health, and between marital status and mental health. Various studies have shown that the highest incidence of mental disorders, for males and females, occurs above age 65, and, indeed, that the highest of all occurs above 75.[25] Other studies have shown that the incidence rates for single, separated, widowed and divorced persons are higher than the rates for married persons. Rates per thousand, for single persons, are about one and a half times as high as the rates for married persons, while rates for divorced and widowed persons are between two and three times as high.[26]

Of course the disorders among old people may be partly organic, but there is no getting away from the fact that old people are almost always more lonely than the young, and that it is usually hard for them to sustain substantial contacts with other people. In the same way, although the disorders among divorced and single people could actually be the sources of their isolation, not the causes of it, the fact that the rate is equally high for widowers and widows makes this very unlikely. In both cases we are dealing with populations of individuals who are exceptionally prone to isolation. The simplest possible explanation, once again, is that the loss of intimate contact causes the disorders.

So far we have discussed only cases of adult isolation. It is very likely that the effects of social isolation on children are even more acute; but here the published evidence is thinner.

The most dramatic available results come from Harlow's work on monkeys. Harlow has shown that monkeys isolated from other infant monkeys during the first six months of life are incapable of normal social, sexual, or play relations with other monkeys in their later lives:

> "They exhibit abnormalities of behavior rarely seen in animals born in the wild. They sit in their cages and stare fixedly into space, circle their cages in a repetitively stereotyped manner, and clasp their heads in their hands or arms and rock for long periods of time . . . the animal may chew and tear at its body until it bleeds . . . similar symptoms of emotional pathology are observed in deprived children in orphanages and in withdrawn adolescents and adults in mental hospitals.[27]

It is well known that infant monkeys—like infant human beings—have these defects if brought up without a mother or a mother surrogate. It is not well known that the effects of separation from other infant monkeys are even stronger than the effects of maternal deprivation. Indeed, Harlow showed that although monkeys can be raised successfully without a mother, provided that they have other infant monkeys to play with, they cannot be raised successfully by a mother alone, without other infant monkeys, even if the mother is entirely normal. He concludes: "It seems possible that the infant-mother affectional system is dispensable, whereas the infant-infant system is a *sine qua non* for later adjustment in all spheres of monkey life."[28]

In Harlow's experiments, the first six months of life were critical. The first six months of a rhesus monkey's life correspond to the first three years of a child's life. Although there is no formal evidence to show that lack of contact during these first three years damages human children—and as far as I know, it has never been studied—there is very strong evidence for the effect of isolation between the ages of four to ten. There is also an informal account by Anna Freud, which shows how powerful the effect of contact among tiny children can be on the emotional development of the children.

Anna Freud describes five young German children who lost their parents during infancy in a concentration camp, and then looked after one another inside the camp until the war ended, at which point they were brought to England.[29] She describes the beautiful social and emotional maturity of these tiny children. Reading the account, one feels that these children, at the age of three, were more aware of each other and more sensitive to each other's needs than many people ever are.

The most telling study is that by Herman Lantz.[30] Lantz questioned a random sample of 1,000 men in the United States Army, who had been referred to a mental hygiene clinic because of emotional difficulties. Army psychiatrists classified each of the men as normal, suffering from mild psychoneurosis, severe psychoneurosis, or psychosis.

Lantz then put each man into one of three categories: those who reported having five friends or more at any typical moment when they were between four and ten years old, those who reported an average of about two friends, and those who reported having no friends at that time. The following table shows the relative percentages in each of the three friendship categories separately. The results are astounding:

	5 OR MORE FRIENDS	ABOUT 2 FRIENDS	NO FRIENDS
Normal	39.5	7.2	0.0
Mild psychoneurosis	22.0	16.4	5.0
Severe psychoneurosis	27.0	54.6	47.5
Psychosis	0.8	3.1	37.5
Other	10.7	18.7	10.0
	100.0	100.0	100.0

Among people who have five friends or more as children, 61.5 per cent have mild cases, while 27.8 per cent have severe cases. Among people who have no friends, only 5 per cent have mild cases, and 85 per cent have severe cases.

It is almost certain then, that lack of contact, when it is extreme, has extreme effects on people. There is a considerable body of literature beyond which I have quoted.[31] Even so, the evidence is sparse. We cannot be sure that the effect is causal, and we have found evidence only for those relatively extreme cases which can be counted unambiguously. From a strictly scientific point of view, it is clearly necessary to undertake a special, extensive study to test the hypothesis in the exact form that I have stated it.

However, just because the scientific literature doesn't happen to contain the relevant evidence, that doesn't mean that we don't know whether the hypothesis is true or not. From our own lives we know that intimate contact is essential to life; and that the whole meaning of life shows itself only in the process of our intimate contacts.[32] The loss of intimate contacts touches each one of us—each one of you who reads this book. The evidence I have quoted happens to concern only people who are suffering from some form of extreme social isolation. But the loss of intimate contacts is not restricted to these people. It applies equally to the man who is happily married, a father of four children and a member of numerous local groups. This man may seem to have many contacts—indeed, he does—but the way that our society works today, he is still most likely lacking intimate contact as I have defined it, and therefore, if my hypothesis is right, even this lucky man is still suffering from disorders which are different only in degree from the extreme disorders I have mentioned. The way of life we lead today makes it impossible for us to be as close to our friends as we really want to be. The feeling of alienation, and the modern sense of the "meaninglessness" of life, are direct expressions of the loss of intimate contact.

3. THE AUTONOMY-WITHDRAWAL SYNDROME

As far as we can judge, then, people need three or four intimate contacts at every moment of their lives, in order to survive. If they don't have these contacts they undergo progressive deterioration and disintegration. It is therefore clear that every human society must provide social mechanisms which sustain these intimate contacts, in order to survive as a society. Yet as we know, the historic mechanisms which once performed this function for our own society are breaking down.

I shall now try to show that we are faced not merely with the collapse of one or two social mechanisms, but rather with a massive syndrome, a huge net of cause and effect in which the breakdown of primary groups, the breakdown of intimacy itself, the growth of individualism, and the withdrawal from the stress of urbanized society are all interwoven. I shall call this syndrome *the autonomy-withdrawal syndrome.*

To study the syndrome, let us begin with the most obvious mechanical reasons for the breakdown of intimate contacts. I have already named them. In preindustrial societies the two institutions which sustained intimate contacts between adults were the extended family and the local neighborhood community. These two primary groups have almost entirely disappeared. The family has shrunk; friends have scattered.

The modern metropolis is therefore a collection of many scattered households, each one small. In the future, individual households will probably be even smaller, and the average size of urban areas even larger.[33] Under these circumstances the three or four intimate contacts which each individual needs are no longer available in his immediate physical surroundings: not in his shrunken family, nor in his neighborhood. We must therefore ask how, in a society of scattered, mobile individuals, these individuals can maintain intimate contact with one another.

Let us go back to the two conditions which intimate contact requires: (1) the people concerned must see each other very often, almost daily; and (2) they must see each other under informal conditions, not controlled by single role relationships or social rules. How can a society of scattered, mobile individuals meet these two conditions?

The first answer which comes to mind is this: since friendships in modern society are mostly based on some community of interest, we should expect the institutions which create such friendships—workplace, golf club, ski resort, precinct headquarters—to provide the necessary meeting ground. It sounds good; but it doesn't work. Though people do meet each other in such groups, the meetings are too infrequent, and the situation too clearly prescribed. People achieve neither the frequency nor the informality which intimacy requires. Further, *people can reach the true intimacy and mutual trust required for self-revelation only when they are in private.*

Frequent, private, almost daily meeting between individuals under conditions of extreme informality, unencumbered by role prescriptions or social rules, will take place only if the people visit one another in their own homes. It is true that occasional meetings in public places may also be very intimate: but the regular, constant meetings which are required to build up the possibility of intimacy cannot happen in public places. In a society of scattered mobile individuals people will therefore be able to maintain intimate contacts with one another only if they are in the habit of constant informal visiting or "dropping-in."

In modern American society dropping-in is thought of as a peculiarly European custom. Yet in fact, it is a normal part of life in every preindustrial society. In part It has to be, because there are no telephones. But dropping-in is not merely the preindustrial version of what we do by phone. The very notion of friendship demands that people be almost totally exposed to one another. To be friends, they must have nothing to hide; and for this reason, informal dropping-in is a natural and essential part of friendship. This is so fundamental that we may even treat it as a definition of true friendship. If two people feel free to drop in on each other knowing that they will be welcome, no matter what is happening, we can be sure that they are intimate friends; if two people feel inhibited about dropping in on each other, we can be sure they are not truly intimate. Why is dropping-in so rare in mobile, urban society?

The first reason, of course, is still mechanical. Two people will not sustain a pattern of daily dropping-in unless they live within a few minutes of each other, ten minutes at the most. Although the car has enormously enlarged the number of people within ten minutes' distance of any given household, most of the people in the metropolis are still outside this distance. If we remember that we are concerned with the half dozen individuals who are potentially most intimate with any given individual, we must face the fact that in a metropolis these individuals are very likely to live as much as half an hour or an hour apart. At this distance, intimate contact can't develop. They see each other very rarely—at most once or twice a month for dinner—and when they do meet, it is after careful invitation, worked out in advance. These kinds of evening contact have neither the frequency, nor the informality, which intimacy requires.

However, distance alone, though it is a serious obstacle, does not fully explain the loss of intimacy. There is another reason for it, far more devastating, and far more profound: when people get home, they want to get away from all the stress outside. They feel more private than they used to feel. They treasure their quiet moments. A visitor who drops in unasked, at such a moment, even if he is a friend, is an intruder. People do not want to be perpetually exposed; they often want to be withdrawn. But withdrawal soon becomes a habit. People reach a point where they are permanently withdrawn, they lose the habit of showing themselves to others as they really are, and become unable and unwilling to let other people into their own world.

At this stage people don't like others dropping in on them, because they don't want to be caught when they aren't ready: the housewife who doesn't like anyone coming around except when she has carefully straightened out her house; the family who don't like to mix their friends, and entertain their friends one couple at a time in case the couples shouldn't get along. Truly intimate contact is not possible to such people. They live behind a social facade. Afraid of showing themselves as they really are, they never reach a truly intimate degree of contact with others.

This fear is partly caused by stress. The man who lives in modern urban society is exposed to innumerable stresses: danger, noise, too many strangers, too much information, and above all, the need to make decisions about the complexities of personal life without the help of traditional mores. These stresses are often too much too bear; so he withdraws from them. He draws a cloak of impenetrability around him, to ward off the too many strangers he meets in the street; he locks his door; he lives buried beneath a system of elaborated social and behavioral defenses against unwelcome and unbidden intrusions from outside. The houses of a century ago were outward-looking; the porch had people on it; the front garden was occupied. Today only the slum-dwellers—who sit on the stoop because it is too grim inside —face toward the city. Everyone else has turned away. Even when they are in public, people behave as though the other people who surround them were not there. A man walks down the street with a glazed look, not looking at people's eyes, but focused determinedly on nothing. A woman cheerfully wears curlers in the street because, although she is curling her hair for people who are real to her, the people who surround her don't exist: she has shut them out.

In its extreme form, this withdrawal turns into schizophrenia: that total withdrawal into the self which takes place when the outside world is so confusing, or so hard to deal with, that the organism finally cannot cope with it and turns away.[34] In the process of withdrawing into the self, the schizophrenic loses sight, entirely, of his dependence on other people. Schizophrenics are completely individualistic: the world they live in is their own world; they do not perceive themselves as dependent on the outside world in any way, nor do they perceive any interaction between themselves and the outside world. Nor indeed, do they enter into any interaction with the world outside.[35]

The stress of urban life has not yet had this extreme and catastrophic effect on many people. Nevertheless, what is nowadays considered "normal" urban behavior is strikingly like schizophrenia: it is also marked by extreme withdrawal from stress, and this withdrawal has also led to unrealistic belief in individualism and the self-sufficiency of individuals.

Any objective observer comparing urban life with rural or preindustrial life must be struck by the extreme individualism of the people who live in cities.[36] This individualism has reached its most extreme form in the urban areas of the United States. Though it has often been criticized by non-Americans as a peculiarity of American culture, I believe this view mistaken. Individualism of an extreme kind is an inevitable by-product of urbanization—it occurs as part of the withdrawal from stress. This individualism is very different from healthy democratic respect for the individual's rights. It is a pathological overbelief in the self-sufficiency and independence of the individual and the individual family, and a refusal to permit dependence of any emotional weight to form. Where contact with others reaches very high proportions—beyond the capacity of the individual organism—the organism is forced to shut these contacts out, and therefore to maintain an unreal belief in its own powers of self-sufficiency.[37]

An obvious expression of individualism is the huge amount of space which people need around them in the United States. Edward Hall has shown that each person carries an inviolable "bubble" of personal space around with him and that the size of the bubble varies according to the intimacy of the situation which the person is involved in.[38] He has also shown that the size of the bubble required varies from culture to culture. It is remarkable that people need a larger bubble in the United States, for any given situation, than in any other country; this is clearly associated with the fear of bodily contact, and with the fact that people view themselves as isolated atoms, separate from everybody else.

This isolation of the individual is also expressed clearly by the love of private property in the United States, and the wealth of laws and institutions which keep people's private property inviolate.

Another recent, and extreme, form of this worship of the individual exists in certain communities on the west coast of the United States, like Canyon, east of Oakland. The people in Canyon have a cult of honesty—about their individual wants—which leads to total disregard for others. Each one of them eats when he chooses to—in order to be "honest"—which means that groups no longer eat communally around a table. They are highly unresponsive to one another: when they meet, instead of moving physically toward each other as normal people do, they merely incline their heads, or nod with their eyelids. Each individual comes and goes as he pleases: there is no mutuality, no interplay of reaction and response.

Another form of extreme individualism, which threatens the development of intimate contacts, is the exaggerated accent on the nuclear family. In modern urban society it is assumed that the needs for intimate contact which any one individual has can be completely met in marriage. This concentration of all our emotional eggs in one basket has gone so far that true intimacy between any friends except man and wife is regarded with extreme suspicion. As Camus says: in Greece a man and his friend walk down the street holding hands—in Paris people would snigger at the sight.

Perhaps the most vivid of all expressions of individualism is the song *People who need people are the luckiest people in the world,* top of the U.S. hit parade in 1964. A society where this statement needs to be made explicitly has reached a low ebb indeed.

Where has this exaggerated arrogant view of the individual's strength come from? It is true that it is a withdrawal from stress. But it could never have happened if it weren't for the fact that urbanization makes individuals autonomous. The extreme differentiation of society in an urban area means that literally any service can be bought, by anyone. In material terms, any individual is able to survive alone. Women can make a living on their own; teenagers no longer need their families; old people can fend for themselves; men are able to get meals from the local automat, or from the freezer in the supermarket. Insurance is not provided by the extended family, but by the insurance companies. Autonomous trailer houses can exist in the wilderness without community facilities.

Of course these isolated, apparently autonomous individuals are in fact highly dependent on society—but only through the medium of money. A man in a less differentiated rural economy is constantly reminded of his dependence on society, and of the fact that his very being is totally intertwined with the being of the social order, and the being of his fellows. The individual who is technically autonomous, whose dependencies are all expressed in money terms, can easily make the mistake of thinking that he, or he and his family, are self-sufficient.

Now, naturally, people who believe that they are self-sufficient create a world which reinforces individualism and withdrawal. In central cities, this is reflected in the concept of apartments. Though collected together at high densities, these apartments are in fact, like the people themselves, totally turned inward. High density makes it necessary to insulate each apartment from the world outside; the actual dwelling is remote from the street; it is virtually impossible to drop in on someone who lives in an apartment block. Not surprisingly, recent studies report that people who live in apartments feel more isolated than people who live in any other kinds of dwelling.[39]

But autonomy and withdrawal, and the pathological belief in individual families as self-sufficient units, can be seen most vividly in the physical pattern of suburban tract development. This is Durkheim's dust-heap in the flesh. The houses stand alone: a collection of isolated, disconnected islands. There is no communal land, and no sign of any functional connection between different houses.

If it seems far-fetched to call this aspect of the suburb pathological, let us examine the results of a study undertaken in Vienna in 1956. The city planning department gave a questionnaire to a random sample of 4,000 Viennese, to find out what their housing preferences were. Most of them, when asked whether they would rather live in apartments or in single-family houses, said that they preferred apartments, because they wanted to be near the center where everything was happening.[40]

A Viennese psychiatrist then gave the same questionnaire to 100 neurotic patients in his clinic. He found that a much higher majority of these patients wanted to live in one-family houses, that they wanted larger houses relative to the size of their families, that they wanted more space per person, and that more of them wanted their houses to be situated in woods and trees. In other words, they wanted the suburban dream. As he says: "The neurotic patients are marked by a strong desire to shun reality and to isolate themselves."[41]

Most people who move to suburbs are not sick in any literal sense. However, there can be no question that their move is a withdrawal. The four main reasons which people give for moving to the suburbs are: (1) Open space for children, because children can't play safely in central urban areas.[42] (2) Wanting more space inside the house than they can afford in the central city.[43] (3) Wanting to own a house of their own.[44] Ownership protects the owner from the uncertainties of tenancy, from reliance on others, and from the dangers of the future. It creates the illusion that the owner and his family have a world of their own, where nobody can touch them. (4) Wanting more grass and trees.[45]

Each of these is a withdrawal from stress. The withdrawal is understandable; but the suburb formed by this withdrawal undermines the formation of intimate contacts in a devastating way. It virtually destroys the children's play-group.

As we saw earlier, the intimate contacts in preindustrial society were maintained by three primary groups: the extended family, the neighborhood group, and the children's play-group. The first two, those which maintain intimate contacts between adults, are obsolete, and need to be replaced. But the third primary group—the children's play-group—is not obsolete at all. Little children, unlike adults, do choose their friends from the children next door. It is perfectly possible for children's play-groups to exist in modern society, just as they always have; and indeed, it is essential. The children's play-group sets the whole style of life for later years. Children brought up in extensive play-groups will be emotionally prepared for intimate contacts in later life; children brought up without play-groups will be prone to individualism and withdrawal.

On the face of it, the suburb ought to be a very good place for children's play-groups. People move to a suburb specifically for the sake of their children. It has open space, and safety, and good schools. Yet, paradoxically, this children's paradise is not a paradise at all for little children. Children begin to seek other children at about ten months.[46] Remembering that Harlow's monkeys required play with other monkeys during the first six months of life in order to be normal, and that these first six months correspond to the first three years in the life of a human child, let us ask: "How well does a suburban subdivision cater for the play-groups of the one and two and three-year-olds?"

If you drive through a subdivision, watching children play, you will see that children who are old enough to have school friends do have local play-groups of a sort. (Even these groups are sparse; in summer many of the children have to be sent off to summer camp.) But what happens to the smallest children? If you look carefully, you see them squatting forlornly outside their houses—occasionally playing with an elder brother or sister, and occasionally in groups of two or three, but most often alone. Compare this with the situation in a primitive village, or with a crowded urban slum: there the little children are out on the street fending for themselves as soon as they can walk; heaps of children are playing and falling and rolling over one another.

The need for preschool play-groups is so desperate and urgent that many mothers try to get their children into nursery school.[47] But even nursery school lasts only 15 hours a week. For a child the week is 100 waking hours long. The 15 hours of nursery school do little to relieve the damage of the other 85 hours.

Why are suburban play-groups small? There are several different reasons. First of all, suburban density is low and little children can't walk very far. Even if every house has children in it, the number of two and three-year-olds that a given two-year-old can reach is very small. Secondly, even though the suburb is safer than the central city, the streets still aren't entirely safe. Mothers keep their two and three-year-olds off the street, inside the individual yards, where they can keep an eye on them. This cuts the children's freedom to meet other children. Further, many suburbs have no common land at all in them, not even sidewalks. There isn't any natural place where children go to find each other: they have to go and look for each other in one another's houses. For a child this is a much more formidable enterprise than simply running out to see who's on the street. It also makes the children hard to find, and keeps the size of play-groups down, especially since many parents won't allow large groups of children in the house. And finally, when children play in one another's yards, parents can control the playmates they consider suitable: "Johnny isn't nice, you mustn't play with him." One young mother told me that her son, four years old, had to be driven to the nearest child he was allowed to play with, and had to come home by taxi.

It is small wonder that children who grow up in these conditions learn to be self-reliant in the pathological sense I have described. As they become adults they are even less able than their parents to live lives with intimate contacts; they seek even more exaggerated forms of individualism and withdrawal. As adults who suffer from withdrawal they create a world which creates children who are even more prone to suffer from withdrawal, and more prone to create such worlds. This closes the cycle of the sundrome, and makes it self-perpetuating.

We may summarize the syndrome briefly. Stress forces people to withdraw into themselves; autonomy allows them to. Pushed by stress, pulled by autonomy, people have withdrawn into a private world where they believe that they are self-sufficient. They create a way of life, and an environment, which reflects this belief; and this way of life, and this environment, then propagate the same illusion. It creates more people who believe in self-sufficiency as an ideal, it makes intimate contact seem less necessary, and it makes it more and more difficult to achieve in practice.

The autonomy-withdrawal syndrome is not a unique American

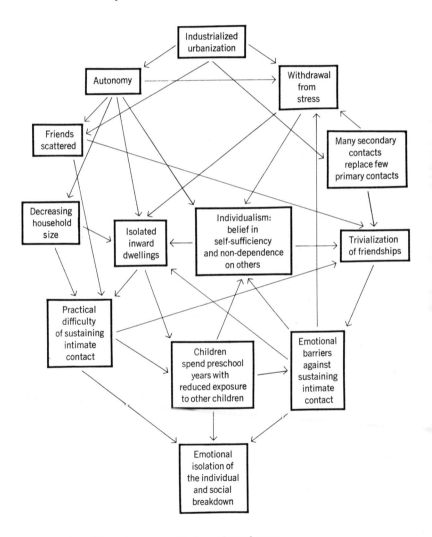

FIGURE 1. The autonomy-withdrawal syndrome.

phenomenon. It is true that it is, so far, more acute in the United States than in any other country; but this is merely because urbanization is more advanced in the United States than anywhere else. As massive urbanization spreads, the syndrome will spread with it. I believe this syndrome is the greatest threat to social human nature which we face in this century. We have already seen that it can create misery and madness. But in the long run its effects are far more devastating. An individual human organism becomes a self only in the process of intimate contacts with other selves. Unless we overcome the syndrome, the loss of intimate contacts may break down human nature altogether.

4. SOLUTION

How can cities help to overcome the syndrome? If the city is to be a mechanism for sustaining intimate human contact, what geometric pattern does the mechanism need?

Of course, no amount of geometric pattern in the environment can overcome the syndrome on its own. The syndrome is a social and psychological problem of massive dimensions: it will be solved only when people decide to change their way of life. But the physical environment needs changing too. People can change their way of life only if the environment supports their efforts.

There are two fundamentally different approaches to the problem. On the one hand, we may decide that intimate contact can be sustained properly only by primary groups, as it always has been in the past; we shall then try to create new kinds of primary groups which might work in our society. On the other hand, we may decide that adult primary groups are gone forever, and that it is unrealistic to try to recreate them in any form whatever in modern society; in this case we must try a more radical approach, and create a social mechanism which is able to sustain informal, daily contact between people without the support of a primary group.

It may be that the first of these approaches is the more hopeful one. This is what T-groups try to do, it is the idea behind the groups of families which Aldous Huxley describes in *Island,* and above all, it is the idea behind group work. If work can be reorganized so that people band together in small work groups of about a dozen and each group is directed toward a single concentrated socially valuable objective, then the dedication and effort which develop in the group are capable of creating great intimacy, which goes far beyond the working day.

However, so far none of these methods has met with any great success. So far the forces which are breaking primary groups apart have been stronger than the efforts to construct artificial primary groups. I shall, therefore, assume that much more radical steps will have to be taken: that although children's play-groups can be saved, adult primary groups are doomed, and adults will have to sustain their intimate contacts in a new way, by frequent casual visiting. I shall now describe the reorganization of the housing pattern which is required by this approach.

At present, people have two main kinds of housing open to them: either they live in apartments, or they live in single-family houses. Neither helps them overcome the autonomy-withdrawal syndrome. I shall now try to show that, in order for them to overcome the syndrome, the houses in a city must have twelve specific geometric characteristics, and that these twelve characteristics, when taken together, define a housing pattern different from any of those which are available today. The detailed reasons for the twelve characteristics are described in notes *a–l*, beginning on page 265. I recommend strongly that you read these reasons in detail. The characteristics themselves are these:

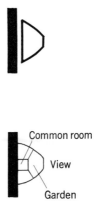

1 Every dwelling must be immediately next to a vehicular through street. If there are any multistory buildings with dwellings in them —like apartments—then there must be vehicular through streets at every level where there are entrances to dwellings.[a]

2 Each dwelling must contain a transparent communal room with the following properties: on one side the room is directly adjacent to the street, on the opposite side the room is directly adjacent to a private open air court or garden. Since the room is transparent its interior, seen against the garden, and the garden itself, are both visible from the street.[b]

3 This transparent communal room is surrounded by free-standing, self-contained enclosed pavilions, each functioning as a bed-living unit, so arranged that each person in the family, or any number of people who wish to be undisturbed, can retire to one of these pavilions and be totally private.[c]

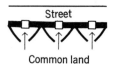

Major artery

1000'

Major artery

4 The street immediately outside the dwelling be no more than about 1,000 feet long, and connected to a major traffic artery at each end.[d]

Common land

5 There must be a continuous piece of common land, accessible and visible from every dwelling.[e]

Street

Common land

6 This common land must be separated from the streets by houses, so that a child on the common land has to go through a house to get to the street.[f]

7 The common land, though continuous, must be broken into many small "places," not much larger than outdoor "rooms," each surfaced with a wide variety of ground surfaces, especially "soft" surfaces like earth, mud, sand, grass, bushes.[g]

8 Each house must be within 100 yards' walk of 27 other houses.[h]

9 Over-all residential densities throughout the metropolitan area must be as high as possible.[i]

10 The entire exterior surface of the residential area is an undulating hillside, covered with grass and flowers and trees: the houses are set immediately under the surface of this hillside.[j]

11 Each house is on an individual load-bearing pad, which doesn't touch any other pad, and may be clearly visualized as a piece of private property. The pad has its own open space, and allows the owner to build and modify his house as he wishes.[k]

Center ⟶

12 The hills vary in height and slope according to their location in the urban region. They are highest and steepest near commercial centers, and low and flat near the periphery.[l]

It now remains to find a single concrete configuration of dwellings in which all of these twelve relations are simultaneously present. The accompanying drawings show such a configuration.

The residential area of the city is a continuous series of rolling linear hills. The hills are about 700 feet long, connected at each end to major traffic arteries. They change in height and slope according to their distance from the major urban centers. The outer surface of these hills is publicly-owned common land, covered by grass and trees and bushes and flowers. Each house is built on a pad, immediately under the surface of the hill. The outer half of this pad is a private, fenced garden, which connects directly with the outer surface of the hill. Daylight for the house comes from the garden. The common part of the hill, which surrounds the private gardens, is broken down to form a series of small places, connected by slopes and stairs. Each house is served by a street inside the hill, at its own level. The house is immediately next to its street. Each house has two basic components: a communal room and a number of private pavilions. The communal room, which is next to the street, between the street and the garden, is open to the street, and transparent, so that the gar-

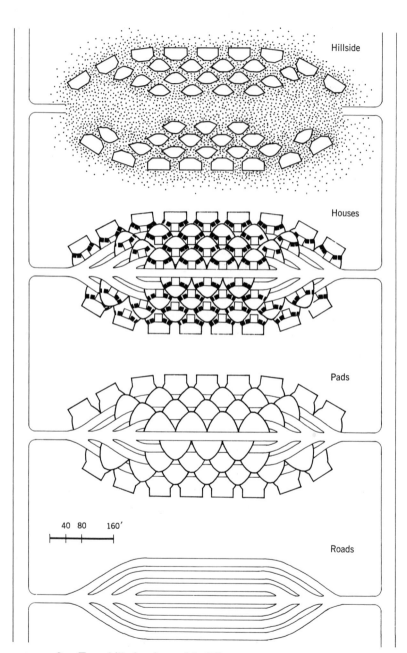

FIGURE 2. Four hills in plan, with different amounts cut away.

den is visible through it, and so that people inside this room are visible against the light. The private pavilions are arranged around this communal room, under the roof provided by the hillside above.

This configuration contains all twelve relations specified. Although it can be varied in many details without damaging any of the twelve relations, I do not believe that it is possible to find a configuration which differs *fundamentally* from the one I have described and still contains all of the twelve. However, I should not like this configuration to be thought of as a building. Many problems still need to be worked out before it can be built. The configuration must be thought of simply as a partial specification of what a city has to be, to function as a mechanism for sustaining human contact.

Let me once more repeat the central argument. It is inevitable that urban concentrations creates stress. People in cities are exposed to stress more than people in small towns and villages. Our first reaction to this urban stress is to move away from it; to turn our backs on it; to try and escape it. This is very natural. Yet the remedy is worse than the disease. The ills of urban life which are commonly attributed to density and stress are in fact produced not by the original stress itself, but by our own actions in turning away from that stress. The stress is making us turn inward. If urban society is to survive, we must overcome this overreaction. There is only one way to overcome it. We must take our lives in our hands, we must overcome the temptation to turn away; we must make ourselves vulnerable. Each individual in society must once more expose himself to those dangers which, in his eagerness to escape from stress, he has shut out altogether. If people do not expose themselves, if they do not dare to make themselves vulnerable, life will become more and more intolerable, and we shall see more and more of the signs of dissociation which are already far too evident. The pattern of twelve relations which I have presented has only this one objective. It brings people out of hiding, and lets them expose themselves to the larger fabric of the city and to society, and to their friends. In such a city there is some chance of breaking down the autonomy-withdrawal syndrome. In our own cities there is no chance at all.

NOTES

a. In the modern city, many houses, and almost all apartments, are some distance off the street. Yet people live so far apart that they have to move around by car or motor-bike. Informal dropping-in will work properly only if all dwellings are directly on the street, so that people in the dwelling can be seen directly from a passing car.

It may be said that this is unnecessary since people who want to visit one another informally can telephone ahead, and ring the doorbell when they get there. This argument is superficial. People will make a regular habit of informal visiting only if they can be certain that they are really wanted when they get there. A phone call in advance, though useful for less subtle kinds of communication, does not convey enough information to make this possible. If you call someone, you cannot be sure from what he says on the phone whether it is really a good time to go around or not. This will be true even with TV-telephones. To be sure, you need to see him: you need to know who else is there, what they are doing, what kind of mood everyone is in, what the children have been doing, whether they are tired or not, whether the whole family would rather be alone. You can find these things out only by seeing for yourself.

But if you go and knock on someone's door, and it turns out to be a bad moment, your visit is already too far advanced for you to withdraw gracefully. Once you are on the doorstep, the hosts feel obliged to invite you in.

It is therefore essential to see the people you intend to visit inside their house, from your car. You wave to them; you sound the horn; you shout a few words. By then you have had a chance to assess the situation, and they have had a chance to react. If it is the right moment for a visit, they will invite you in. If it is not, you talk for a few moments, without leaving your car—and you can then drive on, without embarrassment to either side. It is therefore essential that the house be directly on a through street, and that some part of the house be transparent and directly visible from passing cars.

b. The part of the house which is visible must be indoors, so that it can be used year round and since it is indoors it must have windows both on the street side and the far side, so that people inside can be seen from the street. It must therefore be a transparent room. The room must be designed in such a way that people will go there whenever they are feeling sociable, and likely to welcome a casual visitor. But if the room is merely facing the street, people won't want to sit there; the street is far less pleasant than it used to be. That is why the porch is obsolete. Nowadays people tend to build their living rooms facing away from the street, toward some kind of view or garden. The transparent room, though visible from the street, must therefore be oriented toward a private court or garden, with a view beyond. Under these circumstances it will be a natural place for people to go for family meals, when they want to read the paper, have a drink, or gossip. In warm seasons they may also sit in the court beyond, where they will still be visible from the street.

c. If the communal room of the house is visible from the street, and open to passing friends, then the private rooms of the house must be far more private than they are today, so that their privacy is not infected by the openness of the communal room. Each of these private rooms must be a more or less self-contained pavilion, where people can be entirely undisturbed—either alone, or two, or as a group. People who live in such a house must learn to distinguish deliberately between being accessible and being inaccessible.

When they want to be accessible, they go to the communal room; when they want to be inaccessible, they go to one of the private pavilions.

d. The house must be so placed that people can drive past it easily, without having to go too far out of their way. This means that the house must be on a street which is reasonably short, and connected at each end to a traffic artery that plays a major part in the over-all traffic system.

e. Suburban yards are far too private. They allow only small groups to form, they make it hard for children to find each other, and they allow parents to regulate the other yards their own children may visit. In order to overcome these difficulties, and to give children the chance to meet freely in groups, there must be common land where they can always go to find each other.

In some of the older and denser suburbs, the wide sidewalks provide such common land. However, most suburban tract developments have very narrow sidewalks, or no sidewalks at all: and anyway most middle-class parents consider even the sidewalk dangerous, or rule it out on the ground that "well brought up children don't play in the street." Most important of all, even in the suburbs, parents still feel very protective about the smallest children. They will allow these children to play freely on common land only if they are convinced that the children will be completely safe while they are playing there.

This means, first of all, that the access to the common land must be direct from every house; it must not be necessary to cross streets or other public thoroughfares to get there. Secondly, the common land must be visible from the house itself, so that the parent can, if they want to, watch their children playing there. Third, the common land must be so placed that a child cannot get to any vehicular street without going through a house. Finally, the common land must be disassociated from the street, and clearly meant for play, so that it has no connotation of "playing in the street." If all of these conditions are met, parents will allow the little children—even toddlers—to roam freely on and off the common land, and the play-groups have a good chance of forming.

f. See previous note.

g. One condition must be met, to make sure that the children really like the common land, and don't end up preferring their own yards, or other places. Little children do not enjoy playing in great big open areas. They seek small corners, and opportunities for secrecy; and they seek plastic materials—water, earth, and mud. L. E. White, "The Outdoor Play of Children Living in Flats," *Living in Towns,* ed. Leo Kuper (London, 1953), pp. 235–64. The common land, then, must be broken up into many tiny places, which have natural earth and mud and plants in them.

h. Let us assume that there are two children per household in the areas where children live (the modal figure for suburban households), and that these children are evenly distributed, in age, from 0 to 18. Roughly speaking, a given preschool child who is x years old will play with children who are $x - 1$ or x or $x + 1$ years old. In order to have a reasonable amount of contact, and in order for play-groups to form, each child must be able to reach at least five children in this age range. Statistical analysis shows that in order for each child to have a 95 per cent chance of reaching five such potential playmates, each child must be in reach of 27 households.

(The problem may be stated as follows: In an infinite population of children, one-sixth are the right age and five-sixths are the wrong age. A group of r children is chosen at random. The probability, $P_{r,k}$ that these r children contain exactly k right-age children is given by the hypergeometric distribution. The probability that r has 5 or more right-age children in it is $1 - \sum\limits_{k=0}^{4} P_{r,k}$. If we now ask what is the least r which makes $1 - \sum\limits_{k=0}^{4} P_{r,k} \geq .95$, r turns out to be 54, requiring 27 households.)

If we assume that preschool children are not able, or allowed, to go more than about 100 yards in search of playmates, this means that each house must be within 100 yards of 27 other houses. To achieve this density in a conventional suburban layout, house lots would have to be less than 40 feet wide, about half the width and twice the density they are today.

i. There is a second reason why residential densities must be higher than today. Informal daily dropping-in will not take place between two households that are more than about ten minutes apart. Since average door-to-door speeds in urban areas are about 15 mph, ten minutes is about 2½ miles, thus putting each person in reach of about twenty square miles, or about 100,000 people at current metropolitan densities. This is a tiny fraction of the population of a metropolitan area—a twentieth of a small one, a hundredth of a large one. Since we have started out with the axiom that a person's best friends may live anywhere in the metropolitan area, this means that people are within dropping-in distance of no more than a twentieth of their potentially closest friends.

Obviously vehicle speeds and streets can be improved. But it seems unlikely that average door-to-door speeds will more than double in this century. This means that people in the largest metropolitan areas will still be within informal distance of less than one-twentieth of the population. While transportation must clearly be improved, it is clear that over-all mean densities must *also* be raised as far as they can be.

Many planners believe that high density is bad for man. This is based on the fact that high density is often correlated with the incidence of crime, delinquency, ill health, and insanity. If this belief were justified, any attempt to increase the density of population would obviously be ill advised. However, though the belief has a long history, the evidence available today does not support it.

Let us try to disentangle the evidence. First of all, there seems little doubt that overcrowding—too little living space per person—does cause damage. Calhoun has shown this dramatically for rats. J. B. Calhoun, "Population Density and Social Pathology," *Scientific American,* 206 (Feb., 1962), pp. 139–46. Loring, Chombard de Lauwe, and Lander have shown that it is true for humans. William C. Loring, "Housing Characteristics and Social Disorganization," *Social Problems* (January, 1956); Chombard de Lauwe, *Famille et habitation* (Paris: Editions du Centre National de la Recherche Scientifique, 1959); B. Lander, *Towards an Understanding of Juvenile Delinquency* (New York: Columbia University Press, 1954). This finding makes it clear that people who are now forced to live in crowded conditions either need more income, or need ways of reducing the square foot costs of living space. But it does not imply that the density of population per square mile should be reduced. Even dwellings which are individually very large can still be arranged at very high population densities without overcrowding.

What evidence is there that high population density itself causes ill effects? It is true that there is often a positive correlation between high population density and various indices of social disorder, like crime, delinquency, ill health, and insanity rates. Robert C. Schmitt, "Delinquency and Crime in Honolulu," *Sociology and Social Research,* 41 (March–April, 1957), pp. 274–76, and "Population Densities and Mental Disorders in Honolulu," *Hawaii Medical Journal,* 16 (March–April, 1957), pp. 396–97. However, it seems almost certain that these effects are caused by intervening variables, and are not directly caused by density. There are places—Boston's North End and Hong Kong, for instance—which have exceptionally high densities and exceptionally low indices of social disorder. Jane Jacobs, *The Death and Life of Great American Cities* (New York, 1961), pp. 10 and 206; Robert C. Schmitt, "Implications of Density in Hong Kong," *Journal of the American Institute of Planners,* 29 (1963), pp. 210–17. Unless we assume that Italian-Americans and Chinese are organically different from other people, this means that density, as such, cannot be the source of trouble in the cases where a correlation does exist.

The following hypothesis fully explains all the observed correlations: Those social disorders apparently caused by density are in fact caused by low income, poor education, and social isolation. It is known that people who are poor and badly educated tend to live in high density areas. It is also known that people who are socially isolated tend to live in high density areas. Both variables are associated with high indices of social disorder. Although some published studies of density have controlled for one or the other of these variables, no study has controlled them both. Lander (p. 46) has shown that the correlation between *overcrowding* and delinquency, when controlled for these two variables, vanishes altogether. Schmitt has published a table showing that the correlations persist when income-education is controlled, but also showing a strong negative correlation between household size and social disorder (large households are less prone to social disorders), which suggests strongly that social isolation may be responsible for the persistent correlation. Robert C. Schmitt, "Density, Health and Social Disorganization," *Journal of the American Institute of Planners,* 32 (January, 1966), pp. 38–40. The fact that there are very few social disorders in Boston's North End and in Hong Kong is clearly due to the existence of close-knit extended families: the lack of social isolation. I predict that the partial correlation between density and social disorder, when controlled for income-education *and* for social isolation, will disappear altogether.

This hypothesis explains all the available data. Although it is untested, there is no published evidence which contradicts it. As far as we can tell, the high density characteristics called for by the need for contact are perfectly safe.

j. We cannot expect people to live at high density, just because it has certain social benefits. The low density of suburban tracts is not due to chance; it has been created by a number of insatiable demands, far more important to consumers than the point of view I have presented. These demands are so basic, and play such a basic role in the operation of the urban land market, that low residential density is a universal feature of emerging metropolitan areas throughout the world. Unless these demands can be satisfied equally well at higher densities, there is not the slightest hope that over-all densities will ever be increased. There are five main demands: (1) People seek more open space for their children than they can find in central urban areas. (2) People want to live in a house which is their very own property. (3) People seek more space per person than they can afford in central areas. (4) People want a house which is different from the next man's—not simply one of hundreds of identical apartments. (5) People seek grass and trees as symbols of stability and peace.

All of these demands lead to the same basic tendency: the desire for land. The pattern of density in an urban region is created by the conflict between this one basic tendency and another equally basic tendency: the desire for easy access to central areas. For a given income, each person can choose less land at the center, or more land further from the center. When a population of individuals tries to resolve this conflict for themselves, a characteristic pattern of density comes into being: density declines exponentially with distance from the center according to the equation: $d_r = d_o e^{-br}$. Brian J. L. Berry, James W. Simmons, and Robert J. Tennant, "Urban Population Densities: Structure and Change," *Geographical Review,* 53 (1963), pp. 389–405; John Q. Stewart and William Warntz, "Physics of Population Distribution," *Journal of Regional Science,* Vol. I (1958), pp. 99–123. This relation holds for cities all over the world. Colin Clark, "Urban Population Densities," *Journal of the Royal Statistical Society,* Series A, 114 (1951), Part 4, pp. 490–96; Berry, cited. What is even more surprising, the relation is almost entirely fixed by absolute population, and by the age of the city. This means that in a free market, neither the over-all mean density of a city nor the densities at different distances from the center can be controlled by planning action.

They can, however, be controlled indirectly. The density pattern comes into being as a result of millions of peoples' efforts to resolve the conflict between their desire for access and their desire for land. If we can make land more useful, so that a person can get a given level of satisfaction from a smaller piece of land than he needs to get that satisfaction now, then the desire for access will balance differently against the desire for land, and densities will increase.

Land is valuable for two basic reasons. First of all, it is the prime building surface. Secondly, it provides open space. The first is replaceable. The second is not. It is easy to create artificial building surfaces at many levels. But the area of open space cannot be increased beyond the area of the land. This is a basic natural resource. Yet this resource is almost entirely wasted and destroyed in urban areas today. Fifty per cent is wasted on roads and parking lots, which really don't require it: 25 per cent is wasted on roofs, which get no benefit from it at all. The 25 per cent of open space left over is chopped up and useless.

If a city were built so as to conserve this resource, with all roofs covered with grass and trees, and all roads roofed over, so that the total exterior surface of the city was a parkland of grass and flowers and bushes and trees, people could have the very same amenities they have today, at far higher densities.

How much useful open land does a family in a suburban tract command? At a gross density of 5,000 persons per square mile, each family has a lot about 70′ by 100′, 7,000 square feet in all. Of this, 2,000 square feet go to the house, and another 1,000 square feet to the driveway, leaving about 4,000 square feet of open land, or about 1,000 square feet per person. If the entire exterior surface of the city were artificial open land, it would be possible to house 25,000 people per square mile, and still give them the same 1,000 square feet of open land per person.

To make it work, the surface must undulate like a range of rolling hills, so that windows in the hillsides can get daylight to the houses under the surface.

k. So that people can get the same feeling of ownership, and the same opportunity to build what they want and the same private open space that they get in the suburbs, the houses under the hillside must be built on individual artificial lots. To avoid the half-hearted feeling of ownership which condominium apartments offer, each lot must be totally separate from the other lots, and so made that the owner can build what he wants to on his own lot. Each lot is an individual load-bearing pad, large enough to hold a 2,000-square-foot house with a private garden.

l. Since density will still vary with distance from urban centers, even if the land-access equation changes, the hills must vary in height and slope. The highest and steepest hills, whose density is greatest, will be near the urban centers; the low flat hills at the periphery.

1. Emile Durkheim, *The Division of Labor in Society* (Paris, 1893), trans. by George Simpson (Free Press, 1933).
2. Melvin M. Webber, "Order in Diversity: Community without Propinquity," *Cities and Space,* ed. Lowdon Wingo, Resources for the Future (Baltimore, 1963); Webber, "The Urban Place and the Nonplace Urban Realm," in Webber et al., *Explorations into Urban Structure* (Philadelphia, 1964), pp. 79–153; Marshall McLuhan, *Understanding Media* (New York, 1964); Richard Meier, *A Communications Theory of Urban Growth* (Cambridge: MIT Press, 1960).
3. Of course, people do occasionally have intimate contact with one another, even when these two conditions are not fulfilled. This happens between old friends, who now live 3,000 miles apart and see each other every few years for a day or two. But even in these cases, there must have been some period in the past when the two conditions *were* satisfied.
4. C. H. Cooley, *Social Organization* (first published New York, 1909; reprinted Free Press, 1956), pp. 23–31.
5. Edward A. Shils, "The Study of Primary Groups," in Lerner and Lasswell, *The Policy Sciences* (Stanford University Press, 1951), pp. 44–69; W. I. Thomas, *Social Behavior and Personality,* ed. E. H. Volkart (New York, 1951); George Homans, *The Human Group* (New York, 1950).

6. Homans, pp. 456–57.
7. Ralph Linton, *The Study of Man* (New York, 1936), p. 230.
8. For instance, Clarence Stein, *Towards New Towns for America* (Chicago, 1951).
9. Webber, cited; Ikumi Hoshin, "Apartment Life in Japan," *Marriage and Family Living*, Vol. 26 (1964), pp. 312–17; Rudolf Heberle, "The Normative Element in Neighborhood Relations," *Pacific Sociological Review*, Vol. 3, No. 1 (Spring, 1960), pp. 3–11.
10. Ruth Glass and F. G. Davidson, "Household Structure and Housing Needs," *Population Studies*, Vol. 4 (1951), pp. 395–420; S. P. Brown, *Population Studies*, Vol. 4 (1951), pp. 380–94. This is also the same as saying that one-fifth of all adults in urban areas are either single, separated, widowed, or divorced. See U. S. Census, Vol. I, *General U. S. Statistics* (1960), Table 176.
11. Durkheim, cited; Cooley, cited; Louis Wirth, "Urbanism as a Way of Life," *American Journal of Sociology*, Vol. 40 (1938), pp. 1–24; J. Beshers, *Urban Social Structure* (New York, 1964); Janet Abu-Lughod, *The City Is Dead, Long Live the City* (Berkeley: Center for Planning and Development Research, 1966).
12. H. Gans, *The Urban Villagers* (Free Press, 1962); Michael Young and Peter Willmott, *Family and Kinship in East London* (London, 1957); M. Fried and P. Gleicher, "Some Sources of Residential Satisfaction in an Urban Slum," *Journal of the American Institute of Planners* (1961), pp. 305–15.
13. Abu-Lughod, cited.
14. The numbers three and four have no special significance. I have chosen the range three to four, simply because one or two are too few, and more than about five too many to sustain at the level of intimacy I have defined.
15. R. E. L. Faris and H. W. Dunham, *Mental Disorders in Urban Areas* (Chicago, 1939), pp. 82–109.
16. Ibid., pp. 54–57.
17. Alexander Leighton, *My Name is Legion*, The Stirling County Study, Vol. I (New York, 1959); Charles C. Hughes, Marc-Adelard Tremblay, Robert N. Rapoport, and Alexander Leighton, *People of Cove and Woodlot*, The Stirling County Study, Vol. II (New York, 1960); Dorothea Leighton, John S. Harding, David B. Macklin, Allister M. Macmillan, and Alexander Leighton, *The Character of Danger*, The Stirling County Study, Vol. III (New York, 1963).
18. Hughes et al., p. 267.
19. Ibid., p. 297.
20. Leighton et al. (1963), p. 338.
21. T. S. Langner and S. T. Michael, *Life Stress and Mental Health* (New York, 1963), p. 285.
22. A. M. Rose, "Mental Disorder and Socio-economic Status," *Mental Health and Mental Disorder* (New York, 1955), Summary Table 4, pp. 102–4.
23. Langner and Michael, p. 286.
24. Ibid., pp. 287–89.

25. Neil A. Dayton, *New Facts on Mental Disorders* (Springfield, Ill., 1940), p. 464; C. Landis and J. D. Page, *Modern Society and Mental Disease* (New York, 1938), p. 163; Benjamin Malzberg, *Social and Biological Aspects of Mental Disease* (Utica, 1940), p. 70; Benjamin Malzberg, "Statistical Analysis of Ages of First Admission to Hospitals for Mental Disease in New York State," *Psychiatric Quarterly,* Vol. 23 (1949), p. 344; H. F. Dorn, "The Incidence and Future Expectancy of Mental Disease," *U.S. Public Health Reports,* Vol. 53 (1938), pp. 1991–2004; E. M. Furbush, "Social Facts Relative to Patients with Mental Disease," *Mental Hygiene,* Vol. 5 (1921), p. 597.
26. Malzberg (1940), p. 116; C. Landis and J. D. Page, *Modern Society and Mental Disease* (New York, 1938), p. 69; L. M. Adler, "The Relationship of Marital Status to Incidence of and Recovery from Mental Illness," *Social Forces,* Vol. 32 (1953), p. 186; Neil A. Dayton, "Marriage and Mental Disease," *New England Journal of Medicine,* Vol. 215 (1936), p. 154; F. J. Gaudet and R. I. Watson, "Relation between Insanity and Marital Conditions," *Journal of Abnormal Psychology,* Vol. 30 (1935), p. 368.
27. Harry F. Harlow and Margaret K. Harlow, "The Effect of Rearing Conditions on Behavior," *Bull. Menninger Clinic,* Vol. 26 (1962), pp. 213–24.
28. Harry F. Harlow and Margaret K. Harlow, "Social Deprivation in Monkeys," *Scientific American,* Vol. 207, No. 5 (1962), pp. 136–46.
29. Anna Freud and Sophie Dann, "An Experiment in Group Upbringing," *Readings in Child Behavior and Development,* ed. Celia Stendler (New York, 1964), pp. 122–40.
30. Herman R. Lantz, "Number of Childhood Friends as Reported in the Life Histories of a Psychiatrically Diagnosed Group of 1000," *Marriage and Family Living* (May, 1956), pp. 107–8.
31. R. E. L. Faris, "Cultural Isolation and the Schizophrenic Personality," *American Journal of Sociology,* Vol. 40 (Sept. 1934), pp. 155–69; R. E. L. Faris, *Social Psychology* (New York, 1952), pp. 338–62; R. E. L. Faris, *Social Disorganization* (New York, 1948), chap. 8; Paul Halmos, *Solitude and Privacy* (New York, 1952), pp. 88–92; Carle C. Zimmerman and Lucius F. Cervantes, S.J., *Successful American Families* (New York, 1960); R. Helanko, "The Yard Group in the Socialization of Turku Girls," *Acta Sociologica,* Vol. 4, No. 1 (1959), pp. 38–55; D. Kimball, "Boy Scouting as a Factor in Personality Development," Ph.D. Thesis, Dept. of Education, University of California, Berkeley, 1949; Melvin L. Kohn and John A. Clausen, "Social Isolation and Schizophrenia," *American Journal of Sociology,* Vol. 20 (1955), pp. 265–73; Dietrich C. Reltzes, "The Effect of Social Environment on Former Felons," *Journal of Criminal Law Criminology,* Vol. 46 (1955), pp. 226–31; E. Gartly Jaco, "The Social Isolation Hypothesis and Schizophrenia," *American Journal of Sociology,* Vol. 19 (1954), pp. 567–77; Aldous Huxley, *Island* (New York: Bantam, 1963), pp. 89–90; Arthur T. Jersild and Mary D. Fite, "The Influence of Nursery School Experience on Children's Social Adjustments," *Child Development Monographs,* Vol. 25 (1939); Helena Malley, "Growth in Social Behavior and Mental Activity after Six Months in Nursery School,"

Child Development, Vol. 6 (1935), pp. 303–9; Louis P. Thorpe, Child Psychology and Development (New York, 1955); K. M. B. Bridges, Social and Emotional Development of the Pre-school Child (London, 1931); W. R. Thompson and R. Melzack, "Early Environment," Scientific American, Vol. 194, No. 1 (1956), pp. 38–42.

32. This is, in effect, the same as the classic thesis of Cooley and George Herbert Mead, which says that the individual self appears only as a result of interaction with others, and that it is liable to disintegrate when these interactions are not available. Mead, Mind, Self and Society (Chicago, 1934); Cooley, cited.

33. Glass and Davidson, p. 400.

34. "The person who is diagnosed as suffering from schizophrenia perceives himself as bombarded by a multiplicity of personal and family problems he is not able to handle." L. H. Rogler and A. B. Hollingshead, Trapped: Families and Schizophrenia (New York, 1965).

35. Robert Sommer and Humphrey Osmond, "The Schizophrenic No-Society," Psychiatry, Vol. 25 (1962), pp. 244–55.

36. Durkheim, pp. 283–303.

37. J. G. Miller, "Input Overload and Psychopathology," American Journal of Psychiatry, Vol. 116 (1960), pp. 695–704; Richard Meier, cited.

38. E. T. Hall, The Hidden Dimension (New York, 1966).

39. Ministry of Housing, Families Living at High Density (London, 1966), pp. 29–33; John Madge, "Privacy," Transactions of the Bartlett Society, University College, London, Vol. 3 (1965), p. 139.

40. Leopold Rosenmayr, Wohnverhltnisse und Nachbarschaftsbeziehungen, Der Aufbau, Monograph No. 8 (Vienna, 1956), pp. 39–91.

41. Hans Strotzka, Spannungen und Losungsversuche in Stadtischer Umgebung, Wohnen in Wien, Der Aufbau, Monograph No. 8 (Vienna, 1956), pp. 93–108.

42. Nelson Foote, Janet Abu-Lughod, Mary Mix Foley, and Louis Winnick, Housing Choices and Housing Constraints (New York, 1960), pp. 107 and 392.

43. Ibid., pp. 223–63, and Peter H. Rossi, Why Families Move (Free Press, 1955).

44. Ibid., pp. 187–93, and Irving Rosow, "Homeownership Motives," American Sociological Review, Vol. 13 (1948), pp. 751–56.

45. Center for Urban Studies, Aspects of Change (London, 1964), Chap. 8, "Tall Flats in Pimlico." Santa Clara County Study, unpublished, 1966.

46. Charlotte Buhler, Proceedings and Papers of the Ninth International Congress of Psychology (1929), pp. 99–102.

47. A few of the mothers who try to get their children into nursery school are, of course, trying to get greater freedom for themselves. However, at least one survey has shown that the majority of mothers do so, not because they want more freedom for themselves, but because they want their children to have more contact with other children. Cambridge Association for Advancement of State Education, Report on Nursery Schools (Cambridge, England, 1966).